THE
NAG HAMMADI LIBRARY
IN ENGLISH

THE
NAG HAMMADI LIBRARY
IN ENGLISH

TRANSLATED AND INTRODUCED BY

MEMBERS OF THE COPTIC GNOSTIC LIBRARY PROJECT
OF THE INSTITUTE FOR ANTIQUITY AND CHRISTIANITY,
CLAREMONT, CALIFORNIA

James M. Robinson, General Editor

THIRD, COMPLETELY REVISED EDITION

WITH AN AFTERWORD BY

Richard Smith, Managing Editor

1817

Harper & Row, Publishers, San Francisco

Cambridge, Hagerstown, New York, Philadelphia, Washington
London, Mexico City, São Paulo, Singapore, Sydney

CONTRIBUTORS

Harold W. Attridge

Hans-Gebhard Bethge

Alexander Böhlig

James Brashler

Roger A. Bullard

Peter A. Dirkse

Stephen Emmel

Joseph A. Gibbons

Søren Giversen

James E. Goehring

Charles W. Hedrick

Wesley W. Isenberg

Howard M. Jackson

Karen L. King

Helmut Koester

Thomas O. Lambdin

Bentley Layton

George W. MacRae †

Marvin W. Meyer

Dieter Mueller †

William R. Murdock

Elaine H. Pagels

Douglas M. Parrott

Birger A. Pearson

Malcolm L. Peel

Michel Roberg

James M. Robinson

William C. Robinson, Jr.

William R. Schoedel

Maddalena Scopello

John H. Sieber

John D. Turner

Francis E. Williams

R. McL. Wilson

Orval S. Wintermute

Antoinette Clark Wire

Frederik Wisse

Jan Zandee

Richard Smith, Managing Editor

THE NAG HAMMADI LIBRARY IN ENGLISH. Revised edition. Copyright © 1978, 1988 by E. J. Brill, Leiden, The Netherlands. All rights reserved. Printed in the United States of America. No part of this book may be used or reproduced in any manner whatsoever without written permission except in the case of brief quotations embodied in critical articles and reviews. For information address Harper & Row, Publishers, Inc., 10 East 53rd Street, New York, NY 10022.

Library of Congress Cataloging-in-Publication Data

The Nag Hammadi library in English.

   1. Gnosticism.   2. Gnostic literature.   I. Coptic
Gnostic Library Project.   II. Nag Hammadi codices.
BT1391.A3   1988b   299'.932   88-45154
ISBN 0-06-066934-9

Composition by E. J. Brill, The Netherlands

TABLE OF CONTENTS

PREFACE

This volume is a thorough revision of *The Nag Hammadi Library in English*. The first edition, published in 1977, marked the end of one stage of Nag Hammadi scholarship and the beginning of another. The first stage was concerned with making this library of texts available; the second stage has been characterized by the discussion and interpretation of the texts.

The library of fourth-century papyrus manuscripts consists of twelve codices plus eight leaves from a thirteenth and contains fifty-two separate tractates. Due to duplications there are forty-five separate titles. Because the majority of the library's tractates derive from the Hellenistic sects now called gnostic, and survive in Coptic translations, it is characterized as the Coptic Gnostic Library. Scholarly rivalries and the situation in Egypt in the years following the library's discovery in 1945 hindered work on the manuscripts. Twenty years after the discovery only a small percentage of the texts had been edited and translated, mostly by European scholars, and less than ten percent had become available in English translations. In 1966 the team responsible for the present volume began to come together into "The Coptic Gnostic Library Project" under the auspices of the Institute for Antiquity and Christianity, Claremont, California.

The editing and translating of the library could only proceed as the manuscripts became accessible. In 1970 the Ministry of Culture of the Arab Republic of Egypt, together with UNESCO, named an International Committee for the Nag Hammadi Codices. The representative of the United States, James M. Robinson, was elected secretary. The primary task of the committee was to oversee the publication of photographic facsimiles. Between 1972 and 1977 the entire library was thus published by E.J. Brill of Leiden as *The Facsimile Edition of the Nag Hammadi Codices*. These were followed in 1979 with the publication of the *Cartonnage* volume and in 1984 with an *Introduction* volume, completing the twelve-volume *Facsimile Edition*. That edition was facilitated by members of The Coptic Gnostic Library Project working in the Coptic Museum in Old Cairo between 1971 and 1977 to reconstruct and conserve the manuscripts.

In 1977, coinciding with the availability of the library's complete contents in facsimile form, E.J. Brill and Harper & Row published the first edition of *The Nag Hammadi Library in English*. The one-volume English translation was brought out as the project was beginning to publish its major scholarly work, a complete critical edition, *The Coptic Gnostic Library*. This series of volumes contains the edited Coptic text with English translations, introductions, notes, and indices. It includes the entire Nag Hammadi library plus three similar manuscripts housed in Berlin, London, and Oxford. The volumes and the editors of *The Coptic Gnostic Library*, published by E.J. Brill, are as follows: *Nag Hammadi Codex I (The Jung Codex)*, Volume 1: *Introduction, Texts and Translation*; Volume 2: *Notes*, volume editor Harold W. Attridge, 1985; *Nag Hammadi Codices II,1 and IV,1: The Apocryphon of John, Long Recension*, edited by Frederik Wisse, forthcoming; *Nag Hammadi Codex II,2-7, together with XIII,2*, Brit. Lib. Or. 4926 (I) and P. Oxy. 1,654,655*, Volume I: *Gospel of Thomas, Gospel of Philip, Hypostasis of the Archons, Indexes*; Volume 2: *On the Origin of the World, Exegesis on the Soul, Book of Thomas, Indexes*, edited by Bentley Layton, in the press; *Nag Hammadi Codex III,1 and Papyrus Berolinensis 8502,2: The Apocryphon of John, Short Recension*, edited by Peter Nagel, volume editor Frederik Wisse, forthcoming; *Nag Hammadi Codices III,2 and IV,2: The Gospel of the Egyptians (The Holy Book of the Great Invisible Spirit)*, edited by Alexander Böhlig and Frederik Wisse in cooperation with Pahor Labib, 1975; *Nag Hammadi Codices III,3-4 and V,1 with Papyrus Berolinensis 8502,3 and Oxyrhynchus Papyrus 1081: Eugnostos and The Sophia of Jesus Christ*, edited and translated by Douglas M. Parrott, in the press; *Nag Hammadi Codex III,5: The Dialogue of the Savior*, volume editor Stephen Emmel, 1984; *Nag Hammadi Codices V,2-5 and VI with Papyrus Berolinensis 8502,1 and 4*, volume editor Douglas M. Parrott, 1979; *Nag Hammadi Codex VII*, volume editor Frederik Wisse, forthcoming; *Nag Hammadi Codex VIII*, volume editor John Sieber, forthcoming; *Nag Hammadi Codices IX and X*, volume editor Birger A. Pearson, 1981; *Nag Hammadi Codices XI, XII and XIII*, volume editor Charles W. Hedrick, in the press; *Nag Hammadi Codices: Greek and Coptic Papyri from the Cartonnage of the Covers*, edited by J.W.B. Barns †, G.M. Browne, and J.C. Shelton, 1981; *Pistis Sophia*, text edited by Carl Schmidt, translation and notes by Violet MacDermot, volume editor R. McL. Wilson, 1978; *The Books of Jeu and the Untitled Text in the Bruce Codex*, text edited by Carl Schmidt, translation and notes by Violet MacDermot, volume editor R. McL. Wilson, 1978.

In 1981 and 1984 respectively, Harper & Row and E.J. Brill published paperback editions of *The Nag Hammadi Library in English*. These included an addition to the translation of *The Dialogue of the Savior* based on fragments (144,15-146,24) discovered by Stephen Emmel in the Beinecke Library at Yale University.

At the time of the publication of *The Nag Hammadi Library in English* more than a decade ago, only one title in the Coptic Gnostic Library series had appeared in print. Now, with that series nearing completion, the present book has been extensively revised to bring the translations into conformity with the critical edition's final translations. In the case of the earlier volumes to appear, an occasional improvement on the critical edition has been made. Research in the field of Gnosticism, greatly stimulated by the work of The Coptic Gnostic Library Project, has also developed during the past ten years. New tractate introductions have been written to acknowledge the ongoing discussion. Since several titles appear in the library in more than one version, it has been possible to combine fragmentary versions of some texts to produce more complete translations. Two titles from the closely related Berlin Gnostic Papyrus are also included.

Since the original manuscripts of the library are fragmentary in many places, ellipsis dots (. . .) are included to indicate the place, but not the extent, of all lacunae. The page and line numbers of the papyrus codex, given in the translations, should indicate the extent of the damage. A complete portrayal of the physical condition of the manuscripts is given in *The Facsimile Edition* and in the critical edition, *The Coptic Gnostic Library*. The textual signs that appear in *The Nag Hammadi Library in English* are those found in the critical edition; the reader is referred to those volumes for more scholarly matters. An ongoing bibliography in the field of gnostic studies is provided by David M. Scholer, *Nag Hammadi Bibliography 1948-1969*, volume one of the series *Nag Hammadi Studies*, published by E.J. Brill in 1971, with annual updates in the journal *Novum Testamentum*. All these supplements are soon to be merged with each other and published in *Nag Hammadi Studies* in a volume entitled *Nag Hammadi Bibliography 1970-1985*. Two books recently published by Harper & Row present discussions of ancient Gnosticism and its modern scholarship: *Gnosis: The Nature and History of Gnosticism*, 1983, by Kurt Rudolph; and *The Jesus of Heresy and History: The Discovery and Meaning of the Nag Hammadi Gnostic Library*, 1988, by John Dart.

The Coptic Gnostic Library Project has been generously supported over the years by many organizations which we would like to thank: The

Egyptian Antiquities Organization, UNESCO, the American Research Center in Egypt, the National Endowment for the Humanities, the John Simon Guggenheim Memorial Foundation, the American Philosophical Society, the Smithsonian Institution, and The Claremont Graduate School. In final appreciation, it should be said that the preparation of this thoroughly revised new edition was rendered considerably easier by the work done in the preparation of the first edition by its Managing Editor, Marvin W. Meyer.

Richard Smith
Managing Editor

TABLE OF TRACTATES IN THE
COPTIC GNOSTIC LIBRARY

The following table lists, for the thirteen Nag Hammadi Codices and Papyrus Berolinensis 8502, the codex and tractate numbers, the tractate titles as used in this edition (the titles found in the tractates themselves, sometimes simplified and standardized, or, when the tractate bears no surviving title, one supplied by the editors), and the abbreviations of these titles.

References to the Nag Hammadi tractates, and to the texts in Berlin Gnostic Papyrus, are to page and line number, except for references to *The Gospel of Thomas*, which are to saying number.

TEXTUAL SIGNS

| Small strokes above the line indicate line divisions. Every fifth line a small number is inserted in place of a stroke; the frequency of these numbers, however, may vary in tractates which are quite fragmentary. A new page is indicated with a number in bold type. When the beginning of a new line or page coincides with the opening of a paragraph, the line divider or number is placed at the end of the previous paragraph.

[ ] Square brackets indicate a lacuna in the manuscript. When the text cannot be reconstructed, three dots are placed within the brackets, regardless of the size of the lacuna; a fourth dot, if appropriate, may function as a period. An exception to this rule is the occasional use of a different number of dots to estimate the extent of the missing portion of a proper noun. In a few instances the dots are used without brackets to indicate a series of Coptic letters which do not constitute a translatable sense unit. A bracket is not allowed to divide a word, except for a hyphenated word or a proper noun. Other words are placed entirely inside or outside the brackets, depending on the certainty of the Coptic word and the number of Coptic letters visible.

⟨ ⟩ Pointed brackets indicate a correction of a scribal omission or error. The translator has either inserted letters unintentionally omitted by the scribe, or replaced letters erroneously inserted with what the scribe presumably intended to write.

{ } Braces indicate superfluous letters or words added by the scribe.

( ) Parentheses indicate material supplied by the editor or translator. Although this material may not directly reflect the text being translated, it provides useful information for the reader.

INTRODUCTION

by

JAMES M. ROBINSON

1. The Stance of the Texts

The Nag Hammadi library is a collection of religious texts that vary widely from each other as to when, where, and by whom they were written. Even the points of view diverge to such an extent that the texts are not to be thought of as coming from one group or movement. Yet these diversified materials must have had something in common that caused them to be chosen by those who collected them. The collectors no doubt contributed to this unity by finding in the texts hidden meanings not fully intended by the original authors. After all, one of them, *The Gospel of Thomas*, begins with a word to the wise: "Whoever finds the interpretation of these sayings will not experience death." Thus the texts can be read at two levels: what the original author may have intended to communicate and what the texts may subsequently have been taken to communicate.

The focus that brought the collection together is an estrangement from the mass of humanity, an affinity to an ideal order that completely transcends life as we know it, and a life-style radically other than common practice. This life-style involved giving up all the goods that people usually desire and longing for an ultimate liberation. It is not an aggressive revolution that is intended, but rather a withdrawal from involvement in the contamination that destroys clarity of vision.

As such, the focus of this library has much in common with primitive Christianity, with eastern religion, and with "holy men" (and women) of all times, as well as with the more secular equivalents of today, such as the counter-culture movements coming from the 1960s. Disinterest in the goods of a consumer society, withdrawal into communes of the like-minded away from the bustle and clutter of big-city distraction, non-involvement in the compromises of political process, sharing an in-group's knowledge both of the disaster-course of the culture and of an ideal, radical alternative not commonly known — all this in modern garb is the real challenge rooted in such materials as the Nag Hammadi library.

To be sure, these roots, fascinating and provocative as they are, can also be confusing and even frustrating, not only for the person scarcely open to what they have to say, but also to the more attentive who seek to follow the light glimmering through the flow of language. For the point of the Nag Hammadi library has been battered and fragmented by the historical process through which it has finally come to light. A salvage operation is needed at many levels if that point is to be grasped clearly today. The ancient world's religious and philosophical traditions and mythology were all that was available to express what was in fact a quite untraditional stance. Indeed the stance was too radical to establish itself within the organized religions or philosophical schools of the day, and hence was hardly able to take advantage of the culture's educational institutions to develop and clarify its implications. Gnostic schools began to emerge within Christianity and Neoplatonism, until both agreed in excluding them as the "heresy" of Gnosticism. Thus meaningful and eloquent myths and philosophic formulations of that radical stance became in their turn garbled traditions, re-used by later and lesser authors whose watered-down, not to say muddied, version may be most of what has survived ... though there are several "classics" in the Nag Hammadi library.

The texts were translated one by one from Greek into Coptic, and not always by translators capable of grasping the profundity or sublimity of what they sought to translate. The translator of a brief section of Plato's *Republic* clearly did not understand the text, though it obviously seemed edifying and worth translating. Fortunately, most texts are better translated, but when there are duplications one can sense what a difference the better translation makes in comparison to the poor translation — which leads one to wonder about the bulk of the texts that exist only in a single version.

There is the same kind of hazard in the transmission of the texts by a series of scribes who copied them, generation after generation, from increasingly corrupt copies, first in Greek and then in Coptic. The number of unintentional errors is hard to estimate, since such a thing as a clean control copy does not exist; nor does one have, as in the case of the Bible, a quantity of manuscripts of the same text that tend to correct each other when compared. Only when the error can be detected as such in the sole copy we have can it be corrected. In addition there is the physical deterioration of the books themselves, which began no doubt before they were buried around 400 C.E., advanced steadily while they remained buried, and unfortunately was not completely halted in the period between their discovery in 1945 and their final conservation some thirty years later. When only a few letters are missing, they can often be filled in adequately, but larger holes must simply remain a blank.

The reader should not be misled by such impediments to understanding into thinking that the stance inherent in these essays is unworthy of serious consideration. Rather, we have to do here with an understanding of existence, an answer to the human dilemma, an attitude toward society, that is worthy of being taken quite seriously by anyone able and willing to grapple with such ultimate issues. This basic stance has until now been known almost exclusively through the myopic view of heresy-hunters, who often quote only to refute or ridicule. Thus the coming to light of the Nag Hammadi library gives unexpected access to the gnostic stance as Gnostics themselves presented it. It may provide new roots for the uprooted.

Those who collected this library were Christians, and many of the essays were originally composed by Christian authors. In a sense this should not be surprising, since primitive Christianity was itself a radical movement. Jesus called for a full reversal of values, advocating the end of the world as we have known it and its replacement by a quite new, utopian kind of life in which the ideal would be real. He took a stand quite independent of the authorities of his day . . . and did not last very long before they eliminated him. Yet his followers reaffirmed his stand – for them he came to personify the ultimate goal. Yet some of his circle, being a bit more practical, followed a more conventional way of life. The circle gradually became an established organization with a quite natural concern to maintain order, continuity, lines of authority, and stability. But this concern could encourage a commitment to the status quo, rivaling, and at times outweighing, the commitment to the ultimate goal far beyond any and every achievement. Those who cherished the radical dream, the ultimate hope, would tend to throw it up as an invidious comparison to what was achieved, and thus seem to be disloyal, and to pose a serious threat to the organization.

As the cultural situation changed with the passage of time and the shift of environments, the language for expressing such radical transcendence itself underwent change. The world of thought from which Jesus and his first followers had come was the popular piety of the Jewish synagogue, focused in terms of John the Baptist's rite of transition from the old regime to the new ideal world whose dramatic arrival was forthcoming. In this way of thinking, the evil system that prevails is not the way things inherently are. In principle, though not in practice, the world is good.

The evil that pervades history is a blight, ultimately alien to the world as such. But for some, the outlook on life increasingly darkened; the very origin of the world was attributed to a terrible fault, and evil was given status as the ultimate ruler of the world, not just a usurpation of authority. Hence the only hope seemed to reside in escape. Because humans, or at least some humans, are at heart not the product of such an absurd system, but by their very nature belong to the ultimate. Their plight is that they have been duped and lured into the trap of trying to be content in the impossible world, alienated from their true home. And for some, concentrated inwardness undistracted by external factors came to be the only way to attain the repose, the overview, the merger into the All which is the destiny of one's spark of the divine.

Christian Gnosticism thus emerged as a reaffirmation, though in somewhat different terms, of the original stance of transcendence central to the very beginnings of Christianity. Such Gnostic Christians surely considered themselves the faithful continuation, under changing circumstances, of that original stance which made Christians Christians. But the "somewhat different terms" "under changing circumstances" also involved real divergences, and other Christians clearly considered Gnosticism a betrayal of the original Christian position. This was the conviction of not just those who had accommodated themselves to the status quo, but no doubt also of some who retained the full force of the original protest and ultimate hope. The departure from the original language could be exploited to unite opposition across the breadth of the church. Thus Gnostics came to be excluded from the church as heretics.

In the New Testament two such Gnostic Christians are repudiated at the beginning of the second century (2 Timothy 2:16-18):

> Avoid empty and worldly chatter; those who indulge in it will stray further and further into godless courses, and the infection of their teaching will spread like a gangrene. Such are Hymenaeus and Philetus; they have shot wide of the truth in saying that our resurrection has already taken place, and are upsetting people's faith.

This view, that the Christian's resurrection has already taken place as a spiritual reality, is advocated in *The Treatise on the Resurrection*, *The Exegesis on the Soul*, and *The Gospel of Philip* in the Nag Hammadi library!

But the Nag Hammadi library also documents the fact that the rejection was mutual, in that Christians described there as "heretical" seem to be more like what is usually thought of as "orthodox." *The*

Apocalypse of Peter has Jesus criticize mainstream Christianity as follows:

> They will cleave to the name of a dead man, thinking that they will become pure. But they will become greatly defiled and they will fall into the name of error and into the hand of an evil, cunning man and a manifold dogma, and they will be ruled heretically. For some of them will blaspheme the truth and proclaim evil teaching. And they will say evil things against each other ... But many others, who oppose the truth and are the messengers of error, will set up their error and their law against these pure thoughts of mine, as looking out from one (perspective), thinking that good and evil are from one (source). They do business in my word ... And there shall be others of those who are outside our number who name themselves bishop and also deacons, as if they have received their authority from God. They bend themselves under the judgement of the leaders. These people are dry canals.

With the conversion of the Roman Empire to Christianity of the more conventional kind, the survival chances of Gnostic Christianity, such as that reflected in the Nag Hammadi library, were sharply reduced. The Bishop of Cyprus, Epiphanius, whose main work was a "medicine chest" against all heresies, describes his encounter with Gnosticism in Egypt about the same time the Nag Hammadi library was being collected:

> For I happened on this sect myself, beloved, and was actually taught these things in person, out of the mouths of practising Gnostics. Not only did women under this delusion offer me this line of talk, and divulge this sort of things to me. With impudent boldness moreover, they tried to seduce me themselves ... But the merciful God rescued me from their wickedness, and thus − after reading them and their books, understanding their true intent and not being carried away with them, and after escaping without taking the bait − I lost no time reporting them to the bishops there, and finding out which ones were hidden in the church. Thus they were expelled from the city, about eighty persons, and the city was cleared of their tarelike, thorny growth.

Gnosticism was ultimately eradicated from Christendom, except for occasional underground movements, some affinities in medieval mysticism, and an occasional tamed echo that stays just within the limits of propriety, for example within English romanticism:

> Our birth is but a sleep and a forgetting:
> The Soul that rises with us, our life's Star,
> Hath had elsewhere its setting
> And Cometh from afar.
> . . .
> The world is too much with us; late and soon,
> Getting and spending, we lay waste our powers.

Gnosticism of sorts was also able to continue beyond the frontiers of the Roman-Empire-become-Christendom. It is still extant in the war-torn area of Iraq and Iran in the form of a small sect called Mandeans, which is their word for "knowers," that is to say, "Gnostics."

This same withdrawal to inwardness or despair of the world from which the Gnostic stance emerged, swept not only through early Christianity to produce Christian Gnosticism, but also through late antiquity in general, thus producing forms of Gnosticism outside of Christianity. There is a long-standing debate among historians of religion as to whether Gnosticism is to be understood as only an inner-Christian development or as a movement broader than, and hence independent of, and perhaps even prior to Christianity. This debate seems to be resolving itself, on the basis of the Nag Hammadi library, in favor of understanding Gnosticism as a much broader phenomenon than the Christian Gnosticism documented by the heresiologists.

There is, to begin with, the question of Jewish Gnosticism. It would seem that there is considerable historical truth to the view of the heresiologists, to the effect that some Christian heresies go back to Jewish sects. After all, Christianity itself grew up within Judaism, and it would be surprising if it did not reflect various strands of the Judaism of the day. Primitive Christianity was itself not a unified movement. The Jewish Christianity of the first generation in Galilee that developed the collection of sayings imbedded in the Gospels of Matthew and Luke may well have been considered heretical even by Paul and the Hellenists, and the feeling may have been mutual. Paul clearly rejected as heretical the Christian "Judaizers." Then later in the first century all the various strands of Jewish Christianity were excluded from Judaism, as "normative" Judaism emerged in response to the threat to Jewish identity posed by the destruction of Jerusalem in 70 C.E.

Some of the gnostic essays in the Nag Hammadi library do not seem to reflect Christian tradition, but do build upon the Old Testament, which was of course also the Jewish Bible. But the very idea of Jewish Gnosticism is at times rejected as a contradiction in terms. How could Jews designate their God as the malevolent force whose misguided blunder produced the world, a God who was ignorant of the hidden good God beyond? Since Christians worship the same God as do Jews, this argument could also be made against the very idea of Christian Gnosticism. But since the early Christian heresy-hunters clearly identified Gnostics as Christians, though of course heretical Christians, the concept of Christian Gnosticism is firmly established. To use another analogy, Simon Magus, one of the earliest known Gnostics, was from Samaria, although the Samaritans worshipped in their own way the same God as did the Jews and Christians. Hence the concept of Jewish Gnostics is intelligible, even if, from a given normative point of view, the validity of using the word Jewish, Christian, or Samaritan for such a person or text may be contested. Of course we do not actually know the Gnostics who built upon Jewish or Old Testament traditions, other than through the texts containing such traditions, so that all one really has in view in speaking of Jewish Gnosticism is just Jewish cultural traditions lacking visible Christian overlay, without necessarily any further identification of the bearers of these traditions.

The discovery of the Dead Sea Scrolls has already drawn attention to the fact that first-century Judaism was quite pluralistic in its theological positions, and contained a number of divergent groups or sects. The Essenes, prior to the discovery of the Dead Sea Scrolls, were in a situation much like the Gnostics prior to the discovery of the Nag Hammadi library: they too were a movement about which too little was known to be treated with the seriousness it deserved. Now we know that the Essenes were a Jewish sect that had broken with the official Judaism of the Jerusalem temple and had withdrawn to the desert at the Wadi Qumran. They understood their situation in terms of the antithesis of light and darkness, truth and lie, a dualism that ultimately went back to Persian dualism – and then moved forward toward Gnosticism. The history of Gnosticism, as documented in the Nag Hammadi library, takes up about where the history of the Essenes, as documented by the Dead Sea Scrolls, breaks off. Later Jewish mystical traditions, traced especially by Gershom Scholem, have shown that, inconsistent though it seems, gnostic trends have continued to carry on a clandestine existence within the context of normative Judaism.

Some traits previously thought to be characteristic of Christian Gnosticism have been shown by the Nag Hammadi library to be originally non-Christian, though a Jewish ingredient is unmistakable. Irenaeus presents Barbelo as the leading mythological figure of a Christian Gnostic group designated "Barbelo-Gnostics." But *The Three Steles of Seth* is a Gnostic text without Christian ingredients that nonetheless gives Barbelo a prominent position. Hippolytus cites a "Paraphrase of Seth" as a Christian Gnostic text. But a very similar Nag Hammadi text, *The Paraphrase of Shem*, lacks a Christian ingredient. It is understandable that Christian heresiologists were primarily concerned to refute the Christian form of gnostic texts and movements. But this should not be taken to indicate that the Christian form is the original form, especially when the Nag Hammadi discovery gives documentation of a non-Christian form.

Another instance, though in this case not necessarily gnostic, is the mythological birth narrative in Revelation 12, which commentators have had the greatest difficulty in deriving from any version of the birth stories about Jesus. But *The Apocalypse of Adam* has a series of non-Christian narrations of the coming of the savior that have much the same outline, and thus show a shared mythological background that is not Christian.

It is especially the Sethian texts in the Nag Hammadi library that as a group attest a non-Christian Gnosticism that had not been previously documented so clearly. The Sethian corpus spans the transition from non-Christian to Christianized Gnosticism, as has been summarized by the leading expert on Sethianism as follows: "Most writings of our text group contain no Christian elements at all (*The Three Steles of Seth, Allogenes, Marsanes, The Thought of Norea*); others contain barely Christian motifs (*Zostrianus, The Apocalypse of Adam*) or display only here and there a Christian veneer (*Trimorphic Protennoia, The Gospel of the Egyptians*); while only a few (*The Hypostasis of the Archons, Melchizedek, The Apocryphon of John*) come near to being what is called Christian Gnosis."

In none of these Sethian instances can one derive the texts or their mythology primarily from Christian tradition. For the Christian ingredient seems so external to the main thrust of the text that one is inclined to think it was added by a Christian editor, translator, or scribe to what had been originally composed as a non-Christian text, even though the purely non-Christian form is no longer extant. For example, the *Trimorphic Protennoia*, where a secondary Christianizing has taken place, has nonetheless its roots in the same Jewish wisdom speculation as does the Prologue of the Gospel of John. It is also part of this Christianizing trend when "the Holy Book of the Great Invisible Spirit" is given by some scribe the secondary title "The Gospel of the Egyptians." Thus one concludes that though the Sethian corpus was obviously usable by Christians (as were other non-Christian texts such as the Old Testament), it derives from non-Christian "Jewish" Gnosticism.

The Nag Hammadi library even presents one instance of the Christianizing process taking place almost before one's eyes. The non-Christian philosophic treatise *Eugnostos the Blessed* is cut up somewhat arbitrarily into separate speeches, which are then put on Jesus' tongue, in answer to questions (which sometimes do not quite fit the answers) that the disciples address to him during a resurrection appearance. The result is a separate tractate entitled *The Sophia of Jesus Christ*. Both forms of the text occur side by side in Codex III.

Some of the Nag Hammadi texts, and again often the Sethian traditions, seem to have appropriated a philosophic and Neoplatonic orientation. Plotinus, the leading Neoplatonist of the third century C.E., does in fact refer to Gnostics within his school: "We feel a certain regard for some of our friends who happened upon this way of thinking before they became our friends, and, though I do not know how they manage it, continue in it." But the school turned against Gnosticism, as Plotinus' polemics indicate. His pupil Porphyry reports in his *Life of Plotinus*:

> There were in his time many Christians and others, and sectarians who had abandoned the old philosophy, men ... who ... produced revelations by Zoroaster and Zostrianos and Nicotheus and Allogenes and Messos and other people of the kind, themselves deceived and deceiving many, alleging that Plato had not penetrated to the depths of intelligible reality. Plotinus hence often attacked their position in his lectures, and wrote the treatise to which we had given the title "Against the Gnostics"; he left it to us to assess what he passed over. Amelius went to forty volumes in writing against the book of Zostrianos.

The Nag Hammadi library contains treatises with two such titles, *Zostrianos* and *Allogenes*, which hence may well be those refuted by Amelius and other Neoplatonists. And such Nag Hammadi texts as the *Trimorphic Protennoia* and *Marsanes* are quite similar in philosophic orientation. Plotinus' own attack on gnostic "magic chants" addressed to the "higher powers" may have in view hymnic texts like *The Three Steles of Seth*. Thus the Nag Hammadi library makes an important contribution not only to the history of religion, but also to the history of philosophy.

The Nag Hammadi library also includes material drawing upon other religious traditions than the Judeo-Christian heritage. There are, for example, Hermetic texts that build on Egyptian lore. Typically they present dialogues of initiation between the deities Hermes Trismegistus and his son Tat. *The Discourse on the Eighth and Ninth* in the Nag Hammadi library is such a previously unknown Hermetic text. And, whereas one could debate whether a good number of texts in the library are actually gnostic or not, depending on how one defines Gnosticism and interprets texts, a few, such as *The Sentences of Sextus*, clearly are not gnostic. But, just as a gnostic interpretation of the Bible became possible, one may assume that these moralistic maxims could also be fitted into a gnostic orientation.

Since the Nag Hammadi library seems to have been collected in terms of Christian Gnosticism, it is sometimes difficult to conceive of some of the texts, such as the Hermetic ones, being used by persons who thought of themselves as Christian. One text even claims a Zoroastrian heritage, in that it is ascribed to his grandfather (or, possibly, uncle) Zostrianos and in a cryptogram even mentions Zoroaster. Yet Gnostics were more ecumenical and syncretic with regard to religious traditions than were orthodox Christians, so long as they found in them a stance congenial to their own. If they could identify Seth with Jesus, they probably could produce Christianizing interpretations of Hermes and Zoroaster as well.

Thus Gnosticism seems not to have been in its essence just an alternate form of Christianity. Rather it was a radical trend of release from the dominion of evil or of inner transcendence that swept through late antiquity and emerged within Christianity, Judaism, Neoplatonism, Hermetism, and the like. As a new religion it was syncretistic, drawing upon various religious heritages. But it was held together by a very decided stance, which is where the unity amid the wide diversity is to be sought.

2. The Manuscripts

The Nag Hammadi library is important for the content of the many lost Greek works it has preserved in Coptic translation. It also sheds significant light upon the production of the Coptic books themselves, and hence upon those who copied, read, and buried them.

The Nag Hammadi library consists of twelve books, plus eight leaves removed from a thirteenth book in late antiquity and tucked inside the front cover of the sixth. These eight leaves comprise a complete text, an independent treatise taken out of a book of collected essays. In fact, each of the books, except the tenth, consists of a collection of relatively brief works. Thus there is a total of fifty-two tractates. Since a single book usually contains several tractates, one may suspect that, like the books of the Bible, the texts were composed with a small format in mind, but that a larger format had come into use by the time these extant copies were made. This can be explained in terms of the history of the manufacture of books.

The roll was the usual form of a book up until the first centuries C.E., when it began to be replaced by a more economical format that permitted writing on both sides, namely the modern book with individual leaves. Technically speaking, a book in the firm of a roll is a "scroll" or "volume" (from the Latin verb meaning "to roll"). But a book in the form of a modern book is a "codex" (plural: "codices"), the Latin word for a set of wooden waxed tablets tied together as a scratch pad, which was the ancestor of the book with papyrus, parchment, or paper leaves. Whereas literary works continued to be written in the more prestigious form of the scroll, Christians (but not Jews) soon came to prefer the more economical codex. The codex was also more practical than the scroll, as anyone who has worked with microfilm knows. The inconvenience and wear-and-tear of unrolling and then rerolling the scroll every time one wanted to resume reading or look up a reference led to the replacement of the scroll with the codex, just as today there is a trend away from rolls of microfilm and toward microfiche.

In Egypt the most common writing material was papyrus. The triangular stalk of the papyrus plant is filled with fibrous pith that can be cut or peeled off in long thin strips. These strips are laid side by side and then a second layer is placed at right angles on top. When this is pressed, dried, and polished it becomes a flexible, smooth, and durable writing surface. Whereas these papyrus sheets were usually only about twenty centimeters long, those used in the Nag Hammadi library were often over a meter in length. Since this was a technological feat for that time, it indicated the importance of the books for those who made them.

A series of such papyrus writing surfaces was placed side by side so as to overlap a couple of centimeters where they were pasted together. The result was a papyrus roll, often about three meters long. Sheets ranging in breadth from twenty to forty centimeters would be cut from such rolls, from the right end of the roll to the left. Enough rolls would be thus cut up to produce a stack of from twenty to forty sheets, which, when folded down the middle, formed the quire of a codex. The fact that from two to six rolls were used to manufacture a single codex helps to explain the fact that a codex could contain more than one text, if each text had originally been composed with the size of the roll in view.

Since each strip of papyrus has a fiber pattern as distinctive as a fingerprint, the more fragmentary books in the Nag Hammadi library were reassembled by locating the position of the fibers of a fragment or a leaf on the original papyrus sheet that had been made from the papyrus strips. Then its position within the roll and ultimately within the codex could be calculated.

The Coptic Museum in Cairo, where the Nag Hammadi library is kept, has assigned a number to each book. At the time this was done, the numeration was thought to be the order in which they would be published, which in turn reflected a value judgment in terms of their importance and state of preservation. Only the very fragmentary fourth book is an exception to this tendency — it was given its relatively high position because the two tractates it contains are duplicates of tractates in the third book. For convenience of reference the tractates are numbered consecutively in each book. Although the numeration systems used for the books, tractates, and even pages have varied widely over the past generation, the numeration used here is that of the Coptic Museum and of *The Facsimile Edition of the Nag Hammadi Codices* and hence should supersede older numerations.

Of the fifty-two tractates, six that are duplicates (III,*1*; IV,*1* and *2*; V,*1*; XII,*2*; and XIII,*2*) are not included in the present work since there is a better copy that is included. Six more were already extant when the Nag Hammadi library was discovered, either in the original Greek (VI,*5* and *7*, and XII,*1*), or in translation, in Latin (VI,*8*) or Coptic (II,*1* and III,*4*). The two in Coptic are from a papyrus codex, now in Berlin, called BG 8502, which to this extent is a codex similar to the Nag Hammadi library. For this reason the other two tractates it contains are included at the end of the present work. To get an impression of the amount of literature that has survived only in the Nag Hammadi library, one may subtract the total of twelve duplications inside or outside the Nag Hammadi library and thus reach the figure of forty newly recovered texts. To be sure, a few fragments existed of three of these, one in Greek (II,*2*) and two in Coptic (II,*5* and VII,*4*), but they had not been identified as such until the complete text became available in the Nag Hammadi library. Now that the whole library is accessible, fragments of still others may be identified. But such vestiges of a tractate are more tantalizing than useful. Hence a more serious limitation on the figure of forty new texts is the fact that some of these are themselves quite fragmentary (VIII,*1*; IX,*1*, *2*, and *3*; XI,*1*, *2*, *3*, and *4*; and XII,*3*). It would be safe to think of the Nag Hammadi library as adding to the amount of literature that has survived from antiquity thirty fairly complete texts, and ten that are more fragmentary.

Although the Nag Hammadi library is in Coptic, the texts were originally composed in Greek. Hence the fact that they were discovered in Upper Egypt may be misleading. Some of course have been composed in Egypt, for several contain specific allusions to Egypt: *Asclepius* calls Egypt the "image of heaven"; *On the Origin of the World* appeals to "the water hydri in Egypt" and "the two bulls in Egypt" as witnesses; and *The Discourse on the Eighth and Ninth* instructs the son to "write this book for the temple at Diospolis (Magna near Luxor or Parva near

Nag Hammadi) in hieroglyphic characters." Yet the Greek-writing authors may have been located anywhere in the ancient world where Greek was used, such as Greece itself (VI,5), or Syria (II,2), or Jordan (V,5). Much the same is the case with the Bible and other ancient texts written in various parts of the ancient world and preserved in the "dry sands of Egypt." Thus the Nag Hammadi library involves the collecting of what was originally a Greek literary productivity by largely unrelated and anonymous authors spread through the eastern half of the ancient world and covering a period of almost half a millennium (or more, if one takes into consideration a brief section of Plato's *Republic*, VI,5).

Almost nothing is known about the different persons who translated the tractates into Coptic, or those who copied, used, and buried them, other than what may be inferred from the books themselves. The Egyptian reading public in this period was largely familiar with Greek, and hence Greek literature was imported and copied extensively. A Roman garrison town, Diospolis Parva, with Greek-speaking Galatian troops from Asia Minor, was just across the Nile from the site where the Nag Hammadi library was buried. A Greek inscription reading "In behalf of the [good] fortune of Emperor [Caesar] Trajan Hadrian [Augustus]" has been found at Chenoboskia, on the right bank of the Nile in sight of the place of the burial. Greek prayers to Zeus Sarapis mentioning Antioch are found in two caves in the cliff near where the books were buried. But, more and more, Greek texts such as the Bible and the Nag Hammadi library were translated into the native Egyptian language. This can be illustrated for the region in which the library was produced, read, and buried, and for approximately the same period of time, from *The Life of St. Pachomius*. This text, which itself exists in both Greek and Coptic, tells that a Greek-speaking monk from Alexandria came to Pachomius, who "made him live in the same dwelling with an old brother who knew the Greek language," while he learned the native tongue. Meanwhile Pachomius "made every effort to learn Greek by the grace of God in order to discover the way of offering him solace frequently. Then Pachomius appointed him house manager of the Alexandrian and other foreign brothers who came after him."

When the Egyptian language is written with the Greek alphabet (plus a few letters for sounds Greeks did not make), it is called Coptic. The Nag Hammadi library is written in two Coptic dialects. Even among the texts translated into the same dialect, minor divergences point to a plurality of translators, who do not correspond to the plurality of scribes responsible for surviving copies. In the case of duplicates, different translators were involved, working from divergent Greek texts. The translation process may have been spread over a wide area of Egypt, and more than a single century.

Each codex was bound in leather. The outline of the desired book size was often scored onto the leather, whereupon the flesh side of the outlined area was lined with used papyrus pasted into thick cardboards called cartonnage, producing a hardback effect. This used papyrus consisted of Greek and Coptic letters and business documents, and has produced names of persons and places as well as dates that help to determine the time and place of the manufacture of the covers. After a cover was thus lined with cartonnage, a strip of the cover was turned in at the head and foot of the front and back cover and at the fore edge of the back cover. Since the line of the animal's spine usually ran horizontally across the cover, the narrowing of the skin leading to the animal's tail could be retained to form a flap extending from the fore edge of the front cover. To this was added a thong to encircle horizontally the closed book. This may have been a practice taken over from the manufacture of a papyrus scroll, where a parchment wrapper and thong were traditionally used to protect it and hold it closed. A thong was also needed to hold a codex closed. Each of the Nag Hammadi books has a single quire, that is to say, a single stack of sheets folded down the center to produce the writing surfaces (although in Codex I the main quire is supplemented with two smaller quires). Such large quires would tend to gape at the fore edge unless securely tied. Shorter thongs extending from the head and foot of the front and back covers were tied together to aid in holding the codex closed.

Two of the covers (IV and VIII) lack a flap on the fore edge of the front cover, though they do have the usual thong. A third cover of a similar construction (V) has such a flap added to the fore edge of the front cover. These three books thus seem to have been made from smaller skins, and the poor quality of the papyrus used for their quires confirms the impression of economy. Other covers include a leather reinforcement (called by bookbinders a "mull") that lines the spine and protects the cover and the quire from the pressure of the binding thongs that run through the fold at the center of the quire, as well as two horizontal supportive thongs lying between the cover and the mull. Three covers have such a construction (VI, IX, and X). They form a second group among the covers, together with another similarly constructed cover (II), which however is now lacking whatever lining it may have had. This group is characterized both by such advances in technique as have just been mentioned and by a higher aesthetic quality. Indeed, the cover of Codex II has rather beautiful tinted tooling. The four other covers (I, III, VII, XI) do not share distinctive traits, except for a certain primitiveness, which would make it possible to assign them to a group.

The scribes involved in producing the thirteen codices can be distinguished by their handwriting. There seem to be few clear instances of a single scribe working on more than one codex: One scribe copied most of Codex I, but a second scribe copied tractate 4 of Codex I; this second scribe also copied tractates 1 and 2 of Codex XI. A third scribe copied in a different dialect tractates 3 and 4 of Codex XI and also Codex VII. Thus three of the four books that seem unrelated to each other in terms of the way the covers were made do seem interrelated in terms of the scribes who wrote them. Conversely it was earlier thought that one scribe copied Codices IV, V, VI, VIII and IX, which would mean that the two groups distinguished in terms of leather covers must have been related by scribal hand. But more recent study of the hands has indicated that one has to do with different, even if similar, hands, that diverge most clearly just where the bookbinding divergences take place, thereby belatedly confirming, rather than relativizing, the distinction into groups based initially only on the leather covers.

The two groups of covers plus four miscellaneous covers, and the one group of scribal hands plus miscellaneous scribes, may indicate that the Nag Hammadi library is a secondary merging of what was originally a series of smaller libraries or isolated books. This would seem to be confirmed by the distribution of the duplicates. No one codex contains two copies of the same work, nor is there a duplicate tractate among the books of one group of covers. Nor did the same scribe, with but one exception, copy the same text twice. The one exception would seem to be II,*4* and XIII,*2*, which are the same text in the same scribal hand and with almost identical wording. Yet the second copy was discarded, when Codex XIII was torn apart and only one tractate (XIII,*1*) preserved inside the front cover of Codex VI — together with a few opening lines of XIII,*2* on the back of the last leaf, which could not be discarded without mutilating the text one was seeking to preserve (XIII,*1*). The fact that this scribal duplication was nullified by separating off XIII,*2* (except for the unavoidable opening lines) may attest to what seems to have been an awareness of the unnecessariness of such duplication. A scribal note in Codex VI expresses concern not to displease whoever commissioned the work by duplicating something already owned. Hence when duplication does turn up in terms of the whole library, one is inclined to think the books with the duplication were not produced with the whole library of thirteen books in view. Both the tractates in Codex IV are also in Codex III, so that Codex IV is wholly superfluous in the present library. And there is a total of three copies of the *Apocryphon of John* (II,*1*; III,*1*; and IV,*1*), one from each of the three classifications of covers. Thus one may conjecture that the present library derives from at least three smaller collections.

The dating of Coptic literary hands, such as those attested in the texts before us, is much less certain than is the dating of Greek literary hands, or the dating of the cursive business hands of the day. A thorough study of the hands of the Nag Hammadi library has not yet been made, although dates ranging at least from early to late fourth century C.E. have been proposed. The texts themselves do not normally contain dates or datable historical references. But *The Concept of Our Great Power* may provide one reference that can serve as a point of departure for dating Codex VI: "Cease from the evil lusts and desires and (the teachings of) the Anomoeans, evil heresies that have no basis!" While the Archbishop of Alexandria, Athanasius, was in hiding in the Pachomian monasteries in the late 350s C.E., "Anomoean" heretics were flourishing for a brief period in Alexandria. Probably this text received its final form no earlier than at this time.

The papyrus used for letters and business documents and reused to thicken the leather covers may be located in time and space with more ease than can the leaves that comprise the quires bound with the help of these covers. Dates found in such "cartonnage" of Codex VII are 341, 346, and 348 C.E. This indicates that the cover of Codex VII was manufactured no earlier than the latest date, but perhaps as much as a generation after these dates. A document found in the cartonnage of Codex I mentions "Diospol[is] near Chenobos[kia]." Other locations in the same general region also occur in the cartonnage of the other covers. Some of the cartonnage in the cover of Codex VII seems to have belonged to a monk named Sansnos who was in charge of the cattle of a monastery, which would no doubt account for his close relationship to the manufacture of the leather covers. The headquarters of the monastery of the Pachomian order at Pabau, where the Basilica of Saint Pachomius was located, as well as the third Pachomian monastery at Chenoboskia, where Pachomius himself began his Christian life as a hermit, are only 8.7 and 5.3 kilometers (5.4 and 3.3 miles) respectively from the place where the library was buried. Thus the provenience of the Nag Hammadi codices has often been identified with the Pachomian Monastic Order, which among other things involved a large-scale literary program at the appropriate time and place of the production of the Nag Hammadi codices. But the publication of this cartonnage in 1981 involved a critical sifting of the evidence, which proved to be less conclusive than had been previously maintained. The relation of the Nag Hammadi codices to the Pachomian movement remains a tantalizing possibility, more concrete than any other that has been suggested, and yet far from assured.

In view of the orthodoxy of the Pachomian monasteries reflected in *The Life of St. Pachomius* and other monastic legends, some have hesitated to associate the Nag Hammadi library with these monasteries, unless it be that such texts were copied for ready reference in refuting heresy. But a defender of Christian orthodoxy would hardly bother to collect the non-Christian texts that are in the Nag Hammadi library. And some of the Christian texts are not explicitly "heretical" and hence would hardly have been included in such a backlist. The very fact that the library seems to have been made up by combining several smaller collections tends to point toward individual Christian Gnostics or monasteries producing individual books or small collections for their own spiritual enlightenment, rather than to a heresy-hunting scribal campaign. Since the familiar heresy-hunting literature is in Greek, one should hesitate to postulate such a widespread heresy-hunting activity in Coptic. And the Pachomian literature transmitted through monastic channels is much more pedestrian.

Of course it is conceivable that book manufacture could have been one of the handicrafts common in monasteries to produce commodities to trade or sell for the necessities of life. Hence one could conjecture that uninscribed books were produced in the monastery and sold to Gnostics (or anyone else) to inscribe as they saw fit. But there is some evidence from that period that books were first inscribed and then bound, as when a line of writing passes through the fold at the spine. And in the Nag Hammadi library blotting is usually present on the first and last pages but not elsewhere, which may perhaps be explained as due to the dampness of the paste in the cartonnage at the time of the binding, in which case the quire would have had to have been inscribed before being bound.

The care and religious devotion reflected in the manufacture of the Nag Hammadi library hardly suggest that the books were produced out of antagonism or even disinterest in their contents, but rather reflect the veneration accorded to holy texts. The leather covers are not very ornate, compared, for example, with reports that Manichaean books were studded with jewels (though the very plain extant wooden covers of the Manichaean codices of Medinet Madi are even simpler than the Nag Hammadi covers). Yet simplicity would be appropriate to the Pachomian monasteries. *The Life of St. Pachomius* reports: "He also taught the brothers to pay no attention to the loveliness and beauty of this world, whether it be beautiful food or clothing, or a cell, or an outwardly seductive book." The simple tooling of some of the leather covers does include crosses (II, IV, VIII). The *ankh* hieroglyph of life that became the Christian cross *ansata* is on the beautifully tooled cover of Codex II and at the end of *The Prayer of the Apostle Paul*. The acrostic "fish" symbol standing for the creed "Jesus Christ, Son of God, Savior" occurs in two scribal notes (in codices III and VII). In the first case the name of the scribe is preserved in the comment "in the flesh my name is Gongessos," which is probably the Latin name Concessus. He also had a spiritual name or title of Eugnostos. Thus he had some spiritual status, and referred to his "fellow lights in incorruptibility." Within this spiritual circle he described the text as "God-written." Even if such a scribal note was not composed by the scribe who copied the codex that has survived, but rather came from an earlier scribe who wrote an ancestor of the copy that survived, nevertheless the scribe of Codex III did not feel called upon to eliminate it, much less to replace it with a warning against heresy in the text. Some scribal notes, however, since they were written at the end of an extant codex, may be assumed to have been composed by the scribe of that particular codex. They reflect the godliness the scribe found in what he or she was copying. Codex II concludes with this note: "Remember me also, my brethren, [in] your prayers: Peace to the saints and those who are spiritual." Codex VII ends on a similar note: "The book belongs to the fatherhood. It is the son who wrote it. Bless me, O father. I bless you, O father, in peace. Amen." These scribal notes, together with the scribe's care to correct errors, tend to indicate that the scribes were of a religious persuasion congenial to the contents they were copying.

Perhaps the common presentation of the monastic movement of the fourth century C.E. as solidly orthodox is an anachronism, and more nearly reflects the situation of the later monasticism that recorded the legends about the earlier period. When a hermit withdrew from civilization into the desert, he also tended to be out of contact with the Church, for example with its fellowship, sacraments, and authority. Early in the fourth century there was a monk in the delta named Hierakas, a scribe by trade and a learned interpreter of the Bible, who was so ascetic in his views as to argue that marriage was limited to the old covenant, for no married person "can inherit the kingdom of heaven." Although this led to him being classified as a heretic, it did not prevent him from having a following. *The Testimony of Truth* in the Nag Hammadi library represents a similar view:

> For no one who is under the law will be able to look up to the truth, for they will not be able to serve two masters. For the defilement of the Law is manifest; but undefilement belongs to the light. The Law commands (one) to take a husband (or) to take a wife, and to beget, and to multiply like the sand of the sea. But passion which is a delight to them constrains the souls of those who are begotten in this place, those who defile and those who are defiled, in order that the Law might be fulfilled through them. And they show that they are assisting the world; and they [turn] away from the light, who are unable [to pass by] the archon of [darkness] until they pay the last [penny].

The Life of St. Pachomius narrates that a "philosopher" from Panopolis (Akhmim), where Pachomius built a monastery just 108 kilometers (67 miles) downstream from where the Nag Hammadi library was buried, came to test the monk's "understanding of the scriptures." Pachomius sent his assistant Theodore to meet him:

> The philosopher queried him on something for which the answer was not difficult to find, "Who was not born but died? Who was born but did not die? And who died without giving off the stench of decomposition?" Theodore replied that Adam was not born but died, Enoch was born but did not die, and Lot's wife died but, having become a pillar of salt, did not give off the stench of decomposition. The philosopher accepted these answers and departed.

This may well be a faint echo of Pachomian debates with Christian Gnostics before the middle of the fourth century C.E. Epiphanius' efforts to run Christian Gnostics out of town took place in Egypt about the same time.

In 367 C.E. Archbishop Athanasius wrote an Easter letter that condemns heretics and their "apocryphal books to which they attribute antiquity and give the name of saints." Theodore, by then head of the Pachomian monasteries, had the letter translated into Coptic, and "deposited it in the monastery to serve them as a rule." There must still have been heretics or heretical books influencing the Pachomian monastic movement which made this act necessary. Of course many of the Nag Hammadi texts are indeed pseudonymous, that is to say, ascribed in their titles to some "saint" of the past. In another of the Pachomian legends one of "these books that the heretics write" but "give out under the name of saints" is quoted: "After Eve was deceived and had eaten the fruit of the tree, it is of the devil that she bore Cain." *The Hypostasis of the Archons* in the Nag Hammadi library has a narrative that points in this direction:

> Then the authorities came to their Adam. And when they saw his female counterpart speaking with him, they became agitated with great agitation; and they became enamored of her. They said to one another, "Come let us sow our seed in her," and they pursued her. And she laughed at them for their witlessness and their blindness; and in their clutches, she became a tree, and left them her shadowy reflection resembling herself; and they defiled [it] foully. – And they defiled the stamp of her voice, so that by the form they had modelled, together with [their] (own) image, they made themselves liable to condemnation.

Early in the fifth century C.E. Shenoute, Abbot of the White Monastery at the same Panopolis where Pachomius had founded monasteries and from which the "philosopher" had come, attacked a group at the nearby temple of Pneueit that called itself "kingless," worshipped the "demiurge," and would not accept Cyril, Archbishop of Alexandria, as their "illuminator." These terms, which Shenoute seems to borrow from the group, are so well-known in the Nag Hammadi library that it may have been a Christian Gnostic, perhaps a Sethian group, even though in his polemic Shenoute calls them pagan heretics. He seized their "books full of abomination" and "of every kind of magic." Indeed, series of vowels and unintelligible magic words (Plotinus called it "hissing") occur in the Nag Hammadi library itself. Actually Pachomius himself wrote to the heads of his monasteries using a code that even his successors could not decipher! Hence the Nag Hammadi library and Pachomius' "books of spiritual letters" may not have been entirely different in appearance from what Shenoute would call a book of magic. Shenoute threatened the heretics: "I shall make you acknowledge ... the Archbishop Cyril, or else the sword will wipe out most of you, and moreover those of you who are spared will go into exile." Just as the Dead Sea Scrolls were put in jars for safekeeping and hidden at the time of the approach of the Roman Tenth Legion, the burial of the Nag Hammadi library in a jar may also have been precipitated by the approach of Roman authorities, who by then had become Christian.

The fact that the Nag Hammadi library was hidden in a jar suggests the intention not to eliminate but to preserve the books. For not only were the Dead Sea Scrolls put in such jars for safekeeping, but biblical manuscripts have been found similarly preserved up and down the Nile, in some cases dating from the same period and buried in the Nag Hammadi region.

In fact, a second discovery, made in 1952, of manuscripts buried in a jar a couple of centuries later than the Nag Hammadi codices, is much more certainly the remains of a library of the Pachomian monastic order than is the Nag Hammadi discovery. For this discovery included archival copies of formal letters of abbots of the Pachomian Order. And the rest of the holdings are also what one would expect of a Pachomian library: biblical, apocryphal, martyriological, and other edifying material. To be sure, there are also some Greek (and Latin) classical texts, whose presence may be explained by the assumption that persons who joined the Pachomian movement gave their worldly possessions to the Order, which would thus have acquired non-Christian texts. Later they would have been taken to be venerable texts like the others in the archives, fragile and fragmentary relics to be preserved and no longer texts to be read.

This second discovery is known locally as the Dishnā Papers, since Dishnā near the river and railroad is the large town through which the texts were marketed. But the site of the discovery was at the foot of the Jabal Abū Manāʿ, 5.5 km (3.4 miles) northwest of Dishna, and, more significant, 5 km (3.1 miles) northeast of the headquarters of the Pachomian Order and 12 km (7.5 miles) east of the site of the discovery of the Nag Hammadi codices. This manuscript discovery has been known for the past generation in scholarly circles as the Bodmer Papyri, since the largest part of it was acquired by the Bibliothèque Bodmer near Geneva. But it is only recently, in the process of tracking down the provenience of the Nag Hammadi codices, that the provenience of the Bodmer Papyri has been identified beyond the reports of the antiquities dealers and made public to the scholarly world.

The Bible refers to burial in a jar as a way to preserve a book and to burning as the way to eliminate one (Jer 32:14-15; 36:23). *The Life of St. Pachomius* reports that he got rid of a book by Origen, whom he considered a heretic, by throwing it in the water, with the comment that if the Lord's name had not been in it he would have burned it. The burning of the greatest library in antiquity at Alexandria by Christians late in the fourth century C.E. suggests that such a ready solution would hardly have been overlooked if the intent had been to get rid of the Nag Hammadi library. If the codices had been part of a Pachomian library, they must have been removed not by heresy-hunters, but by devotees who cherished them enough to bury them in a jar for safekeeping, perhaps for posterity.

Two of the texts in the Nag Hammadi library refer to their being stored for safekeeping in a mountain until the end of time. *The Gospel of the Egyptians* concludes:

The Great Seth wrote this book with letters in one hundred and thirty years. He placed it in the mountain that is called Charaxio, in order that, at the end of the times and the eras, ... it may come forth and reveal this incorruptible, holy race of the great savior, and those who dwell with them in love, and the great, invisible, eternal Spirit, and his only begotten Son ...

Near the end of *Allogenes* a similar idea occurs:

Write down [the things that I] shall [tell] you and of which I shall remind you for the sake of those who will be worthy after you. And you will leave this book upon a mountain and you will adjure the guardian, "Come Dreadful One."

On each side of the Nile Valley cliffs rise abruptly to the desert above. The section of the cliff on the right bank marking the limit of the Nile Valley and the arable land between Chenoboskia and Pabau is called the Jabal al-Ṭārif. A protruding boulder shaped somewhat like a stalagmite had broken off in prehistoric times from the face of the cliff and fallen down onto the talus (the inclined plane of fallen rock that over the ages naturally collects like a buttress at the foot of a cliff). Under the northern flank of one of the huge barrel-shaped pieces of this shattered boulder the jar containing the Nag Hammadi library was secreted.

In the face of the cliff, just at the top of the talus, which can be climbed without difficulty, sixth-dynasty tombs from the reigns of Pepi I and II (2350-2200 B.C.E.) had in antiquity long since been robbed. Thus they had become cool solitary caves where a monk might well hold his spiritual retreats, as is reported of Pachomius himself, or where a hermit might have his cell. Greek prayers to Zeus Sarapis, opening lines of biblical Psalms in Coptic, and Christian crosses, all painted in red onto the walls of the caves, show that they were indeed so used. Perhaps those who cherished the Nag Hammadi library made such use of the caves, which would account for the choice of this site to bury them. The jar rested there a millennium and a half ...

3. The Discovery

In the month of December peasants of the Najʿ Ḥammādī region of Upper Egypt fertilize their crops by carrying nitrates from the talus of the Jabal al-Ṭārif to their fields, using the saddlebags of their camels. Two brothers, Muḥammad and Khalīfah ʿAlī of the al-Sammān clan, hobbled their camels on the south side of the fallen boulder and came upon the jar as they were digging around its base. Muḥammad ʿAlī

reports that at first he was afraid to break the jar, whose lid may have
been sealed on with bitumen, for fear that a jinn might be closed up inside it; but, on reflecting that the jar might contain gold, he recovered
his courage and smashed it with his mattock. Out swirled golden-like particles that disappeared into the sky — neither jinns nor gold but perhaps
papyrus fragments! He wrapped the books in his tunic, slung it over his
shoulder, unhobbled his camel, and carried the books home, a hovel in
the hamlet of al-Qaṣr, which was the ancient site of Chenoboskia where
Pachomius had begun his life as a Christian.

Half a year earlier, during the night of 7 May 1945, the father of the
two brothers, whose name was ʿAlī, while on his job as night watchman
guarding irrigation equipment in the fields, had killed a marauder. By
mid-morning he had in turn been murdered in blood vengeance. About
a month after the discovery of the books, a peasant named Aḥmad fell
asleep sitting in the heat of the day on the side of the dirt road near
Muḥammad ʿAlī's house, a jar of sugar-cane molasses for sale beside
him. A neighbor pointed him out to Muḥammad ʿAlī as the murderer of
his father. He ran home and alerted his brothers and widowed mother,
who had told her seven sons to keep their mattocks sharp. The family fell
upon their victim, hacked off his limbs bit by bit, ripped out his heart,
and devoured it among them, as the ultimate act of blood revenge.

Aḥmad was the son of the sheriff, Ismāʿīl Husayn, a strong man imposed on al-Qaṣr from outside, indeed, a member of the Hawāra tribe,
who is so alienated from society that it considers itself non-Arabic
though directly descended from the Prophet. The village of the Hawāra,
Ḥamrah Dūm, is just at the foot of the Jabal al-Ṭārif, for which reason
Muḥammad ʿAlī has been afraid to return to the site of the discovery lest
his vengeance be in turn avenged. In fact Aḥmad's brother did avenge
the death at the time by killing two members of the al-Sammān clan.
Even a decade later, Aḥmad's young son, who by then was a teenager,
heard that at dusk there was to be in al-Qaṣr a funeral procession of the
family of Muḥammad ʿAlī. He proved his manhood by sneaking into
town and shooting up the procession, with a score killed and wounded.
Muḥḥammad ʿAlī proudly shows a wound just above his heart, to prove
that they tried but failed in vengeance. But he stoutly refused to return
to the cliff to identify the site of the discovery until a camouflage cos-
tume, a governmental escort, and of course a financial consideration
combined to persuade him to change his mind.

The village of al-Qaṣr was so glad to be rid of the sheriff's son that no
eye witnesses could be found to testify at the hearing. But during this pe-

riod the police tended to search Muḥammad ʿAlī's home every evening for weapons. Having been told that the books were Christian, no doubt simply on the basis of the Coptic script, Muḥammad ʿAlī asked the Coptic priest of Al-Qaṣr, Bāsīlīyūs ʿAbd al-Masīḥ, if he could deposit the books in his house. A priest's home would hardly be searched. Coptic priests marry, and this priest's wife had a brother, Rāghib Andrawus, who went from village to village in a circuit teaching English and history in the parochial schools of the Coptic Church. Once a week when he taught in al-Qaṣr he stayed in his sister's home. On seeing one of the books (Codex III), he recognized its potential value and persuaded the priest to give it to him. He took it to Cairo and showed it to a Coptic physician interested in the Coptic language, George Sobhi, who called in the authorities from the Department of Antiquities. They took control of the book, agreeing to pay Rāghib £300. After what seemed endless delays, Rāghib finally received £250 upon agreeing to make a gift of the balance of £50 to the Coptic Museum, where the book was deposited. The Register of the Museum records the date as 4 October 1946.

Thinking the books were worthless, perhaps even a source of bad luck, the widow of ʿAlī had burned part of them in the oven (probably Codex XII, of which only a few fragmentary leaves remain). Illiterate Muslim neighbors bartered or purchased the remainder for next to nothing. Nāshid Bisādah had one, and entrusted it to a gold merchant of Nag Hammadi to sell in Cairo, whereupon they divided the profit. A grain merchant is reported to have acquired another and sold it in Cairo at such a high price that he was able to set up his shop there. The villagers of al-Qaṣr identify him as Fikrī Jabrāʾīl, today the proprietor of the "Nag Hammadi Store" in Cairo; however, he stoutly denies any involvement, though familiar with this story. Bahīj ʿAlī, a one-eyed outlaw of al-Qaṣr, got most of the books. Escorted by a well-known antiquities dealer of the region, Dhakī Basṭa, he went to Cairo. They first offered the books to Mansoor's shop at Shepherds Hotel, and then to the shop of Phokion J. Tano, who bought their whole stock and then went to Nag Hammadi to get whatever was left.

Most of Codex I was exported from Egypt by a Belgian antiquities dealer in Cairo, Albert Eid. It was offered for sale unsuccessfully in New York and Ann Arbor in 1949, and then on 10 May 1952 was acquired in Belgium from Eid's widow Simone by the Jung Institute of Zürich and named the "Jung Codex." It was returned to Cairo bit by bit after publication, where it is conserved in the Coptic Museum. Meanwhile Tano's collection was taken into custody by the Egyptian Department of Antiquities to prevent it from leaving the country. After Nasser came to power it was nationalized, with a token compensation of £4,000. Today the Nag Hammadi library is back together again, conserved in the Coptic Museum.

The Director of the Coptic Museum at the time of the discovery, Togo Mina, had studied in Paris under the Abbot Étienne Drioton, who had subsequently become Director of the Department of Antiquities of Egypt. Togo Mina had been a classmate of the wife of Jean Doresse, a young French scholar who came to Egypt to study Coptic monasteries. Togo Mina was glad to give him access to Codex III and to make plans with him for a predominantly French edition of the library, plans cut short by Mina's death in 1949. In 1956 a meeting of some members of an international committee in Cairo led to the publication of *The Gospel of Thomas* in 1959. And the Jung Codex was gradually published in six volumes from 1956 through 1975. Meanwhile the new Director of the Coptic Museum, Pahor Labib, made plans to publish the better part of the library with the German scholars Alexander Böhlig and Martin Krause.

The General Director of UNESCO, René Maheu of France, worked out an agreement in the early 1960s with the Minister of Culture and National Guidance of the United Arab Republic, Saroite Okacha, to publish a complete edition through an international committee jointly chosen by Egypt and UNESCO. But when it was discovered that many of the choicest texts had already been assigned for publication, the UNESCO plan was limited to a facsimile edition. The project was rather dormant until the International Committee for the Nag Hammadi Codices was appointed at the end of 1970. *The Facsimile Edition of the Nag Hammadi Codices* was published by E.J. Brill in twelve volumes from 1972 through 1984. A number of the earlier assignments have by now been published, and complete editions in English, German and French are currently being prepared. The present volume makes use of the translations from the seventeen-volume English edition, entitled *The Coptic Gnostic Library* (see p. x).

With the publication of *The Nag Hammadi Library in English* the work has only just begun, for it marks a new beginning in the study of Gnosticism. Over a century ago students began to study Gnosticism in order to know what the heresy-hunting Church fathers were talking about. Around the turn of this century the History of Religions School broadened this issue by seeking the origins of Gnosticism throughout the ancient Near East. Between the two world wars, Hans Jonas produced a philosophical interpretation of Gnosticism that for the first time made sense of it as a possible way to understand existence. Rudolf Bultmann then reinterpreted the New Testament in terms of an interaction with Gnosticism involving appropriation as well as confrontation. Yet the results of this century of research into the origin, nature, and influence of Gnosticism stand in a certain ambivalence, as if hanging in suspense. One cannot fail to be impressed by the clairvoyance, the constructive power, the learned intuitions of scholars who, from limited and secondary sources, were able to produce working hypotheses that in fact worked so well. Yet the discovery of the Nag Hammadi library has drawn attention to how meager those sources were. For even though the discovery of the Nag Hammadi library was quite accidental and its contents somewhat arbitrary, the flood of new source material it contains cannot fail to outweigh the constructions and conjectures of previous scholarship. But, for the first generation after the discovery, the new source material was at best a trickle, and the suspense produced stagnation, as the scholarly community waited and waited. Now the time has come for a concentrated effort, with the whole Nag Hammadi library accessible, to rewrite the history of Gnosticism, to understand what it was really all about, and of course to pose new questions. Rarely has a generation of students had such an opportunity! May the readers of *The Nag Hammadi Library in English* share this exhilaration, and this responsibility, with those who produced it.

THE PRAYER OF THE APOSTLE PAUL (I,*1*)

Introduced and translated by

Dieter Mueller

The Prayer of the Apostle Paul occupies the front flyleaf of Codex I, also known as the Jung Codex. The scribe apparently added this prayer to the collection of tractates in the codex after he had finished copying *The Tripartite Tractate* (I,*5*). The title, followed by a brief colophon, is placed at the end of the prayer. The Greek language retained in that title was no doubt the original language of the prayer as a whole. The short text is of unknown provenance. Its general gnostic affinities are clear. Details such as the reference to the "psychic God" (A,31) may indicate Valentinian connections. That association in turn suggests a date of origin between the second half of the second century and the end of the third century.

In form and content *The Prayer of the Apostle Paul* echoes various other compositions. It displays a striking resemblance not only to prayers in the *Corpus Hermeticum* (1.31-32; 5.10-11; 13.16-20) but also to invocations found in magical texts. Furthermore, its beginning is rather similar to that of the hymn of the First Stele of *The Three Steles of Seth* (VII,*5*). Both documents may use a common tradition. There are also similarities within *The Gospel of Philip* (II,*3*). In general, *The Prayer of the Apostle Paul* is heavily indebted to the Psalms and the Pauline letters. The most striking echo of the apostle, and at the same time a clear index of gnostic orientation, is the request to be granted "what no angel-eye has seen and no archon-ear has heard and what has not entered into the human heart" (cf. 1 Co 2:9).

THE PRAYER OF THE APOSTLE PAUL

I A, 1-B, 10

A.1 (*Approximately two lines are missing.*) ¹ [your] light, give me your [mercy! My] ¹ Redeemer, redeem me, for ⁵ [I am] yours; the one who has come ¹ forth from you. You are [my] mind; bring me forth! ¹ You are my treasure house; open for me! You ¹ [are] my fullness; take me to you! ¹ You are (my) repose; give me ¹⁰ [the] perfect thing that cannot be grasped! ¹

I invoke you, the one who is ¹ and who pre-existed in the name ¹ [which is] exalted above every name, through Jesus Christ, ¹ [the Lord] of Lords, the King of the ages; ¹⁵ give me your gifts, of which you do

not repent, ' through the Son of Man, ' the Spirit, the Paraclete of '
[truth]. Give me authority ' [when I] ask you; give [20] healing for my
body when I ask ' you through the Evangelist, ' [and] redeem my eternal light soul ' and my spirit. And the First-born of the Pleroma of
grace − [25] reveal him to my mind!

Grant ' what no angel eye has ' [seen] and no archon ear ' (has) heard
and what ' has not entered into the human heart [30] which came to be
angelic and (modelled) ' after the image of the psychic God ' when it
was formed ' in the beginning, since I have ' faith and hope.[35] And
place upon me your ' beloved, elect, ' and blessed greatness, the ' First-
born, the First-begotten, [B.I] and the [wonderful] mystery ' of your
house; [for] ' yours is the power [and] ' the glory and the praise [5] and
the greatness ' for ever and ever. [Amen.] '

Prayer of Paul ' (the) Apostle. '

In Peace.

[10] Christ is holy.

THE APOCRYPHON OF JAMES (I,2)

Introduced and translated by

FRANCIS E. WILLIAMS

The Apocryphon of James is a pseudonymous work translated from Greek to Coptic, which professes to be a letter written by James, the Lord's brother; the alleged recipient's name is illegible but might have been that of the early Christian heterodox teacher, Cerinthus. The letter in turn introduces a secret writing, or "apocryphon" – hence our title for the entire tractate. This apocryphon is meant for an elect few – even among the disciples, for James and Peter only – but salvation is promised to those who receive its message.

"James'" letter states that the apocryphon is written in the Hebrew alphabet, and mentions another even more secret apocryphon, which James has already sent. These details are presumably inserted for the sake of atmosphere.

The apocryphon, which comprises the bulk of our tractate, makes Jesus appear to the disciples 550 days after the resurrection, take Peter and James aside to "fill" them, and give them, in a series of speeches, his final and definitive teaching, heretofore delivered only "in parables." He then ascends to the Father's right hand, with James and Peter unsuccessfully attempting to follow. This closes the apocryphon; the letter now resumes, and states that the revelation just given was meant, not for the disciples of Jesus, but for the "children" who would be "born" later. While the disciples believed the revelation, they were angry over these later children, and James therefore dispatched them to other places. This, presumably, is meant to explain why our tractate formed no part of the apostolic preaching (or the canonical scripture?).

Jesus' speeches in the apocryphon are partly the author's composition, but incorporate older material, which seems to be the product of complex oral and perhaps written transmission; some of it can be compared with the material underlying the canonical gospels. The speeches show Jesus announcing that he has descended to save God's "beloved" sons, and inviting them to follow him back to the place from which he (and they?) came. He assures them of salvation in the strongest terms, while at the same time urging them to earnestness and zeal, and warning them that they can be lost. The first and longest of the speeches, however, is a two-page exhortation to martyrdom. Its distinctive style, manner, and subject matter suggest that it may be a later interpolation.

It is clear that the persons for whom this tractate was written made a distinction between themselves and the larger Christian church. Probably they rejected the doctrine of the atonement; they certainly ignored the second coming of Christ and the general resurrection, and hoped to ascend, in soul or spirit, to the kingdom of heaven, which they meanwhile felt to be within themselves. This outlook, together with the large amount of typically gnostic terminology in the tractate, has led most investigators to conclude that the work is Christian Gnostic, even though it lacks the Valentinian, and other well-known gnostic theologies. The reporting of a special postresurrection appearance of Jesus, and the appeal to James as a source of secret and superior tradition, are means Gnostics often used to legitimate their message.

The exhortation to martyrdom, James' letter, and the description of Jesus' appearance to the disciples, may be secondary; these and other questions relating to the document's literary history have been investigated and deserve further investigation. It has been urged that the tractate must have been written before 150 C.E., while it was still possible to speak of "remembering" orally delivered sayings of Jesus and writing them down; this language, it is argued, would not have been used after the fixing of the Gospel canon. The apocryphon's many resemblances to the Fourth Gospel's "farewell discourses" might also help to establish its date. To use these as a criterion, however, one must decide whether they are allusions to the actual text of the Fourth Gospel, or independent discussions of the same questions. In any case the tractate cannot be later than 314 C.E., when the persecution of the church, and with it the risk of martyrdom, came to an end.

THE APOCRYPHON OF JAMES

I 1, 1-16, 30

[James] writes to ' [. . .]thos: Peace ' [be with you from] Peace, ' [love from] Love, [5] [grace from] Grace, ' [faith] from Faith, ' life from Holy Life! '

Since you asked ' that I send [10] you a secret book ' which was revealed to me ' and Peter by the Lord, ' I could not turn you away ' or gainsay (?) you; [15] but [I have written] it in ' the Hebrew alphabet and ' sent it to you, and you ' alone. But since you are ' a minister of the salvation [20] of the saints, endeavor earnestly ' and take care not to rehearse ' this text to many – this ' that the Savior did not wish ' to tell to all of us, his [25] twelve disciples. ' But blessed will they be ' who will be saved through ' the faith of this discourse.

I ' also sent you, [30] ten months ago, another secret ' book which the Savior ' had revealed to me. Under the circumstances, however, ' regard that one ' as revealed [35] to me, James; but this one 2 [*untranslatable fragments*] ' the twelve disciples ' [were] all sitting together [10] and recalling ' what the Savior had said ' to each one of them, whether ' in secret or openly, ' and [putting it] [15] in books – [But I] ' was writing that which was in [my book] – ' lo, the Savior appeared, [after] ' departing from [us while we] gazed ' after him. And five hundred [20] and fifty days since he had risen ' from the dead, we said 'to him, "Have you departed and removed yourself from us?" '

But Jesus said, "No, but ' I shall go to the place from whence I came.[25] If you wish to come ' with me, come!"

They all answered ' and said, "If you bid ' us, we come."

He said, ' "Verily I say unto you,[30] no one will ever enter ' the kingdom of heaven at my ' bidding, but (only) because ' you yourselves are full. Leave ' James and Peter to me [35] that I may fill them." And ' having called these two, ' he drew them aside and bade ' the rest occupy themselves ' with that which they were about.[40]

The Savior said, "You have received mercy 3 [7] [*untranslatable fragments*] ' Do you not, then, desire to be filled? ' And your heart is drunken; [10] do you not, then, desire to be sober? ' Therefore, be ashamed! Henceforth, waking ' or sleeping, remember ' that you have seen ' the Son of Man, and [15] spoken with him in person, ' and listened to him in person. ' Woe to those who have seen the ' Son [of] Man; ' blessed will they be who [20] have not seen the man, and they ' who have not consorted with him, and ' they who have not spoken with him, ' and they who have not listened to ' anything from him; yours is [25] life! Know, then, that he healed ' you when you were ill ' that you might reign. Woe ' to those who have found relief from ' their illness, for they will [30] relapse into illness. Blessed are ' they who have not been ill, and ' have known relief before ' falling ill; yours is the ' kingdom of God. Therefore, I [35] say to you, 'Become ' full and leave no space within ' you empty, for he who is coming ' can mock you.'"

Then ' Peter replied, "Lo, [40] three times you have told us, 4 'Become [full]; but' ' we are full."

The [Savior answered] ' and said, ["For this cause I have said] ' to you, ['Become full,'] that 5 [you] may not [be in want. They who are in want], ' however, will not [be saved]. For it is good to be full, ' and bad to be in want. Hence, just as ' it is good that you (sg.) be in want and, ' conversely, bad that you be full, so [10] he who is full is in want, ' and he who is in want does not become full as ' he who is in want becomes full, and ' he who has been filled, in turn, attains ' due perfection. Therefore, you must be in want [15] while it is possible to fill you (pl.), and ' be full while it is possible for you to be in want, ' so that you may be able [to fill] ' yourselves the more. Hence become ' full of the Spirit, [20] but be in want of ' reason, for reason ⟨belongs to⟩ the soul; ' in turn it is (of the nature of) soul." '

But I answered and said to him, "Lord, ' we can obey you [25] if you wish, for we have forsaken ' our fathers ' and our mothers and our villages ' and followed you. Grant us, therefore, ' not to be tempted [30] by the devil, the evil one." '

The Lord answered ' and said, "What is your (pl.) merit ' if you do the will of the Father ' and it is not given to you from him [35] as a gift while ' you are tempted by ' Satan? But if ' you (pl.) are oppressed by ' Satan and [40] persecuted and you do his (i.e. the Father's) **5** will, I [say] that he will ' love you, and make you equal ' with me, and reckon ' [you] to have become [5] beloved through his providence ' by your own choice. So ' will you not cease ' loving the flesh and being ' afraid of sufferings? Or do [10] you not know that you have yet ' to be abused and to be ' accused unjustly; ' and have yet to be shut ' up in prison, and [15] condemned ' unlawfully, and ' crucified ⟨without⟩ ' reason, and buried ' ⟨shamefully⟩, as (was) I myself, [20] by the evil one? ' Do you dare to spare the flesh, ' you for whom the Spirit is an ' encircling wall? If you consider ' how long the world existed [25] ⟨before⟩ you, and how long ' it will exist after you, you will find ' that your life is one single day ' and your sufferings one ' single hour. For the good [30] will not enter into the world. ' Scorn death, therefore, ' and take thought for life! ' Remember my cross ' and my death, and you will [35] live!"

But I answered and ' said to him, "Lord, ' do not mention to us the cross ' and death, for they are far **6** from you."

The Lord answered ' and said, "Verily I say ' unto you, none will be saved ' unless they believe in my cross. [5] But those who have believed in my ' cross, theirs is the kingdom of ' God. Therefore, become seekers ' for death, like the dead ' who seek for life; [10] for that which they seek is revealed to them. ' And what is there ' to trouble them? As for you, when you examine ' death, it will ' teach you election. Verily [15] I say unto you, none ' of those who fear death will be saved; ' for the kingdom ⟨of God⟩ ' belongs to those who put themselves to death. ' Become better than I; make [20] yourselves like the son of the Holy Spirit!" '

Then I asked him, ' "Lord, how shall we be able ' to prophesy to those who request ' us to prophesy [25] to them? For there are many who ' ask us, and look ' to us to hear an oracle ' from us."

The Lord ' answered and said, "Do you not [30] know that the head of ' prophecy was cut off with John?" '

But I said, "Lord, ' can it be possible to remove ' the head of prophecy?"

The Lord [35] said to me, "When you (pl.) ' come to know what 'head' means, and ' that prophecy issues from the ' head, (then) understand the meaning of 'Its head was **7** removed.' At first I spoke ' to you (pl.) in parables ' and you did not understand; ' now I speak to [5] you openly, and ' you (still) do not perceive. Yet ' it was you who served me ' as a parable in | parables, and as that which is open [10] in the (words) that are open.

"Hasten | to be saved without being urged! | Instead, be | eager of your own accord and, | if possible, arrive even before me; [15] for thus | the Father will love you. |

"Come to hate | hypocrisy and the evil | thought; for it is the thought [20] that gives birth to hypocrisy; | but hypocrisy is far from | truth.

"Do not allow | the kingdom of heaven to wither; | for it is like a palm shoot [25] whose fruit has dropped down | around it. They (i.e., the fallen fruit) put forth | leaves, and after they had sprouted, | they caused their womb to dry up. | So it is also with the fruit which [30] had grown from this single root; | when it had been picked (?), | fruit was borne by many (?). | It (the root) was certainly good, (and) if | it were possible for you to produce the [35] new plants now, ⟨you⟩ (sg.) would find it.

"Since | I have already been glorified in this fashion, | why do you (pl.) hold me back | in my eagerness to go? **8** For after the [labor], you have | compelled me to stay with | you another eighteen days for | the sake of the parables. It was enough [5] for some ⟨to listen⟩ to the | teaching and understand 'The Shepherds' and | 'The Seed' and 'The Building' and 'The Lamps of | the Virgins' and 'The Wage of the | Workmen' and 'The Didrachmae' and 'The [10] Woman.'

"Become earnest about | the word! For as to the word, | its first part is faith; | the second, love; the | third, works; [15] for from these comes life. | For the word is like a | grain of wheat; when someone | had sown it, he had faith in it; and | when it had sprouted, he loved it because he had seen [20] many grains in place of one. And | when he had worked, he was saved because he had | prepared it for food, (and) again he | left (some) to sow. So also | can you yourselves receive [25] the kingdom of heaven; | unless you receive this through knowledge, | you will not be able to find it.

"Therefore, | I say to you, | be sober; do not be deceived! [30] And many times have I said to you all together, | and also to you alone, | James, have I said, | 'Be saved!' And I have commanded | you (sg.) to follow me, [35] and I have taught you | what to say before the archons. | Observe that I have descended | and have spoken and undergone tribulation | and carried off my crown **9** after saving you (pl.). For | I came down to dwell with | you (pl.) so that you (pl.) in turn | might dwell with me. And, [5] finding your houses | unceiled, I have made my abode | in the houses that could receive me | at the time of my descent. |

"Therefore, trust [10] in me, my brethren; understand | what the great light is. The Father ' has no need of me, ' – for a father does not need a son, ' but it is the son who needs [15] the father – though I go to him. ' For the Father ' of the Son has no need of you. '

"Hearken to the word; ' understand knowledge; love [20] life, and no one will persecute ' you, nor will anyone ' oppress you, other ' than you yourselves. '

"O you wretches; O [25] you unfortunates; O ' you pretenders to the truth; ' O you falsifiers of knowledge; ' O you sinners against the Spirit: ' can you still bear to [30] listen, when it behooved you ' to speak from the first? ' Can you still bear to ' sleep, when it behooved you to be awake ' from the first, so that [35] the kingdom of heaven might receive you? **10** Verily I say unto you, ' it is easier for a pure one ' to fall into defilement, and for ' a man of light to fall [5] into darkness, than for you to reign ' or not reign.

"I have remembered ' your tears and your mourning ' and your anguish, (while you say) 'They are far ' behind us.' But now, you who are [10] outside of the Father's inheritance, ' weep where it is necessary ' and mourn and ' preach what is good, ' as the Son is ascending as he should. [15] Verily I say ' unto you, had I been sent ' to those who listen to me, and ' had I spoken with them, ' I would never have come [20] down to earth. So, ' then, be ashamed for these things. '

"Behold, I shall depart from you ' and go away, and do not wish ' to remain with you any longer, just as [25] you yourselves have not wished it. ' Now, therefore, follow ' me quickly. This is why ' I say unto you, 'for your sakes ' I came down.' You are [30] the beloved; you are they ' who will be the cause of life ' in many. Invoke the Father, ' implore God often, ' and he will give to you. Blessed [35] is he who has seen you with Him ' when He was proclaimed among the ' angels, and glorified among ' the saints; yours (pl.) is life. ' Rejoice and be glad as **11** sons of God. Keep his will ' that you may be saved; ' accept reproof from me and ' save yourselves. I intercede [5] on your behalf with the Father, and he will ' forgive you much.''

And when we ' had heard these words, we became glad, ' for we had been grieved ' at the words we have mentioned [10] before. But when he saw us ' rejoicing, he said, "Woe to you (pl.) ' who lack an advocate! ' Woe to you, who stand in need ' of grace! Blessed will they be [15] who have ' spoken out and obtained ' grace for themselves. Liken ' yourselves to foreigners; ' of what sort are they in the eyes of your [20] city? Why are you disturbed ' when you cast yourselves away ' of your own accord and ' separate yourselves from your city? Why ' do you abandon your dwelling place [25] of your own accord, | making it ready for those who want | to dwell in it? O you | outcasts and fugitives, woe | to you, for you will be caught! Or [30] do you perhaps think that the Father | is a lover of mankind, or that he is | won over without prayers, or that he | grants remission to one on another's behalf, or | that he bears with one who asks? — [35] For he knows the desire and | also what it is that the flesh needs! — | (Or do you think) that it is not this (flesh) that desires | the soul? For without the soul | the body does not sin, just as **12** the soul is not saved without | [the] spirit. But if the soul | is saved (when it is) without evil, and | the spirit is also saved, then the body [5] becomes free from sin. For it is the spirit | that raises the soul, but the body that | kills it; | that is, it is it (the soul) which kills | itself. Verily I say unto you, [10] he will not forgive the soul the sin | by any means, nor the flesh | the guilt; for none of those who have | worn the flesh will be saved. | For do you think that many have [15] found the kingdom of heaven? | Blessed is he who has seen himself as | a fourth one in heaven!" |

When we heard these words, we were distressed. | But when he saw that we were distressed, [20] he said, "For this cause I tell | you this, that you may | know yourselves. For the kingdom | of heaven is like an ear of grain after it | had sprouted in a field. And [25] when it had ripened, it scattered its | fruit and again filled the field | with ears for another year. You | also, hasten to reap | an ear of life for yourselves that [30] you may be filled with the kingdom! |

"And as long as I am | with you, give heed to me | and obey me; but | when I depart from you, [35] remember me. And remember me | because when I was with you, | you did not know me. | Blessed will they be who have | known me; woe to those who have [40] heard and have not believed! | Blessed will they be who **13** have not seen, [yet have believed]! |

"And once more I [prevail upon] you, | for I am revealed to you (pl.) | building a house which is of great value to [5] you when you find shelter | beneath it, just as it will be able | to stand by your neighbors' house | when it threatens to fall. Verily | I say unto you, woe [10] to those for whose sakes I was sent | down to this place; blessed | will they be who ascend | to the Father! Once more I | reprove you, you who are; [15] become like those who are not, | that you may be with those who | are not.

"Do not make | the kingdom of heaven a desert | within you. Do not be proud [20] because of the light that illumines, but | be to yourselves |

as I myself am ¹ to you. For your sakes I have ¹ placed myself under the curse, that you ²⁵ may be saved.'' ¹

But Peter replied ¹ to these words and said, ¹ ''Sometimes you urge ¹ us on to the kingdom of ³⁰ heaven, and then again you turn ¹ us back, Lord; sometimes ¹ you persuade and draw ¹ us to faith and promise ¹ us life, and then again you cast ³⁵ us forth from the kingdom ¹ of heaven.''

But the Lord answered ¹ and said to us, ''I have given you (pl.) ¹ faith many times; moreover, ¹ I have revealed myself to you (sg.), **14** James, and you (pl.) have not ¹ known me. Now again I ¹ see you (pl.) rejoicing many times; ¹ and when you are elated ⁵ at the promise of life, ¹ are you yet sad, and do you ¹ grieve, when you are instructed ¹ in the kingdom? But you, through ¹ faith [and] knowledge, have received ¹⁰ life. Therefore, disdain ¹ the rejection when you ¹ hear it, but when you hear ¹ the promise, rejoice the more. ¹ Verily I say unto you, ¹⁵ he who will receive life and ¹ believe in the kingdom will ¹ never leave it, not even if ¹ the Father wishes ¹ to banish him.

''These are the things that I shall tell ²⁰ you so far; now, however, I shall ¹ ascend to the place from whence I came. ¹ But you, when I was eager ¹ to go, have cast me out, and ¹ instead of accompanying me, ²⁵ you have pursued me. ¹ But pay heed to the glory that awaits ¹ me, and, having opened ¹ your heart, listen to the hymns ¹ that await me up in the heavens; ³⁰ for today I must ¹ take (my place at) the right hand of the Father. ¹ But I have said (my) last word to ¹ you, and I shall depart from you, ¹ for a chariot of spirit has borne me aloft, ³⁵ and from this moment on I shall strip myself ¹ that I may clothe myself. ¹ But give heed; blessed ¹ are they who have proclaimed ¹ the Son before his descent ⁴⁰ that, when I have come, I might ascend (again). ¹ Thrice blessed **15** are they who [were] ¹ proclaimed by the Son ¹ before they came to be, that ¹ you might have a portion ⁵ among them.''

Having said these words, ¹ he departed. But we bent (our) knee(s), ¹ I and Peter, and gave thanks ¹ and sent our heart(s) upwards ¹ to heaven. We heard with ¹⁰ our ears, and saw with ¹ our eyes, the noise of wars ¹ and a trumpet blare ¹ and a great turmoil.

And ¹ when we had passed beyond ¹⁵ that place, we sent our ¹ mind(s) farther upwards and ¹ saw with our eyes and heard ¹ with our ears hymns ¹ and angelic benedictions and ²⁰ angelic rejoicing. And ¹ heavenly majesties were ¹ singing praise, and we too ¹ rejoiced.

After this ¹ again, we wished to send our ²⁵ spirit upward to the ¹ Majesty, and after ascending we ¹ were not permitted to see or hear ¹ anything, for the other ¹ disciples called us and ³⁰ asked us, ''What did you (pl.) | hear from the | Master? And what has | he said to you? And where | did he go?''

But we answered [35] them, "He has ascended and | has given us a pledge and | promised life to us all and | revealed to us children (?) | who are to come after us, after bidding **16** [us] love them, as we would be | [saved] for their sakes.''

And | when they heard (this), they indeed believed | the revelation, but were displeased [5] about those to be born. And so, not wishing | to give them offense, | I sent each one to another | place. But I myself went | up to Jerusalem, praying that I [10] might obtain a portion among the beloved, | who will be made manifest. |

And I pray that | the beginning may come from you, | for thus I shall be capable of [15] salvation, since they will be | enlightened through me, by my faith – | and through another (faith) that is | better than mine, for I would that | mine be the lesser. [20] Endeavor earnestly, then, to make | yourself like them and | pray that you may obtain a portion | with them. For because of what | I have said, the Savior did [25] not make the revelation to us | for their sakes. We do, indeed, proclaim | a portion with those | for whom the proclamation was made, | those whom the Lord has made his [30] sons.

THE GOSPEL OF TRUTH (I,*3* AND XII,*2*)

Introduced and translated by

HAROLD W. ATTRIDGE and GEORGE W. MACRAE

The Gospel of Truth is a Christian Gnostic text with clear affinities to the Valentinian school, offering a subtle yet moving reflection on the person and work of Jesus. The tractate has no explicit title in the manuscript and is known by its *incipit*. Many other works in antiquity, such as the "gospel" of Mark and the "revelation" of John, were similarly identified by their opening words. A Valentinian work entitled the "Gospel of Truth" is attested in the *Adversus Haereses* (3.11.9) of Irenaeus. Unfortunately the heresiologist reveals little about the content of the work, except that it differed significantly from the canonical gospels. Given the general Valentinian affinities of the text of Codex I, it is quite possible that it is identical with the work known to Irenaeus. If so, a date of composition in the middle of the second century (between 140 and 180 C.E.) would be established. On the basis of literary and conceptual affinities between this text and the exiguous fragments of Valentinus, some scholars have suggested that the Gnostic teacher himself was the author. That remains a distinct possibility, although it cannot be definitively established. Whatever its precise date and authorship, the work was certainly composed in Greek in an elaborate rhetorical style, by a consummate literary artist.

Despite its title, this work is not a gospel of the sort found in the New Testament, since it does not offer a continuous narration of the deeds, teachings, passion, and resurrection of Jesus. The term "gospel" in the *incipit* preserves its early sense of "good news." It defines the text's subject, not its genre, which is best understood as a homily. Like other early Christian homilies, such as the Epistle to the Hebrews, *The Gospel of Truth* alternates doctrinal exposition with paraenesis (e.g., 32,31-33,32) and, like that canonical work, it reflects on the significance of the salvific work of Jesus from a special theological perspective.

Identification of the work as a homily says little about its literary or theological dynamics. Analysis of both surface structure and underlying conceptual scheme is made difficult by the elusive character of the discourse, which combines allusions to familiar elements of early Christian tradition, sometimes in unusual associations, with references to less familiar notions. Similarly elusive is the frame of reference of the text, which seems to slip quite easily from cosmic to historical, then to personal or psychological perspectives. These qualities of the work may indicate something of its intended function. Traditions familiar from the New Testament are given a new meaning by being set in a conceptual environment, the structure of which remains artfully obscured. Nonetheless, certain key themes and perspectives characteristic of Valentinian theology, such as the principle that knowledge of the Father destroys ignorance (18,10-11; 24,30-32), are emphasized. The work was thus probably designed to introduce Valentinian soteriological insights to members of the great church.

The work is divided into three large blocks of exposition separated by two formally distinct units, a festive "Litany on the Word" (23,18-24,9) and a paraenetic appeal (32,31-33,32). Each of the three blocks of exposition also contains three thematically distinct sections. After an introduction (16,31-17,4), the first block begins with a description of the generation of Error (17,4-18,11), which comes forth from the Father, but for which the Father is not responsible, and by which he is not diminished. A mythological account, like that of the fall of Sophia, found in many gnostic texts (c.f., e.g., *The Hypostasis of the Archons* or *On the Origin of the World*), no doubt underlies this description of Error. The text then (18,11-19,27) turns to Jesus and his work as revealer and teacher. To illustrate the last notion, the text appeals to traditions like that of Jesus in the temple in Luke 2, although the allusion may be to noncanonical accounts of the youth of Jesus. The final segment of the first block (19,27-24,9) mentions, without any docetic qualifications, the death of Jesus (20,25), then interprets that event, with images drawn from Colossians and the Apocalypse, as an act of revelation. That act reveals the essence of the Father and the origin and destiny of the human self in Him. Through that insight the powers of Error are overcome.

The second major block of exposition (24,9-33,32) describes the effects of the revelation of the "gospel of truth." It produces unity with the Father (24,9-27,7). It makes possible authentic human existence, imaged in traditional gnostic terms as a state of wakefulness (27,7-30,16), a condition of joy and delight graphically contrasted with the nightmarish existence of those in ignorance. Finally the revelation opens the way to ultimate return to the Father (30,16-32,30).

The final block of exposition focuses on the process of reintegration to the primordial source. The return begins (33,33-36,39) as gentle attraction, imaged as an alluring perfume. That attractive fragrance is in fact the spirit of incorruptibility which produces forgiveness. The agent of the return (36,39-40,23) is the Son, who is the name of the Father. The identification of Son and Name involves the most subtle of the reflections of the text (38,6-40,23), combining ancient Jewish-Christian exaltation patterns with philosophical semantics. The final portion of the text (40,23-41,14) describes in festive terms the ultimate goal of the process of return, rest in the Father. Those who recognize that their destiny is in the source from which they have come are the children whom the Father loves.

The Gospel of Truth's combination of literary and conceptual sophistication with genuine religious feeling suggests much better than the rather dry accounts of gnostic systems in the heresiologists why the teaching of Valentinus and his school had such an appeal for many Christians of the second century.

The following translation is based on the text of Codex I; the text of Codex XII is very fragmentary.

THE GOSPEL OF TRUTH

I 16, 31-43, 24

The gospel of truth is joy ' for those who have received from ' the Father of truth the grace of knowing him, ' through the power of the Word that came forth from [35] the pleroma, the one who is in the thought ' and the mind of the Father, that is, ' the one who is addressed as ' the Savior, (that) being the name of the work he is ' to perform for the redemption of those who were [17] ignorant of the Father, while in the name [of] ' the gospel is the proclamation ' of hope, being discovery ' for those who search for him.

When [5] the totality went about searching for the one ' from whom they had come forth — and the totality was ' inside of him, the ' incomprehensible, inconceivable one ' who is superior to every thought — [10] ignorance of the Father brought about anguish ' and terror; and the anguish ' grew solid like a fog, ' so that no one was able to see. ' For this reason error [15] became powerful; it worked on its own matter ' foolishly, ' not having known the truth. It set about with a creation, ' preparing with power and [20] beauty the substitute for the truth. '

This was not, then, a humiliation for him, ' the incomprehensible, inconceivable one, ' for they were nothing, the anguish and the oblivion and the creature [25] of deceit, while the established ' truth is immutable, ' imperturbable, perfect in beauty. ' For this reason, despise ' error.

Thus [30] it had no root; it fell into ' a fog regarding the Father, while it was involved in ' preparing works and ' oblivions and terrors, in order that ' by means of these it might entice those [35] of the middle and capture ' them.

The oblivion of error was ' not revealed. It is not a [18] [. . .] from the Father. Oblivion ' did not come into existence from the Father, ' although it did indeed come into existence because of him. ' But what comes into existence in him is knowledge, [5] which appeared in ' order that oblivion might vanish ' and the Father might be known. Since ' oblivion came into existence because ' the Father was not known, then if [10] the Father comes to be known, oblivion ' will not exist from that moment on.

Through this, ' the gospel of the one who is searched ' for, which ⟨was⟩ revealed to those who ' are perfect through the mercies [15] of the Father, the hidden mystery, ' Jesus, the Christ, ' enlightened those who were in darkness ' through oblivion. ' He enlightened ' them; he showed (them) a way; [20] and the way is the truth ' which he taught them.

For this reason ' error grew angry at him, ' persecuted him, was distressed at him ' (and) was brought to naught. He was nailed to a tree (and) he [25] became a fruit of the knowledge of ' the Father. It did not, however, cause destruction because ' it was eaten, but to those who ate it ' it gave (cause) to become glad ' in the discovery, and he [30] discovered them in himself, ' and they discovered him in themselves.

As for the ' incomprehensible, inconceivable one, the ' Father, the perfect one, the one who ' made the totality, within him is [35] the totality and of him the totality has need. ' Although he retained their perfection ' within himself which he did not give ' to the totality, the Father was not jealous. ' What jealousy indeed (could there be) [40] between himself and his members? **19** For, if this aeon had thus [received] ' their [perfection], they could not have come [...] ' the Father. He retains within himself their perfection, [5] granting it to them as a return to him ' and a perfectly unitary ' knowledge. It is he who fashioned ' the totality, and within him is the totality ' and the totality was in need [10] of him.

As in the case of ' a person of whom some ' are ignorant, he ' wishes to have them know him and ' love him, so — [15] for what did the totality have need of ' if not knowledge regarding ' the Father? — he became a guide, ' restful and leisurely. ' In schools he appeared (and) he spoke [20] the word as a teacher. ' There came the men wise ' in their own estimation, ' putting him to the test. ' But he confounded them because they [25] were foolish. They hated ' him because they were not really ' wise.

After all these, ' there came the little ' children also, those to whom [30] the knowledge of the Father belongs. Having been strengthened, ' they learned about the impressions ' of the Father. They knew, ' they were known; they were glorified, they ' glorified. There was manifested in their [35] heart the living book ' of the living — the one written ' in the thought and the mind **20** [of the] Father, which from before the ' foundation of the totality was within ' his incomprehensibility — that (book) ' which no one was able to take, [5] since it remains for the one who will take it ' to be slain. No one could have become manifest ' from among those who have believed ' in salvation unless ' that book had appeared. [10] For this reason the merciful one, the faithful one, ' Jesus, was patient in accepting sufferings ' until he took that book, ' since he knows that his death ' is life for many. [15]

Just as there lies hidden in a will, before ' it is opened, the fortune ' of the deceased master of the house, ' so (it is) with the totality, which ' lay hidden while the Father of the totality was [20] invisible, being something which is | from him, from whom | every space comes forth. | For this reason Jesus appeared; | he put on that book; [25] he was nailed to a tree; | he published the edict | of the Father on the cross. O | such great teaching! He draws | himself down to death though life [30] eternal clothes him. Having stripped | himself of the perishable rags, | he put on imperishability, | which no one | can possibly take away from him. Having entered [35] the empty spaces of | terrors, he passed through | those who were stripped naked by | oblivion, being knowledge | and perfection, proclaiming the things that are in the heart, 21 [. . .] | teach those who will receive teaching. |

But those who are to receive teaching [are] | the living who are inscribed in the book [5] of the living. It is about themselves that they receive instruction, | receiving it | from the Father, turning | again to him. Since the | perfection of the totality is in the Father, [10] it is necessary for the totality to | ascend to him. Then, if | one has knowledge, he receives what are | his own and draws | them to himself. For he who is [15] ignorant is in need, and | what he lacks is great, | since he lacks that which will | make him perfect. Since the perfection of | the totality is in the Father [20] and it is necessary for the totality to | ascend to him and for each | one to receive what are his own, | he enrolled them in advance, having | prepared them to give to those [25] who came forth from him.

Those | whose name he knew in advance | were called at the end, | so that one who has knowledge is | the one whose name the Father [30] has uttered. For he whose name | has not been spoken is ignorant. | Indeed, how is one | to hear if his name has not | been called? For he who is [35] ignorant until the end is a creature | of oblivion, and he will | vanish along with it. If not, | how is it that these miserable ones have 22 no name, (how is it that) they do not have | the call? Therefore, | if one has knowledge, he is | from above. If he is called, [5] he hears, he answers, | and he turns to him who is calling | him, and ascends to him. And | he knows in what manner he | is called. Having knowledge, he does [10] the will of the one who called | him, he wishes to be pleasing to him, he | receives rest. Each one's name | comes to him. He who is to have knowledge | in this manner knows where he comes [15] from and where he is going. | He knows as one | who having become drunk has turned away from | his drunkenness, (and) having returned to himself, | has set right what [20] are his own.

He has brought many | back from error. He has gone | before them to their places, | from which they had moved away, | since it was on account [25] of the depth that they received error, the depth of the one who encircles | all spaces while there is none | that encircles him. It was a great | wonder that they were in the Father, | not knowing him, and (that) they were [30] able to come forth by themselves, | since they were unable to | comprehend or to know the one | in whom they were. For if | his will had not thus emerged from him — [35] for he revealed it | in view of a knowledge in which | all its emanations concur. |

This is the knowledge of | the living book which he revealed to the **23** aeons, at the end, as [his letters], | revealing how | they are not vowels | nor are they [5] consonants, | so that one might read them and | think of something foolish, | but they are letters of the | truth which they alone speak [10] who know them. | Each letter is a complete ⟨thought⟩ | like a complete | book, since they are | letters written by [15] the Unity, the Father having | written them for the aeons in order that by | means of his letters | they should know the Father.

While his wisdom | contemplates [20] the Word, and his teaching | utters it, his knowledge | has revealed ⟨it⟩. | While forebearance is | a crown upon it, [25] and his gladness is in harmony | with it, his glory | has exalted it, his image | has revealed it, | his repose has [30] received it into itself, his love | has made a body over it, | his fidelity has embraced | it. In this way the Word | of the Father goes [35] forth in the totality, as the fruit **24** [of] his heart and | an impression of his will. | But it supports the totality; it | chooses them and also receives [5] the impression of the totality, | purifying them, bringing them back | into the Father, into the Mother, | Jesus of the infinite | sweetness.

The Father reveals [10] his bosom. — Now his bosom | is the Holy Spirit. — He | reveals what is hidden of him — | what is hidden of him is | his Son — so that through [15] the mercies of the Father | the aeons may know him | and cease laboring in search of | the Father, resting there | in him, knowing [20] that this is the rest. Having | filled the deficiency, he abolished | the form — the form of | it is the world, that | in which he served. — [25] For the place where there is envy | and strife is deficient, | but the place where (there is) Unity | is perfect. Since the deficiency | came into being because the [30] Father was not known, therefore, when | the Father is known, | from that moment on the deficiency will no longer exist. As | in the case of the ignorance | of a person, when he comes [35] to have knowledge, his ignorance | vanishes of itself, | as the darkness vanishes | when light appears, **25** so also | the deficiency vanishes | in the perfection. So | from that moment on the form is not apparent, [5] but it will vanish | in the fusion of Unity, | for now their works

lie scattered. In | time Unity will perfect [10] the spaces. It is within |
Unity that each one | will attain himself; within | knowledge he will
purify himself | from multiplicity into [15] Unity, consuming | matter
within himself | like fire, and | darkness by light, death by | life.

If indeed these things have happened [20] to each one of us, | then we
must | see to it above all that | the house will be holy | and silent for the
Unity. [25] (It is) as in the case of some people | who moved out of dwell-
ings | having | jars that in | spots were not good. [30] They would break
them, and | the master of the house would not suffer loss. | Rather ⟨he⟩
is glad because | in place of the bad jars | (there are) full ones which are
made [35] perfect. For such is | the judgment which has come from **26**
above. It has passed judgment on | everyone; it is a drawn sword, | with
two edges, cutting | on either side. When the [5] Word appeared, the one
that is | within the heart of those who utter it — | it is not a sound alone
| but it became a body — a great | disturbance took place among [10] the
jars because some had | been emptied, others filled; | that is, some had
been supplied, | others poured out, | some had been purified, still [15]
others broken up. All the spaces | were shaken and disturbed | because
they had no order | nor stability. | Error was upset, not knowing [20]
what to do; | it was grieved, in mourning, | afflicting itself because it
knew | nothing. When | knowledge drew near it — this [25] is the
downfall of (error) and all its emanations — | error is empty, | having
nothing inside. |

Truth appeared; | all its emanations knew it. [30] They greeted the
Father in truth | with a perfect power | that joins them with the Father.
| For, as for everyone who loves the truth — | because the truth is the
mouth [35] of the Father; his tongue is the | Holy Spirit — he who is
joined **27** to the truth is joined | to the Father's mouth | by his tongue,
whenever he is to | receive the Holy Spirit, [5] since this is the manifesta-
tion of the | Father and his revelation | to his aeons.

He manifested | what was hidden of him; he explained it. | For who
contains, [10] if not the Father alone? | All the spaces are his emanations.
| They have known that they came forth | from him like children | who
are from a grown [15] man. They knew | that they had not yet | received
form nor yet | received a name, each one of which | the Father begets.
[20] Then, when they receive form | by his knowledge, | though truly
within him, they | do not know him. But the Father | is perfect, know-
ing [25] every space within him. | If he wishes, | he manifests whomever
he wishes | by giving him form and giving | him a name, and he gives a
name [30] to him and brings it about | that those come into existence who,

' before they come into existence, are ' ignorant of him who fashioned them. '

I do not say, then, that [35] they are nothing (at all) who have not ' yet come into existence, but they are **28** in him who will wish ' that they come into existence when he ' wishes, like ' the time that is to come. [5] Before all things appear, ' he knows what he will ' produce. But the fruit ' which is not yet manifest ' does not know anything, nor [10] does it do anything. Thus, ' also, every space which is ' itself in the Father is from ' the one who exists, who ' established it [15] from what does not exist. ' For he who has no ' root has no ' fruit either, but ' though he thinks to himself, [20] "I have come into being," yet ' he will perish by himself. ' For this reason, he who did not exist ' at all will ' never come into existence. What, then, did he [25] wish him to think of himself? ' This: "I have come into being like the ' shadows and phantoms ' of the night." When ' the light shines on the terror [30] which that person had experienced, ' he knows that it is nothing. '

Thus they were ignorant ' of the Father, he being the one **29** whom they did not see. Since ' it was terror and disturbance ' and instability ' and doubt and [5] division, there were many ' illusions at work ' by means of these, and ' (there were) empty fictions, as if ' they were sunk in sleep [10] and found themselves in ' disturbing dreams. Either (there is) a place ' to which they are fleeing, or ' without strength they come (from) having chased ' after others, or they are involved in [15] striking blows, or they are receiving ' blows themselves, or they have fallen from high places, ' or they take off into ' the air though they do not even have wings. [20] Again, sometimes (it is as) if people ' were murdering them, though there is ' no one even pursuing them, or they themselves ' are killing their neighbors, ' for they have been stained with [25] their blood. ' When those who ' are going through ' all these things wake up, they see nothing, ' they who were in the midst [30] of all these disturbances, ' for they are nothing. ' Such is the way ' of those who have cast ' ignorance aside [35] from them like sleep, ' not esteeming it as anything, ' nor do they esteem its **30** works as solid ' things either, but they ' leave them behind like a dream in the night. The [5] knowledge of the Father they value ' as the dawn. This is the way ' each one has acted, ' as though asleep at the time ' when he was ignorant. [10] And this is the way ' he has ⟨come to knowledge⟩, as if ' he had awakened. {and} Good ' for the man who will return ' and awaken. And [15] blessed is he who has opened ' the eyes of the blind.

And ' the Spirit ran after him, ' hastening from ' waking him up.

Having extended his hand [20] to him who lay upon the | ground, he set him up | on his feet, for | he had not yet risen. | He gave them the means of knowing [25] the knowledge of the Father and the | revelation of his Son. | For, when they had seen him and had | heard him, he granted them to | taste him and [30] to smell him and | to touch the | beloved Son.

When he had appeared | instructing them about the Father, | the incomprehensible one, when he had breathed into them [35] what is in the thought, doing | his will, when many had | received the light, they turned **31** to him. For the material ones were strangers | and did not see his likeness | and had not known | him. For he came [5] by means of fleshly | form, while nothing blocked | his course because | incorruptibility is irresistible, | since he, again, spoke [10] new things, still speaking about | what is in the heart of the Father, having | brought forth the flawless word. |

When light had spoken | through his mouth, [15] as well as his voice | which gave birth to life, he | gave them thought and understanding | and mercy and salvation and the powerful spirit | from the infiniteness [20] and the sweetness of the Father. | Having made punishments | and tortures cease — for it was they which | were leading astray from his face some | who were in need of mercy, in [25] error and in bonds — | he both destroyed them with power | and confounded them with knowledge. | He became a | way for those who were gone astray [30] and knowledge for those who were | ignorant, a discovery for those | who were searching, and a support | for those who were wavering, | immaculateness for those who [35] were defiled.

He is the shepherd | who left behind the ninety- **32** nine sheep which were not lost. | He went searching for the one which | had gone astray. He rejoiced when he | found it, for ninety-nine [5] is a number that is in the left hand | which holds it. But | when the one is found, | the entire number | passes to the right (hand). As [10] that which lacks the one — that is, | the entire right (hand) — | draws what was deficient and | takes it from the | left-hand side and brings (it) to the [15] right, so too the number | becomes one hundred. It is the sign of the one who is in | their sound; it is the Father. | Even on the Sabbath, he labored for the sheep | which he found fallen into the [20] pit. He gave life to | the sheep, having brought it up | from the pit in order that you | might know interiorly — [38] you, the sons of interior [39] knowledge — | what is the Sabbath, on which it is not fitting [25] for salvation to be idle, | in order that you may speak | from the day from above, | which has no night, | and from the light [30] which does not sink because it is perfect. |

Say, then, from the heart that ' you are the perfect day ' and in you
dwells ' the light that does not fail. [35] Speak of the truth with those who
' search for it and (of) knowledge to those ' who have committed sin in
their error. **33** Make firm the foot of those ' who have stumbled and
stretch out ' your hands to those who are ill. Feed ' those who are hungry and [5] give repose to those who are weary, and ' raise up those who
wish to ' rise, and awaken those who ' sleep. For you are the ' understanding that is drawn forth. If [10] strength acts thus, it becomes ' even
stronger. Be concerned with yourselves; ' do not be concerned with '
other things which you have ' rejected from yourselves. [15] Do not return
to what you have vomited ' to eat it. Do not be moths. ' Do not be
worms, for you have already ' cast it off. Do not become a [20] (dwelling)
place for the devil, for ' you have already destroyed him. ' Do not
strengthen (those who are) obstacles to you ' who are collapsing, as
though (you were) a support (for them). ' For the lawless one is someone to treat [25] ill rather than the just one. ' For the former ' does his
work as a ' lawless person; the latter as ' a righteous person does his [30]
work among others. So ' you, do the will of the Father, ' for you are
from him. '

For the Father is sweet and in ' his will is what is good. [35] He has taken cognizance of ' the things that are yours that you might find rest '
in them. For by the ' fruits does one take cognizance of ' the things that
are yours because the children of the Father **34** are his fragrance, for '
they are from the grace of his ' countenance. For this reason the Father
loves ' his fragrance and manifests it [5] in every place, and if it mixes '
with matter he gives his fragrance ' to the light and in his repose ' he
causes it to surpass every form ' (and) every sound. For it is not the ears
that [10] smell the fragrance, but ' (it is) the breath that has ' the sense of
smell and attracts the fragrance ' to itself and is submerged ' in the fragrance of the Father, so that he [15] thus shelters it and takes it to the place
' where it came from, ' from the first fragrance which ' is grown cold.
It is something in a ' psychic form, being [20] like cold water ' which has
frozen (?), which is on earth ' that is not solid, of which those ' who see
it think it ' is earth; afterwards it dissolves [25] again. If a breath ' draws
it, it gets hot. The fragrances, ' therefore, that are cold are from the
division. ' For this reason faith came; ' it dissolved the division, [30] and
it brought the warm pleroma ' of love in order that ' the cold should not
come again ' but there should be the unity of ' perfect thought. [35]

This ⟨is⟩ the word of the gospel ' of the discovery of the pleroma, for
' those who await **35** the salvation which is coming ' from on high.

While their ' hope, for which they ' are waiting, is in waiting – they whose image [5] is light with no shadow ' in it – then, at that time, ' the pleroma ' is proceeding to come. The ⟨deficiency⟩ ' of matter came to be not through [10] the limitlessness of ' the Father, who is coming to give time for ' the deficiency, although no one ' could say that the incorruptable one would ' come in this way. But [15] the depth of the Father was multiplied ' and the thought of ' error did not exist ' with him. It is a thing that falls, ' it is a thing that easily stands upright (again) [20] in the discovery of him ' who has come to him whom he shall bring back. ' For the bringing back ' is called repentance. '

For this reason incorruptibility [25] breathed forth; it pursued the one ' who had sinned in order that he might ' rest. For forgiveness is ' what remains for the light in the deficiency, ' the word of the pleroma. [30] For the physician runs to the place ' where sickness is, because ' that is the will that is ' in him. He who has a deficiency, then, does not ' hide it, because one has what [35] the other lacks. So the pleroma, ' which has no deficiency, ' but fills up the deficiency, is what he **36** provided from himself for filling up ' what he lacks, in order that ' therefore he might receive the grace. For when ' he was deficient, he did not have [5] the grace. That is why ' there was diminution existing in ' the place where there is no grace. ' When that which was diminished ' was received, he revealed what he [10] lacked, being (now) a pleroma; ' that is the discovery of the light ' of truth which rose upon him because ' it is immutable.

That is why ' Christ was spoken of in their [15] midst, so that those who were disturbed ' might receive a bringing back, and he ' might anoint them with the ointment. The ointment is ' the mercy of the Father who will have mercy ' on them. But those whom he has anointed [20] are the ones who have become perfect. ' For full jars are the ' ones that are usually anointed. But when ' the anointing of one (jar) is dissolved, ' it is emptied, and the [25] reason for there being a deficiency is the thing ' by which its ointment goes. ' For at that time ' a breath draws it, a thing ' in the power of that which is with it. [30] But from him who ' has no deficiency, no seal is removed ' nor is anything emptied, ' but what he lacks ' the perfect Father fills again. [35] He is good. He knows ' his plantings, because it is he ' who planted them in his paradise. ' Now his paradise ' is his place of rest.

This **37** is the perfection in the thought ' of the Father, and these are ' the words of his meditation. ' Each one of his words [5] is the work of his ' one will in the revelation ' of his Word. While they were still ' depths of his thought, the Word ' which was first to come forth revealed [10] them along with a mind that ' speaks, the one Word in ' silent grace. He was called ' thought, since they ' were in it before being revealed. [15] It came about then, that he ' was first to come forth at the time when the will of him ' who willed desired it. ' And the will is what the Father [20] rests in and ' is pleased with. Nothing ' happens without him nor does anything ' happen without the will of ' the Father, but his will [25] is unsearchable. His trace ' is the will and no one ' will know him nor is it possible ' for one to scrutinize him in order to ' grasp him. But [30] when he wills, ' what he wills is this — even if ' the sight does not please them ' in any way before God — ' desiring the Father. For he knows the [35] beginning of all of them and their end. ' For at their end he will question them ' directly. Now, the end is receiving knowledge ' about the one who is hidden, and this is the Father, **38** from whom the beginning came ' forth, to whom all will ' return who have ' come forth from him. [5] And they have appeared for the glory and the ' joy of his name. '

Now the name of the Father is the Son. It is he ' who first gave a name to the one ' who came forth from him, who was himself, [10] and he begot him as a son. ' He gave him his name which ' belonged to him; he is the one to whom ' belongs all that exists around ' him, the Father. His is the name; [15] his is the Son. It is possible ' for him to be seen. The name, however, ' is invisible because ' it alone is the ' mystery of the invisible [20] which comes to ears that are completely filled ' with it by him. For indeed, ' the Father's name is not spoken, ' but it is apparent through a ' Son.

In this way, then, the name is a great thing. [25] Who, therefore, will be able to utter a name for him, ' the great name, except him ' alone to whom ' the name belongs and the sons of the name ' in whom rested [30] the name of the Father, ' (who) in turn themselves rested ' in his name? Since the ' Father is unengendered, he alone is the one ' who begot him for him(self) as a name, [35] before he brought forth the ' aeons, in order that the name ' of the Father should be over their head as ' lord, that is the **39** name in truth, which is firm in his ' command through perfect power. ' For the name is not from ' (mere) words, nor [5] does his name consist of appellations, ' but it is invisible. ' He gave a name to him alone, ' since he alone sees him, he ' alone having [10] the power to give him a name. ' For he who does not exist ' has no name. ' For what name is given to him ' who does not exist? [15] But the one who exists ' exists also with his name, and ' he alone knows it, ' and alone (knows how) to give him a name. ' It is the Father. The Son [20] is his name. He did ' not, therefore, hide it in the thing, ' but it ' existed; as for the Son, he alone gave a name. ' The name, therefore, is that of the Father, [25] as the name of ' the Father is the Son. Where ' indeed would compassion find a name ' except with the Father?

But ' no doubt one will say [30] to his neighbor: "Who is it ' who will give a name to him who ' existed before himself, ' as if offspring did not receive a name **40** from those ' who begot ⟨them⟩?" First, ' then, it is fitting for us ' to reflect on this matter: What [5] is the name? It is the name ' in truth; it is not therefore ' the name from the Father, for ' it is the one which is the proper ' name. Therefore, he did not receive the name ' on loan as (do) ' others, according to the form ' in which each one ' is to be produced. ' But this is the proper name. [15] There is no one else who gave it to him. ' But he ⟨is⟩ unnamable, ' indescribable, ' until the time when he ' who is perfect spoke of him alone. [20] And it is he who ' has the power to speak ' his name and to see ' it.

When, therefore, it pleased ' him that his name [25] which is loved should be his Son, and ' he gave the name to him, that is, him ' who came forth from the depth, he ' spoke about his secret things, knowing ' that the Father is a being without evil. [30] For that very reason he brought him ' forth in order to speak ' about the place and his ' resting-place from which he had come forth, **41** and to glorify the pleroma, ' the greatness of his name and ' the sweetness of the Father. About ' the place each one came from [5] he will speak, and to the ' region where he received his establishment ' he will hasten to return ' again and to take from ' that place – the place where he [10] stood – receiving a taste ' from that place and ' receiving nourishment, receiving growth. And ' his own resting-place ' is his pleroma.

Therefore, [15] all the emanations of the Father ' are pleromas, and ' the root of all his emanations is in ' the one who made them all ' grow up in himself. He assigned them [20] their destinies. Each one then ' is manifest, ' in order that through their ' own thought ⟨...⟩. ' For the place to which they send [25] their thought, that place, ' their root, is what takes them ' up in all the heights ' to the Father. They possess his ' head, which is rest for them, [30] and they are supported, ' approaching him, ' as though to say that ' they have participated in his face ' by means of kisses. [35] But they do not become manifest **42** in this way, ' for they were not themselves exalted; ' (yet) neither did they lack the glory ' of the Father nor did they think of him as [5] small nor that he is harsh ' nor that he is wrathful, but ' (that) he is a being without evil, imperturbable, ' sweet, knowing ' all spaces before they have come into existence, and [10] he had no need to be instructed. '

This is the manner of ¹ those who possess (something) ¹ from above of the ¹ immensurable greatness, as they ¹⁵ wait for the one alone ¹ and the perfect one, the one who is ¹ there for them. And they do not go down ¹ to Hades nor have they ¹ envy nor ²⁰ groaning nor death ¹ within them, but they ¹ rest in him who is at rest, ¹ not striving nor ¹ being twisted around ²⁵ the truth. But they ¹ themselves are the truth; and ¹ the Father is within them and ¹ they are in the Father, being perfect, ¹ being undivided in ³⁰ the truly good one, being ¹ in no way deficient in anything, but ¹ they are set at rest, refreshed in the ¹ Spirit. And they will heed their ¹ root. They will be concerned with those (things) ³⁵ in which he will find his root ¹ and not suffer loss to his ¹ soul. This is the place of the ¹ blessed; this is their place. ¹

For the rest, then, may they ⁴⁰ know, in their places, that ¹ it is not fitting for me, **43** having come to be in the resting-place, ¹ to speak of anything else. But ¹ it is in it that I shall come to be, and (it is fitting) to ¹ be concerned at all times with the Father of ⁵ the all and the true brothers, ¹ those upon whom the love of ¹ the Father is poured out and ¹ in whose midst there is no lack of him. ¹ They are the ones who appear ¹⁰ in truth, since they exist in ¹ true and eternal life and ¹ speak of the light which ¹ is perfect and filled with ¹ the seed of the Father, and ¹⁵ which is in his heart and in the ¹ pleroma, while his ¹ Spirit rejoices in it and glorifies ¹ the one in whom it existed ¹ because he is good. And ²⁰ his children are perfect and ¹ worthy of his name, ¹ for he is the Father: it is children ¹ of this kind that he ¹ loves.

THE TREATISE ON THE RESURRECTION (I,*4*)

Introduced and translated by

MALCOLM L. PEEL

The importance of this short, eight-page, didactic letter lies in its witness to a distinctively unorthodox interpretation of Christian teaching about survival after death. By the late second century, the probable time of its composition, Christians – whether Gnostic or orthodox – were struggling with certain challenges and questions. Was such survival philosophically demonstrable (as Socrates had argued in the *Phaedo*)? What form might it take? (Immortality of the soul? Resurrection of the body? Reincarnation?) When would such survival be experienced? (At death? At Christ's final return? Perhaps even before death?) The New Testament teaching was somewhat ambiguous on several of these points, though within the great church there seemed general agreement on at least two matters: the prototype and basis of hope for such survival was the resurrection of Jesus Christ, and the resurrection of individuals would entail their retention of personal identity.

The anonymous author of *The Treatise on the Resurrection*, however, claimed a Christ-given knowledge (49,41-50,2) that enabled him to offer direct and unambiguous answers to such questions, questions which in this case had been put to him by his pupil, Rheginos (43,25). First, the resurrection is a matter of faith in the reality of Jesus Christ's resurrection and his destruction of death (46,14-19). Such cannot be the result of philosophical "persuasion," and most philosophers of the world are in fact sceptics.

Second, the form of survival will be the "resurrection," which is *not* understood as the re-creation of a spiritual body at Christ's Parousia (cf. 1 Co 15 *passim*). Rather, at the point of biological death, the "elect" believer experiences the separation of the inward, "living members," whose intellectual nature is clarified by reference to the "mind" and its "thought," *from* the external "body" of "perishable," "visible," outward "members" (47,38-48,2; 45,39-46,2; 45,19-21). Even so, this "resurrection body," covered with a new "flesh" (47,4-8) or "garment of light" ("rays" in 45,30-31), retains personally identifiable features, as the appearance of Elijah and Moses at Christ's transfiguration (Mk 9:2-8) makes clear. Such is the "spiritual resurrection" which "swallows up" (i.e., renders nonsensical or destroys) the "resurrection" of either the naked "soul" or of the crudely literal "flesh" (45,39-46,2). Implied is a dualistic doctrine of outer/inner that goes beyond Pauline anthropology.

Third, unlike the early church, which in its resurrection hope held to an "eschatological reservation" (i.e., the notion that the full benefit of individual Christians' participation in the resurrection would wait the final return of Christ), the author of *The Treatise on the Resurrection* held that for the elect believer who had proleptically participated in Christ's suffering (death), resurrection, and ascension (45,24-28), the new reality should be clear: one already *has* the resurrection in the present. In sum, our author, like the Hymenaeus and Philetus condemned in 2 Timothy 2:18, teaches that the resurrection has already occurred! He reinforces it by means of a kind of existential proof: the believer who knows of death's inevitability should consider himself as dead already and thus as already participating in the resurrected state (49,16-30). Thus, the believer is to have "faith" in the reality of Christ's victory over death and its guarantee (45,14-46, 4,14-17; 46,8-13), to avoid all "doubt" (47,36-48,3), to "know" the "Son of Man" and the truth proclaimed about his resurrection (46,13-17, 30-32), to "practise" one's release from the inimical power of this cosmos (49,30-33) through correct thought, and to realize the mystical unity between the experience of the Savior and that of the believer (45,15-46,2).

Major studies of the text have clarified that the author is a Christian Gnostic teacher who is clearly influenced by Valentinian Gnosticism. The evidence for this is found in the close parallels between the treatise's teaching that the spiritual resurrection has already occurred and the reports of Valentinian "realized eschatology" in Tertullian (*De praes. haer.* 33.7; *De res. mort.* 19,2-7) and Irenaeus (*Haer.* 2.31.2). Also, certain conceptual complexes unique to Valentinianism appear in *Treat. Res.*, such as the idea of a primordial pleroma which suffered a devolution and resulting "deficiency" (46,35-47,1; 49,4-5) which the Savior must "restore" (44,30-33).

Only to be expected, then, is the presence of Middle Platonic ideas which, as prior scholarship has shown, influenced Valentinianism. Such ideas include a distinction between a world of being (including the Good itself) and the sphere of becoming and corruption (48,20-27), as well as between an "intelligible world" and a "sensible" world (46,35-47,1). Also Platonic are notions of the pre-existence of souls (46,38-47,1; cf. 47,4-6; 49,30-36) and of "practising" for dying (49,28-33).

Rather un-Platonic, however, is the absence of any mention of an ultimate quest for ecstatic vision/union with the ultimate One, as well as our treatise's stress on retention of identifiable personal characteristics in the *post mortem* resurrected state.

Because of the centrality of Jesus Christ in the text, however, and because the author appeals to the New Testament as highest authority for his proofs (cf. 43,34; 45,4, 24-28; 48,6-11), we conclude that the author is a Christian Gnostic whose thought displays the influence of Middle Platonism as filtered through a late and somewhat vaguely articulated Valentinian Gnosticism.

Critical opinion now generally holds that *Treat. Res.* is not written by Valentinus himself. Studies of the stage of the New Testament canon of which the anonymous author seems aware, of the place of *Treat. Res.* teaching in the context of debates over the resurrection in the early church, and of the type of Middle Platonic ideas found in it all converge in pointing toward the late second century as the probable time of composition. As to its provenance, neither internal nor external evidence provides any clues.

Debate continues over whether the writing is a genuine didactic letter lacking a *praescriptio* naming its author (such as are the *Epistula Apostolorum* or the *Letter of Ptolemy to Flora*) and incorporating elements of the diatribe style, or whether it is principally a philosophical discourse decisively shaped by the Cynic-Stoic diatribe. As yet, the last named is lacking a convincing demonstration.

Most scholars do seem to reject the suggestions, however, that the text is the result of combining two originally separate letters or that it is the result of a gnostic redaction of an originally Christian text.

THE TREATISE ON THE RESURRECTION

I 43, 25-50, 18

Some there are, my son Rheginos, ' who want to learn many things. ' They have this goal ' when they are occupied with questions ' whose answer is lacking. [30] If they succeed with these, they usually ' think very highly of ' themselves. But I do not think ' that they have stood within ' the Word of Truth. They seek [35] rather their own rest, which ' we have received through our ' Savior, our Lord Christ. **44** We received it (i.e., Rest) when we came to know ' the truth and rested ' ourselves upon it. But ' since you ask us [5] pleasantly what is proper ' concerning the resurrection, I am writing ' you (to say) that it is necessary. ' To be sure, many are ' lacking faith in it, but there are a few [10] who find it. ' So then, let us discuss ' the matter. '

How did the Lord proclaim ' things while he existed [15] in flesh and after ' he had revealed himself as Son ' of God? He lived ' in this place where you ' remain, speaking [20] about the Law of Nature − but I call ' it "Death!" Now the Son ' of God, Rheginos, ' was Son of Man. ' He embraced them [25] both, possessing the ' humanity and the divinity, ' so that on the one hand he might vanquish ' death through his ' being Son of God, [30] and that on the other through the Son of ' Man the restoration ' to the Pleroma ' might occur; because ' he was originally from above, [35] a seed of the Truth, before ' this structure (of the cosmos) had come into being. ' In this (structure) many dominions and ' divinities came into existence. '

I know that I am presenting **45** the solution in difficult terms, ' but there is nothing ' difficult in the Word ' of Truth. But since [5] the Solution appeared ' so as not to leave anything hidden, ' but to reveal all ' things openly concerning ' existence − the destruction [10] of evil on the one hand, the revelation ' of the elect on the other. This (Solution) is ' the emanation of Truth and ' Spirit, Grace is of the Truth. '

The Savior swallowed up [15] death − (of this) you are not reckoned as being ignorant − ' for he put aside the world ' which is perishing. He transformed [himself] ' into an imperishable Aeon ' and raised himself up, having [20] swallowed the visible ' by the invisible, ' and he gave us ' the way of our immortality. Then, | indeed, as the Apostle [25] said, "We suffered | with him, and we arose | with him, and we went to heaven | with him." Now if we are | manifest in [30] this world wearing | him, we are that one's beams, | and we are | embraced by | him until our setting, that is [35] to say, our death in this life. | We are drawn to heaven | by him, like beams | by the sun, not being restrained | by anything. This is [40] the spiritual resurrection | **46** which swallows up the psychic | in the same way as the fleshly. |

But if there is one who | does not believe, he does not have [5] the (capacity to be) persuaded. For it is the domain of faith, | my son, and not that which belongs | to persuasion: the dead shall | arise! There is one who believes | among the philosophers who are in this world. [10] At least he will arise. And let not the philosopher | who is in this world have cause to | believe that he is one who returns himself | by himself — and (that) because of our faith! | For we have known the Son of [15] Man, and we have believed | that he rose from among the | dead. This is he of whom we say, | "He became the destruction | of death, as he is a great one [20] in whom they believe." | ⟨Great⟩are those who believe. |

The thought of those | who are saved shall not perish. | The mind of those who have known him shall not perish. [25] Therefore, we are elected to | salvation and redemption since | we are predestined from the beginning | not to fall into the | foolishness of those who are without knowledge, [30] but we shall enter into the | wisdom of those who have known the | Truth. Indeed, the Truth which is kept | cannot be abandoned, | nor has it been. [35] "Strong is the system of the | Pleroma; small is that which | broke loose (and) became | (the) world. But the All is | what is encompassed. It has not **47** come into being; it was existing." So, | never doubt concerning | the resurrection, my son Rheginos! | For if you were not existing [5] in flesh, you received flesh when you | entered this world. Why | will you not receive flesh when you | ascend into the Aeon? | That which is better than the flesh is that which is [10] for it (the) cause of life. | That which came into being on your account, is it not | yours? Does not that which is yours | exist with you? | Yet, while you are in this world, what is it that you [15] lack? This is what | you have been making every effort to learn. |

The afterbirth of the body is | old age, and you | exist in corruption. You have [20] absence as a gain. | For you will not give up what | is better if you depart. That which is worse | has diminution, | but there is grace for it.

Nothing, [25] then, redeems us from | this world. But the All which |

we are, we are saved. We have received $^|$ salvation from end $^|$ to end. Let us think in this way! ^{30} Let us comprehend in this way!

But $^|$ there are some (who) wish to understand, $^|$ in the enquiry about $^|$ those things they are looking into, whether $^|$ he who is saved, if he leaves ^{35} his body behind, will $^|$ be saved immediately. Let $^|$ no one doubt concerning this. $^|$ ... indeed, the visible members $^|$ which are dead **48** shall not be saved, for (only) the living [members] $^|$ which exist within $^|$ them would arise.

What, $^|$ then, is the resurrection? ^{5} It is always the disclosure of $^|$ those who have risen. For if you $^|$ remember reading in the Gospel $^|$ that Elijah appeared $^|$ and Moses ^{10} with him, do not think the resurrection $^|$ is an illusion. $^|$ It is no illusion, but $^|$ it is truth! Indeed, it is more $^|$ fitting to say that ^{15} the world is an illusion, $^|$ rather than the resurrection which $^|$ has come into being through $^|$ our Lord the Savior, $^|$ Jesus Christ. ^{20}

But what am I telling $^|$ you now? Those who are living $^|$ shall die. How $^|$ do they live in an illusion? $^|$ The rich have become poor, ^{25} and the kings have been overthrown. $^|$ Everything is prone $^|$ to change. The world $^|$ is an illusion! — lest, $^|$ indeed, I rail at ^{30} things to excess!

But $^|$ the resurrection does not have $^|$ this aforesaid character, for $^|$ it is the truth which stands firm. $^|$ It is the revelation of ^{35} what is, and the transformation $^|$ of things, and a $^|$ transition into $^|$ newness. For imperishability **49** [descends] upon $^|$ the perishable; the light flows $^|$ down upon the darkness, $^|$ swallowing it up; and the Pleroma ^{5} fills up the deficiency. $^|$ These are the symbols and $^|$ the images of the resurrection. $^|$ He (Christ) it is who makes the $^|$ good.

Therefore, do not ^{10} think in part, O Rheginos, $^|$ nor live $^|$ in conformity with this flesh for the sake of $^|$ unanimity, but flee $^|$ from the divisions and the ^{15} fetters, and already you have $^|$ the resurrection. For if $^|$ he who will die knows $^|$ about himself that he $^|$ will die — even if he spends many ^{20} years in this life, he is $^|$ brought to this — $^|$ why not consider yourself $^|$ as risen and (already) $^|$ brought to this? ^{25} If you have $^|$ the resurrection but continue as if $^|$ you are to die — and yet that one knows $^|$ that he has died — why, then, $^|$ do I ignore your ^{30} lack of exercise? It is fitting for each $^|$ one to practice $^|$ in a number of ways, and $^|$ he shall be released from this Element $^|$ that he may not fall into error but shall himself ^{35} receive again $^|$ what at first was. $^|$

These things I have received from $^|$ the generosity of my **50** Lord, Jesus Christ. [I have] taught $^|$ you and your [brethren], my sons, concerning them, $^|$ while I have not omitted any of $^|$ the things suitable for strengthening you (pl.). [5] But if there is one thing written ' which is obscure in my exposition of ' the Word, I shall interpret it for you (pl.) ' when you (pl.) ask. But now, ' do not be jealous of anyone who is in your number [10] when he is able to help. '

Many are looking into ' this which I have written ' to you. To these I say: ' peace (be) among them and grace. [15] I greet you and those who love ' you (pl.) in brotherly love. '

The Treatise on the ' Resurrection

THE TRIPARTITE TRACTATE (I,5)

Introduced by

HAROLD W. ATTRIDGE and ELAINE H. PAGELS

Translated by

HAROLD W. ATTRIDGE and DIETER MUELLER

The final tractate of Codex I is an elaborate, but untitled, Valentinian theological treatise which gives an account of the whole process of devolution from and reintegration into the primordial godhead. The text is divided by scribal decoration into three segments which contain the major acts of the cosmic drama; hence its modern title.

The date of composition can only be determined within broad limits. Since the doctrine of the text represents a revised form of Valentinian theology which may be a response to the criticism of orthodox theologians such as Irenaeus or Hippolytus, the work was probably written in the early to mid third century. The text displays some affinities with Origen's doctrines, although these may be due to common theological and philosophical sources.

The tractate offers no information about the identity of its author. Some scholars have speculated that the Valentinian teacher Heracleon could have written the work. While there are affinities with Heracleon and the Western or Italian school of Valentinianism, the work departs from classical Valentinian doctrine more radically than any known representative of the tradition.

Like the other tractates of Codex I and most of the works in the Nag Hammadi collection, *The Tripartite Tractate* was originally composed in Greek. The Coptic translation presents numerous difficulties and obscurities, many of which probably reflect the style of the original.

The theological purview of the tractate is comprehensive. The first part (51,1-104,3) describes the emanation of all supernatural entities from their primal source. It begins with the Father (51,1-57,8), described primarily through a *via negativa* as an utterly transcendent entity. What can be affirmed is that he is unique and monadic. The insistence on the unitary character of the Father distinguishes the text from most other Valentinians who posit a primal masculine-feminine dyad, although some members of the school, such as those mentioned by Hippolytus (*Ref.* 6.29.2-8), also hold to a monadic first principle.

Emanating from the Father are two other entities, the Son and the Church (57,8-59,38). At this point the tractate again differs from other Valentinian sources, which regularly posit a more complex godhead. The pleroma or "fullness of deity" usually consists of an ogdoad, a set eight syzygies, or pairs of divine entities, a similarly composed decad, and duodecad. Instead, *The Tripartite Tractate* posits an initial trinity.

Some elements of the complex traditional Valentinian picture are retained in the description of the components or "aeons" of the third element of the trinity, the Church (50,1-74,18). The dependence on, as well as revision of, Valentinian sources is clear in the stage of the text which describes the problems created by one of the aeons (74,18-80,11). In other Valentinian accounts, which are based on earlier, non-Christian speculation, the problem in the godhead arises because of a female aeon, Sophia (Wisdom), who attempts to do the impossible. According to different versions of the story, she either tries to produce offspring without her consort or tries to know the unknowable primal source. In either case, she falls outside the divine pleroma and produces the world of psychic and material forces. In *The Tripartite Tractate* the agent of the rupture in the pleroma is a masculine aeon, the Logos (Word). His fall, which includes elements of both traditional explanations of Sophia's catastrophe, is presented in remarkably positive terms, as a result of his own "abundant love" (76,19-20). It is also, remarkably enough, in accordance with the Father's will (76,24-77,1). Most importantly, it proceeds from the Logos' free choice (75,35-76,1), a quality which all entities dependent on him share.

The fall of the Logos produces two orders of beings which are outside the pleroma (80,11-85,15). From his confused and defective procreative activity emerge hylic forces. When the Logos, on his own initiative, repents, he produces psychic forces. These supernatural forces will play a role in creation of the first human and in cosmic governance.

The most important result of the conversion of the Logos is the generation of the Savior (85,15-90,13). This transpires when the Logos splits in two. His better, masculine self returns to the pleroma to intercede for his defective, feminine self. That better self, along with the aeons who have never left the pleroma, produce the Savior. That being is also called, by analogy with the highest level of reality, the Son, because as the Son reveals the Father to the aeons of the pleroma, the Savior will provide revelatory insight to those outside the pleroma.

The brief second part of the tractate (104,4-108,12) offers an interpretation of Genesis 1-3. The first human being is produced on the one hand by the Demiurge and on the other hand by the Logos. The former provides Adam's psychic and material components and the latter his spiritual component. The three potencies of the first human being will later be actualized in three classes of human beings at the coming of the Savior.

The third part of the tractate (108,13-138,27) focuses on soteriological issues. The Savior's appearance divides humankind into three classes (118,14-122,12). The pneumatic or spiritual recognize the Savior immediately and respond to him, while the hylic or material reject him utterly. Between these two extremes the psychic or soulful types hesitate, and only gradually come to join the Savior. As is usual in Valentinian texts, the three types have clear social referents. The pneumatics are the Valentinians themselves, the hylics are non-Christians and the psychics are ordinary Christians. The attention lavished on the detailed description of the psychics is indicative of the apologetic and irenic tendencies of the work.

In its final section (129,34-138,27) the text returns to the issue of the psychic and the process of their salvation. It then proceeds to sketch an eschatological tableau, the last portions of which are quite fragmentary. It concludes with a hymn to "the Savior, the Redeemer of all those who belong to the one filled with love, through his Holy Spirit, from now on through all generations forever" (138,20-25).

The Tripartite Tractate has revised traditional Valentinianism on several key points: in its insistence on the unity of the first principle; in the substitution of a trinity for a more complex godhead; in its portrait of the Logos as the element of the godhead responsible for the rupture in the divine; in its moderate assessment of the psychic demiurge; in its detailed analysis of the tripartition of humanity as a result of the freely chosen response of each individual to the appearance of the Savior; and in the hope of final redemption held out to ordinary Christians. This bold revision of Valentinian speculation serves as the basis for a comprehensive theological statement designed to appeal not simply to an isolated sect, but to the church as a whole.

THE TRIPARTITE TRACTATE

I 51, 1-138, 27

Part I

1. *Introduction*

As for what we can say about the things which are exalted, | what is fitting is that we | begin with the Father, who is the root of | the Totality, the one from whom we have received [5] grace to | speak about him.

2. *The Father*

He existed | before anything other than himself | came into being. The Father is a | single one, like a [10] number, for he is the first one and the one who | is only himself. Yet he is | not like a solitary individual. | Otherwise, how could he be a father? | For whenever there is a "father," [15] the name "son" follows. But the single | one, who alone is | the Father, is like a root | with tree, branches | and fruit. It is said [20] of him that he is | a father in the proper sense, since he is | inimitable | and immutable. Because of | this he is single in the proper sense [25] and is a god, because no | one is a god for him nor | is anyone a father to him. | For he is unbegotten and there is no other | who begot him, nor [30] another who created him. | For whoever is someone's father | or his creator, | he, too, has a father and | creator. It is certainly possible [35] for him to be father and creator | of the one who came into being | from him and the one whom he created, | for he is not a father in the proper sense, nor [40] a god, because he has [52] someone who begot [him and] who | created him. It is, then, | only the Father and God in the proper sense

' that no one else begot. As for [the] Totalities, [5] he is the one who begot them and ' created them. He is without beginning ' and without end.

Not only ' is he without end – He is immortal for this reason, ' that he is unbegotten – [10] but he is also invariable in ' his eternal existence, ' in his identity, in that ' by which he is established and in that ' by which he is great. Neither [15] will he remove himself from that by which he ' is, nor will anyone else ' force him to produce ' an end which he has not ever desired. ' He has not had [20] anyone who initiated his own existence. ' Thus, he is himself unchanged ' and no one else ' can remove him from his ' existence and [25] his identity, that in which he is, ' and his greatness, so that ' he cannot be grasped; nor is it possible ' for anyone else to change him into a different ' form or to reduce him, or alter him [30] or diminish him, – since this is so ' in the fullest sense of the truth – ' who is the unalterable, immutable one, ' with immutability clothing him. '

Not only is he the one [35] called ' "without a beginning" and "without an end," ' because he is unbegotten ' and immortal; ' but just as he has [40] no beginning and no ' end as he is, he is ' unattainable [53] in his greatness, inscrutable ' in his wisdom, incomprehensible ' in his power, ' and unfathomable in his [5] sweetness.

In the proper sense ' he alone, the good, ' the unbegotten Father and the ' complete perfect one, is the one filled ' with all his offspring [10] and with every virtue and with ' everything of value. And he has ' more, that is, lack of any ' malice, in order that it may be discovered ' that whoever has [anything] is indebted to him, [15] because he gives it, being ' himself unreachable and unwearied ' by that which he gives, since he is wealthy ' in the gifts which he bestows ' and at rest [20] in the favors which he grants. '

He is of such a kind and ' form and great magnitude ' that no one else has been with ' him from the beginning; nor is there a place [25] in which he is, or from which he has come forth, ' or into which he will go; ' nor is there a primordial form, ' which he uses as a model ' as he works; nor is there any difficulty [30] which accompanies him in what ' he does; nor is there any material which ' is at his disposal, from which ⟨he⟩ creates ' what he creates; ' nor any substance within him from [35] which he begets what he begets; ' nor a co-worker ' with him, working with him on the things at which he works. ' To say anything of this sort ' is ignorant. Rather, (one should speak of him) as [40] good, faultless, perfect, [54] complete, being himself the Totality. '

Not one of ' the names which are conceived, ' or spoken, seen or [5] grasped, ' not one of them applies to him, ' even though they are exceedingly glorious, magnifying ' and honored. However, ' it is possible to utter these names for his glory [10] and honor, in accordance with the capacity ' of each of those who give him glory. ' Yet as for him, in his own ' existence, being ' and form, [15] it is impossible for mind to conceive ' him, nor can any speech ' convey him, nor can any eye ' see him, nor can any body ' grasp him, because of [20] his inscrutable greatness ' and his incomprehensible depth, ' and his immeasurable height, ' and his illimitable will. ' This is the nature of the [25] unbegotten one, which does not touch ' anything else; nor is it joined (to anything) ' in the manner of something which is limited. ' Rather, he possesses this constitution, ' without having a [30] face or a form, things which ' are understood through ' perception, whence also comes (the epithet) "the incomprehensible." ' If he is incomprehensible, ' then it follows that [35] he is unknowable, that he is the one who is inconceivable ' by any thought, ' invisible by any thing, ' ineffable by any word, ' untouchable by any hand. [40] He alone ' is the one who knows himself as he [55] is, along with his form ' and his greatness and his magnitude, ' and since he has the ability to ' conceive of himself, to see himself, to name [5] himself, to comprehend himself, he ' alone is the one who is his own mind, ' his own eye, ' his own mouth, his own ' form, and he is what he thinks, [10] what he sees, ' what he speaks, ' what he grasps, himself, ' the one who is inconceivable, ' ineffable, incomprehensible, immutable, [15] while sustaining, joyous, ' true, delightful, ' and restful is that which he conceives, ' that which he sees, that about which he speaks, ' that which he has as thought. [20] He transcends ' all wisdom, and is ' above all intellect, and is ' above all glory, and is ' above all beauty, and [25] all sweetness, and all greatness, ' and any depth and any height. '

If this one, who is ' unknowable in his ' nature, to whom pertain all the greatnesses which [30] I already mentioned, ' if out of the abundance of his sweetness he wishes to grant knowledge ' so that he might be known, ' he has the ability to do so. ' He has his power, [35] which is his will. Now, however, ' in silence he himself holds back, ' he who is ' the great one, who is the cause ' of bringing the Totalities into their [40] eternal being. [56]

It is in ' the proper sense that he begets ' himself as ineffable, ' since he alone is self-begotten, [5] since he conceives of himself, and since he ' knows himself as he is. ' What is worthy of ' his admiration and glory and honor ' and praise, he produces [10] because of the boundlessness ' of his greatness, and the ' unsearchability of his ' wisdom, and the immeasurability ' of his power and his [15] untasteable sweetness. ' He is the one who projects himself ' thus, as generation, having ' glory and honor ' marvelous and lovely; the one who [20] glorifies himself, ' who marvels, ⟨who⟩ ' honors, who also loves; ' the one who has ' a Son, who subsists [25] in him, who is silent concerning him, who is ' the ineffable one ' in the ineffable one, the ' invisible one, the incomprehensible one, ' the inconceivable one in [30] the inconceivable one. Thus, ' he exists in him forever. ' The Father, in the way we mentioned earlier, ' in an unbegotten way, is the one in whom ' he knows himself, [35] who begot him having ' a thought, ' which is the thought ' of him, that is, the **57** perception of him, which is the [...] ' of his constitution ' forever. That is, ' however, in the proper sense, [5] [the] silence and the wisdom ' and the grace, if it is designated ' properly ' in this way.

3. *The Son and the Church*

Just as [the] ' Father exists in the proper sense, [10] the one before whom [there was no one] ' else and [the one] ' apart from [whom] there is no other unbegotten one, so ' too the [Son] ' exists in the proper sense, [15] the one before whom there was no other, ' and after whom ' no other son exists. ' Therefore, he is a firstborn ' and an only Son, [20] "firstborn" because no one ' exists before him and "only Son" ' because no one is after ' him. Furthermore, he has ' his fruit, [25] that which is unknowable because ' of its surpassing greatness. Yet ' he wanted it to be known, ' because of the riches of his ' sweetness. [30] And he revealed the unexplainable power and ' he combined with it ' the great abundance of his generosity. '

Not only did the Son exist ' from the beginning, but the Church, [35] too, existed from the beginning. ' Now, he who thinks that the discovery ' that the Son is an only son ' opposes the statement (about the Church) − ' because of the mysterious quality of the matter [40] it is not so. For just as **58** the Father is a unity ' and has revealed himself ' as Father for him ' alone, so too [5] the Son was found ' to be a brother to himself alone, ' in virtue of the fact that he is unbegotten ' and without beginning. He ' wonders at himself [10] [along with the] Father, and he gives ' [him(self)] glory and honor and ' [love.] Furthermore, he too ' is the one whom he conceives of ' as Son, in accordance with the [15] dispositions: "without ' beginning" and "without end." ' Thus is the matter ' something which is fixed. ' Being innumerable and [20] illimit-

able, his offspring ' are indivisible. Those ' which exist have come '
forth from the Son and the Father ' like kisses, because of the multitude
25 of some who kiss one ' another with a ' good, insatiable thought, '
the kiss being a unity, although it involves ' many kisses. This is to say,
it is the 30 Church consisting of many men that ' existed before the
aeons, ' which is called, in the proper ' sense, "the aeons of the aeons."
' This is the nature of the 35 holy imperishable spirits, ' upon which the
Son rests, ' since it is his essence, just as ' the Father rests **59** upon the
Son.

4. *Aenoic Emanations*

[...] ' the Church exists in the ' dispositions and properties ' in which
the Father and the Son exist, 5 as I have said from the start. ' Therefore,
it subsists ' in the procreations of innumerable aeons. ' Also in an un-
countable way [they] ' too beget, by [the] properties [and] 10 the dispositions in which it (the Church) [exists.] ' [For] these [comprise its] '
association which [they form] ' toward one another and [toward those]
' who have come forth from [them] 15 toward the Son, for whose glory
they exist. ' Therefore, ' it is not possible for mind to conceive of ' him
– He was the perfection of that place – ' nor can speech 20 express
them, for they are ineffable ' and unnameable ' and inconceivable.
They ' alone have the ability ' to name themselves and to conceive 25 of
themselves. For they have not been rooted ' in these places.

Those of that place ' are ineffable, ' (and) innumerable in ' the system
which is 30 both the manner and the ' size, the joy, the gladness ' of the
unbegotten, ' nameless, unnameable, ' inconceivable, invisible, 35 incomprehensible one. ' It is the fullness of paternity, ' so that his abundance ' is a begetting **60** [...] of the aeons.

They ' were forever in ' thought, for the Father ' was like a thought
5 and a place for them. When their ' generations had been established,
the one who is completely in control ' wished to lay hold of and to bring
forth that which was deficient in the 10 [..., and he brought] forth those
' [...] him. But since he is ' [as] he is, ' [he is] a spring, which is not '
diminished by the water which 15 abundantly flows from it. ' While they
were ' in the Father's thought, that ' is, in the hidden depth, ' the depth
knew them, 20 but they ' were unable to know ' the depth in which they
were; ' nor was it ' possible for them to know 25 themselves, nor ' for
them to know anything else. That ' is, they were ' with the Father; they
did not exist for ' themselves. Rather, 30 they only had ' existence in the

manner ' of a seed, so that it has been discovered ' that they existed like a ' fetus. Like the word [35] he begot them, subsisting ' spermatically, and ' the ones whom he was to beget had not yet come into being **61** from him. The one who ' first thought of them, the Father, ' – not only so that they might exist for him, ' but also that they might exist for themselves as well, [5] that they might then exist in [his] thought ' as mental substance ' and that they might exist for themselves too, – ' sowed a thought like a [spermatic] seed. ' Now, in order that [they] [10] might know [what exists] ' for them, he graciously [granted the] ' initial form, while in order that they might [recognize] ' who is the Father who exists [for them]. ' he gave them the name "Father" [15] by means of a voice proclaiming to them ' that what exists exists through ' that name, which they have ' by virtue of the fact that they came into being, because the exaltation, ' which has escaped their notice, is in the name. [20]

The infant, while in the ' form of a fetus ' has enough for itself, ' before ever seeing the one who ' sowed it. Therefore, they had [25] the sole task ' of searching for him, realizing ' that he exists, ever wishing to find out ' what exists. Since, however, ' the perfect Father is good, [30] just as he did not hear ' them at all so that they would exist (only) ' in his thought, but rather granted that ' they, too, might come into being, so ' also will he give them grace [35] to know what exists, ' that is, the one who knows ' himself eternally, **62** [. . .] ' form to [know] what ' exists, just as people are begotten in this ' place: when they are born, they are in [5] the light, so that they see those who have begotten them. '

The Father brought forth everything, ' like a little child, ' like a drop from a ' spring, like a blossom [10] from a [vine], like a ' [flower], like a ⟨planting⟩ ' [. . .] in need of gaining ' [nourishment] and growth and ' faultlessness. He withheld it [15] for a time. He who had thought ' of it from the very beginning, ' possessed it from the very beginning, ' and saw it, but he closed it off ' to those who first came from [20] him. (He did this,) not out of envy, but ' in order that the aeons might not receive their faultlessness ' from the very beginning ' and might not exalt themselves to the ' glory, to the Father, and might think [25] that from themselves alone ' they have this. But ' just as he wished ' to grant that they might come into being, so ' too, in order that they might come into being as [30] faultless ones, when he wished, he gave them ' the perfect idea of ' beneficience ' toward them.

The one whom he raised up ' as a light for those who came [35] from himself, the one ' from whom they take their name, ' he is the Son, who is full, complete ' and faultless. He brought him forth ' mingled with

what came forth from **63** him [. . .] | partaking of the [. . .] | the Totali-
ty, in accordance with [. . .] by which each | one can receive [him] for
himself, [5] though such was not his greatness | before he was received by
it. Rather, | he exists by himself. As | for the parts in which he exists in
his own manner and | form and greatness, [10] it is possible for ⟨them⟩ to
see him | and speak about that which they know | of him, since they
wear | him while he wears them, [because] | it is possible for them to
comprehend him. [15] He, however, is as he is, | incomparable. | In order
that the Father might receive | honor from each one | and reveal
himself, [20] even in his ineffability, | hidden, and invisible, | they marvel
at him mentally. | Therefore, the | greatness of his loftiness consists in
the fact that they [25] speak about him and see him. | He becomes
manifest, | so that he may be hymned because of the abundance | of his
sweetness, with the grace | of ⟨. . .⟩. And just as [30] the admirations | of
the silences | are eternal generations | and they are mental offspring, |
so too the dispositions [35] of the word are spiritual | emanations. Both of
them [admirations and dispositions], | since they belong to a word, **64**
are [seeds] and | thoughts [of] his offspring, | and roots which live |
forever, appearing [5] to be offspring which have come forth from |
themselves, being minds and | spiritual offspring to | the glory of the
Father.

There is no need | for voice and spirit, mind and [10] word, because
there is no need to | [work at] that which they desire | [to do], but on the
pattern | by which [he was] existing, so | are those who have come forth
from him, [15] begetting everything which they desire. And | the one
whom they conceive of, and | whom they speak about, and the one |
toward whom they move, and | the one in whom they are, and [20] the
one whom they hymn, thereby glorifying him, | he has | sons. For this
is their procreative | power, like | those from whom they have come, [25]
according to their mutual assistance, | since they assist one another |
like the unbegotten ones. |

The Father, in accordance with his | exalted position over the
Totalities, being [30] an unknown and incomprehensible one, | has such
greatness | and magnitude, that, | if he had revealed himself | suddenly,
quickly, [35] to all the exalted ones among the aeons | who had come
forth from him, they | would have perished. Therefore, he | withheld
his power and his inexhaustibility | within that in which he **65** is. [He is]
| ineffable [and] unnameable | and exalted above every mind | and every
word. This one, however, stretched [5] himself out | and it was that which
he stretched out | which gave a foundation and | a space and a dwelling

place for ' the universe, a name of his being "the ¹⁰ one through whom," since he is ' Father of the All, out of his ' laboring for those who exist, ' having sown into their thought that [they] ' might seek after him. The abundance of their [. . .] ¹⁵ consists in the fact that they understand that he ' exists and in the fact that they ask what it is ' [that] was existing. This one was ' given to them for enjoyment and ' nourishment and joy and an abundance ²⁰ of illumination, which ' consists in his fellow laboring, ' his knowledge and his mingling ' with them, that is, the one ' who is called and is, in fact, ²⁵ the Son, since he is the Totalities ' and the one of whom they know both who he is ' and that it is he who clothes. ' This is the one who is called ' "Son" and the one of whom they understand ³⁰ that he exists and they were seeking ' after him. This is the one who exists ' as Father and (as) the one about whom they cannot speak, ' and the one of whom they do not conceive. ' This is the one who first came into being. ³⁵

It is impossible for anyone to conceive ' of him or think of him. Or can anyone ' approach there, toward the exalted one, ' toward the pre-existent in the proper ' sense? But all the names conceived **66** or spoken ' about him are presented ' in honor, as a trace ' of him, according to the ability of each ⁵ one of those who glorify him. Now he ' who arose from him when he stretched ' himself out for begetting and ' for knowledge on the part of the Totalities, he ' [. . .] all of the names, without falsification, ¹⁰ and he is, ' in the proper sense, the sole first one, ' [the] man of the Father, that is, the one whom I ' call

the form of the formless, '
the body of the bodiless,
the face ¹⁵ of the invisible,
the word of [the] ' unutterable,
the mind of the inconceivable, '
the fountain which flowed from ' him,
the root of those who are planted, '
and the god of those who exist,
the light ²⁰ of those whom he illumines,
the love of those ' whom he loved,
the providence of those for whom he ' providentially cares,
the wisdom ' of those whom he made wise,
the power ' of those to whom he gives power,
the assembly ²⁵ [of] those whom he assembles to him,
the revelation ' of the things which are sought after,
the eye ' of those who see,

the breadth of those who breathe, |
the life of those who live,
the unity | of those who are mixed with the Totalities. [30]

All of them exist in the single one, | as he clothes himself completely | and by his single name | he is never called. | And in [35] this unique way they are equally | the single one and the Totalities. | He is neither divided as a body, | nor is he separated into the names | which he has [received], [40] (so that) he is one thing in this way and another [67] in [another way.] Also, neither | does he change in [...], nor | does he turn into [the names] which he | [thinks of,] and become now this, now [5] something else, this thing now being one thing | and, at another time, something else, | but rather he is wholly himself to the uttermost. [He] | is each and every one of the Totalities | forever at the same time. He is what [10] all of them are. He brought | the Father to the Totalities. He also is the Totalities, | for he is the one who is knowledge | for himself and he is | each one of the properties. He [15] has the powers and [he is] beyond | all that which he knows, | while seeing himself in himself | completely and having a | Son and form. Therefore, [20] his powers and properties are innumerable | and inaudible, | because of the begetting [by] which he | begets them. Innumerable | and indivisible are [25] the begettings of his words, and | his commands and his Totalities. | He knows them, which things he himself is, | since they are in | the single name, and [30] are all speaking in it. And | he brings (them) forth, in order that | it might be discovered that they | exist according to their individual properties in a unified way. | And he did not reveal the multitude [35] to the Totalities at once | nor did he reveal his equality | to those who had come forth from him. |

5. Aeonic Life

All those who came forth from him, | ⟨who⟩ are the aeons of the aeons, [68] being emanations and offspring of | ⟨his⟩ procreative nature, | they too, in their procreative | nature, have ⟨given⟩ glory to [5] the Father, as he was | the cause of their establishment. This is what | we said previously, namely that he creates | the aeons as roots and [10] springs and fathers, and that he | is the one to whom they give glory. They have begotten, for | he has knowledge | and wisdom | and the Totalities knew [15] that it is from knowledge | and wisdom that they have come forth. | They would have brought forth | a seeming honor: "The Father is the one | who is the Totalities," [20] if the aeons had risen

up to give ' honor individually. ' Therefore, in the ' song of glorification and ' in the power of the unity [25] of him from ' whom they have
come, they were drawn into a mingling ' and a combination and a unity
' with one another. ' They offered glory worthy of [30] the Father from
the pleromatic ' congregation, which is a ' single representation although many, ' because it was brought forth as a glory ' for the single
one and because [35] they came forth toward the one who ' is himself the
Totalities. Now, this **69** was a praise [. . .] ' the one who brought forth
the Totalities, ' being a first-fruit of the immortals ' and an eternal one,
because, [5] having come forth from the living aeons, being ' perfect and
full because of the one who is perfect ' and full, it left full ' and perfect
those who have given glory in ' a perfect way because of the [10] fellowship. For, like the faultless Father, ' when he is glorified he ' also hears
the glory which glorifies him, ' so as to make them manifest as that
which ' he is.

The cause of the second [15] honor which accrued to them ' is that
which was returned ' to them from the Father when they had known '
the grace by which they bore fruit with one another ' because of the
Father. [20] As a result, just as they ' ⟨were⟩ brought forth in glory for
the Father, ' so too in order to appear ' perfect, they appeared ' acting
by giving glory.

They [25] were fathers of the third glory ' according to the in-
dependence and ' the power which was begotten with them, ' since each
one of them individually does not ' exist so as to give glory [30] in a unitary way to him whom he loves. '

They are the first and the ' second and thus both of them are perfect
and ' full, for they are manifestations ' of the Father who is perfect [35]
and full, as well as of those who came forth, ' who are perfect by the
fact that they glorify ' the perfect one. The fruit of the third, however,
' consists of honors of ' the will of each one of the aeons [40] and each
one of the properties. − ' The Father has power. − It exists **70** fully, '
perfect in [the thought] which is a product of ' agreement, since it is a
product ' of the individuality [5] of the aeons. It is this which he loves '
and over which he has power, ' as it gives glory to the Father by means
of it. '

For this reason, they are minds of ' minds, which are found to be [10]
words of words, ' elders of ' elders, degrees ' of degrees, which are exalted above ' one another. Each one [15] of those who give glory has ' his
place and his ' exaltation and his dwelling and his ' rest, which consists
of the glory ' which he brings forth. [20]

All those who glorify the Father ' have their begetting ' eternally, —
they beget in ' the act of assisting one another — ' since the emanations
are limitless and [25] immeasurable and since there is ' no envy on the part
' of the Father toward those who came forth from ' him in regard to
their begetting something ' equal or similar to him, since he is the one
who [30] exists in the Totalities, begetting ' and revealing himself. '
Whomever he wishes, he makes into a father, ' of whom he in fact is
Father, ' and a god, of whom he in fact [35] is God, and he makes them
' the Totalities, whose ' entirety he is. In the proper sense all the names
which **71** are great are kept there, ' these (names) which ' the angels
share, ' who have come into being in [5] the cosmos along with the archons, although [they] do not have ' any resemblance ' to the eternal
beings.

The entire system ' of the aeons has ' a love and a longing [10] for the
perfect, complete discovery ' of the Father and this is their unimpeded
agreement. ' Though the Father reveals ' himself eternally, ' he did not
wish [15] that they should know him, since he grants that he be ' conceived of in such a way as to be sought for, while ' keeping to himself
his unsearchable ' primordial being.

It is he, ' [the] Father, who gave root impulses [20] to the aeons, since
they are places ' on the path which leads toward him, ' as toward a
school of ' behavior. He has extended to them ' faith in and prayer to
him whom [25] they do not see; and a firm hope ' in him of whom they do
not conceive; ' and a fruitful love, ' which looks toward that which it
does not ' see; and an acceptable understanding [30] of the eternal mind;
' and a blessing, ' which is riches and freedom; ' and a wisdom of the
one ' who desires the glory of the Father [35] for ⟨his⟩ thought.

It is by virtue of his will that the Father, ' the one who is exalted, is
known, **72** that is, ' (by virtue of) the spirit which breathes in the Totalities ' and it gives them an ' idea of seeking after the [5] unknown one, '
just as one is drawn ' by a pleasant ' aroma to search for the thing '
from which the aroma arises, ' since the aroma [10] of the Father surpasses these ordinary ones. ' For his sweetness ' leaves the aeons in ' ineffable pleasure ' and it gives them their idea [15] of mingling with him
who ' wants them to know him in ' a united way and to assist ' one
another in the spirit which ' is sown within them. Though existing [20]
under a great weight, ' they are renewed in an inexpressable way, ' since
it is impossible ' for them to be separated from that ' in which they are
set in an uncomprehending way, [25] because they will not speak, ' being
silent about the Father's glory, ' about the one who has power ' to

speak, and yet they will take form from ' him. He revealed [himself, though] [30] it is impossible to speak of him. ' They have him, hidden in ' a thought, since from ' this one [...]. They are silent about ' the way the Father is [35] in his form and his nature ' and his greatness, **73** while the aeons have become worthy of knowing ' through his spirit ' that he is unnameable and ' incomprehensible. It is through [5] his spirit, which is the trace ' of the search for him, that he provides ' them the ability to conceive of him and ' to speak about him.

Each one ' of the aeons is a name, ⟨that is⟩, each of [10] the properties and powers of ' the Father, since he exists in many names, which are ' intermingled and harmonious with one another. ' It is possible to speak of him because ' of the wealth of speech, just as the Father [15] is a single name, because ' he is a unity, yet is innumerable ' in his properties and ' names.

The emanation of ' the Totalities, which exist from the one [20] who exists, did not occur according ' to a separation from one another, ' as something cast off from the one who begets ' them. Rather, their begetting is like ' a process of extension, [25] as the Father extends himself ' to those whom he loves, so that ' those who have come forth from him might ' become him as well.

Just as ' the present aeon, though a [30] unity, is divided by units of time ' and units of time are divided into ' years and years are divided into ' seasons and seasons into months, ' and months into days, and days [35] into hours, and hours ' into moments, so **74** too the aeon of the Truth, ' since it is a unity ' and multiplicity, receives honor in the small ' and the great names according to the [5] power of each to grasp it − by way ' of analogy − like a spring ' which is what it is, ' yet flows into streams ' and lakes and canals [10] and branches, or like a ' root spread out beneath ' trees and branches with ' its fruit, or like a ' human body, which is partitioned [15] in an indivisible way into members ' of members, primary members ' and secondary, great [and] ' small.

6. *The Imperfect Begetting by the Logos*

The aeons have brought [themselves] forth ' in accord with the third [20] fruit by the ' freedom of the will ' and by the wisdom ' with which he favored them for their thought. ' They do not wish to give honor [25] [with] that which is from an agreement, [though] ' it was produced for words of [praise] ' for each of the Pleromas. ' Nor do they wish ' to give honor with the Totality. Nor do [30] they wish (to do so) with anyone else

' who was originally above ' the depth of that one, or (above) his '
place, except, however, for the one who exists ' in an exalted name and
[35] in the exalted place, and only if he receives ' from the one who
wished (to give honor), **75** and takes it to him(self) for the one above '
him, and (only if) he begets ' him(self), so to speak, himself, and, '
through that one, begets him(self) [5] along with that which he is, and
himself ' becomes renewed along with the one who came upon him, ' by
his brother, and sees him ' and entreats him about the matter, ' namely,
he who wished to ascend to him. [10]

So that it might be in this way, ' the one who ' wished to give honor
does not say anything to him about this, ' except only that there is a
limit ' to speech set in the Pleroma, so [15] that they are silent about the
incomprehensibility ' of the Father, but they speak about the one ' who
wishes to comprehend him. It came to ' one of the aeons that he should
attempt ' to grasp the incomprehensibility [20] and give glory to it and '
especially to the ineffability of the Father. ' [Since] he is a Logos of the
unity, ' he is one, though he is not from ' the agreement of the
Totalities, nor [25] from him who brought them forth, ' namely, the one
who brought forth the Totality, the Father. '

This aeon was among those ' to whom was given wisdom, so that he
could become ' pre-existent in each one's [30] thought. By that which he
wills ' will they be produced. Therefore, ' he received a wise nature ' in
order to examine the hidden basis, ' since he is a wise fruit; [35] for, the
free will ' which was begotten with ' the Totalities was a cause ' for this
one, such as to make him do **76** what he desired, with no one ' to restrain him.

The ' intent, then, of the Logos, who ' is this one, was good. [5] When
he had come forth, he gave ' glory to the Father, even if it led ' to
something beyond possibility, ' since he had wanted to bring forth one
' who is perfect, from an [10] agreement in which he had not been, ' and
without having the ' command. '

This aeon was last to have ' ⟨been⟩ brought forth by [15] mutual assistance, and he was small ' in magnitude. And before ' he begot anything
else for the glory ' of the will and in agreement with the Totalities, ' he
acted, magnanimously, [20] from an abundant love, ' and set out ' toward
that which surrounds ' the perfect glory, for ' it was not without the will
of the Father [25] that the Logos was produced, which ' is to say, not
without it ' will he go forth. But ' he, the Father, had brought him forth
' for those about whom he knew that it was [30] fitting that they should
come into being.

The Father ' and the Totalities drew away from him, ' so that the limit ' which the Father had set ' might be established — for [35] it is not from grasping the incomprehensibility ' but by the will **77** of the Father, — and furthermore, (they withdrew) so that ' the things which have come to be might become ' an organization which would come into being. ' If it were to come, it would not come into being [5] by the manifestation of the Pleroma. ' Therefore, it is not fitting to ' criticize the movement which is the Logos, ' but it is fitting that we should say about ' the movement of the Logos that it is a cause [10] of an organization which has been destined to ' come about.

The Logos himself caused it to happen, ' being complete and unitary, ' for the glory of the Father, whom ' he desired, and (he did so) being content with it, [15] but those whom he wished to take hold of ' firmly he begot in shadows ' [and] copies and likenesses. ' For, he was not able to bear the sight ' of the light, but he looked into [20] the depth and he doubted. ' Out of this there was a division — he became ' deeply troubled — and a turning away because of his ' self-doubt and division, forgetfulness ' and ignorance of himself and [25] ⟨of that⟩ which is.

His self-exaltation and ' his expectation of comprehending ' the incomprehensible became firm for him ' and was in him. But the sicknesses ' followed him [30] when he went beyond ' himself, having come into being ' from self-doubt, namely from the fact ' that he did not ⟨reach the attainment of⟩ ' the glories of the Father, the one whose exalted status [35] is among things unlimited. This one ' did not attain him, for he did not receive him. '

The one whom he himself brought forth **78** as a unitary aeon ' rushed up to ' that which is his and this kin of his ' in the Pleroma abandoned [5] him who came to be in the defect along with ' those who had come forth from him in ' an imaginary way, since they are not his. '

When he who produced ' himself as perfect actually did bring [10] himself forth, ' he became weak like a female nature ' which has abandoned its ' virile counterpart.

From that ' which was deficient in itself there [15] came those things which came into being ' from his thought and [his] ' arrogance, but from that ' which is perfect in him he left it and raised [himself] ' up to those who are his. He was [20] in the Pleroma as ' a remembrance for him so that he [would be] ' saved from his arrogance. '

The one who ran on high and ' the one who drew him to himself were not [25] barren, but in bringing ' forth a fruit in the Pleroma, ' they upset those who ' were in the defect. '

Like the Pleromas are the things which came into being from the [30] arrogant thought, | which are their (the Pleromas') | likenesses, | copies, shadows, | and phantasms, lacking [35] reason and the light, these | which belong to the vain thought, | since they are not products of anything. Therefore, **79** their end will be like | their beginning: from that which did | not exist (they are) to return once again to | that which will not be. It is they, however, [5] by themselves | who are greater, more powerful, | and more honored than the names | which are given to them, which are [their] shadows. | In the manner of a reflection are they beautiful. [10] For the [face] of the copy normally takes its beauty | from that of which it is a copy. |

They thought of themselves | that they are beings existing by themselves | and are without a source, [15] since they do not see anything else | existing before them. Therefore, they | [lived] in disobedience | [and] acts of rebellion, without | having humbled themselves before the one because of whom they came into being. [20]

They wanted to command | one another, overcoming one another | [in] their vain ambition, | while the glory which they possess | contains a cause [25] [of] the system which was to be. |

They are likenesses of the things which are exalted. | They were brought to a lust for power | in each one of them, | according to the greatness of the name [30] of which each is a shadow, | each one imagining that it is superior | to his fellows.

The thought of these | others was not barren, | but just like ⟨those⟩ [35] of which they are shadows, all that | they thought about they have as | potential sons; **80** those of whom they thought | they had | as offspring. Therefore, | it happened that many offspring came forth from them, [5] as fighters | as warriors, as | troublemakers, as apostates. | They are disobedient beings, | lovers of power. [10] All [the] other beings of this sort were [brought] | forth from these.

7. *The Conversion of the Logos*

The Logos was | a cause of those [who] | came into being and he continued all the more | to be at a loss and he was astonished. [15] Instead of perfection, he saw a defect; | instead of unification, he saw division; | instead of stability, he [saw] disturbances; instead of [rests,] | tumults. Neither was it [possible] [20] for him to make them cease from [loving] | disturbance, nor was it possible for him | to destroy it. He was completely powerless, | once his totality and his exaltation | abandoned him.

Those who had come into being [25] not knowing themselves | both did not know | the Pleromas from which they came forth | and did not know | the one who was the cause of [30] their existence.

The Logos, | being in | such unstable conditions, | did not continue to bring | forth anything like emanations, [35] the things which are in the Pleroma, | the glories which exist for the honor | of the Father. Rather, he brought **81** forth little weaklings, | [hindered] by the illnesses | by which he too was hindered. | It was the likeness of the disposition which was [5] a unity, that which | was the cause of the things | which do not themselves exist from the first. |

Until the one who brought | forth into the defect these things which were thus [10] in need, until he | judged those who came into being because | of him contrary to reason — which is the judgment | which became a condemnation — | he struggled against them unto destruction, [15] that is, the ones who struggled against the condemnation | and whom the wrath pursues, while | it (the wrath) accepts and | redeems (them) from their (false) opinion and | apostasy, since from it [20] [is] the conversion which is | also called "metanoia." | The Logos turned to [another] opinion | and another thought. | Having turned away from evil, [25] he turned toward the good things. | Following the conversion came | the thought of the things which exist | and the prayer for the one who converted | himself to the good. [30]

The one who is in the Pleroma | was what he first prayed to and | remembered; then (he remembered) his brothers | individually and (yet) always | with one another; then all of them together; [35] but before all of them, the Father. **82** The prayer of the agreement | was a help for him | in his own return | and (in that of) the Totality, for a cause [5] of his remembering | those who have existed from the first was | his being remembered. This | is the thought which calls out | from afar, bringing him back. [10]

All his prayer and | remembering were | numerous powers according to that limit. | For there is nothing | barren in his thought. [15]

The powers were good | and were greater than those of the | likeness. For those belonging to the | likeness also belong to a nature of [falsehood]. | From an illusion [20] of similarity and a thought | of arrogance has [come about] | that which they became. And they | originate from the thought | which first knew [them.] [25]

To what do the former beings pertain? | They are like forgetfulness | and heavy sleep; being | like those who dream | troubled dreams, to whom [30] sleep comes while they — | those who dream — are oppressed.

' The others are ' like some creatures of light ' for him, looking for ³⁵ the rising of the sun, since it happened that ' they saw in him dreams ' which are truly sweet. **83** It immediately put a stop ' [to] the emanations of the thought. ' They [did] not any longer have ' their substance and also they did ⁵ not have honor any longer. '

Though he is not equal to those who ' pre-existed, if they were superior to ' the likenesses, it was he alone ' through whom they were more exalted than those, ¹⁰ for they are not from a good intent. '

It was not ' from the sickness which came into being that they were produced, ' from which is the good intent, ' but (from) the one who ¹⁵ sought after the pre-existent. ' Once he had prayed, he both raised ' himself to the good ' and sowed in them ' a pre-disposition to seek ²⁰ and pray to the ' glorious pre-existent one, ' and he sowed in them a thought ' about him and an idea, so that they should ' think that something greater than themselves ²⁵ exists prior to them, although they did not understand ' what it was. Begetting ' harmony and mutual love ' through that thought, ' they acted in ³⁰ unity and unanimity, ' since from ' unity and from unanimity ' they have received their very being. '

They were stronger than them ³⁵ in the lust for power, ' for they were more honored **84** than the first ones, who had been raised ' above them. Those had not ' humbled themselves. They thought about themselves ' that they were beings originating from themselves ⁵ alone and were ' without a source. As they brought [forth] ' at first according to their own birth, ' the two orders assaulted one another, ' fighting for ¹⁰ command because of their manner of ' being. As a result, they were submerged in ' forces and natures ' in accord with the condition of mutual assault, ' having ¹⁵ lust for power ' and all other things ' of this sort. It is from these that the ' vain love of glory draws ' all of them to ²⁰ the desire of the lust ' for power, while none ' of them has the exalted ' thought nor acknowledges ' it.

The powers ²⁵ of this thought are prepared ' in the works of the pre-existent ' ⟨ones⟩, those of which they are ' the representations. For the order ' of those of this sort ³⁰ had mutual ' harmony, but it ' fought against the order ' of those of the likeness, while the order ' of those of the likeness wages war ³⁵ against the representations and acts ' against it alone, because of its ' wrath. **85** From this it [...] ' them [...] ' one another, many [...] ' necessity appointed them [...] ⁵ and might prevail [...] ' was not a multitude, [...] ' and their envy and their [...] ' and their wrath and violence and ' desire and prevailing ignorance ¹⁰ produce empty matters and ' powers of various sorts, mixed in ' great number with one another; while the mind of the Logos, who was | a cause of their begetting, was open | to a revelation of the hope [15] which would come to him from above.

8. *The Emanation of the Savior*

The Logos | which moved had | the hope and the expectation of him | who is exalted. As for those of the shadow, he separated | himself from them in every way, [20] since they fight against him and are not at all humble | before him. He was content | with the beings of the thought. And as for the one who is set up | in this way and who is within the | exalted boundary, remembering [25] the one who is defective, the Logos brought him forth | in an invisible way, | among those who came into being according to the thought, according | to the one who was with them, | until the light shone upon him from [30] above as a lifegiver, the one who was begotten | by the thought of brotherly love | of the pre-existent Pleromas. |

The stumbling, which happened to the aeons | of the Father of the Totalities who did [35] not suffer, was brought to them, as if it were their own, | in a careful and non-malicious | and immensely sweet way. **86** [It was brought to the] Totalities so that they might be instructed about the | [defect] by the single one, | from whom [alone] they all [received strength] | to eliminate the defects.

The order [5] [which] was his came into being from | him who ran [on] high and that which brought itself forth | from him and from the entire perfection. | The one who ran on high became | for the one who was defective an intercessor with the [10] emanation of the aeons which had come into being in accord with | the things which exist. When he prayed | to them, they consented joyously and | willingly, since they were in agreement, and with harmonious | consent, to aid the [15] defective one. They gathered together, | asking the Father with beneficent intent | that there be aid from | above, from the Father, for his glory, | since the defective one could not become perfect in any other way, [20] unless it was the will of | the Pleroma of the Father, which he had drawn to himself, | revealed, and given to the defective | one. Then from the harmony, in a | joyous willingness which had come into being, they [25] brought forth the fruit, which was a begetting | from the harmony, a | unity, a possession of the Totalities, | revealing the countenance of | the Father, of whom the aeons thought [30] as they gave glory and prayed for help for their | brother with a wish in which the Father counted himself | with them. Thus, it was willingly and ' gladly that they bring forth ' the fruit. And he made manifest the agreement of the [35] revelation of his union ' with them — which is his beloved ' Son. **87** But the Son in whom the Totalities are pleased ' put himself on them as a garment, ' through which ' he gave perfection to the defective one, [5] and gave confirmation to those who are perfect, ' the one who is properly called ' "Savior" and "the Redeemer" ' and "the Well-Pleasing one" and "the Belov-ed," ' "the one to whom prayers have been offered" and "the Christ" and [10] "the Light of those appointed," in accordance with the ones from whom ' he was brought forth, since he has become ' the names of the positions [which] were given ' to him. Yet, what other name may be ap-plied ' to him except "the Son," as we previously [15] said, since he is the knowledge ' of the Father, whom he wanted them ' to know?

Not only did the aeons ' generate the countenance of the Father to whom ' they gave praise, which was written previously, but also [20] they generated their own; for the aeons ' who give glory generated their countenance ' and their face. They were produced as an army ' for him, as for a king, ' since the beings of the thought have a [25] powerful fel-lowship and an intermingled ' harmony. They came forth ' in a multi-faceted form, in ' order that the one to whom help was to be given might ' see those to whom he had prayed [30] for help. He also sees the one who gave ' it to him.

The fruit ' of the agreement with him, of which we previously spoke, ' is subject to the power of the Totalities. ' For the Father has set the Totalities within him, [35] both the ones which pre-exist ' and the ones which are, and the ones which will be. **88** He was capable (of doing it). He revealed ' those which he had placed within him. ' He did not give them, when he entrusted (them) to him. ' He directed the organization of the universe [5] according to the authority which was given him ' from the first and (according to) the power of the task. ' Thus, he began and effected ' his revelation.

The one ' in whom the Father is and the one [10] in whom the Totalities are ⟨was⟩ created ' before the one who lacked ' sight. He instructed him about those who searched ' for their sight, by ' means of the shin-ing of that perfect light. [15] He first perfected him ' in ineffable joy. He ' perfected him for himself as a perfect one ' and he also gave him what is appropriate to each ' individual. For this is the determination of [20] the first joy. And ⟨he⟩ sowed ' in him in an invisible way ' a word which is destined to be ' knowledge. And he gave him power ' to separate and cast out from himself [25] those who are disobedient to him.

Thus, he made himself manifest ' to him. But to those ' who came into being because of him he ' revealed a form surpassing [30] them. They acted in a hostile way ' toward one another. Suddenly he revealed himself to them, ' approaching them ' in the form of lightning. And ' in putting an end to the entanglement which they have with [35] one another he stopped it **89** by the sudden revelation, ' which they were not informed about, ' did not expect, ' and did not know of. Because of this, they [5] were afraid and fell down, since they were not able to bear ' the appearance of the light which struck ' them. The one who appeared was an ' assault for the two orders. Just as ' the beings of thought had been given the name [10] "little one," so they have ' a faint notion that they have the ' exalted one, – he exists before them, – and they ' have sown within them an attitude of ' amazement at the exalted one who [15] will become manifest. Therefore, they welcomed ' his revelation and ' they worshipped him. They became ' convinced witnesses to ⟨him⟩. They acknowledged ' the light which had come into being as [20] one stronger than those who fought against them. The ' beings of the likeness, however, were exceedingly afraid, ' since they were not able to hear about him ' in the beginning, that there is a vision of this sort. ' Therefore they fell down [25] to the pit of ignorance ' which is called "the Outer Darkness," ' and "Chaos" and ' "Hades" and "the Abyss." He set up what ' was beneath the order of the beings [30] of thought, as it was ' stronger than they. They were worthy of ' ruling over the unspeakable darkness, ' since it is theirs ' and is the lot which was assigned to them. He [35] granted them that they, too, should be of use ' for the organization which was to come, **90** to which he had [assigned] them.

There is a great ' difference between the revelation of the one who came into being ' to the one who was defective and to those things which are to come into being because of ' him. For he revealed himself to him within [5] him, since he is with him, is ' a fellow sufferer with him, gives ' him rest little by little, makes ' him grow, lifts him up, gives himself ' to him completely for enjoyment from [10] a vision. But to those who fall outside, ' he revealed himself quickly and ' in a striking way and he withdrew to himself suddenly ' without having let them see him. '

9. *The Pleroma of the Logos*

When the Logos which was defective was illumined, [15] his Pleroma began. ' He escaped those who had disturbed ' him at first. He became ' unmixed with them. He stripped off ' that arrogant thought. [20] He received mingling with the Rest, ' when those who had been disobedient to him at first ' bent down and humbled themselves before him. ' And [he] rejoiced ' over the visitation of his brothers 25 who had visited him. He gave ' glory and praise to those who had become manifest ' as a help to him, while he gave thanks, ' because he had escaped those who revolted against him, ' and admired and honored the greatness 30 and those who had appeared to him in a ' determined way. He generated manifest images ' of the living visages, pleasing ' among [things] which are good, existing ' among the things which exist, resembling 35 them in beauty, but unequal to them ' in truth, since they [are] not from ' an agreement with him, between the one who brought them 91 forth and the one who revealed himself to him. But ' in wisdom and knowledge ' he acts, mingling the Logos with ' him(self) entirely. Therefore, those which came 5 forth from him are great, just as ' that which is truly great. '

After he was amazed at the beauty ' of the ones who had appeared to him, ' he professed gratitude for this 10 visitation. The Logos performed this activity, ' through those from whom he had received ' aid, for the stability ' of those who had come into being because of him and ' so that they might receive something good, 15 since he thought to pray for the organization ' of all those who came forth from him, ' which is stabilized, so that it might make them established. ' Therefore, those whom he intentionally produced ' are in chariots, 20 just as those who came into being, those who ' have appeared, so that they might pass through ' every place of things which are below, ' so that each one might be given the place ' which is constituted as he 25 is. This is destruction ' for the beings of the likeness, yet is an act of beneficence ' for the beings of the thought, a revelation ' *[Dittography]* ' of those who are from 30 the ordinance, which was a unity ' while suffering, while they are seeds, ' which have not come to be by themselves. '

The one who appeared was a countenance ' of the Father and of the harmony. He was 35 a garment (composed) of every grace, and food ' which is for those whom the Logos ' brought forth while praying and [giving] glory and ' honor. 92 This is the one whom he glorified and honored ' while looking to those to whom he prayed, ' so that he might perfect them through the ' images which he had brought forth.

The Logos added 5 even more to ' their mutual assistance and ' to the hope of the promise, since ' they have joy and abundant rest ' and undefiled pleasures. 10 He generated those whom he ' remembered at first, when they ' were not with him, (he generated them) having the perfection. | *[Dittography]* | Now, while he who belongs to the vision is with him, [15] he exists in hope and | faith in the perfect Father, as much as the Totalities. | He appears to him before he | mingles with him in order that the things which have | come into being might not perish by looking [20] upon the light, for they can | not accept the great, exalted stature. |

The thought of the Logos, | who had returned to his stability | and ruled over those who had [25] come into being because of him, was called | "Aeon" and "Place" of | all those whom he had brought forth | in accord with the ordinance, and it is also called | "Synagogue of [30] Salvation," because he healed him(self) from | the dispersal, which is the multifarious thought | and returned to | the single thought. Similarly, | it is called "Storehouse," [35] because of the rest which he | obtained, giving (it) to himself alone. **93** And it is also called "Bride," | because of the joy of the one | who gave himself to him in the hope of fruit | from the union, and who appeared to him. [5] It is also called "Kingdom," | because of the stability which he received, while he | rejoices at the domination over those who fought him. | And it is called "the Joy | of the Lord," because of the gladness in [which he] [10] clothed himself. With him is the light, | giving him recompense for the | good things which are in him | and (with him is) the thought of freedom. |

The aeon, of whom we previously spoke, [15] is above the two orders | of those who fight against one another. | It is not a companion of those who hold dominion and | is not implicated in the illnesses and weaknesses, | things belonging to the thought and to the likeness. [20]

That in which the Logos set | himself, perfect in joy, | was an aeon, having | the form of matter, but also having | the constitution of the cause, which [25] is the one who revealed himself. (The aeon was) an image | of those things which are in the Pleroma, | those things which came into being from the abundance | of the enjoyment of the one who exists | joyously. It, moreover, the [30] countenance of the one who revealed himself, was | in the sincerity and the attentiveness | and the promise concerning | the things for which he asked. It had | the designation of the Son [35] and his essence and his power and his | form, who is the one whom he loved | and in whom he was pleased, **94** who was entreated in a loving way. | It was light and was a desire | to be established and an openness | for instruction and an eye for vision, [5] qualities which it had | from the exalted ones. It was also wisdom | for his thinking in opposition to the things beneath the | organization. It was also a word for | speaking and the perfection of the things [10] of this sort. And it is these who ' took form with him, but according to the image ' of the Pleroma, having ' their fathers who are the ones who gave them life, ' each one being a copy [15] of each one of the faces, ' which are forms of maleness, ' since they are not from the illness which ' is femaleness, but are from ' this one who already has left behind [20] the sickness. It has the name ' "the Church," for in harmony ' they resemble the harmony in the assembly ' of those who have revealed themselves.

That ' which came into being in the image of the [25] light, it too is perfect, ' inasmuch as it is an image of the ' one existing light, which is the ' Totalities. Even if it was inferior to the one of whom ' it is an image, nevertheless it has [30] its indivisibility, because ' it is a countenance of the ' indivisible light. Those, however, ' who came into being in the image ' of each one of the aeons, [35] they in essence are in the one whom we ' previously mentioned, but in power they are not equal, ' because it (the power) is in each ' of them. In ' this mingling with one another [40] they have equality, **95** but each one has not cast off what is peculiar to itself. ' Therefore, they are passions, ' for passion is sickness, since ' they are productions not of the agreement [5] of the Pleroma, but of this one, ' prematurely, before he received the Father. Hence, ' the agreement with his Totality and will ' was something beneficial for the organization ' which was to come. It was granted them [10] to pass through the places which are below, ' since the places are unable ' to accommodate their ' sudden, hasty coming, unless (they come) individually, ' one by one. [15] Their coming is necessary, since ' by them will everything be perfected. '

In short, the Logos received the vision of all things, ' those which pre-exist and those which are now ' and those which will be, [20] since he has been entrusted ' with the organization of all that which ' exists. Some things are already ' in things which are fit for ' coming into being, but the seeds which are to [25] be he has within himself, ' because of the promise which belonged to that ' which he conceived, as something belonging ' to seeds which are to be. And ' he produced his offspring, that [30] is, the revelation of that which ' he conceived. For a while, however, the seed of ' promise is guarded, ' so that those who have been appointed for a ' mission might be appointed [35] by the coming of the Savior and of those who ' are with him, the ones who are first ' in knowledge and glory of ' the Father.

10. *The Organization*

It is fitting, from **96** the prayer which he made and the ' conversion which occurred because of it, ' that some should perish ' while others benefit [5] and still others be ' set apart. He first prepared ' the punishment of those who are ' disobedient, making use of a power ' of the one who appeared, the one from whom he received [10] authority over all things, ' so as to be separate from him. He is ' the one who is below and he also keeps himself ' apart from that which is exalted, until he ' prepares the organization of all those things [15] which are external, and gives to each the place ' which is assigned to it. '

The Logos established him(self) at ' first, when he beautified the Totalities, as ' a basic principle and cause [20] and ruler of the things which ' came to be, like the Father, the one who ' was the cause of the establishment, ' which was the first to exist after him. ' He created the pre-existent images, [25] which he brought forth ' in thanks and glorification. Then ' he beautified the place of those whom he had ' brought forth in glory, which is called ' "Paradise" and [30] "the Enjoyment" and "the Joy full ' of sustenance" and "the Joy," which ' pre-exist. And of ' every goodness which exists in ' the Pleroma, it preserves the image. [35] Then he beautified the kingdom, ' like a city ' filled with everything pleasing, ' which is brotherly love and ' the great generosity, which is filled **97** with the holy spirits and [the] ' mighty powers which govern ' them, which the Logos ' produced and established [5] in power. Then (he beautified) the place of ' the Church which assembles in this place, ' having the form of the ' Church which exists in the aeons, which glorifies ' the Father. After these (he beautified) the place [10] of the faith and obedience (which arises) from ' hope, which things the Logos received ' when the light appeared; ' then (he beautified the place of) the disposition, which is prayer [and] ' supplication, which were followed by forgiveness [15] and the word concerning ' the one who would appear.

All the spiritual places ' are in spiritual power. ' They are separate from the beings ' of the thought, since the power is established in [20] an image, which is that which separates ' the Pleroma from the Logos, while the power ' which is active in prophesying about ' the things which will be, directs the beings of the thought ' which have come into being toward that which is pre-existent, [25] and it does not permit them to mix with the things which ' have come into being through a vision of the things which are ' with him.

The beings of the thought which | is outside are humble; they | preserve the representation of the pleromatic, [30] especially because of the sharing | in the names by which they are beautiful. |

The conversion is | humble toward the beings of the thought, and the law, | too, is humble toward them, [35] (the law) of the judgment, which is the condemnation and | the wrath. Also humble toward them | is the power which separates those who | fall below them, sends them | far off and does not allow them **98** [to] spread out over the beings of the thought and | the conversion, which (power) consists in fear and | perplexity and forgetfulness and astonishment and | ignorance and the things which have come into being [5] in the manner of a likeness, through phantasy. | And these things, too, which were in fact lowly, | are given the exalted names. | There is no knowledge for those who have come | forth from them with arrogance [10] and lust for power | and disobedience and false-hood. |

To each one he gave | a name, since the two orders are | in a name. Those belonging to the thought and those of the representation [15] are called | "the Right Ones" and "Psychic" and | "the Fiery Ones" and "the Middle Ones." | Those who belong to the arrogant thought and those of the likeness | are called "the Left," [20] "Hylic," "the Dark Ones," and "the Last." |

After the Logos established | each one in his order, | both the images and the representations and the likenesses, | he kept the aeon of the images [25] pure from all those who | fight against it, since it is a place of joy. | However, to those of the thought he revealed | the thought which he had stripped | from himself, desiring to draw them [30] into a material union, for the sake | of their system and dwelling place | and in order that they might also bring forth | an impulse for diminution from | their attraction to evil, so that they might not any more [35] rejoice in the glory | of their environment and be dissolved, | but might rather see | their sickness in which they suffer, **99** so that they might beget love | and continuous searching after | the one who is able to heal them | of the inferiority. Also over those [5] who belong to the likeness, he set | the word of beauty, so that he might | bring them into a form. He also set | over them the law of judgment. | Again, he set over them [the] [10] powers which the roots had produced | [in] their lust for power. He [ap-pointed] | them as rulers over them, so that | either by the support of the word which is beautiful | or by the threat of the [law] [15] or by the power of lust for | power the order might be preserved | from those who have reduced it to evil, | while the Logos is pleased with them, | since they are useful for the organization.

The Logos knows the agreement [20] in the lust for power of the ' two orders. ' To these and to all the others, he ' graciously granted their desire. He gave ' to each one the appropriate rank, [25] and it was ordered ' that each one ' be a ruler over a ' place and an activity. He yields to the place ' of the one more exalted than himself, in order to command [30] the other places in an activity ' which is in the allotted activity ' which falls to him to have control over ' because of his mode of being. ' As a result, there are commanders and [35] subordinates in positions of domination ' and subjection among the angels **100** and archangels, while the activities ' are of various types and are different. ' Each one of the archons with his ' race and his perquisites to which his lot [5] has claim, just as they ' appeared, each was on guard, since they have been entrusted ' with the organization and none ' lacks a command and ' none is without kingship from [10] the end of the heavens to the end of the ' [earth], even to the foundations of the [earth] ' and to the places beneath the earth. There are ' kings, there are lords and those who give ' commands, some [15] for administering punishment, others ' for administering justice, still others for ' giving rest and healing, others ' for teaching, others for guarding. '

Over all the archons he appointed an Archon [20] with no one commanding ' him. He is the lord of all of them, ' that is, the countenance which the Logos ' brought forth in his thought ' as a representation of the Father of the Totalities. Therefore, [25] he is adorned with every ⟨name⟩ ' which ⟨is⟩ a representation of him, since he is characterized by every property ' and glorious quality. For he too is called ' "father" and "god" and "demiurge" and ' "king" and "judge" and "place" [30] and "dwelling" and "law." '

The Logos uses him ' as a hand, to beautify and ' work on the things below and he ' uses him as a mouth, [35] to say the things which will be prophesied. '

The things which he has spoken he does. ' When he saw that they were great and ' good and wonderful, he was ' pleased and rejoiced, as **101** if he himself in his own thought ' had been the one to say them and do ' them, not knowing that the movement ' within him is from the spirit who moves [5] him in a determined way toward those things which he wants. '

In regard to the things which came into being from him, he spoke of them ' and they came into being as a representation of the spiritual ' places which we mentioned previously ' in the discussion about the images.

Not only ^{10} ⟨did⟩ he work, but also, as ' the one who is appointed as father of [his] organization, ' he engendered by himself and by the seeds, yet also [by ' the spirit] which is elect and which will descend ' through him to the places which are below. ^{15} Not only does he speak spiritual words ' of his own, ⟨but⟩ in ' an invisible way, ' (he speaks) through the spirit which calls out ' and begets things greater than his own essence. ^{20}

Since in his ' essence he is a "god" ' and "father" [and] all the rest of ' the honorific titles, he was ' thinking that they were elements ^{25} of his own essence. He established ' a rest for those who obey ' him, but for those who ' disobey him, he also established punishments. ' With him, too, ^{30} there is a paradise and a ' kingdom and everything else ' which exists in the aeon ' which exists before him. They are more valuable ' than the imprints, because of the thought which ^{35} is connected with them, which is like **102** a shadow and a garment, so to ' speak, because he does not see ' in what way the things which exist actually do exist.

He established ' workers and ^{5} servants, assisting in ' what he will do and what he will say, ' for in every place where he worked ' he left his countenance ' in his beautiful name, ^{10} effecting and speaking of ' the things which he thinks about.

He ' established in his place ' images of the light ' which appeared and of [those things which are] ^{15} spiritual, though they were of ' his own essence. For, thus they were ' honored in every place by him, ' being pure, from the countenance ' of the one who appointed them, and they were ^{20} established: paradises ' and kingdoms and rests ' and promises and multitudes ' of servants of his will, ' and though they are lords of dominions, ^{25} they are set beneath the one who is ' lord, the one who appointed them. '

After he listened to him ' in this way, properly, about the lights, ' which are the source ^{30} and the system, he set them over ' the beauty of the things below. ' The invisible spirit moved him in this way, ' so that he would **103** wish to administer through ' his own servant, ' whom he too used, ' as a hand and ^{5} as a mouth and as if ' he were his face, (and his servant is) the things which he brings, ' order and threat and ' fear, in order that those [with] whom he has done ' what is ignorant ^{10} might despise the order which [was given for them to] ' keep, since they are fettered in the [bonds of ' the] archons which are on them [securely]. '

The whole establishment of matter ' [is divided] into three. The [strong] powers ^{15} which the spiritual Logos ' brought forth from phantasy ' and arrogance, he established ' in the first spiritual rank. ' Then those (powers) which these produced by [20] their lust for power, he set ' in the middle area, since they are powers ' of ambition, so that they ' might exercise dominion and give commands with compulsion and force ' to the establishment which is beneath them. [25] Those ' which came into being through envy ' and jealousy and all the other offspring ' from dispositions of this sort, he set ' in a servile order [30] controlling the extremities, commanding ' all those which exist and all (the realm of) generation, ' from whom come ' rapidly destroying illnesses, ' who eagerly desire begetting, who are something [35] in the place where they are from ' and to which they will return. ' And therefore, he appointed over ' them authoritative powers, ' acting [continuously] on matter, in order that **104** the offspring of those which exist might also exist ' continuously. For this is their ' glory. '

Part II

11. *The Creation of Material Humanity*

The matter which flows through its form [5] (is) a cause by which the ' invisibility which exists through the powers ' [...] for them all, for ' [...], as they beget before them and ' [destroy.]

The thought which is set [10] between those of the right [and] ' those of the left is a power of [begetting]. ' All those which the [first ones] ' will wish to make, so to ' speak, a projection of theirs, [15] like a shadow cast from ' and following a body, those things which ' [are] the roots of the visible creations, ' namely, the entire preparation of the ' adornment of the images and representations [20] and likenesses, have come ' into being because of those who need ' education and teaching and formation, ' so that the smallness ' might grow, little [25] by little, as through a mirror image. ' For it was for this reason that he created ' mankind at the end, having first ' prepared and ' provided for him the things which he had created [30] for his sake. '

Like that of all else is the creation of mankind as well. ' The spiritual Logos ' moved him ' invisibly, as he perfected [35] him through the **105** Demiurge and his angelic servants, ' who shared in the act of fashioning in [multitudes, when he] ' took counsel with his archons. ' Like a shadow is earthly man, [5] so that he might be like [those] ' who are cut off from the Totalities. Also ' he is something prepared by all of them, those of the right ' and those of the left, since each one in [the] ' orders gives a form to the [. . .], [10] in which it exists.

The [. . .] which ' the Logos [who was] ' defective brought forth, who [was] ' in the sickness, did not resemble him ' because he brought it forth [forgetfully,] [15] ignorantly, and [defectively,] ' and in all the other weak ways, ' although the Logos gave the first form ' through the Demiurge ' out of ignorance, so that he [20] would learn that the exalted one exists ' and would know that he needs [him]. ' This is what the prophet called ' "Living Spirit" and "Breath ' of the exalted aeons" and "[the] [25] Invisible" and this is the living soul ' which has given life to the power ' which was dead at first. For that which ' is dead is ignorance. '

It is fitting that we explain [30] about the soul of the first human being, ' that it is from the spiritual Logos, ' while the creator thinks ' that it is his, since it is from ' him, as from a mouth through which [35] one breathes. The creator also sent ' down souls ' from his substance, since he, ' too, has a power of procreation, **106** because he is something which has come into being from the representation ' of the Father. Also those of the left brought forth, ' as it were, men ' of their own, since they have [5] the likeness of ⟨being⟩. '

The spiritual substance is a ' [single thing] and a single representation, ' [and] its weakness is the determination ' [in many] forms. As for the substance [10] of the psychics, its determination ' is double, since it has the knowledge ' and the confession of the exalted one, ' and it is not inclined to evil, because of ' the inclination of the thought. As for the material substance [15] its way is different ' and in many forms, and it was a weakness ' which existed in many types ' of inclination.

The first human being is a ' mixed formation, and a [20] mixed creation, and a deposit ' of those of the left and those of the right, ' and a spiritual word ' whose attention is divided between each of the two ' substances from which he takes [25] his being. Therefore, ' it is said that ' a paradise was planted for him, so that he might ' eat of the food of three ' kinds of tree, since it is a garden of the [30] threefold order, ' and since it is that which gives enjoyment.

The ' noble elect substance ' which is in him was more exalted. ' It created and it did not wound [35] them. Therefore they issued ' a command, making a threat ' and bringing upon him a great **107** danger, which is death. Only the ' enjoyment of the things which are evil ' did he allow him to taste, ' and from the other tree with [5] the double (fruit) he did not allow him ' to eat, much less from the tree of life, so that [they would not] | acquire honor [...] | them and so that [they would not be ...] [10] by the evil power [which] | is called "the serpent." And he is more cunning | than all the evil powers. | He led man astray [through] | the determination of those things which belong to the thought [15] and the desires. ⟨He⟩ made him transgress | the command, so that he would die. | And he was expelled from | every enjoyment of that place. |

This is the expulsion which was made [20] for him, when he was expelled from the enjoyments | of the things which belong to the likeness and those of the representation. | It was a work of providence, so that | it might be found that it is a short time | until man will receive the enjoyment [25] of the things which are eternally good, | in which is the place of rest. | This the spirit ordained when | he first planned | that man should experience the [30] great evil, which is death, | that is complete ignorance of the Totality, | and that he should experience | all the evils which | come from this and, [35] after the deprivations and cares which are in these, | that he should receive of the greatest **108** good, which is | life eternal, that is, | firm knowledge of the Totalities | and the reception of all good things. [5] Because of the transgression of the first man | death ruled. It was accustomed | to slay every man | in the manifestation of its | [domination] which had been given it [10] [as] a kingdom, because of the organization | of the Father's will, | of which we spoke previously. |

Part III

12. *The Variety of Theologies*

If both the orders, | those on the right and those on the left, [15] are brought together with one another by | the thought which is set between them, | which gives them their organization | with each other, it happens | that they both act with the same [20] emulation of their deeds, with | those of the right resembling those of the left | and those of the left resembling | those of the right. And if at times the evil order | begins to do [25] evil in a | foolish way, | the ⟨wise⟩ order emulates, | in the form of a man of violence, | also doing what is evil, [30] as if it were a power of a man | of violence. At other times | the foolish order | attempts to do good, | making itself like it, since the hidden order, [35] too, is zealous to do it. | Just as it is in | the things which are established, [so] (it is) in the **109** things which have come to be. Since they bring | things unlike one another, ' those who were not instructed were ' unable to know the cause of the things which exist. ⁵ Therefore, ' they have introduced other types (of explanation), ' some saying that ' it is according to providence that the things which exist have their being. ' These are the people who observe ¹⁰ the stability and the conformity of the movement of creation. ' Others say ' that it is something alien. ' These are people who observe the ' diversity and the lawlessness and the evil of the powers. ¹⁵ Others say ' that the things which exist are what ' is destined to happen. These are the people who were ' occupied with this matter. Others say ' that it is something in accordance with nature. ²⁰ Others say that ' it is a self-existent. The majority, however, ' all who have reached as far as the visible elements, ' do not know anything more ' than them.

Those who were wise ²⁵ among the Greeks and the barbarians ' have advanced to the powers which have ' come into being by way of imagination and ' vain thought. Those who have ' come from these, in accord with the mutual conflict ³⁰ and rebellious manner ' active in them, ' also spoke in a likely, ' arrogant and ' imaginary way concerning the things ³⁵ which they thought of as wisdom, ' although the likeness deceived them, ' since they thought that they had attained the truth, **110** when they had (only) attained error. ' (They did so) not simply in minor appellations, but ' the powers themselves seem to hinder them, ' as if they were the Totality. ⁵ Therefore, the ' order was caught up in fighting ' itself alone, because of the ' arrogant hostility of ' one [of the offspring] of the archon who is ¹⁰ superior, who exists before him. ' Therefore, nothing ' was in agreement with its fellows, ' nothing, neither ' philosophy nor types of medicine ¹⁵ nor types of rhetoric nor types ' of music nor types of ' logic, but they are opinions and ' theories. ' Ineffability held sway ²⁰ in confusion, because of the indescribable quality ' of those who hold sway, who give them ' thoughts.

Now, as for the things which came ' forth from the ⟨race⟩ of the ' Hebrews, things which are written by ²⁵ the hylics who speak in the fashion of the Greeks, ' the powers of those who think about all ' of them, so to speak, the "right ones," the powers ' which move them all to think of ' words and a representation, they ⟨brought⟩ them, and ³⁰ they grasped so as to attain ' the truth and used the confused powers ' which act in them. ' Afterwards they attained to the order ' of the unmixed ones, the one which is established, the ³⁵ unity which exists as a ' representation of the representation of the Father. It is not invisible **111** in its nature, but ' a wisdom envelops it, so that ' it might preserve the form of the ' truly invisible one. Therefore, ⁵ many angels have not been able to see it. ' Also, other men of ' the Hebrew race, of whom we ' already spoke, namely the righteous ones ' and the prophets, did not think of anything [10] and did not say anything ' from imagination or through a ' likeness or from esoteric thinking, ' but each one ' by the power which was at work in him, [15] and while listening to the things which he saw ' and heard, spoke of them in [...]. ' They have a unified harmony ' with one another after the manner ' of those who worked in them, [20] since they preserve the connection and the ' mutual harmony primarily ' by the confession of the one more exalted ' than they. And there is one who is greater than they, ' who was appointed since they have need [25] of him, and whom the spiritual Logos ' begot along with them as one who needs ' the exalted one, in hope and ' expectation in accord with the thought which ' is the seed of salvation. [30] And he is an illuminating word, which ' consists of the thought and his offspring and ' his emanations. Since the righteous ones and ' the prophets, whom we have previously mentioned, ' preserve the confession and the [35] testimony concerning ' the one who is great, made by their fathers who were **112** looking for the hope and ' the hearing, in them is sown ' the seed of prayer and the searching, ' which is sown in many [5] who have searched for strengthening. ' It appears and draws them to ' love the exalted one, to proclaim ' these things as pertaining to a unity. ' And it was a unity which [10] worked in them when they spoke. ' Their vision and their words do not differ ' because of the multitude ' of those who have given them the vision and ' the word. Therefore, those who have [15] listened to what they have said ' concerning this do not reject any ' of it, but have accepted the scriptures ' in an altered way. By interpreting ' them they established [20] many heresies which ' exist to the present among the ' Jews. Some ' say that God is one, ' who made a proclamation [25] in the ancient scriptures. Others ' say that he is many. ' Some say ' that God is simple ' and was a single mind [30] in nature. Others say ' that his activity is linked with ' the establishment of good ' and evil. Still others ' say that he is the [35] creator of that which has come into being. Still others ' say that **113** it was by the angels that he created. '

The multitude of ideas of ' this sort is the multitude of forms and the abundance ' of types of scripture, that which produced [5] their teachers of the Law. The ' prophets, however, did not say anything of ' their own accord, ' but each one of them ' (spoke) of the things which he had seen and [10] heard through the proclamation of ' the Savior. This is what he proclaimed, ' with the main subject of their ' proclamation being that which each said concerning ' the coming of the Savior, which is this coming. [15] Sometimes the prophets speak about it | as if it will be. | Sometimes (it is) as if the Savior speaks | from their mouths, saying that the Savior will come | and show favor to those who have not [20] known him. They have not all joined | with one another in confessing anything, | but each one, on the basis of the | thing from which he received power | to speak about him [25] and on the basis of the place which he saw, | thinks that it is from it | that he will be begotten and that he will | come from that place. Not | one of them knew [30] whence he would come nor by whom he | would be begotten, but he alone | is the one of whom it is worthy to speak, the one who | will be begotten and | will suffer. Concerning [35] that which he previously was | and that which he is eternally, | an unbegotten, impassible one from | the Logos, who came into being in flesh, **114** he did not come into their thought. And this | is the account which they received an impulse | to give concerning his flesh | which was to appear. They say that [5] it is a production from all of them, | but that before all things it is from | the spiritual Logos | who is the cause of the things which | have come into being, from whom the Savior received [10] his flesh. He had | conceived ⟨it⟩ at the revelation | of the light, according to the | word of the promise, at his revelation | from the seminal state. [15] For the one who exists is not a seed of the things which exist, | since he was begotten at the end. But to the one | by whom the Father ordained the manifestation | of salvation, who is | the fulfillment of the promise, [20] to him belonged all these instruments for | entry into life, through which he | descended. His Father is one | and alone is | truly a father to him, the [25] invisible, unknowable, | the incomprehensible in his nature, who | alone is God in his will | and his form, who | has granted that he might be seen, [30] known and comprehended. |

13. *The Incarnate Savior and his Companions*

He it is who was our Savior | in willing compassion, | who is that which | they were. For it was for their sake that he became [35] manifest in an involuntary suffering. | They became flesh and soul, − | that is, eternally − which (things) hold | them and with corruptible things | they die. And as for those who [came into being] **115** [the] invisible one | taught them invisibly about himself. |

Not | only did he take upon ⟨himself⟩ the death of [5] those whom he thought | to save, but he also accepted their smallness | to which they had descended when they were ⟨born⟩ | in body and soul. | (He did so), because he had let himself be conceived [10] and born as an infant, in | body and soul.

Among all the others | who shared in them | and those who fell and received the light, | he came being exalted, because [15] he had let himself be conceived without sin, | stain and | defilement. | He was begotten in life, being in life | because the former and the latter are in [20] passion and changing opinion | from the Logos who moved, | who established them to be body | and soul. He it is ⟨who⟩ has taken | to himself the one who came from those whom we previously [25] mentioned.

He came into being from the | glorious vision and the unchanging thought | of the Logos who | returned to himself, after his movement, | from the organization, just as [30] those who came with him took body and soul | and a confirmation | and stability and judgment of | things. They too intended | to come.

When they thought of [35] the Savior they came, and [they came] when he knew; | they also came more exalted in the | emanation according to the flesh than those | who had been brought forth from a defect, because **116** in this way | they, too, received their bodily emanation along with | the body of the Savior, through | the revelation and [5] the mingling with him. These | others were those of one substance | and it indeed is the spiritual (substance). | The organization | is different. This is one thing, [10] that is another. Some | come forth from passion | and division, needing | healing. Others are from | prayer, so that they heal [15] the sick, when they have been appointed | to treat those who have fallen. These | are the apostles and the evangelists. | They are the disciples | of the Savior, and teachers [20] who need instruction. Why, then, | did they, too, share in the passions | in which | those who have been brought forth | from passion share, if indeed they are bodily productions [25] in accordance with the organization and | ⟨the⟩ Savior, who did not | share in the passions? |

The Savior was an image | of the unitary one, he who [30] is the Totality in bodily form. | Therefore, he preserved the form of | indivisibility, from which | comes impassibility. | They, however, are images [35] of each thing which | became manifest. Therefore, they | assume division from | the pattern, having taken form for the planting which | exists beneath [the heaven.] This also **117** is what shares in the evil which exists | in the places which they have reached. | For the will | held the Totality under sin, so that [5] by that will he might have mercy | on the Totality and they might be saved, while a single one | alone is appointed to give life and all the rest | need salvation. Therefore, | it was from (reasons) of this sort that [10] it began to receive grace to give the | honors which were proclaimed | by Jesus, which were suitable for | him to proclaim to the rest, | since a seed of the [15] promise of Jesus Christ was set up, whom we have | served in (his) revelation and union. | Now the promise possessed | the instruction and the return | to what they are from [20] the first, from which they possess | the drop, so as to return | to him, which is that which is called | "the redemption." And it is the release | from the captivity and the acceptance [25] of freedom. In its places the captivity of | those who were slaves of ignorance | holds sway. | The freedom is the knowledge of | the truth which existed before [30] the ignorance was ruling, | forever without beginning and | without end, being something good | and a salvation of things | and a release from [35] the servile nature | in which they have suffered.

Those | who have been brought forth in a lowly thought | of vanity, | that is, (a thought) which goes to things which are evil **118** through the thought which [draws] them | down to the lust for power, these have | received the possession which is freedom, | from the abundance of the grace which looked [5] upon the children. It was, however, a disturbance of the | passion and a destruction of | those things which he cast off from | himself at first, when the Logos separated them | from himself, (the Logos) who [10] was the cause of their being destined for | destruction, though he kept ⟨them⟩ at ⟨the⟩ end of the organization | and allowed them to exist | because even they were useful for the things which were | ordained.

14. *The Tripartition of Mankind*

Mankind came [15] to be in three essential types, | the spiritual, the psychic | and the material, conforming | to the triple disposition | of the Logos, from which [20] were brought forth the material ones and the | psychic ones and the spiritual ones. Each | of the three essential types | is known by its fruit. | And they were not known at first [25] but only at the coming of the Savior, | who shone upon the saints | and revealed what each | was.

The | spiritual race, being [30] like light from | light and like spirit from | spirit, when its head | appeared, it ran toward him | immediately. It immediately became a body [35] of its head. It suddenly received knowledge | in the revelation. | The psychic race is like light | from a fire, since it hesitated to accept knowledge **119** of him who appeared to it. (It hesitated) even | more to run toward him in faith. | Rather, through a voice it was instructed ' and this was sufficient, since it is not far ⁵ from the hope according to the promise, ' since it received, so to speak as a ' pledge, the assurance of the things ' which were to be. The material ' race, however, is alien in ¹⁰ every way; since it is dark, it ' shuns the shining of the light ' because its appearance destroys ' it. And since it has not received its unity, ' it is something excessive and ¹⁵ hateful toward the Lord at his ' revelation.

The spiritual race ' will receive complete salvation in ' every way. The material will receive ' destruction in every way, just as ²⁰ one who resists him. The psychic ' race, since it is in the middle ' when it is brought forth and also when it is created, ' is double according to its determina- tion ' for both good and evil. It takes its ²⁵ appointed departure ' sud- denly and its complete escape ' to those who are good. ' Those whom the Logos brought forth ' in accordance with the first element of his ³⁰ thought, when he remembered the ' exalted one and prayed for salva- tion, ' have salvation [suddenly.] ' They will be saved completely [be- cause of] ' the salvific thought. As he ³⁵ was brought forth, so, [too], ' were these brought forth from ' him, **120** whether angels or men. ' In accordance with the confession that there is ' one who is more exalted than themselves, ' and in accordance with the prayer and the search for ⁵ him, they also will attain the ' salvation of those who have been brought forth, since ' they are from the disposition ' which is good. They were appointed for ' service in proclaiming the coming ¹⁰ of the Savior who was to be and ' his revelation which had come. ' Whether angels or men, when ' he was sent as a service to them, they received, ' in fact, the essence of their being. ¹⁵ Those, however, who are from ' the thought of lust for ' power, who have come into being from ' the blow of those who fight ' against him, those whom the thought ²⁰ brought forth, from these, ' since they are mixed, they will receive their end ' suddenly. Those who will be brought forth ' from the lust for ' power which is given to them for a ²⁵ time and for certain periods, and who will give glory to ' the Lord of glory, and who will relinquish ' their wrath, they will receive the reward for ' their humility, which is to re- main ' forever. Those, however, who ³⁰ are proud because of the desire ' of ambition, and who love temporary ' glory and who forget that ' it was only for certain periods and times which they have ' that they were entrusted with power, ³⁵ and for this reason ' did not acknowledge that the Son of God **121** is the Lord of all and ' Savior, and were not brought ' out of wrath and the ' resemblance to the evil ones, they ⁵ will receive judgment for their ignorance ' and their senselessness, ' which is suffering, along with those ' who went astray, anyone ' of them who turned away; and [10] even more (for) wickedness in ' doing to the Lord things ' which were not fitting, ' which the powers of the left did to him, ' even including his death. They persevered [15] saying, "We shall become rulers ' of the universe, if ' the one who has been proclaimed king of the universe ' is slain," (they said this) when they labored to do ' this, namely the men and angels [20] who are not from the good disposition ' of the right ones but ' from the mixture. And ' they first chose for themselves ' honor, though it was only a temporary wish [25] and desire, while the ' path to eternal rest is by way ' of humility for salvation of ' those who will be saved, those of ' the right ones. After they confess [30] the Lord and the thought of that which ' is pleasing to the church and the song of ' those who are humble along with her to the full extent ' possible, in that which is pleasing to do ' for her, in sharing in her sufferings [35] and her pains in the manner of ' those who understand what is good ' for the church, they will have a share ' in [her] hope. This is to be said **122** on the subject of how men and angels ' who are from the ' order of the left ' have a path to error: [5] not only did they deny the Lord ' and plot evil against him, ' but also toward the Church did they direct ' their hatred ' and envy and jealousy; [10] and this is the reason for the condemnation ' of those who have moved and have aroused themselves ' for the trials of the Church.

15. *The Process of Restoration*

The election ' shares body ' and essence with [15] the Savior, since it is like a bridal ' chamber because of its unity ' and its agreement with him. For, before ' every place, the Christ came for her sake. ' The calling, [20] however, has the place ' of those who rejoice at the bridal chamber ' and who are glad and happy ' at the union of the bridegroom ' and the bride. [25] The place which the calling will have is the aeon ' of the images, where ' the Logos has not yet joined with the Pleroma. And ' since the man of the Church was happy and ' glad at this, as he was hoping for [30] it, ' he separated spirit, soul, and body in ' the organization of the one who thinks that ' he is a unity, though within him ' is the man who is [35] the Totality – and he is all of them. ' And, though he has ' the escape from the [. . .] which **123** the places will receive, he also has ' the members about which we spoke ' earlier. When the redemption was proclaimed, ' the perfect man received knowledge [5] immediately, ' so as to return in haste to his ' unitary state, to the place from ' which he came, to return ' there joyfully, to the place [10] from which he came, to the place from which ' he flowed forth. His ' members, however, needed a place of instruction, ' which is in the places which ' are adorned, so that [they] might receive from them resemblance [15] to the images and archetypes, ' like a mirror, until ' all the members of the body of ' the Church are in a single place ' and receive the restoration at one [20] time, when they have been manifested as the ' whole body, – namely the restoration ' into the Pleroma. – ' It has a preliminary concord ' with a mutual agreement, [25] which is the concord which belongs to the Father, ' until the Totalities receive a countenance ' in accordance with him. The restoration is ' at the end, after the Totality ' reveals what it is, the Son, [30] who is the redemption, that ' is, the path toward the ' incomprehensible Father, that is, the return to ' the pre-existent, and (after) ' the Totalities reveal themselves [35] in that one, in the proper way, who ' is the inconceivable one and the ' ineffable one, **124** and the invisible one and the ' incomprehensible one, so that it ' receives redemption. It was not only release ' from the domination of the [5] left ones, nor was it only [escape] ' from the power ' of those of the right, to each of which ' we thought ' that were slaves and [10] sons, from whom none ' escapes without quickly ' becoming theirs again, but ' the redemption also is an ascent ' [to] the degrees which are in the [15] Pleroma and [to] those who have named ' themselves and who conceive of themselves ' according to the power of each of ' the aeons, and (it is) an entrance ' into what is silent, where there is no [20] need for voice nor for ' knowing nor for forming a concept ' nor for illumination, ' but (where) all things are ' light, while they do not need to be [25] illumined.

Not only ' do humans need ' redemption, but also the angels, ' too, need redemption along with ' the image and the rest of the Pleromas of [30] the aeons and the wondrous powers of ' illumination. So that we might not be in doubt in regard to ' the others, even the Son ' himself, who has the position of ' redeemer of the Totality, [needed] redemption **125** as well, – he who had become ' man, – since he gave ' himself for each thing which we need, ' we in the flesh, who are [5] his Church. Now, when he ' first received redemption from ' the word which had descended upon him, ' all the rest received redemption from ' him, namely those who had taken him to themselves. [10] For those who received the one who had received (redemption) ' also received what was in him.

Among ' the men who are in the flesh redemption ' began to be given, his first-born, ' and his love, the [15] Son who was incarnate, while the ' angels who are in heaven ' asked to associate, so that they might form an association ' with him upon the earth. Therefore, ' he is called "the Redemption [20] of the angels of the Father," he who ' comforted those who were laboring ' under the Totality for his knowledge, ' because he was given the grace ' before anyone else.

The Father had foreknowledge [25] of him, since he was ' in his thought before ' anything came into being and since he had ' those to whom he has revealed him. ' He set the deficiency on the one who [30] remains for certain periods and times, ' as a glory for his Pleroma, since ' the fact that he is unknown ' is a cause ' of his production from his [35] agreement [. . .] **126** of him. Just as reception of ' knowledge of him is a manifestation of his lack ' of envy and the revelation ' of the abundance of his sweetness, [5] which is the second glory, ' so, too, he has been found ' to be a cause ' of ignorance, although he is also ' a begetter of knowledge.

In a [10] hidden and incomprehensible wisdom ' he kept the knowledge to the end, ' until the Totalities became weary while searching for ' God the Father, whom no one ' found through his own wisdom [15] or power. ' He gives himself, so that they might receive knowledge of the abundant thought about ' his great glory, which ' he has given, and (about) the cause, which he has ' given, which is his unceasing thanksgiving, [20] he who, from ' the immobility of his counsel, ' reveals himself eternally ' to those who have been worthy of the Father ' who is unknown in his nature, so that they [25] might receive knowledge of him, through his desire ' that they should come to experience the ' ignorance and its pains. '

Those of whom he first thought ' that they should attain knowledge and [30] the good things which are in it, ' they were planning — which is the wisdom ' of the Father, — that they might experience ' the evil things and might ' train themselves in them, [35] as a [. . .] for a time, ' [so that they might] receive the enjoyment ' [of good things] for ' eternity. **127** They hold change and ' persistent renunciation and the ' cause of those who fight against them as an adornment ' and marvelous quality of those who [5] are exalted, so that it is manifest ' that the ignorance of ' those who will be ignorant of the Father was ' something of their own. He who gave them ' knowledge of him was one of his powers [10] for enabling them to grasp that ' knowledge in the fullest sense is ' called "the knowledge of ' all that which is thought of" and "the ' treasure" and "the addition for the [15] increase of knowledge," "the revelation ' of those things which were known at first," ' and "the path toward harmony ' and toward the ' pre-existent one," which is the [20] increase of those who have ' abandoned the greatness which was theirs ' in the organization of ˈ the will, so that the end ˈ might be like the beginning. [25]

As for the baptism which exists ˈ in the fullest sense, into ˈ which the Totalities will descend ˈ and in which they will be, there is no other ˈ baptism apart from this one alone, [30] which is the redemption into ˈ God, Father, Son and ˈ Holy Spirit, when ˈ confession is made through ˈ faith in those names, [35] which are a single name of ˈ the gospel, **128** when they have come to believe what has been said to them, ˈ namely that they exist. From ˈ this they have their ˈ salvation, those who have [5] believed that they exist. This ˈ is attaining in an invisible way ˈ to the Father, Son, ˈ and Holy Spirit in an ˈ undoubting faith. And when they [10] have borne witness to them, it is also with a ˈ firm hope that they ˈ attained them, so that the return to them might ˈ become the perfection of those who have believed ˈ in them and (so that) [15] the Father might be one with them, the Father, ˈ the God, whom they have confessed ˈ in faith and who ˈ gave (them) their union with him in ˈ knowledge.

The baptism which we [20] previously mentioned is called ˈ "garment of those who do not ˈ strip themselves of it," for those who ˈ will put it on and those who have ˈ received redemption wear it. It is also [25] called "the confirmation of the ˈ truth which has no fall." ˈ In an unwavering and ˈ immovable way it grasps those ˈ who have received the [restoration] [30] while they grasp it. (Baptism) is ˈ called "silence" because of ˈ the quiet and the tranquility. ˈ It is also called "bridal chamber" ˈ because of the agreement and the [35] indivisible state of those who know ˈ they have known him. It is also called **129** "the light which does not set ˈ and is without flame," since it does not give light, ˈ but those who have worn it ˈ are made into light. They [5] are the ones whom he wore. ˈ (Baptism) is also called, "the ˈ eternal life," which is ˈ immortality; and it is called ˈ "that which is, entirely, simply, [10] in the proper sense, what is pleasing, ˈ inseparably and irremovably ˈ and faultlessly and ˈ imperturbably, for the one who exists ˈ for those who have received a beginning." For, what else is there [15] to name it ˈ apart from "God," since it is the Totalities, ˈ that is, even if it is given ˈ numberless names, ˈ they are spoken simply as a reference to it. [20] Just as he transcends every word ˈ and he transcends every voice ˈ and he transcends every mind ˈ and he transcends everything ˈ and he transcends every silence, [25] so it is ˈ *[Dittography]* ˈ with those who are that ˈ which he is. This is that which they find ˈ it to be, [30] ineffably and ˈ inconceivably in (its) visage, for the coming into being in those who ˈ know, through him whom they have comprehended, ˈ who is the one to whom ˈ they gave glory.

16. *Redemption of the Calling*

Even if on the matter of the election **130** there are many more things for ' us to say, as it is fitting to ' say, nonetheless, on the ' matter of those of the calling — for [5] those of the right are so named ' — it is necessary ' for us to return once again to them ' and it is not profitable ' for us to forget them. We have spoken [10] about them, — If there is enough in ' what preceded at some length, how have we ' spoken? In a partial way, — ' since I said about all those who came ' forth from the Logos, [15] either from the judgment of ' the evil ones or from ' the wrath which fights against them and the ' turning away from them, which ' is the return to [20] the exalted ones, or from the prayer and ' the remembrance of those who pre-existed ' or from hope and ' faith that [they] would receive their salvation ' from good work [25] since they have been deemed worthy because ' they are beings from the good ' dispositions, (that) they have ' cause of their begetting ' which is an opinion from the one who [30] exists. Still further (I said) that before the ' Logos concerned himself with ' them in an invisible way, ' willingly, the exalted one added ' to this thought, because [35] they were [in need] of him, **131** who was the cause of ' their being. They did not exalt themselves, ' when they were saved, as if there were nothing ' existing before them, but they [5] confess that they have a beginning ' to their existence and they ' desire this: to know him ' who exists before them. ' Most of all (I said) that they worshipped [10] the revelation of the light ' in the form of lightning and ' they bore witness that it appeared ' as ⟨their⟩ salvation. '

Not only those who have come forth [15] from the Logos, about whom ' alone we said that ' they would accomplish the good work, ' but also those whom these brought forth ' according to the good dispositions [20] will share ' in the repose according to the abundance ' of the grace. Also those who have been ' brought forth from the desire ' of lust for [25] power, having the ' seed in them which is the ' lust for power, will receive ' the reward for (their) good deeds, ' namely those who acted and those [30] who have the predisposition ' toward the good, if they ' intentionally desire and wish ' to abandon the ' vain, temporal ambition [35] and [they] keep the commandment of the Lord **132** of glory, instead of the momentary ' honor, and inherit ' the eternal kingdom.

Now, ' it is necessary that we unite [5] the causes and the effects on them ' of the grace and the impulses, ' since it is fitting that we say what ' we mentioned previously about the salvation ' of all those of the right, [10] of all those unmixed and those mixed, ' to join them ' [with] one

another. And as for the repose, [which] ' is the revelation of [the] form
⟨in⟩ which they believed, [15] (it is necessary) that we should treat it with
a ' suitable discussion. For when we ' confessed the kingdom ' which is
in Christ, ⟨we⟩ escaped from ' the whole multiplicity of forms and
from [20] inequality and change. For the end ' will receive a unitary existence ' just as the beginning is unitary, ' where there is no ' male nor female, nor slave [25] and free, nor circumcision ' and uncircumcision,
neither angel ' nor man, but ' Christ is all in all. What is the form ' of
the one who did not exist at first? [30] It will be found that he will exist.
And ' what is the nature of the one who was a slave? ' He will take a
place with a **133** free man. For, they will receive the vision ' more and
more by nature ' and not only by a little word, ' so as to believe, only
through [5] a voice, that this is the way ' it is, that ' the restoration to that
which used to be is a unity. ' Even if some are ' exalted because of the
organization, since they have been appointed [10] as causes of the things
which have come into being, ' since they are more active as natural
forces ' and since they are desired because of these things, ' angels and
men will receive the kingdom and the confirmation ' [and] the salvation. [15] These, then, are the causes. '

About the ⟨one⟩ who appeared in flesh they believed ' without any
doubt ' that he is the Son of the unknown ' God, who [20] was not previously spoken of ' and who could not be seen. ' They abandoned their
gods ' whom they had previously worshipped ' and the lords who are [25]
in heaven and on ' earth. Before ' he had taken them up, and while he
was still ' a child, they testified that he had already ' begun to preach,
[30] and when he was in the tomb ' as a dead man the ' [angels] thought
that he was alive, ' [receiving] life **134** from the one who had died. '
They first desired their numerous services ' and wonders, ' which were
in the temple on their behalf, [5] to be performed continuously ⟨as⟩ the
confession. ' That is, it can ' be done on their behalf through ' their approach to him. '

That preparation which they did not accept [10] they rejected ' because
of the one who had not been sent ' from that place, but [they granted
to] ' Christ, of whom they thought ' that he exists in [that] place [15] from
which they had come ' along with him, a place of gods ' and lords
whom they served, ' worshipped ' and ministered to [20] in the names
which they had received on loan. ' — They were given to the one who
is designated ' by them properly. — ' However, after his ' assumption,
they had the experience [25] to know that he is their Lord, ' over whom
no one else is lord. ' They gave him their kingdoms; ' they rose from

their thrones; ' they were kept from their [30] crowns. He, however, revealed himself to them, ' for the reasons which we have already spoken
of, ' their salvation and the [return to a] ' good thought until [. . .] **135**
[. . .] companion and the angels ' [. . .] and the abundance of good '
[which they did] with it. Thus, ' they were entrusted with the services, [5]
which benefit the elect, ' bringing their iniquity ' up to heaven. They
tested them eternally ' for the lack of humility from the inerrancy ' of
the creation, continuing on their [10] behalf until all come to life and '
leave life, while their ' bodies [remain] on earth, serving ' all their [. . .],
sharing ' [with them] in their sufferings [15] [and] persecutions and '
tribulations, which were brought ' upon the saints in [every] place. '

As for the servants of the ' evil ⟨one⟩, though [20] evil is worthy of destruction, they are in ' [. . .]. But because of the ' [. . .] which is above
' all the worlds, which is ' their good thought [25] and the fellowship, ' the
Church will remember them ' as good friends ' and faithful servants,
once she has received ' redemption [from the one who gives] requital. [30]
Then the [grace] which is in ' the bridal [chamber] and [. . . ' . . .] in her
house [. . . ' . . .] in this thought ' of the giving and the one who [. . .]
136 Christ is the one with her [and the] ' expectation of the Father [of]
' the Totality, since she will produce for them ' angels as guides and [5]
servants.

They will ' think pleasant thoughts. ' They are services for her. She
will ' give them their requital for all that which ' the aeons will think
about. [10] He is an emanation from them, so that, ' just as Christ [did]
his ' will which he brought [forth and] ' exalted the greatnesses of the
Church [and] ' gave them to her, so [15] will she be a thought for ' [these.]
And to men he gives [their] ' eternal dwelling places, in ' which they will
dwell, [leaving] ' behind the attraction toward [20] the defect, while ' the
power of the Pleroma pulls them up ' in the greatness of the ' generosity
and [the] sweetness of ' the aeon which pre-exists. This [25] is the nature
of the entire begetting of those ' whom he had when he shone ' on them
[in] a [light] which he ' revealed [. . .]. ' Just as his [. . .] [30] which will be
[. . .] ' so too his [lord] ' [while] the change alone is ' in those who have
changed. **137** which [. . .] by ' him [. . .] ' [. . .] said, ' while the hylics
will remain until [10] the end for destruction, since they will not give '
forth for their [names], if ' [they would] return once again to that which
' [will not be]. As they were ' [. . .] they were not [15] [. . .] but they were
of use ' [in the] time that they were ' [in it] among them, although they
were not ' [. . .] at first. If ' [. . .] to do something else concerning [20] the
control which ' they have of the preparation, ' [. . .] before them. ' —

For though I continually use ' these words, I have not understood [25] his meaning. – Some ' [elders . . .] him ' [greatness.] **138** all [. . .] angels ' [. . .] word ' and [the sound of] a trumpet ' he will proclaim the great [10] complete amnesty ' from the beauteous east, in the ' bridal chamber which is the love ' of God the Father [. . .] ' according to the power which [. . .] [15] of the greatness [. . .] ' the sweetness of [. . .] ' of him, since he reveals ' himself to the greatnesses [. . .] ' his goodness [. . .] [20] the praise, the dominion, [and] the [glory] ' through [. . .] the Lord the ' Savior, the Redeemer of all those belonging to the one filled ' with Love, ' through his Holy Spirit [25] from now through all ' generations forever ' and ever. Amen.

THE APOCRYPHON OF JOHN
(II,*1*, III,*1*, IV,*1*, AND BG 8502,*2*)

Introduced and translated by

FREDERIK WISSE

The Apocryphon of John is an important work of mythological Gnosticism. Using the framework of a revelation delivered by the resurrected Christ to John the son of Zebedee, this tractate offers a remarkably clear description of the creation, fall, and salvation of humanity; the mythological description is developed largely in terms of the early chapters of Genesis. Reports of the church fathers indicate that some of them were familiar with the contents of *The Apocryphon of John*: the teachings of certain Gnostics described by Irenaeus are very similar to the cosmological teachings of the present tractate. Though Irenaeus apparently did not know *The Apocryphon of John* in its present form, it is certain that the main teachings of the tractate existed before 185 C.E., the date of Irenaeus' work *Against Heresies*. *The Apocryphon of John* was still used in the eighth century by the Audians of Mesopotamia.

The Apocryphon of John supplies answers to two basic questions: What is the origin of evil? How can we escape from this evil world to our heavenly home? The cosmogeny, in spite of its exotic details, also seeks to answer these questions. The highest deity is defined in terms of an abstract Greek concept of perfection, a perfection which excludes all anthropomorphism and all involvement in the world. From this supreme deity emanates a series of light-beings, including Christ and Sophia.

According to *The Apocryphon of John*, the fall occurs when Sophia desires to bring forth a being without the approval of the great Spirt or her consort. Consequently, she produces the monstrous creator-god Yaldabaoth, who still possesses some of the light-power of his mother. Yaldabaoth creates angels to rule over the world and aid in the creation of man; man himself is fashioned after the perfect Father's image, which was mirrored on the water. Man comes to life when Yaldabaoth is tricked into breathing light-power into him. Thus begins a continuous struggle between the powers of light and the powers of darkness for the possession of the divine particles in man. The evil powers put man in a material body to keep him imprisoned, and also create woman and sexual desire to spread the particles of light and make escape more difficult. Finally Christ is sent down to save humanity by reminding people of their heavenly origin. Only those who possess this knowledge and have lived ascetic lives can return to the realm of light; the others are reincarnated until they also come to saving knowledge.

Three versions of *The Apocryphon of John* are known. III,*1* and BG,*2* represent independent translations into Coptic of a short Greek recension of the work. II,*1* and IV,*1* are copies of the same Coptic translation of a long Greek recension. The English translation presented here is of the long recension. Page and line numbers are given for II,*1*, except where IV,*1* preserved text which was omitted in II,*1* through scribal error.

THE APOCRYPHON OF JOHN

II 1, 1-32, 9 = IV 1, 1-49, 28

The teaching [of the savior], and [the revelation] ' of the mysteries, [and the] things hidden in ' silence, [even these things which] he taught ' John, [his] disciple. [5]

[And] it happened one [day], when ' John, [the brother] of James ' – who are the sons of Zebedee – had come up to ' the temple, that a Pharisee ' named Arimanius approached him and said [10] to him, "Where is your master [whom] ' you followed?" And he [said] to him, ' "He has gone to the [place] from which he came." The Pharisee ' [said to him, "With deception ' did this Nazarene] deceive you (pl.), [15] and he filled [your ears with lies], ' and closed [your hearts (and) turned you] ' from the traditions [of your fathers."]

[When] ' I, [John], heard these things [I turned] ' away from the temple [to a desert place]. [20] And I grieved [greatly in my heart saying], ' "How [then was] the savior [appointed], ' and why was he sent [in to the world] ' by [his Father, and who is his] ' Father who [sent him, and of what sort] [25] is [that] aeon [to which we shall go?] ' For what did he [mean when he said to us], ' 'This aeon to [which you will go is of the] type ' of the [imperishable] aeon,' [but he did not teach] ' us concerning [the latter of what sort it is."] [30]

Straightway, [while I was contemplating these things,] ' behold, the [heavens opened and] the whole creation [which is] below heaven shone, ' and [the world] was shaken. **2** [I was afraid, and behold I] saw in ' the light [a youth who stood] by me. ' While I looked [at him he became] like an ' old man. And he [changed his] likeness (again) becoming [5] like a servant. There was [not a plurality] before me, ' but there was a [likeness] with multiple forms ' in the light, and the [likenesses] appeared ' through each other, [and] the [likeness] had three ' forms.

He said to me, "John, John, [10] why do you doubt, or why [are you] ' afraid? You are not unfamiliar with this image, are you? ' – that is, do not [be] timid! – I am the one who ' is [with you (pl.)] always. I ' [am the Father], I am the Mother, I am the Son. [15] I am the undefiled and incorruptible one. ' Now [I have come to teach you] what is ' [and what was] and what will come to ' [pass], that [you may know the] things which are not revealed ¹ [and those which are revealed, and to teach you] concerning the ²⁰ [unwavering race of] the perfect [Man]. Now, ¹ [therefore, lift up] your [face, that] you may ¹ [receive] the things that I [shall teach you] today, [and] ¹ may [tell them to your] fellow spirits who [are ¹ from] the [unwavering] race of the perfect ²⁵ Man.''

[And I asked] to ¹ [know it, and he said] to me, ''The Monad ¹ [is a] monarchy with nothing above it. ¹ [It is he who exists] as [God] and Father of ¹ everything, [the invisible] One who is above ³⁰ [everything, who exists as] incorruption, which is ¹ [in the] pure light into which no ¹ [eye] can look. ¹

He [is the] invisible [Spirit] of whom it is not right ¹ [to think] of him as a god, or something ³⁵ similar. For he is more than a god, ¹ since there is nothing above him, for no one 3 lords it over him. [For he does] not [exist] in something ¹ inferior [to him, since everything] exists in him. ¹ (IV 4, 9-10: [For it is he who establishes]) himself. [He is eternal] since ¹ he does [not] need [anything]. For [he] is total ⁵ perfection. [He] did not [lack anything] that he might ¹ be completed by [it; rather] he is always completely perfect ¹ in [light]. He is [illimitable] since ¹ there is no one [prior to him] to set limits to him. ¹ He is unsearchable [since there] exists no one ¹⁰ prior to him to [examine him. He is] immeasurable ¹ since there [was] no one [prior to him to measure] ¹ him. [He is invisible since no] ¹ one saw [him. He is eternal] since he [exists] ¹ eternally. He is [ineffable since] ¹⁵ no one was able to comprehend him to speak [about him]. ¹ He is unnameable since [there is no one prior to him] ¹ to give [him] a name.

He is [immeasurable light] ¹ which is pure, holy [(and) immaculate]. ¹ He is ineffable [being perfect in] incorruptibility. ²⁰ (He is) [not] in perfection, nor in ¹ blessedness, nor in ¹ divinity, but he is far superior. ¹ He is not corporeal [nor] is he incorporeal. ¹ He is neither large [nor] is he small. [There is no] ²⁵ way to say, 'What is his quantity?' or, 'What [is his quality?'], ¹ for no one can [know him]. ¹ He is not someone among (other) [beings, rather he is] ¹ far superior. [Not] that [he is (simply) superior], but his ¹ essence does not [partake] in the aeons nor ³⁰ in time. For he who partakes in [an aeon] ¹ was prepared beforehand. Time [was not] ¹ apportioned to him, [since] he does not ¹ receive anything from another, [for it would be received] ¹ on loan. For he who precedes someone does not [lack] ³⁵ that he may receive from [him]. ¹ For [rather] it is the latter that looks expectantly at him in 4 his light.

For the [perfection] is majestic. ¹ He is pure, immeasurable [mind]. ¹

He is an aeon-giving aeon. ' He is [life]- ' giving life. He is a blessed-
ness-giving [5] blessed one. He is knowledge-giving ' knowledge. [He is]
goodness-giving ' goodness. [He is] mercy and redemption-[giving mer-
cy]. ' He is grace-giving grace, [not] because ' he possesses it, but because he gives [the] immeasurable, [10] incomprehensible [light].

[How am I to speak] with you about him? His ' [aeon] is indestructible, at rest and ' existing in [silence, reposing] (and) being ' prior [to
everything. For he] is the head of [all] the aeons, ' [and] it is he who
gives them strength in [15] his goodness. For [we know] not ' [the ineffable things, and we] do not understand what ' [is immeasurable], except for him who came forth ' [from] him, namely (from) [the] Father.
For it is he ' who [told] it to us [alone]. For it is he who looks [20] at
him[self] in his light which surrounds ' [him], namely the spring [of the]
water of life. And ' it is he who gives to [all] the [aeons] and in every
way, (and) who ' [gazes upon] his image which he sees ' in the spring of
the [Spirit]. It is he who puts his desire in his [25] [water]-light [which is
in the] spring of the ' [pure light]-water [which] surrounds him.

And ' [his thought performed] a deed and she came forth, ' [namely]
she who had [appeared] before him ' in [the shine of] his light. This is
[30] the first [power which was] before all of them ' (and) [which came]
forth from his mind, She ' [is the forethought of the All] − her light '
[shines like his] light − the [perfect] ' power which is [the] image of the
invisible, [35] virginal Spirit who is perfect. ' [The first power], the glory
of Barbelo, the perfect **5** glory in the aeons, the glory of the ' revelation, she glorified the virginal ' Spirit and it was she who praised him,
because thanks to him ' she had come forth. This is the first thought, [5]
his image; she became the womb of everything ' for it is she who is prior
to them all, the ' Mother-Father, the first man, the holy Spirit, ' the
thrice-male, the thrice-powerful, ' the thrice-named androgynous one,
and the [10] eternal aeon among the invisible ones, and ' the first to come
forth.

"⟨She⟩ requested from ' the invisible, virginal Spirit − ' that is
Barbelo − to give her foreknowledge. ' And the Spirit consented. And
when he had [consented], [15] the foreknowledge came forth, and ' it
stood by the forethought; it originates from ' the thought of the invisible, ' virginal Spirit. It glorified him [and] ' his perfect power, Barbelo,
for [20] it was for her sake that it had come into being.

"And she requested again ' to grant her [indestructibility], and he
consented. ' When he had [consented], indestructibility ' [came] forth,
and it stood by ' the thought and the foreknowledge. It glorified [25] the

invisible One and Barbelo, ˈ the one for whose sake they had come into being.

"And Barbelo requested ˈ to grant her eternal life. And ˈ the invisible Spirit consented. And ˈ when he had consented, eternal life [30] came forth, and [they attended] and glorified ˈ the invisible [Spirit] and Barbelo, ˈ the one for whose sake they had come into being.

"And she requested again ˈ to grant her truth. And the invisible Spirit ˈ consented. (IV 8, 24f.: And [when he had] consented) truth came forth, [35] and they attended and glorified the invisible, **6** excellent Spirit and his Barbelo, ˈ the one for whose sake they had come into being.

"This is the pentad of the aeons ˈ of the Father, which is the first ˈ man, the image of the invisible Spirit; [5] it is the forethought, which is Barbelo, ˈ and the thought, and the foreknowledge, and ˈ the indestructibility, and the eternal life, and ˈ the truth. This is the androgynous pentad of the aeons, ˈ which is the decad of the aeons, which is [10] the Father.

"And he looked at Barbelo ˈ with the pure light which surrounds the invisible ˈ Spirit and (with) his spark, and she conceived ˈ from him. He begot a spark of light with a light ˈ resembling blessedness. But it does not equal [15] his greatness. This was an only-begotten child ˈ of the Mother-Father which had come forth; ˈ it is the only offspring, the only-begotten one of ˈ the Father, the pure Light.

"And ˈ the invisible, virginal Spirit rejoiced [20] over the light which came forth, that which ˈ was brought forth first by the first power ˈ of his forethought which is Barbelo. ˈ And he anointed it with his goodness ˈ until it became perfect, not lacking [25] in any goodness, because he had anointed it ˈ with the goodness of the invisible Spirit. And ˈ it attended him as he poured upon ˈ it. And immediately when it had received from ˈ the Spirit, it glorified the holy Spirit [30] and the perfect forethought [32] for whose sake it had ˈ come forth.

"And it requested to give it a fellow worker, ˈ which is the mind, and he consented (IV 10, 14: [gladly]). [35] And when the invisible Spirit had consented, **7** the mind came forth, and it attended ˈ Christ glorifying him and ˈ Barbelo. And all these came into being ˈ in silence.

"And the mind wanted [5] to perform a deed through the word ˈ of the invisible Spirit. And his will became ˈ a deed and it appeared with ˈ the mind; and the light glorified it. ˈ And the word followed the will. [10] For because of the word, Christ ˈ the divine Autogenes created everything. And the ˈ eternal life ⟨and⟩ his will and the mind ˈ and the foreknowledge attended and glorified ˈ the invisible Spirit and Barbelo, [15] for whose sake they had come into being.

"And the holy ' Spirit completed the divine Autogenes, ' his son, together with Barbelo, ' that he may attend the mighty and invisible, ' virginal Spirit as the divine [20] Autogenes, the Christ whom he had ' honored with a mighty voice. He came forth ' through the forethought. And the invisible, ' virginal Spirit placed the ' divine Autogenes of truth over everything. [25] And he subjected to him every authority, ' and the truth which is in him, ' that he may know the All which ' had been called with a name exalted above ' every name. For that name will be mentioned [30] to those who are worthy of it.

"For from the light, ' which is the Christ, and the indestructibility, ' through the gift of the Spirit the four ' lights (appeared) from the divine Autogenes. ' He expected that they might attend **8** him. And the three (are) will, ' thought, and life. And the four ' powers (are) understanding, grace, perception, ' and prudence. And grace belongs to [5] the light-aeon Armozel, which ' is the first angel. And there are ' three other aeons with this aeon: grace, ' truth, and form. And the second ' light (is) Oriel, who has been placed [10] over the second aeon. And there are ' three other aeons with him: conception, perception, ' and memory. And the third light ' is Daveithai, who has been placed ' over the third aeon. And there are [15] three other aeons with him: understanding, ' love, and idea. And the fourth ' aeon was placed over the fourth ' light Eleleth. And there are ' three other aeons with him: perfection, [20] peace, and wisdom. These are the four lights ' which attend the divine Autogenes, ' (and) these are the twelve aeons which attend ' the son of the mighty one, the Autogenes, the Christ, ' through the will and the gift of the invisible [25] Spirit. And the twelve aeons belong to ' the son of the Autogenes. And all things were ' established by the will of the holy Spirit ' through the Autogenes.

"And from ' the foreknowledge of the perfect mind, [30] through the revelation of the will of the invisible ' Spirit and the will of the Autogenes, ' ⟨the⟩ perfect Man (appeared), the first revelation, ' and the truth. It is he whom ' the virginal Spirit called Pigera- [35] Adamas, and he placed him over **9** the first aeon with the mighty one, the Autogenes, ' the Christ, by the first light Armozel; ' and with him are his powers. ' And the invisible one gave him a spiritual, [5] invincible power. And he spoke ' and glorified and praised the invisible ' Spirit, saying, 'It is for thy sake that everything ' has come into being and everything will return to thee. ' I shall praise and glorify thee and [10] the Autogenes and the aeons, the three: the Father, ' the Mother, and the Son, the perfect power.'

"And he ' placed his son Seth over the second ' aeon in the presence of the second light ' Oriel. And in the third aeon [15] the seed of Seth was placed ' over the third light Daveithai. ' And the souls of the saints were placed (there). ' And in the fourth aeon ' the souls were placed of those who do not know the [20] Pleroma and who did not repent at once, ' but who persisted for a while and repented ' afterwards; they are by the fourth ' light Eleleth. These are ' creatures which glorify the invisible Spirit. [25]

"And the Sophia of the Epinoia, being an aeon, ' conceived a thought from herself and ' the conception of the invisible Spirit and ' foreknowledge. She wanted to bring forth ' a likeness out of herself without the consent of the Spirit, [30] − he had not approved − and without her consort, ' and without his consideration. And though the person of her ' maleness had not approved, ' and she had not found her agreement, ' and she had thought without the consent of the Spirit [35] and the knowledge of her agreement, (yet) she brought forth. **10** And because of the invincible power which is in her, ' her thought did not remain idle and ' something came out of her ' which was imperfect and different from her appearance, [5] because she had created it without her consort. ' And it was dissimilar to the likeness of its mother ' for it has another form.

"And when she saw (the consequences of) her ' desire, it changed into a form ' of a lion-faced serpent. And its eyes [10] were like lightning fires which ' flash. She cast it away from her, outside ' that place, that no one ' of the immortal ones might see it, for she had created it ' in ignorance. And she surrounded it with [15] a luminous cloud, and she placed a throne ' in the middle of the cloud that no ' one might see it except the holy Spirit ' who is called the mother of the living. ' And she called his name Yaltabaoth.

"This [20] is the first archon who took a great ' power from his mother. And he ' removed himself from her and moved ' away from the places in which he was born. He ' became strong and created for himself other aeons with [25] a flame of luminous fire which (still) exists ' now. And he joined with his arrogance ' which is in him and begot ' authorities for himself. The name of the first one ' is Athoth, whom the generations call [30] [the reaper]. The second one is Harmas, ' who [is the eye] of envy. The third one ' is Kalila-Oumbri. The fourth one is Yabel. ' The fifth one is Adonaiou, who is called ' Sabaoth. The sixth one is Cain, [35] whom the generations of men call ' the sun. The seventh is Abel. The ' eighth is Abrisene. The ninth is Yobel. **11** The tenth is Armoupieel. The eleventh is Melceir-Adonein. The twelth is Belias, it is he who is over the depth of Hades. And he placed seven kings [5] – each corresponding to the firmaments of heaven – over the seven heavens, and five over the depth of the abyss, that they may reign. And he shared his fire with them, but he did not send forth from the power of the light which he had taken from his mother, [10] for he is ignorant darkness.

"And when the light had mixed with the darkness, it caused the darkness to shine. And when the darkness had mixed with the light, it darkened the light and it became neither light nor dark, but it became [15] dim.

"Now the archon who is weak has three names. The first name is Yaltabaoth, the second is Saklas, and the third is Samael. And he is impious in his arrogance which is in him. For he said, [20] 'I am God and there is no other God beside me,' for he is ignorant of his strength, the place from which he had come.

"And the archons created seven powers for themselves, and the powers created for themselves six angels for [25] each one until they became 365 angels. And these are the bodies belonging with the names: the first is Athoth, he has a sheep's face; the second is Eloaiou, he has a donkey's face; the third is Astaphaios, he has a [hyena's] face; the [30] fourth is Yao, he has a [serpent's] face with seven heads; the fifth is Sabaoth, he has a dragon's face; the sixth is Adonin, he had a monkey's face; the seventh is Sabbede, he has a shining fire-face. This is the [35] sevenness of the week.

"But Yaltabaoth had a multitude **12** of faces more than all of them so that he could put a face before all of them, according to his desire, when he is in the midst of seraphs. He shared [5] his fire with them; therefore he became lord over them. Because of the power of the glory he possessed of his mother's light, he called himself God. And he did not [10] obey the place from which he came. And he united the seven powers in his thought with the authorities which were with him. And when he spoke it happened. And he named each power beginning [15] with the highest: the first is goodness with the first (authority), Athoth; the second is foreknowledge with the second one, Eloaio; and the third is Astraphaio (II has been corrected by a later hand to read: and the third is divinity with the third one, Astraphaio); the fourth is [20] lordship with the fourth one, Yao; the fifth is kingdom with the fifth one, Sabaoth; the sixth is envy with the sixth one, Adonein; the seventh is understanding with the seventh one, [25] Sabbateon. And these have a firmament corresponding to each aeon-heaven. They were ¹ given names according to the glory which belongs to heaven ¹ for the [destruction of the] powers. And in the names which were ¹ given to [them by] their Originator ³⁰ there was power. But the names which were given ¹ them according to the glory which belongs to heaven mean ¹ for them destruction and powerlessness. ¹ Thus they have two names. ¹

"And (IV 20, 11: having created [   ]) everything he organized according to the model of the first ³⁵ aeons which had come into being, so that he might **13** create them like the indestructible ones. Not because ¹ he had seen the indestructible ones, but the power ¹ in him, which he had taken from ¹ his mother, produced in him the likeness of ⁵ the cosmos. And when he saw the creation which surrounds ¹ him and the multitude of the angels around ¹ him which had come forth from him, ¹ he said to them, 'I am a jealous God ¹ and there is no other God beside me.' But by ¹⁰ announcing this he indicated to the angels ¹ who attended him that there exists another God. ¹ For if there were no other one, of whom ¹ would he be jealous?

Then the mother began ¹ to move to and fro. She became aware of the deficiency when ¹⁵ the brightness of her light diminished. And she ¹ became dark because her consort ¹ had not agreed with her."

And I ¹ said, "Lord, what does it mean that she moved to and fro?" But he ¹ smiled and said, "Do not think it is, as ²⁰ Moses said, 'above ¹ the waters.' No, but when she had seen ¹ the wickedness which had happened, and the theft which ¹ her son had committed, she repented. ¹ And she was overcome by forgetfulness in the darkness of ²⁵ ignorance and she began to be ashamed. (IV 21, 13-15: And she did not dare ¹ to return, but she was moving) ¹ about. And the moving is the going to and fro.

"And the ¹ arrogant one took a power from ¹ his mother. For he was ignorant, ¹ thinking that there existed no other except ³⁰ his mother alone. And when he saw the multitude ¹ of the angels which he had created, then he exalted ¹ himself above them.

"And when ¹ the mother recognized that the garment of darkness ¹ was imperfect, then she knew ³⁵ that her consort had not agreed ¹ with her. She repented **14** with much weeping. And the whole ¹ pleroma heard the prayer of her repentance ¹ and they praised on her behalf ¹ the invisible, virginal ⁵ Spirit. (IV 22, 5-7: And ¹ he consented; and when the invisible Spirit ¹ had consented), the holy Spirit poured ¹ over her from their whole pleroma. ¹ For it was not her consort who came to her, ¹ but he came to her through the pleroma ¹ in order that he might correct her deficiency. And she was taken ¹⁰ up not to her own aeon ¹ but above her son, that she might be ' in the ninth until she has corrected her ' deficiency.

"And a voice came forth from the exalted ' aeon-heaven: 'The Man exists and [15] the son of Man.' And the chief archon, Yaltabaoth, ' heard (it) and thought that the ' voice had come from his mother. ' And he did not know from where it came. And ' he taught them, the holy and perfect Mother-Father, [20] the complete foreknowledge, ' the image of the invisible one who is the Father ' of the all (and) through whom everything came into being, ' the first Man. For he revealed his likeness ' in a human form.

"And the [25] whole aeon of the chief archon trembled, ' and the foundations of the abyss shook. And ' of the waters which are above ' matter, the underside was illuminated by ' the appearance of his image which [30] had been revealed. And when all the authorities ' and the chief archon looked, they ' saw the whole region of the underside which was ' illuminated. And through the light they saw ' the form of the image in the water. **15**

"And he said to the authorities which attend him, ' 'Come, let us create a man according to ' the image of God and according to our likeness, that ' his image may become a light for us.' [5] And they created by means of their respective powers ' in correspondence with the characteristics which were given. And ' each authority supplied a characteristic ' in the form of the image which he had seen ' in its natural (form). He created a being [10] according to the likeness of the first, perfect Man. ' And they said, 'Let us call him ' Adam, that his name may become ' a power of light for us.'

"And the powers ' began: the first one, goodness, created [15] a bone-soul; and the second, foreknowledge, ' created a sinew-soul; the third, ' divinity, created a flesh-soul; ' and the fourth, the lordship, created ' a marrow-soul; the fifth, kingdom [20] created a blood-soul; the sixth, ' envy, created a skin-soul; ' the seventh, understanding, created ' a hair-soul. And the multitude ' of the angels attended him and they received [25] from the powers the seven substances ' of the natural (form) in order to create ' the proportions of the limbs and the proportion of the rump ' and the proper working together of each ' of the parts.

"The first one began to create [30] the head. Eteraphaope-Abron created ' his head; Meniggesstroeth created ' the brain; Asterechme (created) the right eye; ' Thaspomocha (created) the left eye; ' Yeronumos (created) the right ear; Bissoum (created) [35] the left ear; Akioreim (created) the nose; **16** Banen-Ephroum (created) the lips; Amen (created) ' the teeth; Ibikan (created) the molars; Basiliademe (created) ¹ the tonsils; Achcha (created) the uvula; Adaban (created) ¹ the neck; Chaaman (created) the vertebrae; ⁵ Dearcho (created) the throat; Tebar (created) the (IV 25, 4-5: right shoulder; ¹ [.... (created) the]) left ¹ shoulder; Mniarcon (created) the (IV 25, 6-7: right ¹ elbow; [.... (created) the]) left elbow; ¹ Abitrion (created) the right underarm; ¹ Evanthen (created) the left underarm; Krys (created) the right hand; ¹ Beluai (created) the left hand; Treneu ¹⁰ (created) the fingers of the right hand; Balbel ¹ (created) the fingers of the left hand; Kriman (created) the nails ¹ of the hands; Astrops (created) the right breast; ¹ Barroph (created) the left breast; Baoum (created) the right ¹ shoulder joint; Ararim (created) the left shoulder joint; Areche (created) ¹⁵ the belly; Phthave (created) the navel; Senaphim (created) ¹ the abdomen; Arachethopi (created) the right ¹ ribs; Zabedo (created) the left ribs; ¹ Barias (created) the (IV 25, 19-20: right ¹ hip; Phnouth the) left hip; Abenlenarchei (created) ¹ the marrow; Chnoumeninorin (created) the bones; ²⁰ Gesole (created) the stomach; Agromauna (created) ¹ the heart; Bano (created) the lungs; Sostrapal (created) ¹ the liver; Anesimalar (created) the spleen; Thopithro ¹ (created) the intestines; Biblo (created) the kidneys; ¹ Roeror (created) the sinews; Taphreo (created) the spine ²⁵ of the body; Ipouspoboba (created) the veins; ¹ Bineborin (created) the arteries; Atoimenpsephei, ¹ theirs are the breaths which are in all the limbs; ¹ Entholleia (created) all the flesh; Bedouk (created) ¹ the right buttock (?); Arabeei (created) the left penis; ³⁰ Eilo (created) the testicles; Sorma (created) the genitals; Gorma-Kaiochlabar ¹ (created) the right thigh; Nebrith (created) ¹ the left thigh; Pserem (created) the kidneys of ¹ the right leg; Asaklas (created) the left ¹ kidney; Ormaoth (created) the right leg; ³⁵ Emenun (created) the left leg; Knyx (created) the 17 right shin-bone; Tupelon (created) the left shin-bone; ¹ Achiel (created) the right knee; Phnene (created) the ¹ left knee; Phiouthrom (created) the right foot; ¹ Boabel (created) its toes; Trachoun (created) ⁵ the left foot; Phikna (created) its toes; ¹ Miamai (created) the nails of the feet; Labernioum − . ¹

"And those who were appointed over all of these ¹ are: Zathoth, Armas, Kalila, Jabel, (IV 26, 19-20: Sabaoth, Cain, ¹ Abel). And ¹ those who are particularly active in the limbs ¹⁰ (are) the head Diolimodraza, the neck Yammeax, ¹ the right shoulder Yakouib, the ¹ left shoulder Verton, the right hand ¹ Oudidi, the left one Arbao, the fingers of the right hand ¹ Lampno, the fingers of the left hand ¹⁵ Leekaphar, the right breast Barbar, the ¹ left breast Imae, the chest Pisandriaptes, ¹ the right shoulder joint Koade, the left shoulder joint | Odeor, the right ribs Asphixix, the left | ribs Synogchouta, the belly Arouph [20] the womb Sabalo, the right thigh | Charcharb, the left thigh Chthaon, | all the genitals Bathinoth, the right | leg Choux, the left leg Charcha, | the right shin-bone Aroer, the left shin-bone [25] Toechtha, the right knee Aol, the left | knee Charaner, the right foot | Bastan, its toes Archentechtha, the | left foot Marephnounth, its toes | Abrana.

"Seven have power over [30] all of these: Michael, Ouriel, | Asmenedas, Saphasatoel, Aarmouriam, | Richram, Amiorps. And the ones who are in charge over the senses | (are) Archendekta; and he who is in charge over the receptions | (is) Deitharbathas; and he who is in charge over the imagination [35] (is) Oummaa; and he who is over the composition **18** Aachiaram, and he who is over the whole impulse | Riaramnacho.

"And the origin of the demons | which are in the whole body is determined to be four: | heat, cold, wetness, [5] and dryness. And the mother of all of them is matter. | And he who reigns over the heat (is) Phloxopha; | and he who reigns over the cold | is Oroorrothos; and he who reigns over | what is dry (is) Erimacho; and he who reigns [10] over the wetness (is) Athuro. And the mother of all of these, | Onorthochrasaei, stands in their midst | since she is illimitable, and she mixes | with all of them. And she is truly matter, | for they are nourished by her.

"The four [15] chief demons are: Ephememphi who | belongs to pleasure, Yoko who belongs to desire, | Nenentophni who belongs to grief, Blaomen | who belongs to fear. And the mother of them all is | Aesthesis-Ouch-Epi-Ptoe. And from the four [20] demons passions came forth. | And from grief (came) envy, jealousy, | distress, trouble, pain, | callousness, anxiety, mourning, | etc. And from pleasure [25] much wickedness arises, and empty | pride, and similar things. | And from desire (comes) anger, wrath, | and bitterness, and bitter passion, | and unsatedness, and similar things. [30] And from fear (comes) dread, | fawning, agony, and shame. All of these | are like useful things as well as evil things. | But the insight into their true (character) is Anaro, | who is the head of the material soul, **19** for it belongs with the seven senses, Ouch-Epi-Ptoe. |

"This is the number of the angels: | together they are 365. They | all worked on it until, [5] limb for limb, the natural and | the material body was completed by them. Now there are | other ones in charge over the remaining passions | whom I did not mention to you. But if you | wish to know them, it is written in [10] the book of Zoroaster. And | all the angels and demons worked | until they had constructed the natural body.

And their product was completely inactive and motionless for a long time. [15]

"And when the mother wanted to retrieve the power which she had given to the chief archon, she petitioned the Mother-Father of the All who is most merciful. He sent, by means of the holy decree, the five lights [20] down upon the place of the angels of the chief archon. They advised him that they should bring forth the power of the mother. And they said to Yaltabaoth, 'Blow into his face something of your spirit and [25] his body will arise.' And he blew into his face the spirit which is the power of his mother; he did not know (this), for he exists in ignorance. And the power of the mother went out of [30] Yaltabaoth into the natural body which they had fashioned after the image of the one who exists from the beginning. The body moved and gained strength, and it was luminous.

"And in that moment the rest of the powers **20** became jealous, because he had come into being through all of them and they had given their power to the man, and his intelligence was greater than that of those who had made him, and [5] greater than that of the chief archon. And when they recognized that he was luminous, and that he could think better than they, and that he was free from wickedness, they took him and threw him into the lowest region of all matter.

"But the blessed One, the Mother-Father, [10] the beneficent and merciful One, had mercy on the power of the mother which had been brought forth out of the chief archon, for they (the archons) might gain power over the natural and perceptible body. And he [15] sent, through his beneficent Spirit and his great mercy, a helper to Adam, luminous Epinoia which comes out of him, who is called Life. And she assists the whole creature, [20] by toiling with him and by restoring him to his fullness and by teaching him about the descent of his seed (and) by teaching him about the way of ascent, (which is) the way he came down. [25] And the luminous Epinoia was hidden in Adam, in order that the archons might not know her, but that the Epinoia might be a correction of the deficiency of the mother.

"And the man came forth because of the shadow of the light [30] which is in him. And his thinking was superior to all those who had made him. When they looked up they saw that his thinking was superior. And they took counsel with the whole array of archons [35] and angels. They took fire and earth **21** and water and mixed them together with the four fiery winds. And they wrought them together and caused a great disturbance. And they brought him (Adam) into the shadow [5] of death in order that they might form (him) again ' from earth and water and fire ' and the spirit which originates in matter, which is ' the ignorance of darkness and desire, ' and their counterfeit spirit. This [10] is the tomb of the newly-formed body ' with which the robbers had clothed the man, ' the bond of forgetfulness; and he became a ' mortal man. This is the first one who came down ' and the first separation. But the [15] Epinoia of the light which was in him, ' she is the one who was to awaken his thinking.

"And ' the archons took him and placed ' him in paradise. And they said to him, ' 'Eat, that is at leisure,' for [20] their luxury is bitter and their beauty is depraved. ' And their luxury is deception and ' their trees are godlessness and their fruit ' is deadly poison and their ' promise is death. And the tree of their [25] life they had placed in the midst of paradise. '

"And I shall teach you (pl.) ' what is the mystery of their life, ' which is the plan which they made together, ' which is the likeness of their spirit. [30] The root of this (tree) is bitter and its branches ' are death, its shadow is hate ' and deception is in its leaves, ' and its blossom is the ointment of evil, ' and its fruit is death and [35] desire is its seed, and ' it sprouts in darkness. The **22** dwelling place of those who taste from it is ' Hades and the darkness is their place of rest. '

"But what they call ' the tree of knowledge of good and [5] evil, which is the Epinoia of the light, ' they stayed in front of it in order that he (Adam) might not ' look up to his fullness and ' recognize the nakedness of his shamefulness. ' But it was I who brought about that they ate.''

And [10] I said to the savior, "Lord, was it not the serpent ' that taught Adam to eat?'' ' The savior smiled and said, "The serpent taught them ' to eat from wickedness of begetting, ' lust, (and) destruction, that he (Adam) might [15] be useful to him. And he (Adam) knew that he was ' disobedient to him (the chief archon) due to light of the Epinoia ' which is in him, which made him more correct in his ' thinking than the chief archon. And (the latter) ' wanted to bring about the power which he himself had given [20] him. And he brought a forgetfulness ' over Adam.

And I said to the savior, "What is ' the forgetfulness?'' And he said, "It is not the way Moses ' wrote (and) you heard. For he said in ' his first book, 'He put him to sleep' (Gn 2: 21), but [25] (it was) in his perception. For also he said through the ' prophet, 'I will make their ' hearts heavy that they may not pay attention and may not ' see' (Is 6: 10).

"Then the Epinoia of the light ' hid herself in him (Adam). And the chief archon wanted [30] to bring her out of his rib. | But the Epinoia of the light cannot be grasped. | Although darkness pursued her, it did not catch her. And | he brought a part of his power | out of him. And he made another creature [35] in the form of a woman according to the likeness of the Epinoia | which had appeared to him. And he brought **23** the part which he had taken from the power | of the man into the female creature, | and not as Moses said, | 'his rib-bone.'

"And he (Adam) saw the woman beside [5] him. And in that moment | the luminous Epinoia appeared, and she lifted | the veil which lay over his mind. | And he became sober from the drunkenness of darkness. | And he recognized his counter-image, and he said, [10] 'This is indeed bone of my bones | and flesh of my flesh.' Therefore | the man will leave his father and his | mother and he will cleave to his wife and they will | both be one flesh. For they [15] will send him his consort, | and he will leave his father and his mother. {....} [20]

"And our sister | Sophia (is) she who came down in innocence | in order to rectify her deficiency. | Therefore she was called Life, which is | the mother of the living, by the foreknowledge [25] of the sovereignty of heaven (IV 36, 18-20: and [   ] to him [   ].) And through her | they have tasted the perfect Knowledge. I appeared | in the form of an eagle on | the tree of knowledge, which is the Epinoia | from the foreknowledge of the pure light, [30] that I might teach them and awaken | them out of the depth of sleep. For they | were both in a fallen state and they | recognized their nakedness. The Epinoia | appeared to them as a light (and) she awakened [35] their thinking.

"And when Yaldabaoth | noticed that they withdrew from him, | he cursed his earth. He found the woman as she was **24** preparing herself for her husband. He was lord | over her though he did not know the mystery | which had come to pass through the holy decree. | And they were afraid to blame him. And [5] he showed his angels his | ignorance which is in him. And | he cast them out of paradise and | he clothed them in gloomy darkness. And the | chief archon saw the virgin who stood [10] by Adam, and that the luminous | Epinoia of life had appeared in her. | And Yaldabaoth was full of ignorance. | And when the foreknowledge of the All | noticed (it), she sent some and they snatched [15] life out of Eve.

"And the chief archon | seduced her and he begot in her | two sons; the first and the second | (are) Eloim and Yave. Eloim has a bear-face | and Yave has a cat-face. The one [20] is righteous but the other is unrighteous. (IV 38, 4-6: Yave | is righteous but Eloim is | unrighteous.) |

Yave he set ' over the fire and the wind, and Eloim he set ' over the water and ' the earth. And these he called with the names ²⁵ Cain and Abel with a view to deceive. '

"Now up to the present day ' sexual intercourse continued due to the chief archon. ' And he planted sexual desire ' in her who belongs to Adam. And he produced through ³⁰ intercourse the copies of the bodies, ' and he inspired them with his counterfeit spirit. '

"And the two archons he set ' over principalities so that ' they might rule over the tomb. ³⁵ And when Adam recognized the likeness of his own ' foreknowledge, he begot the likeness **25** of the son of man. He called him Seth ' according to the way of the race in the aeons. Likewise ' the mother also sent down her spirit ' which is in her likeness and a ⁵ copy of those who are in the pleroma, for she will ' prepare a dwelling place for the aeons which will come ' down. And he made them drink water of forgetfulness, ' from the chief archon, in order that they might not ' know from where they came. Thus ¹⁰ the seed remained for ' a while assisting (him) in order that, when ' the Spirit comes forth from ' the holy aeons, he may raise up and ' heal him from the deficiency, that the ¹⁵ whole pleroma may (again) become holy and ' faultless."

And I said to the savior, ' "Lord, will all the souls then be brought safely ' into the pure light?" He answered ' and said to me, "Great things ²⁰ have arisen in your mind, for it is ' difficult to explain them to others ' except to those who are from ' the immovable race. Those on whom the Spirit of life ' will descend and (with whom) he will be with the power, ²⁵ they will be saved and become perfect ' and be worthy of the greatness and ' be purified in that place from ' all wickedness and the involvements in evil. ' Then they have no other care than ³⁰ the incorruption alone, to which they direct their attention ' from here on, without anger or envy or jealousy ' or desire and greed of ' anything. They are not affected by ' anything except the state of being in ³⁵ the flesh alone, which they bear while looking expectantly ' for the time when they will be met **26** by the receivers (of the body). Such ' then are worthy of the imperishable, ' eternal life and the calling. For they endure ' everything and bear up under ⁵ everything, that they may finish ' the good fight and inherit ' eternal life."

I said to him, "Lord, ' the souls of those who did not do these works, ' (but) on whom the power and Spirit ¹⁰ descended, (IV 40, 24-25: will they be rejected?" He ' answered and said to me, "If) the ' Spirit (IV 40, 24-25: descended upon them), they will in any case be saved ' and they will change (for the better). For the ' power will descend on every man, ' for without it no one can stand. [15] And after they are born, then, ' when the Spirit of life increases and ' the power comes and strengthens that soul, ' no one can lead it astray ' with works of evil. [20] But those on whom the counterfeit spirit ' descends are drawn by ' him and they go astray.''

And I ' said, "Lord, where will the souls of these go ' when they have come out of their [25] flesh?'' And he smiled ' and said to me, "The soul, in which the power ' will become stronger than the counterfeit spirit, ' is strong and it flees from ' evil and, through [30] the intervention of the incorruptible one, it is saved ' and it is taken up to the rest ' of the aeons.''

And I said, "Lord, ' those, however, who have not known ' to whom they belong, where will their souls [35] be?'' And he said to me, ' "In those the despicable spirit has [27] gained strength when they went astray. And he ' burdens the soul and draws it ' to the works of evil, and he casts ' it down into forgetfulness. And after it [5] comes out of (the body), it is handed over to the authorities, ' who came into being through the archon, and ' they bind it with chains and cast ' it into prison and consort with it ' until it is liberated from the forgetfulness and [10] acquires knowledge. And if thus it ' becomes perfect, it is saved.''

And I ' said, "Lord, how can the soul become smaller ' and return in-to the nature ' of its mother or into man?'' Then [15] he rejoiced when I asked him this, and ' he said to me, "Truly, you are blessed, ' for you have understood! That soul ' is made to follow another one (fem.), since the Spirit of ' life is in it. It is saved through [20] him. It is not again cast ' into another flesh.''

And I said, ' "Lord, these also who did not know but ' have turned away, where will their ' souls go?'' Then he said to me, "To that place [25] where the angels of poverty go ' they will be taken, the place ' where there is no repentance. And ' they will be kept for the day on which ' those who have blasphemed the spirit will be tortured, [30] and they will be punished with eternal punishment.'' '

And I said, "Lord, ' from where did the counterfeit spirit come?'' ' Then he said to me, "The Mother-Father ' who is rich in mercy, the ho-ly Spirit [35] in every way, the One who is merciful and [28] who sympathizes with you (pl.), i.e. the ' Epinoia of the foreknowledge of light, ' he raised up the offspring of the perfect ' race and its thinking and the eternal [5] light of man. When ' the chief archon realized that they were exalted ' above him in the height — and they surpass ' him in thinking

– then he wanted to seize their ¦ thought, not knowing that they surpassed ¹⁰ him in thinking and that he will not be able ¦ to seize them.

"He made a plan ¦ with his authorities, which are his powers, and ¦ they committed together adultery with Sophia, and ¦ bitter fate was begotten through them, ¹⁵ which is the last of the changeable bonds. ¦ And it is of a sort that ¦ is interchangeable. And it is harder and ¦ stronger than she with whom ¦ the gods united and the angels and the demons ²⁰ and all the generations until this day. ¦ For from that fate ¦ came forth every sin and ¦ injustice and blasphemy and the chain ¦ of forgetfulness and ignorance and every ²⁵ severe command and serious sins ¦ and great fears. And thus ¦ the whole creation was made blind, ¦ in order that they may not know God who is ¦ above all of them. And because of the chain of forgetfulness ³⁰ their sins were hidden. For they are bound with ¦ measures and times and moments, ¦ since it (fate) is lord over everything.

"And he (the chief archon) ¦ repented for everything which had come into being ¦ through him. This time he planned ³⁵ to bring a flood **29** upon the work of man. But the greatness ¦ of the light of the foreknowledge informed ¦ Noah, and he proclaimed (it) to all the offspring ¦ which are the sons of men. But ⁵ those who were strangers to him did not listen to him. ¦ It is not as Moses said, ¦ 'They hid themselves in an ark' (Gn 7: 7), but ¦ they hid themselves in a place, not ¦ only Noah but also many other people ¹⁰ from the immovable race. They went ¦ into a place and hid themselves in a ¦ luminous cloud. And he (Noah) recognized his authority, ¦ and she who belongs to the light was with him, ¦ having shone on them because ¹⁵ he (the chief archon) had brought darkness upon the whole earth. ¦

"And he made a plan with his powers. ¦ He sent his angels to the daughters ¦ of men, that they might take some of them for themselves ¦ and raise offspring ²⁰ for their enjoyment. And at first they did not succeed. ¦ When they had no success, they gathered ¦ together again and they made ¦ a plan together. They created ¦ a counterfeit spirit, who resembles the Spirit who had descended, ²⁵ so as to pollute the souls through it. ¦ And the angels changed themselves in their ¦ likeness into the likeness of their (the daughters of men) mates, ¦ filling them with the spirit of darkness, ¦ which they had mixed for them, and with evil. ³⁰ They brought gold and silver ¦ and a gift and copper and iron ¦ and metal and all kinds ¦ of things. And they steered the people ¦ who had followed them **30** into great troubles, by leading them astray ¦ with many deceptions. They (the people) became old without having enjoyment. | They died, not having found truth and | without knowing the God of truth. And [5] thus the whole creation became enslaved forever, | from the foundation of the world | until now. And they took women | and begot children out of the darkness according to | the likeness of their spirit. And they closed their hearts, [10] and they hardened themselves through the hardness | of the counterfeit spirit until now.

"I, | therefore, the perfect Pronoia of the all, | changed myself into my seed, for I existed | first, going on every road. [15] For I am the richness of the light; | I am the remembrance of the pleroma.

"And I | went into the realm of darkness and | I endured till I entered the middle | of the prison. And the foundations of chaos [20] shook. And I hid myself from them because of | their wickedness, and they did not recognize me.

"Again | I returned for the second time | and I went about. I came forth from those who belong to the light, | which is I the remembrance of the Pronoia. [25] I entered into the midst of darkness and | the inside of Hades, since I was seeking (to accomplish) | my task. And the foundations of chaos | shook, that they might fall down upon those who | are in chaos and might destroy them. [30] And again I ran up to my root of light | lest they be destroyed before | the time.

"Still for a third time | I went — I am the light | which exists in the light, I am [35] the remembrance of the Pronoia — that I might | enter into the midst of darkness and the inside [31] of Hades. And I filled my face with | the light of the completion of their aeon. | And I entered into the midst of their prison | which is the prison of the body. And [5] I said, 'He who hears, let him get up from the deep | sleep.' And he wept and shed tears. | Bitter tears he wiped from | himself and he said, 'Who is it that calls my | name, and from where has this hope come to me, [10] while I am in the chains of the prison?' And | I said, 'I am the Pronoia of the pure light; | I am the thinking of the virginal | Spirit, who raised you up to the honored | place. Arise and remember [15] that it is you who hearkened, and follow | your root, which is I, the merciful one, and | guard yourself against | the angels of poverty and the demons | of chaos and all those who ensnare you, [20] and beware of the | deep sleep and the enclosure of the inside | of Hades.'

"And I raised him up | and sealed him in the light | of the water with five seals, in order that [25] death might not have power over him from this time on.

"And | behold, now I shall go up to the perfect | aeon. I have completed everything for you | in your hearing. And I | have said everything to you that you might write [30] them down and give them secretly to your fellow spirits, | for this is the mystery of the immovable race." |

And the savior presented these things to him that | he might write them down and keep them | secure. And he said to him, "Cursed be [35] everyone who will exchange these things for a gift | or for food or for | drink or for clothing or for any other such thing." **32** And these things were presented to him | in a mystery, and immediately | he disappeared from him. | And he went to his fellow disciples and related [5] to them what the savior had told him. |

Jesus Christ, Amen. |

The | Apocryphon | According to John

THE GOSPEL OF THOMAS (II,*2*)

Introduced by

HELMUT KOESTER

Translated by

THOMAS O. LAMBDIN

The Gospel of Thomas is a collection of traditional sayings of Jesus. These sayings, or small groups of sayings (the numeration of the 114 sayings is not found in the manuscript, but is followed by most scholars today) are introduced in most instances by "Jesus said (to them)," sometimes by a question or a statement of the disciples. Only in one instance (13) is a saying expanded into a longer discourse between Jesus and the disciples. The sayings preserved in *The Gospel of Thomas* are of several types: wisdom sayings (proverbs), parables, eschatological sayings (prophecies), and rules for the community. They appear in this document in arrangement that does not reveal any overall plan of composition. On occasion, small groups of sayings are kept together by similarity in form or by catchword association.

The Coptic *Gospel of Thomas* was translated from the Greek. Fragments of this gospel in the original Greek version are extant in the Oxyrhynchus Papyri 1, 654 and 655, which had been discovered and published at the beginning of this century, but were identified as parts of *The Gospel of Thomas* only after the discovery of the Coptic Nag Hammadi library. The first of these Greek papyri contains sayings 26-30, 77, 31-33 (in this order!), the other two the sayings 1-7 and 36-40, respectively. At least one of these Greek fragments comes from a manuscript that was written before 200 C.E.; thus the Greek version of this gospel was used in Egypt as early as the second century.

The authorship of this gospel is attributed to Didymos Judas Thomas, that is, Judas "the twin" (both the Aramaic *thomas* and the Greek *didymos* mean "twin"). In the Syrian church, (Judas) Thomas was known as the brother of Jesus who founded the churches of the East, particularly of Edessa (in a somewhat later tradition, he even travels to India). Other Christian writings of the eastern churches have been attributed to the same apostle; to these belong the *Acts of Thomas* and most likely also *The Book of Thomas*, which was discovered as part of the Nag Hammadi library (II,*7*). The latter writing, as well as *The Gospel of Thomas*, were most likely written in Syria. It is doubtful, however, whether it was originally composed in Aramaic and then translated into Greek, although many of the sayings, like the oldest sayings of the canonical gospels, were certainly first circulated in Aramaic, the language of Jesus.

A large number of the sayings of *The Gospel of Thomas* have parallels in the gospels of the New Testament, in the Synoptic Gospels (Matthew, Mark, and Luke), as well as the Gospel of John (parallels with the latter are especially striking; cf., e.g., sayings 13, 19, 24, 38, 49, 92). Some of the sayings are known to occur also in noncanonical gospels, especially in the *Gospel According to the Hebrews* (cf. saying 2) and the *Gospel of the Egyptians* (cf. saying 22), which are both attested for the second century by Clement of Alexandria (floruit 180-200). However, a direct dependence of *The Gospel of Thomas* upon another noncanonical gospel is very unlikely. More problematic is the relationship of *The Gospel of Thomas* to the canonical gospels. Whereas the latter all contain large segments of narrative materials, no traces of such materials are found in the former. Already this makes it unlikely that our document can be considered as an eclectic excerpt from the gospels of the New Testament. If one considers the form and wording of the individual sayings in comparison with the form in which they are preserved in the New Testament, *The Gospel of Thomas* almost always appears to have preserved a more original form of the traditional saying (in a few instances, where this is not the case, the Coptic translation seems to have been influenced by the translator's knowledge of the New Testament gospels), or presents versions which are independently based on more original forms. More original and shorter forms are especially evident in the parables of Thomas (cf. sayings 8, 9, 57, 63, 64, 65, 96, cf. 109).

In its literary genre, *The Gospel of Thomas* is more akin to one of the sources of the canonical gospels, namely the so-called Synoptic Sayings Source (often called "Q" from the German word *Quelle*, "source"), which was used by both Matthew and Luke. Indeed, many of the sayings found in our document were also parts of this source of the gospels of the New Testament. On the other hand, *The Gospel of Thomas* also contains quite different older sayings, paralleled in the Gospel of John, in Mark 4:21-25, and even in 1 Corinthians (cf. saying 17 with 1 Co 2:9). Moreover, the sayings about the future coming of the Son of Man, so characteristic for "Q" (cf. Lk 12:8, 10; 17:22, 24, 26), are completely missing. *The Gospel of Thomas* is, therefore, a closely related but independent collection of sayings. In its most original form, it may well date from the first century (the middle of the first century is usually considered the best date for the composition of "Q").

Neither the Coptic translation nor the Greek fragments seem to have preserved this gospel in its oldest form. Even the comparison of the extant Coptic and Greek texts demonstrates that the text was subject to change in the process of transmission. The oldest form most likely contained wisdom sayings and eschatological sayings of Jesus, including a number of parables. The sayings of this type, even those which have no parallels in the gospels of the New Testament (especially the parables 97 and 98), may belong to the oldest strata of the tradition. Whereas "Q" emphasized the eschatological expectation of the future coming of the "Kingdom of God," *The Gospel of Thomas* in its oldest form, stressed the finding of wisdom, or of the "Kingdom of the Father," in the knowledge (*gnosis*) of oneself (cf. saying 3), guided by the sayings of Jesus. This understanding of salvation is similar to that expressed in many passages of the Gospel of John in which the finding of truth and life is bound to the words of Jesus (Jn 6:63; 8:51). The first saying of *The Gospel of Thomas* states this programmatically: the interpretation of the sayings is identical with the finding of eternal life.

In the further history and growth of *The Gospel of Thomas*, this wisdom interpretation of the sayings of Jesus is more clearly developed under the influence of gnostic theology, though it is not possible to ascribe the work to any particular gnostic school or sect. The theme of recognizing oneself is further elaborated in sayings (cf. 50, 51) which speak of the knowledge of one's divine origin which even Adam did not share, although "he came into being from a great power" (saying 85). Salvation is obtained in stripping off everything that is of this world (cf. sayings 21a, 37, 56). The disciples must "pass by" the present corruptible existence (saying 42). The existence of the ideal gnostic disciple is characterized by the term "solitary one," which describes the one who has left behind everything that binds human beings to the world (cf. sayings 16, 23, 30, and 76). Even women can obtain this goal, if they achieve the "maleness" of the solitary existence (saying 114).

THE GOSPEL OF THOMAS

II 32, 10-51, 28

These are the secret sayings which the living Jesus [1] spoke and which Didymos Judas Thomas wrote down. [1]

(1) And he said, [1] "Whoever finds the interpretation of these sayings will [1] not experience death."

(2) Jesus said, [15] "Let him who seeks continue seeking until he [1] finds. When he finds, he will [1] become troubled. When he becomes troubled, he will [1] be astonished, and he will [1] rule over the all."

(3) Jesus said, "If [20] those who lead you say to you, [1] 'See, the kingdom is in the sky,' [1] then the birds of the sky will precede you. [1] If they say to you, 'It is in the sea,' [1] then the fish will precede you. [25] Rather, the kingdom is inside of you, and [1] it is outside of you. When you come to [1] know yourselves, then you will become known, **33** and you will realize that it is you who are [1] the sons of the living father. But if [1] you will not know yourselves, you [1] dwell in poverty and it is you [5] who are that poverty."

(4) Jesus said, "The man old in days will not [1] hestitate to ask [1] a small child seven [1] days old about the place of life, and [1] he will live. For many who are first will become last, [10] and they will become one and the same."

(5) Jesus said, [1] "Recognize what is in your (sg.) sight, [1] and that which is hidden from you (sg.) will become plain [1] to you (sg.). For there is nothing hidden which will [1] not become manifest."

(6) His disciples questioned him [15] and said to him, "Do you want us to fast? [1] How shall we pray? Shall we give alms? [1] What diet shall we observe?"

Jesus said, "Do not tell lies,' ' and do not do what you hate, for [20] all things are plain in the sight ' of heaven. For nothing hidden will not ' become manifest, and nothing covered ' will remain without being uncovered."

(7) Jesus said, ' "Blessed is the lion which [25] becomes man when consumed by ' man; and cursed is the man ' whom the lion consumes, and ' the lion becomes man."

(8) And he said, ' "The man is like a wise fisherman [30] who cast his net ' into the sea and drew it up ' from the sea full of small fish. ' Among them the wise fisherman found a fine large fish. ' He threw [35] all the small fish **34** back into the sea and chose the large ' fish without difficulty. Whoever has ears ' to hear, let him hear."

(9) Jesus said, "Now ' the sower went out, took a handful (of seeds), [5] and scattered them. Some fell on the road; ' the birds came and gathered them up. Others ' fell on rock, did not take root ' in the soil, and did not produce ears. ' And others fell on thorns; [10] they choked the seed(s) and worms ate them. ' And others fell on the good soil ' and it produced good fruit: ' it bore sixty per measure and a hundred and twenty per measure."

(10) Jesus said, "I have cast fire upon [15] the world, and see, I am guarding it ' until it blazes."

(11) Jesus said, "This heaven will ' pass away, and the one above it will pass away. ' The dead are not alive, and the living ' will not die. In the days when you consumed [20] what is dead, you made it what is alive. ' When you come to dwell in the light, ' what will you do? On the day when you ' were one you became two. But when ' you become two, what [25] will you do?"

(12) The disciples said to Jesus, ' "We know that you will depart from us. Who is ' to be our leader?"

Jesus said to them, ' "Wherever you are, you are to ' go to James the righteous, [30] for whose sake heaven and earth came into being."

(13) Jesus said ' to his disciples, "Compare me to someone and ' tell me whom I am like."

Simon Peter ' said to him, "You are like a ' righteous angel."

Matthew said to him, [35] "You are like a wise philosopher."

Thomas said to him, ' "Master, my mouth is wholly incapable ' of saying whom you are like."

Jesus said, [5] "I am not your (sg.) master. Because you (sg.) have drunk, you (sg.) have become intoxicated ' from the bubbling spring which I ' have measured out."

And he took him and withdrew ' and told him three things. ' When Thomas returned to his companions, they asked him, [10] "What did Jesus say to you?"

Thomas said to them, ' "If I tell you one of the things ' which he told me, you will pick up stones and ' throw them at me; a fire will come out of ' the stones and burn you up." [15]

(14) Jesus said to them, "If you fast, you will ' give rise to sin for yourselves; and if you ' pray, you will be condemned; and ' if you give alms, you will do ' harm to your spirits. When you [20] go into any land and ' walk about in the districts, if they receive ' you, eat what they will set before you, ' and heal the sick among them. ' For what goes into your mouth [25] will not defile you, but that which ' issues from your mouth – it is that which ' will defile you."

(15) Jesus said, "When ' you see one who was not born ' of woman, prostrate yourselves on [30] your faces and worship him. That one ' is your father."

(16) Jesus said, ' "Men think, perhaps, that it is peace which I have come to cast ' upon the world. ' They do not know that it is dissension which I have come to cast [35] upon the earth: fire, sword, ' and war. For there will be five **36** in a house: three will be against ' two, and two against three, the father ' against the son, and the son against the father. ' And they will stand solitary." [5]

(17) Jesus said, "I shall give you what ' no eye has seen and what no ' ear has heard and what no hand has touched ' and what has never occurred to the human ' mind."

(18) The disciples said to Jesus, "Tell [10] us how our end will be." '

Jesus said, "Have you discovered, then, ' the beginning, that you look for ' the end? For where the beginning is, ' there will the end be. Blessed is [15] he who will take his place in the beginning; ' he will know the end and will not experience ' death."

(19) Jesus said, "Blessed is ' he who came into being before he came into being. ' If you become my disciples [20] and listen to my words, these stones ' will minister to you. ' For there are five trees for you in Paradise ' which remain undisturbed summer and winter ' and whose leaves do not fall. [25] Whoever becomes acquainted with them will not experience death." '

(20) The disciples said to Jesus, "Tell ' us what the kingdom of heaven is ' like."

He said to them, "It is like ' a mustard seed. It is the smallest of [30] all seeds. But when it ' falls on tilled soil, it ' produces a great plant and becomes ' a shelter for birds of the sky."

(21) Mary said to Jesus, "Whom are your disciples [35] like?"

He said, "They are like **37** children who have settled in a field | which is not theirs. When the owners of the field come, | they will say, 'Let us have back our field.' | They (will) undress in their presence [5] in order to let them have back their field and to give | it back to them. Therefore I say, | if the owner of a house knows that the thief is coming, | he will begin his vigil before he comes and will not | let him dig through into his house of his [10] domain to carry away his goods. You (pl.), | then, be on your guard against the world. Arm | yourselves with great strength | lest the robbers find a way to come | to you, for the difficulty which you expect [15] will (surely) materialize. Let there be | among you a man of understanding. | When the grain ripened, he came quickly | with his sickle in his hand and reaped it. | Whoever has ears to hear, let him hear." [20]

(22) Jesus saw infants being suckled. He said to | his disciples, "These infants being suckled | are like those who enter the | kingdom."

They said to him, "Shall we then, as children, | enter the kingdom?"

Jesus said to them, [25] "When you make the two one, and | when you make the inside like the outside | and the outside like the inside, and the above | like the below, and when | you make the male and the female one and the same, [30] so that the male not be male nor | the female female; and when you fashion | eyes in place of an eye, and a hand | in place of a hand, and a foot in place | of a foot, and a likeness in place of a likeness; [35] then will you enter [the kingdom]." **38**

(23) Jesus said, "I shall choose you, one out | of a thousand, and two out of ten thousand, and | they shall stand as a single one." |

(24) His disciples said to him, "Show us the place [5] where you are, since it is necessary for us | to seek it."

He said to them, "Whoever has | ears, let him hear. There is light | within a man of light, | and he lights up the whole world. If he [10] does not shine, he is darkness."

(25) Jesus said, "Love | your (sg.) brother like your soul, guard him | like the pupil of your eye."

(26) Jesus said, "You (sg.) see the mote | in your brother's eye, | but you do not see the beam in your own eye. When [15] you cast the beam out of your own | eye, then you will see clearly to cast the mote | from your brother's eye."

(27) ⟨Jesus said,⟩ "If you do not fast | as regards the world, you will not find the kingdom. | If you do not observe the Sabbath as a Sabbath, [20] you will not see the father." |

(28) Jesus said, "I took my place in the midst of the world, ' and I appeared to them in flesh. ' I found all of them intoxicated; I found none ' of them thirsty. And my soul became afflicted [25] for the sons of men, because they are blind ' in their hearts and do not have sight; ' for empty they came into the world, ' and empty too they seek to leave the world. ' But for the moment they are intoxicated. [30] When they shake off their wine, then they will ' repent."

(29) Jesus said, "If the flesh ' came into being because of spirit, it is a wonder. ' But if spirit came into being because of the body, ' it is a wonder of wonders. Indeed, I am amazed **39** at how this great wealth ' has made its home in this poverty."

(30) Jesus said, ' "Where there are three gods, ' they are gods. Where there are two or one, I [5] am with him."

(31) Jesus said, "No prophet ' is accepted in his own village; no physician heals ' those who know him."

(32) Jesus said, ' "A city being built on a high mountain ' and fortified cannot fall, [10] nor can it be hidden."

(33) Jesus said, "Preach from your (pl.) housetops ' that which you (sg.) will ' hear in your (sg.) ear. ' For no one lights a lamp and ' puts it under a bushel, nor does he put it in a [15] hidden place, but rather he sets it on a lampstand ' so that everyone who enters ' and leaves will see its ' light."

(34) Jesus said, "If a blind man leads ' a blind man, they will both fall [20] into a pit."

(35) Jesus said, "It is not possible ' for anyone to enter the house of a strong man ' and take it by force unless he binds ' his hands; then he will (be able to) ransack ' his house."

(36) Jesus said, "Do not be concerned from [25] morning until evening and from evening ' until morning about what you will wear." '

(37) His disciples said, "When ' will you become revealed to us and when ' shall we see you?"

Jesus said, "When [30] you disrobe without being ' ashamed and take up your garments ' and place them under your feet ' like little children and ' tread on them, then [will you see] **40** the son of the living one, and you will not be ' afraid."

(38) Jesus said, "Many times have you ' desired to hear these words ' which I am saying to you, and you have [5] no one else to hear them from. There will be days ' when you will look for me and ' will not find me."

(39) Jesus said, "The pharisees ' and the scribes have taken the keys

of knowledge (gnosis) and hidden them. They themselves have not entered, [10] nor have they allowed to enter those who wish to. You, however, be as wise as serpents and as innocent as doves.''

(40) Jesus said, ''A grapevine has been planted outside of the father, but being [15] unsound, it will be pulled up by its roots and destroyed.''

(41) Jesus said, ''Whoever has something in his hand will receive more, and whoever has nothing will be deprived of even the little he has.''

(42) Jesus said, ''Become passers-by.'' [20]

(43) His disciples said to him, ''Who are you, that you should say these things to us?''

⟨Jesus said to them,⟩ ''You do not realize who I am from what I say to you, but you have become like the Jews, for they (either) love the tree and hate [25] its fruit (or) love the fruit and hate the tree.''

(44) Jesus said, ''Whoever blasphemes against the father will be forgiven, and whoever blasphemes against the son will be forgiven, but whoever blasphemes against the holy spirit [30] will not be forgiven either on earth or in heaven.''

(45) Jesus said, ''Grapes are not harvested from thorns, nor are figs gathered from thistles, for they do not produce fruit. A good man brings forth **41** good from his storehouse; an evil man brings forth evil things from his evil storehouse, which is in his heart, and says evil things. For out of [5] the abundance of the heart he brings forth evil things.''

(46) Jesus said, ''Among those born of women, from Adam until John the Baptist, there is no one so superior to John the Baptist that his eyes should not be lowered (before him). [10] Yet I have said, whichever one of you comes to be a child will be acquainted with the kingdom and will become superior to John.''

(47) Jesus said, ''It is impossible for a man to mount two horses or to stretch two bows. And it is impossible [15] for a servant to serve two masters; otherwise, he will honor the one and treat the other contemptuously. No man drinks old wine and immediately desires to drink new wine. And new wine is not put into old wineskins, [20] lest they burst; nor is old wine put into a new wineskin, lest it spoil it. An old patch is not sewn into a new garment, because a tear would result.''

(48) Jesus said, ''If two make peace with [25] each other in this one house, they will say to the mountain, 'Move away,' and it will move away.''

(49) Jesus said, "Blessed are the | solitary and elect, for you will | find the kingdom. For you are from it, [30] and to it you will return." |

(50) Jesus said, "If they say to you, | 'Where did you come from?', say to them, | 'We came from the light, the place | where the light came into being on [35] its own accord and established [itself] **42** and became manifest through their image.' | If they say to you, 'Is it you?', say, | 'We are its children, and we are the elect | of the living father.' If they ask you, [5] 'What is the sign of your father in | you?', say to them, 'It is movement and | repose.' "

(51) His disciples said to him, | "When will the repose of | the dead come about, and when [10] will the new world come?"

He said to them, | "What you look forward to has already come, but | you do not recognize it." |

(52) His disciples said to him, "Twenty-four | prophets spoke in Israel, [15] and all of them spoke in you." |

He said to them, "You have omitted the one living in | your presence and have spoken (only) of the | dead."

(53) His disciples said to him, | "Is circumcision beneficial or not?"

He said [20] to them, "If it were beneficial, their father | would beget them already circumcised from their mother. | Rather, the true circumcision in spirit has | become completely profitable."

(54) Jesus said, "Blessed are the poor, | for yours is the kingdom of heaven." [25]

(55) Jesus said, "Whoever does not hate his father | and his mother cannot become a disciple to me. | And whoever does not hate his brothers and | sisters and take up his cross in my way | will not be worthy of me." [30]

(56) Jesus said, "Whoever has come to understand the world has found (only) | a corpse, and whoever has found a corpse | is superior to the world." |

(57) Jesus said, "The kingdom of the father is like | a man who had [good] seed. [35] His enemy came by night **43** and sowed weeds among the good seed. | The man did not allow them to pull up | the weeds; he said to them, 'I am afraid that | you will go intending to pull up the weeds [5] and pull up the wheat along with them.' | For on the day of the harvest the weeds will be plainly visible, | and they will be pulled up and burned."

(58) Jesus said, | "Blessed is the man who has suffered | and found life."

(59) Jesus said, "Take heed of the [10] living one while you are alive, lest you die | and seek to see him and be unable | to do so."

(60) ⟨They saw⟩ a Samaritan carrying ǀ a lamb on his way to Judea. ǀ He said to his disciples, "That man is round about the [15] lamb."

They said to him, "So that he may ǀ kill it and eat it."

He said to them, "While ǀ it is alive, he will not eat it, but only when he has ǀ killed it and it has become a corpse."

They said to him, ǀ "He cannot do so otherwise."

He said to them, [20] "You too, look for a ǀ place for yourselves within repose, ǀ lest you become a corpse and be ǀ eaten."

(61) Jesus said, "Two will rest ǀ on a bed: the one will die, and the other [25] will live."

Salome said, "Who are you, ǀ man, that you ... have come up on ǀ my couch and eaten from my ǀ table?"

Jesus said to her, "I am he ǀ who exists from the undivided. [30] I was given some of the things of my father."

⟨...⟩ "I ǀ am your disciple."

⟨...⟩ "Therefore I say, ǀ if he is destroyed he will be filled ǀ with light, but if he is ǀ divided, he will be filled with darkness."

(62) Jesus said, "It [35] is to those [who are worthy of **44** my] mysteries that I tell my mysteries. Do not let your (sg.) left hand know ǀ what your (sg.) right hand is doing."

(63) Jesus said, ǀ There was a rich man who had ǀ much money. He said, 'I shall put [5] my money to use so that I may sow, reap, ǀ plant, and fill my storehouse with produce, ǀ with the result that I shall lack nothing.' Such were ǀ his intentions, but ǀ that same night he died. Let him who has ears [10] hear."

(64) Jesus said, "A man ǀ had received visitors. And when he had prepared ǀ the dinner, he sent his servant to ǀ invite the guests. He went to ǀ the first one and said to him, 'My master invites [15] you.' He said, 'I have claims ǀ against some merchants. They are coming to me this evening. ǀ I must go and give them my orders. I ask to be excused ǀ from the dinner.' He went to another ǀ and said to him, 'My master has invited you.' [20] He said to him, 'I have just bought a house and ǀ am required for the day. I shall not have any spare time.' ǀ He went to another and said to him, 'My master ǀ invites you.' He said to him, 'My friend ǀ is going to get married, and I am to prepare the banquet. [25] I shall not be able to come. I ask to be excused from the dinner.' ǀ He went to another and said to him, 'My master ǀ invites you.' He said to him, 'I have just bought ǀ a farm, and I am on my way to collect the rent. I shall not be able to come. ǀ I ask to be excused.' The servant returned and said [30] to his master, 'Those whom you invited to ǀ the din-

ner have asked to be excused.' The master said to ' his servant, 'Go outside to the streets ' and bring back those whom you happen to meet, so that ' they may dine.' Businessmen and merchants [35] [will] not enter the places of my father.'' **45**

(65) He said, "There was a good man who owned ' a vineyard. He leased it to tenant farmers ' so that they might work it and he might collect the produce ' from them. He sent his servant so that [5] the tenants might give him the produce of ' the vineyard. They seized his servant ' and beat him, all but killing him. ' The servant went back and told his master. ' The master said, 'Perhaps he did not recognize them.' [10] He sent another servant. The tenants beat ' this one as well. Then the owner sent ' his son and said, 'Perhps they will show respect ' to my son.' Because the tenants ' knew that it was he who was the heir [15] to the vineyard, they seized him and killed him. ' Let him who has ears hear.'' '

(66) Jesus said, "Show me the stone which ' the builders have rejected. That one is the ' cornerstone.''

(67) Jesus said, "If one who knows the all [20] still feels a personal deficiency, he is completely deficient.'' '

(68) Jesus said, "Blessed are you when ' you are hated and persecuted. ' Wherever you have been persecuted ' they will find no place.'' [25]

(69) Jesus said, "Blessed are they who have been persecuted ' within themselves. It is they ' who have truly come to know the father. ' Blessed are the hungry, for ' the belly of him who desires will be filled.''

(70) Jesus said, [30] "That which you have will save you ' if you bring it forth from yourselves. ' That which you do not have within you [will] kill you ' if you do not have it within you.'' '

(71) Jesus said, "I shall [destroy this] house, [35] and no one will be able to build it [. . .]'' **46**

(72) [A man said] to him, "Tell my brothers ' to divide my father's possessions ' with me.''

He said to him, "O man, who ' has made me a divider?''

He turned to [5] his disciples and said to them, "I am not a divider, ' am I?''

(73) Jesus said, "The harvest ' is great but the laborers are few. ' Beseech the lord, therefore, to send out laborers ' to the harvest.''

(74) He said, "O lord, there are [10] many around the drinking trough, but there is nothing in ' the cistern.''

(75) Jesus said, "Many are standing ' at the door, but it is the solitary who will enter ' the bridal chamber.''

(76) Jesus said, | "The kingdom of the father is like a [15] merchant who had a consignment of merchandise | and who discovered a pearl. That merchant | was shrewd. He sold the merchandise | and bought the pearl alone for himself. | You too, seek [20] his unfailing and enduring treasure | where no moth comes near | to devour and no worm destroys." |

(77) Jesus said, "It is I who am the light which is above | them all. It is I who am the all. [25] From me did the all come forth, and unto me did the all | extend. Split a piece of wood, and I | am there. Lift up the stone, and you will | find me there."

(78) Jesus said, "Why | have you come out into the desert? To see a reed [30] shaken by the wind? And to see | a man clothed in fine garments | [like your] kings and your great **47** men? Upon them are the fine garments, | and they are unable to discern | the truth."

(79) A woman from the crowd said to him, | "Blessed are the womb which [5] bore you and the breasts which | nourished you."

He said to [her], | "Blessed are those who have heard | the word of the father and have truly kept it. | For there will be days [10] when you (pl.) will say, 'Blessed are the womb | which has not conceived and the breasts which have not | given milk.' "

(80) Jesus said, "He who has recognized | the world has found the body, but he who has found | the body is superior to the world." [15]

(81) Jesus said, "Let him who has grown rich | be king, and let him who possesses power | renounce it."

(82) Jesus said, "He who is near | me is near the fire, and he who is far | from me is far from the kingdom."

(83) Jesus said, [20] "The images are manifest to man, | but the light in them remains concealed | in the image of the light of the father. He will | become manifest, but his image will remain concealed | by his light."

(84) Jesus said, [25] "When you see your likeness, you | rejoice. But when you see | your images which came into being before you, | and which neither die nor become manifest, | how much you will have to bear!"

(85) Jesus said, [30] "Adam came into being from a great | power and a great wealth, | but he did not become worthy of you. | For had he been worthy, [he would] not [have experienced] | death."

(86) Jesus said, "[The foxes **48** have their holes] and the birds have | their nests, but the son of man | has no place to lay his head and | rest."

(87) Jesus said, "Wretched [5] is the body that is dependent upon a body, | and wretched is the soul that is dependent | on these two."

(88) Jesus said, "The angels ' and the prophets will come to you and ' give to you those things you (already) have. And ¹⁰ you too, give them those things which you have, ' and say to yourselves, 'When ' will they come and take what is theirs?' " '

(89) Jesus said, "Why do you wash the outside ' of the cup? Do you not realize that ¹⁵ he who made the inside is the same one ' who made the outside?"

(90) Jesus said, ' "Come unto me, for my yoke is easy ' and my lordship is mild, ' and you will find repose for ²⁰ yourselves."

(91) They said to him, "Tell us ' who you are so that we may believe in you." '

He said to them, "You read the face of the sky ' and of the earth, but you have not recognized ' the one who is before you, and ²⁵ you do not know how to read this moment." '

(92) Jesus said, "Seek and you will find. Yet, what ' you asked me about in former times and which I did not ' tell you then, now ' I do desire to tell, but you do not inquire after ³⁰ it."

(93) ⟨Jesus said,⟩ "Do not give what is holy to dogs, lest ' they throw them on the dung heap. Do not throw the ' pearls [to] swine, lest they ... it ' [...]."

(94) Jesus [said], "He who seeks will find, ' and [he who knocks] will be let in." ³⁵

(95) [Jesus said], "If you have money, **49** do not lend it at interest, but give [it] to one ' from whom you will not get it back."

(96) Jesus said, ' "The kingdom of the father is like [a certain] woman. She ' took a little leaven, [concealed] it in ⁵ some dough, and made it into large loaves. ' Let him who has ears hear." '

(97) Jesus said, "The kingdom of the [father] is like ' a certain woman who was carrying a [jar] full of meal. While she was walking [on the] road, ¹⁰ still some distance from home, the handle of the jar broke ' and the meal emptied out behind her [on] the road. ' She did not realize it; she had noticed no ' accident. When she reached her house, ' she set the jar down and found it ¹⁵ empty."

(98) Jesus said, "The kingdom of the father ' is like a certain man who wanted to kill ' a powerful man. In his own house he drew ' his sword and stuck it into the wall ' in order to find out whether his hand could carry through. ²⁰ Then he slew the powerful man." '

(99) The disciples said to him, "Your brothers ' and your mother are standing outside.' '

He said to them, "Those here ' who do the will of my father are ²⁵ my brothers and my mother. It is they who will | enter the kingdom of my father." |

(100) They showed Jesus a gold coin and said to him, | "Caesar's men demand taxes from us." |

He said to them, "Give Caesar what belongs ³⁰ to Caesar, give God what belongs to God, | and give me what is mine." |

(101) ⟨Jesus said,⟩ "Whoever does not hate his [father] and his | mother as I do cannot become a [disciple] to me. | And whoever does [not] love his [father and] his ³⁵ mother as I do cannot become a [disciple to] | me. For my mother [...], **50** but [my] true [mother] gave me life." |

(102) Jesus said, "Woe to the pharisees, for | they are like a dog sleeping in the | manger of oxen, for neither does he eat ⁵ nor does he [let] the oxen eat."

(103) Jesus said, | "Fortunate is the man who knows | where the brigands will enter, | so that [he] may get up, muster his | domain, and arm himself ¹⁰ before they invade." |

(104) They said to Jesus, "Come, let us pray today | and let us fast."

Jesus said, "What | is the sin that I have committed, or wherein have I been defeated? | But when the bridegroom leaves ¹⁵ the bridal chamber, then let them | fast and pray."

(105) Jesus said, | "He who knows the father and the mother will be called | the son of a harlot."

(106) Jesus said, | "When you make the two one, you will become ²⁰ the sons of man, and when you | say, 'Mountain, move away,' it will | move away."

(107) Jesus said, "The kingdom is like | a shepherd who had a hundred | sheep. One of them, the largest, went astray. ²⁵ He left the ninety-nine and looked for that one | until he found it. When he had gone to such trouble, he said | to the sheep, 'I care for you more than the ninety-nine.' " |

(108) Jesus said, "He who will drink from my mouth | will become like me. I myself shall become ³⁰ he, and the things that are hidden will be revealed to him." |

(109) Jesus said, "The kingdom is like a man | who had a | [hidden] treasure in his field without knowing it. | And [after] he died, he left it to his ³⁵ [son]. The son [did] not know (about the treasure). He inherited **51** the field and sold [it]. And the one who bought it | went plowing and [found] the treasure. | He began to lend money at interest to whomever he wished." |

(110) Jesus said, "Whoever finds the world [5] and becomes rich, let him renounce the world." [1]

(111) Jesus said, "The heavens and the earth will be rolled up [1] in your presence. And the one who lives from [1] the living one will not see death." Does not Jesus [1] say, "Whoever finds himself [10] is superior to the world"?

(112) Jesus said, "Woe [1] to the flesh that depends on the soul; woe [1] to the soul that depends on the flesh." [1]

(113) His disciples said to him, [1] "When will the kingdom come?"

⟨Jesus said,⟩ "It will not come by [15] waiting for it. It will not be a matter of saying 'here [1] it is' or 'there it is'. Rather, the kingdom [1] of the father is spread out upon the earth, and [1] men do not see it."

(114) Simon Peter said [1] to them, "Let Mary leave us, [20] for women are not worthy of life."

Jesus said, [1] "I myself shall lead her [1] in order to make her male, so that [1] she too may become a living spirit resembling [1] you males. For every woman who will make herself [25] male will enter the kingdom [1] of heaven." [1]

The Gospel [1]
According to Thomas

THE GOSPEL OF PHILIP (II,3)

Introduced and translated by

WESLEY W. ISENBERG

The Gospel of Philip is a compilation of statements pertaining primarily to the meaning and value of sacraments within the context of a Valentinian conception of the human predicament and life after death.

Like the gospels of the New Testament canon these statements employ a variety of literary types: aphorism, analogy, parable, paraenesis, polemic, narrative dialogue, dominical sayings, biblical exegesis, and dogmatic propositions. However, *The Gospel of Philip* is not a gospel like one of the New Testament gospels. To be sure, it does provide the occasional word or deed of Jesus. It contains seventeen sayings of Jesus, nine of which are citations and interpretations of Jesus' words already found in the canonical gospels (55,33-34; 57,3-5; 68,8-12; 68,26-27; 72,33-73,1; 77,18; 83,11-13; 84,7-9; 85,29-31). The new sayings (55,37-56,3; 58,10-14; 59,25-27; 63,29-30; 64,2-9; 64,10-12; 67,30-35; and 74,25-27), identified by the formula introducing them ("he said," "the Lord said," or "the Savior said") are brief and enigmatic and are best interpreted from a gnostic perspective. There are also a few stories about Jesus; they are similar to those in the early Christian apocryphal gospels. During a revelation on a mountain he appeared larger than life to his disciples (57,28-58,10). His three female companions were each named Mary (59,6-11), though he had an apparent preference for Mary Magdalene (63,32-36). After he had put seventy-two colors into a single vat in the dye-works of Levi, they coalesced into white (63,25-30). Philip the apostle is said to be the source of the story that Joseph the carpenter made the cross on which his offspring later hung (73,8-15).

These few sayings and stories about Jesus, however, are not set in any kind of narrative framework like one of the New Testament gospels. In fact, *The Gospel of Philip* is not organized in a way that can be conveniently outlined. Although some continuity is achieved through an association of ideas (cf. 51,29-52,35), a series of contrasts) or by catchwords (cf. 77,15-78,24, the word *love*), the line of thought is rambling and disjointed. Complete changes of subject are common.

The text gives the impression of logical coherence because of the recurrence of certain themes (e.g., the meaning of the names of Jesus, 56,3-15; 62,7-17; 63,21-24; the need to experience resurrection before one dies, 56,15-20; 56,26-57,22; 66,16-23; 73,1-8; putting on light to escape the hostile powers, 70,5-9; 76,22-77-1; 86,4-10), but this coherence is probably more coincidental than planned.

It is possible that the compiler of this collection purposely disjoined what were once whole paragraphs of thought and distributed the pieces in various places in this work. A clear thought results if one joins 70,5-9 with 76,22-77,1 and 66,7-29, in that order. Indefinite pronouns gain proper antecedents in the process. Similarly 75,13-14 seems to provide the theme amplified by 61,36-62,5. In 63,5-11 one has the analogy prefacing the point made in 70,22-29.

Since *The Gospel of Philip* is eccentrically arranged, its contents can best be considered by reference to summarizing statements. The statement at 69,1-4 reflects a dominant concern, the mysteries of the bridal chamber, and distinguishes those who may participate – the free men and virgins – from those who may not – the animals, slaves, and defiled women.

Those excluded from the bridal chamber are described entirely in negative terms. We learn, *inter alia*, that animals and men must remain separate (78,25-28; 75,25-26). But "there are many animals in the world which are in human form" (81,7-8). If one is an "animal" he belongs "outside or below" rather than "above" or "within" (79,5-11). "Slaves" are to be contrasted with "sons" (52,2-6), with "children" (81,12-14) and with the "free" (79,13-18). A "slave" is one who commits sin (77,18), who is ignorant of the inner wickedness which enslaves him (83,18-29; 85,24). "Defiled women" are all women who participate in sexual intercourse, i.e., in "the marriage of defilement," which is fleshly and lustful (81,34-82,10). Unclean spirits seek to defile men and woman sexually (65,1-23).

"Free men and virgins" are the opposite of "animals, slaves, and defiled women." A virgin has never been defiled by sexual intercourse (55,27-28; cf. 81,34-82,8). The "free man" does not sin (77,15-18). He neither fears the flesh nor loves it (66,4-6). He is endangered by the deceptions of the archons who seek to enslave him (54,16-31). "Free men and virgins" are those called "Christians" (74,13-16), who possess "the resurrection, the light, the cross, the holy spirit" (74,18-21).

According to this gospel the existential malady of humanity results from the differentiation of the sexes. When Eve was separated from Adam, the original androgynous unity was broken (68,22-26). The purpose of Christ's coming is to reunite Adam and Eve (70,12-17). Just as a husband and wife unite in the bridal chamber, so also the reunion effected by Christ takes place in a bridal chamber, the sacramental one (70,17-22), where a person receives a foretaste and assurance of ultimate union with an angelic, heavenly counterpart (cf. 58,10-14).

This leads us to another summarizing statement (67,27-30), "The lord did everything in a mystery, a baptism and a chrism and a eucharist and a redemption and a bridal chamber." The sentence probably describes five stages of a complete initiation, rather than five separate, unrelated sacraments. It is possible that "bridal chamber" is a covering term for the whole initiation, since a particular benefit of one stage of the initiation (e.g., "light," associated usually with chrism, 67,5-6; 69,12-14; 57,27-28) is also connected with bridal chamber (86,4-11; cf. 70,5-9). In 74,12-24 the person anointed in chrism is said to possess everything – resurrection, light, the cross, the holy spirit – but then the author adds, "the father gave him this in the bridal chamber." Conversely, what one expects to be connected with bridal chamber appears in reference to eucharist (58,10-14) or baptism and chrism (69,4-14).

The Gospel of Philip does not describe, step by step, the ritual of all or any of the five stages of initiation. It does explain, however, that in baptism one "goes down into the water and comes up" with the gift of the name "Christian," so that one can say, "I am a Christian" (64,22-31; cf. 77,9-12). The analogy of God as a dyer suggests that baptism was by immersion (61,12-20). The initiate takes off his clothes before entering the water so that he may put on the perfect man as a new garment (75,21-25). That the chrism was a warm perfumed oil is apparent from references to the chrism as fire (67,5-9; 57,27-28) and to the oil as being fragrant (77,36-78,7; 82,15-23). Perhaps a trinitarian formula was used at the moment of anointing (67,19-24). The priest consecrates the bread and the cup for the eucharist (77,2-8). The consecrated cup contains wine mixed with water (75,14-21). The consecrated bread is "bread from heaven," food fit for the initiate (55,10-14). To partake of the bread and the cup is to receive "the flesh and the blood" of Jesus (56,26-57,22; cf. 63,21-24). A further ritual called ransom, or redemption, is mentioned, but no details are given. This stage of the initiation is compared to "the holy of the holy" in the Jerusalem temple and is said to take place in the bridal chamber (69,23-27).

Because of the contents, the eccentric arrangement, and the literary types exhibited, it is likely that *The Gospel of Philip* is a collection of excerpts mainly from a Christian Gnostic sacramental catechesis. It explains the significance of sacramental rites of initiation, the meaning of sacred names, especially names of Jesus, and provides paraenesis for the life of the initiated. It interprets Biblical passages, particularly from the book of Genesis, makes use of typology, both historical and sacramental, and, as catechists do, argues on the basis of analogy and parable. In these and other ways *The Gospel of Philip* resembles the orthodox catechisms from the second through fourth centuries.

The title of this text may be derived merely from the fact that Philip is the only apostle named in it (73,8), though Philip, along with Thomas and Matthew, had an eminence among Gnostics as a privileged recipient and custodian of dominical revelation. The Coptic text is undoubtedly a translation of a Greek text which was written perhaps as late as the second half of the third century C.E. Because of the interest in the meaning of certain Syriac words (63,21-23; 56,7-9), its affinities to Eastern sacramental practice and catecheses, and its ascetic ethics, an origin in Syria is probable.

THE GOSPEL OF PHILIP

II 51, 29-86, 19

A Hebrew makes another Hebrew, [30] and such a person is called | "proselyte." But a proselyte does not | make another proselyte. [...] | just as they [...] | and make others like themselves, **52** while [others] simply exist. |

The slave seeks only to be | free, but he does not hope to acquire the estate | of his master. But the son is not only [5] a son but lays claim to the inheritance of the father. | Those who are heirs | to the dead are themselves dead, | and they inherit the dead. Those | who are heirs to what is living are alive, [10] and they are heirs to both what is living and the dead. | The dead are heirs to | nothing. For how can he who is dead inherit? | If he who is dead inherits | what is living he will not die, but he who is dead [15] will live even more.

A gentile ' does not die, for he has never lived in order that ' he may die. He who has believed in the truth ' has found life, and this one is in danger of dying, for he is alive. ' Since Christ came the world has been [20] created, the cities adorned, ' the dead carried out. When we were ' Hebrews we were orphans and ' had only our mother, but when we became ' Christians we had both father and mother. [25]

Those who sow in winter reap in summer. ' The winter is the world, the summer the other eternal realm (aeon). ' Let us sow in the world that ' we may reap in the summer. Because of this it is fitting ' for us not to pray in the winter. Summer [30] follows winter. But if any man reap ' in winter he will not actually reap but only ' pluck out, since it will not provide ' a harvest for such a person. It is not only [...] that it ' will [...] come forth, but also on the Sabbath [35] [...] is barren.

Christ came [53] to ransom some, ' to save others, to ' redeem others. He ransomed those who were strangers and ' made them his own. And he set [5] his own apart, those whom he gave as a pledge ' according to his plan. It was not only when he ' appeared that he voluntarily laid down his life, ' but he voluntarily laid down his life ' from the very day the world came into being. [10] Then he came first in order to take it, since ' it had been given as a pledge. It fell into the hands of ' robbers and was taken captive, but he ' saved it. He redeemed the good people ' in the world as well as the evil.

Light and darkness, [15] life and death, right and left, ' are brothers of one another. They are inseparable. ' Because of this neither are the good ' good, nor the evil evil, ' nor is life life, nor death death. [20] For this reason each one will dissolve ' into its earliest origin. But those who are exalted ' above the world are indissoluble, ' eternal.

Names given ' to the worldly are very deceptive, [25] for they divert our thoughts ' from what is correct to what is incorrect. ' Thus one who hears the word "God" does not perceive ' what is correct, but perceives ' what is incorrect. So also with "the father" [30] and "the son" and "the holy spirit" and ' "life" and "light" and "resurrection" ' and "the church" and all the rest — ' people do not perceive what is correct but they ' perceive what is incorrect, [unless] they [35] have come to know what is correct. The [names which are heard] ' are in the world [... [54] deceive. If they] were in the eternal realm (aeon), they would ' at no time be used as names in the world. ' Nor were they set among ' worldly things. They have an end in [5] the eternal realm.

One single name is not uttered ' in the world, the name which the father gave ' to the son; it is the name above all things: ' the name of the father. For the son ' would not become father unless he wore [10] the name of the father. ' Those who have this name know it, but they do ' not speak it. But those who do not have it ' do not know it.

But truth brought names into existence ' in the world for our sakes because it is not possible [15] to learn it without these names. Truth is one single thing; ' it is many things and for our sakes to ' teach about this one thing in love through ' many things. The rulers (archons) wanted to deceive ' man, since they saw that he had [20] a kinship with those that are ' truly good. They took the name of those that are good ' and gave it to those that are not good, ' so that through the names they might deceive ' him and bind them to those that are [25] not good. And afterward, what a ' favor they do for them! They make them be removed ' from those that are not good and place them ' among those that are good. These things they knew, ' for they wanted to [30] take the free man and make him a ' slave to them forever.

There are powers ' which [. . .] man, not wishing ' him to be [saved], in order that they may ' [. . .]. For if man [35] is [saved, there will not] be any sacrifices ' [. . .] and animals will not be offered [55] to the powers. Indeed the animals were ' the ones to whom they sacrificed. They were indeed offering ' them up alive, but when they ' offered them up they died. As for man, they offered [5] him up to God dead, and he lived. '

Before Christ came there was no bread ' in the world, just as Paradise, the place ' where Adam was, had many trees ' to nourish the animals but no wheat [10] to sustain man. Man used to feed ' like the animals, but when Christ ' came, the perfect man, he brought bread ' from heaven in order that man might be nourished ' with the food of man. The rulers [15] thought that it was by their own power and will ' that they were doing what they did, ' but the holy spirit in secret ' was accomplishing everything through them ' as it wished. Truth, [20] which existed since the beginning, is sown everywhere. And ' many see it being sown, ' but few are they who see it being reaped. '

Some said, "Mary conceived by ' the holy spirit." They are in error. [25] They do not know what they are saying. When ' did a woman ever conceive by a woman? ' Mary is the virgin whom no ' power defiled. She is a ' great anathema to the Hebrews, who [30] are the apostles and [the] apostolic men. ' This virgin whom no power defiled [. . .] the powers ' defile themselves. And the lord [would] not have said ' "My [father who is in] heaven" (Mt 16:17) [35] unless [he] had had another father, ' but he would have said simply "[My father]." '

The lord said to the disciples, "[. . .] [56] from every house. Bring into

the house ' of the father. But do not take (anything) in the house ' of
the father nor carry it off.''

"Jesus" is a hidden name, ' "Christ" is a revealed name. [5] For this
reason "Jesus" is not particular ' to any language; rather he is always
called ' by the name "Jesus." While as for "Christ," in Syriac it is
"Messiah," ' in Greek it is "Christ." Certainly [10] all the others have it
' according to their own language. ' "The Nazarene" is he who reveals
' what is hidden. Christ has everything ' in himself, whether man or
angel [15] or mystery, and the father.

Those who say ' that the lord died first and (then) ' rose up are in error, for he rose up ' first and (then) died. If one does not first attain '
the resurrection he will not die. As God [20] lives, he would . . .

No one ' will hide a large valuable object ' in something large, but
many a time ' one has tossed countless thousands ' into a thing worth a
penny. Compare [25] the soul. It is a precious thing and it came to be ' in
a contemptible body.

Some ' are afraid lest they rise naked. ' Because of this they wish to
rise ' in the flesh, and [they] do not know that it is those who [30] wear the
[flesh] who are naked. ' [It is] those who [. . .] to unclothe ' themselves
who are not naked. "Flesh ' [and blood shall] not inherit the kingdom
' [of God]" (1 Co 15:50). What is this which will **57** not inherit? This
which is on us. But what ' is this, too, which will inherit? It is that
which belongs to Jesus ' and his blood. Because of this he said, ' "He
who shall not eat my flesh and drink [5] my blood has not life in him" (Jn
6:53). What ' is it? His flesh is the word, and his blood ' is the holy
spirit. He who has received these has ' food and he has drink and
clothing. ' I find fault with the others who say [10] that it will not rise.
Then both of them ' are at fault. You (sg.) say ' that the flesh will not
rise. But tell me ' what will rise, that we may honor you (sg.). ' You
(sg.) say the spirit in the flesh, [15] and it is also this light in the flesh. (But)
this too is a matter ' which is in the flesh, for whatever you (sg.) shall,
say, ' you (sg.) say nothing outside the flesh. ' It is necessary to rise in
this flesh, since ' everything exists in it. In this world [20] those who put
on garments are better than the ' garments. In the kingdom of heaven
the garments ' are better than those who have put them on.

It is through ' water and fire that the whole place is purified — ' the
visible by visible, [25] the hidden by the hidden. There are some things '
hidden through those visible. ' There is water in water, there is fire ' in
chrism.

Jesus took them all by stealth, ' for he did not appear as [30] he was, but ' in the manner in which [they would] be able to see ' him. He appeared to [them all. ' He appeared] to the great ' as great. He [appeared] [35] to the small as small. He [appeared 58 to the] angels as an angel, and ' to men as a man. Because of this his ' word hid itself from everyone. Some ' indeed saw him, thinking that they were seeing [5] themselves, but when he appeared ' to his disciples in glory ' on the mount he was not small. He ' became great, but he made the disciples ' great, that they might be able to see [10] him in his greatness.

He said on that day ' in the thanksgiving, "You who have joined ' the perfect light with the holy spirit, ' unite the angels with us also, ' as being the images." Do not despise the lamb, for without it [15] it is not possible to see the king. No one ' will be able to go in to the king if he is ' naked.

The heavenly man has many more sons ' than the earthly man. If the sons of Adam ' are many, although they die, [20] how much more the sons of the perfect man, ' they who do not die but are ' always begotten. The father makes a son, ' and the son has not the power to make ' a son. For he who has been begotten has not the power [25] to beget, but the son gets ' brothers for himself, not sons. All who ' are begotten in the world ' are begotten in a natural way, and ' the others [are nourished] from [the place] whence they have been born. [30] It is from ' being promised to the heavenly place ' that man [receives] nourishment. ' [. . .] him from the mouth. ' [And had] the word gone out from that place 59 it would be nourished from the mouth and ' it would become perfect. For it is ' by a kiss that the perfect conceive and give birth. For this reason ' we also kiss one another. [5] We receive conception from the grace which is in ' one another.

There were three who always walked with ' the lord: Mary his mother ' and her sister and Magdalene, the one ' who was called his companion. [10] His sister and his mother ' and his companion were each a Mary.

"The father" and "the son" ' are single names, "the holy spirit" ' is a double name. For they are ' everywhere: they are above, they are below; [15] they are in the concealed, they are in the revealed. ' The holy spirit is in the revealed: ' it is below. It is in the concealed: ' it is above.

The saints are served ' by evil powers, [20] for they are blinded by the holy spirit ' into thinking that they are serving ' an (ordinary) man whenever they do so for the saints. ' Because of this a disciple ' asked the lord one day for something [25] of this world. He said to him, ' "Ask your mother, and she will give you ' of the things which are another's."

The apostles said ' to the disciples, "May our entire offering ' obtain salt.'' [30] They called [Sophia] "salt." Without it ' no offering [is] acceptable. But Sophia ' is barren, [without] child. For this reason ' she is called "a trace of ' salt.'' Wherever they will [. . .] [35] in their own way, the holy spirit [. . . , **60** and] her children are many.

What the father possesses ' belongs to the son, and the son ' himself, so long as he is small, is not ' entrusted with what is his. But when [5] he becomes a man his father gives him ' all that he possesses.

Those who have gone astray, whom ' the spirit (itself) begets, usually go astray also ' because of the spirit. Thus, by one and the same breath, ' the fire blazes and is put out. [10]

Echamoth is one thing and Echmoth another. ' Echamoth is Wisdom simply, ' but Echmoth is the Wisdom of death which is ' the one which ' knows death, which is called [15] "the little Wisdom."

There are ' domestic animals, like the bull ' and the ass and others of this kind. ' Others are wild ' and live apart in the deserts. Man ploughs [20] the field by means of the domestic animals, ' and from this he is nourished (both) he and ' the animals, whether tame or ' wild. Compare the perfect ' man. It is through powers which are submissive [25] that he ploughs, preparing for everything to come into being. ' For it is because of this that the whole place stands, ' whether the good or the evil, ' the right and the left. The holy spirit ' shepherds every one and rules [30] [all] the powers, the "tame" ones ' and the "wild" ones, as well as those which are unique. ' For indeed he [. . . (and)] shuts them in, ' in order that [if . . .]wish, they will not be able [to escape].

[He who] has been created is [35] [beautiful, but] you (sg.) would ⟨not⟩ find his sons **61** noble creations. If he were not ' created but begotten, you (sg.) would find ' that his seed was noble. But now ' he was created, (and) he begot. What [5] nobility is this? First adultery ' came into being, afterward murder. And he ' was begotten in adultery, for he was the child ' of the serpent. So he became ' a murderer, just like his father, and [10] he killed his brother. Indeed every act of sexual intercourse ' which has occurred between those unlike ' one another is adultery.

God ' is a dyer. As the good dyes, ' which are called "true," dissolve [15] with the things dyed in them, so ' it is with those whom God has dyed. ' Since his dyes are immortal, they become immortal by means of his colors. ' Now God dips what he dips [20] in water.

It is not possible ' for anyone to see anything of the things that actually exist ' unless he becomes like ' them. This is not the way with man ' in the world: he sees the sun without being a sun; [25] and he sees the heaven and the earth and ' all other things, but he is not these

things. ' This is quite in keeping with the truth. But you (sg.) saw '
something of that place, and you became ' those things. You saw the
spirit, you ³⁰ became spirit. You saw Christ, you became ' Christ. You
saw [the father, you] shall become father. ' So [in this place] you see '
everything and [do] not [see] yourself, ' but [in that place] you do see
yourself – and what ³⁵ you see you shall [become]. '

Faith receives, love gives. [No one will be able **62** to receive] without
faith. No one will be able to give without ' love. Because of this, in
order that we may indeed receive, ' we believe, and in order that we
may love, we give, since ' if one gives without love, he has no ⁵ profit
from what he has given. He who ' has received something other than
the lord is still a Hebrew. '

The apostles who were before us had these names for him: ' "Jesus,
the Nazorean, Messiah," that ' is, "Jesus, the Nazorean, the Christ."
The last ¹⁰ name is "Christ," the first is "Jesus," that in ' the middle is
"the Nazarene." "Messiah" ' has two meanings, both "the Christ" '
and "the measured." "Jesus" in Hebrew is ' "the redemption." "Na-
zara" is "the truth." "The ¹⁵ Nazarene," then, is "the truth." "Christ"
' ... been measured. It is "the Nazarene" and "Jesus" ' who have
been measured.

When the pearl is cast ' down into the mud it becomes greatly despised, ²⁰ nor if it is anointed with balsam oil ' will it become more
precious. But it always has ' value in the eyes of its owner. ' Compare
the sons of ' God, wherever they may be. ²⁵ They still have value in the
eyes of their ' father.

If you (sg.) say, "I am a Jew," ' no one will be moved. If you say, "I
am a ' Roman," no one will be disturbed. If you say, "I am a Greek,
a barbarian, ³⁰ a slave, [a] free man," no one ' will be troubled. [If] you
[say], "I am a ' Christian," the [...] will tremble. Would ' that I might
[...] like that – the person whose name ' [...] will not be able to endure ³⁵ [hearing].

God is a **63** man-eater. For this reason men are [sacrificed] ' to him.
Before men were sacrificed ' animals were being sacrificed, since those
' to whom they were sacrificed were not gods. ⁵

Glass decanters and earthenware ' jugs are both made by means of
fire. ' But if glass decanters break ' they are done over, for ' they came
into being through a breath. If earthenware jugs ¹⁰ break, however, they
are destroyed, ' for they came into being without breath.

An ass ' which turns a millstone did a hundred miles ' walking. When
it was loosed ' it found that it was still at the same place. ¹⁵ There are

men who make many journeys, | but make no progress towards | any
destination. When evening came upon them, | they saw neither city nor
| village, neither human artifact nor natural phenomenon, [20] power nor
angel. In vain have the wretches | labored.

The eucharist is Jesus. For | he is called in Syriac "Pharisatha," |
which is "the one who is spread out," | for Jesus came to crucify the
world. [25]

The lord went into the dye works | of Levi. He took seventy-two dif-
ferent colors | and threw them into the vat. He took them | out all
white. And he said, "Even so | has the son [30] of man come [as] a dyer."

As for the Wisdom | who is called "the barren," she | is the mother
[of the] angels. And the | companion of the [. . .] Mary Magdalene. |
[. . . loved] her [35] more than [all] the disciples [and used to] | kiss her
[often] on her [. . .]. | The rest of [the disciples **64** . . .]. They said to
him, | "Why do you love her more than all of us?" The | savior an-
swered and said to them, | "Why do I not love you [5] like her? When a
blind man and one who sees | are both together in darkness, they are no
different from | one another. When the light comes, then | he who sees
will see the light, and | he who is blind will remain in darkness." [10]

The Lord said, "Blessed is he who | is before he came into being. For
he who | is, has been and shall be."

The superiority | of man is not obvious to the eye, but | lies in what
is hidden from view. Consequently he [15] has mastery over the animals
which are stronger than he is and | great in terms of the obvious and the
hidden. | This enables them to survive. But if | man is separated from
them, they slay | one another and bite one another. [20] They ate one
another because they did not find | any food. But now they have found
food because | man tilled the soil.

If one | go down into the water and come up without | having re-
ceived anything and says, "I am a Christian," [25] he has borrowed the
name at interest. But if he | receive the holy spirit, he has | the name as
a gift. He who has received a | gift does not have to give it back, but of
him who | has borrowed it at interest, payment is demanded. This is the
way [30] [it happens to one] when he experiences | a mystery.

Great is | the mystery of marriage! For [without] it the world | would
[not exist]. Now the existence of | [the world . . .], and the existence [35]
[. . . marriage]. Think of the [. . . relationship], for it possesses | [. . .]
power. Its image **65** consists of a [defilement].

The forms of evil spirit | include male ones and | female ones. The
males are they that | unite with the souls which inhabit [5] a female form,

but the females ' are they which are mingled with those in a ' male form, though one who was disobedient. And none ' shall be able to escape them, since they detain him ' if he does not receive a male power or a [10] female power, the bridegroom and ' the bride. – One receives them from the ' mirrored bridal chamber. – When the wanton women ' see a male sitting ' alone, they leap down on him and [15] play with him and defile him. So ' also the lecherous men, when they see a ' beautiful woman sitting alone, ' they persuade her and compel her, ' wishing to defile her. But if they see [20] the man and his wife sitting ' beside one another, the female cannot come ' in to the man, nor can the male ' come in to the woman. So ' if the image and the angel are united [25] with one another, neither can any venture ' to go in to the man or the woman. '

He who comes out of the world ' and so can no longer be detained on the grounds that he was in ' the world evidently is above [30] the desire of the [. . .] and fear. ' He is master over [. . .]. He is superior to ' envy. If [. . .] comes, they seize ' him and throttle [him]. And how will [this one] be able to escape the [great . . .] powers? [35] How will he be able to [. . .] ' There are some [who say], ' "We are faithful," in order that [. . . **66** the unclean spirits] and the demons. ' For if they had the holy spirit, ' no unclean spirit would cleave ' to them. Fear not the flesh nor [5] love it. If you (sg.) fear it, it will gain mastery ' over you. If you love it, it will swallow and paralyze you. '

And so he dwells either in this world or in the ' resurrection or in the middle place. ' God forbid that I be found there! [10] In this world there is good ' and evil. Its good things ' are not good, and its evil things ' not evil. But there is evil after ' this world which is truly evil – [15] what is called "the middle." It ' is death. While we are in this world ' it is fitting for us to acquire the resurrection, ' so that when we strip off the flesh ' we may be found in rest and not [20] walk in the middle. For many go astray ' on the way. For it is good to come forth ' from the world before one ' has sinned.

There are some who neither will ' nor have the power to; and others who, [25] if they will, do not profit: for ' they did not act since, (they believe,) [. . .] makes them ' sinners. And if they do not will, justice ' will elude them in both cases: ' and [it is] always a matter of the will, not the act.

An [30] apostolic man in a vision saw some people ' shut up in a house of fire and ' bound with fiery [. . .], lying ' [. . .] flaming [. . .]. them in ' [. . .] faith [. . .]. And they said to them, [35] "[. . .] able to be saved?" ' [. . .] "They did not desire it. They received ' [. . .] punishment, what is called **67** 'the [. . .] darkness,' because he [. . .]" '

It is from water and fire that the soul ' and the spirit came into being. It is from water and ' fire and light that the son of ⁵ the bridal chamber (came into being). The fire is the chrism, the light ' is the fire. I am not referring to that fire ' which has no form, but to the other fire whose ' form is white, which is bright and beautiful, ' and which gives beauty.

Truth did not come ¹⁰ into the world naked, but it came in ' types and images. The world will not receive truth in ' any other way. There is a rebirth and an ' image of rebirth. It is certainly necessary ' to be born again through the image. Which ¹⁵ one? Resurrection. The image must ' rise again through the image. The bridal chamber and ' the image must enter through the image into ' the truth: this is the restoration. Not only must those who produce the name of ²⁰ the father and the son and the holy spirit do so, ' but ⟨those who⟩ have produced them for you. If one does not acquire ' them, the name ("Christian") will also be taken from him. ' But one receives the unction of the [...] ' of the power of the cross. This power the apostles ²⁵ called "the right and the left." ' For this person is no longer a Christian but ' a Christ.

The lord [did] everything in a ' mystery, a baptism and a chrism ' and a eucharist and a redemption ³⁰ and a bridal chamber.

[...] he said, ' "I came to make [the things below] ' like the things [above, and the things] ' outside like those [inside. I came to unite] ' them in the place." [...] ³⁵ here through [types ...]. ' Those who say, "[There is a heavenly man and] ' there is one above [him," are wrong. ' – For it is the first of these two heavenly [men], the one who is revealed, **68** that they call ' "the one who is below"; and he to whom the hidden belongs ' is (supposed to be) that one who is above him. ' For it would be better for them to say, "The inner ⁵ and the outer, and what ' is outside the outer." Because of this the ' lord called destruction "the outer darkness": ' there is not another outside of it. He said, ' "My father who is in secret." He said, ¹⁰ "Go into your (sg.) chamber and shut ' the door behind you, and pray to your father ' who is in secret" (Mt 6:6), the one who is ' within them all. But that which is within ' them all is the fullness. ¹⁵ Beyond it there is nothing else within it. ' This is that of which they say, "That which is ' above them."

Before Christ some ' came from a place they were no longer ' able to enter, and they went where they were no longer ²⁰ able to come out. Then Christ came. ' Those who went in he brought out, and ' those who went out he brought in.

When ' Eve was still in Adam death did not exist. ' When she was separated from him death came into being. ²⁵ If he enters again and attains his former self, ' death will be no more.

"My God, my God, ' why, O lord, have you forsaken me?" (Mk 15:34 and parallels). It was ' on the cross that he said these words, for he had departed from that place.

[. . .] who has been begotten through [30] him who [. . .] from God. ' The [. . .] from the dead. ' [. . .] to be, but now ' [. . .] perfect. ' [. . .] flesh, but this [35] [. . .] is true flesh. ' [. . .] is not true, but ' [. . .] only an image of the true. **69**

A bridal chamber is not for the animals, ' nor is it for the slaves, nor for defiled ' women; but it is for free ' men and virgins.

Through [5] the holy spirit we are indeed begotten ' again, but we are begotten through ' Christ in the two. We are anointed through ' the spirit. When we were begotten we were united. None ' can see himself either in water or in [10] a mirror without light. Nor again can you (sg.) ' see in light without water or mirror. ' For this reason it is fitting to baptize in the two, ' in the light and the water. Now the light ' is the chrism.

There were three buildings specifically for [15] sacrifice in Jerusalem. The one ' facing west was called ' "the holy." Another facing ' south was called "the holy of ' the holy." The third facing [20] east was called "the holy ' of the holies," the place where only the high priest ' enters. Baptism ' is "the holy" building. Redemption is "the holy ' of the holy." "The holy of the holies" [25] is the bridal chamber. Baptism includes ' the resurrection [and the] redemption; the redemption ' (takes place) in the bridal chamber. But the bridal chamber ' is in that which is superior to [. . .] ' you (sg.) will not find [. . .] [30] are those who pray [. . .] ' Jerusalem. [. . .] ' Jerusalem who [. . .] ' Jerusalem, [. . .] ' those called "the holy [35] of the holies" [. . . the] ' veil was rent [. . .] ' bridal chamber except the image [. . .] **70** above. Because of this its ' veil was rent from top to bottom. For it was fitting for some ' from below to go upward. [5]

The powers do not see ' those who are clothed in the perfect light, ' and consequently are not able to detain them. ' One will clothe himself in this light ' sacramentally in the union.

If the [10] woman had not separated from the man, she should not die ' with the man. His separation became ' the beginning of death. Because of this ' Christ came to repair ' the separation which was from the beginning [15] and again unite the two, and to give life to those ' who died as a result of the separation ' and unite them. But the woman is united ' to her husband in the bridal chamber. ' Indeed those who have united in the bridal chamber will [20] no longer be separated. Thus Eve ' separated from Adam because it was not in the bridal chamber ' that she united with him.

The soul of Adam ' came into being by means of a breath. The ' partner of his soul is the spirit. His mother [25] is the thing that was given to him. His soul was taken from him and ' replaced by a [spirit]. When ' he was united (to the spirit), [he spoke] words incomprehensible ' to the powers. They envied him ' [...] spiritual partner [30] [...] hidden ' [...] opportunity ' [...] for themselves alone ' [...] bridal chamber so that ' [...]

Jesus appeared [35] [...] Jordan — the ' [fullness of the kingdom] of heaven. He who ' [was begotten] before everything **71** was begotten anew. He [who was] once [anointed] ' was anointed anew. He who was redeemed ' in turn redeemed (others).

Indeed, one must utter a ' mystery. The father of everything united [5] with the virgin who came down, and ' a fire shone for him on that day. ' He appeared in the great bridal chamber. ' Therefore, his body came into being ' on that very day. It left the bridal chamber [10] as one who came into being ' from the bridegroom and the bride. So ' Jesus established everything ' in it through these. ' It is fitting for each of the disciples [15] to enter into his rest. '

Adam came into being from two virgins, ' from the spirit and from ' the virgin earth. Christ, therefore, ' was born from a virgin [20] to rectify the fall which ' occurred in the beginning. '

There are two trees growing in Paradise. ' The one bears [animals], the other bears ' men. Adam [ate] from the tree [25] which bore animals. [He] became an animal ' and he brought forth animals. For this reason ' the children of Adam worship [animals]. The tree [...] ' fruit is [...] [30] increased. [...] ate the [...] ' fruit of the [...] ' bears men, [...] man. [...] [35] God created man. [... men] **72** create God. That is the way it is in the world — ' men make gods and worship their creation. It would be fitting for the gods ' to worship men!

Surely [5] what a man accomplishes ' depends on his abilities. ' For this reason we refer to one's accomplishments as ' ''abilities.'' Among his accomplishments are his children. They ' originate in a moment of ease. [10] Thus his abilities determine ' what he may accomplish, but this ease ' is clearly evident in the children. ' You will find that this applies directly to the image. ' Here is the man made after the image [15] accomplishing things with his physical strength, ' but producing his children with ease. '

In this world the slaves ' serve the free. In the ' kingdom of heaven the free will [20] minister to the slaves: the children of ' the bridal chamber will minister to the children ' of the marriage. The children of the bridal chamber ' have [just one] name: rest. ' [Altogether] they need take no (other) [25] form [because they have] contemplation, ' [...]. They are numerous ' [...] in the things ' [...] the glories ' [...]

Those [30] [... go] down into the water. ' [...] out (of the water), will consecrate it, ' [...] they who have ' [...] in his name. For he said, ' "[Thus] we should fulfill at **73** righteousness" (Mt 3:15).

Those who say they will ' die first and then rise ' are in error. If they do not first receive the ' resurrection while they live, when they die they will receive nothing. [5] So also when speaking about ' baptism they say, "Baptism ' is a great thing," because if people receive it they will ' live.

Philip the apostle ' said, "Joseph the carpenter planted [10] a garden because he needed wood ' for his trade. It was he who ' made the cross from the ' trees which he planted. His own offspring hung ' on that which he planted. His offspring was [15] Jesus and the planting was the cross." But the tree ' of life is in the middle of the garden. ' However, it is from the olive tree ' that we get the chrism, and from the chrism, ' the resurrection.

This world is a corpse-eater. [20] All the things eaten ' in it themselves die also. Truth ' is a life-eater. Therefore no one ' nourished by [truth] will die. It was ' from that place that Jesus came and brought [25] food. To those who ' so desired he gave [life, that] ' they might not die.

God [...] a garden. ' Man [...] garden. ' There are [...] [30] and [...] ' of God. [...] ' The things which are in [...] ' I wish. This garden [is the place where] ' they will say to me, "... eat] [35] this or do not eat [that, just as you (sg.)] **74** wish." In the place where I will eat all things ' is the tree of knowledge. ' That one killed Adam, ' but here the tree of knowledge made men alive. [5] The law was the tree. It has power ' to give the knowledge of good ' and evil. It neither removed him from ' evil, nor did it set him in the good, ' but it created death for those who [10] ate of it. For when he said, ' "Eat this, do not eat that," it became ' the beginning of death.

The chrism is superior ' to baptism, for it is from the word "chrism" ' that we have been called "Christians," certainly not because [15] of the word "baptism." And it is because of the chrism that "the ' Christ" has his name. For the father anointed ' the son, and the son anointed the apostles, ' and the apostles anointed us. He who ' has been anointed possesses everything. He possesses [20] the resurrection, the light, the cross, ' the holy spirit. The father gave him this ' in the bridal chamber;

he merely accepted (the gift). The father was ' in the son and the son in the father. ' This is [the] kingdom of heaven. [25]

The lord said it well: "Some have entered the kingdom ' of heaven laughing, and they have come out ' [...] because [...] a Christian, ' [...] And as soon as ' [... went down into] the water he came [30] [...] everything (of this world), [...] because ' [...] a trifle, but ' [... full of] contempt for this ' [...] the kingdom of ' [heaven ...]. If he despises [35] [...] and scorns it as a trifle, ' [...] out laughing. So it is also **75** with the bread and the cup and the oil, ' even though there is another one superior to these.

The ' world came about through a mistake. ' For he who created it wanted to create [5] it imperishable and immortal. ' He fell short of attaining his desire. ' For the world never was imperishable, ' nor, for that matter, was ' he who made the world. [10] For things are not imperishable, ' but sons are. Nothing ' will be able to receive imperishability if it does not ' first become a son. But he who has not the ability ' to receive, how much more will he be unable to give?

The cup [15] of prayer contains wine and ' water, since it is appointed as the type of ' the blood for which thanks is given. And ' it is full of the holy spirit, and ' it belongs to the wholly perfect man. When [20] we drink this, we shall receive for ourselves the perfect ' man. The living water is a body. ' It is necessary that we put on the living man. ' Therefore, when he is about to go down into the water, ' he unclothes himself, in order that he may put on the living man. [25]

A horse sires a horse, a ' man begets man, a god ' brings forth a god. Compare ' [the] bridegroom and the [bride]. They have come from the [...]. [30] No Jew [...] ' [...] ' has existed. And ' [...] ' from the Jews. [...] ' Christians, [...] [35] these [...] are referred to as ' "the chosen people of [...]" **76** and "the true man" and "the son of ' man" and "the seed of the son of man." ' This true race is renowned ' in the world. ... that [5] the sons of the bridal chamber dwell. '

Whereas in this world the union ' is one of husband with wife — a case of strength complemented by ' weakness (?) — in the eternal realm (aeon) the form of the union ' is different, although we refer to them by the same names. There are [10] other names, however; they are superior to every name ' that is named and are ' stronger than the strong. For where there is a show of strength, ' there those who excel in strength appear. ' These are not separate things, [15] but both of them are this one ' single thing. This is the one which will not be able to rise ' above the heart of flesh.

Is it not necessary for all those who possess | everything to know themselves? | Some indeed, if they do not know [20] themselves, will not enjoy what they | possess. But those who have come to know themselves will | enjoy their possessions.

Not only | will they be unable to detain the perfect man, | but they will not be able to see him, for if they see him [25] they will detain him. There is no other way | for a person to acquire this quality except by putting on the perfect light | [and] he too becoming perfect light. He who has [put it] on will enter [30] [...]. This is the perfect | [...] that we [...] become | [...] before we leave | [...]. Whoever receives everything | [...] hither [...] be able [35] [...] that place, but will | [... the middle] as imperfect. **77** Only Jesus knows the end of this person. |

The priest is completely holy, down | to his very body. For if he has taken the bread, | he will consecrate it. Or the cup [5] or anything else that he gets, | he will consecrate. Then how will he not consecrate | the body also?

By perfecting | the water of baptism, Jesus | emptied it of death. Thus we do go [10] down into the water, but we do not go | down into death in order that we may not be poured | out into the spirit of the world. When | that spirit blows, it brings the winter. | When the holy spirit breathes, [15] the summer comes.

He who has | knowledge of the truth is a free man, | but the free man does not sin, | for "he who sins is the slave of sin" (Jn 8:34). | Truth is the mother, knowledge [20] the father. Those who think that sinning does not apply to them | are called "free" by the world. | "Knowledge" of the truth merely "makes | such people arrogant," which | is what the words "it makes them free" mean. [25] It even gives them a sense of superiority over the whole world. But "love | builds up" (1 Co 8:1). In fact, he who is really free through | knowledge is a slave because of love | for those who have not yet been able to attain to the | freedom of knowledge. Knowledge [30] makes them capable of becoming | free. Love [never calls] | something its own, [...] it [...] possess [...]. | It never [says "This is yours"] | or "This is mine," [but "All these] [35] are yours." Spiritual love | is wine and fragrance. **78** All those who anoint themselves with it take pleasure in it. | While those who are anointed are present, | those nearby also profit (from the fragrance). | If those anointed with ointment withdraw from them [5] and leave, then those not anointed, | who merely stand nearby, still | remain in their bad odor. The Samaritan | gave nothing but | wine and oil to the wounded man. It is nothing other than [10] the ointment. It healed the wounds, | for "love covers a multitude of sins" (1 P 4:8). |

The children a woman bears ' resemble the man who loves her. If her ' husband loves her, then they resemble her husband. If it is an adulterer, ¹⁵ then they resemble the adulterer. Frequently, ' if a woman sleeps with her ' husband out of necessity, while her heart is with the adulterer ' with whom she usually has intercourse, the child ' she will bear is born resembling ²⁰ the adulterer. Now you who live together with the son ' of God, love not the world, ' but love the lord, in order that those you will ' bring forth may not resemble the world, ' but may resemble the lord. ²⁵

The human being has intercourse with the human being. ' The horse has intercourse with the horse, the ass ' with the ass. Members of a race usually have associated ' [with] those of like race. So spirit ' mingles with spirit, and thought ³⁰ consorts with thought, ' and [light] shares ' [with light. If you (sg.)] are born a human being, ' it is [the human being] who will love you. If you become ' [a spirit], it is the spirit which will be joined to you. If you become ³⁵ thought, it is thought which will mingle **79** with you. If you become light, ' it is the light which will share ' with you. If you become one of those who belong above, ' it is those who belong above who will rest ⁵ upon you. If you become horse ' or ass or bull or dog or sheep ' or another of the animals which are outside ' or below, then ' neither human being nor spirit ¹⁰ nor thought nor light will be able to love you. Neither ' those who belong above nor those who belong within ' will be able to rest in you, ' and you have no part in them.

He ' who is a slave against his will will be able to become free. ¹⁵ He who has become free by the favor ' of his master and has sold ' himself into slavery will no longer be able ' to be free.

Farming in the ' world requires the cooperation of four essential elements. A harvest is gathered ²⁰ into the barn only as a result of the natural action of water, ' earth, wind, and light. ' God's farming likewise ' has four elements — faith, ' hope, love, and ²⁵ knowledge. Faith is our earth, that in which we ' take root. [And] hope ' is the water through which we are ' nourished. Love is the wind through ' which we grow. Knowledge then is the light ³⁰ through which we [ripen]. ' Grace exists in [four ways: it is] ' earthborn; it is [heavenly; ...] ' the highest heaven; [...] in [...].

Blessed ' is the one who on no occasion caused a soul [...]. **80** That person is Jesus Christ. He came to ' the whole place and did not burden anyone. ' Therefore, blessed is the one who is like ' this, because he is a perfect man. For ⁵ the word tells us that this kind is difficult ' to define. How shall we be able to accomplish ' such a great thing? How will he give everyone comfort? ' Above all, it is not proper ' to cause anyone distress — whether the person is great or small, [10] unbeliever or believer — and then give comfort ' only to those who take satisfaction in good deeds. ' Some find it advantageous to give ' comfort to the one who has fared well. He who does ' good deeds cannot give comfort [15] to such people; for he does not seize whatever he likes. ' He is unable to cause distress, ' however, since he does not afflict them. To be sure, the one who ' fares well sometimes causes people distress — ' not that he intends to do so; rather it is their own wickedness [20] which is responsible for their distress. He who possesses ' the qualities (of the perfect man) bestows joy upon the good. ' Some, however, are terribly distressed by all this. '

There was a householder who had ' every conceivable thing, be it son or slave or [25] cattle or dog or pig or corn ' [or] barley or chaff or grass or ' [...] or meat and acorn. [Now he was] a sensible fellow ' and he knew what the food of each ' one was. He served the children bread [30] [...]. He served the slaves ' [... and] meal. And ' [he threw barley] and chaff and grass to the cattle. ' He threw bones to [the] dogs, ' and to the pigs he threw acorns **81** and slop. Compare the disciple ' of God: if he is a sensible fellow he ' understands what discipleship is all about. The ' bodily forms will not deceive him, [5] but he will look at the condition ' of the soul of each one and speak ' with him. There are many animals in the world ' which are in human form. When ' he identifies them, to the swine he will throw [10] acorns, to the cattle he will throw ' barley and chaff and grass, to the ' dogs he will throw bones. To the slaves ' he will give only the elementary lessons, to the children he will give ' the complete instruction.

There is the son of man [15] and there is the son of the son of man. ' The lord is the son of man, ' and the son of the son of ' man is he who creates through the son ' of man. The son of man received [20] from God the capacity to create. He also has the ability ' to beget. He who has received ' the ability to create is a creature. He who has received ' the ability to beget is an offspring. He who creates cannot ' beget. He who begets also has power to create. [25] Now they say, "He who creates begets." ' But his so-called "offspring" is merely a creature. Because of [...] ' of birth, they are not his offspring but [...]. ' He who creates works openly ' and he himself is visible. [30] He who begets begets in [private] ' and he himself is hidden, since [...] ' image. Also, he who creates [creates] ' openly. But one who begets [begets] ' children in private. No [one can] [35] know when [the husband] **82** and the wife have intercourse with one another | except the two of them. Indeed marriage in the | world is a mystery for those who have taken | a wife. If there is a hidden quality to the marriage of defilement, [5] how much more is the undefiled marriage | a true mystery! It is not fleshly | but pure. It belongs not to desire | but to the will. It belongs not to the darkness | or the night but to the day and [10] the light. If a marriage is open to the public, | it has become prostitution, and the bride | plays the harlot not only when she is impregnated by another man | but even if she slips out of her bedroom | and is seen. [15] Let her show herself only to her father and her | mother and to the friend of the bridegroom and | the sons of the bridegroom. These are permitted | to enter every day into the bridal chamber. | But let the others yearn just [20] to listen to her voice and to enjoy | her ointment, and let them feed from the | crumbs that fall from the table, like the | dogs. Bridegrooms and | brides belong to the bridal chamber. No one shall be able [25] to see the bridegroom with the bride unless | [he become] such a one.

When Abraham | [. . .] that he was to see what he was to see, | [he circumcised] the flesh of the foreskin, teaching | us that it is proper to destroy the flesh. [30]

[Most things] in the world, as long as their | [inner parts] are hidden, stand upright and live. | [If they are revealed] they die, as | is illustrated by the visible man: | [as long as] the intestines of the man are hidden, the man is alive; **83** when his intestines are exposed | and come out of him, the man will die. | So also with the tree: while its root | is hidden it sprouts and grows. If its [5] root is exposed, the tree dries up. | So it is with every birth that is in the world, | not only with the revealed | but with the hidden. For so long as the root | of wickedness is hidden, it is strong. But when it is recognized [10] it is dissolved. When it is revealed | it perishes. That is why the word says, | "Already the ax is laid at the root | of the trees" (Mt 3:10). It will not merely cut — what | is cut sprouts again — but the ax [15] penetrates deeply until it | brings up the root. Jesus pulled out | the root of the whole place, while others did it only | partially. As for ourselves, let each | one of us dig down after the root [20] of evil which is within one, and let one pluck it | out of one's heart from the root. It will be plucked out | if we recognize it. But if we | are ignorant of it, it takes root in | us and produces its fruit [25] in our heart. It masters us. | We are its slaves. It takes us captive, | to make us do what we do [not] want; | and what we do want we do [not] do. It | is powerful because we have not recognized it. While [it exists] [30] it is active. Ignorance ' is the mother of [all evil]. ' Ignorance will result in [death, because] ' those that come from [ignorance] ' neither were nor [are] [35] nor shall be. [...] **84** will be perfect when all the truth ' is revealed. For truth is like ' ignorance: while it is hidden it rests ' in itself, but when it is revealed [5] and is recognized, it is praised inasmuch as ' it is stronger than ignorance and error. ' It gives freedom. The word said, ' "If you (pl.) know the truth, ' the truth will make you free" (Jn 8:32). [10] Ignorance is a slave. Knowledge is ' freedom. If we know the truth, ' we shall find the fruits of the truth within ' us. If we are joined to it, it will bring our fulfillment. '

At the present time we have the manifest things [15] of creation. We say, ' "The strong who are held in high regard are great people. ' And the weak who are despised are the obscure." Contrast the manifest things ' of truth: they are weak and ' despised, while the hidden things are strong and [20] held in high regard. The mysteries of truth are ' revealed, though in type and image. The bridal chamber, ' however, remains hidden. It is the holy in ' the holy. The veil at first ' concealed how God controlled [25] the creation, but when the veil is rent ' and the things inside are revealed, ' this house will be left ' desolate, or rather will be ' [destroyed]. And the whole (inferior) godhead will flee [30] [from] here but not into the holies ' [of the] holies, for it will not be able to mix with the ' unmixed [light] and the ' [flawless] fullness, but will be under the wings of the cross ' [and under] its arms. This ark will be [35] [their] salvation when the flood **85** of water surges over them. If ' some belong to the order of the priesthood ' they will be able to go ' within the veil with the high priest. [5] For this reason the veil was not ' rent at the top only, since it ' would have been open only to those above; nor ' was it rent at the bottom only, since ' it would have been revealed only to those below. [10] But it was rent from top to bottom. Those ' above opened to us the things below, ' in order that we may go in to the secret ' of the truth. This truly is what is ' held in high regard (and) what is strong! But we shall go in there [15] by means of lowly types and forms of weakness. ' They are lowly indeed when compared with the perfect glory. ' There is glory which surpasses glory. There is power which surpasses ' power. Therefore the perfect things have opened ' to us, together with the hidden things of truth. The holies [20] of the holies were revealed, and ' the bridal chamber invited us in.

As long ' as it is hidden, wickedness is indeed ineffectual, but ' it has not been removed from the midst of the seed of the holy spirit. ' They are slaves of evil. But when [25] it is revealed, then the ' perfect light will flow out on every ' one. And all those who are in it will [receive the chrism]. ' Then the slaves will be free [and] ' the captives ransomed. "[Every] plant [which] [30] my father who is in heaven [has not] planted [will be] ' plucked out" (Mt 15:13). Those who are separated will unite [. . .] and ' will be filled. Every one who will [enter] ' the bridal chamber will kindle the [light], for [. . .] ' just as in the marriages which are [. . .] happen [35] at night. That fire [. . .] only **86** at night and is put out. But the mysteries ' of that marriage are perfected rather in ' the day and the light. Neither that day ' nor its light ever sets. If anyone becomes a son [5] of the bridal chamber, he will receive the light. ' If anyone does not receive it while he is here, he will not be able to receive it ' in the other place. He who will receive that light ' will not be seen, nor can he be detained. ' And none shall be able to torment [10] a person like this even while he dwells ' in the world. And again when he leaves ' the world he has already received the truth in ' the images. The world has become the eternal realm (aeon), ' for the eternal realm is fullness for him. [15] This is the way it is: it is revealed ' to him alone, not hidden in the darkness and the ' night, but hidden in a perfect day ' and a holy light.

The Gospel '
According to Philip

THE HYPOSTASIS OF THE ARCHONS (II,*4*)

Introduced by

ROGER A. BULLARD

Translated by

BENTLEY LAYTON

The Hypostasis of the Archons ("Reality of the Rulers") is an anonymous tractate presenting an esoteric interpretation of Genesis 1-6, partially in the form of a revelation discourse between an angel and a questioner. While the treatise illustrates a wide-ranging Hellenistic syncretism, the most evident components are Jewish, although in its present form *The Hypostasis of the Archons* shows clearly Christian features and thus can be considered a Christian work. Its theological perspective is a vigorous Gnosticism of perhaps Sethian affiliation.

It is generally assumed that *The Hypostasis of the Archons*, like all the other Nag Hammadi texts, is a translation from Greek. The possibility of a Coptic pun on the phrase "beside me" (Is 46:9) and "blind" (*Hyp. Arch.* 86,30; 94,22), as well as the description of animal-headed Rulers (87,29) suggests that the provenance may have been Egypt.

The document is tentatively dated in the third century C.E. It is obviously no later than the fourth century, to which the Nag Hammadi collection is dated. But the well-developed gnostic treatment of the material in this document as well as the midrashic handling of scriptural material argue against an early date. Further, the philosophical orientation of 96,11-14 has been identified as typical of third-century Neoplatonism.

The questions of date and provenance are complicated by the possibility that the work as it stands is a result of a Christian editor's having combined a narrative source (interpreting parts of Genesis) with a revelation discourse concerned with soteriology and eschatology, and placing them both within a Christian framework.

The Hypostasis of the Archons is certainly the work of a gnostic teacher instructing an audience. While using previous material, he writes from a position of authority, even in the angelic revelation where a character in the discourse is ostensibly speaking. The audience is a Christian Gnostic community, aware of material of both testaments and accepting the authority of Paul. They are familiar with Jewish literary traditions, including apocalyptic. A traditional function of apocalyptic – providing reassurance for an insecure community – is operative here. *The Hypostasis of the Archons* is thus an esoteric work, written for a self-conscious community which probably felt pressure from a Christian community that defined itself as orthodox and others as heretical.

There is clearly some literary relationship between *The Hypostasis of the Archons* and *On the Origin of the World*, which follows this tractate in Codex II.

Both seem to draw from common sources. The latter mentions a *Book* or *Books of Norea* (102,11, 24-25), to which Epiphanius also refers. It has been suggested that *The Hypostasis of the Archons* is to be identified with that source, but without compelling evidence.

After a brief introduction quoting "the great apostle" Paul, *The Hypostasis of the Archons* offers its mythological narrative. The main characters in the mythological drama which unfolds include the blind ruler Samael, also called Sakla ("fool") and Yaldabaoth, who blasphemes against the divine; the spiritual Woman, who rouses Adam and outwits the rapacious rulers; the Snake, the Instructor, who counsels the man and woman to eat of the fruit forbidden by the rulers; and Norea, the daughter of Eve, a virgin pure in character and exalted in knowledge. On page 93 of the tractate the focus changes somewhat: on center stage now is the great angel Eleleth, who reveals to Norea the origin and destiny of the archontic powers.

The Hypostasis of the Archons proclaims, as its title indicates, the reality of the archontic rulers: far from being merely fictitious, imaginary powers, the archons are all too real. These rulers indeed exist. This is a grim reality for the Christian Gnostics, who define their own spiritual nature in opposition to that of the ruling and enslaving authorities. Yet, as this document promises, the Christian Gnostics can have hope, for their spiritual nature will be more lasting than the archons, and their heavenly destiny will be more glorious. In the end the rulers will perish, and the Gnostics, the children of the light, will know the Father and praise him.

THE HYPOSTASIS OF THE ARCHONS

II 86, 20-97, 23

On account of the reality (*hypostasis*) of the authorities (*eksousiai*), (inspired) by the spirit ¦ of the father of truth, the great ¦ apostle − referring to the "authorities of the darkness" (Col 1:13) − told us ¦ that "our contest is not against flesh and ¦ [blood]; rather, the authorities of the universe ²⁵ and the spirits of wickedness" (Ep 6:12). ¦ [I have] sent (you) this because you (sg.) inquire about the reality ¦ [of the] authorities.

Their chief is blind; ¦ [because of his] power and his ignorance ¦ [and his] arrogance he said, with his ³⁰ [power], "It is I who am God; there is none ¦ [apart from me]."

When he said this, he sinned against ¦ [the entirety]. And this speech got up **87** to incorruptibility; then there was a voice that came ¦ forth from incorruptibility, saying, ¦ "You are mistaken, Samael" − which is, "god ¦ of the blind."

His thoughts became blind. And, having expelled ⁵ his power − that is, the blasphemy he had spoken – ' he pursued it down to chaos and ' the abyss, his mother, at the instigation of Pistis ' Sophia (Faith Wisdom). And she established each of his offspring ' in conformity with its power – after the pattern [10] of the realms that are above, for by starting from the ' invisible world the visible world was invented.

As incorruptibility ' looked down into the region of the waters, ' her image appeared in the waters; ' and the authorities of the darkness became enamored of her. [15] But they could not lay hold of that image, ' which had appeared to them in the waters, ' because of their weakness – since beings that merely possess a soul ' cannot lay hold of those that possess a spirit – for ' they were from below, while it was from [20] above.

This is the reason why "incorruptibility ' looked down into the region (etc.)'': ' so that, by the father's will, she ' might bring the entirety into union with the light. The rulers (*archontes*) laid ' plans and said, "Come, [25] let us create a man that will be soil from ' the earth." They modelled their creature ' as one wholly of the earth.

Now the rulers ... ' body ... they have ... female ... is ... ' with the face of a beast. They had taken [some soil] [30] from the earth and modelled their [man], ' after their body and [after the image] ' of God that had appeared [to them] ' in the waters.

They said, "[Come, let] us ' lay hold of it by means of the form that we have modelled, [so that] [35] it may see its male counterpart [...], **88** and we may seize it with the form that we have modelled" – not ' understanding the force of God, because of ' their powerlessness. And he breathed into ' his face; and the man came to have a soul (and remained) [5] upon the ground many days. But they could not ' make him arise because of their powerlessness. ' Like storm winds they persisted (in blowing), that they might ' try to capture that image, which had appeared ' to them in the waters. And they did not know [10] the identity of its power.

Now all these (events) came ' to pass by the will of the father of the entirety. Afterwards, ' the spirit saw the soul-endowed man ' upon the ground. And the spirit came forth from ' the Adamantine Land; it descended and came to dwell within [15] him, and that man became a living soul. '

It called his name Adam since he ' was found moving upon the ground. A voice ' came forth from incorruptibility for the assistance of Adam; ' and the rulers gathered together [20] all the animals of the earth and all the ' birds of heaven and brought them in to Adam ' to see what

Adam would call them, ' that he might give a name to each of the birds ' and all the beasts.

They took Adam [25] [and] put him in the garden, that he might cultivate ' [it] and keep watch over it. And the rulers issued a command ' to him, saying, "From [every] tree ' in the garden shall you (sg.) eat; ' yet – [from] the tree of recognizing good [30] and evil do not eat, nor ' [touch] it; for the day you (pl.) eat ' [from] it, with death you (pl.) are going to die."

They ' [. . .] this. They do not understand what ' [they have said] to him; rather, by the father's will, **89** they said this in such a way that he ' might (in fact) eat, and that Adam might ⟨not⟩ regard them as would a man of an exclusively ' material nature.

The rulers took counsel ' with one another and said, "Come, let us cause [5] a deep sleep to fall upon Adam." And he slept. ' – Now the deep sleep that they ' "caused to fall upon him, and he slept" is Ignorance. – They opened ' his side like a living woman. ' And they built up his side with some flesh [10] in place of her, and Adam came to be endowed ' only with soul.

And the spirit-endowed woman ' came to him and spoke with him, saying, ' "Arise, Adam." And when he saw her, ' he said, "It is you who have given me life; [15] you will be called 'Mother of the living.' ' – For it is she who is my mother. It is she who is the physician, ' and the woman, and she who has given birth."

Then the ' authorities came up to their Adam. ' And when they saw his female counterpart speaking with him, [20] they became agitated with great agitation; ' and they became enamored of her. They said to one another, ' "Come, let us sow our seed ' in her," and they pursued her. And ' she laughed at them for their witlessness [25] and their blindness; and in their clutches, she became a tree, ' and left before them her shadowy reflection resembling herself; ' and they defiled [it] ' foully. – And they defiled the stamp of ' her voice, so that [30] by the form they had modelled, together with [their] (own) image, they made themselves liable to condemnation. '

Then the female spiritual principle came [in] ' the snake, the instructor; and it taught [them], ' saying, "What did he [say to] ' you (pl.)? Was it, 'From every tree in the garden [35] shall you (sg.) eat; yet – from [the tree] **90** of recognizing evil and good ' do not eat'?"

The carnal woman said, ' "Not only did he say 'Do not eat,' but even ' 'Do not touch it; for the day you (pl.) eat from it, with death you (pl.) are going to die.'" '

And the snake, the instructor, said, "With death ' you (pl.) shall not die; for it was out of jealousy ' that he said this to you (pl.). Rather your (pl.) eyes ' shall open and you (pl.) shall come to be like gods, recognizing [10] evil and good." ' And the female instructing principle was taken away from the snake, ' and she left it behind merely a thing of the earth. '

And the carnal woman took from the tree ' and ate; and she gave to her husband as well as herself; and [15] these beings that possessed only a soul, ate. And their imperfection ' became apparent in their lack of acquaintance; and ' they recognized that they were naked of the spiritual element, ' and took fig leaves and bound them ' upon their loins.

Then the chief ruler came; [20] and he said, "Adam! Where are you?" – for he did not ' understand what had happened.

And Adam ' said, "I heard your voice and was ' afraid because I was naked; and I hid." '

The ruler said, "Why did you (sg.) hide, unless it is [25] because you (sg.) have eaten from the tree ' from which alone I commanded you (sg.) not to eat? ' And you (sg.) have eaten!" '

Adam said, "The woman that you gave me, ' [she gave] to me and I ate." And the arrogant [30] ruler cursed the woman.

The woman ' said, "It was the snake that led me astray and I ate." ' [They turned] to the snake and cursed its shadowy reflection, ' [. . .] powerless, not comprehending ' [that] it was a form they themselves had modelled. From that day, **91** the snake came to be under the curse of the authorities; ' until the all-powerful man was to come, ' that curse fell upon the snake.

They turned ' to their Adam and took him and expelled him from the garden [5] along with his wife; for they have no ' blessing, since they too are ' beneath the curse.

Moreover they threw mankind ' into great distraction and into a life ' of toil, so that their mankind might be [10] occupied by worldly affairs, and might not have the opportunity ' of being devoted to the holy spirit.

Now afterwards, ' she bore Cain, their son; and Cain ' cultivated the land. Thereupon he knew his ' wife; again becoming pregnant, she bore Abel; and Abel [15] was a herdsman of sheep. Now Cain brought ' in from the crops of his field, but ' Abel brought in an offering (from) among ' his lambs. God looked upon the ' votive offerings of Abel; but he did not accept the votive offerings [20] of Cain. And carnal Cain ' pursued Abel his brother.

And God | said to Cain, "Where is Abel your brother?" |
He answered, saying, "Am I, then, | my brother's keeper?"
God said to [25] Cain, "Listen! The voice of your brother's blood | is crying up to me! You have sinned with | your mouth. It will return to you: anyone who | kills Cain will let loose seven | vengeances, and you will exist groaning and [30] trembling upon the earth."

And Adam [knew] | his female counterpart Eve, and she became pregnant, and bore [Seth] | to Adam. And she said, "I have borne [another] | man through God, in place [of Abel]." |

Again Eve became pregnant, and she bore [Norea]. [35] And she said, "He has begotten on [me a] virgin [92] as an assistance [for] many generations | of mankind." She is the virgin whom the | forces did not defile.

Then mankind began | to multiply and improve.

The rulers took counsel [5] with one another and said, "Come, let | us cause a deluge with our | hands and obliterate all flesh, from man | to beast."

But when the ruler of the forces | came to know of their decision, he said to Noah, [10] "Make yourself an ark from some wood | that does not rot and hide in it − you | and your children and the beasts and | the birds of heaven from small to large − and set it | upon Mount Sir."

Then Orea came [15] to him wanting to board the ark. | And when he would not let her, she blew upon the | ark and caused it to be consumed by fire. Again he | made the ark, for a second time.

The rulers went to meet her | intending to lead her astray. [20] Their supreme chief said to her, "Your mother | Eve came to us."

But Norea turned to | them and said to them, "It is you who are the rulers of | the darkness; you are accursed. And you did not know | my mother; instead it was your female [25] counterpart that you knew. For I am not your descendant; | rather it is from the world above that I am come." |

The arrogant ruler turned, with all his might, | [and] his countenance came to be like (a) black | [...]; he said to her presumptuously, [30] "You must render service to us, | [as did] also your mother Eve; for I have been given (?) | [...]."

But Norea turned, with the might of | [...]; and in a loud voice [she] cried out | [up to] the holy one, the God of the entirety, [93] "Rescue me from the rulers of unrighteousness | and save me from their clutches − forthwith!"

The ⟨great⟩ angel | came down from the heavens | and said to her, "Why are you crying up [5] to God? Why do you act so boldly towards the | holy spirit?"

Norea said, "Who are you?" |

The rulers of unrighteousness had withdrawn from | her. He said, "It is I who am Eleleth, | sagacity, the great angel, who stands [10] in the presence of the holy spirit. | I have been sent to speak with you and | save you from the grasp of the lawless. And I | shall teach you about your root."

– Now as for that angel, | I cannot speak of his power: his appearance is like [15] fine gold and his raiment is like snow. | No, truly, my mouth cannot bear | to speak of his power and the appearance of his face! |

Eleleth, the great angel, spoke to me. | "It is I," he said, "who am understanding. [20] I am one of the four light-givers, | who stand in the presence of the great | invisible spirit. Do you think | these rulers have any power over you (sg.)? None | of them can prevail against the root [25] of truth; for on its account he appeared | in the final ages; and | these authorities will be restrained. And these authorities | cannot defile you and that generation; | for your (pl.) abode is in incorruptibility, [30] where the virgin spirit dwells, | who is superior to the authorities of chaos | and to their universe."

But I said, | Sir, teach me about the [faculty of] | these authorities – [how] did they come into being, [35] and by what kind of genesis, [and] of **94** what material, and who | created them and their force?"

And the | great angel Eleleth, understanding, spoke to me: | "Within limitless realms [5] dwells incorruptibility. Sophia, | who is called Pistis, wanted to | create something, alone without her consort; and | her product was a celestial thing. |

"A veil exists between the world above [10] and the realms that are below; and | shadow came into being beneath the veil; | and that shadow became matter; | and that shadow was projected | apart. And what she had created became [15] a product in the matter, like an aborted fetus. | And it assumed a plastic form molded out of shadow, and became | an arrogant beast resembling a lion." | It was androgynous, as I have already said, | because it was from matter that it derived.

"Opening his [20] eyes he saw a vast quantity of matter without limit; | and he became arrogant, saying, 'It is I who am God, and there | is none other apart from me.'

"When he said | this, he sinned against the entirety. | And a voice came forth from above the realm of absolute power, [25] saying, 'You are mistaken, Samael' – | which is, 'god of the blind.'

"And he | said, 'If any other thing exists before | me, let it become visible to me!' And | immediately Sophia stretched forth her finger [30] and introduced light into | matter; and she pursued it down | to the region of chaos. And she returned | up [to] her light; once again darkness | [. . .] matter.

"This ruler, by being androgynous, [35] made himself a vast realm, **95** an extent without limit. And he contemplated | creating offspring for himself, and created | for himself seven offspring, androgynous just like | their parent.

"And he said to his offspring, [5] 'It is I who am the god of the entirety.'

"And Zoe (Life), | the daughter of Pistis Sophia, cried | out and said to him, 'You are mistaken, Sakla!' — | for which the alternate name is Yaltabaoth. She | breathed into his face, and her breath became [10] a fiery angel for her; and | that angel bound Yaldabaoth | and cast him down into Tartaros | below the abyss.

"Now when his offspring | Sabaoth saw the force of that angel, [15] he repented and | condemned his father and his | mother matter.

"He loathed her, but he | sang songs of praise up to Sophia and her daughter Zoe. | And Sophia and Zoe caught him up [20] and gave him charge of the seventh heaven, | below the veil between | above and below. And he is | called 'God of the forces, Sabaoth,'' | since he is up above the forces [25] of chaos, for Sophia established | him.

"Now when these (events) had come to pass, he made | himself a huge four-faced chariot of cherubim, | and infinitely many angels | to act as ministers, [30] and also harps and | lyres.

"And Sophia took her daughter | Zoe and had her sit upon his right to teach him about the things that exist | in the eighth (heaven); and the angel [of] wrath [35] she placed upon his left. [Since] that day, [his right] has been called **96** life; and the left has come to represent | the unrighteousness of the realm of absolute power | above. It was before your (sg.) time that they came into being (text corrupt?).

"Now when | Yaldabaoth saw him in this [5] great splendor and at this height, he envied him; | and the envy became an androgynous product. | and this was the origin of | envy. And envy engendered death; and death | engendered his offspring and gave each [10] of them charge of its heaven; and all the heavens | of chaos became full of their multitudes.

"But it was | by the will of the father of the entirety that they all came into being — | after the pattern of all the things above — | so that the sum of chaos might be attained. [15]

"There, I have taught you (sg.) about the pattern | of the rulers; and the matter in which it was expressed; | and their parent; and their universe.''

But I ' said, "Sir, am I also ' from their matter?"

– "You, together with your offspring, are from [20] the primeval father; ' from above, out of the imperishable light, ' their souls are come. Thus the authorities ' cannot approach them because of ' the spirit of truth present within them; [25] and all who have become acquainted with this way ' exist deathless in the midst ' of dying mankind. Still that sown element (*sperma*) ' will not become known now.

"Instead, ' after three generations it will come to be known, [30] and has freed them from the bondage of the ' authorities' error."

Then I said, ' "Sir, how much longer?"

He said ' to me, "Until the moment when the true man, ' within a modelled form, reveals the existence of (?) [35] [the spirit of] truth, which the father has sent. **97**

"Then he will teach them about ' everything: And he will anoint them with the ' unction of life eternal, ' given him from the un-dominated generation. [5]

"Then they will be freed of ' blind thought: And they will trample under foot ' death, which is of the authorities: And they will ascend ' into the limitless light, ' where this sown element belongs. [10]

"Then the authorities will relinquish their ' ages: And their angels will weep ' over their destruction: And their demons ' will lament their death.

"Then all the children ' of the light will be truly acquainted with the truth [15] and their root, and the father ' of the entirety and the holy spirit: They will all say ' with a single voice, ' 'The father's truth is just, and the son ' presides over the entirety': And from everyone [20] unto the ages of ages, 'Holy – holy – holy! Amen!'" '

The Reality '
Of the Rulers

ON THE ORIGIN OF THE WORLD (II,5 AND XIII,2)

Introduced by

Hans-Gebhard Bethge

Translated by

Hans-Gebhard Bethge, Bentley Layton,
Societas Coptica Hierosolymitana

The text of this tractate is quite well preserved. It is a compendium of central gnostic ideas, especially on cogmogony, anthropogony, and eschatology. Based on various sources and traditions, the treatise is in part presented in a semischolarly style, with numerous etiologies and etymologies. It is in the form of an apologetic tract designed for public effectiveness in attracting adherents. Earthly history, but also the presentation of the world above, including its development, are largely ignored. On the basis of the unnamed and unknown author's intention, stated at the beginning and then carried through in the text itself, scholarship has assigned the document the hypothetical title *On the Origin of the World*.

There are good reasons to assume that we have to do with a conscious, wellplanned literary composition without extensive secondary alterations, rather than with the product of a rather long process in the transmission of tradition. The early fourth century could possibly be the time of composition. The remarkable mixture of various kinds of Jewish views, Manichaean elements, Christian ideas, Greek philosophical conceptions, and figures of Greek or Hellenistic mythology, magic, and astrology, as well as a clear emphasis on Egyptian thought, all point to Alexandria as the probable place of origin for the Greek original of *On the Origin of the World*. The process of translating into Coptic may have involved several stages. The seemingly corrupt condition of many passages that invite emendation, along with other difficult, often barely intelligible, parts could be explained by assuming that the text as it lies before us still represents a provisional stage in the process of translation. *On the Origin of the World* would thus be an "opus imperfectum" (B. Layton).

The author uses various sources and traditions, some gnostic, some not, that are difficult to define more closely in terms of literary criticism, much less to reconstruct. In the process there are on occasion tensions, unevenness, and contradictions, since at least a few of these traditions or works presuppose a very special system all their own, or contain other tendencies, e.g., Sethian, or Valentinian, or even Manichaean. *On the Origin of the World* itself offers no closed system of its own, nor does it represent one of the known gnostic systems. The author works with direct or indirect quotations, references, summaries, explanations, and etymologies, which stand in sharp contrast to the otherwise dominant narrative style. This way of working, defending one's own view by appeal or reference to other works, is intended as a demonstration of a substantive and convincing argumentation. *On the Origin of the World* has many parallels with *The Hypostasis of the Archons*, indicating a close relation between the two texts. Yet the dissimilar nature of both documents, the diverging world views, and numerous differences in details, indicate that direct literary relationships are rather improbable. The parallelism probably results from the use of the same source material.

The cosmogony and anthropogony that follow upon the semi-philosophical beginning are in part oriented to Genesis 1-2, but beyond that to concepts such as those known from Jubilees or the Enoch literature. In general, characteristically Jewish influences dominate, e.g., in the angelology, demonology, and eschatology, as well as in etymologies. The gnostic reinterpretation of the received material varies considerably. It extends from complete reevaluation, e.g., in the case of the demiurge's presumption (making use of Is 45:5; 46:9 LXX), and what took place in Genesis 3, on to relatively unbroken appropriation of Jewish ideas and motifs, such as the presentation of paradise.

The primordial history emphasizes the creation of the earthly man by the Archons, in connection with the doctrine of the primal man, which to be sure is hard to understand, due to varying motifs and heterogeneous concepts. On the other hand, the primordial history initiates already the story of redemption on the part of Pistis Sophia or Sophia Zoe, who are encountered or act in various ways. In this complex soteriology, however, Jesus Christ has no central function, but rather a marginal role. For these reasons *On the Origin of the World* belongs to the gnostic Nag Hammadi texts that are essentially non-Christian.

On the Origin of the World is oriented towards universal eschatology. This is shown by the many allusions to the end, as well as by the broad presentation of the final events with a massive appropriation of thoughts, terms, and motifs from apocalypticism. The final state, brought about by the higher world, distinguishing the redemption of the gnostics from the destruction of the creation together with its creator, surpasses the primal condition, and renders impossible a repetition of events such as these presented in *On the Origin of the World*.

On the Origin of the World is a significant gnostic work. We attain through this relatively long document a good insight into an educated author's thinking, work habits, and argumentation on fundamental themes. Furthermore, *On the Origin of the World* shows to what a high degree and with what freedom and authority a gnostic author makes use of foreign, even non-gnostic and heterogenous thoughts. It thus attests the greater importance ascribed to the gnostic stance toward the world and existence than to its mythological formulation. *On the Origin of the World* can help us understand how the gnostic world view, in debate with other intellectual currents, but also making use of them, could maintain itself or perhaps at times even win the field.

ON THE ORIGIN OF THE WORLD

II 97, 24-127, 17

Seeing that everybody, gods of the world [25] and mankind, says that nothing [1] existed prior to chaos, I [1] in distinction to them shall demonstrate that they are ' all mistaken, because they are not acquainted with the origin ' of chaos, nor with its root. Here is the demonstration. [30] How well it suits **98** all men, on the subject of chaos, to say that ' it is a kind of darkness! But in fact it comes from a shadow, ' which has been called by the name darkness. And the shadow ' comes from a product that has existed [5] since the beginning. It is, moreover, clear that it (viz., the product) ' existed before chaos came into being, and that the latter ' is posterior to the first product.

Let us therefore concern ourselves ' with the facts of the matter; and furthermore, with the first ' product, from which chaos was projected. [10] And in this way the truth will be clearly demonstrated. '

After the natural structure of the immortal beings ' had completely developed out of the infinite, ' a likeness then emanated from Pistis (Faith); ' it is called Sophia (Wisdom). It exercised volition [15] and became a product resembling ' the primeval light. And ' immediately her will manifested itself ' as a likeness of heaven, having ' an unimaginable magnitude; [20] it was between the immortal beings and those things that ' came into being after them, like ... : she (Sophia) ' functioned as a veil dividing ' mankind from the things above.

Now the eternal realm (aeon) ' of truth has no shadow outside it, [25] for the limitless light is everywhere ' within it. But its exterior is shadow, ' which has been called by the name darkness. From ' it there appeared a force, presiding over ' the darkness. And the forces [30] that came into being subsequent to them called the shadow ' "the limitless chaos." From it, ' every [kind] of divinity sprouted up ' ... together with the entire place, [so that] ' also, [shadow] is posterior to the first **99** product. It was ⟨in⟩ the abyss that [it] (shadow) appeared, ' deriving from the aforementioned Pistis.

Then ' shadow perceived that there was something ' mightier than it, and felt envy; and when it had become pregnant [15] of its own accord, suddenly it ' engendered jealousy. Since that day, ' the principle of jealousy amongst ' all the eternal realms and their worlds has been apparent. Now as for that jealousy, ' it was found to be an abortion without [10] any spirit in it. Like a shadow it came into existence ' in a vast watery substance. Then ' the bile that had come into being out of the shadow ' was thrown into a part of chaos. ' Since that day, a watery substance [15] has been apparent. And what sank within ' it flowed away, being visible ' in chaos: as with a woman giving birth to a child ' — all her superfluities flow out; ' just so, matter came into being out of [20] shadow and was projected apart. And it (viz., matter) did not ' depart from chaos; rather, matter was in chaos, ' being in a part of it. '

And when these things had come to pass, then Pistis came ' and appeared over the matter of [25] chaos, which had been expelled like an ' aborted fetus – since there was no spirit in it. For all of it (viz., chaos) ' was limitless darkness ' and bottomless water. ' Now when Pistis saw what had resulted [30] from her defect, she became disturbed. ' And the disturbance appeared, as a ' fearful product; it rushed [to] her in ' the chaos. She turned to it and [blew] into ' its face in the abyss, which is below **100** all the heavens.

And when Pistis ' Sophia desired to cause the thing ' that had no spirit to be formed into a likeness ' and to rule over matter and over all her [5] forces, there appeared for the first time ' a ruler, out of the waters, ' lionlike in appearance, androgynous, ' having great authority within ' him, and ignorant of whence he had come into being. [10] Now when Pistis Sophia ' saw him moving about in the depth of the waters ' she said to him, "Child, ' pass through to here," whose equivalent is *"yalda baōth."*

Since that day there appeared the principle [15] of verbal expression, which reached ' the gods and the angels and mankind. ' And what came into being as a result of verbal expression, ' the gods and the angels and mankind finished. ' Now as for the ruler Yaltabaoth, [20] he is ignorant of the force of Pistis: ' he did not see her face, rather he saw ' in the water the likeness that spoke with him. ' And because of that voice, he called ' himself Yaldabaoth. But [25] Ariael is what the perfect call him, for he was like ' a lion. Now when he had come to have authority over matter, ' Pistis Sophia withdrew up ' to her light.

When the ruler saw [30] his magnitude – and it was only himself ' that he saw: he saw nothing else, ' except for water and darkness – then he supposed ' that it was he alone who existed. His ' [. . .] was completed by verbal expression: it **101** appeared as a spirit moving to and fro ' upon the waters. And when that spirit ' appeared, the ruler set apart the watery substance. ' And what was dry [5] was divided into another place. And from matter ' he made for himself an abode, and he called ' it heaven. And from matter, ' the ruler made a footstool, ' and he called it earth.

Next, [10] the ruler had a thought – consistent with his nature – and ' by means of verbal expression he created an androgyne. ' He opened his mouth and cooed to ' him. When his eyes had been opened, he looked ' at his father, and he said to him, "Eee!" Then his [15] father called him Eee-a-o (Yao). Next he ' created the second son. He cooed ' to him. And he opened his eyes and said ' to his father, "Eh!" His father called ' him Eloai. Next he created [20] the third son. He cooed to him. And he opened his ' eyes and said to his father, "Asss!" His ' father called him Astaphaios. These ' are the three sons of their father. '

Seven appeared in chaos, androgynous. [25] They have their masculine names ' and their feminine names. The feminine name ' is Pronoia (Forethought) Sambathas, which ' is "week." And his son is called ' Yao: his feminine name is Lordship. [30]

Sabaoth: his feminine name is Deity. '

Adonaios: his feminine name is Kingship. '

Eloaios: his feminine name is Jealousy. '

Oraios: his feminine name is Wealth. '

And Astaphaios: his feminine name **102** is Sophia (Wisdom). These are the [seven] forces ' of the seven heavens of [chaos]. And they were born ' androgynous, consistent with the immortal pattern ' that existed before them, according to the wish [5] of Pistis: so that the likeness of what had ' existed since the beginning might reign to ' the end.

You (sg.) will find the effect of these names ' and the force of the male entities in the *Archangelic (Book)* ' *of the Prophet Moses*, and the [10] names of the female entities in the first *Book (biblos)* ' *of Noraia.*

Now the prime parent Yaldabaoth, ' since he possessed great authorities, ' created heavens for each of his ' offspring through verbal expression — created them beautiful, as dwelling places [15] — and in each heaven he created great glories, ' seven times excellent. Thrones and ' mansions and temples, and also ' chariots and virgin spirits up ' to an invisible one and their glories, each one [20] has these in his heaven; mighty ' armies of gods and lords and angels ' and archangels — countless myriads ' — so that they might serve.

The account of these matters you (sg.) will find ' in a precise manner in the first *Account* [25] *of Oraia.*

And they were completed from this heaven to as far up as ' the sixth heaven, namely that of Sophia. ' The heaven and his earth were destroyed by ' the troublemaker that was below them all. ' And the six heavens shook violently; [30] for the forces of chaos knew who it was ' that had destroyed the heaven that was below them. ' And when Pistis knew about the breakage ' resulting from the disturbance, she sent forth her breath and ' bound him and cast him down into Tartaros. [35] Since that day, the heaven, along with **103** its earth, has consolidated itself through Sophia the daughter of Yaldabaoth, ' she who is below them all. '

Now when the heavens had consolidated themselves along with their forces ¹ and all their administration, the prime parent ⁵ became insolent. And he was honored by ¹ all the army of angels. And ¹ all the gods and their angels ¹ gave blessing and honor to him. And for his part he ¹ was delighted and continually boasted, ¹⁰ saying to them, ¹ "I have no need of anyone." He said, ¹ "It is I who am God, and there is no other one that exists ¹ apart from me." And when he said this, he sinned against ¹ all the immortal beings who give answer. And they laid it ¹⁵ to his charge.

Then when Pistis saw the impiety ¹ of the chief ruler she was filled with anger. ¹ She was invisible. She said, "You are mistaken, ¹ Samael," that is, "blind god." ¹ "There is an immortal man of light who ²⁰ has been in existence before you and who will appear ¹ among your modelled forms; he will trample you to scorn ¹ just as potter's clay is pounded. And you will descend ¹ to your mother, the abyss, along with those that belong to you. ²⁵ For at the consummation of your (pl.) works ¹ the entire defect that has become visible ¹ out of the truth will be abolished, and it will cease to be and will be ¹ like what has never been." ¹ Saying this, Pistis revealed ³⁰ her likeness of her greatness in the waters. And ¹ so doing she withdrew up ¹ to her light.

Now when Sabaoth the son ¹ of Yaldabaoth heard the ¹ voice of Pistis, he sang praises to her, and [he] ³⁵ condemned the father ... **104** at the word of Pistis; and he praised her ¹ because she had instructed them about the immortal man ¹ and his light. Then Pistis Sophia ¹ stretched out her finger and poured upon him ⁵ some light from her light, to be a condemnation ¹ of his father. Then when Sabaoth ¹ was illumined, he received great authority ¹ against all the forces of chaos. ¹ Since that day he has been called ¹⁰ "Lord of the Forces."

He hated his father, the darkness, ¹ and his mother, the abyss, and loathed ¹ his sister, the thought of the prime parent, ¹ which moved to and fro upon the waters. And because of ¹ his light all the authorities of chaos were jealous ¹⁵ of him. And when they had become disturbed, ¹ they made a great war in the seven ¹ heavens. Then when Pistis Sophia ¹ had seen the war, she dispatched ¹ seven archangels to Sabaoth from her light. ²⁰ They snatched him up to the seventh ¹ heaven. They stood before him as attendants. ¹ Furthermore she sent him three more ¹ archangels and established the kingdom for him ¹ over everyone so that he might dwell ²⁵ above the twelve gods ¹ of chaos.

Now when Sabaoth had taken up the place ¹ of repose in return for his repentance, ¹ Pistis also gave him her daughter Zoe (Life) ¹ together with great authority so that she might ³⁰ instruct him about all things that exist in the eighth heaven. ¹ And as he had authority, ¹ he made himself first of all a mansion. ¹ It is huge, magnificent, ¹ seven times as great as all those that exist ³⁵ in the seven heavens.

And before **105** his mansion he created a throne, ¹ which was huge and was upon a ¹ four-faced chariot called ¹ "Cherubin." Now the Cherubin has ⁵ eight shapes per each of ¹ the four corners, lion forms and ¹ calf forms and human forms ¹ and eagle forms, so that all the forms ¹ amount to sixty-four forms ¹⁰ − and (he created) seven archangels that stand ¹ before it; he is the eighth, and has ¹ authority. All the forms amount to ¹ seventy-two. Furthermore, from this chariot ¹ the seventy-two gods took shape; ¹⁵ they took shape so that they might rule over the seventy-two ¹ languages of the peoples. And by that throne ¹ he created other, ¹ serpent-like angels, called ¹ "Saraphin," which praise him at all times. ²⁰

Thereafter he created a congregation (*ekklesia*) of angels, thousands and myriads, numberless, ¹ which resembled the congregation in ¹ the eighth heaven; and a firstborn ¹ called Israel − which ²⁵ is, "the man that sees God"; and another being, ¹ called Jesus Christ, who resembles the savior ¹ above in the eighth heaven and who ¹ sits at his right upon a ¹ revered throne, and at his left, there ³⁰ sits the virgin of the holy spirit, ¹ upon a throne and glorifying him. ¹ And the seven virgins stand before her, ¹ ... possessing thirty harps, ¹ and psalteries and **106** trumpets, glorifying him. And ¹ all the armies of the angels glorify him, ¹ and they bless him. Now where he sits is upon a ¹ throne of light ⟨within a⟩ great cloud that covers ⁵ him. And there was no one with him ¹ in the cloud except Sophia ⟨the daughter of⟩ Pistis, ¹ instructing him about all the things that exist in the eighth heaven, ¹ so that the likenesses of those things might be created, ¹ in order that his reign might endure ¹⁰ until the consummation of the heavens of chaos ¹ and their forces.

Now Pistis Sophia ¹ set him apart from the darkness and summoned him to her right, ¹ and the prime parent she put at her left. ¹ Since that day, right has been called ¹⁵ justice, and left called ¹ wickedness. Now because of this they all received ¹ a realm (*kosmos*) in the congregation of justice ¹ and wickedness, ... stand ... upon a creature ... ¹ all.

Thus when the prime parent of chaos ²⁰ saw his son Sabaoth and the glory ¹ that he was in, and perceived that he was greatest of all the authorities ¹ of chaos, he envied him. And ¹ having become wrathful he engendered Death out of his ¹ death: and he (viz., Death) was established over the sixth ²⁵ heaven, ⟨for⟩ Sabaoth had been snatched up from there. | And thus the number | of the six authorities of chaos was achieved. Then Death, | being androgynous, mingled with his (own) nature | and begot seven androgynous offspring. [30] These are the names of the male ones: Jealousy, Wrath, | Tears, Sighing, Suffering, Lamentation, | Bitter Weeping. And these are the names | of the female ones: Wrath, Pain, Lust, | Sighing, Curse, Bitterness, Quarrelsomeness. [35] They had intercourse with one another, and each | one begot seven, so that they amount to **107** forty-nine androgynous demons. |

Their names and their effects you will find | in the *Book of Solomon.* |

And in the presence of these, Zoe, who [15] was with Sabaoth, created seven | good androgynous forces. | These are the names of the male ones: the Unenvious, | the Blessed, the Joyful, the True, | the Unbegrudging, the Beloved, [10] the Trustworthy. Also, as regards the female ones, these are their | names: Peace, Gladness, Rejoicing, Blessedness, | Truth, Love, Faith (Pistis). And | from these there are many good | and innocent spirits.

Their influences [15] and their effects you will find in | the *Configurations of the Fate of Heaven That Is | Beneath the Twelve.* |

And having seen the likeness | of Pistis in the waters, the prime parent grieved very much, [20] especially when he heard her voice, | like the first voice that had | called to him out of the waters. And | when he knew that it was she who had given a name | to him, he sighed. He was ashamed on account of his [25] transgression. And when he had come to know in truth | that an immortal man | of light had been existing before him, he was greatly disturbed; | for he had previously said | to all the gods and their angels, [30] "It is I who am god. No other one | exists apart from me." For he had been afraid | they might know that another | had been in existence before him, and might condemn him. But he, being devoid of understanding, [35] scoffed at the condemnation | and acted recklessly. He said, "If **108** anything has existed before me, let it appear, | so that we may see its light."

And | immediately, behold! Light came out of the eighth heaven | above and passed through all of the heavens [5] of the earth. When the prime parent saw that the light was beautiful as it radiated, | he was amazed. And he was greatly ashamed. As | that light appeared, a human likeness | appeared within it, very wonderful. [10] And no one saw it except for | the prime parent and Pronoia, | who was with him. Yet its light appeared | to all the forces of the heavens. Because of this | they were all troubled by it.

Then [15] when Pronoia saw that emissary, she became enamored of him. | But he hated her because she was on the darkness. | But she desired to embrace him, and she was not | able to. When she was unable to assuage her love, | she poured out her light upon the earth. Since [20] that day, that emissary has been called | "Adam of Light," whose rendering | is "the luminous man of blood," and the earth spread over him, holy Adaman, | whose rendering is "the Holy Land of Adamantine." [25] Since that day, | all the authorities have honored the blood of the virgin. | And the earth was purified on account of | the blood of the virgin. But most of all, | the water was purified through the likeness of Pistis [30] Sophia, who had appeared to | the prime parent in the waters. | Justly, then, it has been said: "through the waters." | The holy water, since it vivifies the all, **109** purifies it.

Out of that first blood | Eros appeared, being androgynous. | His masculinity is Himireris (i.e., Himeros), being | fire from the light. His femininity, [5] that is with him — a soul of blood — is from | the stuff of Pronoia. He is very lovely | in his beauty, having a charm beyond | all the creatures of chaos. Then all the gods | and their angels, when they beheld [10] Eros, became enamored of him. And appearing | in all of them he set them afire: just as | from a single lamp many lamps | are lit, and one and the same light is there, but the lamp | is not diminished. And in this way Eros [15] became dispersed in all the created beings of chaos, | and was not diminished. Just as from | the midpoint of light and darkness | Eros appeared and at the midpoint | of the angels and mankind [20] the sexual union of Eros was consummated, so | out of the earth the primal pleasure blossomed. | The woman followed earth. | And marriage followed woman. | Birth followed marriage. Dissolution [25] followed birth.

After that Eros, | the grapevine sprouted up | out of that blood, which had been shed over | the earth. Because of this, those who drink of it | conceive the desire of sexual union. [30] After the grapevine, a fig tree | and a pomegranate tree sprouted up from | the earth, together with the rest of the trees, | all species, having | within them their seed from the **110** seed of the authorities and their angels. |

Then Justice created Paradise, | being beautiful and being outside the orbit | of the moon and the orbit of the sun in [15] the Land of Wantonness, in the East in the midst | of the stones. And desire is in the midst of | the beautiful, appetizing trees. And | the tree of eternal life is as it | appeared by God's will, [10] to the north of Paradise, so that it might make | eternal the souls of the pure, | who shall come forth from the modelled forms of poverty | at the consummation of the age. Now the color ' of the tree of life is like the sun. And [15] its branches are beautiful. Its leaves are like ' those of the cypress. Its fruit is like ' a bunch of grapes when it is white. Its height ' goes as far as heaven. And next to it (is) the tree ' of acquaintance (*gnosis*), having the strength [20] of God. Its glory is like the moon ' when fully radiant. And its branches are beautiful. ' Its leaves are like fig leaves. ' Its fruit is like a good appetizing date. ' And this tree is to the north of Paradise, [25] so that it might arouse the souls from ' the torpor of the demons, in order that they might approach ' the tree of life and eat of ' its fruit and so condemn the ' authorities and their angels.

The effect [30] of this tree is described in the *Sacred Book*, ' to wit: "It is you who are the tree of acquaintance, ' which is in Paradise, from which the first ' man ate and which opened his mind; ' and he loved his female counterpart and condemned **111** the other, alien likenesses and loathed them." '

Now after it, the olive tree sprouted up, ' which was to purify the kings and the ' high priests of righteousness, who were to [5] appear in the last days, since ' the olive tree appeared out of the light ' of the first Adam for the sake of the unguent ' that they were to receive.

And the first soul (*psyche*) loved ' Eros, who was with her, and poured her blood [10] upon him and upon the earth. ' And out of that blood the rose first sprouted up, ' out of the earth, out of ' the thorn bush, to be a source of joy for the light that ' was to appear in the bush. [15] Moreover after this the beautiful, good-smelling flowers ' sprouted up from the earth, ' different kinds, from every single virgin ' of the daughters of Pronoia. ' And they, when they had become enamored of Eros, poured out [20] their blood upon him and upon the earth. ' After these, every plant sprouted up ' from the earth, different kinds, containing ' the seed of the authorities and their ' angels. After these, the authorities [25] created out of the waters all species of beast, ' and the reptiles and birds – different kinds – containing ' the seed of the authorities and their angels. '

But before all these, when he had appeared [30] on the first day, he remained upon the earth, something like two days, and ' left the lower Pronoia in ' heaven, and ascended towards his light. And ' immediately darkness covered all the universe. **112** Now when she wished, the Sophia who was in the lower heaven ' received authority from ' Pistis, and fashioned great luminous bodies ' and all the stars. And she put them in the sky to [5] shine upon the earth and to render ' temporal signs and seasons and ' years and months and days ' and nights and moments and so forth. [|] And in this way the entire region upon the sky was adorned. [10]

Now when Adam of Light conceived the wish [|] to enter his light —
i.e., [|] the eighth heaven — he was unable to do so because of [|] the
poverty that had mingled with his light. Then [|] he created for himself a
vast eternal realm. And within [15] that eternal realm he created six eternal
realms [|] and their adornments, six in number, that were seven times bet-
ter [|] than the heavens of chaos and their adornments. [|] Now all these
eternal realms and their [|] adornments exist within the infinity [20] that is
between the eighth heaven and the chaos below [|] it, being counted with
the universe that belongs to [|] poverty.

If you (sg.) want to know the arrangement [|] of these, you will find it
written in the *Seventh [|] Universe of the Prophet Hieralias.* [25]

And before Adam of Light had [|] withdrawn in the chaos, the
authorities saw him [|] and laughed at the prime parent because he had [|]
lied when he said, "It is I who am God. [|] No one exists before me."
When they came to [30] him, they said, "Is this not the god who [|] ruined
our work?" He answered and said, [|] "Yes. If you do not want him to
be able [|] to ruin our work, come let us [|] create a man (i.e., human be-
ing) out of earth, according to [35] the image of our body and according
to the likeness **113** of this being (viz., Adam of Light), to serve us; so that
when he (viz., Adam of Light) [|] sees his likeness he might become
enamored of it. No longer will he [|] ruin our work; rather, [|] we shall
make those who are born out of the light our servants [5] for all the dura-
tion of this eternal realm. Now all of this [|] came to pass according to
the forethought of Pistis, [|] in order that man should appear after [|] his
likeness, and should condemn them [|] because of their modelled form.
And their modelled form [10] became an enclosure of the light.

Then the authorities [|] received the acquaintance (*gnosis*) necessary to
create [|] man. Sophia [|] Zoe — she who is with Sabaoth — had anticipat-
ed them. And she laughed [|] at their decision. For they are blind: [15]
against their own interests they ignorantly created him. [|] And they do
not realise what they are about to do. [|] The reason she anticipated them
and made her own man (i.e., human being) [|] first, was in order that he
might instruct [|] their modelled form how to despise [20] them and thus to
escape from them. [|]

Now the production of the instructor came about [|] as follows. When
Sophia let fall a droplet [|] of light, it flowed onto the water, [|] and imme-
diately a human being appeared, being androgynous. [25] That droplet she
molded [|] first as a female body. Afterwards, [|] using the body she
molded it [|] in the likeness of the mother which had appeared. [|] And he

finished it in twelve months. [30] An androgynous human being was produced, | whom the Greeks call Hermaphrodites; | and whose mother the Hebrews call | Eve of Life (Eve of Zoe), namely, the female instructor | of life. Her offspring is the creature [35] that is lord. Afterwards, the authorities **114** called it "Beast," so that it might lead astray | their modelled creatures. The interpretation of "the beast" | is "the instructor." For it was found to be the wisest | of all beings.

Now, Eve is the first [5] virgin, the one who without a husband bore her first offspring. | It is she who served as her own midwife.

For | this reason she is held to have said: |

"It is I who am the part of my mother;
And it is I who am | the mother;
It is I who am the wife;
It is I who am the virgin; [10]
It is I who am pregnant;
It is I who am the midwife;
It is I who am the one that | comforts pains of travail;
It is my husband who bore me;
And | it is I who am his mother,
And it is he who is my father | and my lord.
It is he who is my force;
What he desires, | he says with reason.
I am in the process of becoming.
Yet [15] I have borne a man as lord."

Now these through the will | ⟨...⟩. The souls | that were going to enter the modelled forms of the authorities were manifested to Sabaoth and his Christ. | And regarding these the holy voice | said, "Multiply and improve! Be lord [20] over all creatures." And it is they who were | taken captive, according to their destinies, by | the prime parent. And thus | they were shut into the prisons of the modelled forms. | Or: at the consummation of the age. And at that time, [25] the prime parent | then rendered an opinion concerning man to those who were with him. | Then each of them cast | his sperm into the midst of the navel of | the earth. Since that day, the seven rulers [30] have fashioned man with his body | resembling their body, but his likeness | resembling the man that had appeared to them. | His modelling took place by parts, | one at a time. And their leader fashioned [35] the brain and the nervous system. Afterwards | he appeared as prior to him. He became **115** a soul-endowed man. And he was called | Adam, that is, "father," according to | the name of the one that existed before him.

And when they had finished | Adam, he abandoned him as an inanimate vessel, since he had taken form [5] like an abortion, in that no spirit was in him. | Regarding this thing, when the chief ruler | remembered the saying of Pistis, he was afraid | lest the true man enter his | modelled form and become its lord. For this reason he [10] left his modelled form forty days without | soul, and he withdrew and abandoned it. Now on the fortieth | day, Sophia Zoe sent | her breath into Adam, who had no | soul. He began to move upon the ground. [15] And he could not stand up.

Then when the seven | rulers came, they saw him and | were greatly disturbed. They went up to | him and seized him. And he (viz., the chief ruler) said to | the breath within him, "Who are you? And [20] whence did you come hither?" It answered | and said, "I have come from the force | of the man for the destruction of your work." | ⟨...⟩ When they heard, they glorified him, since he | gave them respite from the fear and the anxiety in which they found themselves. [25] Then they called that day | "Rest," in as much as they had rested | from toil. And when they saw that Adam | could not stand up, they were glad, and they took him | and put him in Paradise. And they withdrew [30] up to their heavens.

After | the day of rest Sophia | sent her daughter Zoe, being called | Eve, as an instructor in order that she might | make Adam, who had no soul, arise [35] so that those whom he should engender might become | containers of light. When **116** Eve saw her male counterpart prostrate she had pity | upon him, and she said, "Adam! Become alive! | Arise upon the earth!" Immediately her word | became accomplished fact. For Adam, having [5] arisen, suddenly opened his eyes. | When he saw her he said, "You shall be called | 'Mother of the Living'. For it is you who have | given me life."

Then the authorities were informed | that their modelled form was alive and had arisen, and they [10] were greatly troubled. They sent seven archangels | to see what had happened. They came | to Adam. When they saw Eve talking to | him they said to one another, "What sort of thing is this luminous woman? | For she resembles that likeness which appeared [15] to us in the light. Now come, | let us lay hold of her and cast our | seed into her, so that when she becomes soiled | she may not be able to ascend into her light. | Rather, those whom she bears will be under [20] our charge. But let us not tell Adam, for he is not one | of us. Rather let us bring a deep sleep | over him. And let us instruct him in his | sleep to the effect that she came from | his rib, in order that his wife may obey, [25] and he may be lord over her."

Then Eve, ' being a force, laughed at their decision. ' She put mist into their eyes and secretly left ' her likeness with Adam. She entered ' the
tree of acquaintance and remained there. [30] And they pursued her, and
she revealed ' to them that she had gone into the tree and become ' a
tree. Then, entering a great ' state of fear, the blind creatures fled.

Afterwards, ' when they had recovered from the daze, they came [35]
[to Adam]; and seeing the likeness of this woman **117** with him, they were
greatly disturbed, thinking it was she ' that was the true Eve. And they
acted rashly; they came ' up to her and seized her and cast ' their seed
upon her. They did so [5] wickedly, defiling not only ' in natural ways but
also in foul ways, ' defiling first the seal of her voice ' – that had
spoken with them, saying, "What is it that exists ' before you?" – in-
tending to defile those who might say [10] at the consummation (viz., of
the age) that they had been born ' of the true man through verbal expression. ' And they erred, not knowing ' that it was their own body
that they had defiled: it was the likeness that ' the authorities and their
angels defiled in every way. [15]

First she was pregnant with Abel, ' by the first ruler. And it was ' by
the seven authorities and their angels ' that she bore the other offspring.
And all this ' came to pass according to the forethought of the prime
parent, [20] so that the first mother ' might bear within her every seed, '
being mixed and being fitted to the fate ' of the universe and its confi-
gurations, and ' to Justice. A prearranged plan came into effect [25] regarding Eve, so that the modelled forms of the authorities ' might
become enclosures of the light, whereupon ' it (viz., the light) would
condemn them through their ' modelled forms.

Now the first Adam, (Adam) of Light, ' is spirit-endowed (*pneumati-
kos*), and appeared [30] on the first day. The second ' Adam is soul-
endowed (*psychikos*), and appeared ' on the sixth day, which is called
Aphrodite. The third ' Adam is a creature of the earth (*choikos*), that
is, [35] the man of the law, and he appeared on ' the eighth day [... the]
tranquility **118** of poverty, which is called ' Sunday. And the progeny of
the ' earthly Adam became numerous and was completed, ' and produced within itself every kind of scientific information of [5] the soul-
endowed Adam. But all were in ' ignorance.

Next let me say ' that once the rulers had seen him and ' the female
creature who was with him erring ignorantly ' like beasts, they were
very glad. [10] ⟨...⟩ When they learned that the immortal man was not
going to ' neglect them, rather that they would even have to fear ' the
female creature that had turned into a tree, they were disturbed, and said,

¹ "Perhaps this is the true man ¹ — this being who has brought a fog upon us and ¹⁵ has taught us that she who was soiled is like ¹ him — and so we shall be conquered!"

Then ¹ the seven of them together laid plans. They came up to Adam ¹ and Eve timidly: they said to him, ¹ "The fruit of all the trees created for you in Paradise ²⁰ shall be eaten; but as for the tree ¹ of acquaintance, control yourselves and do not eat ¹ from it. If you eat you ¹ will die." Having imparted great fear to them ¹ they withdrew up to their authorities.

Then ²⁵ came the wisest of all creatures, ¹ who was called Beast. ¹ And when he saw the likeness of their mother ¹ Eve he said to her, "What did God ¹ say to you (pl.)? Was it 'do not eat from the tree ³⁰ of acquaintance (*gnosis*)'?" She said, "He said, 'Not only ¹ do not eat from it, but ¹ do not touch it, lest you (sg.) die'." He said ¹ to her, "Do not be afraid. In death you (pl.) shall not ¹ die. For he knows that when you eat **119** from it, your intellect will become sober and ¹ you will come to be like gods, ¹ recognizing the difference that obtains between evil ¹ men and good ones. ⁵ Indeed, it was in jealousy that he said this to you, so that you ¹ would not eat from it."

Now Eve had confidence ¹ in the words of the instructor. She gazed ¹ at the tree and saw that it was beautiful and ¹ appetizing, and liked it; she took some of ¹⁰ its fruit and ate it; and she gave some also to her ¹ husband, and he too ate it. Then their intellect ¹ became open. For when they had eaten, the light of ¹ acquaintance had shone upon them. When they clothed ¹ themselves with shame, they knew that they were naked ¹⁵ of acquaintance. When they became sober, they saw that ¹ they were naked and became enamored of one another. When ¹ they saw that the ones who had modelled them had the form ¹ of beasts, they loathed them: they were very aware. ¹

Then when the rulers knew that they had broken ²⁰ their commandments, they entered Paradise ¹ and came to Adam and Eve with earthquake and great threatening, ¹ to see ¹ the effect of the aid. Then ¹ Adam and Eve trembled greatly ²⁵ and hid under the trees in Paradise. ¹ Then the rulers did not know where they were ¹ and said, "Adam, where are you?" He said, "I am here, ¹ for through fear of you I hid, ¹ being ashamed." And they said to him ignorantly, ³⁰ "Who told you about ¹ the shame with which you clothed yourself? — unless ¹ you have eaten from that tree!" He said, ¹ "The woman whom you gave me — it is she that ¹ gave to me and I ate." Then they said to the latter, **120** "What is this that you have done?" She answered and said, ¹ "It is the instructor that urged me on, and I ¹ ate."

Then the rulers came up to the instructor. ' Their eyes became misty because of him, [5] and they could not do anything to him. They cursed him, ' since they were powerless. Afterwards, they came up to the woman ' and cursed her and her offspring. After ' the woman, they cursed Adam, and (cursed) the land because of him, ' and the crops; and all things that they had created [10] they cursed. They have no blessing. ' Good cannot result from ' evil.

From that day, the authorities ' knew that truly there was something mightier than ' they: they recognized only that [15] their commandments had not been kept. Great ' jealousy was brought into the world solely because of ' the immortal man. Now when the rulers saw ' that their Adam had entered into an alien state of acquaintance they ' desired to test him, and they gathered together [20] all the domestic animals and the wild beasts ' of the earth and the birds of heaven and brought them to Adam ' to see what he would call them. ' When he saw them he gave names to their ' creatures.

They became troubled because Adam had recovered from [25] all the trials. They assembled and ' laid plans, and they said, "Behold Adam! ' He has come to be like one of us, so that he ' knows the difference between the light and the darkness. ' Now perhaps he will be deceived as in the case of [35] the tree of acquaintance and also will come to ' the tree of life and eat from it ' and become immortal and become lord and despise ' us and disdain [us] and all our glory. ' Then he will denounce [35] [us along with our] universe. Come let us expel him **121** from Paradise down to the land ' from which he was taken, so that henceforth he might not ' be able to recognize anything better ' than we can."And so they expelled Adam from [5] Paradise, along with his wife. And this deed ' that they had done was not enough for them. Rather, they were afraid. ' They went in to the tree of life and surrounded it ' with great fearful things, fiery living creatures ' called "Cheroubin," and they put [10] a flaming sword in their midst, fearfully ' twirling at all times, so that ' no earthly being might ever enter ' that place.

Thereupon ' since the rulers were envious of Adam they wanted to diminish [15] their (viz., Adam's and Eve's) lifespans. They could not because of ' fate, which had been fixed since the beginning. ' For to each had been alotted a lifespan ' of 1,000 years according to the course of the luminous bodies. ' But although the rulers could not [20] do this, each of the evil doers ' took away ten years. ' And all this lifespan (which remained) amounted to 930 years: and these are in pain and ' weakness and evil [25] distraction. And so ' life has turned out to be, from that day until the consummation ' of the age.

Then when Sophia Zoe ' saw that the rulers of the darkness had ' laid a curse upon her counterparts, she was indignant. [30] And coming out of the first heaven with ' full power she chased those rulers out of ' [their] heavens, and cast them down into ' the sinful [world], so that there they ' should dwell, in the form of evil [35] spirits (*daimones*) upon the earth.

[...], **122** so that in their world it might pass the thousand years in Paradise ' − a soul-endowed living creature ' called "phoenix." It ' kills itself and brings itself to life as a witness [5] to the judgment against them, for they did wrong to Adam and his ' generation, unto the consummation of the age. ⟨...⟩ There are ... three ' men, and also his posterities unto the consummation ' of the world: the spirit-endowed of eternity, and the soul-endowed, and the earthly. Likewise, [10] the three phoenixes ⟨in⟩ Paradise − the first ' [is] immortal; the second lives 1,000 ' years; as for the third, it is written in the *Sacred Book* ' that it is consumed. So too there are ' three baptisms − the first is the spiritual, [15] the second is by fire, the third ' is by water. Just as the phoenix ' appears as a witness concerning the angels, ' so the case of the water hydri in Egypt, ' which has been a witness to those going down [20] into the baptism of a true man. ' The two bulls in Egypt possess ' a mystery, the sun and moon, being ' a witness to Sabaoth: namely, that over ' them Sophia received the universe; from [25] the day that she made the sun and the moon she ' put a seal upon her heaven, unto eternity. '

And the worm that has been born out of the phoenix ' is a human being as well. It is written (Ps 91:13 LXX) concerning it, "the just man ' will blossom like a phoenix." And [30] the phoenix first appears ' in a living state, and dies, and rises again, ' being a sign of what has become apparent ' at the consummation of the age. It was only in Egypt that these great signs appeared [35] − nowhere else − as an indication **123** that it is like God's Paradise. '

Let us return to the aforementioned rulers, ' so that we may offer ' some explanation of them. Now, when the seven rulers [5] were cast down from their heavens ' onto the earth, they made for themselves angels, ' numerous, demonic, to serve ' them. And the latter instructed mankind in many kinds of error ' and magic and potions and worship of [10] idols and spilling of blood and altars and ' temples and sacrifices and libations to all the spirits ' of the earth, having their coworker ' fate, who came into existence by ' the concord between the gods of injustice [15] and justice.

And thus when the world ' had come into being, it distractedly erred ' at all times. For all men ' upon earth worshipped the spirits (*daimo-*

nes) from ' the creation to the consummation − both the angels [20] of righteousness and the men of unrighteousness. ' Thus did the world come to exist in distraction, ' in ignorance, and in a stupor. ' They all erred, until the appearance (*parousia*) ' of the true man.

Let this suffice [25] so far as the matter goes. Now we shall proceed to consideration of our world, ' so that we may accurately finish the description of its structure ' and management. ' Then it will become obvious how ' belief in the unseen realm, which has been apparent [30] from creation down to the consummation ' of the age was discovered.

I come, therefore, to the main points ' [regarding] the immortal man: I shall ' speak of all the beings that belong to him, explaining how ' they happen to be here.

When a multitude [35] of human beings had come into existence, through the parentage of [the Adam] **124** who had been fashioned, and out of matter, ' and when the world had already become full, the rulers were master ' over it − that is, they kept ' it restrained by ignorance. For what reason? [5] For the following: since the immortal father knows ' that a deficiency of truth came into being amongst the eternal realms ' and their universe, when he wished ' to bring to naught the rulers of perdition through the ' creatures they had modelled he sent your (pl.) likenesses down into the world [10] of perdition, namely, the blessed little ' innocent spirits. They are not alien to ' acquaintance. For all acquaintance is vested in one angel ' who appeared before them; he is not without power ' in the company of the father. And ⟨he⟩ gave them acquaintance. [15] Whenever they appear in the world ' of perdition, immediately and first of all they reveal [20] the pattern of imperishability as a condemnation ' of the rulers and their forces. Thus when the blessed beings ' appeared in forms modelled by authorities, ' they were envied. And out of envy the authorities ' mixed their seed with them, in hopes of [25] polluting them. They could not. Then when the blessed beings ' appeared in luminous form, ' they appeared in various ways. And each one ' of them, starting out in his land, revealed ' his (kind of) acquaintance to the visible church [30] constituted of the modelled forms of perdition. ' It (viz., the church) was found to contain all kinds of seed, because of the seed ' of the authorities that had [mixed with it].

Then ' the savior created [. . .] of ' them all − and the spirits of these [are manifestly] [35] superior, being blessed **125** and varying in election − and ' also (he created) many other beings, which have no king and are superior ' to everyone that was before them. Consequently, four ' races exist. There are three that belong to the kings [5] of the eighth heaven. But the fourth ' race is kingless and perfect, being ' the highest of all. For these shall enter ' the holy place of their father. ' And they will gain rest in repose ¹⁰ and eternal, unspeakable glory ' and unending joy. Moreover they are ' kings within the mortal domain, in that they are immortal. They ' will condemn the gods of chaos and ' their forces.

Now the Word (*Logos*) that is superior to ¹⁵ all beings was sent for this purpose alone: ' that he might proclaim the unknown. ' He said (Mk 4:22 par.), "There is nothing hidden that is ' not apparent, and what has not been recognized ' will be recognized." And these were sent ²⁰ to make known what is hidden, and ' the seven authorities of chaos and their ' impiety. And thus they were condemned ' to death.

So when all the perfect ' appeared in the forms modelled ²⁵ by the rulers and when they revealed ' the incomparable truth, ' they put to shame all the wisdom of the gods. ' And their fate was found ' to be a condemnation. And their force ³⁰ dried up. Their lordship was dissolved. ' Their forethought became [emptiness, ' along with] their glory.

Before the consummation ' [of the age], the whole place will shake ' with great thundering. Then the rulers ³⁵ will be sad, [...] their **126** death. The angels will mourn for their mankind, ' and the demons will weep over their seasons, ' and their mankind will wail and scream ' at their death. Then the age ⁵ will begin, and they will be disturbed. Their kings will ' be intoxicated with the fiery sword, and they will ' wage war against one another, so that ' the earth is intoxicated with bloodshed. ' And the seas will be disturbed by ¹⁰ those wars. Then the sun will become dark. ' And the moon will cause its light to cease. ' The stars of the sky will cancel their circuits. ' And a great clap of thunder will come out ' of a great force that is above ¹⁵ all the forces of chaos, where ' the firmament of the woman is situated. ' Having created the first product, she will ' put away the wise fire of intelligence ' and clothe herself with witless wrath. ²⁰ Then she will pursue the gods ' of chaos, whom she created along with the prime parent. ' She will cast them down into the abyss. ' They will be obliterated because of their wickedness. For they will ' come to be like volcanoes ²⁵ and consume one another until they perish ' at the hand of the prime parent. ' When he has destroyed them, he will turn against himself ' and destroy himself until he ceases to exist.

And ' their heavens will fall one upon the next ³⁰ and their (the rulers') forces will be consumed by fire. Their eternal realms, too, ' will be overturned. And his (the prime parent's) heaven will ' fall and break in two. His ... will ' fall down upon the [...] ' support them; they will fall into the abyss, ³⁵ and the abyss will be overturned.

The light will ¹ [. . . the] darkness and obliterate it: it will be like **127** something that has never been. And the product ¹ to which the darkness had been posterior will dissolve. And ¹ the deficiency will be plucked out by the root (and thrown) down into ¹ the darkness. And the light will withdraw up ⁵ to its root. And the glory of the unbegotten ¹ will appear. And it will fill ¹ all the eternal realm. When the prophecy and ¹ the account of those that are king becomes known and ¹ is fulfilled by those who are called ¹⁰ perfect, those who − in contrast − have not become perfect ¹ in the unbegotten father will receive their glory ¹ in their realms and in the kingdoms of the ¹ immortals: but they will never enter ¹ the kingless realm.

For everyone must ¹⁵ go to the place from which he has come. ¹ Indeed, by his acts and his ¹ acquaintance each person will make his nature known.

THE EXEGESIS ON THE SOUL (II,6)

Introduced by

MADDALENA SCOPELLO

Translated by

WILLIAM C. ROBINSON, JR.

The Exegesis on the Soul is a short tale (ten pages of papyrus) narrating the gnostic myth of the soul from her fall into the world to her return to heaven. The soul, whose nature is feminine — she even had a womb — was virginal and androgynous in form when she was alone with her Father in heaven, but when she fell into the world and into a body she polluted herself with many lovers. These lovers are brigands and bandits who treat the soul as a whore, then abandon her. In her suffering, she seeks for other lovers who also deceive her, making her the slave of their sexual pleasure. Ashamed, the soul remains in slavery, living in a brothel, going from one market place to another. The only gift she receives from her lovers is their polluted seed: her children are dumb, blind, sick and feeble-minded.

The soul remains in this sexual and psychic captivity until the day she perceives her situation and repents. She asks help from the Father who has mercy on her. He performs two actions to help the soul: first, he makes her womb turn inward so that the soul regains her proper character: "the womb of the soul is around the outside like the male genitalia, which are external" (131,19-27). This turning inward protects the soul from further sexual contaminations by her lovers. Secondly, the Father sends a bridegroom from heaven to the soul. The bridegroom is her brother, the firstborn of the house of the Father.

Renewed and purified, the soul adorns herself in the bridal chamber waiting for the fiancé. At his arrival, they love each other passionately. Their love, which is spiritual and eternal, is described with a vivid sensuality normally used for carnal intercourse. The fruit of this marriage are good and beautiful children (i.e., in allegory, the good, virtuous ideas: cf. Philo, *Cher.* 44). Finally the soul regenerates herself and returns to her former state.

In its main lines, the story of the soul in *Exeg. Soul* follows the Valentinian myth of Sophia, the last aeon who leaves the Pleroma searching for new horizons. From prostitution to repentance in tears and from repentance to her return to the house of the Father, the itinerary of the soul closely recalls Sophia's journey.

Nevertheless, much of the originality of *Exeg. Soul* is to be found in the theatrical approach to the myth, now presented not in a philosophical and complex way but in a novelistic adaptation, capable of capturing the reader's attention.

Two close literatures and traditions have certainly influenced the author in the composition of his treatise: Hellenistic and Jewish romance literature. Love and adventures are the chief ingredients of Hellenistic novels, love being the first cause of the action. These novels are governed by a single motif: the tragic separation of two lovers and their final reunion after thousands of misadventures (tricks, brigands, ambiguous figures tempting the soul's chastity; cf. the Greek novels of Achilles Tatius, Chariton, Heliodorus, Longus, and Xenophon of Ephesus).

However, two features having no connection with the Greek novel can be observed in the gnostic story: first, the heroine in *Exeg. Soul* is unique. The fiancé has little part in the narration, while in the Greek novel the primary role is always given to a couple. Second, if Greek heroines are always chaste and pure, the heroine in *Exeg. Soul* (as in other gnostic novels) has led a life of prostitution. Only later will she attain virginity.

The Jewish influence is deeper. *Exeg. Soul* is a female story, the soul in fact is presented as a woman. This is quite rare in ancient literature. We find women's stories in Jewish writings, however, especially in Apocrypha and Pseudepigrapha. The story of the soul from prostitution to virginity through repentance recalls the stories of Jewish sinners such as Rahab, Tamar, Ruth, and Bathsheba (cf., Joshua, *Jubilees, Testament of Judah*, Ruth, 2 Kings).

Exeg. Soul is not the only Nag Hammadi treatise consecrated to a female figure. Comparisons exist also with *Auth. Teach, Thund., Norea, Trim. Prot.*, and with other gnostic texts recounting short women's stories. Under the different names and physiognomies of all these women there is hidden one and only one personnage: soul searching for her heavenly origin. The common feature linking these female figures is the opposition, the polarity ''virginity-prostitution.'' Rehabilitation consists in recovering original purity which is essential to attain knowledge.

In *Exeg. Soul* emphasis on pollution shows how the author was influenced by Apocryphal Judaism. This intense focus on pollution is typical of Essenic psychology (cf., *Testaments of the Twelve Patriarchs* and Qumran literature). In *Exeg. Soul* as well as in Essenic spirituality, purification and repentance are the only remedies for impurity. The turning inward of the womb is to be compared with spiritual circumcision; both express the will to abandon the outside, symbol of worldly temptations.

The author of *Exeg. Soul* illustrates the myth of the soul by a series of biblical quotations and two Homeric references. These quotations are part of the narrative and strictly linked to it: they even give the writer the occasion to develop themes related to the myth of the soul. Part of these quotations are grouped together in order to point out the three stages of the soul's journey: prostitution, repentance, return to the Father. These groups of quotations were not gathered by the author but drawn from an anthology of which traces had been preserved by some Christian authors of Alexandria: Clement, Didymos and Origen.

This helps to determine the author's milieu. He is dependent on an academic culture in which florilegia and anthologies formed an important part of an intellectual education.

The use of biblical as well as of Homeric references shows that Greek and Jewish wisdom had the same prophetical value for the author. Both of them expound the gnostic doctrine in a comprehensible way to a Christian, Jewish, or pagan public. These elements show that the gnostic author of *Exeg. Soul* was part of a cultivated, syncretistic milieu where Jewish and Greek scriptures were well known, probably Alexandria at the beginning of the third century C.E. Even though the author borrowed traditions from Judaism and, partly, from Christianity and Paganism, nonetheless he was able to reinterpret them in the light of a new message, the gnostic one.

THE EXEGESIS ON THE SOUL

II 127, 18-137, 27

The Expository Treatise on the Soul [1]

Wise men of old gave [20] the soul a feminine name. [1] Indeed she is female in her nature as well. [1] She even has her womb.

As long as [1] she was alone with the father, [1] she was virgin and in form androgynous. [25] But when she fell [1] down into a body and came to this life, then she [1] fell into the hands of many robbers. And [1] the wanton creatures passed her from one to another [1] and [...] her. Some made use of [30] her [by force], while others did so by seducing [1] her with a gift. In short, [1] they defiled her, and she [... her] **128** virginity.

And in her body she prostituted herself [1] and gave herself to one and all, [1] considering each one she was about to embrace [1] to be her husband. When she had given herself [5] to wanton, unfaithful adulterers, [1] so that they might make use of her, then she sighed [1] deeply and repented. But even when she [1] turns her face from those adulterers, she runs [1] to others and they compel her [10] to live with them and render service to them [1] upon their bed, as if they were her masters. [1] Out of shame she no longer dares [1] to leave them, whereas they deceive [1] her for a long time, pretending to be faithful, true husbands, [15] as if they greatly respected [1] her. And after all this [1] they abandon her and go.

She then [1] becomes a poor desolate widow, [1] without help; not even a measure of food [20] was left her from the time of her affliction. [1] For from them she gained nothing except [1] the defilements they gave her while they had [1] sexual intercourse with her. And her offspring [1] by the adulterers are dumb, [25] blind, and sickly. [1] They are feebleminded.

But when [1] the father who is above visits her [1] and looks down upon her and sees her [1] sighing — with her sufferings and disgrace [30] — and repenting of the prostitution [1] in which she engaged, and when she begins to call [1] upon [his name] [1] so that he might help her, [...] all [1] her heart, saying, "Save [35] me, my father, for behold I will render an account | [to thee, for I abandoned] my house and **129** fled from my maiden's quarters. | Restore me to thyself again.'' When he sees her | in such a state, then he will count | her worthy of his mercy upon her, for many are the afflictions [5] that have come upon her because she abandoned her house.

Now concerning | the prostitution of the soul the holy spirit prophesies in | many places. For he said | in the prophet Jeremiah (3:1-4),

If | the husband divorces his wife and she [10] goes and takes another man, can she return to him after | that? Has not that woman utterly | defiled herself? "And you (sg.) | prostituted yourself to many shepherds and you returned | to me!" said the lord. "Take an honest [15] look and see where you | prostituted yourself. Were you not sitting in the | streets defiling the land with your acts of prostitution | and your vices? And you took many shepherds for a | stumbling block for yourself. You became shameless [20] with everyone. You did not call on me as | kinsman or as father or author of your | virginity."

Again it is written in the prophet Hosea (2:2-7), |

Come, go to law with | your (pl.) mother, for she is not to be a wife to me [25] nor I a husband to her. | I shall remove her prostitution from my presence, | and I shall remove her adultery from | between her breasts. I shall make her naked | as on the day she was born, and [30] I [shall] make her desolate like a land without | [water], and I shall make her [longingly] childless. | [I] shall show her children no pity, for | they are children of prostitution, since their mother | prostituted herself and [put her children to shame]. **130** For she said, "I shall prostitute myself to | my lovers. It was they who gave me my | bread and my water and my garments and my | clothes and my wine and my oil and everything [5] I needed." Therefore behold | I shall shut them up so that she shall not be able | to run after her adulterers. And when she | seeks them and does not find them, she will say, | "I shall return to my former husband, for [10] in those days I was better off than now." |

Again he said in Ezekiel (16:23-26), |

It came to pass after much depravity, said | the lord, you built yourself a brothel | and you made yourself a beautiful place [15] in the streets. And you built yourself | brothels on every lane, and you wasted | your beauty, and you spread your legs | in every alley, and you multiplied your acts of prostitution. | You prostituted yourself to the sons of Egypt, [20] those who are your neighbors, men great of flesh.

But what ꞌ does "the sons of Egypt, men great of flesh" mean ꞌ if not the domain of the flesh and the perceptible realm ꞌ and the affairs of the earth, by which the soul ꞌ has become defiled here, receiving bread from [25] them, as well as wine, oil, clothing, ꞌ and the other external nonsense ꞌ surrounding the body – the things she thinks ꞌ she needs.

But as to this prostitution the ꞌ apostles of the savior commanded (cf. Acts 15:20, 29; 21:25; 1 Th 4:3; 1 Co 6:18; 2 Co 7:1), [30]

Guard yourselves against it, purify yourselves from it, ꞌ
speaking not just of the prostitution of the ꞌ body but especially of that of the soul. For this reason ꞌ the apostles [write to the churches] of ꞌ God, that such [prostitution] might not [35] occur among [us].

Yet the greatest ꞌ [struggle] has to do with the prostitution **131** of the soul. From it arises the prostitution ꞌ of the body as well. Therefore Paul, ꞌ writing to the Corinthians (1 Co 5:9-10), said,

I wrote ꞌ you in the letter, "Do not associate with prostitutes," [5] not at all (meaning) the prostitutes of this world ꞌ or the greedy or the thieves or the ꞌ idolators, since then you would have to ꞌ go out from the world.

here it is speaking ꞌ spiritually –

For our struggle is [10] not against flesh and blood – as he ꞌ said (Ep 6:12) – but against the world rulers ꞌ of this darkness and the spirits of ꞌ wickedness.

As long as the soul ꞌ keeps running about everywhere copulating with whomever [15] she meets and defiling herself, she exists suffering ꞌ her just deserts. But when ꞌ she perceives the straits she is in ꞌ and weeps before the father and repents, ꞌ then the father will have mercy on her and he will make [20] her womb turn from the external domain ꞌ and will turn it again inward, so that the soul will regain her ꞌ proper character. For it is not so with a woman. ꞌ For the womb of the body is ꞌ inside the body like the other internal organs, but the womb [25] of the soul is around the outside ꞌ like the male genitalia, which are ꞌ external.

So when the womb of the soul, ꞌ by the will of the father, turns itself inward, ꞌ it is baptized and is immediately [30] cleansed of the external pollution ꞌ which was pressed upon it, just as ꞌ [garments, when] dirty, are put into ꞌ the [water and] turned about until their ꞌ dirt is removed and they become clean. And so the cleansing [35] of the soul is to regain the [newness] **132** of her former nature and to turn herself back again. ꞌ That is her baptism.

Then she will ꞌ begin to rage at herself like a woman ꞌ in labor, [5] who writhes and rages in the hour of delivery. ꞌ But since she is female, by herself she is powerless to beget ' a child. From heaven the father sent her ' her man, who is her brother, ' the firstborn. Then the bridegroom came [10] down to the bride. She gave up ' her former prostitution and cleansed herself of the pollutions ' of the adulterers, and she was renewed so as to be a bride. ' She cleansed herself in the bridal chamber; she filled it with perfume; ' she sat in it waiting [15] for the true bridegroom. No longer does she ' run about the market place, copulating with whomever she ' desires, but she continued to wait for him — ' (saying) "When will he come?" — and to fear him, ' for she did not know what he looked like: [20] she no longer remembers since the time she fell ' from her father's house. But by the will ' of the father ⟨ . . . ⟩. And she dreamed of him like ' a woman in love with a man.

But then ' the bridegroom, according to the father's will, [25] came down to her into the bridal chamber, ' which was prepared. And he decorated the bridal chamber. '

For since that marriage is ' not like the carnal marriage, those who are to have intercourse ' with one another will be satisfied with [30] that intercourse. And as if it were a burden ' they leave behind them the annoyance of physical ' desire and they [turn their faces from] ' each other. But this marriage [. . .]. ' But [once] they unite [35] [with one another], they become a single life. **133** Wherefore the prophet said (Gn 2:24) ' concerning the first man and the first woman, '

They will become a single flesh. '

For they were originally joined to one another when they were with the father [5] before the woman led astray the man, who ' is her brother. This marriage ' has brought them back together again and the ' soul has been joined to her true love, her ' real master, as it is written (cf. Gn 3:16; 1 Co 11:1; Ep 5:23), [10]

For the master of the woman is her husband.

Then gradually she recognized him, ' and she rejoiced once more, weeping ' before him as she remembered the ' disgrace of her former widowhood. ' And she adorned herself still more so that [15] he might be pleased to stay with her.

And the ' prophet said in the Psalms (45:10-11),

Hear, ' my daughter, and see and incline your ear ' and forget your people and your father's house, ' for the king has desired your beauty, [20] for he is your lord.

For he requires her ' to turn her face from her ' people and the multitude of her adulterers, ' in whose midst she once was, to devote herself ' only to her king, her real ' lord, and to forget the house of the ' earthly father, with whom things went | badly for her, but to remember her father | who is in heaven. Thus also it was said | (Gn 12:1) to Abraham,

> Come out from your [30] country and your kinsfolk and from | your father's house.

Thus when the soul [had adorned] | herself again in her beauty | [. . .] enjoyed her beloved, | and [he also] loved her. And [35] when she had intercourse with him, she got **134** from him the seed that is the life-giving | spirit, so that by him she bears good children | and rears them. | For this is the great, perfect marvel [5] of birth. And so this marriage is made perfect | by the will of the father.

Now it is fitting that the soul | regenerate herself and become again as | she formerly was. The soul then moves of her own accord. | And she received the divine nature from the father [10] for her rejuvenation, so that she might be restored to | the place where originally she had been. This is | the resurrection that is from the dead. | This is the ransom from captivity. | This is the upward journey of ascent to heaven. This [15] is the way of ascent to the father. Therefore | the prophet said (Ps 103:1-5), |

> Praise the lord, O my soul, and, all that is | within me, (praise) his holy name. My | soul, praise God, who forgave [20] all your sins, who healed | all your sicknesses, who ransomed | your life from death, who crowned | you with mercy, who satisfies your longing | with good things. Your youth will [25] be renewed like an eagle's.

Then when she becomes young | again she will ascend, praising the father | and her brother, by whom she was rescued. | Thus it is by being born again that the soul will | be saved. And this [30] is due not to rote phrases | or to professional skills or to | book learning. Rather it [is] the grace of the [. . . , | it is] the gift of the [. . .]. | For such is this heavenly thing. [35] Therefore the savior cries out (Jn 6:44), **135**

> No one can come to me unless | my Father draws him and brings him to me; | and I myself will raise him up on the last | day.

It is therefore fitting to pray to the father and to call [5] on him with all our soul − not externally with the lips | but with the spirit, | which is inward, which came forth from the | depth − sighing; repenting for | the life we lived; confessing [10] our sins; perceiving the empty deception | we were in, and the empty zeal; | weeping over how we were | in darkness and in the wave; mourning for ourselves, | that he might have pity on us; hating [15] ourselves for how we are now. Again | the savior said (cf. Mt 5:4, 6; Lk 6:12),

> Blessed | are those who mourn, for it is they who will be pitied; | blessed, those who are hungry, for | it is they who will be filled.

Again he said (cf. Lk 14:26),

> If [20] one does not hate his soul he cannot follow | me.

For the beginning of salvation is | repentance. Therefore (cf. Acts 13:24),

> Before | Christ's appearance came John, | preaching the baptism of repentance. [25]

And repentance takes place in distress | and grief. But the father is good and loves | humanity, and he hears the | soul that calls upon him and | sends it the light of salvation. Therefore [30] he said through the spirit to the | prophet (cf. 1 Cl 8:3),

> Say to the children of my people, | "[If your] sins extend | [from earth to] heaven, and if they become | [red] like scarlet and [35] blacker than [sackcloth and if] **136** you return to me with all your | soul and say to me, | "My father," I will heed you as a | holy people."

Again another place (Is 30:15),

> Thus says [5] the lord, the holy one of | Israel: "If you (sg.) return and sigh, | then you will be saved and will know where you were | when you trusted in what is empty."

Again | he said in another place (Is 30:19-20) ,

> Jerusalem wept [10] much, saying, "Have pity on me." He will have pity on the sound | of your (sg.) weeping. And when he saw he heeded you. | And the lord will give you (pl.) bread of | affliction and water of oppression. | From now on those who deceive will not approach you (sg.) again. [15] Your eyes will see those who are deceiving | you.

Therefore it is fitting to pray to | God night and day, spreading out | our hands towards him as do people sailing in the middle | of the sea: they pray to God [20] with all their heart without hypocrisy. | For those who pray | hypocritically deceive only themselves. | Indeed, it is in order that he might know who is worthy of salvation | that God examines the inward parts and [25] searches the bottom of the heart. For no | one is worthy of salvation who still loves | the place of deception. Therefore it is written | in the poet (Homer, *Odyssey* 1.48-59),

> Odysseus sat | on the island weeping and grieving and turning [30] his face from the words of Calypso | and from her tricks, longing to see | his village and smoke coming | forth from it. And had he not [received] | help from heaven, [he would] not [have been able to return] [35] to his village.

Again [Helen] ⟨...⟩ saying (*Odyssey* 4.260-261), |

[My heart] turned itself from me. **137** It is to my house that I want to return.

For she sighed, ' saying (*Odyssey* 4.261-264),

It is Aphrodite who ' deceived me and brought me out of my village. My only daughter ' I left behind me, and my [5] good, understanding, handsome husband.

For when ' the soul leaves her ' perfect husband because of the treachery of Aphrodite, ' who exists here in the act of begetting, then ' she will suffer harm. But if she sighs [10] and repents, she will be restored to her ' house.

Certainly Israel would not have been visited ' in the first place, to be brought out of the land of Egypt, ' out of the house of bondage, if it had not sighed ' to God and wept for the oppression [15] of its labors. Again it is written in the Psalms (6:6-9), '

I was greatly troubled in my groaning. I will ' bathe my bed and my cover each ' night with my tears. I have become old in the midst of all my enemies. ' Depart from me, all [20] you who work at lawlessness, for behold the ' lord has heard the cry of my weeping and ' the lord has heard my prayer."

If ' we repent, truly God will ' heed us, he who is long suffering and abundantly [25] merciful, to whom is the glory for ' ever and ever. Amen. '

The Expository Treatise on the Soul

THE BOOK OF THOMAS THE CONTENDER (II,7)

Introduced and translated by

JOHN D. TURNER

The Book of Thomas the Contender is the seventh and last treatise in Codex II of the Coptic Gnostic library from Nag Hammadi. It is a revelation dialogue between the resurrected Jesus and his twin brother Judas Thomas, ostensibly recorded by Mathaias (the apostle Matthew?) at a time just before Jesus' ascension. It is a literary expression of traditions native to Syrian Edessa about the apostle Jude, surnamed Thomas, the missionary to India. It was likely composed in the first half of the third century C.E. Two products of this tradition have been dated with fair certainty: *The Gospel of Thomas*, composed ca. C.E. 50-125, and the *Acts of Thomas*, composed ca. C.E. 225. Both seem to derive from the ascetic, pre-Manichaean Christianity in the Osrhoëne (eastern Syria, between Edessa [modern Urfù] and Messene). *The Book of Thomas the Contender* seems to occupy a median position between the *Gos. Thom.* and the *Acts* in 1) date of composition, 2) relative dominance of the role played by Thomas in these works, and 3) in developing from a sayings collection preserved by Thomas (*Gos. Thom.*) to a dialogue between Jesus and Thomas (*Thom. Cont.*), to a full-blown romance centered on the missionary exploits of Thomas (*Acts of Thomas*). The present Coptic version was probably translated from Greek; the existence of the text is otherwise unattested in antiquity.

The subscripted title designates the work as a "book" of "Thomas the *athletes* (i.e., "one who struggles" against the fiery passions of the body) writing to the perfect, while the opening lines designate the work as "secret sayings" spoken by Jesus to Judas Thomas and recorded by Mathaias as he heard them speaking. The designation "sayings" does not really correspond to the genre of the work, which is a revelation dialogue. This type of dialogue is unlike the Platonic dialogue in which a conversational process of statement, counterstatement, and clarification leads step by step to the birth of knowledge. It is instead more related to the literature sometimes called *eratapokriseis* ("questions and answers"), in which an initiate elicits revealed truth from a spiritual authority in the form of catachetical answers to topical questions. Such revelation dialogues are found in many pagan Hermetic and gnostic Christian texts, including many from Nag Hammadi (*Ap. John, Soph. Jes. Chr., Dis. 8-9, Dial. Sav., Ep. Pet. Phil.*) These dialogues are set at a time between the resurrection and ascension, when the Savior appeared on earth in his true divine form, so that both he and his teaching were available to select apostles in a form unclouded by the sort of materiality which was believed to obscure the spiritual significance of his rather parabolic earthly, preresurrection teaching. This special teaching might consist of enlightening commentary on his darker earthly teaching, or even new revelations to special apostles. As the Savior's twin, Thomas had a claim to direct insight into the nature of the Savior and his teaching. By "knowing himself," Thomas would also know the "depth of the all," whence the Savior came, and whither he was about to return, and thus become a missionary possessing the true teaching of Jesus.

This true teaching of Jesus turns out to be consistently ascetic. Its basic theme or catchword is "fire," the fire of bodily passions that torment the soul, and its counterpart in the flames of hell: one shall be punished by that by which one sins. Around this principal theme are gathered a number of conceptual oppositions. It is of course the presence of the Savior as the emissary of the light which serves to illumine the eyes to see invisible reality within that which heretofore was only perceptually visible and thus illusory. The treatise thus evinces a Platonic dualism of a radically ascetic stripe, and may be properly considered broadly ascetic rather than gnostic. The gnostic myth of the creation of the world by a divine accident or evil power is neither mentioned nor apparently presupposed, and the dualism of the treatise is much more anthropological (body/soul) than cosmic (the above/below). A more appropriate designation for the doctrine of this work is Christian(ized) wisdom with ascetic application: the wisdom themes of seeking, finding, being troubled, resting, and ruling (cf. *Gospel of Thomas*, saying 2, etc.) are distinctly present and pressed into the service of an exhortation to the ascetic life by means of a Platonic dualism between the visible-passional-illusory and the invisible-spiritual-real.

There are presently two competing theories concerning the composition of *The Book of Thomas the Contender*. The more recent one, developed by H.M. Schenke, holds that its underlying source lay in a probably non-Christian Hellenistic Jewish wisdom treatise. Subsequently, in the Christian orbit, this ascetic treatise was Christianized by the substitution of Jesus for the figure of divine wisdom as the revelatory figure of the work, by the addition to the title of the phrase "The Book of Thomas," and by the attendant recasting of the whole from the genre of expository treatise into the genre of revelation dialogue. That is, the text was dissected into smaller expository sections placed upon the lips of the risen Jesus; these were recast as answers to fictitious questions put to him by the apostle Thomas, which themselves were inserted into the text as pretexts for the ensuing answers of the Savior.

The earlier theory, developed by the author of this article, began with the observation that the actual dialogue between Thomas and Jesus occupies only the first three fifths of the treatise (138,4-142,21), while the remaining two fifths (142,21-end) actually constitute a long monologue of the Savior, in which Thomas no longer plays a role. This and the detection of a transitional editorial seam at 142,21 suggest that *The Book of Thomas the Contender* could have been compiled by a redactor from two separate works, the first three fifths from a dialogue between Thomas and Jesus, perhaps entitled "The Book of Thomas the Contender writing to the Perfect," and the second two fifths from a collection of the sayings of the Savior gathered into a homiletical discourse perhaps entitled "The hidden words which the Savior spoke, which I recorded, even I, Mathaias." A redactor later prefixed the dialogue to the sayings collection, prefaced the whole with the present opening lines, augmented by the reference to Thomas as the recipient of the secret words and Mathaias as the scribe, but then appended a subscript title designating Thomas as the author of the whole.

While a final decision between these two compositional theories is still awaited, there can be no question that *The Book of Thomas the Contender* displays the marks of a redactional history. On either view, it represents a new source for the critical investigation of early Christian literature and for the process by which ever new literary genres were adapted for Christian teaching. It also constitutes another instance in a growing body of Christian wisdom literature, with its emphasis on seeking, finding, resting on, and ruling by the truth, and thus escaping the troubles of life.

THE BOOK OF THOMAS THE CONTENDER

II 138, 1-145, 19
145, 20-23

The secret words that the savior spoke to | Judas Thomas which I, even I Mathaias, | wrote down, while I was walking, listening to them speak with | one another.

The savior said, "Brother Thomas, while [5] you (sg.) have time in the world, listen to me, | and I will reveal to you the things you have pondered | in your mind.

"Now since it has been said that you are my | twin and true companion, examine yourself and learn | who you are, in what way you exist, and [10] how you will come to be. Since you will be called my brother, | it is not fitting that you be ignorant | of yourself. And I know that you have understood, | because you had already understood that I am the knowledge of the truth. | So while you accompany me, although you are uncomprehending, [15] you have (in fact) already come to know, and you will be called 'the one who | knows himself.' For he who has not known himself | has known nothing, but he who has known himself | has at the same time already achieved knowledge about the depth of the all. | So then, you, my brother Thomas, have beheld what is obscure [20] to men, that is, what they ignorantly stumble against." |

Now Thomas said to the lord, | "Therefore I beg you to tell me | what I ask you before your ascension, | and when I hear from you about [25] the hidden things, then I can speak about | them. And it is obvious to me that the truth is difficult to | perform before men."

The savior answered, saying, | "If the things that are visible to you (pl.) are obscure | to you, how can you hear [30] about the things that are not visible? If the deeds of the truth | that are visible in the world are difficult for you (pl.) to perform, | how indeed, then, shall you perform those that pertain to the | exalted height and to the pleroma which are not visible? | And how shall you be called 'laborers'? [35] In this respect-you are apprentices, and have not yet received ' the height of perfection.''

Now Thomas answered ' and said to the savior, ''Tell us about these things ' that you say are not visible, [but are] hidden ' from us.''

The savior said, ''[All] bodies [. . .] [40] the beasts are begotten [. . .] . . . ' it is evident like [. . .] . . . ' [. . .] . . . this, too, those that are above ' [. . .] things that are visible, but [they are] visible **139** in their own root, and it is their fruit ' that nourishes them. But these visible bodies ' survive by devouring creatures similar to them ' with the result that the bodies change. Now that which changes will [5] decay and perish, and has no hope of life from then on, ' since that body is bestial. So just as the body of the beasts ' perishes, so also will these formations ' perish. Do they not derive from intercourse ' like that of the beasts? If it, (the body) too derives from intercourse, [10] how will it beget anything different from ' beasts? So, therefore, you are babes until ' you become perfect.''

And Thomas answered, ' ''Therefore I say to you, lord, that those who speak ' about things that are invisible and difficult [15] to explain are like those who shoot their arrows at a ' target at night. To be sure, they shoot their arrows as ' anyone would — since they shoot at the target — but it is not visible. ' Yet when the light comes forth and ' hides the darkness, then the work of each will appear. [20] And you, your light, enlighten, O lord.'' '

Jesus said, ''It is in light that light exists.'' '

Thomas spoke, saying, ''Lord, ' why does this visible light that shines ' on behalf of men rise and set?''

The savior [25] said, ''O blessed Thomas, of course this visible light ' shines on your (pl.) behalf — not in order [that] ' you (pl.) remain here, but rather that you might come forth ' — and whenever all the elect abandon ' bestially, then this light will withdraw [30] up to its essence, and its essence will welcome it, ' since it is a good servant.''

Then ' the savior continued and said, ''O ' unsearchable love of the light! O bitterness of ' the fire that blazes in the bodies of men and in [35] their marrow, kindling in them night and ' day, and burning the limbs of men and ' [making] their minds become drunk and their souls become deranged ' [. . .] them within males and females ' . . . [. . .] night and moving them, [. . .] [40] . . . secretly and visibly. ' For the males [move . . . upon the females] ' and the females upon [the males. Therefore it is] **140** said, 'Everyone who seeks the truth from ' true wisdom will make himself wings so as to ' fly, fleeing the lust that scorches the spirits ' of men.' And he will make himself wings to flee ⁵ every visible spirit.''

And Thomas answered, ' saying, ''Lord, this is exactly what I am asking ' you about, since I have understood that you ' are the one who is beneficial to us, as you say.''

Again the savior answered and said, ''Therefore it is necessary ¹⁰ for us to speak to you (pl.), since this is the doctrine for the perfect. ' If, now, you (pl.) desire to become perfect, you shall ' observe these things; if not, your (pl.) name is 'Ignorant,' ' since it is impossible for an intelligent man to dwell with a ' fool, for the intelligent man is perfect in all wisdom. ¹⁵ To the fool, however, the good and bad are ' the same — indeed the wise man will be nourished by ' the truth and (Ps 1:3) 'will be like a tree growing by ' the meandering stream' — seeing that there are some who, although having wings, ' rush upon the visible things, things that ²⁰ are far from the truth. For that which guides them, ' the fire, will give them an illusion of truth, ' [and] will shine on them with a [perishable] beauty, ' and it will imprison them in a dark ' sweetness and captivate them with fragrant pleasure. ²⁵ And it will blind them with insatiable lust ' and burn their souls and become ' for them like a stake stuck in their heart ' which they can never dislodge. And like ' a bit in the mouth it leads them according to its ³⁰ own desire.

''And it has fettered them with its ' chains and bound all their limbs ' with the bitterness of the bondage of lust for those ' visible things that will decay and change ' and swerve by impulse. They have ³⁵ always been attracted downwards; as they are killed, ' they are assimilated to all the beasts of ' the perishable realm.''

Thomas answered and said, ''It ' is obvious and has been said, '[Many are ... ' ... those who do not know [...] ... ⁴⁰ soul.'''

And [the savior] answered, saying, ' ''[Blessed is] the wise man who [sought ' after the truth, and] when he found it, he rested **141** upon it forever and was unafraid of those ' who wanted to disturb him.''

Thomas answered ' and said, ''Is it beneficial for us, lord, to rest ' among our own?''

The savior said, ''Yes, it is useful. ⁵ And it is good for you (pl.) since things visible ' among men will dissolve — for the vessel of ' their flesh will dissolve, and when it is brought to naught ' it will come to be among visible things, among things that are seen. ' And then the fire which they see gives them pain ¹⁰ on account of love for the faith they ' formerly possessed. They will be gathered back to that which is visible. ' Moreover, those who have sight among things that are not visible, without ' the first love they will perish in the concern for this ' life and the scorching of the fire. Only a little while longer, [15] and that which is visible will dissolve; then ' shapeless shades will emerge and ' in the midst of tombs they will forever dwell upon the corpses ' in pain and corruption of soul." '

Thomas answered and said, "What have we [20] to say in the face of these things? What shall we say to ' blind men? What doctrine should we express to these miserable ' mortals who say, 'We came to [do] ' good and not to curse,' and yet [claim], ' 'Had we not been begotten in the flesh, we would not have known [25] [iniquity]'?"

The savior said, "Truly, as for ' [those], do not esteem them as men, but regard them [as] ' beasts, for just as beasts devour one another, ' so also men of this sort ' devour one another. On the contrary, they are deprived of [the kingdom] [30] since they love the sweetness of the fire and are ' servants of death and rush to the works of corruption. ' They fulfill the lust of their fathers. They will ' be thrown down to the abyss and be afflicted ' by the torment of the bitterness of their evil nature. [35] For they will be scourged so as to make them ' rush backwards, whither they do not know, and ' they [will recede] from their limbs not patiently, but ' [with] despair. And they rejoice over [...] ' [...] madness and derangement ... [40] [They] pursue [this] derangement without realizing [their ' madness, thinking] that they [are] wise. [They ...] ' ... their body [...] **142** Their mind is directed to their own selves, for their thought is occupied ' with their deeds. But it is the fire that will burn them!" '

And Thomas answered and said, "Lord, what will the one ' thrown down to them do? For I am most anxious [5] about them; many are those who fight them." '

The savior answered and said, 'What is your own ' opinion?"

Judas — the one called ' Thomas — said, "It is you, lord, whom it befits ' to speak, and me to listen." [10]

The savior replied, "Listen to what I am going to tell you (sg.) ' and believe in the truth. That which sows and that which is sown ' will dissolve in their fire — within the fire ' and the water — and they will hide in tombs of darkness. ' And after a long time they shall show forth [15] the fruit of the evil trees, being punished, ' being slain in the mouth of beasts and men ' at the instigation of the rains and winds and air ' and the light that shines above."

Thomas ' replied, "You have certainly persuaded us, lord. [20] We realize in our heart, and it is obvious, that this ' [is so], and that your word is sufficient. But these words ¹ that you speak to us are ridiculous and contemptible to the world ¹ since they are misunderstood. ¹ So how can we go ²⁵ preach them, since we are [not] esteemed ¹ [in] the world?''

The savior answered and said, ¹ ''Truly I tell you (pl.) that he who will listen to ¹ [your] word and turn away his face or sneer ¹ at it or smirk at these things, truly ³⁰ I tell you that he will be handed over to ¹ the ruler above who rules over ¹ all the powers as their king, and he will turn ¹ that one around and cast him from heaven down to ¹ the abyss, and he will be imprisoned in a narrow ³⁵ dark place. Moreover, he can neither turn nor move on account of ¹ the great depth of Tartaros and the [heavy bitterness] ¹ of Hades that is steadfast [. . .] ¹ [. . .] them to it . . . ¹ [. . .] they will not forgive . . . ⁴⁰ [. . .] pursue you (pl.). They will hand ¹ [. . .] over [to. . .] angel Tartarouchos ¹ [. . .] fire pursuing them 143 [. . .] fiery scourges that cast a shower of sparks into ¹ the face of the one who is pursued. If he flees westward, he ¹ finds the fire. If he turns southward, he finds it there as well. ¹ If he turns northward, the threat ⁵ of seething fire meets him again. Nor does he find the way to the east ¹ so as to flee there and be saved, for he did not find it in the day ¹ he was in the body, so that he might find it in the day of judgment.'' ¹

Then the savior continued, saying, ¹ ''Woe to you, godless ones, who have no hope, ¹⁰ who rely on things that will not happen!

''Woe to you (pl.) ¹ who hope in the flesh and in the prison that will perish! ¹ How long will you be oblivious? And how long will you suppose that the imperishables ¹ will perish too? Your hope is set ¹ upon the world, and your god is this life! ¹⁵ You are corrupting your souls!

''Woe to you (pl.) within ¹ the fire that burns in you, for it is insatiable! ¹

''Woe to you because of the wheel that turns in ¹ your minds!

''Woe to you within the grip of the burning ¹ that is in you, for it will devour your flesh openly ²⁰ and rend your souls secretly, ¹ and prepare you for your companions!

''Woe to ¹ you, captives, for you are bound in caverns! ¹ You laugh! In mad laughter you rejoice! ¹ You neither realize your perdition, nor ²⁵ do you reflect on your circumstances, nor have [you] ¹ understood that you dwell in darkness and [death]! ¹ On the contrary, you are drunk with the fire and [full] ¹ of bitterness. Your mind is deranged on account of the [burning ¹ that is in] you, and sweet to you are the poison and ³⁰ the blows of your enemies! And the darkness rose for ¹ you like the light, for you surrendered your freedom ¹ for servitude! You darkened your hearts ¹ and surrendered your thoughts ¹ to folly, and you

filled your thoughts [35] with the smoke of the fire that is in you! And |
your light [has hidden] in the cloud | [of . . .] and the garment that is
put upon you, you [. . .] | [. . .]. And [you] were seized [by | the hope
that] does not exist. And whom is it [you [40] have] believed? Do you [not
know that you] | all dwell among those who that [. . .] | [. . .] you as
though [you . . .]. **144** You baptized your souls in the water of darkness!
| You walked by your own whims!

"Woe | to you (pl.) who dwell in error, heedless | that the light of the
sun which judges and [5] looks down upon the all will circle around all
things | so as to enslave the enemies. You do not even notice | the
moon, how by night and day it | looks down, looking at the bodies of
your slaughters!

"Woe | to you (pl.) who love intimacy with womankind [10] and pol-
luted intercourse with them!

"Woe to you (pl.) in the grip of the powers of your body, | for they
will afflict you!

"Woe to you (pl.) in the grip of | the forces of the evil demons! |

"Woe to you (pl.) who beguile your limbs with fire! [15] Who is it that
will rain a refreshing dew on you | to extinguish the mass of fire from
you | along with your burning? Who is it that will cause the sun to |
shine upon you to disperse the darkness in you | and hide the darkness
and polluted water?

"The sun [20] and the moon will give a fragrance to you (pl.), together
with the air and | the spirit and the earth and the water. For if the sun
does not | shine upon these bodies, they will wither and perish | just like
weeds or grass. If | the sun shines on them, they prevail and choke [25]
the grapevine; but if the grapevine | prevails and shades those weeds |
[and] all that other brush growing alongside and | [spreads] and flour-
ishes, it alone | inherits the land in which it grows; [30] and every place it
has shaded it dominates. | And when it grows up, it dominates all the
land | and is bountiful for its master, and it pleases him | even more, for
he would have suffered great pains | on account of these plants until he
uprooted them. But the [35] grapevine alone removed them and choked |
them, and they died and became like the soil."

Then | Jesus continued and said to them, "Woe to | you (pl.), for you
did not receive the doctrine, and those who are [. . .] | will labor at
preaching [. . .]. [40] And [you] are rushing into . . . [. . .] | [. . .] will send
[them] down . . . | [. . .] you kill them daily **145** in order that they might
rise from death.

"Blessed are you (pl.) | who have prior knowledge of the stumbling
blocks and who flee | alien things.

"Blessed are you (pl.) who are reviled ˈ and not esteemed on account of the love [5] their lord has for them.

"Blessed are ˈ you (pl.) who weep and are oppressed by ˈ those without hope, for you will be released from ˈ every bondage.

"Watch and pray that you (pl.) not come to be ˈ in the flesh, but rather that you come forth from the bondage of the bitterness [10] of this life. And as you pray, ˈ you will find rest, for you have left behind the suffering and the disgrace. ˈ For when you come forth from the sufferings and ˈ passions of the body, you will receive rest ˈ from the good one, and you will reign with the king, [15] you joined with him and he with you, from now on, ˈ for ever and ever. Amen." ˈ

The Book of Thomas ˈ
The Contender Writing ˈ
To the Perfect (pl.). [20]

****

Remember me also, my brethren, ˈ
[in] your prayers: ˈ
Peace to the saints ˈ
and those who are spiritual.

THE GOSPEL OF THE EGYPTIANS (III,2 AND IV,2)

Introduced and translated by

ALEXANDER BÖHLIG and FREDERIK WISSE

The so-called *Gospel of the Egyptians* is preserved in two Coptic versions which were translated independently from the Greek. It is not related to the apocryphal Gospel of the Egyptians which is cited in Patristic literature. The tractate, which is also entitled "The Holy Book of the Great Invisible Spirit," is an esoteric writing representing a Sethian type of mythological Gnosticism. It may be described as a work which presents a gnostic salvation history. Since the mythological, heavenly Seth is portrayed as the father of the gnostic race, it is appropriate that the tractate lists him as the author of this divinely inspired book.

The tractate is divisible into four main sections. The first section (III 40,12-55,16 = IV 50,1-67,1) deals with the origin of the heavenly world: from the supreme God, dwelling in solitary height as the transcendent Great Invisible Spirit, there evolves and emanates a series of glorious beings, from the mighty trinity of Father, Mother Barbelo, and Son, through the pleroma of heavenly powers, to Adamas' great son Seth, the father and savior of the incorruptible race. The second section (III 55,16-66,8 = IV 67,2-78,10) discusses the origin, preservation, and salvation of the race of Seth: because of the arrogance and hostility of Saklas and the Archons, Seth comes from heaven, puts on Jesus as a garment, and accomplishes a work of salvation on behalf of his children. The third section (III 66,8-67,26 = IV 78,10-80,15) is hymnic in character; and the fourth section (III 68,1-69,17 = IV 80,15-81,end) contains a concluding account of the Sethian origin and transmission of the tractate.

Thus, in a manner analogous to that in which the New Testament gospels proclaim the life of Jesus, *The Gospel of the Egyptians* presents the life of Seth. His pre-history, the origin of his seed, the preservation of his seed by the heavenly powers, the coming of Seth into the world, and his work of salvation, especially through baptism, are proclaimed with drama and praise.

The following translation is based primarily on the text of Codex III; the more fragmentary (though probably more reliable) text of Codex IV has been utilized for the missing pages 45-48, and when the text of III,2 appears to be corrupted.

THE GOSPEL OF THE EGYPTIANS

III 40, 12-44, 28
IV 55, 20-60, 30
III 49, 1-69, 20

The [holy] book [of the Egyptians] ' about the great invisible [Spirit, the] Father ' whose name cannot be uttered, [he who came] [18] forth from the heights of [the perfection, the] light ' of the light of the [aeons of light], ' the light of the [silence of the] providence ' ⟨and⟩ the Father of the silence, the [light] ' of the word and the truth, the light [of the **41** incorruptions, the] infinite light, ' [the] radiance from the aeons of light ' of the unrevealable, unmarked, ' ageless, unproclaimable Father, [5] the aeon of the aeons, Autogenes, ' self-begotten, self-producing, alien, ' the really true aeon.

Three ' powers came forth from him; ' they are the Father, the Mother, (and) the Son, [10] from the living silence, what came forth from ' the incorruptible Father. These came ' [forth from] the silence of the unknown Father. '

[And] from that place ' Domedon Doxomedon came [forth, [15] the aeon of] the aeons and the [light ' of] each one of [their] powers. ' [And] thus the Son came ' [forth] fourth; the Mother [fifth; ' the Father] sixth. He was [20] [...] but unheralded; ' [it is he] who is unmarked among ' all [the powers], the glories, and the ' [incorruptions].

From that place ' the three powers [came] forth, **42** the three ogdoads that [the Father ' brings] forth, in silence with his providence, ' from his bosom, i.e. ' the Father, the Mother, (and) the Son. [5]

The ⟨first⟩ ogdoad, because of which ' the thrice-male child came forth, ' which is the thought, and [the] word, ' and the incorruption, and the eternal ' [life], the will, the mind, [10] and the foreknowledge, the androgynous ' Father.

The second ' ogdoad-power, the Mother, the virginal Barbelon ' epititioch[...] ' ai, memeneaimen[... who] [15] presides over the heaven, karb[...] ' the uninterpretable power, ' the ineffable Mother. [She originated] ' from herself [...]; ' she came forth; [she] [20] agreed with the Father [of the] silent ' [silence].

The third ogdoad-[power], ' the Son of the [silent silence], ' and the crown of the silent silence, [and] ' the glory of the Father, and the virtue [of the **43** Mother. He] brings forth from the bosom ' the seven powers of the great ' light of the seven voices, and the word ' [is] their completion.

These are the three [5] [powers], the three ogdoads that the Father | [through] his providence brought | [forth] from his bosom. He brought them | [forth] at that place.

Domedon | Doxomedon came forth, [10] the aeon of the aeons, and the | [throne] which is in him, and the powers | [which surround] him, the glories and the | [incorruptions. The] Father of the great light | [who came] forth from the silence, he is [15] [the great] Doxomedon-aeon in which | [the thrice]-male child rests. | And the throne | of his [glory] was established [in it, | this one] on which his unrevealable name [20] [is inscribed], on the tablet | [...] one is the word, the [Father | of the light] of everything, he | [who came] forth from the silence, while he rests | in the silence, he whose **44** name [is] in an [invisible] symbol. [A] | hidden, [invisible] mystery | came forth iiiiiiiiiiiiiiiiiiii[iii] | ēēēēēēēēēēē-ēēēēēēēē[ēē o] [5] ooooooooooooooooooooooo uu[uuu] | uuuuuuuuuuuu-uuuuu eeeee | eeeeeeeeeeeeeeeee aaaaaaa[aaaa] | aaaaaaaaaaa ōōōōōōōōō[ōō] | ōōōōōōōōōōō.

And [in this] [10] way the three powers gave praise to the [great], | invisible, unnameable, | virginal, uncallable Spirit, and [his] | male virgin. They asked [for a] | power. A silence of living silence [15] came forth, namely [glories] and | incorruptions in the aeons [... aeons] | myriads added [on ..., the] | three males, [the three] | male offspring, the [male] races (IV 55, 5-7 adds: the [glories of the Father, | the] glories of the great [Christ and | the] male offspring, the [races]) [20] filled the great Doxomedon-[aeon with] | the power of the word of the [whole pleroma]. |

Then the thrice-male [child of the great] | Christ whom the [great] invisible | Spirit had anointed — he [whose] [25] power [was called] Ainon — gave [praise to] | the great invisible Spirit [and his] | male virgin Yoel, [and] | the silence of silent silence, and the [greatness] **IV 55** [20] that [...] | ineffable. [...] | ineffable [...] | unanswerable and | uninterpretable, the [25] first one who has [come forth], | and (who is unproclaimable, [...] **56** which is wonderful | [...] ineffable | [...], he who has | all the greatnesses [of] greatness [5] [of] the silence at | that [place]. The thrice-[male | child] brought | praise and asked [for a | power] from the [great, [10] invisible, virginal] | Spirit.

Then there | appeared at [that] place | [...] who [... | who] sees [glories [15] ...] treasures in a [... | invisible] | mysteries to [...] | of the silence | [who is the male] virgin [20] [Youel].

Then | [the child of the] child | Esephech [appeared]. |

And [thus] he was completed, | namely, the [Father, the] Mother, the

[Son], [25] the [five] seals, the ' unconquerable power which [is] ' the great [Christ] of all the incorruptible 57 ones. [...] ' holy [...] ' the end, [the] incorruptible [...] ' and [...], [5] they are powers [and glories ' and] incorruptions [...] ' they came forth [...]. [13] This one brought [praise] ' to the unrevealable, [15] hidden [mystery ... ' the] hidden [...] [21] him in the [... ' and] the aeons [...] thrones, ' [...] and ' each one [...] [25] myriads of [powers] ' without number surround [them, 58 glories] and ' incorruptions [...] and they ' [... of] the Father, ' [and] the [Mother, and] the Son, and [5] [the] whole [pleroma] which I [mentioned] ' before, [and the] five seals ' [and the mystery] of ' [mysteries]. They [appeared ... [13] who] presides [over ' ...] and the aeons [of [15] ... really] ' truly [...] and the [...] [18] eternal [...] [21] and the ' [really] truly [eternal] aeons.

Then [providence came forth ' from silence], and the [living silence [25] of] the Spirit, [and] ' the Word [of] the Father, and [a] ' light. [She ... the five] 59 seals which [the Father brought] ' forth from his bosom, and she passed [through] ' all the aeons which I mentioned ' before. And she established [5] thrones of glory [and myriads] ' of angels [without] number ' [who] surrounded them, [powers ' and incorruptible] glories, who ' [sing] and give glory, all giving [10] praise with [a single voice], ' with one accord, [with ' one] never-silent [voice ... ' to] the Father, and the [Mother, ' and the] Son [... and [15] all the] pleromas [that I] ' mentioned [before], who is [the ' great] Christ, who is from [silence, ' who] is the [incorruptible] child ' Telmael Telmachael [20] [Eli Eli] Machar Machar ' [Seth, the] power which really truly lives, ' [and the] male ' [virgin] who is with [him], Youel, ' [and] Esephech, [the] holder of glory, [25] the [child] of the child ' [and the crown of] his glory ' [...] of the five ' seals, [the] pleroma [that ' I mentioned before].

There 60 the great self-begotten ' living [Word came forth, ' the] true [god], the ' unborn physis, he whose [5] name I shall tell, saying, ' [...]aia[.....]thaōthōsth[..], ' who [is the] son of the [great] ' Christ, who is the son [of ' the] ineffable silence, [who] [10] came forth from the great [invisible] ' and incorruptible [Spirit]. ' The [son] of the silence and [silence] ' appeared [... [15] invisible ... ' man ' and the] treasures [of] his glory. [Then] ' he appeared in the revealed [...]. ' And he [established] [20] the four [aeons]. ' With a word [he] established ' them.

He brought [praise] ' to the great, [invisible], ' virginal Spirit, [the silence] [25] of the [Father] in a silence [of the] ' living silence [of silence, ' the] place where the man rests. ' [...] ' through [...]. [30]

Then there came forth [at (or: from)] **III 49** that [place] the cloud [of the] great light, the living power, the mother of the holy, incorruptible ones, the great power, the Mirothoe. [5] And she gave birth to him whose name I name, saying, ien ien ea ea ea, three times. **IV 61** [8]

For this one, [Adamas], is [a light] which radiated [from [10] the light; he is] the eye of the [light]. For [this is] the first man, **III 49** [10] he through whom and to whom everything became, (and) without whom nothing became. The unknowable, incomprehensible Father came forth. He [15] came down from above for the annulment of the deficiency.

Then the great Logos, the divine Autogenes, and the incorruptible man Adamas mingled with each other. [20] A Logos of man came into being. However, the man came into being through a word.

He gave praise to the great, invisible, incomprehensible, virginal [25] Spirit, and the male virgin, and the thrice-male child, **50** and the male [virgin] Youel, and Esephech, the holder of glory, the child of the child and the crown of his glory, and the great [5] Doxomedon-aeon, and the thrones which are in him, and the powers which surround him, the glories and the incorruptions, and their whole pleroma which I mentioned before, [10] and the ethereal earth, the receiver of God, where the holy men of the great light receive shape, the men of the Father [15] of the silent, living silence, the Father and their whole pleroma as I mentioned before.

The great Logos, the divine Autogenes, and [20] the incorruptible man Adamas gave praise, (and) they asked for a power and eternal strength for the Autogenes for the completion of the four aeons, in order that, [25] through them, there may appear **51** [. . .] the glory and the power of the invisible Father of the holy men of the great light which will come to the world [5] which is the image of the night. The incorruptible man Adamas asked for them a son out of himself, in order that he (the son) may become father of the immovable, incorruptible race, so [10] that, through it (the race), the silence and the voice may appear, and, through it, the dead aeon may raise itself, so that it may dissolve.

And thus [15] there came forth, from above, the power of the great light, the Manifestation. She gave birth to the four great lights: Harmozel, Oroiael, Davithe, Eleleth, [20] and the great incorruptible Seth, the son of the incorruptible man Adamas.

And thus the perfect hebdomad which exists in hidden mysteries became complete. **52** When she [receives] the [glory] she becomes eleven ogdoads.

And the Father nodded approval; | the whole pleroma of the | lights was well pleased. | Their consorts came forth | for the completion of the ogdoad of | the divine Autogenes: the | Grace of the first light [10] Harmozel, the Perception of the second | light Oroiael, the Understanding | of the third light | Davithe, the Prudence of the | fourth light Eleleth. This [15] is the first ogdoad of the | divine Autogenes.

And | the Father nodded approval; the whole pleroma | of the lights was well pleased. | The ⟨ministers⟩ came forth: [20] the first one, the great | Gamaliel (of) the first great | light Harmozel, and the great | Gabriel (of) the second great | light Oroiael, and the great [25] Samlo of the great light Davithe, | and the great Abrasax of **53** [the great light] Eleleth. And | [the] consorts of these came forth | by the will of the good pleasure | of the Father: the Memory of the great one, [5] the first, Gamaliel; the Love | of the great one, the second, Gabriel; | the Peace of the third one, the great | Samblo; the eternal Life | of the great one, the fourth, Abrasax. [10] Thus were the five ogdoads completed, | a total of forty, | as an uninterpretable power.

Then | the great Logos, the Autogenes, | and the word of the pleroma [15] of the four lights gave | praise to the great, invisible, | uncallable, virginal Spirit, | and the male virgin, | and the great Doxomedon-aeon, [20] and the thrones which are in | them, and the powers which surround them, | glories, authorities, | and the powers, ⟨and⟩ the thrice-male | child, and the male virgin [25] Youel, and Esephech, **54** the holder of glory, [the child] | of the child and the crown of [his] | glory, the whole pleroma, and | all the glories which are there, the [5] infinite pleromas ⟨and⟩ the | unnameable aeons, in | order that they may name the Father | the fourth with the incorruptible | race, (and) that they may call the seed [10] of the Father the seed of the great | Seth.

Then everything shook, | and trembling took hold of the incorruptible | ones. Then the three male | children came forth [15] from above down | into the unborn ones, and the | self-begotten ones, and those who were begotten | in what is begotten. | The greatness came forth, the [20] whole greatness of the great Christ. He | established thrones in glory, | myriads without number, | in the four aeons around them, | myriads without number, [25] powers and glories **55** and incorruptions. And they came | forth in this way.

And | the incorruptible, spiritual | church increased in the four [5] lights of the great, living Autogenes, | the god of truth, praising, | singing, (and) giving glory with one voice, | with one accord, with a mouth | which does not rest, to the Father, and [10] the Mother, and the Son,

and their whole ' pleroma, just as I mentioned ⟨before⟩. ' The five seals
which possess the myriads, and ' they who rule over the aeons and they
who ' bear the glory of the leaders [15] were given the command to reveal
' to those who are worthy. Amen.

Then the great ' Seth, the son of the incorruptible ' man Adamas,
gave praise ' to the great, invisible, uncallable, [20] unnameable, virginal
' Spirit, and the ⟨male virgin, and the thrice-male child, and the male⟩
' virgin Youel, and Esephech, ' the holder of glory, and the ' crown of
his glory, the child of the child, **56** and the great Doxomedon-aeons, '
and the pleroma which I mentioned ' before; and asked for his seed. '

Then there came forth from that place [5] the great power of the great
' light Plesithea, the mother of the angels, ' the mother of the lights, the
' glorious mother, the virgin with the ' four breasts, bringing the fruit [10]
from Gomorrah as spring and Sodom, ' which is the fruit of the spring
of ' Gomorrah which is in her. She came forth ' through the great Seth.

Then ' the great Seth rejoiced about [15] the gift which was granted him
' by the incorruptible ' child. He took his seed ' from her with the four
breasts, the virgin, ' and he placed it with [20] him in the fourth aeon (or,
IV 68, 3: [in] the four aeons), ' in the third great ' light Davithe.

After five ' thousand years the great ' light Eleleth spoke: "Let someone [25] reign over the chaos and Hades." ' And there appeared a cloud
57 [whose name is] hylic Sophia ' [. . . . She] looked out on the parts '
[of the chaos], her face being like ' [. . . in] her form [. . .] [5] blood. And
' [the great] angel Gamaliel spoke ' [to the great Gabriel], the minister
of ' [the great light] Oroiael; ' [he said, "Let an] angel come forth [10] [in
order that he may] reign over the chaos ' [and Hades]." Then the cloud,
being ' [agreeable, came forth] in the two monads, ' each one [of which
had] light. ' [. . . the throne], which she had placed [15] in the cloud
[above. ' Then] Sakla, the great ' [angel, saw] the great demon ' [who is
with him, Nebr]uel. And they became ' [together a] begetting spirit of
the earth. [20] [They begot] assisting angels. ' Sakla [said] to the great '
[demon Neb]ruel, "Let ' [the] twelve aeons come into being in ' [the
. . .] aeon, worlds [25] [. . . ." . . .] the great angel ' [Sakla] said by the
will of the Autogenes, **58** "There shall [be] the [. . .] ' of the number of
seven [. . .]." ' And he said to the [great angels], ' "Go and [let each] [5]
of you reign over his [world]." ' Each one [of these] ' twelve [angels]
went [forth. The first] ' angel is Ath[oth. He is the one] ' whom [the
great] generations [10] of men call [. . . . The] ' second is Harmas, [who]
is [the eye of the fire]. ' The third [is Galila. The] ' fourth is Yobel. [The
fifth is] ' Adonaios, who is [called] [15] Sabaoth. The sixth [is Cain,

whom] ¦ the [great generations of] ¦ men call the sun. The [seventh is Abel]; ¦ the eighth Akiressina; the [ninth Yubel]. ¦ The tenth is Harm[upiael. The] [20] eleventh is Arch[ir-Adonin]. ¦ The twelfth [is Belias. These ¦ are] the ones who preside over Hades [and the chaos]. ¦

And after the founding [of the world] ¦ Sakla said to his [angels], [25] "I, I am a [jealous] god, ¦ and apart from me nothing has [come into being," since he] **59** trusted in his nature.

Then a voice ¦ came from on high, saying, ¦ "The Man exists, and the Son of the Man." ¦ Because of the descent of the image [5] above, which is like its voice in the height ¦ of the image which has looked out, ¦ through the looking out of the image ¦ above, the first creature was ¦ formed.

Because of this [10] Metanoia came to be. She received her ¦ completion and her power by the will ¦ of the Father and his approval with which he ¦ approved of the great, incorruptible, ¦ immovable race of the great, [15] mighty men of the great Seth, ¦ in order that he may sow it in the aeons which ¦ had been brought forth, so that, through her (Metanoia), ¦ the deficiency may be filled up. ¦ For she had come forth from above down [20] to the world which is the image of the night. ¦ When she had come, she prayed for (the repentance of) both the seed ¦ of the archon of this aeon and ⟨the⟩ authorities ¦ who had come forth from him, that ¦ defiled (seed) of the demon-begetting god [25] which will be destroyed, and the seed **60** of Adam and the great Seth, ¦ which is like the sun.

Then the great ¦ angel Hormos came to prepare, ¦ through the virgins of the [5] corrupted sowing of this aeon, in ¦ a Logos-begotten, holy vessel, ¦ through the holy Spirit, ¦ the seed of the great Seth. ¦

Then the great Seth came and brought his [10] seed. And it was sown in the aeons ¦ which had been brought forth, their number being the amount of ¦ Sodom. Some say ¦ that Sodom is the place of pasture ¦ of the great Seth, which is Gomorrah. [15] But others (say) that the great Seth took ¦ his plant out of Gomorrah and ¦ planted it in the second place ¦ to which he gave the name Sodom. ¦

This is the race which came forth through [30] Edokla. For she gave birth through the word ¦ to Truth and Justice, the origin ¦ of the seed of the eternal life ¦ which is with those who will persevere ¦ because of the knowledge of their emanation. [25] This is the great, incorruptible ¦ race which has come forth through three **61** worlds to the world.

And the ¦ flood came as an example ¦ for the consummation of the aeon. But it ¦ will be sent into the world [5] because of this race. A conflagration will ¦ come upon the earth. And grace ¦ will be with those who belong to the race ' through the prophets ' and the guardians who guard the life [10] of the race. Because of this race ' famines will occur and plagues. ' But these things will happen because of the ' great, incorruptible race. Because of ' this race temptations will come, [15] a falsehood of false prophets. '

Then the great Seth saw the activity ' of the devil, and his many ' guises, and his schemes which will come ' upon his incorruptible, immovable race, [20] and the persecutions of his ' powers and his angels, and their ' error, that they acted against themselves. '

Then the great Seth gave ' praise to the great, uncallable, [25] virginal Spirit, and the male **62** virgin Barbelon, ' and the thrice-male child Telmael ' Telmael Heli Heli Machar ' Machar Seth, the power which really truly [5] lives, and the male virgin ' Youel, and Esephech, the ' holder of glory, and the crown of his ' glory, and the great Doxomedon-aeon, ' and the thrones which are in him, and [10] the powers which surround them, and the whole ' pleroma, as I mentioned before. ' And he asked for guards over his ' seed.

Then there came forth from the great ' aeons four hundred ethereal [15] angels, accompanied by the great ' Aerosiel and the great Selmechel, to ' guard the great, incorruptible race, ' its fruit, and the great men ' of the great Seth, from the time and [20] the moment of Truth and Justice ' until the consummation of the aeon and its ' archons, those whom the great judges ' have condemned to ' death.

Then the great Seth was [25] sent by the four ' lights, by the will of the Autogenes **63** and the whole pleroma, through ' ⟨the gift⟩ and the good pleasure of the great invisible ' Spirit, and the five seals, ' and the whole pleroma.

He passed through [5] the three parousias which I mentioned ' before: the flood, and the conflagration, ' and the judgment of the archons and the powers ' and the authorities, to save her (the race) who went astray, ' through the reconciliation of the world, and [10] the baptism through a Logos-begotten ' body which the great Seth ' prepared for himself, ' secretly through the virgin, in order that the ' saints may be begotten by the holy Spirit, through [15] invisible, secret symbols, ' through a reconciliation of the world with the world, ' through the renouncing of the world ' and the god of the thirteen aeons, ' and (through) the convocations of the saints, and [20] the ineffable ones, and the incorruptible bosom, ' and (through) the great light of the Father ' who preexisted with his Providence ' and established through her ' the holy baptism that surpasses [25] the heaven, through the incorruptible, **64** Logos-begotten one, even Jesus the living one, even ' he whom the great Seth has ' put on. And through him he nailed the powers ' of the thirteen aeons, and [5] established those who are brought forth and ' taken away. He armed them ' with an armor of knowledge of this truth, ' with an unconquerable power ' of incorruptibility.

There appeared to them ' the great attendant Yesseus ' Mazareus Yessedekeus, the living ' water, and the great leaders, ' James the great and Theopemptos ' and Isaouel, and they who preside over [15] the spring of truth, Micheus and Michar ' and Mnesinous, and he who presides over ' the baptism of the living, and the ' purifiers, and Sesengenpharanges, ' and they who preside over the gates of the waters, [20] Micheus and Michar, and they who ' preside over the mountain Seldao and Elainos, ' and the receivers of ' the great race, the incorruptible, ' mighty men ⟨of⟩ the great Seth, the [25] ministers of the four lights, ' the great Gamaliel, the great Gabriel, ' the great Samblo, and the great **65** Abrasax, and they who preside over the sun, its ' rising, Olses and Hypneus and ' Heurumaious, and they who preside over the ' entrance into the rest of eternal [5] life, the rulers Mixanther ' and Michanor, and they who guard the ' souls of the elect, Akramas and ' Strempsouchos, and the great power ' Heli Heli Machar Machar Seth, and [10] the great invisible, uncallable, ' unnameable, virginal ' Spirit, and the silence, and the great light ' Harmozel, the place of the living Autogenes, ' the God of the truth, and ⟨he⟩ who is with [15] him, the incorruptible man Adamas, ' the second, Oroiael, the place of the great ' Seth, and Jesus, who possesses the life and who came ' and crucified that which is in the law, ' the third, Davithe, the place of the [20] sons of the great Seth, the fourth, ' Eleleth, the place where the souls ' of the sons are resting, ' the fifth, Yoel, who presides over the name ' of him to whom it will be granted to baptize with [25] the holy baptism that surpasses the heaven, ' the incorruptible one.

But from now on **66** through the incorruptible man Poimael, ' and they who are worthy of (the) invocation, ' the renunciations of the five seals in ' the spring-baptism, these will [5] know their receivers as ' they are instructed about them, and they will ' know them (or: be known) by them. These ' will by no means taste death.

Iē ieus ' ēō ou ēō ōua! Really truly, [10] O Yesseus Mazareus Yessedekeus, ' O living water, O child of the child, ' O glorious name, really truly, ' aiōn o ōn (or: O existing aeon), iiii ēēēē eeee oo ' oo uuuu ōōōō aaaa{a}, really [15] truly, ēi aaaa ōō ' ōō, O existing one who sees the aeons! ' Really truly, aee ēēē iiii ' uuuuuu ōōōōōōōō, ' who is eternally

eternal, [20] really truly, iēa aiō, in ' the heart, who exists, u aei eis aei, '
ei o ei, ei os ei (or: (Son) forever, Thou art what Thou art, Thou art who
Thou art)!

This great name ' of thine is upon me, O self-begotten Perfect one, '
who art not outside me. [25] I see thee, O thou who art visible ' to everyone. For who will be able ' to comprehend thee in another tongue? Now
67 that I have known thee, I have mixed ' myself with the immutable. I
have armed ' myself with an armor of light; ' I have become light. For
the Mother was at [5] that place because of the ' splendid beauty of grace.
Therefore ' I have stretched out my hands while they were ' folded. I
was shaped in the circle ' of the riches of the light which is in [10] my
bosom, which gives shape to the many ' begotten ones in the light into
which no complaint ' reaches. I shall declare thy ' glory truly, for I have
comprehended ' thee, sou iēs ide aeiō aeie ois, O [15] aeon, aeon, O God
of silence! I ' honor thee completely. Thou art my ' place of rest, O son
ēs ēs o e, the ' formless one who exists in the formless ones, ' who exists, raising up the man [20] in whom thou wilt purify me into ' thy life,
according to thine imperishable name. ' Therefore the incense of life ' is
in me. I mixed it with water ' after the model of all archons, [25] in order
that I may live with thee in the peace ' of the saints, thou who existeth
really truly **68** for ever.

This is the book ' which the great Seth wrote, and placed ' in high
mountains on which ' the sun has not risen, nor is it [5] possible. And
since the days of the prophets, ' and the apostles, and the ' preachers,
the name has not at all risen ' upon their hearts, nor is it possible. ' And
their ear has not heard it. [10]

The great Seth wrote this book ' with letters in one hundred and thirty ' years. He placed it in the mountain ' that is called Charaxio, ' in
order that, at the end of the [15] times and the eras, by the ' will of the
divine Autogenes ' and the whole pleroma, through the gift ' of the un-
traceable, unthinkable, ' fatherly love, it may [20] come forth and reveal
this ' incorruptible, holy race ' of the great savior, and those who '
dwell with them in love, and ' the great, invisible, eternal [25] Spirit, and
his only begotten ' Son, and the eternal light, **69** and his great, incorruptible ' consort, and the incorruptible ' Sophia, and the Barbelon,
and the ' whole pleroma in eternity. [5] Amen. '

The Gospel of ⟨the⟩ Egyptians. ' The God-written, holy, secret '
book. Grace, understanding, ' perception, prudence (be) with him [10]
who has written it, Eugnostos the beloved ' in the Spirit — in the flesh

| my name is Gongessos − and my | fellow lights in incorruptibility, |
Jesus Christ, Son of God, [15] Savior, Ichthus, God-written (is) | the holy
book of the great, invisible | Spirit. Amen. |

The Holy Book of the Great |
Invisible Spirit. [20]
Amen.

EUGNOSTOS THE BLESSED (III,*3* and V,*1*)

and

THE SOPHIA OF JESUS CHRIST (III,*4* AND BG 8502,*3*)

Introduced and translated by

DOUGLAS M. PARROTT

Eugnostos begins as a formal letter written by a teacher to his disciples and subsequently shifts to take on qualities of a revelation discourse. It is without apparent Christian influence. With some minor omissions and one major one, it was used by a Christian gnostic editor as he composed *The Sophia of Jesus Christ*. In form, *Soph. Jes. Chr.* is a revelation discourse given by the risen Christ in response to the questions of his disciples. Thus the placing of the two tractates together in the present edition allows one to see the process by which a non-Christian tractate was modified and transformed into a Christian gnostic one. On the basis of the model provided by these two tractates, scholars have conjectured that the same process may have been responsible for other Christian gnostic writings, such as *The Gospel of the Egyptians* and *The Apocryphon of John*.

Eugnostos seems to be directed to a general audience interested in certain religious-philosophical problems. *Soph. Jes. Chr.* was directed to an audience for whom Christianity was an added element in their religious environment. The audience may have been made up of non-Christian Gnostics who already knew the tractate *Eugnostos*. By connecting Christ, in *Soph. Jes. Chr.*, with the prediction at the end of *Eugnostos* (90,6-11), the editor may have hoped to persuade them that Christ was the latest incarnation of the gnostic savior. Or the audience may have consisted of non-gnostic Christians, and the editor may have wanted to persuade them that the religion revealed by Christ was gnostic Christianity. Perhaps the editor had both groups in mind.

The main intent of *Eugnostos* appears to have been to assert and describe the existence of an invisible, supercelestial region beyond the visible world – a region not reflected in the speculations of philosophers (whose views, as they are described, resemble those of Stoics, Epicureans, and Babylonian astrologers). Ruling that region is a hierarchy of five principal divine beings: Unbegotten Father; his reflection, called Self-Father; Self-Father's hypostatized power, Immortal Man, who is androgynous; Immortal Man's androgynous son, Son of Man; and Son of Man's androgynous son, the Savior. The names of the female aspects of the last three include the term Sophia. These divine beings each have their own sphere or aeon, and numerous attendant and subordinate beings. A special group, called "the generation over whom there is no kingdom among the kingdoms that exist," has its origin and true home with Unbegotten Father

(75,12-19). A second group of six divine beings spring from the first five. These are said to resemble the first. Ineffable joy and unutterable jubilation characterize existence in the supercelestial region; and from there come patterns or types for subsequent creations. Following a summary passage (85,9-21), the tractate concludes with an appendix dealing with the realm of Immortal Man, which is our aeon. *Eugnostos* shows the influence of the transcendent realm upon this world. With one brief exception (85,8), which is probably an editorial addition, the influence is benign. *Eugnostos*, then, cannot be considered gnostic in any classic sense.

In the *Soph. Jes. Chr.* the following major points are added: the Savior (Christ) came from the supercelestial region (III 93,8-10; 94,10-14; 107,11-14; 118,15-16). Sophia is the one responsible for the fall of drops of light from the divine realm into the visible world (III 107,16-17; III 114,13/BG 119,9). Furthermore, a god exists who, with his subordinate powers, directly rules this world to the detriment of those who come from the divine realm (III 107,3-11; BG 119,2-121,13). Sex, it is suggested, is the means by which enslavement to the powers is perpetuated (III 108,10-14). But the Savior (Christ) broke the bonds imposed by the powers, and taught others to do the same (III 107,15-108,4; BG 121,13-122,3; III 118,3-25). Two classes of persons will be saved: those who know the Father in pure knowledge (that is, as described in *Soph. Jes. Chr.*), who will go to him; and those who know the Father defectively (III 117,8-118,2), who will go to the Eighth. In addition, it should be noted that the disciples named in *Soph. Jes. Chr.*, Philip, Matthew, Thomas, Bartholomew, and Mary, reflect a tradition within Gnosticism of disciples who are distinctively gnostic, and who are contrasted with some regularity, and in various ways, with "orthodox" or "orthodox turned gnostic" disciples (principally, Peter and John).

The notion of three divine men in the heavenly hierarchy appears to be based on Genesis 1-3 (Immortal Man = God; Son of Man = Adam [81,12]; Son of Son of Man, Savior = Seth). Because of the presence of Seth (although unnamed in the tractate), *Eugnostos* must be thought of as Sethian, in some sense. However, since it is not classically gnostic and lacks other elements of developed Sethian thought, it can only be characterized as proto-Sethian. Egyptian religious thought also appears to have influenced its picture of the supercelestial realm. The probable place of origin for *Eugnostos*, then, is Egypt. A very early date is suggested by the fact that Stoics, Epicureans and astrologers are called "all the philosophers." That characterization would have been appropriate in the first century B.C.E., but not later. *Eugnostos* and *Soph. Jes. Chr.* may have influenced the Sethian-Ophites, as described by Irenaeus. Some have proposed an influence by *Eugnostos* on Valentianism. Because of the dating of *Eugnostos*, it would not be surprising if *Soph. Jes. Chr.* had been composed soon after the advent of Christianity in Egypt – the latter half of the first century C.E. That possibility is supported by the tractate's relatively nonpolemical tone.

The two versions of *Eugnostos* differ from each other at significant points, attesting a long period of usage. The two versions of *Soph. Jes. Chr.* are very close. The translation which follows is based on the versions of Codex III; the other versions have been employed in instances where pages are no longer extant and where the text has required restoration.

EUGNOSTOS THE BLESSED

THE SOPHIA OF JESUS CHRIST

III 70, 1-90, 12;
Supplemented by V 7, 23-9, 9

III 90, 1-119, 18
Supplemented by BG 107, 1-111, 1
and 118, 13-112, 9

Eugnostos, the Blessed, to those |
who are his.

The Sophia of Jesus Christ.

After [15] he rose from the | dead, his twelve | disciples and seven | women continued to be his followers and | went to Galilee onto the mountain **91** called "Divination | and Joy." When they gathered together | and were perplexed about the underlying reality | of the universe and the plan and [5] the holy providence and | the power of the authorities and about | everything that the Savior is doing | with them in the secret | of the holy plan, [10] the Savior appeared, not in his | previous form, but in the | invisible spirit. And his likeness | resembles a great angel of light. | But his resemblance I must not describe. [15] No mortal flesh | could endure it, but only | pure (and) perfect flesh, like | that which he taught us about on the mountain | called [20] "Of Olives" in Galilee. And | he said: "Peace be to you (pl.)! My peace | I give | to you!" And they all marveled | and were afraid.

The Savior **92** laughed and said to them: "What | are you thinking about? (Why) are you perplexed? | What are you searching for?" | Philip said: "For the underlying reality [5] of the universe and the plan." [1]

The Savior said to them: [1] "I want you to know [1] that all men born [1] on earth from the foundation of [10] the world until now, being [1] dust, while they have inquired about God, [1] who he is and what he [1] is like, have not found him. Now the [1] wisest among [15] them have speculated from the ordering of [1] the world and (its) movement. [1] But their speculation has not reached [1] the truth. For it [1] is said that the ordering is directed in three ways [20] by all the philosophers, [1] (and) hence they do not [1] agree. For some of [1] them say about the world [1] that it is directed by itself. **93** Others, [1] that it is providence (that directs it). Others, [1] that it is fate. [1] But it is none of these. [5] Again, of the three voices I have [1] just mentioned, none [1] is close to the truth, and (they are) from [1] man. But I, who came [1] from Infinite Light, [10] I am here — for I know him (Light) — [1] that I might speak to you about the precise nature [1] of the truth. For whatever is from [1] itself is a polluted life; [1] it is self-made. Providence [15] has no wisdom in it. And [1] fate does not discern.

But to you [1] it is given to know; [1] and whoever is worthy of knowledge [1] will receive (it), whoever has not been [20] begotten by the sowing of [1] unclean rubbing but by First [1] Who Was Sent, for [1] he

Rejoice in this, [1] that you know (V [1], 3-4: Greetings! I want [you to know]) that all men [1] born from the foundation [5] of the world until now are [1] dust. While they have inquired about God, [1] who he is and what he is like, [1] they have not found him. The wisest [1] among them have speculated about the truth from the ordering [10] of the world. [1] And the speculation has not reached [1] the truth. For the ordering [1] is spoken of in three (different) opinions [1] by [15] all the philosophers, (and) hence [1] they do not agree. For some [1] of them say [1] about the world that it was directed [1] by itself. Others, [20] that it is providence (that directs it). [1] Others, that it is fate. [1] But it is none of these. [1] Again, of the three voices I have just [1] mentioned, none **71** is true.

For whatever is from itself [1] is an empty [1] life; it is self-made. Providence [1] is foolish. (And) fate [5] is an undiscerning thing.

Whoever, then, is able [1] to get free of [1] these three voices [1] I have just mentioned and come by means [1] of another voice to confess the [10] God of truth and agree [1] in everything concerning him, he is [1] immortal, dwelling in the midst | of mortal men.

He Who | Is is ineffable. [15] No principle knew him, no authority, | no subjection, nor any creature | from the foundation of the world, | except he alone.

For he | is immortal and eternal, [20] having no birth; for everyone | who has birth will perish. | He is unbegotten, having no beginning; | for everyone who has a beginning | has an end. No one rules **72** over him. He has no name; for whoever has | a name is the creation of another. | He is unnameable. He has no | human form; for whoever has [5] human form is the creation | of another. He has his own semblance — | not like | the semblance we have received and seen, | but a strange semblance [10] that surpasses all things | and is better than the totalities. It looks | to every side and sees itself | from itself. | He is infinite; he is incomprehensible. [15] He is ever imperishable | (and) has no likeness (to anything). He is | unchanging good. He is | faultless. He is everlasting. | He is blessed. He is unknowable, [20] while he (none-

is an immortal in the midst of | mortal men."

Matthew said **[9]4** to him: "Lord, | no one can find the truth except | through you. Therefore teach us | the truth." The Savior said: [5] "He Who Is is ineffable. | No principle knew him, no authority, | no subjection, nor any creature | from the foundation of | the world until now, except [10] he alone and anyone to whom he wants | to make revelation through him | who is from First | Light. From now on | I am the Great Savior. For he [15] is immortal and eternal. | Now he is eternal, | having no birth; for everyone | who has birth will perish. He is unbegotten, | having no beginning; [20] for everyone who has a beginning | has an end. Since no one rules | over him, he has no name; for whoever | has a name is the creation of | another. (**BG 84**, 13-17 adds: He is unnameable. He has no human form; for whoever has human form is the creation of another.) And he has a semblance **9[5]** of his own — not like | what you have seen and | received, but a strange semblance | that surpasses all things [5] and is better than the universe. | It looks to every side and sees itself | from itself. Since it is infinite, | he is ever incomprehensible. | He is imperishable and has no likeness (to anything). [10] He is unchanging good. | He is faultless. He is eternal. | He

theless) knows | himself. He is im-
measurable. | He is untraceable.
He is | perfect, having no defect.
73 He is imperishably blessed. |
He is called "Father | of the Uni-
verse."

Before anything is | visible
among those that are visible, [5] the
majesty and the authorities that |
are in him, he embraces the |
totalities of the totalities, and
nothing | embraces him. For he |
is all mind, thought [10] and reflect-
ing, considering, | rationality and
power. | They all are equal pow-
ers. | They are the sources of the
totalities. | And their whole race
⟨from first⟩ to last [15] is in the fore-
knowledge | of Unbegotten, |

is blessed. While he is not known,
| he ever knows | himself. He is
immeasurable. He is [15] untrace-
able. He is perfect, | having no de-
fect. He is imperishably blessed. |
He is called | 'Father of the Uni-
verse.'"

Philip said: "Lord, [20] how,
then, did he appear to the perfect
ones?" | The perfect Savior said
to him: | "Before anything is vis-
ible | of those that are visible, the
| majesty and the authority are
9[6] in him, since he embraces the
whole of the totalities, | while
nothing embraces | him. For he is
| all mind. And he is thought [5]
and considering | and reflecting
and | rationality and power. They
| all are equal powers. | They are
the sources of the totalities. [10] And
their whole race from | first to last
was | in his foreknowledge, (that
of) the infinite | Unbegotten |
Father."

Thomas said to him: [15] "Lord,
Savior, | why did these come to
be, and why | were these re-
vealed?" | The perfect Savior
said: | "I came from the Infinite
[20] that I might tell you all | things.
Spirit Who Is was the begetter, |
who had | the power ⟨of⟩ a beget-
ter **[97]** and form-[giver's] nature,
that | the great | wealth that was
hidden in him might be revealed.
Because of | his mercy and his
love [5] he wished | to bring forth
fruit by himself, that | he might
not ⟨enjoy⟩ his | goodness alone

for they had not yet come to visibility. |

Now a difference existed | among the imperishable aeons. [20] Let us, then, consider (it) this way. |

Everything that came from the perishable will perish, since it came | from the perishable. Whatever came **74** from imperishableness will not | perish but will become | imperishable, since it came from | imperishableness. So, [5] many men went astray | because they had not known this difference; that | is, they died.

But this much is | enough, since it is impossible for anyone | to dispute the nature of the words [10] I have just spoken about the blessed, | imperishable, true God. | Now, if anyone | wants to believe the words | set down (here), let him go [15] from what is hidden to the end of what is visible, | and this Thought | will in-

but (that) other spirits | of the Unwavering Generation might bring forth [10] body and fruit, glory and | honor in imperishableness and | his infinite grace, | that his treasure might be revealed | by Self-begotten God, [15] the father of every imperishableness and | those that came to be afterward. | But they had not yet come to visibility.

Now a great difference | exists among the imperishables." He called [20] out saying: "Whoever | has ears to hear about | the infinities, let him hear"; | and "I have addressed those who are awake." | Still he continued **[98]** and said: "Everything that came | from the perishable will perish, | since it came from | the perishable. But whatever came [5] from imperishableness does not perish | but becomes imperishable (**BG 89**, 16-17 adds: since it is from imperishableness). So, many men | went astray because they had not known this | difference and they died."

Mary said to him: [10] "Lord, | then how will we know that?" | The perfect Savior said: |

"Come (pl.) from invisible | things to the end of those that are visible, [15] and the very emanation

struct him how faith ' in those things that are not visible was ' found in what is visible. This is a [20] knowledge principle.

The Lord ' of the Universe is not rightly ' called "Father" but "Forefather." ' For the Father is the beginning (*or* principle) **7[5]** of what is visible. For he (the Lord) is ' the beginningless ' Forefather. He sees himself ' within himself, like a [5] mirror, having appeared in his ' likeness as Self-Father, that is, ' Self-Begetter, and as Confronter, ' since he confronted ' Unbegotten First Existent. [10] He is indeed of equal age with the one who is before ' him, but he is not equal to him ' in power. '

And the whole multitude [20] of the place over which there is no ' kingdom is called ' "Sons of Unbegotten ' Father."

Now the Unknowable **7[6]** [is] ever [full] of imperishableness [and] ineffable joy. ' They all are at rest '

of ' Thought will reveal to you ' how faith in those ' things that are not visible was found ' in those that are visible, those that belong to [20] Unbegotten Father. ' Whoever has ears to hear, ' let him hear.

The Lord of the Universe ' is not called 'Father' ' but 'Forefather.' ⟨For the Father is⟩ the beginning (*or* principle) of [25] those that will appear, but he (the Lord) **99** is [the] beginningless Forefather. ' Seeing himself ' within himself in a mirror, he appeared ' resembling himself, [5] but his likeness appeared ' as Divine ' Self-Father ' and ⟨as⟩ Confronter 'over the confronted ones,' ' First Existent Unbegotten [10] Father. He is indeed of equal age ' ⟨with⟩the Light that is before ' him, but he is not equal to him ' in power. '

"And afterward was revealed ' a whole multitude of confronting, [15] self-begotten ones, ' equal in age and power, ' being in glory (and) without number, whose race is called ' 'The Generation ' over Whom There Is No Kingdom ' 'from the one [20] in whom you yourselves have appeared ' from these ' men.' And that whole multitude ' over which there is no ' kingdom is called **100** 'Sons of Unbegotten ' Father, God, [Savior], ' Son of God,' ' whose likeness is with you. Now he [5] is the Unknowable, ' who is full of ever imperishable glory ' and ineffable joy. '

in him, [5] ever rejoicing in ineffable joy | over the unchanging glory | and the measureless jubilation | that was never heard or | known among all the aeons [10] and their worlds. But | this much is enough, lest we | go on endlessly. | This is another knowledge principle from | ⟨Self-⟩begotten.

The First [15] who appeared before the universe | in infinity is Self-grown, | Self-constructed Father, | and is full of shining, ineffable light. | In the beginning, he decided [20] to have his likeness become | a great power. | Immediately, | the principle (*or* beginning) of that Light | appeared as Immortal Androgynous Man.

His male name **[77]** is | "[Begotten,] Perfect [Mind]." | And his female name (is) "All-wise | Begettress Sophia." It is also said [5] that she resembles her | brother and her consort. | She is uncontested truth; | for here below error, which exists with truth, | contests it.

They all are at rest | in him, [10] ever rejoicing in ineffable joy | in his unchanging glory | and measureless jubilation; | this was never heard | or known [15] among all the aeons and their worlds | until now."

Matthew said | to him: "Lord, | Savior, how was Man revealed?" | The perfect [20] Savior said: "I want | you to know that he who | appeared before the universe in | infinity, Self-grown **101** Self-constructed Father, being full | of shining light | and ineffable, | in the beginning, when he decided to have his [5] likeness become a great power, | immediately the principle (*or* beginning) | of that Light appeared as Immortal | Androgynous Man, | that through that Immortal [10] Man they might attain | their salvation and awake | from forgetfulness through the interpreter | who was sent, who | is with you until the end [15] of the poverty of the robbers.

"And his | consort is the Great Sophia | who from the first was

Through [10] Immortal Man ' appeared the first designation, ' namely, divinity ' and kingdom, for the Father, who is ' called "Self-Father Man," [15] revealed this. ' He created a great aeon for his own majesty. He gave him ' great authority, and he ruled ' over all creations. He created [20] gods and archangels ' and angels, myriads ' without number for retinue. '

Now through that Man ' originated divinity [78] [and kingdom]. Therefore he was ' called "God of gods," "King ' of kings."

First Man ' is "Faith" for those who will come [5] afterward. He has, within, ' a unique mind (and) thought – just as ' he is it (thought] – (and) reflecting ' and considering, rationality and power. All the attributes [10] that exist are perfect and immortal. ' In respect to imperishableness, they ' are indeed equal. (But) in respect to power, there is a difference, ' like the difference between father ' and son, and son and thought, [15] and the thought and the remainder.

As ' I said earlier, among the things that were created, ' the monad is first, The dyad ' follows it, and the triad, ' up to the tenths. Now the tenths [20] rule the

destined in him ' for union by ' Self-begotten Father, from [20] Immortal Man 'who appeared ' as First and divinity and kingdom,' ' for the Father, who is **102** called 'Man, Self-Father,' ' revealed this. ' And he created a great aeon, ' whose name is Ogdoad, [5] for his own majesty.

"He was given ' great authority, and he ruled ' over the creation of poverty. ' He created gods ' and angels ⟨and⟩ archangels, [10] myriads without number ' for retinue from that Light ' and the ' tri-male Spirit, which is that of Sophia, ' his consort. [15] For from this God originated ' divinity ' and kingdom. Therefore he ' was called 'God of ' gods,' 'King of kings.'

" [20] First Man has ' his unique mind, ' within, and thought ' – just as he is it (thought) – (and) considering, ' reflecting, rationality, **103** power. All the attributes that exist ' are perfect and ' immortal. In respect to ' imperishableness, they are indeed equal. (But) in respect to [5] power, they are different, like the difference ' between father and son, ⟨and son⟩ and thought, ' and the thought and the remainder.

"As ' I said earlier, among ' the things that were created, the monad is [10] first.

hundredths; the hundredths | rule
the thousandths; the thou-
sand⟨th⟩s rule | the ten thou-
sand⟨th⟩s. This is the pattern
⟨among the⟩ | immortals. First
Man | is like this: His monad

(Pages **79** and **80** are missing. They
are replaced here with the corresponding section from Eugnostos
– Codex V, the beginning of
which is somewhat different from
the final partial sentence of **III 78**.)

V **[7]** [23] Again it is this pattern |
[that] exists among the immortals:
the monad [25] and the thought are
those things that belong to [Im-
mortal] Man. | The thinkings [are]
for | ⟨the⟩ decads, and the hun-
dreds are [the teachings,] | [and
the thousands] are the counsels, |
[and] the ten thousands [are] the
powers. [Now] those [who] [30]
come [from the . . .] | exist with
their [. . .] | [in] every aeon [. . .] |
[. . .] **[8]** [. . . In the beginning,
thought] | and thinkings [ap-
peared from] mind, | [then] teach-
ings [from] | thinkings, counsels [5]
[from teachings], (and) power
[from] | [counsels]. And after all
[the attributes,] | all that [was re-
vealed] | appeared from [his
powers.] | And [from what [was]
[10] created, what was [fashioned]
appeared. And | what was formed
appeared | from what was
[fashioned.] | What was named
appeared | from what was form-

And after everything, | all that
was revealed | appeared from his
power. And from what | was
created, | all that was fashioned [15]
appeared; from | what was fash-
ioned | appeared what was form-
ed; | from what was formed, |
what was named. Thus [20] came the
difference among the unbegotten

ed, [15] while the difference among begotten things ' appeared from what was [named], ' from beginning to end, by ' power of all the aeons. Now Immortal Man ' is full of every [20] imperishable glory and ineffable ' joy. His whole kingdom ' rejoices in ' everlasting rejoicing, those who never ' have been heard of or known [25] in any aeon that ' [came] after [them and ' its [worlds].

Afterward [another] ' [principle] came from Immortal [Man], ' who is [called] "Self-perfected [30] [Begetter.]" ' [When he received the consent] of his [consort,] ' [Great Sophia, he] revealed ' [that first-begotten androgyne,] **[9]** [who is called] ' "First-begotten [Son] ' [of God]." His female aspect ' [is "First-]begotten Sophia, [5] [Mother of the Universe]," whom some ' [call] "Love." ' [Now] First-begotten, since he has ' [his] authority from ' his [father], **III [81]** He created angels, ' myriads [without] number, ' for retinue. The whole multitude ' of those angels are called [5] "Assembly of the ' Holy Ones, the

ones ' from beginning to end." '

Then Bartholomew ' said to him: "How (is it that) ⟨he⟩ was designated in **104** the Gospel 'Man' ' and 'Son of Man'? ' To which of ' them, then, is this Son related?" The Holy One [5] said to him:

"I want you ' to know that First Man ' is called ' 'Begetter, Self-perfected ' Mind.' [10] He reflected with Great ' Sophia, his consort, and revealed ' his first-begotten, ' androgynous son. His ' male name [15] is designated 'First Begetter ' Son of God'; his female ' name, 'First ' Begettress Sophia, Mother of the Universe.' ' Some call her [20] 'Love.' Now First- ' begotten is called ' 'Christ.' Since he has authority ' from his father, he created ' a multitude of angels **105** without number for retinue ' from Spirit and Light." '

Shadowless Lights.'' ' Now when these greet ' each other, their embraces ' become angels [10] like themselves.

First Begetter ' Father is called ' ''Adam of the Light.''

And the kingdom ' of Son of Man is ' full of ineffable joy [15] and unchanging jubilation, (they) ever rejoicing ' in ineffable joy ' over their imperishable ' glory, which has ' never been heard nor has it been revealed [20] to all the aeons that came to be ' and their worlds.

Then Son ' of Man consented with ' Sophia, his consort, and ' revealed a great androgynous light. **[82]** [His] masculine name ' is [designated] ''Savior, ' Begetter

His disciples ' said to him: ''Lord, reveal to us [5] about the one ' called 'Man' that ' we also may know his glory exactly.'' ' The perfect ' Savior said: ''Whoever has [10] ears to hear, let him ' hear. First Begetter ' Father is called 'Adam, ' Eye of Light,' because he came ' from shining Light, [15] [and] his holy angels, who are ineffable ' (and) shadowless, ' ever rejoice with joy ' in their reflecting, ' which they received from their Father. The whole kingdom [20] of Son of Man, ' who is called 'Son ' of God,' is full of ' ineffable and shadowless joy, ' and unchanging jubilation, (they) rejoicing [25] over his imperishable **106** glory, which has never been heard until ' now, nor has it been revealed ' in the aeons that came ' afterward and their worlds. [5] I came from Self- ' begotten and First ' Infinite Light that ' I might reveal everything to you.'' '

Again, his disciples said: [10] ''Tell us clearly ' how (it is that) they came down from the ' invisibilities, ' from the immortal (realm) to the world ' that dies?'' The perfect [15] Savior said: ''Son of ' Man consented with Sophia, his ' consort, and revealed ' a great androgynous light. ' His male name [20] is designated 'Savior, '

of All things." His feminine name
is designated [5] "Sophia, All-
Begettress." Some call her
"Pistis."

Then Savior consented with
his consort, Pistis Sophia, and
revealed six androgynous spiritual
beings [10] who are the type of
those who preceded them. Their
male names are these: first, "Unbegotten"; second, "Self-
begotten"; third, [15] "Begetter";
fourth, "First Begetter"; fifth,
"All-Begetter"; sixth, "Arch-
Begetter." Also the names of the
females are these: first, [20] "All-
wise Sophia"; second, "All-
Mother Sophia"; third,
"All-Begettress Sophia";
fourth, "First Begettress
Sophia"; fifth, "Love Sophia";
[83] [sixth], "Pistis Sophia."

[From the] consenting of those
I have just mentioned, thoughts
appeared in the aeons that exist.
[5] From thoughts, reflectings;
from reflectings, considerings;
from considerings, rationalities;
from rationalities, wills; from [10]
wills, words.

Then the twelve powers,
whom I have just discussed, consented with each other. ⟨Six⟩
males (each) (and) ⟨six⟩ females
(each) were revealed, so that
there are seventy- [15] two powers.
Each one of the seventy-two revealed five spiritual (powers),
which (together) are the three hundred sixty powers. The union of
them all is [20] the will.

Begetter of All Things.' His
female name is designated 'All-Begettress Sophia.' Some call her
'Pistis.'

Therefore our aeon came to be as the type | of Immortal Man. | Time came to be as | the type of First Begetter, **[84]** his son. [The year] came to be as | the type of [Savior. The] twelve | months came to be as the type | of the twelve powers. The three ⁵ hundred sixty days of the year | came to be as the type of the three hundred | sixty powers who appeared | from Savior. Their hours | and moments came to be as the ¹⁰ type of the angels who came | from them (the three hundred sixty powers) (and) who are without number. |

All who come ²⁵ into the world, like **107** a drop from the Light, | are sent by him | to the world of Almighty, | that they might be guarded ⁵ by him, And the bond of | his forgetfulness bound him by the will | of Sophia, that the matter might be ⟨revealed⟩ through it | to the whole world in poverty | concerning his (Almighty's) arrogance ¹⁰ and blindness and | the ignorance that he was named. But I | came from the places | above by the will of the great | Light, (I) who escaped from that bond; ¹⁵ I have cut off the work of the | robbers; I have wakened that drop | that was sent from Sophia, | that it | might bear much fruit ²⁰ through me and be perfected and not again be | defective but be ⟨joined⟩ through | me, the Great Savior, that his | glory might be revealed, so that ' Sophia might also be justified in regard to that [25] defect, that her **108** sons might not again become defective but ' might attain honor and ' glory and go up to their ' Father and know the words of the masculine Light. And [5] you ' were sent by ' the Son, who was sent ' that you might receive Light and ' remove yourselves from the forgetfulness of [10] the authorities, and that it might not again come to appearance ' because of you, namely, the unclean rubbing ' that is ' from the fearful fire that ' came from their fleshly part. [15] Tread upon their ' malicious intent.''

Then Thomas said to [him]: ' ''Lord, Savior ' how many are the aeons of those ' who surpass the heavens?'' The perfect [20] Savior said: ''I praise ' you (pl.) because you ask about ' the great aeons, for your roots ' are in the infinities. Now when ' those whom I have discussed earlier were revealed, [25] he [provided]

(Pages **109** and **110** are missing. They are replaced here with the corresponding section from the Berlin Gnostic Codex [no. 8502], the beginning of which is somewhat different from the final partial sentence of **III 108**.)

And when those whom I have discussed appeared, ' All-Begetter, their father, very soon '

BG 107 Now when ' those whom I have discussed earlier were revealed, ' Self-Begetter ' Father created [15] twelve aeons | for retinue for the twelve | angels.

And in | each aeon there were six (heavens), | so [20] there are seventy-two heavens of the seventy-two | powers who appeared | from him. And in each of the heavens | there were five firmaments, | so there are (altogether) three hundred sixty [85] [firmaments] of the three hundred | sixty powers that appeared | from them.

When the firmaments | were complete, they were called [5] "The Three Hundred Sixty Heavens," according to the name of the | heavens that were before them. And all these | are perfect and good. And in this | way the defect | of femaleness appeared.

The first [10] aeon, then, is that of Immortal Man. | The second aeon is that of Son of | Man, who is called | "First Begetter," (**V 13**, 12-13 adds here: The third is that of son of Son of Man), who | is called "Savior." [15] That which embraces these is the aeon | over which there is no kingdom, (the aeon) of the | Eternal Infinite God, the | aeon of the aeons of the immortals | who are in it, (the aeon) above the Eighth [20] that ap-

very soon created [5] twelve | aeons for retinue | for the twelve | angels.

All | these are perfect [10] and good. | Thus | the defect | in the female appeared."

And ⟨he⟩ said | to him: "How many are the [15] aeons of the immortals, | starting from the infinities?" | The perfect Savior said: | "Whoever has | ears to hear, let him **108** hear. The first aeon | is that of Son of Man, | who is called | 'First Begetter,' [5] who is called | 'Savior,' | who has appeared. | The second aeon (is) that of | Man, who is called [10] 'Adam, Eye | of Light.'

That which embraces | these is the aeon | over which there is no kingdom, | (the aeon) of the Eternal [15] Infinite God, | the Self-begotten aeon | of the aeons | that are in it, (the aeon) of the immor-

peared in | chaos.

Now Immortal Man | revealed aeons | and powers and kingdoms | and gave authority to everyone **[86]** who [appeared from] him | to make [whatever they desire] | until the days that are above chaos. | For these consented with each other [5] and revealed | every magnificence, even from spirit, | multitudinous lights | that are glorious and without number. These | received names in the beginning, that [10] is, the first, the middle, ⟨and⟩ the perfect; | that is, the first aeon and | the second and the third. | The first was called | "Unity and Rest." [15] Since each one has its (own) | name, the | ⟨third⟩ aeon was designated "Assembly" | from the great multitude that | appeared in the multitudinous one. [20] Therefore, when the multitude | gathers and comes to a unity, | they are called "Assembly," | from the Assembly that surpassed | heaven. Therefore, the Assembly of **[87]** the [Eighth was] revealed | as [androgynous] and was named | partly as male and partly | as female. The male was called "Assembly," [5] the female, "Life," that | it might be shown that from | a female came the life | in all the aeons. Every name was received, | starting from the beginning.

tals, | whom I described earlier, **109** (the aeon) above the Seventh | that appeared from | Sophia, which is the | first aeon.

"Now [5] Immortal Man revealed | aeons | and powers and kingdoms | and gave authority | to all who appear [10] in him that they might | exercise their desires until | the last things that are above | chaos. For these | consented with each [15] other and revealed | every magnificence, even | from spirit, | multitudinous lights that are glorious | and without number. These **110** were called | in the beginning, that is, | the first aeon | and ⟨the second⟩ and ⟨the third⟩. [5] The first ⟨is⟩ called | 'Unity | and Rest.' Each one has | its (own) name; for [10] the ⟨third⟩ aeon | was designated 'Assembly' | from the | great multitude that | appeared: [15] in one, a multitude revealed themselves. | Now because | the multitudes **111** gather **III 111** and come to a unity, (**BG 111**, 2-5 adds here: therefore ⟨they⟩ are called 'Assembly,' from that Assembly that surpasses heaven) we call | them 'Assembly | of the Eighth.' It appeared | as androgynous and was named [5] partly as male and | partly as female. The male | is called 'Assembly,' while the | female is called 'Life,' | that it might be shown that from [10] a female came the life for | all the aeons. And every name was | received, starting from the beginning.

From his [10] concurrence with his thought, | the powers appeared who were called | "gods"; and the gods | from their considerings revealed | divine gods; [15] and the gods from their | considerings revealed lords; | and the lords of the lords from | their words revealed lords; | and the lords from [20] their powers revealed | archangels; the archangels | revealed angels; from | ⟨them⟩ the semblance appeared [88] with structure [and form] for naming | [all] the aeons [and] their worlds. |

All the immortals, whom | I have just described, have authority – all of them – [5] from the power of | Immortal Man and Sophia, | his consort, who was | called "Silence," (and) who was named | "Silence" because by reflecting [10] without speech she perfected her | own majesty. Since the imperishabilities had | the authority, each provided | great kingdoms in all the immortal heavens [15] and their firmaments, | thrones, (and) temples, | for their own majesty.

Some, indeed, | (who are) in dwellings and in chariots, | being in ineffable glory [20] and not able to be sent into any creature, | provided for themselves | hosts of angels, myriads | without number

"For from | his concurrence with his thought, the powers | very soon appeared who [15] were called 'gods'; | and [the] gods of the gods from their | wisdom revealed gods; | ⟨and the gods⟩ from their wisdom revealed | lords; and the lords of [20] the lords from their thinkings revealed lords; | and the lords from | their power revealed archangels; | the archangels | from their words revealed angels; 112 from them | semblances appeared with structure and form | and name for all the aeons | and their worlds.

"And the immortals, [5] whom I have just described, all have | authority from | Immortal Man, 'who | is called 'Silence' | because by reflecting without [10] speech all her own majesty was perfected.' | For since the imperishabilities had | the authority, each created | a great kingdom | in the Eighth [15] and (also) thrones and | temples (and) firmaments for | their own majesties. For these all | came by the will | of the Mother of the Universe."

Then [20] the Holy Apostles said | to him: "Lord, Savior, | tell us about those who are in the aeons, | since it is necessary for us to ask | about them." The perfect 113 Savior said: "If you ask | about anything, I will tell you. | They created hosts of | angels, myriads without number [5] for retinue and their glory. They created | virgin for retinue **[89]** and glory, even virgin ' spirits, the ineffable lights. ' They have no sickness ' nor weakness, but it is only will: [5] it comes to be in an instant. ' Thus were completed ' the aeons with their heavens and firmaments ' for the glory of Immortal ' Man and Sophia, his consort: [10] the area which ⟨contained the pattern of⟩ every aeon and ' their worlds and those that came ' afterward, in order to provide ' the types from there, their ' likenesses in the heavens of chaos and [15] their worlds.

And all natures ' from the Immortal One, from Unbegotten ' to the revelation of ' chaos, are in the light that shines without shadow ' and (in) ineffable joy [20] and unutterable jubilation. ' They ever delight themselves ' on account of their glory that does not change ' and the rest that is not measured, ' which cannot be described **90** or conceived ' among all the aeons ' that came to be and their powers. ' But this much is enough. All [5] I have just said to you, ' I said in the way you might ' accept, until the one who need not be taught ' appears among you, ' and he will speak all these things to you [10] joyously and in ' pure knowledge. '

spirits, the ' ineffable and unchangeable lights. ' For they have no sickness ' nor weakness, [10] but it is will. (**BG 115**, 14 adds here: And they came to be in an instant.)

"Thus the aeons were completed ' quickly with the heavens ' and the firmaments in the glory ' of Immortal Man and Sophia, ' his consort: the area from which [15] every aeon and the world ' and those that came afterward ' took (their) pattern for their creation ' of likenesses in the heavens of chaos ' and their worlds. And all natures, [20] starting from the revelation of chaos, ' are in the Light that shines without shadow ' and joy that cannot be described ' and ' unutterable jubilation. They ever [25] delight themselves on account of their unchanging glory **114** and the immeasurable rest, ' which cannot be described ' among all the aeons that ' came to be afterward and all their [5] powers. Now all that ' I have just said to you, I ' said that you might shine in ' Light more than these."

Mary said ' to him: "Holy Lord, [10] where did your disciples ' come from and where are they going and (what) should they ' do here?" ' The perfect Savior said to them: "I want ˈ you to know that Sophia, [15] the Mother of the Universe and the consort, ˈ desired by herself ˈ to bring these to existence without ˈ her male (consort). But by the will ˈ of the Father of the Universe, that his [20] unimaginable goodness might be revealed, ˈ he created that curtain ˈ between the immortals ˈ and those ˈ that came afterward, [25] that the consequence might follow

(Pages **115** and **116** are missing. They are replaced here with the corresponding section from the Berlin Gnostic Codex [no. 8502].)

BG 118 every aeon ˈ and chaos, [15] that the defect of the female ˈ might ⟨appear⟩, and it might come about that ˈ Error would contend with ˈ her. And these became **119** the curtain ˈ of spirit. From ⟨the⟩ aeons ˈ above the emanations ˈ of Light, as [5] I have said already, a ˈ drop from Light ˈ and Spirit came down to the lower regions ˈ of Almighty [10] in chaos, that ˈ their molded forms might appear ˈ from that drop, ˈ for it is a judgment ˈ on him, Arch-Begetter, [15] who is called ˈ 'Yaldabaoth.' ˈ That drop revealed ˈ their molded forms ˈ through the breath, as a **120** living soul. It was withered ˈ and it slumbered in the ignorance ˈ of the soul. When it ˈ became hot from the breath [5] of the Great Light ˈ of the Male, and

it took ' thought, (then) ' names
were received by all who ' are in
the world of chaos [10] and all things
that are in ' it through that ' Immortal One, when the breath '
blew into him. ' But when this
came about [15] by the will of
Mother ' Sophia — so that Immortal Man ' might piece together
121 the garments there ' for a
judgment ' on the robbers — '
⟨he⟩ then welcomed the blowing [5]
of that breath; ' but since he was
soul-like, ' he was not able to take
' that power for himself ' until [10]
the number of chaos should be
complete, (that is,) when the time
' determined by the great ' angel is
complete.

"Now I have taught ' you
about Immortal [15] Man and have
loosed ' the bonds of the robbers '
from him. ' I have broken the
gates of **122** the pitiless ones in
their presence. ' I have humiliated
their ' malicious intent, and they
all have been shamed ' and have
risen [5] from their ignorance. Because ' of this, then, I came here,
' that they might be joined with '
that Spirit and ' Breath, **III 117**
that [. . .] and Breath, and might '
from two become one, just as from
' the first, that you might yield
much fruit ' and go up to [5] Him
Who Is from the Beginning, in '
ineffable joy and glory ' and
[honor and] grace of ' [the Father
of the Universe].

"Whoever, [then], knows ' [the

Father in pure] knowledge [10] [will depart] to the Father | [and repose in] Unbegotten | [Father]. But [whoever knows] [him defectively] will depart | [to the defect] and the rest [15] [of the Eighth. Now] whoever knows | Immortal [Spirit] | of Light in silence, through reflecting | and consent in the truth, | let him bring me signs [20] of the Invisible One, and he will become | a light in the Spirit of Silence. | Whoever knows Son of Man | in knowledge and love, | let him bring me a sign **118** of Son of Man, that he might depart | to the dwelling-places with those in the Eighth. |

"Behold, I have revealed to you | the name of the Perfect One, the whole will [5] of the Mother of the Holy Angels, | that the masculine [multitude] | may be completed here, | that there [might appear, in the aeons,] | [the infinities and] [10] those that [came to be in the] untraceable | [wealth of the Great] | Invisible [Spirit, that they] all [might take] | [from his goodness,] | even the wealth [of their rest] [15] that has no [kingdom over it]. I | came [from First] Who | Was Sent, that I might reveal | to you Him Who Is from | the Beginning, because of the arrogance [20] of Arch-Begetter and his angels, | since they say about themselves that | they are gods. And I | came to remove them from their blindness | that I might tell everyone [25] about the God who is above the universe. **119** Therefore, tread upon their | graves, humiliate their malicious intent | and break their yoke | and arouse my own. I have given [5] you authority over all things | as Sons of Light, | that you might tread upon their power with | [your] feet."

These are the things [the] blessed | Savior [said,] [10] [and he disappeared] from them. Then | [all the disciples] were in | [great, ineffable joy] in | [the spirit from] that day on. | [And his disciples] began to preach [15] [the] Gospel of God, | [the] eternal, imperishable [Spirit]. | Amen. |

EUGNOSTOS, THE BLESSED　　　THE SOPHIA OF JESUS

THE DIALOGUE OF THE SAVIOR (III,5)

Introduced by

HELMUT KOESTER and ELAINE H. PAGELS

Translated by

STEPHEN EMMEL

The title *The Dialogue of the Savior* appears in the *incipit* and the *explicit* of the manuscript and is apparently a later addition. No specific author is indicated anywhere in the text. But the speaker is the "Savior" or the "Lord" (he is never called Jesus or Jesus Christ) in conversation with his disciples Judas, Mary, and Matthew. In this respect, the title "dialogue" is appropriate, except for the first section of the text (120,3-124,22) which is an uninterrupted monologue of the Savior. The text is preserved only in this somewhat fragmentary manuscript, and it is not referred to or quoted in any ancient source. Thus, no external attestation for the date of its composition is available.

The Dialogue of the Savior is a writing of considerable complexity, and its several parts exhibit a great variety in style and content. It is best seen as a compilation of various generations of Christianity and composed in its extant form, originally in Greek, some time during the 2nd century. Parallels to the author's understanding of baptism in deutero-Pauline epistles suggest a date close to the turn of the first century.

The primary source was a dialogue between the Lord and three disciples. This source is preserved in the following sections of the extant work: 124,23-127,19; 128,23-129,16; 131,19-133,21(?); 137,3-146,20, i.e., in about 65% of the present text. These sections are characterized by brief questions, usually from one of the named disciples (sometimes by all disciples) and equally brief answers of the Lord. Sometimes these questions and answers are expanded into longer units discussing a particular topic. Traditional sayings of Jesus used in these questions and answers have parallels in the Gospels of Matthew, Luke, and John, and particularly in *The Gospel of Thomas*. However, a literary dependence upon any of these writings seems unlikely. Rather, the sayings tradition used here appears to be an independent parallel to the one used in *The Gospel of Thomas* and the Gospel of John.

The form of these brief dialogue units parallels the dialogues found in the Gospel of John. In contrast to some gnostic dialogues which are actually secondarily arranged theological discourses (such as *The Sophia of Jesus Christ* and *Pistis Sophia*), the dialogues of the Gospel of John and of *The Dialogue of the Savior* are not free compositions of an author, but elaborations and interpretations of traditional sayings. In some instances, the dialogical development of the sayings tradition in our document is less advanced and theologically less complex than the Johannine parallels. This would argue for a date of the original dialogue source of this document before the end of the first century.

The sequence of the topics explored in these dialogues has close parallels in sayings of *The Gospel of Thomas*, especially in its saying 2 about the seeking, finding, marvelling, ruling and resting. That saying presents an eschatological timetable which is further explored in the dialogues of this writing. The disciples have sought and found and marvelled, but their ruling and resting will come only in the future. At the present time, they still carry the burden of the flesh, i.e., the body and earthly labor or, in the words of this writing, of "the works of womanhood." Mary who recognizes this receives the highest praise. This theme, the continuation of the works of the female, i.e., the continuation of the human race through childbirth, is prominent in the last portion of the dialogue. It deals with the role of the female in the process of salvation more explicitly than most other early Christian writings (close parallels can be found in *The Gospel of the Egyptians*, quoted by Clement of Alexandria), and it gives Mary a very high estimate as "a woman who had understood completely" (139,11-13).

In the final form of the document, several other traditional pieces have been added to the original dialogue: 1) Fragments of a creation myth (127,19-131,18) which is based upon Gen 1-2. The myth relates how water, originally separated from the earth by a wall of fire, made the world fruitful. In 128,1-129,12, the author has interrupted the account of this myth in order to interpret the term spirit. 2) A cosmological wisdom list (133,23-134,24). The author has added comments about the root of wickedness and about baptism. 3) An apocalyptic vision of which fragments are still recognizable in 134,24-137,3. The vision, taking place on a high mountain from where the whole of heaven and earth can be seen, originally spoke about the rescue of a soul and its installation before God in a new garment. The process is explained by an angelic figure called "Son of Man," a title which *The Dialogue of the Savior* never uses for Jesus.

The final author opened his compilation of these materials with an intriguing section (120,2-124,22), consisting of an exhortation, a prayer of thanksgiving and a gnostic discourse about the passage of the soul through the heavenly powers. This section employs established Christian soteriological language with allusions to passages from the New Testament epistles; it also contains a reference to the Gospel of John (Jn 1:18). With this introduction the entire dialogue is placed into a new context: baptismal initiation. The baptismal theology resolves the conflict between the "already" of a realized eschatology and the "not yet" of a futuristic eschatology. As baptism is understood in the same way as in Eph 2:1-6 and Col 3:1-4, those who are baptized have already passed through death into true life. Metaphorical and mythical language is thus related to a cultic act for the expression of realized eschatology.

Yet, receiving visions in the context of baptism is not the culmination of the experience of redemption. Instead, through the utilization and interpretation of the older dialogue used in the composition, the author presents a discussion of the complex eschatological situation of the disciples. Although the disciples have already sought and found and have marvelled at visions, have experienced the indwelling of the living God and passed through the powers in the experience of baptism, their final entry into ruling and resting is still to come. Their present existence is defined as work in behalf of the revelation, so that they, like their Lord, may save others and "reveal the greatness of the revealer," while they are still wearing the flesh, carrying a burden just as the Lord himself. This also indicates that the "Lord" who is speaking in this dialogue is not the exalted Lord but the "earthly" Jesus. The "place of truth" is not defined in terms of other-worldly existence, but as the place where the Lord is. This emphasis upon the tasks of a Christian life in this world implies that the "dissolution of the works of womanhood" does not suggest a metaphysically motivated sexual asceticism, but speaks of the secret birth through the one who "is coming from the Father." In spite of the evident employment of gnostic language in the description of the baptismal experience, *The Dialogue of the Savior* cannot be understood as the simple product of gnostic theology. Rather, it resembles the Gospel of John in its attempt to reinterpret the sayings of Jesus in the horizon of gnostic thought.

THE DIALOGUE OF THE SAVIOR

III 120, 1-147, 23

The Dialogue of the Savior |

(1) The Savior said to his disciples, | "Already the time has come, | brothers, for us to abandon [5] our labor and stand at | rest. For whoever stands | at rest will rest | forever. And I | say to you, [be] always [10] [above ...] | time ... [...] | ... you [...] | be afraid [of ...] | ... you ... [...] [15] ... anger [is] fearful [...] | arouse anger ... [... is ...] | but since you have ... [...] | ... [...] | they accepted these words [concerning it] with [fear] [20] and trembling, and it set | them up with governors, | for from it nothing was forthcoming. | But when I came, I | opened the path and I taught them about [25] the passage which they will traverse, | the elect and solitary, **121** [who have known the Father, having | believed] the truth and [all] the praises | while you offered praise. |

(2) "So when you offer praise, do so like this: [5] Hear us, Father, just as | you heard your only-begotten | son and received him | [and] gave him rest from many ... | [.... You are the one] whose power [10] [... your] armor ... | [... is ...] ... light | [...] ... living | [...] ... touch ... | [...] ... the word ... [15] [...] repentance ... life | [...] ... you. You are | [the] thinking and the [entire] serenity | of the solitary. Again: [Hear] | us just as you heard [20] your elect. Through your [sacrifice | these] will enter; through their | [good] works these have saved | their souls from these | blind [limbs] so that they might exist **122** eternally. Amen.

(3) "I will | teach you. When | the time of dissolution arrives, | the first power of darkness will [5] come upon you. Do not be afraid | and

say, 'Behold! The time ' has come!' But when you see ' a single staff
... [...] ' ... this ... [...] ... [...] ¹⁰ ... [...] ' ... [...] ' understand ... [...] ' ... the work ... [...] ' and the governors ... [...]
¹⁵ come upon you ... [...]. ' Truly, fear is the [power ...] ' .... So
if you are going to be [afraid] ' of what is about to come upon [you], '
it will engulf you. ²⁰ For there is not one among them who will ' spare
you or show [you] mercy. ' But in this way, look at [the ...] ' in it,
since you have mastered every word ' on earth. It **123** [... take] you up
to the ... ' [... place] where there is no rule ' [... tyrant]. When you
' [... you] will see those who ⁵ [...] ... and also ... ' [... tell] you
... ' [...] ... the reasoning power ' [...] reasoning power ... ' [...
place] of truth ¹⁰ [...] ... but ... ' [...]. But you ' [...] ... truth,
this ' [...] ... living ... ' [... and] your joy ¹⁵ [...]. So [...] ... in
order that ' [...] your souls ' [...] lest it ' [...] the word [... ' ...]
... raise ... ²⁰ [...] ... [...] ... ' [...] ... [...] ... your ... ' [...]
... [...] ... ' [...] .... For the crossing place **124** is fearful [before
you]. ' But you, [with a] ' single mind, pass [it] by! ' For its depth is
great; [its] ⁵ height [is] enormous [...] ' a single mind ... [...] ' and
the fire ... [...] ' ... [... ' all] the powers [...] ¹⁰ ... you, they ...
[...] ' and the [powers ...] ' they ... [...] ' ... [...] ' ... soul ...
[...] ¹⁵ ... [...] ' in everyone [... you] ' are the ... [...] ' and ...
[...] ' ... forget ... [...] ²⁰ ... son ... [...] ' and you [...] ...
[...] ' you ... [...] ... [...]." '

(4) [Matthew] said, "[How ... ' ... **125** ...]?"

(5) The Savior said, ' "[...] ... the things inside you ' [...] ... will
remain, you ' [...]."

(6) Judas [said], "Lord, ⁵ [...] ... the works ' [... these] souls,
these ' [...] these little ones, when ' [...]where will they be? ' [...] ...
[...] ... the spirit ¹⁰ [...]."

(7) The Lord [said], ' "[...] ... ' [... receive] ' them. These do not
die, ' [...] ... they are not destroyed, for they have known ¹⁵ [their]
consorts and him who would [receive ' them]. For the truth seeks ' [out
the] wise and the righteous." '

(8) The Savior [said], "The lamp ' [of the body] is the mind. As long
as ²⁰ [the things inside] you are set in order, that is, ' [...] ... , your
bodies are [luminous]. ' As long as your hearts ' are [dark], the luminosity you **126** anticipate [...] ' I have ... [...] ' ... I will go ...
[...] ' ... my word ... [...] ⁵ I send ... [...]." '

(9) His [disciples said, "Lord], ' who is it who seeks, and [...] '
reveals?"

(10) [The Lord said to them,] ' "He who seeks [...] ^{10} reveals ... [...]." '

(11) [Matthew said, "Lord, when] ' I [...] ' and [when] I speak, who is it who ... [...] ' ... who listens?"

(12) [The Lord] said, ^{15} "It is the one who speaks who also [listens], ' and it is the one who can see who also ' reveals."

(13) [Mary] said, ' "Lord, behold! ' Whence [do I] bear the body [while I] ^{20} weep, and whence while I [...]?" '

(14) The Lord said, "[...] ' weep on account of its works [...] ' remain and the mind laughs [...] ... [... **127** ...] ... spirit. If one does not ' [...] darkness, he will be able to see ' [...]. So I tell you ' [...] light is the darkness ^{5} [...] ... stand in ' [...] not see the light ' [...] the lie [...] ... they brought them from ' [...] ... [...] .... You will give ' [...] ... and ^{10} [... exist] forever. ' [...] ... ' [...] ... ' [...] ever. Then ' [all] the powers ^{15} which are above as well as those ' [below] will [...] you. In that place ' [there will] be weeping and ' [gnashing] of teeth over the end of [all] these things." '

(15) Judas [said], "Tell ^{20} [us, Lord], what was [...] before ' [the heaven and the] earth existed." '

(16) The Lord said, ' "There was darkness and water and **128** spirit upon [water]. ' And I say [to you, ... ' what] you seek [after ...] ' inquire after ... [...] ^{5} within you ... [...] ' ... the power and the [mystery ...] ' spirit, for from ... [...] ' wickedness [...] come ... [...] ' mind ... [...] ^{10} behold ... [...] ' ... [...]." '

(17) [...] said, "[Lord], ' tell us ' where [the ... is established] and ^{15} where [the true mind] exists." '

(18) The Lord [said], "The fire [of the] ' spirit came into existence ... [...] ' both. On this account, the [...] ' came into existence, and ^{20} the [true] mind came into existence [within] them [...]. ' If someone [sets his soul] ' up high, [then he will] ' be exalted."

(19) And Matthew [asked him **129** ...] ... took ... ' [...] ... it is he who ... ' [...]."

(20) The Lord [said], ' "[... stronger] than ... ^{5} [...] ... you ... ' [...] ... [...] ... to follow ' [you] and all the works ' [...] your hearts. For just as ' your hearts [...], so ^{10} [...] the means to overcome the powers ' [above] as well as those below ' [...]. I say to you, ' let him [who possesses] power renounce ' [it and repent]. And ^{15} [let] him who [...] seek and find and [rejoice]." '

(21) Judas [said], "Behold! ' [I] see that all things exist ' [...] like signs upon ' [...]. On this account did they happen thus." ^{20}

(22) The Lord [said], "When the [Father ' established] the cosmos, he ' [...] water from it ' [and his] Word came forth from it **130** and it inhabited many ... [...]. ' It was higher than the [path ... surround] ' the entire earth ... [...] ' ... the [collected] water [...] [5] existing outside them. [...] ' ... the water, a great fire [encircling] ' them like a wall. ... [...] ' ... time once many things had become separated [from what] ' was inside. When the [...] [10] was established, he looked ... [...] ' and said to it, 'Go, and ... [...] ' from yourself in order that ... [...] ' be in want from generation to [generation, and] ' from age to age.' [Then it] [15] cast forth from itself [fountains] ' of milk and [fountains of] ' honey and oil and [wine] ' and [good] fruits ' and sweet flavor and [20] good roots, [in order that] ' it might not be deficient from generation [to] ' generation, and from age [to age]. '

(23) "And it is above ... [... **131** ...] standing ' [...] ... its beauty ... ' [...] ... and outside ' [there was a great] light, powerful [5] [...] ... resemble it, for it ' [...] ... rules over [all] the aeons ' [above] and below. ' [... was] taken from the fire ... ' [...] ... it was scattered in the [10] [...] ... above and ' [below. All] the works ' [which] depend on them, it is they ' [...] over the heaven above ' [and over] the earth [below]. [15] On them depend ' all [the works]."

(24) [And] when [Judas] ' heard these things, he bowed down and he ' [...] and he offered praise to the Lord. '

(25) [Mary] hailed her brethren, [20] [saying], "Where are you going to put [these things] about which you ask the son ... ' [...]?" '

(26) [The Lord said] to her, "Sister, ' [...] will be able to inquire about these things [except ' for someone who] has somewhere **132** to put them in his [heart ...] ' ... to come [forth ...] ' and enter ... [...] ... [...] ' so that they might not hold back ... [...] [5] this impoverished cosmos."

(27) [Matthew] said, ' "Lord, I want [to see] ' that place of life [...] ' where there is no wickedness, [but rather] ' there is pure [light]!"

(28) The Lord [said], [10] "Brother [Matthew], ' you will not be able to see it [as long as you are] ' carrying flesh around."

(29) [Matthew] said, ' "Lord, [even if I will] ' not [be able] to see it, let me [know it]!" [15]

(30) The Lord [said], "[Everyone] ' who has known himself has seen [it in] ' everything given to him to do [...] ' ... and has come to [...] ' it in his [goodness]."

(31) [Judas] [20] responded, saying, ' "Tell me, Lord, [how it is that ...] ' ... which shakes the earth ' moves."

(32) The Lord picked up a [stone and] ' held it in his hand, [saying,
133 "What] am I holding ' [in] my [hand]?"

(33) He said, "[It is] a stone." '

(34) He [said] to them, "That which supports ' [the earth] is that
which supports the heaven. [5] When a Word comes forth ' from the
Greatness, it will come on what ' supports the heaven and the earth. For
the earth ' does not move. Were it to move, it would ' fall. But it neither
moves nor falls, in order that the First Word might not [10] fail. For it was
that which established ' the cosmos and inhabited ' it and inhaled fragrance from ' it. For, ... [...] ... which do not move I ' [...] ...
you, all the sons of [men. [15] For] you are from [that] place. ' [In] the
hearts of those who speak out of [joy] ' and truth you exist. ' Even if it
comes forth in ' [the body] of the Father among men [20] and is not received, still ' it [...] return to its place. Whoever [does not] know ' [the
work] of perfection [knows] ' nothing. If one does not stand ' in the
darkness, he will not be able to see the light. **134**

(35) "If [one] does not [understand ' how] fire came into existence, '
he will burn in it, because ' he does not know the root of it. [5] If one
does not first understand ' water, he knows nothing. For what ' use is
there for him to be baptized ' in it? If one does not understand ' how
blowing wind [10] came into existence, he will blow away ' with it. If one
does not understand ' how body, which he bears, ' came into existence,
he will [perish] with ' it. And how will someone who does [not] know
[the Son] [15] know the [Father]? ' And to someone who will not know
the [root] ' of all things, they remain hidden. Someone who ' will not
know the root of wickedness ' is no stranger to it. Whoever [20] will not
understand how ' he came will not understand how ' he will go, and he
is no [stranger] ' to this cosmos which [will ...], ' which will be humiliated."

(36) Then he [... Judas] [25] and Matthew and [Mary **135** ...] ... [...]
... the edge of heaven ' [and] earth. [And] when he placed his ' [hand]
upon them, they hoped that they might ' [...] ... it. Judas raised his
eyes [5] and saw an exceedingly high place, ' and he saw the place of the
abyss ' below. Judas said to ' Matthew, "Brother, who will ' be able to
climb up to such a height or down to the [10] bottom of the abyss? For there
is a tremendous ' fire there and something very fearful!" ' At that moment, a Word came forth from ' it. As it stood there, ' he saw how it
had come [15] [down]. Then he said to it, "[Why] ' have you come
down?"

(37) And the Son ' of Man greeted them and said to them, ' "A seed

from a power was ' deficient and it went down to [20] [the] abyss of the earth. And the Greatness ' remembered [it] and he sent the [Word ' to] it. It brought it up into ' [his presence] so that **136** the First Word might not fail." [Then his disciples] were ' amazed at [all the things] ' he had said to them, and they accepted them on [faith]. ' And they concluded that it is useless [5] to regard wickedness.

(38) Then he said to ' his disciples, "Have I not told ' you that like a visible voice and flash of ' lightning ' will the good be taken up to [10] the light?"

(39) Then all his disciples ' offered him praise and said, "Lord, ' before you appeared ' here, who was it who offered you praise? ' For all praises exist on your account. [15] Or who is it who will bless [you]? ' For all blessing derives [from] ' you."

(40) As they stood there, he saw ' two spirits bringing a single soul ' with them in a great flash of lightning. [20] And a Word came forth from ' the Son of Man, saying, ' "Give them their garment!" [And] ' the small one became like the big one. They were [...] ... [...] ' ... those who received **137** them. ... [...] each other. ' Then ... [...] disciples, ' [whom] he had ... [...].

(41) Mary [said, ' "...] see [5] [evil ...] ... them from the ' first [...] each other." '

(42) The [Lord] said, "[...] ... when you see ' them ... [...] become huge, they ' will ... [...] .... But when you [10] see the Eternal Existent, that ' is the great vision."

(43) Then they all said to him, ' "Tell us about it!"

(44) He said to them, ' "How do you wish to see it? ' [By means of a] transient vision or an [15] eternal [vision]?" He went on and said, ' "[Strive] to save that ' [which] can follow ' [you], and to seek it out, and to ' speak from within it, so that, [20] as you seek it out, [everything] ' might be in harmony with you! For ' I [say] to you, truly, ' the living God [...] ... in you **138** ... [...] ... in ' him."

(45) [Judas said, "Truly], I ' want [...]." '

(46) The [Lord said] to him, "[...] living [...] [5] dwells [...] ... entire ' ... the [deficiency ...]."

(47) [Judas said], ' "Who ... [...]?" '

(48) The Lord said, "[...] all [the] works ' which ... [...] the remainder, [10] it is they [which you ...] ... [...] ...." '

(49) Judas said, "Behold! ' The governors dwell above ' us, so it is they who will rule ' over us!"

(50) The Lord said, [15] "It is you who will rule over them! ' But when

you rid yourselves of ' jealousy, then ' you will clothe yourselves in light
' and enter the bridal chamber.'' [20]

(51) Judas said, ' ''How will [our] garments be brought to us?'' '

(52) The Lord said, ''There are ' some who will provide for you, and
' there are others who will receive [. . .]. **139** For [it is] they [who will
give you] your ' garments. [For] who [will] be able to reach ' that place
[which] is [the] reward? ' But the garments of life were given to [5] man
because he knows the ' path by which he will leave. And ' it is difficult
even for me to reach it!'' '

(53) Mary said, ''Thus with respect to 'the ' wickedness of each day,'
and 'the laborer [10] is worthy of his food,' and ' 'the disciple resembles
his teacher.''' ' She uttered this as a woman who had understood ' completely.

(54) The disciples said to him, ' ''What is the fullness and [15] what is
the deficiency?''

(55) He said to them, ' ''You are from the fullness ' and you dwell in
the place ' where the deficiency is. And lo! His light has poured [down]
[20] upon me!''

(56) [Matthew] said, ' 'Tell me, Lord, ' how the dead die ' [and] how
the living live.'' **140**

(57) The [Lord] said, ''[You have] asked ' me about a saying [. . .]
which ' eye has not seen, [nor] have I heard it ' except from you. But I
say [5] to you that when ' what invigorates a man is removed, ' he will be
called 'dead.' And when ' what is alive leaves what is dead, ' what is
alive will be called upon.''

(58) Judas said, [10] ''Why else, for the sake of truth, do they ' ⟨die⟩
and live?''

(59) The Lord said, ' ''Whatever is born of truth ' does not die.
Whatever is born of woman ' dies.''

(60) Mary said, [15] ''Tell me, Lord, why ' I have come to this place to
profit ' or to forfeit.''

(61) The Lord said, ''You make clear ' the abundance of the revealer!'' '

(62) Mary said to him, [20] ''Lord, is there then a place which is . . . ,
' or lacking truth?'' '

(63) The Lord said, ''The place where I ' am not!''

(64) Mary said, ' ''Lord, you are fearful and [wonderful], **141** and
. . . [. . .] . . . ' . . . those who do not know [you].'' '

(65) Matthew said, ''[Why] do we ' not rest [at once]?'' [5]

(66) The Lord said, ''When you lay down ' these burdens!''

(67) Matthew said, ' "How does the small ' join itself to the big?"

(68) The Lord said, ' "When you abandon [10] the works which will not be able ' to follow you, then you will rest." '

(69) Mary said, ' "I want to understand all things, ' [just as] they are."

(70) The [Lord] said, [15] "He who will seek out life! ' For [this] is their wealth. ' For the ... [...] ... of this cosmos ' is [...], and its gold and its silver ' are [misleading]."

(71) His [disciples] said to him, [20] "What should we do to ensure that ' our work will be perfect?" '

(72) The Lord [said] to them, "Be ' [prepared] in face of everything. ' [Blessed] is the man who has found **142** ... [...] ... the contest ... ' his eyes. [Neither] did he kill, nor ' was [he] killed, but he came forth victorious." '

(73) [Judas] said, "Tell me, Lord, [5] what the beginning of the path is."

(74) He said, ' "Love and goodness. For if ' one of these existed among the ' governors, wickedness would never have come into existence." '

(75) Matthew said, "Lord, [10] you have spoken about the end of everything without concern." '

(76) The Lord said, "You have understood all the things ' I have said to you ' and you have accepted them on faith. ' If you have known them, then they are [yours]. [15] If not, then they are not yours." '

(77) They said to him, "What is the place ' to which we are going?"

(78) The [Lord] said, ' "Stand in ' the place you can reach!" [20]

(79) Mary said, "Everything ' established thus is seen." '

(80) The Lord [said], "I have told you [that] ' it is the one who can see who [reveals]." '

(81) His [disciples], numbering twelve, asked him, [25] "Teacher, [... **143** ... serenity ...] teach ' us ... [...]." '

(82) The Lord said, "... [...] ... everything ' which I have ... [...] you will ... [5] ... [...] ... you [...] ... everything." '

(83) [Mary] said, "There is but one saying ' I will [speak] to the Lord ' concerning the mystery of truth: ' In this have we taken our stand, and [10] to the cosmic are we transparent." '

(84) Judas said to Matthew, "We ' [want] to understand the sort ' of garments we are to be [clothed] with ' [when] we depart the decay of the [15] [flesh]."

(85) The Lord said, "The governors ' [and] the administrators possess ' garments granted [only for a time,] ' which do not last. [But]

you, ' as children of truth, [20] not with these transitory garments are you to clothe yourselves. ' Rather, I say ' [to] you that you will become [blessed] ' when you strip [yourselves]! ' For it is no great thing **144** . . . [. . .] outside." '

(86) [. . . said . . .] . . . speak, I ' . . . [. . .] . . . ."

(87) The Lord said, ' ". . . [. . .] . . . your Father [5] . . . [. . .] . . . ."

(88) [Mary said, ' "Of what] sort is that [mustard seed]? ' Is it something from heaven or ' is it something from earth?"

(89) The Lord said, ' "When the Father established the [10] cosmos for himself, he left much over from ' the Mother of the All. Therefore, he speaks and ' he acts."

(90) Judas said, "You have ' told us this out of the mind of ' truth. When we pray, [15] how should we pray?"

(91) The Lord said, ' "Pray in the place where there is no woman." '

(92) Matthew said, ' "'Pray in the place where there is [no woman],' he tells us, ' meaning, 'Destroy the [20] works of womanhood,' not because there is any other [manner of birth], ' but because they will cease [giving birth]." '

(93) Mary said, "They will never be obliterated." '

(94) The Lord said, "[Who] ' knows that they will [not] dissolve **145** and . . . [. . .] . . . ' [. . .] . . . [. . .] . . .?" '

(95) Judas said [to Matthew], ' "[The works] of [womanhood] will dissolve [5] [. . .] the governors ' will . . . [. . .] . . . . Thus will we [become] ' prepared [for] them." '

(96) [The] Lord [said], "Right. For do they see ' [you? Do they see] those who receive [10] [you]? Now behold! A [true] Word ' is coming forth from the Father ' [to the abyss], in silence with a [flash of lightning], ' giving birth. Do they see it or [overpower] ' it? But you are even more [15] aware of [the path], this one, [before] ' either [angel or authority has ' . . . . Rather it belongs to the Father] and the [Son ' because they] are both a single ' [. . . . And] you [will] go via [20] [the path] which you have [known]. Even [if] ' the governors become huge ' [they will] not be able to reach it. [But listen!] I ' [tell] you [that] it is difficult ' even [for] me [to reach] it!" **146**

(97) [Mary] said [to the Lord], "When ' the works [. . .] . . . ' . . . [. . . which] dissolves ' a [work]."

(98) [The Lord said, "Right. For] you [5] know [. . .] . . . if I ' dissolve [. . .] . . . will go to ' his [place]."

(99) Judas said, "How ' is the [spirit] apparent?" '

(100) The Lord said, "How [is] [10] the sword [apparent]?"

(101) [Judas] said, ' "How is the [light] apparent?" '

(102) The Lord said, "... [...] ' in it forever."

(103) [Judas] said, ' "Who forgives the [works] ¹⁵ of whom? [The works] which ... [...] ' the cosmos [...] ... [... ' who] forgives the [works]." '

(104) The Lord [said], "[Who ...] ...? ' It behooves whomever has understood [the works] ²⁰ to do the [will] of the Father. ' And as for [you, strive] to rid [yourselves] of [anger] ' and [jealousy], ' and [to strip] yourselves ' of your [...] ...s, and not to ... [... **147** ... ⁸ ...] ... ' [...] ... ¹⁰ [...] ... ' [...] ... ' [...] ... ' [...] ... reproach ' [...]. For I say ... ¹⁵ [...] ... you take ... ' [...] ... you ... ' [...] who has sought, having ' [...] ... this, will ... ' [...] he will live [forever. ²⁰ And] I say to ' [you ...] ... so that you will not lead ' [your] spirits and your souls into error." '

[The Dialogue] of the Savior

THE APOCALYPSE OF PAUL (V,*2*)

Introduced and translated by

GEORGE W. MACRAE and WILLIAM R. MURDOCK

Edited by

DOUGLAS M. PARROTT

The first of the four apocalypses in Codex V is a highly syncretistic, gnostic version of the ascension of Paul through the heavens. It bears no literary relationship to the Greek work of the same name, though the latter also deals with Paul's vision of judgment in the heavens. Whether it had affinities with the now lost "Ascension of Paul" used by the "Gnostics" according to Epiphanius, it is impossible to tell, but it should be noted that in Epiphanius' account the "Ascension" refers only to three heavens, whereas it is the uniqueness of the present work that it describes Paul's experience of the fourth to the tenth heavens; the third is mentioned only as a starting point.

Apoc. Paul begins with a narrative of Paul's encounter with a small child on the "mountain of Jericho" en route to Jerusalem. The child, who is Paul's guiding spirit or interpreting angel, sometimes called the Holy spirit in the text, takes him to the heavens to meet his fellow apostles, who accompany him during his further ascent. In the fourth heaven Paul witnesses the judgment of souls; in the fifth, angels driving souls to judgment. The sixth heaven is illuminated by a light from above, and in the seventh Paul meets an old man on a shining throne who threatens to block his further ascent. He continues, however, into the Ogdoad and the ninth and tenth heavens, and when he reaches the last he has been transformed so that he greets, no longer his fellow-apostles, but his fellow-spirits. The language of the narrative fluctuates from third person to first at 19,8, back to third person at 19,18, and finally to first person again from 20,5 on. The inconsistency may perhaps be attributed to literary carelessness rather than to multiple sources, for at these points in the narrative no clear "seams" can be detected on other grounds.

For purposes of analysis, the contents of *Apoc. Paul* may be divided into three distinct episodes: an epiphany scene, a scene of judgment and punishment, and a heavenly journey. In the first, the little child who meets Paul on the mountain and gives him a revelation most naturally suggests an epiphany of the risen Christ, who is sometimes described as a small child (e.g., in *Ap. John* (BG,*2*) 20,19-21,4, *Act. Jn.* 88). This experience, as the allusion to Gal 1:15 (Jer 1:5) in 18,15-16 suggests, functions as the calling of Paul to be an apostle and thus interprets Gal 1:11-17. The heavenly visitor not only reveals to Paul but conducts him above to (the heavenly) Jerusalem, to the apostles, thus interpreting Gal 2:1-2 also. The ascent itself builds on 2 Co 12:2-4.

The scene of the judgment and punishment of souls in the fourth and fifth heavens has its closest parallel in Jewish apocalyptic literature, notably in the *Testament of Abraham* 10 (long recension) and even more closely in the Coptic version of the short recension, which has several details peculiar to it. The author of *Apoc. Paul* is indebted to other traditions, however, for his picture of the three angels who rival one another in whipping the souls forward to judgment (22,5-10). This is clearly an evocation of the Erinyes of Greek mythology. Likewise the toll-collector who is also judge belongs to Babylonian and Hellenistic astrology. The scene is thus the result of popular syncretism.

The third main element of the work, the heavenly journey, is concentrated for the most part in the sixth and seventh heavens. The ascent theme may have been borrowed from Jewish apocalyptic tradition, but its gnostic coloring is obvious in the depiction of the "old man" on the throne in the seventh heaven (Dan 7:13; 1 Enoch 46-47) as a hostile figure who tries to block the gnostic soul's ascent to the Ogdoad and the higher heavens. And the interrogation of Paul also recalls similar dialogues or formulas in other gnostic works (e.g., 1 *Apoc. Jas.* (V,*3*), *Gos. Mary* (BG,*1*), *Gos. Thom.* (II,2, saying 50).

The date and provenance of the document cannot be determined with any certainty. That it comes from gnostic circles with a typical anti-Jewish bias seems assured by the negative view of the deity in the seventh heaven. The portrayal of Paul as exalted even above the other apostles is at home in second-century Gnosticism, especially Valentinianism, and, according to Irenaeus (*Haer*. II.30.7), there was a gnostic tradition of interpreting Paul's experience in 2 Co 12:2-4. Nothing in *Apoc. Paul* demands any later date than the second century for its composition.

THE APOCALYPSE OF PAUL

V 17, 19-24, 9

[The Apocalypse of] Paul [1]

[...] **18**[3] the road. And [he spoke to him], [1] saying, "[By which] [5] road [shall I go] up to [Jerusalem]?" [1] The little child [replied, saying], [1] "Say your name, so that [I may show] [1] you the road." [The little child] [1] knew [who Paul was]. [10] He wished to make conversation with [1] him through his words [in order that] he [1] might find an excuse for speaking [1] with him.

The little child spoke, [1] saying, "I know [15] who you are, Paul. [1] You are he who was blessed from [1] his mother's womb. For I have [come] [1] to you that you may [go up to Jerusalem] [1] to your fellow [apostles. And] [20] for this reason [you were called. And] [1] I am the [Spirit who accompanies] [1] you. Let [your mind awaken, [1] Paul], with [...]. **19** For [...] [1] whole which [...] [1] among the [principalities and] these authori-

ties [and] | archangels and powers [5] and the whole race of demons, |
[. . .] the one that reveals | bodies to a soul-seed." |

And after he brought that speech | to an end, he spoke, saying [10] to
me, "Let your mind awaken, | Paul, and see that this mountain | upon
which you are standing is the mountain | of Jericho, so that you may
know the | hidden things in those that are visible. [15] Now it is to the
twelve apostles | that you shall go, | for they are elect spirits, and they
will | greet you." He raised | his eyes and saw them [20] greeting him.

Then the | Holy [Spirit] who was speaking | with [him] caught him up
| on high to the third | heaven, and he passed [25] beyond to the fourth
[heaven]. | The [Holy] Spirit spoke to him, | saying, "Look | and see
your [likeness] | upon the earth." And he [looked] [30] down and saw
those [who were upon] | the earth. He stared [and saw] | those who were
upon the [. . . . Then **20** he] gazed [down and] saw | the [twelve] apostles
| [at] his right [and] at his left | in the creation; and the Spirit was [5] go-
ing before them.

But I saw | in the fourth heaven according to class − I | saw the an-
gels resembling | gods, the angels bringing | a soul out of the land of [10]
the dead. They placed it at the gate | of the fourth heaven. And | the
angels were whipping it. | The soul spoke, saying, | "What sin was it
that I committed [15] in the world?" | The toll-collector who dwells in the
| fourth heaven replied, saying, | "It was not right to commit all those
lawless deeds | that are in the world [20] of the dead." | The soul replied,
saying, | "Bring witnesses! Let them [show] you | in what body I com-
mitted lawless deeds. | [Do you wish] to bring a book [25] [to read
from]?"

And | the three witnesses came. | The first spoke, saying, | "Was I
[not | in] the body the second hour [30] [. . .]? I rose up against you **21** un-
til [you fell] into anger [and | rage] and envy." And | the second spoke,
saying, | "Was I not [5] in the world? And I entered at | the fifth hour,
and I saw you | and desired you. And behold, | then, now I charge you
with the | murders you committed." [10] The third spoke, saying, | "Did
I not come to you at | the twelfth hour of the day when | the sun was
about to set? I gave you darkness | until you should accomplish your
sins." [15] When the soul heard these things, | it gazed downward in | sor-
row. And then it gazed | upward. It was cast down. | The soul that had
been cast down [20] [went] to [a] body which had been prepared | [for it.
And] behold | [its] witnesses were finished.

[Then I | gazed] upward and [saw | the] Spirit saying [to me], [25]
"Paul, come! [Proceed | toward] me!" Then as I [went], | the gate

opened, [and] ' I went up to the fifth [heaven]. ' And I saw my fellow apostles [30] [going with me] **22** while the Spirit accompanied us. ' And I saw a great angel ' in the fifth heaven holding ' an iron rod in his [5] hand. There were three other angels with ' him, and I stared into ' their faces. But they were rivalling ' each other, with whips ' in their hands, goading the [10] souls on to the judgment. ' But I went with the Spirit ' and the gate opened for me. '

Then we went up to the sixth heaven. ' And I saw my fellow apostles [15] going with me, and the Holy Spirit ' was leading me before them. ' And I gazed up on high and saw a ' great light shining down ' on the sixth heaven. I spoke, [20] saying to the toll-collector ' who was in the sixth heaven, "[Open] ' to me and the [Holy] Spirit [who ' is] before [me]." He opened [to me].

[Then ' we went] up to the seventh [heaven [25] and I saw] an old man [. . .] ' light [and ' whose garment] was white. [His throne], ' which is in the seventh heaven, ' [was] brighter than the sun [30] by [seven] times. **23** The old man spoke, saying to [me], ' "Where are you going, Paul, ' O blessed one and the one who was ' set apart from his mother's womb?" [5] But I looked at the Spirit, ' and he was nodding his head, saying ' to me, "Speak with him!" ' And I replied, saying ' to the old man, "I am going to the place [10] from which I came." And ' the old man responded to me, "Where are you from?" ' But I replied, saying, ' "I am going down to the world of ' the dead in order to lead captive [15] the captivity ' that was led captive ' in the captivity of Babylon." ' The old man replied to me, ' saying, "How will you be [20] able to get away from me? Look ' and see the principalities and ' authorities." [The] ' Spirit spoke, saying, "Give him [the] ' sign that you have, and [he will] [25] open for you." And then I gave [him] ' the sign. He turned his face ' downwards to his creation ' and to those who are his own authorities. '

And then the [30] ⟨seventh⟩ heaven opened and we went up to [the] **24** Ogdoad. And I saw the ' twelve apostles. They ' greeted me, and we went ' up to the ninth heaven. I [5] greeted all those who were in the ' ninth heaven, and we went up ' to the tenth heaven. And I ' greeted my fellow spirits. '

The Apocalypse of Paul

THE (FIRST) APOCALYPSE OF JAMES (V,3)

Introduced and translated by

WILLIAM R. SCHOEDEL

Edited by

DOUGLAS M. PARROTT

The manuscript names this writing *The Apocalypse of James*. We refer to it here as *The (First) Apocalypse of James* to distinguish it from the next writing (V,4) which the manuscript also entitles *The Apocalypse of James*. Our apocalypse is an excellent example of a "revelation dialogue." The partners in the dialogue are the Lord and James the Lord's brother (though the latter is said to be the Lord's brother only in a purely spiritual sense). In the first part of the writing (24,10-30,11) James addresses questions to the Lord that reflect his anxiety at the suffering soon to overtake both himself and the Lord, and the Lord provides James consolation in terms of standard gnostic teaching about the place of man in the universe. An oblique and very brief reference to the crucifixion in 30,12-13 serves as the turning point in the account. After the reappearance of the Lord, the story is dominated by a series of formulae transmitted to James to enable him to meet the challenges of the hostile powers who will attempt to block his ascent to "the Pre-Existent One" after his martyrdom (32,23-36,1). These formulae represent a dramatized version of texts that appear elsewhere in the context of rites for the dying in forms of Valentinian Gnosticism (Irenaeus, *Haer.* 1.21.5; Epiphanius, *Pan.* 36.3.1-6). It is worth noting, however, that at least one characteristic line that appears here ("I am an alien, a son of the Father's race") has a close parallel in the *Corpus Hermeticum* (13.3). Other interesting matters taken up in the second part of our apocalypse include the directions concerning the handing on of the teaching in secret (36,13-38,11), the comments about the value of women as disciples (38,15-41,18), the mention of James' rebuke of the twelve disciples (42,20-24), and the relatively lengthy account (now much mutilated) of James' martyrdom at the conclusion of the writing.

The designation of James as "James the Just" (32,2-3; cf. 43,19) indicates contact with Jewish Christian tradition (cf. Hegesippus, in Eusebius, *H.E.* 2.23.4,7; *Gospel according to the Hebrews*, in Jerome, *De viris inl.* 2; *Gos. Thom.*, saying 12). The inclusion of Addai (36,15-24) in the list of figures who will hand on the teaching in secret points to contact with Syria and thereby possibly also to a Semitic form of Christianity (cf. Eusebius, *H.E.* 1.13). Some scholars have argued that numerous other themes in our apocalypse also betray the influence of Jewish Christian theology. But apart from the importance attributed to James the Just there is little in the writing that can with any confidence be attributed to the influence of Jewish Christianity in particular. There is a good possibility, then, that the figure of James was chosen by a circle of Gnostics as a convenient peg on which to hang their teaching.

One reason for the appeal of the figure of James was the fact that he stood outside the circle of twelve disciples and because of his relationship to Jesus (here understood in purely spiritual terms) could be appealed to as the originator of a purer form of Christian teaching than that represented by the twelve. In this connection, the command to hand on the teaching in secret presumably served to explain why it was that Gnosticism appeared to the uninitiated as a relatively late flowering of the religion of Jesus. Our apocalypse, in short, was attempting to present an alternative to the apostolic authority claimed for the teaching of a steadily advancing catholic form of Christianity. It appears, however, that whereas Jerusalem and Judaism are associated with the darker powers of the universe, the twelve (and thus catholic Christianity) move within the more beneficent spheres of the activity of Achamoth, the lesser Sophia.

Another reason for the appeal that the figure of James had for some Gnostics was that it enabled them to make more sense of the history of the first century. The fall of Jerusalem was an event that cried out for explanation. And though it soon seemed natural to attribute the disaster to the treatment of Jesus by the Jews (cf. Origen, *Contra Celsum* 2.13; Eusebius, *H.E.* 3.7), it was even more natural to connect the fall of Jerusalem with the treatment meted out to James by Jewish authorities just before the great war with Rome (Hegesippus, in Eusebius, *H.E.* 2.23). A careful Christian scholar was bound to find this disquieting (cf. Origen, *Contra Celsum* 1.47). Our apocalypse, however, has no such uneasiness and finds it possible to exploit the role of James for two reasons. First, the difference between the redeemer (the Lord) and the redeemed (James, the prototypical disciple) is significantly less pronounced in Gnosticism (cf. 27,8-10 where James is flatly identified with "Him-who-is"). Consequently, the two figures complement rather than rival one another in ways that are difficult for catholic Christianity to contemplate. Second, the general gnostic view that martyrdom could be (and in the minds of some Gnostics inevitably was) embraced for the wrong reasons made the emergence of resolve in this regard only after a long period of fear and anxiety a perfectly natural expectation. Thus the crucifixion of Jesus and the martyrdom of James are seen as complementary events, both of which are required for the full exemplification of the victory over the powers of darkness. In this connection, the defeat of the archons by James during his ascent to God is presumably connected with the fall of Jerusalem, the dwelling place (according to 25,15-19) of many archons.

A guide to the place of James the Just in early Christianity is provided by a fragment of Clement of Alexandria: "To James the Just and John and Peter the Lord transmitted the *gnosis* after the resurrection. They transmitted it to the other apostles. And the other apostles transmitted it to the seventy ..." (Eusebius, *H.E.* 2.1.4). The passage strongly suggests that there were three main (no doubt overlapping) stages in the development of the image of James: 1) as James the Just, a symbol of Jewish-Christian values; 2) as the recipient of postresurrection revelation in a Gnosticizing milieu; and 3) as a colleague of the apostles of the Lord in a catholicizing milieu. Our apocalypse presumably reflects an interest in James that corresponds to the second main stage of the development of his image.

It should be noted finally that there is some evidence of the direct influence of esoteric Jewish speculation in our apocalypse. For it is only through an unusual manipulation of numbers and an awareness of the importance of the number 72 in Jewish lore that we can account for the fact that "twelve hebdomads" (12×7) amount to "seventy-two heavens (26,2-18).

THE (FIRST) APOCALYPSE OF JAMES

V 24, 10-44, 10

The Apocalypse of James |

It is the Lord who spoke with me: | "See now the completion of my redemption. | I have given you a sign of these things, James, | my brother. For not without reason have I called [15] you my brother, although you are not my brother | materially. And I am not ignorant | concerning you; so that | when I give you a sign — know and | hear.

"Nothing existed except [20] Him-who-is. He is unnameable | and ineffable. | I myself also am unnameable, | from Him-who-is, just as I have been | [given a] number of names — two [25] from Him-who-is. And I, | [I] am before you. Since you have | [asked] concerning femaleness, femaleness existed, | but femaleness was | not [first]. And [30] [it] prepared for itself powers and gods. | But [it did] not exist [when] I came forth, **25** since I am an image of Him-who-is. | But I have brought forth the image of [him] | so that the sons of Him-who-is | might know what things are theirs [5] and what things are alien (to them). Behold, | I shall reveal to you everything | of this mystery. For they will seize | me the day after tomorrow. But my | redemption will be near." [10]

James said, "Rabbi, you have said, | 'They will seize me.' But I, | what can I do?" He said to me, | "Fear not, James. | You too will they seize. [15] But leave Jerusalem. | For it is she who always gives the cup of bitterness | to the sons | of light. She is a dwelling place | of a great number of archons. [20] But your redemption will be preserved | from them. So that | you may understand who they are [and] | what kinds they are, you will [...]. | And listen. They [are] not [...] [25] but [archons ...]. | These twelve | [...] down [...] [29] archons [...] **26** upon his own hebdomad." |

James said, "Rabbi, are there then | twelve hebdomads | and not seven as [5] there are in the scriptures?" | The Lord said, "James, he who spoke | concerning this scripture had a limited understanding. | I, however, shall reveal to you | what has come forth from him [10] who has no number. I shall give a sign concerning their | number. As for what has come forth from him ' who has no measure, I shall give a sign concerning their ' measure.''

James said, ' "Rabbi, behold then, I have received [15] their number. There are seventy-two measures!" ' The Lord said, "These ' are the seventy-two heavens, which ' are their subordinates. These are the powers of ' all their might; and they were [20] established by them; ' and these are they who were distributed ' everywhere, existing under the [authority] ' of the twelve archons. ' The inferior power among them [25] [brought forth] for itself angels ' [and] unnumbered hosts. ' Him-who-is, however, has been given ' [...] on account of ' [...] Him-who-is [30] [...] they are unnumbered. **27** If you want ' to give them a number now, you [will] ' not be able to (do so) until you cast away ' from yourself blind thought, [5] this bond of flesh which encircles you. ' And then you will reach ' Him-who-is. ' And you will no longer be ' James; rather you are [10] the One-who-is. And all those who are ' unnumbered will ' all have been named.'' '

⟨James said, "Then,⟩ ' Rabbi, in what way shall I reach [15] Him-who-is, since ' all these powers and these ' hosts are armed against me?" ' He said to me, "These powers ' are not armed against you specifically, [20] but are armed against another. ' It is against me that they are armed. ' And they are armed with other [powers]. ' But they are armed against me [in] ' judgment. They did not give [...] [25] to me in it [...] ' through them [...]. ' In this place [...] ' suffering, I shall [...]. ' He will [...] **28** and I shall not rebuke them. But there shall ' be within me a silence and ' a hidden mystery. But I ' am fainthearted before their anger.'' [5]

James said, "Rabbi, ' if they arm themselves against you, then ' is there no blame?

> You have come with knowledge,
> that ' you might rebuke their forgetfulness.
> You have come with ' recollection,
> that you might rebuke their [10] ignorance.

But I was concerned ' because of you.

> For you descended into a ' great ignorance,
> but ' you have not been defiled by anything in it. '
> For you descended into a great mindlessness, [15]
> and your recollection remained. '

> You walked in mud, '
> and your garments were not soiled, '

and you have not been buried ˈ in their filth,
and ²⁰ you have not been caught.

And I was ˈ not like them, but I clothed myself with everything ˈ of theirs.

There is in me ˈ forgetfulness,
yet I ˈ remember things that are not theirs. ²⁵
There is in me [...], ˈ
and I am in their ˈ [...].

[...] knowledge ˈ [...] not in their sufferings ˈ [...]. But I have become afraid ³⁰ [before them], since they rule. For what 29 will they do? What will I be able ˈ to say? Or what word will I be able ˈ to say that I may escape them?" ˈ

The Lord said, "James, I praise ⁵ your understanding and your fear. ˈ If you continue to be distressed, ˈ do not be concerned for anything else ˈ except your redemption. ˈ For behold, I shall complete this destiny ¹⁰ upon this earth as ˈ I have said from the heavens. ˈ And I shall reveal to you ˈ your redemption."

James said, ˈ "Rabbi, how, after these things, ¹⁵ will you appear to us again? ˈ After they seize you, ˈ and you complete this destiny, ˈ you will go up to Him- ˈ who-is." The Lord said, "James, ²⁰ after these things I shall reveal to you ˈ everything, not for your sake ˈ alone but for the sake of [the] ˈ unbelief of men, ˈ so that [faith] may ²⁵ exist in them. ˈ For [a] multitude will [attain] ˈ to faith [and] ˈ they will increase [in ...]. 30 And after this I shall appear ˈ for a reproof to the archons. And I shall ˈ reveal to them that ˈ he cannot be seized. If they ⁵ seize him, then ˈ he will overpower each of them. ˈ But now I shall go. Remember ˈ the things I have spoken and let them ˈ go up before you." ¹⁰ James said, "Lord, I shall hasten ˈ as you have said." ˈ The Lord said farewell to him and fulfilled ˈ what was fitting.

When James ˈ heard of his sufferings ¹⁵ and was much distressed, ˈ they awaited the sign ˈ of his coming. And he came after ˈ several days. And James ˈ was walking upon the mountain, ²⁰ which is called "Gaugelan," ˈ with his disciples, ˈ who listened to him ˈ [because they had been distressed], and he was ˈ [...] a comforter, ²⁵ [saying], "This is ˈ [...] the (or: a) second [....]" ˈ Then the] crowd dispersed, ˈ but James remained ˈ [...] prayer ³⁰ [...], as 31 was his custom. ˈ

And the Lord appeared to him. ˈ Then he stopped (his) prayer ˈ and embraced him. He kissed ⁵ him, saying, "Rabbi, ˈ I have found you! I

have heard of your ' sufferings, which you endured. And ' I have been
much distressed. My ' compassion you know. [10] Therefore, on reflection, I was wishing ' that I would not see this people. They must ' be
judged for these things that they have done. ' For these things that they
have done are contrary to ' what is fitting.''

The Lord said, [15] "James, do not be concerned ' for me or for ' this
people. I am he who ' was within me. Never ' have I suffered in any
way, [20] nor have I been distressed. ' And this people has done ' me no
harm. ' But this (people) existed [as] ' a type of the archons, [25] and it
deserved to be [destroyed] ' through them. But [...] ' the archons,
[...] ' who (or: which) has [...] ' but since it (fem.) [...] [30] angry with
[.... ' The] just [...] **132** is his servant. Therefore ' your name is
'James ' the Just.' You see ' how you will become sober when you see
[5] me. And you stopped this prayer. ' Now since you are a just ' man of
God, you have ' embraced me and kissed me. ' Truly I say to you that
[10] you have stirred up great anger and ' wrath against yourself. But '
(this has happened) so that these others might come to be.'' '

But James was timid ' (and) wept. And he was very distressed. [15] And
they both sat down ' upon a rock. The Lord said ' to him, "James, thus
' you will undergo these sufferings. But do not ' be sad. For the flesh is
[20] weak. It will receive what has been ' ordained for it. But as for you,
do not ' be [timid] or afraid.'' ' The Lord [ceased].

[Now] when James ' heard these things, he [25] wiped away [the] tears
in ' [his eyes] and very bitter (?) ' [...] which is ' [...]. The Lord [said]
to [him, ' "James], behold, I shall **33** reveal to you your redemption. '
When [you] are seized, ' and you undergo these sufferings, ' a multitude
will arm themselves against you [5] that ⟨they⟩ may seize you. And in particular ' three of them ' will seize you − they who ' sit (there) as toll collectors. Not ' only do they demand toll, but [10] they also take away souls
' by theft. When ' you come into their power, ' one of them who is their
guard will say ' to you, [15] 'Who are you or where are you from?' ' You
are to say to him, 'I am ' a son, and I am from ' the Father.' He will say
to you, ' 'What sort of son are you, and [20] to what father do you
belong?' You are to ' say to him, 'I am from ' the Pre-existent Father,
' and a son in the ' Pre-existent One.' [When he says] [25] to you, [...],
' you are to [say to him, ...] ' in the [...] ' that I might [...].

"[... **34** of] alien things?'' You are to say to him, ' 'They are not entirely alien, ' but they are from Achamoth, ' who is the female. And
these [5] she produced as she brought down the race ' from the ' Pre-
existent One. So then ' they are not alien, but they are ours. ' They are

indeed ours because she who [10] is mistress of them is from [the Pre-existent One.] At the same time they are alien because [the Pre-existent One did not [have intercourse with her, when she [15] produced them.' When he also says to you, ["Where will you go?,' you are to [say to him, 'To the place from which I have come, [there shall I return.'] And if you say these things, you will [20] escape their attacks.

"But when [you come to [[these] three detainers [[who] take away souls by [theft in that place [25] [. . .] these. You [[. . .] a vessel [[. . .] much more than [. . .] [35] of the one (fem.) whom [you [. . .] for [. . .] [her root. You [too will [5] be sober [. . .]. But I shall call [[upon] the imperishable knowledge, [which is Sophia who [is in the Father (and) who is the mother [of Achamoth. [10] Achamoth had no father nor [male consort, but [she is female from a [female. She produced you (pl.) [without a male, since she was alone [15] (and) in ignorance as to what [[lives through] her mother because she thought [that she alone existed. [But [I] shall cry out [to her mother. And then [20] they will fall into confusion (and) will [blame their [root and the race [of] [their mother. [But] you [will go up to [what is] [25] yours [. . .] [you will [. . .] [36] the [Pre-existent One].

"[They are [a] type [of the] twelve [disciples and [the] twelve [pairs, [. . .] [5] Achamoth, which is [translated 'Sophia.' [And who I myself am, [and (who) the imperishable Sophia (is) [through whom you will be redeemed, [10] and (who are) all the sons of Him-who- [is — these things they have known [and have hidden within [them. You are to hide ⟨these things⟩ within you, [and you are to keep silence. [15] But you are to reveal them to [Addai. When you [depart], [immediately war will be [made] [with this land. [Weep], [then, for him who dwells in Jerusalem. [20] But let Addai take these things [to heart. In the tenth [year let Addai sit [and write them down. [And when he writes them down [25] [. . .] and they are to give them [[. . .] he has the [. . .] [37⁶] he is [called] [Levi. Then he is to bring [[. . .] word [[. . .] from [10] [what I] said earlier [[. . .] a woman [[. . .] Jerusalem in her [[. . . and] he begets [[two] sons through her. [15] [They are to] inherit these things [[and] the understanding of him who [[. . .] exalts. And they are to receive [[. . .] through him from his [intellect. Now, the younger of them [20] is greater. And [may these things remain [hidden in him until [he] [comes to the age of [seventeen years [. . .] [38³] beginning [. . .] [5] through [them]. They will pursue [him exceedingly, since [they are] from [his [. . .] companions. He will be [proclaimed [through] them, [and [they will] proclaim this word. [10] [Then he will become] [a seed of [. . .]." [

James said, "[I am] ' satisfied [. . .] ' and they are [. . .] [15] my soul.
Yet [another thing] ' I ask of you: who are the [seven] ' women who
have [been] your disciples? ' And behold, ' all women bless you. [20] I
also am amazed ' how [powerless] vessels ' have become strong by a
perception ' which is in them." ' [The] Lord [said], "You [. . .] well
[. . .] 39[3] a spirit [of . . .], ' a [spirit] of thought, [a spirit] [5] of counsel
of [a . . .], ' a spirit [. . . , a] spirit ' of knowledge [. . .] of their ' fear.
[. . .] when we had passed ' through [the breath] of [10] [this] archon who
' is [named] Adonaios ' [. . .] him and ' [. . .] he was ignorant ' [. . .]
when I came forth from him, [15] [he] remembered that I ' am [a] son of
his. He was gracious ' [to me] at that time as ' his son. And then, '
before ⟨I⟩ [20] appeared here, ⟨he⟩ ' cast them among [this] ' people.
And from the [place] ' of heaven the prophets [. . .]." 40[4]

James [said], "Rabbi, [. . .] [6] I [. . .] all together ' [. . .] in them '
especially [. . .]." ' The Lord said, "[James], I [10] praise [you . . .] ' walk
upon the earth [. . .] ' the words while he [. . .] ' on the [. . .]. ' For cast
away from [you the] [15] cup, which is bitterness. ' For some from [. . .]
' set themselves against you. For [you have begun] ' to understand [their
roots] ' from beginning to end. Cast [20] away from yourself all
lawlessness. ' And beware lest ' they envy you. When you ' speak these
words of this ' [perception], encourage these [25] [four]: Salome and
Mariam ' [and Martha and Arsinoe . . .] 41[6] since he takes ' some
[. . .]to me ' he is [. . .] burnt offerings ' and [. . .]. But I [10] [. . .] not in
this way; but ' [. . .] first-fruits of the ' [. . .] upward ' [. . .] so that ' the
power [of God might] appear. [15] The perishable has [gone ' up] to the
imperishable and ' the female element has ' attained to this male element." '

James said, [20] "Rabbi, into these three (things), then, ' has their [. . .]
been cast. ' For they have been reviled, [and they have been] ' persecuted [. . .]. 42[5] Behold ' [. . .] everything ' [. . .] from ' anyone [. . .]. '
For you have received [. . .] of [10] knowledge. [And . . .] ' that what is
the [. . .] ' go [. . .] ' you will [find . . .]. ' But I shall go [forth] [15] and
shall reveal ' that they believed in you [that they may] ' be content with
their [blessing] ' and salvation, and ' this revelation may come to pass."
[20] And he went at that time ' [immediately] and rebuked the ' twelve,
and cast ' [out] of them contentment ' [concerning the] way of knowledge [. . .].

[. . .]. 43[7] And the majority ' of [them . . .] when they ' [saw, the]
messenger took in [10] [. . .]. The others [. . .] [12] said, "[. . .] [14] him from
this earth. ' For [he is] not [worthy] of life." ' These, then, [were]

afraid. They arose, [|] saying, "We [|] have no part in this blood, [|] for a just man ²⁰ will perish through [|] injustice." James departed [|] so that [. . .] **44**⁶ look [|] [. . .] for [|] we (?) [. . .] him. [|]

The Apocalypse ¹⁰
of James

THE (SECOND) APOCALYPSE OF JAMES (V,*4*)

Introduced and translated by

CHARLES W. HEDRICK

Edited by

DOUGLAS M. PARROTT

The fourth tractate in Codex V has been given the modern title *The (Second) Apocalypse of James* in order to distinguish it from the preceding tractate, since both documents have the same ancient title: *The Apocalypse of James*. The twenty pages comprising the tractate are preserved in a fragmentary state. The literary form is difficult to describe. The title of the text calls it an apocalypse, and the first line describes it as a discourse. In the sense that James relates a revelation received from the resurrected Jesus, it may be called a revelation discourse. However, its actual structure is cast in the form of a two-part report to Theuda, the father of James, by Mareim, a priest and relative of Theuda, who apparently was present at the stoning of James.

The tractate contains at least four sections artistically arranged. Because of their balance and stylized form they have been described as "harmonic prose" possessing a "hymnic" quality. Three of these units are aretalogies. One (49,5-15) is a series of self-assertions by the resurrected Jesus in the "I am" style. Another (58,2-20) is a series of predications about the resurrected Jesus made by James in the third person (i.e., "he is"). In a further aretalogy (55,15-56,13) the resurrected Jesus describes James' special role in the second person (i.e., "you are"). The entire description in the third aretalogy suggests that James is intended to perform the function of gnostic redeemer.

The fourth unit (62,16-63,29) is a prayer attributed to James. Its present setting requires that one read it as the prayer of a martyr shortly before death. However, it is by no means certain that the present setting of the prayer was its original setting. Apart from its context, it has the character of a prayer that one might pray if one were facing some future period of persecution or trial. The request in 62,21-22 suggests that there was a prospect of continued existence in the world. The material in 63,23-24 speaks of something other than a painful death, already mentioned in 63,5-6, and in fact suggests trials and tribulations such as one might anticipate in one's daily experience.

The tractate as a whole is clearly gnostic in character, yet it shows remarkable restraint in treating usual gnostic themes. Nor can it be identified with any of the known gnostic systems of the second century. On the other hand, the author has made extensive use of Jewish-Christian traditions. James, who held a position of special prominence in Jewish-Christian circles, is regarded as the possessor of a special revelation from Jesus and is assigned a role in the gnostic tradition that rivals, and perhaps exceeds, that of Peter in the canonical tradition. For example,

James is the "escort" who guides the Gnostic through the door of the heavenly kingdom and even rewards him (55,6-14; cf. 55,15-56,13). The description is similar to Peter's charge as the keeper of the keys of heaven (Mt 16:19).

As to the date and place of composition, little can be said with certainty. Because of the basic Jewish-Christian traditions out of which the tractate is composed, it is probable that its origin is to be associated with Jewish-Christian circles. The absence of allusions to the later developed gnostic systems, and the almost total absence of allusions to the New Testament tradition suggest an early date for the origin of the tractate.

The presence and order of the two James apocalypses in Codex V are undoubtedly due to deliberate scribal organization. The two apocalypses stress different aspects of the James tradition and actually complement one another. The setting of *1 Apoc. Jas.* emphasizes the period prior to the suffering of James, while *2 Apoc. Jas.* describes his suffering and death in line with the predictions in *1 Apoc. Jas.*

THE (SECOND) APOCALYPSE OF JAMES

V 44, 11-63, 32

The Apocalypse |
of [James] |

This is [the] discourse that James | [the] Just spoke [15] in Jerusalem, [which] | Mareim, one [of] the priests, | wrote. He had told it to | Theuda, the father of the Just One, | since he was a relative [20] of his. He said, | "[Hasten]! Come with | [Mary], your wife and | your relatives [...] **45** therefore [...] [5] of this [...] | to [him, he will] understand. | For behold, a multitude [10] are disturbed over | his [...], and they are greatly | angry [at him. ...] | and they pray [...]. [15] For | [he would] often say these words | and others | also.

"He used to speak these words | while the multitude of people [20] were seated. But (on this occasion) he entered | and did ⟨not⟩ sit down | in the place, as was his custom. | Rather he sat above | the fifth flight of steps, [which] [25] is (highly) esteemed, while all our people [...] [27] the words [...].

"'[...]. **46**[6] I am he who | received revelation from | the Pleroma [of] Imperishability. | (I am) he who was first summoned [10] by him who is great, and | who obeyed the [Lord] − | he who passed [through] | the [worlds ...] | he who [... he who] [15] stripped [himself and] | went about naked, | he who was found in a | perishable (state), though he was about to be brought | up into imperishability. − [20] This Lord who is present ' [came] as a son who sees, ' and as a brother ' [was he sought]. He will come to ' [...] produced him because [25] [...] and he unites ' [...] make him free [...] **47** in [...] ' he who came [to ...]. [7]

' 'Now again am I rich in ' knowledge [and] I have ' a unique [understanding], [10] which was produced only from ' above and the [...] ' comes from a [...]. ' I am the [...] [15] whom I ' knew. That which was revealed ' to me was hidden from everyone ' and shall (only) be revealed ' through him. These [20] two who see I ⟨...⟩ ' (and) they have already proclaimed ' through these [words]: ' "He shall be judged with the [unrighteous]." ' He who lived [without] [25] blasphemy died by means of [blasphemy]. ' He who was cast out ' they [...].

' ' ' '[... **48**[5] the] flesh ' [and] it is by knowledge ' that I shall come forth from the [flesh]. ' I am surely dying, ' but it is in life that I shall be found. [10] I entered ' in order that they might judge [... I] ' shall come forth [in ...] ' judge [... I do] ' not bring blame against the [15] servants of his [...] ' I hasten ' to make them free and ' want to take them above ' him who wants to rule [20] over them. If ' they are helped, ' I am the brother in ' secret, who prayed ' to the Father [until [25] he ...] in [...] **49**[2] reign: [... ' imperishability ...] first ' in [...]. [5]

> I [am the] first [son] ' who was begotten. –
> He will destroy ' the dominion of [them] all. – '
> I am the beloved. '
> I am the righteous one. [10]
> I am the son of ' [the Father].
>
> I speak even as ' [I] heard.
> I command ' even as I [received] the order.
> I ' show you (pl.) even as [15] I have [found].

Behold, I speak ' in order that I may come forth. Pay ' attention to me in order that you ' may see me!

' ' ' "If I ' have come into existence, who then am I? [20] For I did ⟨not⟩ come as I am, ' nor would I have appeared ' as I am. ' For I used to exist ' for a brief period [25] of time [...]." **50**[5]

' 'Once when I was sitting ' deliberating, ' [he] opened [the] door. ' That one ' whom you hated [10] and persecuted came in to me. ' He said to me, "Hail, my ' brother; my brother, hail." ' As I raised my [face] ' to stare at him, [15] (my) mother said to me, "Do not ' be frightened, my son, because ' he said 'My brother' to you (sg.). ' For you (pl.) were nourished with ' this same milk. Because of [20] this he calls ' me 'My mother.' ' For he is not a stranger to us. ' He is your [step-brother ...].''

''''[...] **51**² these words [...] ⁵ great [...] ' I shall [find] them, and [they shall come] ' forth. [However], I am the stranger, ' and they have no knowledge ' of me in [their] thoughts, ¹⁰ for they know me in ' [this place]. But it ' was fitting that others ' know through you. '

''''⟨You are⟩ the one to whom I say: ¹⁵ Hear and understand − ' for a multitude, when they ' hear, will be slow witted. ' But you, understand as I ' shall be able to tell you. Your father ²⁰ is not my father. But ' my father has become a father ' to [you].

''''This virgin ' about whom you hear − ' this is how [...] ²⁷ virgin [...] **52** namely, the virgin. ' [...], how ' [...] to me for ' [...] to know ⁵ [...] not as ' [...] whom I [...]. For this one (masc.) ' [...] to him, ' and this also is profitable ' for you. Your father, whom you ¹⁰ consider to be [rich], ' shall grant that you inherit ' all these (things) that you ' see.

''''I proclaim ' to you to tell you ¹⁵ these (words) that I shall speak. When ' you hear, therefore, ' open your ears ' and understand and walk (accordingly)! ' It is because of you that they pass by, ²⁰ activated by ' that one who is glorious. ' And if they want to make a ' disturbance and (seize) possession [...] **53** he began [...] ' not, nor those who are [coming], ' who were sent forth [by] ' him to make this present [creation]. ⁵ After [these things, ' when he] is ashamed, he shall be disturbed ' that his labor, which is far [from] ' the aeons, is nothing. And ' his inheritance, ¹⁰ which he boasted ' to be great, shall appear ' small. And his ' gifts are not ' blessings. His promises are evil ¹⁵ schemes. For you are not an (instrument) ' of his compassion, ' but it is through you ' that he does violence. He wants ' to do injustice to us, and ²⁰ will exercise dominion for a time ' allotted to him.

''''But ' understand and know the Father ' who has compassion. ' He was not given ²⁵ an inheritance that was unlimited, ' [nor] does it (his inheritance) [have] ' a (limited) number of days, ' but it is as [the] eternal [day ...] ³⁰ it is [...] **54** perceive [...]. ' And he used ' [...]. For in fact he is not ' one (come) from [them], (and) because of this he ⁵ [is despised]. Because of this he [boasts], so ' that he may not be reproved. ' For because of this he is superior to ' those who are below, those ' by whom you ¹⁰ were looked down upon. After he imprisoned ' those from [the] Father, ' he seized them ' and fashioned them to resemble ' himself. And it is ¹⁵ with him that they exist.

''''I ' saw from the height ' those (things) that happened, and I have explained ' how they happened. ' They were visited while they [20] were in another form, and, ' while I was watching, ' [they] came to know ⟨me⟩ as I am, ' through those whom I know. '

" " "Now before those (things) [25] [have happened] they will make a ' [...]. I know ' [how] they attempted ' [to come] down to this place **55** [that] he might approach [...] ' the small children, [but ' I] wish to reveal ' through you and the [Spirit [5] of Power], in order that he might reveal ' [to those] who are yours. And ' those who wish to enter, ' and who seek to ' walk in the way that is [10] before the door, ' open the good door through you. And they ' follow you; they enter ' [and you] escort them inside, and give a reward ' to each one who is ready for it. [15]

> For you are not the redeemer '
> nor a helper of strangers. '
> You are an illuminator ' and a redeemer '
>   of those who are mine,
> and now [20] of those who are yours.
> You shall ' reveal (to them);
> you shall bring good ' among them all.
>
> You [they shall] ' admire
>   because of every powerful (deed). '
> You are he whom the heavens [25] bless.
> You ' he shall envy,
>   he [who has] ' called himself your [Lord]. '
> I am the [...] **56**
>   [those who] are instructed in these
>   (things) with [you]. '
>
> For your sake
>   they will be told ' [these (things)],
>   and will come to rest. '
> For your sake
>   they will reign,
>   [and will] [5] become kings.
> For [your] sake '
>   they will have pity
>   on whomever they pity. '
>
> For just as ' you are first
>   having clothed ' yourself,
> you are also the [10] first who will strip himself, '

and you shall become ' as you were '
before you were stripped." '

"'And he kissed [15] my mouth. He took hold of me, saying, ' "My beloved! ' Behold, I shall reveal ' to you those (things) that (neither) ' [the] heavens nor their archons [20] have known. Behold, ' I shall reveal to you ' those (things) that he did not know, ' he who [boasted, '... [26] there is no] **57** other except me. Am I not alive? ' Because I am a father, ' [do] I [not have power] for everything?" ' Behold, I shall reveal to you [5] everything, my beloved. ' [Understand] and know them ' [that] you may come forth just as ' I am. Behold, I ' [shall] reveal to you him who [10] [is hidden]. But now, stretch out your ' [hand]. Now, take hold of me." ' [And] then I stretched out my ' hands and I did not find him ' as I thought (he would be). But [15] afterward I heard him ' saying, "Understand and ' take hold of me." Then I understood, ' and I was afraid. And ' I was exceedingly joyful. [20]

"'Therefore, I tell ' you (pl.), judges, you ' have been judged. And you ' did not spare, but you were spared. ' Be sober and [...] **58** you did not [know]. '

He was that one ' whom he who created ' the heaven and the earth, [5]
and dwelled in it, ' did not see.
He was [this one who] ' is the life.
He ' was the light.
He ' was that one who will come to be. [10]

And again he shall provide
[an] ' end for what ' has begun
and a beginning ' for what is about to be ended. '
He was the Holy Spirit [15] and the Invisible One, ' who did not descend ' upon the earth.
He was ' the virgin, and that which ' he wishes happens [20] to him.
I saw ' that he was naked, ' and there was no garment clothing ' him.
That which he wills ' happens to him [...]. **59**

"'[Renounce] this difficult way, ' which is (so) variable, ' [and] walk in accordance with him who desires ' [that] you become free men [5] [with] me, after you have passed above ' every [dominion]. For he will not [judge] (you) ' for those (things) that you did, ' but will have mercy on you. ' For (it is) not you that did them, but it is [10] [your] Lord (that did them). [He was not] ' a wrathful one, but he was a kind Father. '

"'But you have judged [yourselves], ' and because of this you will remain ᴵ in their fetters. You ¹⁵ have oppressed yourselves, and you ᴵ will repent, (but) you will ᴵ not profit at all. Behold him ᴵ who speaks and seek ᴵ him who is silent. Know him ²⁰ who came to this place, and understand ᴵ him who went forth (from it). I am ᴵ the Just One, and I do ⟨not⟩ judge. ᴵ I am not a master, then, but ᴵ I am a helper. He was cast ²⁵ out before he ᴵ stretched out his hand. I [...].

"'[...] **60** and he allows me to hear. ᴵ And play your trumpets, ᴵ your flutes ᴵ and your harps [of ⁵ this house]. The Lord has taken ᴵ you captive ᴵ from the Lord, having closed ᴵ your ears, that ᴵ they may not hear the sound of ¹⁰ my word. Yet you [will be able to pay] ᴵ heed in your hearts, [and] ᴵ you will call me "the Just One." ᴵ Therefore, I tell ᴵ you: Behold, I gave ¹⁵ you your house, which ᴵ you say that God ᴵ has made – that (house) in which ᴵ he promised to give you ᴵ an inheritance through it. ²⁰ This (house) I shall doom to ᴵ destruction and derision of those ᴵ who are in ignorance. ᴵ For behold, ᴵ those who judge deliberate [...].' **61**

"[On] that day ᴵ all the [people] and the crowd ᴵ were disturbed, and they ᴵ showed that they had not been persuaded. ⁵ And he arose and went ᴵ forth speaking in this [manner]. ᴵ And he entered (again) on that same day and ᴵ spoke a few hours. ᴵ And I was with the priests ¹⁰ and revealed nothing ᴵ of the relationship, ᴵ since all of them were saying ᴵ with one voice, 'Come, ᴵ let us stone the Just One.' ¹⁵ And they arose, ᴵ saying, 'Yes, let ᴵ us kill this man, that ᴵ he may be taken from our midst. ᴵ For he will be of no use to us.' ²⁰

"And they were there and found him ᴵ standing beside the columns of ᴵ the temple beside the mighty corner ᴵ stone. And they decided to throw ᴵ him down from ²⁵ the height, and they cast ᴵ him down. And ᴵ they [...] they [...]. **62** They seized him and [struck] ᴵ him as they dragged him upon the ground. ᴵ They stretched him out, and placed ᴵ a stone on his abdomen. ⁵ They all placed their feet on him, ᴵ saying, ᴵ 'You have erred!'

"Again ᴵ they raised him up, since he was alive, and made him ᴵ dig a hole. They made him stand ¹⁰ in it. After having covered him ᴵ up to his abdomen, they stoned ᴵ him in this manner.

"And ᴵ he stretched out his hands ᴵ and said this prayer – ¹⁵ not that (one) which it is his custom to say: ᴵ

'My God and my Father, ᴵ
    who saved me from ᴵ this dead hope, ᴵ
    who made me alive through a ²⁰ mystery of what he wills, ᴵ

do not let these days of this world ' be prolonged for me, '
but the day of your (sg.) ' [light ...] remains [25]
in [...] **63** salvation.
Deliver me from this ' [place of] sojourn!
Do not let your grace be left behind ' in me,
 but may ' your grace become pure! [5]
Save me from an ' evil death!
Bring me from ' a tomb alive,
 because your grace — ' love — is alive in me '
 to accomplish a work of fullness! [10]
Save me from ' sinful flesh,
 because I trusted ' in you with all my strength!
 Because you ' are the life of the life,
save me ' from a humiliating [15] enemy!
Do not give me into the hand ' of a judge
 who is severe ' with sin!
Forgive me ' all my debts of the ' days (of my life)!
Because I am alive [20] in you, your grace is alive in me. '
 I have renounced everyone, '
 but you I have confessed. '
Save me from evil ' affliction!
But now is the [time] [25] and the hour.
O Holy ' [Spirit], send [me] '
 salvation [...] the light [...] '
 the light [...] ' in a power [...].' [30]

"After he [spoke, he] fell silent [...] ' word [... afterward ' ...] the discourse [...]."

THE APOCALYPSE OF ADAM (V,5)

Introduced and translated by

GEORGE W. MACRAE

Edited by

DOUGLS M. PARROTT

The Apocalypse of Adam is a revelation received by Adam from three heavenly visitors and narrated by him to his son Seth. He explains the loss of saving knowledge by himself and Eve (the fall), its transmission to Seth and his descendants, and its preservation, despite the attempts of the creator-god to destroy mankind by flood and by fire, until the third coming of a savior figure, the "Illuminator." The latter is persecuted by the powers of the world but will ultimately triumph over them. At the mention of his coming there is a long hymnic passage (77,27-83,4), which may be an interpolation into an original apocalypse, in which thirteen false or inadequate explanations of his origin are contrasted with a true one by the "generation without a king," i.e., the Gnostics. This unusual passage is a remarkable example of gnostic syncretism.

In terms of literary form the work embodies a whole succession of the traditional revelation devices. First, the revelation comes to Adam in a dream vision (65,24-66,23) in which it is not clearly stated that he sees the events of the future but perhaps is merely told them. Secondly, Adam's narration to Seth takes the form of a secret *traditio* from father to son (85,19-22). Thirdly, though not written in a book, these words are hidden on a high mountain (85,3-11). Finally, since Adam's revelation takes place just before his death, the work assumes the form of a testament. Though it is clearly dependent on certain episodes of the Genesis story which are often found in gnostic revelation literature, *Apoc. Adam* does not follow closely the text of Genesis as do *Hyp. Arch.* (II,4) and *Ap. John* (II,1), for example.

The most notable feature of this work is the absence of any explicit or clear borrowings from the Christian tradition. This has led several interpreters to see in it a witness to a non-Christian Gnosticism which contains an already well developed redeemer myth. On the other hand, its close dependence on Jewish apocalyptic tradition suggests that it may represent a transitional stage in an evolution from Jewish to gnostic apocalyptic. In this case the document may be a very early one, perhaps first or second century C.E., but no clear indications of its date have been perceived. *Apoc. Adam* is a Sethian work in the sense that Seth and his posterity are the tradents of the saving knowledge; it does not have any uniquely close affinities to the description of the Sethians found in Hippolytus (*Ref.* V.19-21) or Epiphanius (*Pan.* 39). Within the Nag Hammadi collection it has a great deal in common with *Gos. Eg.* (III,2), which seems to suppose a christianized version of the story. Using as a key the three sets of angel names, which are not common in the gnostic writings (Abrasax, Sablo, and Gamaliel, 75,22-23; Micheu, Michar, and Mnesinous, 84,5-6; Iesseus Mazareus Iessedekeus, 85,30-31), we find that *Apoc. Adam* is related to *The Untitled Text* in the Bruce Codex, to *Gos. Eg.*, to *Zostrianos* (VIII,*1*), and to *Trim. Prot.* (XIII,*1*). In addition several of these works share an interest in the personage of Seth and some concern with the interpretation of baptism, thus reflecting at least a remote connection with (Jewish) baptist circles.

There are references to "apocalypses of Adam" in the writings of the heresiologist Epiphanius (4th cent. C.E.) and Manichaean writings refer to "an apocalypse of Adam," but no direct connection with this tractate can be made in either case.

(George W. MacRae †)

The possibility that the third illuminator, described in 76,8-77,18, might be Christ, has continued to be discussed. Some who favor the identification with Christ have argued that the vagueness of the allusions is precisely what one would expect in an apocalyptic work. The apocalyptic tradition, however, did not prevent the writer from being rather precise about the flood. Also, the details that do come through in the illuminator's description only partly resemble the traditional details about Christ: He will come in great glory, bring the knowledge of the eternal God, and perform signs and wonders. The god of the powers will become angry. At that point the glory will withdraw. The flesh of the man, who was the illuminator when he had the glory, will be punished. We are not told the form of the punishment or whether it ended in death. Nor are we told of a subsequent resurrection. Thus the description is that of a charismatic figure who ran afoul of the authorities and was punished. It is difficult to see any compelling reason to identify this figure with Christ.

Seams in the text have invited those interested in source analysis. In addition to the suggestion, noted above, that the long hymnic passage (13 Kingdoms) was originally independent, two other proposals should be mentioned. One is that the tractate originally ended at 84,3 and that the remainder was added later (it seems to have its own theme − opposition to water baptism). The other is that the tractate is the result of the combining of two separate source documents by a redactor, who also made some contributions of his own. One can get a sense of the basis for the latter theory by looking at the following passages, which, it is contended, are the beginning sections of each of the sources: (A) 64,6-65,23; 66,12-67,11; (B) 65,24-66,12; 67,12-67,21.

(Douglas M. Parrott)

THE APOCALYPSE OF ADAM

V 64, 1-85, 32

The Apocalypse of Adam [1]

The revelation which Adam [1] taught his son Seth in [1] the seven hundredth year, saying, [5] "Listen to my words, my [1] son Seth. When [1] god had created me out of [1] the earth along with Eve your mother, [1] I went about with her in a [10] glory which she had seen in [1] the aeon from which we had come [1] forth. She taught me a word [1] of knowledge of the eternal god. [1] And we resembled [15] the great eternal angels, [1] for we were higher than [1] the god who had created us and [1] the powers with him, whom [1] we did not know. [20]

"Then god, [1] the ruler of the aeons [1] and the powers, divided us in wrath. Then [1] we became two aeons. [1] And the glory in our heart(s) [25] left us, [1] me and your mother Eve, [1] along with the first knowledge [1] that breathed within us. And [1] it (glory) fled from us; [30] it entered into [. . .] great [. . .] which (fem.) **65** [had come] forth, not from this aeon from which [we had] [1] come forth, I [1] and Eve your mother. But [1] it (knowledge) entered into the seed of [5] great aeons. For this reason [1] I myself have called you [1] by the name of that man [1] who is the seed of the great generation [1] or from whom (it comes). After [10] those days the eternal knowledge [1] of the God of truth [1] withdrew from me [1] and your mother Eve. [1] Since that time we [15] learned about dead things, [1] like men. Then [1] we recognized the god who had [1] created us. For we were not [1] strangers to his powers. And [20] we served him in fear [1] and slavery. [1] And after these (events) we became [1] darkened in our heart(s). [1] Now I slept in the [25] thought of my heart. [1]

"And I saw three [1] men before me [1] whose likeness I was unable [1] to recognize, since they [30] were not the powers [1] of the god who had [created [1] us]. They surpassed [. . .] [1] glory, and [. . .] [1] men [. . .] **66** saying to me, 'Arise, [1] Adam, from the sleep [1] of death, and hear [1] about the aeon and the seed [5] of that man [1] to whom life has come, [1] who came from you and [1] from Eve, your wife.' [1]

"When I had heard these [10] words from the great men [1] who were standing [1] before me, then we [1] sighed, I and Eve, in [1] our heart(s). And the Lord, the god [15] who had created us, stood [1] before us. He said to us, [1] 'Adam, why were you (pl.) [1] sighing in your heart? [1] Do you not know that I [20] am the god who created [1] you? And I breathed into [1] you a spirit of life ' as a living soul.' ' Then darkness came upon our ²⁵ eyes.

"Then the god, who ' created us, created a ' son from himself [and] Eve, ' [your mother], for [. . . **67** in] the thought [of] ' my [. . .]. I knew ' a sweet desire ' for your mother. Then ⁵ the vigor of ' our eternal knowledge ' was destroyed in us, ' and weakness ' pursued us. ¹⁰ Therefore the days of ' our life became few. ' For I knew that I had ' come under the authority ' of death.

"Now then, ¹⁵ my son Seth, I will ' reveal to you the things ' which those men ' whom I saw ' before me ²⁰ at first ' revealed to me: ' after I have completed ' the times ' of this generation ²⁵ and [the] years of ' [the generation] ' have been accomplished, [then ' . . .] slave [. . .]. (p. 68 blank) **69**²

"For rain-showers ' of [god] the ' almighty ⁵ will be poured forth [so that] he ' might destroy [all] flesh {of ' god the almighty, ' so that he might destroy all flesh} ' from the earth ¹⁰ on account of the things that it seeks ' after, along with [those from] ' the seed [of] the men ' to whom passed ' the life of ¹⁵ the knowledge, which ' came from me [and] Eve, ' your mother. For they were ' strangers to him. ' Afterwards great ²⁰ angels will come ' on high clouds, ' who will bring those men ' into the place ' where the spirit [of] life dwells [. . .] **70** glory ' [. . .] there, ' [. . .] come from heaven ' to earth. [Then] ⁵ the whole [multitude] of flesh ' will be left behind in the [waters].

"Then god ' will rest from ' his wrath. And he will cast ' his power upon the waters, ¹⁰ and [he will] give power to his sons ' and their wives by means of the ark ' along with [the] animals, ' whichever he pleased, and the ' birds of heaven, which he ¹⁵ called and released ' upon the earth. And god ' will say to Noah — ' whom the generations will call ' Deucalion —, 'Behold, ²⁰ I have protected ⟨you⟩ in the ark ' along with your wife and your sons ' and their wives and their ' animals and the birds of ' [heaven], which you called ²⁵ [and released upon the earth]. **71** Therefore I will give the [earth] to you — ' you and your sons. In ' kingly fashion you will rule over it — you ' and your sons. And no ⁵ seed will come from you ' of the men who will not ' stand in my presence in ' another glory.'

"Then they will ' become as the cloud of the ¹⁰ great light. Those ' men will come who have ' been cast forth from the knowledge ' of the great aeons and the ' angels. They will stand ¹⁵ before Noah and the aeons. ' And god will say to ' Noah, 'Why have you departed from ' what I told you? You have ' created another generation so that you ²⁰ might scorn my power.' Then ' Noah will say, 'I shall ' testify before your ' might that the generation ' of these men did not come [25] [from me] nor [from ' my sons. . . .] **72** knowledge.

"And [he] will ' [. . .] those men ' and bring them into their proper ' land and build them a [5] holy dwelling-place. And ' they will be called by that ' name and dwell there ' six hundred years in a ' knowledge of imperishability. [10] And angels of the great ' light will dwell with them. ' No foul deed ' will dwell in their heart(s), but ' only the knowledge of god. [15]

"Then Noah will divide the ' whole earth among his sons, ' Ham and Japheth and Shem. ' He will say to them, 'My sons, ' listen to my words. Behold, [20] I have divided the earth among you. But ' serve him in fear and ' slavery all the days ' of your life. Let not ' your seed depart from the face [25] of god the almighty. ' [. . .] I and your [. . .] **73** son of Noah, '[My] ' seed [will be] pleasing before you ' and before your power. ' Seal it by your ' strong hand with fear and ' commandment, so that the whole ' seed which came forth from me ' may not be inclined away from you ' and god the almighty, [10] but it will serve ' in humility and ' fear of its knowledge.' '

"Then others ' from the seed of Ham and [15] Japheth will come, four hundred ' thousand men, and enter into ' another land and sojourn ' with those men who ' came forth from the great [20] eternal knowledge. For ' the shadow of their power will ' protect those who have sojourned ' with them from every evil thing ' and every unclean desire. [25] Then the seed of Ham and ' Japheth will form twelve ' kingdoms, and their ' seed [also] will enter into ' the kingdom of another people. [30]

"[Then . . .] will take counsel [. . .] ' aeons [. . .] **74** who are dead, of the great ' aeons of imperishability. ' And they will go to Sakla ' their god. They will go in [5] to the powers, accusing the great ' men who are in their ' glory.

"They will say to Sakla, ' 'What is the power of these men who ' stood in your presence, [10] who were taken from the ' seed of Ham and Japheth, ' who will number four hundred ⟨thousand⟩ men? ' They have been received into another aeon ' from which they had come forth, and [15] they have overturned all the glory of your ' power and the dominion of your hand. ' For the seed of Noah through ' his sons has done ' all your will, and (so have) all the powers [20] in the aeons over which your might ' rules, while both those ' men and the ones who are ' sojourners in their glory ' have not done your will. [25] [But] they have turned (aside) your ' whole throng.'

"Then the god ' of the aeons will give them ' (some) of those who serve [him . . .] [30] they will come upon that land **75** where the great men ' will be who ' have not been defiled, nor will be ' defiled by any desire. [5] For their soul did not come ' from a defiled hand, but it ' came from a great commandment ' of an eternal angel. ' Then fire [10] and sulphur and asphalt will be cast upon ' those men, and ' fire and (blinding) mist will come over ' those aeons, and ' the eyes of the powers of the illumi-nators will be darkened, [15] and the aeons will not see ' them in those days. ' And great clouds of light ' will descend, and ' other clouds of light [20] will come down upon them from ' the great aeons. '

"Abrasax and Sablo and ' Gamaliel will descend and bring ' those men out of [25] the fire and the wrath, and ' take them above the aeons ' and the rulers of the [powers], and ' [take] them away [. . .] ' of life [. . .] [30] and take them away [. . .] ' aeons [. . . **76** dwelling place] of the [great . . .] ' there with the holy angels ' and the aeons. ' The men will be like [5] those angels, for they ' are not strangers to them. But ' they work in the imperishable seed. '

"Once again, for the ' third time, the illuminator [10] of knowledge will pass by in great ' glory, in order to leave ' (something) of the seed of Noah ' and the sons of Ham and Japheth — ' to leave for himself [15] fruit-bearing trees. And he will ' redeem their souls from the ' day of death. For the whole creation ' that came from ' the dead earth will be [20] under the authority of death. ' But those who reflect upon the knowl-edge ' of the eternal God ' in their heart(s) will not perish. ' For they have not received spirit [25] from this kingdom alone, ' but they have re-ceived (it) from an ' [. . .] eternal angel. ' [. . .] illuminator ' [. . . will] come upon [30] [. . . that is] dead [. . .] **77** of Seth. And he will perform ' signs and wonders in order to ' scorn the powers and their ruler. '

"Then the god [5] of the powers will be disturbed, saying, 'What ' is the power of this man who ' is higher than we?' Then he will ' arouse a great wrath against ' that man. And [10] the glory will withdraw and ' dwell in holy houses which ' it has chosen for itself. And ' the powers will not see it ' with their eyes, nor will they [15] see the illuminator either. ' Then they will punish the flesh ' of the man upon whom the ' holy spirit came.

"Then ' the angels and all the [20] generations of the powers ' will use the name ' in error, asking, ' 'Where did it (the error) come from?' or ' 'Where did the [25] words of deception, which ' all the powers have failed to discover, come from?

"[Now] the first ' kingdom [says of him] '
    [that] he came [from . . .]. **78** A spirit [. . .] to heaven.
    He was nourished ' in the heavens.
    He received the glory ' of that one and the power. He came ' to
        the bosom of his mother. ⁵
    And thus he came to the water. '

"And the second kingdom says ' about him
    that he came ' from a great prophet. ' And a bird came, took ¹⁰
        the child who was born and brought him ' onto a high moun-
        tain. '
    And he was nourished by ' the bird of heaven. An angel ' came
        forth there. He said to him, ¹⁵ 'Arise! God has given glory ' to
        you.'
    He received glory and strength. '
    And thus he came to the water. '

"The third kingdom says ' of him
    that he came ²⁰ from a virgin womb. ' He was cast out of his ci-
        ty, ' he and his mother; he was brought ' to a desert place.
    He was nourished ' there.
    He came and received ²⁵ glory and power.
    And thus ' he came to the water. '

"[The fourth] kingdom says ' [of him]
    [that] he came ' [from a virgin. ³⁰ . . . Solomon **79** sought] her,
        he and Phersalo ' and Sauel and his armies, ' which had been
        sent out. Solomon ' himself sent his army ⁵ of demons to seek
        out the ' virgin. And they did not find ' the one whom they
        sought, but ' the virgin who was given to them. ' It was she
        whom they fetched. ¹⁰ Solomon took her. ' The Virgin became
        pregnant and gave birth to ' the child there. '
    She nourished him on a border ' of the desert. When ¹⁵ he had
        been nourished,
    he received glory ' and power from the seed ' from which he had
        been begotten. '
    And thus he came to the ' water.

"And the fifth ²⁰ kingdom says of him
    that ' he came from a ' drop from heaven. He was thrown ' into
        the sea. The abyss ' received him, gave birth to him, ²⁵ and
        brought him to heaven.

He received [|] glory and power.
And [|] thus he came to [the water]. [|]

"And [the] sixth kingdom [|] [says]
that a [. . . ³⁰ down] to the aeon **80** which is below, in order to [gather] [|] flowers. She became pregnant from [|] the desire of the flowers. She [|] gave birth to him in that place. ⁵
The angels of the [|] flower garden nourished him.
He received [|] glory there [|] and power.
And thus he came [|] to the water.

"And the ¹⁰ seventh kingdom says [|] of him
that he is a drop. [|] It came from heaven to earth. [|] Dragons brought him down to caves. [|] He became a ¹⁵ child. A spirit came upon him and [|] brought him on high to the place where the [|] drop had come forth. [|]
He received glory and power [|] there.
And thus ²⁰ he came to the water.

"And the [|] eighth kingdom says [|] of him
that a cloud came [|] upon the earth and enveloped a [|] rock. He came ²⁵ from it.
The angels [|] who were above the cloud [|] nourished him.
He [received] glory [|] [and] power [there].
And [thus he] came to [the water]. **81**

"And the [ninth] kingdom says [|] of him
that from the nine [|] Muses one separated away. [|] She came to a high mountain and spent ⁵ (some) time seated there, so that [|] she desired herself alone [|] in order to become androgynous. [|] She fulfilled her desire [|] and became pregnant from her desire. ¹⁰ He was born.
The [|] angels who were over the desire nourished him. [|]
And he received glory there [|] and power.
And [|] thus he came to the water.

"The ¹⁵ tenth kingdom says of him [|]
that his god loved a cloud [|] of desire. He begot him [|] in his hand and cast [|] upon the cloud above him ²⁰ (some) of the drop, and [|] he was born.
He received glory and [|] power there.
And [|] thus he came to the water. [|]

"And the eleventh ²⁵ kingdom says
   that the father ' desired his [own] ' daughter. She herself became pregnant ' [from] her father. She cast [...] ' tomb **82** out in the desert.
   The angel ' nourished him there.
   And thus he came ' to the water.

"The ⁵ twelfth kingdom says ' of him
   that he came from ' two illuminators.
   He was ' nourished there.
   He received glory ' and power.
   And thus he came ¹⁰ to the water.

"And the ' thirteenth kingdom says ' of him
   that every birth ' of their ruler is a word. '
   And his word received ¹⁵ a mandate there.
   He ' received glory and power. '
   And thus he came to the water, '
     in order that the desire ' of those powers might be satisfied.

"But the generation ²⁰ without a king over it says ' that God chose ' him from all the aeons. ' He caused knowledge of the ' undefiled one of truth to come to be ²⁵ [in] him. [He (or: It)] said, '[Out of] ' a foreign air, ' [from a] great aeon, [the ' great] illuminator came forth. [And he made] **83** the generation of those men ' whom he had chosen for himself shine, ' so that they could shine upon the ' whole aeon.'

"Then the seed, ⁵ those who will receive his ' name upon the water and (that) of them all, will fight against the power. ' And a cloud ' of darkness will come upon them.

"Then ' the peoples will cry out with a ¹⁰ great voice, saying, ' 'Blessed is the soul of those ' men because they have known ' God with a knowledge ' of the truth! They shall live forever, ¹⁵ because they have not been ' corrupted by their desire, ' along with the angels, nor ' have they accomplished the works of the ' powers, but they have stood ²⁰ in his presence in a knowledge ' of God like light ' that has come forth from ' fire and blood.

"'But we ' have done every deed of the powers ²⁵ senselessly. We have ' boasted in the transgression ' of [all] our works. ' We have [cried] against [the God] ' of [truth] because all his works [...] **84** is eternal. These are against our ' spirits. For now we have known that ' our souls will die the death.'' '

"Then a voice came to them, [5] saying, 'Micheu and Michar and Mnesinous, who ' are over the holy baptism ' and the living water, why ' were you crying out against the [10] living God with lawless voices ' and tongues without law ' over them, and souls ' full of blood and foul ' [deeds]? You are full of [15] works that are not of the truth, ' but your ways are full of ' joy and rejoicing. ' Having defiled the water of life, ' you have drawn it within [20] the will of the powers ' to whom you have been given ' to serve ' them.

"'And your ' thought is not like that of [25] those men whom ' you persecute [...] [28] desire [...]. **85** Their fruit does not wither. But ' they will be known ' up to the great aeons, because the words ' they have kept, of the God [5] of the aeons, were not committed to ' the book, nor were they written. ' But angelic (beings) will bring ' them, whom all the generations ' of men will not know. [10] For they will be on a high ' mountain, upon a rock of truth. ' Therefore they will be named ' "The Words of Imperishability ' [and] Truth," for those who know [15] the eternal God in ' wisdom of knowledge ' and teaching of angels ' forever, for he knows all things.'" '

These are the revelations which [20] Adam made known to Seth his ' son. And his son taught ' his seed about them. This is the ' hidden knowledge of Adam, ' which he gave to Seth, which is the [25] holy baptism of those who ' know the eternal knowledge ' through those born of the word ' and the imperishable illuminators, who ' came from the holy seed: [30] Yesseus, Mazareus, ' [Yesse]dekeus, [the Living] Water. '

The Apocalypse of Adam

THE ACTS OF PETER
AND THE TWELVE APOSTLES (VI,*1*)

Introduced by

DOUGLAS M. PARROTT

Translated by

DOUGLAS M. PARROTT and R. McL. WILSON

The title appears only at the conclusion of the tractate. At first glance it gives the impression of referring to thirteen apostles (Peter plus the twelve). But a reading of the text makes it clear that the title probably has to do with two different "acts": an act of Peter (1,30-5,5) and an act of the apostolic group (5,5-12,19). The title, however, must nonetheless be secondary, since the number twelve contradicts the explicit statement of the text that the disciples numbered eleven (9,20-21).

The tractate can be divided into four major units:

1. *An introductory section, which sets the stage for the tractate.* The first seven lines probably contained some indication of initial setting and purpose. The narrator is Peter (1,30) and the time is after the crucifixion, since the apostles undertake their journey on their own immediate initiative, and Jesus is not with them. The fact that there are only eleven disciples, however, suggests the preascension period. Having decided to undertake their ministry together, the apostles find a ship and set sail (1,16-26). They appear to leave their destination to the Lord. The ship arrives at an island city called Habitation, and Peter goes to learn about lodgings.

2. *Peter meets a pearl merchant and sees the response of the rich and the poor to him* (2,10-5,18). He observes that the rich turn away from him when he hawks his wares because they think he really has none. The poor, however, flock to him, although they lack the means to buy what he offers. They would be content to see a pearl. But the merchant says he will give them one without cost, if they would go to his city. The poor ask Peter about the hazards of the way to the city. Peter tells them what he has heard and turns to the merchant, asking about his name and the hardships of the way. The merchant tells him his name is Lithargoel, which is interpreted in the text as a lightweight, gazelle-like (i.e., gleaming like a gazelle's eyes) stone, presumably a pearl.

3. *The journey of Peter and his friends to Lithargoel's city* (5,19-8,11), *following instructions by Lithargoel.* The only way to prepare for the journey to the city of "nine gates" is complete renunciation of possessions and a regimen of fasting, so that one will have nothing predators might want (5,19-6,8). All that is needed is the name of Jesus (6,9-19). Then Peter sees a vision of the walls of the city surrounded by waves. The meaning of this is interpreted in a brief dialogue between Peter and an old man. Peter and the disciples then make the journey to the city.

4. *The appearance of Lithargoel as a physician, his revelation of himself as Jesus Christ, and the commissioning of the eleven disciples* (8,11-12,19). Lithargoel comes out of the city disguised as a physician and says that he will show them where Lithargoel lives (8,11-35). Instead of doing that, however, he reveals that he is Jesus Christ (9,1-19), in a dialogue with Peter that has been traced to Matthew 16,13-19. After the disciples prostrate themselves in worship and indicate their willingness to do his will, Christ, who is henceforth called the Lord, gives them a box and pouch of medicine and commissions them to return to Habitation, the city from which they came. They are to teach and minister to the faithful, with special emphasis on the poor (9,1-10,13). Peter objects that they have nothing to give the poor, since they have renounced everything, but the Lord points out that they have his name, which is of more value than anything else (10,13-30). After further discussion, the dialogue concludes with the injunction to avoid the rich. The disciples accept the commission and the Lord departs.

The text is composite. This can be seen by the awkward relationship among the various sections. For example, between sections 2 and 3, the reader expects the poor to go to the pearl merchant's city, but only the disciples do; two differing explanations are given for Peter's request about the way; the reader is unprepared for Peter's asking about the merchant's name; the reader is surprised that journey from the island city can be undertaken by foot. Examples of problems between 4 and the earlier sections are these: the sudden shift to third person narrative; the information that the disciples are expected to *continue* a ministry to *Christians* (10,4-6) (one had the impression at the start that the disciples were embarking on a mission to a non-Christian world), and the presence of explicit rules regarding church life at the conclusion of the tractate.

Four originally independent accounts seem to have been brought together by an editor. Three probably began as parables or allegories, somewhat resembling those found in *The Shepherd of Hermas*: the story of the pearl merchant who is rejected by the rich and accepted by the poor; the account of a city surrounded by walls (in part three, above) called Habitation; and the story of a journey whose successful completion required giving up food and possessions, rather than having enough of them. The fourth is the account of Christ's commissioning of the disciples to undertake a ministry of preaching and healing among poor and sick Christians. These accounts are related to each other by the common presence of Peter and the other disciples, and by the name Lithargoel, which serves to connect the pearl merchant, in section 2, with the one who gives instructions about the way, in section 3, and, then, also, with Christ, in section 4, who commissions the disciples.

The narrative intention of the final editor appears to have been to depict the disciples' preparation for apostolic activity. In the course of the account, he shifts the time frame from the earliest apostolic period to that of his own time. The result is that, at the conclusion of the final segment, it is not really the original disciples who are being commissioned, but their latter day representatives. In view of the shift, it appears that the editor wished to remind contemporary church leaders about their true mission.

Lithargoel may originally have been a non-Christian deity. But since no record of a Lithargoel cult has come down to us, it seems more reasonable to think that identification of Lithargoel with Jesus Christ (9,8-15) was the intention when the word was first coined. (See *Acts of Peter* 20 and Rv 2:17.) The image of Christ as a physician may have been a way of dealing with the popularity of the cult of Asclepius.

It has sometimes been assumed that this tractate is gnostic. But that view has been based more on its presence in the Nag Hammadi library than on the text itself. As has been discussed elsewhere (see introduction to *Asclepius 21-29* [VI,*8*]), the codex in which it is found is not itself gnostic, but rather a miscellaneous collection of spiritual writings reflecting on the ultimate fate of the soul. If one examines the tractate by itself, little is found that would have offended developing orthodoxy. The Christology is that of the divine sonship; the crucifixion and death of Jesus, although not mentioned, may be implied (see 2,14). The theme of apostolic poverty is found in the Gospels, as is the polemic against the rich. A moderate encratite emphasis may be seen in the prohibition on the eating of meat, but there is nothing said about sexual activity or marriage. The tractate, then, does not appear to have sprung from or be directed to a sectarian group within early Christianity. The editor rather seems to be standing within the broad church and to be appealing for a return to apostolic practice on the part of the leaders.

It seems unlikely that this tractate would have been part of the lost portion of the apocryphal *Acts of Peter*, as has been proposed (see introduction to *The Act of Peter* [BG,*4*], for discussion).

The Acts of Peter and the Twelve Apostles is to be grouped with the apocryphal Acts of the second and third centuries, rather than with the later ones, with which it has little in common. The similarity of portions of it to *The Shepherd of Hermas* suggests a second-century date for them.

THE ACTS OF PETER AND THE TWELVE APOSTLES

VI 1, 1-12, 22

[...] which [...] ' purpose [... : ' after ...] ' us [...] [5] apostles [...]. ' We sailed [...] ' of the body. [Others] were not ' anxious in [their ' hearts]. And in our hearts, we were [10] united. We agreed to fulfill ' the ministry to which ' the Lord appointed us. And we made ' a covenant with each other. '

We went down to the sea at [15] an opportune moment, which came ' to us from the Lord. We ' found a ship moored at the shore ' ready to embark, ' and we spoke with the sailors of [20] the ship about our coming aboard with them. ' They showed great ' kindliness toward us as ' was ordained by the Lord. ' And after we had embarked, [25] we sailed a day ' and a night. After that, ' a wind came up behind the ship and ' brought us to a small city ' in the midst of the sea. [30]

And I, Peter, inquired about the name ' of this city from residents ' who were ' standing on the dock. **2** [A man] among [them] answered, [saying, ' "The name] of this [city is ' Habitation, that is], Foundation [...] ' endurance." And [5] the leader [among them ' holding] the palm branch at the edge of [the dock]. ' And after we had gone ashore [with the] ' baggage, I [went] ' into [the] city, to seek [advice] [10] about lodging.

A man came out ' wearing a cloth ' bound around his waist, ' and a gold belt girded [it]. ' Also a napkin was tied over [his] [15] chest, extending over ' his shoulders and covering his head ' and his hands.

I was staring at the ' man, because he was beautiful in his ' form and stature. There were four [20] parts of his body that ' I saw: the soles of his ' feet and a part of his ' chest and the palms of his ' hands and his visage. [25] These things I was able to see. ' A book cover like (those of) my ' books was in his left hand. ' A staff of styrax wood was in ' his right hand. His [30] voice was resounding as he slowly spoke, ' crying out in the city, ' "Pearls! Pearls!"

I, ' indeed, thought he was a man [of] ' that city. I said [35] to him, "My brother and my friend!" **3** [He answered] me, [then, saying, ' "Rightly] did you say, '[My brother ' and] my friend.' What is it you [seek] ' from me?" I said to him, "[I [5] ask] you [about] lodging for me ' [and the] brothers also, because we ' are strangers here." He said [to] me, ' "For this reason have I myself just said, ' 'My brother and my friend,' [10] because I also am a fellow stranger ' like you."

And ' having said these things, he cried out, ' "Pearls! Pearls!" ' The rich men of that [15] city heard his voice. ' They came out of their hidden storerooms. ' And some were ' looking out from the storerooms ' of their houses. Others [20] looked out from their ' upper windows. And they did not see (that they could gain) ' anything from him, because ' there was no pouch on his back nor ' bundle inside his cloth [25] and napkin. And because of their ' disdain they did not ' even acknowledge him. ' He, for his part, did not reveal himself to them. ' They returned to their [30] storerooms, saying, ' "This man is mocking us." '

And the poor [of that city] heard **4** [his voice, ' and they came to] the man [who sells ' this pearl. They said], ' "Please take the trouble to [show us [5] the] pearl [so that we may], then, [see] ' it with our (own) eyes. For we are [the poor]. ' And we do not have this [...] price ' to pay for it. But [show us] ' that we might say to our friends that [we saw] [10] a pearl with our (own) eyes." He ' answered, saying to them, "If ' it is possible, come to my city, ' so that I may not only show it ' before your (very) eyes, but give it to [15] you for nothing."

And indeed they, ' the poor of that city, heard ' and said, "Since we

| are beggars, we surely | know that a man does not give a pearl [20] to a beggar, but (it is) bread | and money that is usually received. | Now then, the kindness which we want to receive | from you (is) that you show | us the pearl before our eyes. [25] And we will say to our friends | proudly that we saw a | pearl with our (own) eyes" — because | it is not found among the poor, especially | such beggars (as these). He answered [30] (and) said to them, "If it is | possible, you yourselves come | to my city, so that I may not only | show you it, but give it | to you for nothing." [35] The poor and the beggars rejoiced because of **5** the man [who gives for] nothing.

[The men | asked Peter] about the hardships. | Peter answered [and | told] those things that he had heard about the [hardships] [5] of [the] way. Because they are [interpreters of the] | hardships in their ministry. |

He said to the man who sells this | pearl, "I want | to know your name and the hardships of [10] the way to your city because we | are strangers and servants of | God. It is necessary for us to spread | the word of God in | every city harmoniously." He [15] answered and said, "If you | seek my name, Lithargoel | is my name, the interpretation of which is, | the light, gazelle-like stone. |

"And also (concerning) the road to the city, [20] which you asked me about, I will tell you | about it. No man is able to go | on that road, except one | who has forsaken everything that | he has and has fasted [25] daily from stage to stage. | For many are the robbers and | wild beasts on that road. | The one who carries bread with him | on the road, the black dogs [30] kill because of | the bread. The one who carries a costly garment | of the world with him, | the robbers kill **6** [because of the] garment. [The one who carries] water | [with him, the wolves kill because | of the water], since they were thirsty [for] it. | [The one who] is anxious about [meat] and [5] green vegetables, the lions eat | because of the meat. [If] he evades | the lions, the bulls | devour him because of the green vegetables." |

When he had said [these] things to me, I sighed [10] within myself, saying, "[Great] | hardships are on the road! If only | Jesus would give us power to walk it!" | He looked at me since my face was sad, and I | signed. He said to me, "Why [15] do you sigh, if you, indeed, know | this name 'Jesus' and believe him? | He is a great power for giving strength. | For I too believe in the Father | who sent him."

I replied, [20] asking him, "What is the name | of the place to which you go, | your city?" He said to me, | "This is the name of my city, | 'Nine Gates.' Let us praise God [25] as we are mindful that the tenth | is the head." After this I went away | from him in peace.

As I was ¹ about to go and call my friends, I ¹ saw waves and large ³⁰ high walls surrounding ¹ the bounds of the city. I ¹ marveled at the great things I saw. ¹ I saw an old man ¹ sitting and I asked him if the name of the ³⁵ city was really **7** [Habitation]. He [. . .], ¹ "Habitation . . .]." ¹ He said to me, "[You ¹ speak] truly, for we [inhabit] here ⁵ because [we] endure."

[I ¹ responded], saying, "Justly ¹ [. . .] have men named it ¹ [. . .], because (by) everyone ¹ [who] endures his trials, ¹⁰ cities are inhabited, ¹ and a precious kingdom ¹ comes from them, because ¹ they endure in the midst of the ¹ apostasies and the difficulties of the storms. ¹⁵ So that in this way, the city of everyone ¹ who endures the burden of his yoke ¹ of faith will be inhabited, ¹ and he will be included in ¹ the kingdom of heaven."

I hurried ²⁰ and went and called my ¹ friends so that we might go to the city ¹ that he, Lithargoel, appointed for us. ¹ In a bond ¹ of faith we forsook ²⁵ everything as ¹ he had said (to do). We evaded ¹ the robbers, because they did not ¹ find their garments with us. ¹ We evaded the ³⁰ wolves, because they did not find the water ¹ with us for which they thirsted. ¹ We evaded the lions, ¹ because they did not find the desire ¹ for meat with us. **8** [We evaded the bulls . . . ³ they did not find] green vegetables. ¹

A great joy [came upon] us [and a] ⁵ peaceful carefreeness [like ¹ that of] our Lord. We [rested ¹ ourselves] in front of the gate, [and] ¹ we talked with each other [about that] ¹ which is not a distraction of this [world]. ¹⁰ Rather we continued in contemplation ¹ of the faith.

As we discussed the ¹ robbers on the road, whom we ¹ evaded, behold ¹ Lithargoel, having changed, came out to ¹⁵ us. He had the appearance of a physician, ¹ since an unguent box was under ¹ his arm, and a young disciple was ¹ following him carrying a pouch ¹ full of medicine. ²⁰ We did not recognize him. ¹

Peter responded and said to him, ¹ "We want you to do ¹ us a favor, because we are ¹ strangers, and take us to the house of ²⁵ Lithargoel before evening comes." ¹ He said, "In uprightness ¹ of heart I will show it to you. ¹ But I am amazed at how ¹ you knew this good man. ³⁰ For he does not reveal himself to ¹ every man, because he himself ¹ is the son of a great king. ¹ Rest yourselves a little so ¹ that I may go and heal this man ³⁵ and come (back)." He hurried and came (back) **9** quickly.

He said to Peter, ¹ "Peter!" And Peter was frightened, ¹ for how did he know ¹ that his name was Peter? ⁵ Peter responded to the Savior, ¹ "How do you know me, ¹ for you called my name?" ¹ Lithargoel an-

swered, "I ' want to ask you who gave the [10] name Peter to you?" He
' said to him, "It was Jesus Christ, the ' son of the living God. He '
gave this name to me." He answered ' and said, "It is I! Recognize me,
[15] Peter." He loosened the garment, ' which clothed him − the one into
which ' he had changed himself because of us − ' revealing to us in
truth that ' it was he.

We prostrated ourselves [20] on the ground and worshipped him. We '
comprised eleven disciples. ' He stretched forth his hand ' and caused us
to stand. We spoke with ' him humbly. Our heads were [25] bowed down
in unworthiness ' as we said, "What you ' wish we will do. But ' give us
power to do ' what you wish at all times." [20]

He gave them the unguent box ' and the pouch ' that was in the hand
of the young disciple. ' He commanded them like this, **10** saying, "Go
into [the] ' city from which you came, ' which is called Habitation. '
Continue in endurance as you [5] teach all those who have believed ' in
my name, because I have endured ' in hardships of the faith. I ' will
give you your reward. To the ' poor of that city give [10] what they need
in order to live ' until I give them what is better, ' which I told you that
I will give ' you for nothing."

Peter answered ' and said to him, [15] "Lord, you have taught us to '
forsake the world and ' everything in it. We have renounced them ' for
your sake. What we are concerned about (now) ' is the food for a single
day. [20] Where will we be able to find the needs that you ask ' us to provide for the poor?" '

The Lord answered and said, ' "O Peter, it was necessary ' that you
understand the parable [25] that I told you! Do you not understand ' that
my name, which you teach, ' surpasses all riches, ' and the wisdom of
God ' surpasses gold, and silver [30] and precious stone(s)?" '

He gave them the pouch ' of medicine and said, ' "Heal all the sick
' of the city who believe **11** [in] my name." Peter was afraid ' [to] reply
to him for the second time. ' He signaled to the one who was beside '
him, who was John: "You [5] talk this time." ' John answered and said,
' "Lord, before you we are afraid ' to say many words. ' But it is you
who asks us [10] to practice this skill. We have not been ' taught to be
physicians. How then ' will we know how to heal bodies ' as you have
told us?" '

He answered them, "Rightly have you [15] spoken, John, for I know '
that the physicians of this world ' heal what belongs to the world. ' The
physicians of souls, however, ' heal the heart. Heal [20] the bodies first,
therefore, so ' that through the ' real powers of healing ' for their

bodies, without medicine of ' the world, they may believe in you, [25] that you have power to heal ' the illnesses of the heart also.

"The ' rich men of the city, however, those ' who did not see fit ' even to acknowledge me, but who [30] reveled in their ' wealth and pride — ' with such as these, therefore, **12** do not dine in [their] houses ' nor be friends with them, ' lest their partiality ' influence you. For many in the churches have [5] shown partiality to the rich, because ' they also are sinful, ' and they give occasion for ' others to sin. But judge ' them with uprightness, so [10] that your ministry may ' be glorified, and that ' my name also, may be glorified in the ' churches." The disciples ' answered and said, "Yes, [15] truly this is what is fitting ' to do."

They prostrated themselves on the ground ' and worshipped him. He caused them ' to stand and departed from ' them in peace. Amen. [20]

The Acts of Peter '
and the Twelve '
Apostles

THE THUNDER: PERFECT MIND (VI,2)

Introduced and translated by

GEORGE W. MACRAE

Edited by

DOUGLAS M. PARROTT

The title appears to be double: "The Thunder" is not syntactically related to "Perfect Mind" but is separated by a mark of punctuation (:). It is nowhere referred to in the body of the work (unless one should reconstruct "[perfect] mind" at 18,9).

In content *Thund.* is virtually unique in the Nag Hammadi library and very unusual. It is a revelation discourse by a female figure who is, except possibly for the title, otherwise not specifically identified. The work has no apparent structural divisions but is written throughout in the first person, interweaving and combining three types of statement: self-proclamation in the "I am" style, exhortations to heed the speaker, and reproaches for failures to heed or love, etc. The most distinctive feature is that the self-proclamations are most often antithetical or even paradoxical. The parallelism of form suggests that originally these may have been part of a hymnic structure.

Parallels for this revelatory genre can be adduced from a variety of sources. In *Orig. World* (II,5) 114,7-15, the heavenly Eve utters a hymnic self-proclamation that is very similar to *Thund.* 13,19-14,9, and a trace of the same material, though not in the form of self-proclamation, occurs in a similar context in *Hyp. Arch.* (II,4) 89,14-17. It may be significant that the *Thund.* passage thus paralleled is not repeated in the work, whereas many of the other self-proclamations occur more than once in *Thund.*, sometimes in varying forms. In such other Nag Hammadi works as *Trim. Prot.* (XIII,1) and the longer ending of *Ap. John* (II,1:30,11-31,25), there are examples of the "I style" of proclamation by a revealer figure, but without the antithetical context. There are three interesting parallels to *Thund.*, in content or in style or in both, outside the Nag Hammadi corpus. One is the well-known "Hymn of Christ" in the *Acts of John* 94-96, in which Christ sings of himself in a succession of antitheses and contrasts, without, however, the use of "I am" formulas. The second example is a passage in the Mandaean Ginza R, Book VI, the so-called "Book of Dinanukht," which is generally thought to be one of the older sections of the Ginza. There the spirit Ewath recites a formula which contains antitheses similar to, but for the most part not identical with, those in *Thund.*: "I am death, I am life. I am darkness, I am light. I am error, I am truth, etc." The third example is a series of passages in ancient Indian literature in which contrasting or contradictory assertions are made of the Deity either in the "I am" form (Bhagavad-Gita IX,16-19) or in the second or third person (Atharva-Veda X, viii,27-28; Śvetāśvatara Upanishad

IV,3). These examples include both personal categories ("Thou art woman, Thou art man") and non-personal ones ("Death am I and deathlessness, What is not and that which is").

In terms of the religious traditions represented in the Nag Hammadi collection, *Thund.* is difficult to classify. It contains no distinctively Christian, Jewish, or gnostic allusions and does not seem clearly to presuppose any particular gnostic myth. There are resemblances to the tone and style of the wisdom hymns in the Biblical and intertestamental wisdom literature, and the self-proclamations are similar to the Isis aretalogy inscriptions. But if the multiple assertions in these works are intended to assert the universality of Isis or of God's wisdom, perhaps the antithetical assertions of *Thund.* are a way of asserting the totally other-worldly transcendence of the revealer.

(George W. MacRae †)

There has been a tendency among scholars to assume that *Thund.* is gnostic, in spite of George MacRae's caution, expressed above. Accordingly it has been proposed that the female figure here is to be understood as a combination of the higher and lower Sophia figures found in gnostic literature. It has also been proposed that the figure is Eve, as she is understood in gnostic writings found in the Nag Hammadi collection (see references above) and mentioned elsewhere.

If one takes *Thund.* at face value and includes the title in consideration, the female figure who is the speaker throughout is named Thunder (feminine in Greek), a figure who must be understood in terms of the parallel phrase in the title: Perfect Mind. Thunder, in Greek myth, in the Hebrew Bible, and elsewhere, comes forth from the highest god (the Greeks sometimes called Zeus "The Thundering One"). It is the way in which the god makes his presence known on earth. In the tractate, Thunder is allegorized as Perfect Mind, meaning the extension of the divine into the world (1,1-2). The understanding of Perfect Mind appears to owe much to the Stoic notion of cosmic Pneuma, the active, intelligent element in all things, made up of air and fire. It was thought of as spanning all worldly divisions and dichotomies and at some level being responsible for everything that occurs. In its manifestation as reason, it was also able to instruct those who listen about the way to true life. (For Thunder's similar role, see 20,26-27; 21,20-32). The tractate as it stands, is not Stoic, since it speaks of a power above Perfect Mind (1,1). But with its conception of the immanence of the divine in all aspects of the world, neither is it gnostic. It still remains "difficult to classify."

(Douglas M. Parrott)

THE THUNDER: PERFECT MIND

VI 13, 1-21, 32

The Thunder: Perfect Mind |

I was sent forth from | [the] power,
    and I have come to those who | reflect upon me,
    and I have been found [5] among those who seek after me. |
Look upon me, you (pl.) who reflect upon me, |
    and you hearers, hear me. |
    You who are waiting for me, take me | to yourselves.
And do not banish me [10] from your sight. |
And do not make your voice hate | me, nor your hearing. |
    Do not be ignorant of me anywhere | or any time. Be on your
        guard! [15]
    Do not be ignorant of me. |

For I am the first and the last.
I | am the honored one and the scorned one. |
I am the whore and the holy one. |
I am the wife and the [20] virgin.
I am ⟨the mother⟩ | and the daughter.
I am the members | of my mother.
I am the barren one |
    and many are her sons.
I | am she whose wedding is great,
    and [25] I have not taken a husband.
I am the midwife | and she who does not bear.
I | am the solace of my labor pains.
I | am the bride and the bridegroom, |
    and it is my husband who [30] begot me.
I am the mother of | my father
    and the sister of my | husband,
    and he is my offspring. |
I am the slave of him who | prepared me.
I am the ruler **14** of my offspring.
    But he is the one who [begot me] | before the time
    on a birthday. |
    And he is my offspring [in] | (due) time,

and my power [5] is from him.
I am the staff | of his power in his youth,
   [and] | he is the rod of my | old age.
   And whatever he wills | happens to me.
I am the silence [10] that is incomprehensible
   and the idea | whose remembrance is frequent. |
I am the voice whose sound is | manifold
   and the word whose appearance | is multiple.
I am the utterance of [15] my name.

Why, you who hate me, | do you love me
   and | hate those who love me? |
You who deny me, confess | me,
   and you who confess [20] me, deny me.
You who tell | the truth about me, lie about me,
   and you | who have lied about me, tell the truth about me. |
You who know me, be ignorant | of me,
   and those who have not [25] known me, let them know me. |

For I am knowledge and | ignorance.
I am | shame and boldness. |
I am shameless; I am [30] ashamed.
I am strength and | I am fear.
I am | war and peace.
Give heed | to me.
I am the one who is disgraced | and the great one.

Give heed to my **15** poverty and my wealth. |
Do not be arrogant to me when I am | cast out upon the earth,
   [and] | you will find me in [those [5] that] are to come.
And do not look | [upon] me on the dung-heap
   nor go | and leave me cast out, |
   and you will find me in | the kingdoms.
And do not look [10] upon me when I am cast out among those who |
   are disgraced and in the least | places,
   nor laugh at me. |
And do not cast me out among those who | are slain in violence. [15]
But I, I am compassionate | and I am cruel.

Be on your guard! |
Do not hate my obedience |
   and do not love my self-control. |

In my weakness, do not [20] forsake me,
    and do ' not be afraid of my power. '
For why do you despise ' my fear
and ' curse my pride? [25]
But I am she who exists in ' all fears
    and strength ' in trembling.
I am she who is ' weak,
    and I am well in a ' pleasant place.
    I am [30] senseless and I am wise. '

Why have you hated me ' in your counsels?
For I shall be ' silent among those who are silent, '
    and I shall appear and speak. **16**
Why then have you hated me, you Greeks? '
    Because I am a barbarian among [the] ' barbarians?
For I am the wisdom ' [of the] Greeks
    and the knowledge of [the] [5] barbarians.
I am the judgment of [the] ' Greeks and of the barbarians.
[I] ' am the one whose image is great in Egypt '
    and the one who has no image among the ' barbarians.
I am the one who has been hated [10] everywhere
    and who has been loved ' everywhere.
I am the one whom they call ' Life,
    and you have ' called Death.
I am the one whom ' they call Law, [15]
    and you have called Lawlessness. '
I am the one whom you have pursued, '
    and I am the one whom you have seized. '
I am the one whom you have scattered, '
    and you have gathered me together. [20]
I am the one before whom you have ' been ashamed,
    and you have been ' shameless to me.
I am she who does not keep festival, '
    and I am she whose festivals are many. '
I, I am godless,
    and [25] I am the one whose God is great. '
I am the one whom you have reflected upon, '
    and you have scorned me.
I am ' unlearned,
    and they learn from ' me.

I am the one whom you have [30] despised,
   and you | reflect upon me.
I am the one | whom you have hidden from,
   and you | appear to me.
   But whenever | you hide yourselves, [35]
      I myself will appear. **17**
   For [whenever] you | [appear],
      I myself | [will hide] from you.
Those who have [. . .] | to it [. . .] [5] senselessly [. . .]. |

Take me [. . . | understanding] from grief, |
   and take me | to yourselves from understanding [10] [and] grief.
And take | me to yourselves from places | that are ugly and in ruin, |
   and rob from those | which are good even though in ugliness. [15]
Out of shame, take me | to yourselves shamelessly; |
   and out of shamelessness | and shame, upbraid my members |
      in yourselves.
And [20] come forward to me, | you who know me
   and you who | know my members,
   and | establish the great ones among the small | first creatures.
Come [25] forward to childhood, |
   and do not despise it | because it is small and it is little. |
And do not turn away | greatnesses in some parts from [30] the
      smallnesses,
   for | the smallnesses are known | from the greatnesses.

Why | do you curse me | and honor me? [35]
You have wounded and you have | had mercy.
Do not separate me from the first **18** ones whom you have [known].
[And] | do not cast anyone [out nor] | turn anyone away
   [. . .] | turn you away and [. . . [5] know] him not.
   [. . .]. |
   What is mine [. . .]. |
I know the [first ones] and | those after them [know] me. |

But I am the mind of [. . .] [10] and the rest of [. . .]. |
I am the knowledge of my inquiry,
   and | the finding of those who seek after me,
   and | the command of those who ask of me, |
   and the power of the powers in my knowledge [15]
      of the angels, who have been | sent at my word,

and of gods ' in their seasons by my counsel, '
   and of spirits of every man who ' exists with me,
     and of women [20] who dwell within me.
I am the one who ' is honored, and who is praised, '
   and who is despised ' scornfully.
I ' am peace,
   and war [25] has come because of me.
And I ' am an alien and a citizen. '
I am the substance and the one who ' has no substance.

Those who are ' without association with me are ignorant [30] of me,
   and those who are in my ' substance are the ones who know me. '
Those who are close to me have been ignorant ' of me,
   and those who are far ' away from me are the ones who have
     known [35] me.
On the day when I am close to [19] [you],
   [you] are far away ' [from me],
   [and] on the day when I ' [am far away] from you,
     [I am ' close] to you.

[I am [5] ...] within.
[I am ' ...] of the natures.
I am ' [...] of the creation of the [spirits]. '
[...] request of the souls. '
[I am] control and the uncontrollable. [10]
I am the union and ' the dissolution.
I am the abiding ' and I am the dissolution.
I ' am the one below,
   and they come ' up to me.
I am the judgment [15] and the acquittal.
I, I ' am sinless,
   and the root ' of sin derives from me. '
I am lust in (outward) appearance, '
   and interior self-control [20] exists within me.
I ' am the hearing which is attainable to ' everyone
   and the speech which cannot be ' grasped.
I am a mute ' who does not speak,
   and great [25] is my multitude of words.

Hear ' me in gentleness, and ' learn of me in roughness. '
I am she who cries out, '

and I am cast [30] forth upon the face of the earth. |
I prepare the bread and | my mind within.
I am the | knowledge of my name.
I am the one | who cries out,
    and I listen. **20**
I appear and [...] | walk in [...] | seal of my [...]. [5]
I am [...] | the defense [...]. |
I am the one who is called | Truth,
    and iniquity [...]. |

You honor me [...] [10] and you whisper against [me].
You [who] | are vanquished,
judge them (who vanquish you) | before they give judgment
    against you, |
    because the judge and partiality | exist in you.
If you are condemned [15] by this one, who will | acquit you?
    Or if you are acquitted | by him, who will be able to | detain
        you?
For what is | inside of you is what is outside of you, [20]
    and the one who fashions you on the outside |
        is the one who shaped | the inside of you.
    And what | you see outside of you, |
        you see inside of you; [25]
        it is visible and it is your garment. |

Hear me, you hearers, |
    and learn of my words, | you who know me.
I am | the hearing that is attainable to everything; [30]
    I am the speech that cannot | be grasped.
I am | the name of the sound
    and the sound | of the name.
I am the sign | of the letter
    and the designation [35] of the division.
And I [...].
[...] **21**[4] light [...].
[...] [6] hearers [...] | to you
[...] | the great power.
And [...] | will not move the name. [10]
[...] to the one who created me. |
    And I will speak his name. |

Look then at his words
   and all ' the writings which have been completed.
Give ' heed then, you hearers
   and [15] you also, the angels ' and those who have been sent, '
   and you spirits who have arisen from ' the dead.
For I am the one who ' alone exists,
   and I have no one [20] who will judge me.

For many ' are the pleasant forms which ' exist in
   numerous sins, '
   and incontinencies, '
   and disgraceful passions, [25]
   and fleeting pleasures, '
      which (men) embrace ' until they become sober
   and ' go up to their resting-place. '
And they will find [30] me there,
   and they will ' live,
   and they will not die ' again.

AUTHORITATIVE TEACHING (VI,3)

Introduced and translated by

GEORGE W. MACRAE

Edited by

DOUGLAS M. PARROTT

The third tractate of Codex VI is not obviously related either to what precedes or to what follows. It is a heavily metaphorical exposition of the origin, condition, and ultimate destiny of the soul. With respect to its contents, there are some reasons for regarding *Auth. Teach.* as a composite or collection of several explanations of the soul's origin, fall, and victory over the material world. There is a major break at 25,26, where the narrative returns to the world of the Father where it has (presumably) begun, and from 26,20 onward there are several sections containing statements in the first person plural. Moreover, a number of different extended metaphors are introduced successively to explain the same phenomenon, the condition of the soul in the world, although some key metaphors such as those of the food, the medicine, the bridal relationship occur in several sections of the work. Some of these metaphors are extremely common in the literature of the Roman Hellenistic era, e.g., the bridegroom and life as an athletic contest, but others are highly distinctive and almost unparalleled in their elaborateness, e.g., the fisherman and the dealers in bodies.

Auth. Teach. contains no typical gnostic cosmogenic myth – unless it is alluded to in the passages now lost through some of the early lacunae – but it seems to presuppose a generally gnostic, i.e., anticosmic dualist, understanding of the fate of the soul in the material world. It has a number of parallels in the remainder of the Nag Hammadi library, notably with *Gos. Phil.* (II,3), *Exeg. Soul* (II,6), *Teach. Silv.* (VII,4), and the Hermetic tractates of Codex VI, as well as with the *Corpus Hermeticum*. There is nothing in *Auth. Teach.*, however, to suggest that it is itself a Hermetic composition. It is also distinctively different from the *De anima* literature of the early Christian centuries, whether of Tertullian and his sources, or of Porphyry or Iamblichus, in that it is totally nonphilosophical in its forms of expression. Apart from a few expressions such as "evangelists," "hearing the preaching," and the like, there is nothing specifically Christian in the document, nor is there any trace of the heavy dependence on Jewish speculation which we find in so many other Nag Hammadi tractates.

Perhaps there is a clue, though a veiled one, to be sure, to its origin in the section 33,4-34,34, which contains a polemic against the senseless who are distinguished both from the "we" with whom the writer identifies and from the pagans, who are more or less excusable on grounds of ignorance. One is tempted to think of a Christian berating the Jews for their failure to heed the message which they have heard preached to them, but again there is no unambiguous al-

lusion to either Christian or Jewish belief or practice. In its emphasis on the evil character of the material world, on the heavenly origin of the spiritual soul, on the role of revealed knowledge as salvific, *Auth. Teach.* appears to be a gnostic work. But it lacks the tone of self-assurance and confidence, almost arrogance, which characterizes many unquestionably gnostic treatises. The soul is in perpetual danger of succumbing to the "adversary," or to the false attraction of the material, and consequently she must maintain a practised vigilance.

(George W. MacRae †)

Since George W. MacRae wrote, attempts have been made to be more precise about the group responsible for the tractate. Some have argued that they were in fact Gnostics, who only expressed as much of the gnostic myth in the tractate as was needed. A fundamental difference may be seen between Gnostics and traditional Christians, it is argued, in 33,4-34,34, where gnostic "seekers" contrast themselves with the "senseless" faith-oriented Christians, who have "found" the way, in sterile creedal religion. Others believe that second-century Christian Middle Platonists produced the tractate. They find numerous echoes to passages in the New Testament. They also find the distinctive Middle Platonic doctrine of two souls (spiritual and rational). Neither of these basically antithetical positions is well enough supported in the text to warrant abandoning the cautious assessment expressed by MacRae.

(Douglas M. Parrott)

AUTHORITATIVE TEACHING

VI 22, 1-35, 24

[...] [6] in heaven [...] | within him [...] | anyone appears [...] | the hidden heavens [...] [10] appear, and [before] | the invisible, ineffable worlds | appeared. | From these the invisible | soul of righteousness [15] came, being | a fellow member, and a fellow | body, and a fellow spirit. | Whether she is in the descent | or is in the Pleroma, [20] she is not separated from them, but they see | her and she looks at them | in the invisible world. |

Secretly her bridegroom | fetched it. He presented it to her mouth [25] to make her eat it like | food, and he applied the word | to her eyes as a medicine | to make her see with her mind | and perceive her kinsmen [30] and learn about her root, | in order that she might cling to her branch | from which she had first come forth, | in order that she might receive what | is hers and renounce [matter].

[...] **23** [5] he [dwelt ...] | having [...] | sons. The sons [...] | truly, those who have | [come] from his seed, [10] call the sons | of the woman

"our brothers." | In this very way, when the spiritual | soul was cast | into the body, it became [15] a brother to lust and hatred | and envy, and a material | soul. So therefore the body | came from lust, | and lust [20] came from material substance. | For this reason the soul | became a brother to them.

And yet | they are outsiders, without power | to inherit from the male, [25] but they will inherit | from their mother only. | Whenever, therefore, the soul | wishes to inherit | along with the outsiders − for the possessions of [30] the outsiders are | proud passions, the pleasures | of life, hateful envies, | vainglorious things, nonsensical things, | accusations 24 [...] [6] for her [... | prostitution], he excludes her [and puts] | her into the brothel. For [...] | [debauchery] for her. [She left] [10] modestly behind. For death | and life are set before | everyone. Whichever of these two they wish, then, | they will choose for themselves.

That one (fem.) then will fall [15] into drinking much wine in | debauchery. For wine is | the debaucher. Therefore she does not remember | her brothers and her father, for | pleasure and sweet profits [20] deceive her.

Having | left knowledge behind, she fell | into bestiality. For a senseless person | exists in | bestiality, not knowing what it is [25] proper to say and what it is proper | not to say. But, on the other hand, the | gentle son inherits | from his father with pleasure, while | his father rejoices over him [30] because he receives honor on account of him from | everyone, as he looks again | for the way to double the things | that he has received. For the outsiders [...].

[...] [25][5] to mix with the [...]. | For if a thought [of] lust | enters into | [a] virgin man, he has | [already] become contaminated. And their [10] gluttony cannot | mix with moderation. | For if the chaff is mixed | with the wheat, it is not the chaff that is | contaminated, but the wheat. [15] For since they are mixed with each other, no | one will buy her wheat because it is contaminated. | But they will coax | him, "Give us this chaff!", | seeing the wheat mixed [20] with it, until they get it and | throw it with all other chaff, | and that chaff | mixes with all other materials. | But a pure seed [25] is kept in storehouses | that are secure. All these things, then, | we have spoken.

And before | anything came into being, | it was the Father alone who existed, [30] before the worlds that are in | the heavens appeared, | or the world that is on | the earth, or principality, or | authority, or the powers. 26 [...] [4] appear [...] | and [.... | And] nothing | came into being without his wish. |

He, then, the Father, wishing ' to reveal his [wealth] [10] and his glory, brought about ' this great contest ' in this world, wishing ' to make the contestants appear, ' and make all those who contend [15] leave behind ' the things that had come into being, and ' despise them with a ' lofty, incomprehensible knowledge, ' and flee to the one who [20] exists.

And (as for) those who contend with us, ' being adversaries who ' contend against us, we are to be victorious over their ' ignorance through our ' knowledge, since we have already known [25] the Inscrutable One from whom we have ' come forth. We have nothing in ' this world, lest ' the authority of the world that ' has come into being should detain us [30] in the worlds that are in the heavens, ' those in which universal death ' exists, ' surrounded by the individual 27 [. . .] [5] worldly. [We have] ' also become ashamed [of the] worlds, ' though we take no interest in them when they ' [malign] us. And we ignore ' them when they curse [10] us. When they cast shame in ' our face, we look at them ' and do not speak.

For they ' work at their business, ' but we go about in hunger (and) [15] in thirst, looking toward ' our dwelling-place, the place which ' our conduct and our conscience ' look toward, ' not clinging to the things [20] which have come into being, but withdrawing ' from them. Our hearts ' are set on the things that exist, though we are ill ' (and) feeble (and) in pain. ' But there is a great strength hidden [25] within us.

Our soul ' indeed is ill because she dwells ' in a house of poverty, while ' matter strikes blows at her eyes, ' wishing to make her blind. [30] For this reason she pursues ' the word and applies it to her eyes ' as a medicine, ⟨opening⟩ ' them, casting away 28 [. . .] [4] thought of a[. . .] ' blindness in [. . .] ' afterwards when ' that one is again in ' ignorance, he is completely [darkened] ' and [is] material. [10] Thus the soul [. . .] ' a word every hour, to apply ' it to her eyes as a medicine ' in order that she may see, ' and her light may conceal the hostile forces [15] that fight with ' her, and she may make them blind with ' her light, and enclose them in ' her presence, ' and make them fall down in sleeplessness, [20] and she may act boldly ' with her strength and with her ' scepter.

While her enemies look ' at her in shame, she runs ' upward into her treasure-house − [25] the one in which her mind ' is − and (into) her ' storehouse which is secure, since nothing ' among the things that have come into being has seized ' her, nor has she received a [30] stranger into her house. ' For many are her ' homeborn ones who fight against her ' by day and by night, ' having no rest 29 by day or by night, ' for their lust oppresses ' them.

For this reason, then, we do ' not sleep, nor do we forget [the] ⁵ nets that are spread out in ' hiding, lying in wait for us to catch ' us. For if we are caught in ' a single net, it will suck us ' down into its mouth, while the water flows ¹⁰ over us, striking our face. And we will ' be taken down into the dragnet, and we ' will not be able to come up from ' it because the waters are high ' over us, flowing from above ¹⁵ downward, submerging our heart down ' in the filthy mud. And we ' will not be able to escape from them. ' For man-eaters will seize ' us and swallow us, rejoicing ²⁰ like a fisherman casting ' a hook into the water. For ' he casts many kinds of food ' into the water because each one ' of the fish has his own ²⁵ food. He smells it ' and pursues its odor. ' But when he eats it, ' the hook ' hidden within the food ³⁰ seizes him and brings him up by ' force out of the deep waters. ' No man is able, then, ' to catch that fish ' down in the deep waters, **30** except for the trap ' that the fisherman sets. ' By the ruse of food he brought the fish ' up on the hook.

In this very ⁵ way we exist in this world, ' like fish. The adversary ' spies on us, lying in wait ' for us like a fisherman, ' wishing to seize us, rejoicing ¹⁰ that he might swallow us. For [he places] ' many foods before ' our eyes, (things) which belong to this ' world. He wishes to make us ' desire one of them ¹⁵ and to taste only a ' little, so that he may seize us ' with his hidden poison and bring ' us out of freedom ' and take us into ²⁰ slavery. For whenever he catches us ' with a single food, ' it is indeed necessary for ⟨us⟩ to ' desire the rest. ' Finally, then, such things ²⁵ become the food of death. '

Now these are the foods with which ' the devil lies in wait for us. ' First he ' injects a pain into your ³⁰ heart until you have heartache ' on account of a small thing of ' this life, and he seizes ⟨you⟩ ' with his poisons. And ' afterwards (he injects) the desire ³⁵ of a tunic so that you will pride yourself **31** in it, and ' love of money, pride, ' vanity, envy that ' rivals another envy, beauty of ⁵ body, fraudulence. ' The greatest of all these ' are ignorance and ease. '

Now all such things ' the adversary prepares ¹⁰ beautifully and spreads out ' before the body, ' wishing to make the mind of the soul ' incline her toward one of them ' and overwhelm her, like a hook ¹⁵ drawing her by force in ' ignorance, deceiving ' her until she conceives evil, ' and bears fruit of matter, ' and conducts herself ²⁰ in uncleanness, pursuing many ' desires, ' covetousnesses, while ' fleshly pleasure draws her in ' ignorance.

But the soul — ²⁵ she who has tasted these things — ' realized that

sweet passions | are transitory. | She had learned about evil: | she went away from them and she entered [30] into a new conduct. | Afterwards she | despises this life, | because it is transitory. And she | looks for those foods that will [35] take her into life, **32** and leaves behind her those deceitful foods. | And she learns about her light, as she | goes about stripping off this | world, while her true garment [5] clothes her within, | (and) her bridal clothing | is placed upon her in beauty of | mind, not in pride of flesh. | And she learns about her depth and [10] runs into her fold, while | her shepherd stands at the door. | In return for all the shame and scorn, then, | that she received in this | world, she receives [15] ten thousand times the grace and | glory.

She gave the body to | those who had given it to her, and they were | ashamed, while the dealers | in bodies sat down and wept [20] because they were not able to | do any business with | that body, nor did they find | any (other) merchandise except it. | They endured great labors [25] until they had shaped the body of this | soul, wishing to strike | down the invisible soul. | They were therefore ashamed of their | work; they suffered the loss of the one [30] for whom they had endured labors. They did not realize | that she has an | invisible spiritual body, | thinking, "We are her | shepherd who feeds her." [35] But they did not realize that she knows **33** another way, which is hidden from them. This | her true shepherd | taught her in knowledge. |

But these — the ones who are ignorant — [5] do not seek after God. | Nor do they inquire about | their dwelling-place, which exists | in rest, but they | go about in bestiality. They [10] are more wicked than the | pagans, because first of all they | do not inquire about God, for | their hardness of heart draws | them down to make them [15] their cruelty. | Furthermore, if they find someone else | who asks about his salvation, | their hardness of | heart sets to work upon [20] that man. | And if he does not stop asking, they | kill him by | their cruelty, | thinking that they have done a [25] good thing for themselves.

Indeed | they are sons of the devil! | For even the pagans give | charity, and they know | that God who is in the heavens [30] exists, the Father of the universe, | exalted over their idols, which | they worship. [34] But they have not heard the word, that | they should inquire about his ways. | Thus the senseless man | hears the call, [5] but he is ignorant of the place | to which he has been called. And | he did not ask during the preaching, | "Where is the temple | into which I should go and worship [10] my hope?" |

On account of his senselessness, then, | he is worse than a pagan, |

for the pagans know ' the way to go to their stone temple, [15] which will perish, and they worship ' their idol, while their hearts ' are set on it because it is their hope. ' But to this senseless man ' the word has been preached, [20] teaching him, "Seek and ' inquire about the ways you should go, ' since there is nothing else ' that is as good as this thing." ' The result is that the substance of hardness [25] of heart strikes a blow upon ' his mind, along with the force ' of ignorance and ' the demon of error. ' They do not allow his mind [30] to rise up, because he was wearying ' himself in seeking that he might learn about his ' hope.

But the rational soul [35] who (also) wearied herself in seeking − ' she learned about God. ' She labored with inquiring, enduring ' distress in the body, wearing out [5] her feet after ' the evangelists, ' learning about the Inscrutable One. ' She found her rising. ' She came to rest in him who [10] is at rest. She reclined ' in the bride-chamber. She ate ' of the banquet for which ' she had hungered. She partook ' of the immortal food. [15] She found what she had sought after. ' She received rest from her labors, ' while the light that shines forth ' upon her does not sink. ' To it belongs the glory [20] and the power and the ' revelation for ever and ' ever. Amen. '

Authoritative '
Teaching

THE CONCEPT OF OUR GREAT POWER (VI,*4*)

Introduced by

Francis E. Williams

Translated by

Frederik Wisse

Edited by

Douglas M. Parrott

The Concept of Our Great Power is a Christian Gnostic "salvation history." Beginning with creation, it recounts the workings of God's justice and mercy in the conflict between good and evil, ending with the final beatitude. Unusually for a gnostic work the tractate is "apocalyptic," that is, its climax is a dramatic description of the end of the world. Even here, however, it betrays its gnostic character; in gnostic fashion it expects no general resurrection, and contemplates the salvation of nothing material.

"Our great power" is the document's supreme God. He is transcendent and "above all powers" — including the Old Testament God, the "Father of the flesh." However, he intervenes in history; it is he who builds the ark and rescues Noah from the flood.

The very first lines of the tractate make it clear that human salvation depends upon knowing our great power. As the title has probably been taken from the first line, it might well be rendered "the perception of our great power," or even "the knowledge of our great power."

In the manner typical of apocalyptic, the tractate divides all history into three "aeons." The first, the "aeon of the flesh," ends with the flood. In the second, or "psychic" aeon, the revealer appears. He is clearly meant to be the New Testament Christ, though the author avoids that title and is careful not to say explicitly that the revealer is crucified.

The second aeon ends with a war among wicked angelic rulers — the "Archons" — the appearance of an antichristlike figure, and the destruction of the world by fire. Though the fire consumes matter, it purifies souls; together with "the saints," the purified souls then live forever in the great power's "indestructible aeon."

While the tractate's message is clear in broad outline, its details are often puzzling. Some figures well known from other gnostic theology — "the Mother," for example — are mentioned but seem to play no part in the story. Incidents sometimes repeat themselves, or come at unexpected places in the narrative — thus the fire can be understood to destroy the universe twice. The transitions between episodes are often abrupt; so, likewise, are the changes in the per-

son of pronouns and the person and tense of verbs. Of a few passages it is even difficult to make connected sense.

Some of the problems can be solved simply by an attentive reading of the trac-
tate, and a recent interpretation has presented the work as a self-consistent whole. Ohther investigators, however, may still feel that the document has undergone more than one redaction, or at least been extensively glossed. In particular, the question whether an original Jewish apocalypse underlies certain por-
tions of the work seems worthy of investigation.

Even the language of the tractate, a mixture of Sahidic and Subakhmimic dia-
lects of Coptic, calls for explanation. It may simply be that a Sahidic-speaking scribe attempted to translate a Subakhmimic writing into his own dialect. Some, however, explain the language as "proto-Sahidic," a stage of Coptic earlier than that of the Sahidic New Testament.

Questions of the tractate's date and provenance are bound up with those of its language and presumed literary history. If the language is felt to be proto-
Sahidic, the document will be dated rather early. There is, however, an apparent reference to the Anhomoean heresy; one who sees this as stemming from the original author, rather than a glossator, will wish to place the document in the fourth century C.E.

Similar uncertainties make it difficult to determine the document's prove-
nance. If the statement that the Word "appeared in the east at the first" is the author's, the tractate might come from Asia Minor. If the words in question are a gloss, there is less reason to hold this view.

THE CONCEPT OF OUR GREAT POWER

VI 36, 1-48, 15

The Perception of Understanding |
The Concept (or: Thought) of the Great Power |

He who will know our great | Power will become invisible, [5] and fire | will not be able to consume him. But it (i.e. the fire) will | purge and destroy | all your (pl.) possessions. For | everyone in whom my form [10] will appear will be | saved, from (the age of) seven days | up to one hun-
dred and twenty years. | (Those) whom I constrained to | gather all that is fallen, — and [15] the writings of our great Power, in order that | he (i.e. the Power) may inscribe your (sg.) name | in our great light — and | their thoughts | and their works may be ended, [20] that they may be purged, | and be scattered, and be | destroyed, and be gathered in | the place which no one | in it sees. But [25] you (pl.) will see me and | you will prepare your dwelling places | in our great Power.

Know | how what has departed | came to be, in order that you [30] may

know how to discern ' what lives to become: ' of what appearance ' that aeon is, or **37** what kind it is, or ' how it [will] come to be. [Why] ' do you not ask what [kind] ' you will become, [5] (or) rather how you came to be? '

Discern what size ' the water is, that it is immeasurable ' (and) incomprehensible, both its beginning ' and its end. It supports the earth; it [10] blows in the air where ' the gods and the angels are. ' But in him who is exalted ' above all these there is the fear ' and the light, and [15] in him are my writings revealed. ' I have given them as a service ' to the creation of the physical things, for ' it is not possible for anyone to stand ' without that One, nor [20] is it possible for the aeon to live ' without him. It is he who possesses ' what is in him by discerning ' (it) in purity.

Then ' behold the Spirit and know [25] where he is. He gave himself to ' men that they may receive life ' from him every day, ' since he has his life within ' him; he gives to them all.

Then [30] the darkness together with Hades ' took the fire. And ' he (i.e. the darkness) will release from himself what is mine. ' His eyes were not able ' to endure my light. [35] After the spirits and the waters moved, **38** the remainder came into being: ' the whole aeon of the creation ' and their ⟨powers⟩. ' [The] fire came forth from [5] them and the Power came in ' the midst of the powers. And the ' powers desired to see my ' image. And the soul became ' its (i.e. my image's) replica.

This is [10] the work that came into being. See ' what it is like, that ' before it comes into being it does not see, ' because the aeon ' of the flesh came to be in the great bodies. [15] And there were apportioned to them ' long days in the creation. ' For when they had polluted themselves ' and had entered into the flesh, ' the father of the flesh, [20] the water, avenged ' himself. For when ' he had found that Noah was pious ' (and) worthy ' − and it is the father of the flesh who holds [25] the angels in subjection. ' And he (i.e. Noah) preached piety ' for one hundred and twenty ' years. And no one ' listened to him. And he [30] made a wooden ark, ' and whom he had found entered ' it. And the flood ' took place. **39** And thus Noah was saved ' with his sons. For if [indeed] ' ⟨the⟩ ark had not been meant for man ' to enter, then the water [5] of the flood would ' not have come. In this way he intended ' (and) planned to save ⟨the⟩ gods ' and the angels, and the powers, ' the greatness of all of these, [10] and the ⟨nourishment⟩ and the way of life. ' And he moves them from ' the aeon (and) nourishes them ' in the permanent places. And the judgment ' of the flesh was unleashed. [15] Only the work of the Power stood up. '

Next the psychic [|] aeon. It is a small one, [|] which is mixed with bodies, [|] by begetting in the souls (and) defiling (them). ²⁰ For the first defilement of the creation [|] found strength. And it begot [|] every work: many works [|] of wrath, anger, [|] envy, malice, hatred, ²⁵ slander, contempt [|] and war, lying and [|] evil counsels, sorrows [|] and pleasures, [|] basenesses and defilements, ³⁰ falsehoods and diseases, [|] evil judgments [|] that they decree according to their [|] desires.

Yet you are sleeping, **40** dreaming dreams. Wake up [|] and return, [|] taste and eat [|] the true food! Hand out the word ⁵ and the water of life! Cease [|] from the evil lusts and [|] desires and (the teachings of) the Anomoeans, [|] evil heresies [|] that have no basis.

And ¹⁰ the mother of the fire was impotent. [|] She brought the fire upon the soul and [|] the earth, and she burned all ⟨the⟩ dwellings [|] that are in it (fem.). [|] And its (fem.) shepherd perished. ¹⁵ Moreover, when she does not find (anything else) to burn, [|] she will destroy herself. And [|] it (the fire?) will become incorporeal, [|] without body, and it will burn matter, [|] until it has cleansed ²⁰ everything, – and all wickedness. [|] For when it does not find [|] anything else to burn, it will turn [|] against itself until it has destroyed itself. [|]

Then, in this aeon, which ²⁵ is the psychic one, [|] the man will come into being [|] who knows the great Power. [|] He will receive (me) and he will know me. [|] He will drink from the milk of ³⁰ the mother, in fact. He will speak [|] in parables; he will proclaim [|] the aeon that is to come, **41** just as he spoke in [|] the first aeon of the flesh [|] as Noah. Now concerning [|] his words, which he uttered, ⁵ he spoke in all of them, [|] in seventy-two tongues. [|] And he opened the gates [|] of the heavens with his words. [|] And he put to shame the ¹⁰ ruler of Hades; he raised [|] the dead, and [|] he destroyed his dominion. [|]

Then a great disturbance [|] took place. ¹⁵ The archons raised up their wrath against him. [|] They wanted to hand him over [|] to the ruler of Hades. [|] Then they recognized one of [|] his followers. ²⁰ A fire took hold of his (i.e. Judas') [|] soul. He handed [|] him over, since no one knew [|] him. They acted and seized [|] him. They brought ²⁵ judgment upon themselves. [|] And they delivered him up [|] to the ruler [|] of Hades. And they handed [|] him over to Sasabek ³⁰ for nine bronze coins. He prepared [|] himself to go down and [|] put them to shame. Then [|] the ruler of Hades took him. **42** And he found that the nature of his flesh [|] could not be seized, [|] in order to show it to the archons. [|] But he was saying: "Who is ⁵ this? What is it? His word has [|] abolished the law of the aeon. [|] He is from the Logos of the power [|] of life." And he was vic-

torious over the command ' of the archons, and [10] they were not able by
their work ' to rule over him.

The archons ' searched after that which had come to pass. ' They did
not know that this is the sign ' of their dissolution, and (that) [15] it is the
change of the aeon. The sun ' set during the day; that day ' became
dark. The evil spirits were ' troubled. And after these things he will appear ' ascending. [20] And ' the sign of the aeon that is to come will appear. ' And the aeons will dissolve, '

And those who would ' know these things [25] that were discussed with
them, will become ' blessed. And they ' will reveal them, and ' they will
become blessed, since ' they will come to know the truth. [30] For you
(pl.) have found rest in ' the heavens.

Then many ' will follow him, and they will ' labor in their birth
places. **43** They will go about; they will write down ' his words according to ⟨their⟩ desire. '

Behold, these aeons have passed. ' What size [5] is the water of ' the
aeon that has ' dissolved? ' What dimensions do aeons have? How ' will
men prepare themselves, [10] and how will they be established, and how
will they become ' indestructible aeons?

But at first, ' after his preaching ' − it is he who proclaims the second aeon, ' and the first. [15] And the first aeon ' perished in the course
of time. ' He made the first aeon, going about ' in it until it perished '
while preaching one hundred and twenty [20] years in number. ' This is
the perfect number ' that is highly exalted. ' He made the border of the
West ' desolate, and he [25] destroyed the East.

Then ' your (sg.) seed and those who wish ' to follow our ' great Logos and his proclamation − . ' Then the wrath of the archons [30] burned.
They were ashamed ' of their dissolution. ' And they fumed and were
angry ' at the life. The cities were ⟨overturned⟩; ' the mountains dissolve. [35] The archon came, with the **44** archons of the western regions,
to ' the East, i.e., that place ' where the Logos appeared ' at first. Then
[5] the earth trembled, and the cities ' were troubled. Moreover, the birds
' ate and were filled ' with their dead. The earth ' mourned together
with the inhabited world; [10] they became desolate.

Then when the ' times were completed, then wickedness ' arose
mightily even until the final ' end of the Logos. Then ' the archon of the
western regions arose, [15] and from the East ' he will perform a work,
and he will instruct ' men in his wickedness. ' And he wants to nullify
' all teaching, the words of true wisdom, [20] while loving the lying wisdom. For ' he attacked the old, wishing ' to introduce wickedness ' and

to put on ' dignity. He was incapable, ²⁵ because the defilement ' ⟨of⟩ his garments is great. Then he ' became angry. He appeared and desired ' to go up and to pass up ' to that place.

Then ³⁰ the appointed time came and drew near. And ' he changed the commands. Then ' the time came until ' the child had grown up. ' When he had come to his maturity, **45** then the archons sent ' the imitator to ' that man in order that they might know ' our great Power. And ⁵ they were expecting from ' him that he would perform for them a ' sign. And he bore ' great signs. And he ' reigned over the whole earth and ¹⁰ ⟨over⟩ all those who are under heaven. ' He placed his throne upon the end ' of the earth, for "I shall ' ⟨make⟩ you (sg.) god of the world." ' He will perform signs ¹⁵ and wonders. Then they ' will turn from me, and they will go astray. '

Then those men ' who will follow after him (i.e. the imitator) ' will introduce circumcision. ²⁰ And he will pronounce judgment upon those who are from the ' uncircumcision, who are ' the (true) people. For in fact he sent many ' preachers beforehand, who preached ' on his behalf.

When ²⁵ he has completed the established ' time of the kingdom ' of the earth, then ' the cleansing of the souls ' will come, since ³⁰ wickedness is stronger than you (pl.). ' All the powers of the sea will tremble ' and dry up. And the firmament ' will not pour down dew. ' The springs will ³⁵ cease. The rivers will not flow **46** down to their springs. And ' the waters of the springs of ' the earth will cease. Then the depths ' will be laid bare and they will open. The stars ⁵ will grow in size, and the sun will cease. '

And I shall withdraw with ' everyone who will know me. ' And they will enter into the ' immeasurable light, (where) there is ¹⁰ no one of the flesh nor ' the wantonness of the first ' to seize them. They will be unhampered ' (and) holy, since nothing ' drags them down. I ¹⁵ myself protect them, ' since they have ' holy garments, which ' the fire cannot touch, ' nor darkness nor ²⁰ wind nor a moment, so as ' to cause one to shut the eyes.

Then ' he will come to destroy all of them. ' And they will be chastised ' until they become pure. ²⁵ Moreover their period, which was ' given to them to have power, which ' was apportioned to them, (is) fourteen ' hundred and sixty years. ' When the fire has ³⁰ consumed them all, and when ' it does not find anything else to burn, ' then it will perish by its own hand. ' Then the [. . .] will be completed **47** [. . .] ' the [second] power [. . .] ' the mercy will come [. . .] ' through wisdom [. . .] ⁵ Then the firmaments [will fall] ' down into the depth. Then [the] ' sons of matter will perish; they ' will not be, henceforth. '

Then the souls will appear, [10] who are holy through the ' light of the Power, who is exalted ' above all powers, the immeasurable, ' the universal one, I and ' all those who will know me. [15] And they will be in the aeon ' of beauty of ' the aeon of judgment, since they are ready ' in wisdom, having given glory ' to him who is in the [20] incomprehensible unity; and they ' see him because of his will, ' which is in them. And ' they all have become as reflections ' in his light. They [25] all have shone, and they have found rest ' in his rest. '

And he will release the souls that ' are being punished, ' and they will come to be [30] in purity. And they will ' see the saints and ' cry out to them, ' "Have mercy on us, O Power who art above ' all powers." For **48** [...] and in the tree ' [of] iniquity that exists ' [...] to him their eyes. ' [And they] do not seek him [5] because they do not seek us ' nor do they believe us, ' but they acted according to the creation of ' the archons and its other rulers. ' But we have acted according to our [10] birth of the flesh, in the creation ' of the archons, which gives law. ' We also have come to be ' in the unchangeable aeon. '

The Concept of Our Great [15]
Power

PLATO, REPUBLIC 588A-589B (VI,5)

Introduced by

HOWARD M. JACKSON

Translated by

JAMES BRASHLER

Edited by

DOUGLAS M. PARROTT

Tractate VI,5 is a Coptic version of part (588A-589B, not, as formerly, 588B) of Socrates' parable in the ninth book of Plato's *Republic*, in which the human soul is likened to a trichotomous hybrid of different forces: a hybrid composed of a many-headed beast, representing the baser passions; a lion, representing the nobler passion courage; and man, representing the outermost element, reason. The fact of the excerption of the parable as an independent unit, perhaps originally in some philosophical anthology, is made understandable by its great popularity among late antique authors, especially Neoplatonists, who frequently cite or allude to it. What has proved more difficult to account for is the extent to which the Coptic version deviates from the Greek original. So much does it deviate from what Plato wrote that the tractate's first editors (1971) did not recognize it for what it is. The deviation has been accounted for in two ways. In the first, it is viewed as the product of inept translation (so Schenke, who first recognized the tractate's Platonic identity in 1974, and Brashler). In the second, it is viewed as the product of gnosticizing redaction of the Greek original, a redacted version which was then translated into Coptic (so Orlandi). These explanations are obviously not mutually exclusive, and the truth may therefore be a mixture of both (so Jackson and Painchaud). An additional element is doubtless also the incapability of the Coptic language to render the complexities and niceties of Plato's style. The question who the gnosticizing redactor may have been is not readily answerable, since many late antique groups with world-denying and ascetic inclinations revered Plato and shared technical terminology. It may have been Hermetists, especially as Hermetic tractates (VI,6,7,8) follow our tractate, in which case VI,5-8 would have come to the Coptic translator as a group. But gnostic tractates precede VI,5, and the repeated allusion, for example, to "images" and the references in 50,24-33 to the weakness of man (or the [primal] Man) with regard to the images of the evil beast and the lion and his initial fall into their clutches, together with the directive to him to cast down and trample the images, suggests a specifically gnostic setting, perhaps even more explicitly a Manichaean one.

PLATO, REPUBLIC 588A-589B

VI 48, 16-51, 23

"Since we have come ᐧ to this point in a discussion, let us again take up ᐧ the first things that were said ᐧ to us. And we will find [20] that he says, 'Good is ᐧ he who has been done injustice completely. ᐧ He is glorified justly.' ᐧ Is not this how he was ᐧ reproached?''

"This is certainly the [25] fitting way!''

And I said, ᐧ "Now then, we have spoken because ᐧ he said that he who does injustice ᐧ and he who does justice ᐧ each has [30] a force.''

"How then?'' ᐧ

"He said, 'An image that has no ᐧ likeness is the rationality of the soul,' ᐧ so that he who said these things will **49** understand. He [...] [3] or not? We [...] ᐧ is for me. But all [...] [5] who told them [...] ᐧ ruler, these now have become natural creatures — even ᐧ Chimaera and Cerberus ᐧ and all the rest that [10] were mentioned. They all ᐧ came down and they cast ᐧ off forms and ᐧ images. And they all became ᐧ a single image. It was [15] said, 'Work now!' ᐧ Certainly it is a ᐧ single image that became ᐧ the image of a complex beast ᐧ with many heads. [20] Some days indeed it is like ᐧ the image of a wild beast. ᐧ Then it is able to cast ᐧ off the first image. And ᐧ all these hard [25] and difficult forms ᐧ emanate from it with ᐧ effort, since these are ᐧ formed now ᐧ with arrogance. And also [30] all the rest that are ᐧ like them are formed ᐧ now through the word. For now ᐧ it is a single image. ᐧ For the image of the lion is one thing [35] and the image of the man is another. **50** [...] single [...] is the [...] of ᐧ [...] join. And this ᐧ [...] much more complex ᐧ [than the first]. And the second [5] [is small].''

"It has been formed.'' ᐧ

"Now then, join them to ᐧ each other and make them a single ᐧ one — for they are three — so ᐧ that they grow together [10] and all are in a ᐧ single image outside of the image ᐧ of the man just like him ᐧ who is unable to see ᐧ the things inside him. But what [15] is outside only is what he sees. ᐧ And it is apparent ᐧ what creature his image is in and ᐧ that he was formed ᐧ in a human image.

"And I spoke [20] to him who said that there is profit ᐧ in the doing of injustice for the man. ᐧ He who does injustice truly ᐧ does not profit nor ᐧ does he benefit. But [25] what is profitable for him is this: that he ᐧ cast down every image of the ᐧ evil beast and trample ᐧ them along with the images of the lion. ᐧ But the man is in weakness [30] in this regard. And

all the things that he ' does a e weak. ' As a result he is drawn to ' the place where he spends time with them. **51** [...]. And he [...] ³ to him in [...]. ' But he brings about [...] ⁵ enmity [...]. ' And with strife they ' devour each other among ' themselves. Yes, all these things ' he said to everyone who ¹⁰ praises the doing of injustice.'' '

"Then is it not ' profitable for him who speaks ' justly?''

"And if he ' does these things and speaks in them, ¹⁵ within the man they ' take hold firmly. ' Therefore especially he strives ' to take care of them and he nourishes ' them just like the ²⁰ farmer nourishes his ' produce daily. And ' the wild beasts ' keep it from growing.''

THE DISCOURSE ON THE EIGHTH AND NINTH
(VI,6)

Introduced by

DOUGLAS M. PARROTT

Translated by

JAMES BRASHLER, PETER A. DIRKSE, and DOUGLAS M. PARROTT

Although its title is lost, this tractate has been identified as Hermetic from the use of the names Trismegistus and Hermes and close similarities with previously known Hermetic tractates. It has been named from its contents, using a phrase found in the tractate itself (53,24-26). It describes in dialogue form the process by which a spiritual guide (mystagogue) leads an initiate to a mystical experience.

The eighth and the ninth indicate the eighth and ninth spheres surrounding the earth. In ancient times it was thought that the first seven spheres were the realms of the sun, moon, and planets, the lower powers whose control over human life was not necessarily benevolent. The eighth and ninth spheres thus designate the beginning of the divine realm, the levels beyond the control of the lower powers. At death the soul would journey through the seven spheres, and after successful passage it would reach the eighth and the ninth, the levels at which the soul could experience true bliss. Furthermore, the eighth and the ninth spheres can also indicate advanced stages of spiritual development. The tractate possibly assumes yet another sphere, a higher, tenth sphere, where God himself dwells, though this is not entirely clear.

The tractate begins with an introductory discussion (52,2-53,21) in which the initiate secures the approval of the mystagogue to request the experience of the eighth and the ninth. He then makes the formal request (53,24-27). The process leading to the experience begins with a period of instruction, which culminates in a carefully constructed prayer, perhaps spoken by both participants (53,28-57,25). At the heart of the prayer is a request for the visionary experience (57,3-9). Following an embrace between initiative and mystagogue, the mystagogue has his vision (57,28-58,22). Then, directed by the mystagogue, the initiate enters first the eighth, and then the ninth (58,22-60,1).

Following that, the mystagogue exhorts the initiate to silence and gives instruction about continuing in the way of the mystical experience (60,1-10). The tractate concludes with a hymn of thanks by the initiate, and instructions for writing and preserving the account of the experience (60,10-63,32).

Assumed in the tractate are earlier levels of spiritual attainment. They are not described in *Disc. 8-9* but it is clear that two things need to have occurred in order to be ready for the experience of the eighth and ninth: the attainment of purity of life according to the standard of divine law (56,27-57,1) and the banishing of ignorance by mastering the knowledge found in certain books (54,6-18).

The attainment of the final two stages for the initiate requires that the mysta-gogue have the experience first and thereby become the embodiment of universal mind, which is the ninth (58,1-22). The initiate then enters the eighth by recogniz-ing the presence of universal mind, and responds to this recognition by joining the chorus of the eighth and singing a silent hymn to universal mind. He reaches the ninth when he experiences his own unity with universal mind and receives the confirmatory vision in which the chorus of the eighth sings to him (59,24-60,1).

This and other Hermetic tractates may well have been used in the context of small groups devoted to secret knowledge and mystical experience, in which those who were more advanced would teach and direct neophytes, and in which certain cultic acts were engaged in (prayers and hymns are found throughout the Hermetic corpus). The tractates would have served as the basis for discussion and as texts for individual meditation.

Evidence that *Disc. 8-9* was composed in Egypt is found in references to the city of Diospolis, as well as to hieroglyphic characters and gods with animal faces – all found in the section beginning 61,18. The designation of the mystagogue as Hermes and Trismegistus also suggests Egypt. A second-century C.E. date for the composition is possible, because of affinities with the thought of the Middle Platonist Albinus.

THE DISCOURSE ON THE EIGHTH AND NINTH

VI 52, 1-63, 32

[...] ¹

"[My father], yesterday you promised [me ¹ that you would bring] my mind into ¹ [the] eighth and ⁵ afterwards you would bring me into the ¹ ninth. You said that this is the ¹ order of the tradition."

"My ¹ son ¹, indeed this is the order. ¹ But the promise was according to ¹⁰ human nature. For I told you ¹ when I initiated the promise, I ¹ said, 'If you hold in mind ¹ each one of the steps.' ¹ After I had received the spirit through the power, ¹⁵ I set forth the action for you. ¹ Indeed the understanding dwells ¹ in you; in me (it is) as though ¹ the power were pregnant. ¹ For when I conceived from the fountain ²⁰ that flowed to me, I gave birth." ¹

"My father, you have spoken every word ¹ well to me. But I am amazed ¹ at this statement that you have just ¹ made. For you said, 'The ²⁵ power that is in me –.'" ¹

He said, "I gave birth to it (the power), as ¹ children are born."

"Then, my ¹ father, I have many brothers, if ¹ I am to be numbered among the offspring." ³⁰

"Right, my son! This ¹ good thing is numbered by 53 [...]. ⁴ And

[...] ' at all times. ' Therefore, my son, ' it is necessary for you to ' recognize your brothers and ' to honor them rightly and [10] properly, because they ' come from the same father. ' For each generation I have ' called. I have named ' it, because they were offspring [15] like these sons.''

"Then, ' my father, do they have ' (a) day?''

"My son, ' they are spiritual ones. For ' they exist as forces that grow [20] other souls. Therefore I say ' that they are immortal.'' ' '

"Your word is true; it has no ' refutation from now on. ' My father, begin the [25] discourse on the eighth and ' the ninth, and include me also ' with my brothers.''

"Let us pray, ' my son, to the father of the ' universe, with your brothers who are my [30] sons, that he may give ' the spirit of eloquence.''

"How ' do they pray, my father, ' when joined with the generations? ' I want to obey, my father.''

54 [...] [3] "But it is [not ...]. ' Nor [is it] a [...]. [5] But he is satisfied [with] it (fem.). ' [...] it (masc.). And it is right ' [for you] to remember the progress ' that came to you as ' wisdom in the books. [10] My son, compare yourself to the ' early years of life. As children (do), ' you have posed senseless, ' unintelligent questions.''

"My ' father, the progress that has come [15] to me now and the foreknowledge, ' according to the books, that has come to me, ' exceeding the deficiency − these things are ' foremost in me.''

"My son, ' when you understand the [20] truth of your statement, you will ' find your brothers, who are my sons, ' praying with you.'' '

"My father, I understand nothing else ' except the beauty that [25] came to me in the books.''

"This is ' what you call the beauty ' of the soul, the edification that ' came to you in stages. ' May the understanding come to you, [30] and you will teach.''

"I have understood, ' my father, each one of ' the books. And especially the (fem.) **55** [...] which is in [...].'' '

'My son, [...] [4] in praises from ' [those who] extolled [them].'' '

"My father, from you ' I will receive the [power] of the ' discourse [that you will] give. As it was told ' to both (of us), let us pray, [10] my father.''

"My son, ' what is fitting is to pray ' to God with all our mind ' and all our heart and our ' soul, and to ask [15] him that the gift of the ' eighth extend to ' us, and that each one ' receive from him what ' is his.

Your part, then, is [20] to understand; my own is | to be able to deliver the discourse | from the fountain that flows to me.'' |

"Let us pray, my father: | I call upon you, who [25] rules over the kingdom | of power, whose word | comes as (a) birth of light. | And his words are immortal. | They are eternal and [30] unchanging. He is the one whose will | begets life for the forms in | every place. His nature gives form | to substance. By him **56** the souls of [the eighth | and] the angels are moved [. . .] [4] those that exist. His providence | extends to everyone [. . .] | begets everyone. He is the one who | [. . .] the aeon among spirits. | He created everything. He who is | self-contained cares [10] for everything. He is perfect, the | invisible God to whom one speaks | in silence — his | image is moved when it is directed, | and it governs — the [15] one mighty power, who is exalted | above majesty, who is better than the | honored (ones), Zoxathazo a ōō | ee ōōō ēēē ōōōō | ēē ōōōō-ōō ooooo [20] ōōōōōō uuuuuu | ōōōōōōōōōōōō | ōōō Zozazoth.

"Lord, | grant us a wisdom from | your power that reaches [25] us, so that we may describe to ourselves the | vision of the eighth and the ninth. | We have already advanced to the seventh, | since we are pious and | walk in your law. [30] And your will | we fulfill | always. For we have walked in **57** [your way, and we have] renounced | [. . .], so that | your [vision] may come. Lord, grant | us the truth in the image. [5] Allow us through the spirit to | see the form of the image | that has no deficiency, | and receive the reflection of the pleroma | from us through our praise. [10]

"And acknowledge the spirit | that is in us. For from | you the universe received soul. | For from you, the unbegotten one, | the begotten one came into being. [15] The birth of the self-begotten one | is through you, | the birth of all begotten things | that exist. Receive | from us these spiritual sacrifices, [20] which we send | to you with all our heart | and our soul and all | our strength. Save that which | is in us and grant us [25] the immortal wisdom.'' |

"Let us embrace | each other affectionately, my son. | Rejoice over this! For already | from them the power, [30] which is light, is coming to us. | For I see! I see | indescribable depths. | How shall I tell you, **58** my son? [. . .] | from the (fem.) [. . .] | the places. How [shall I describe] | the universe? I [am Mind and] [5] I see another Mind, the one that [moves] the | soul! I see the one that moves me | from pure forgetfulness. You give | me power! I see myself! I want | to speak! Fear restrains [10] me. I have found the | beginning of the power that is above | all powers, the one that has no | beginning. I see a fountain bubbling | with life. I have

said, [15] my son, that I am Mind. ' I have seen! Language is not able ' to reveal this. For the entire ' eighth, my son, and ' the souls that are in it, and the [20] angels, sing a hymn in ' silence. And I, Mind, ' understand."

"What is the way to sing ' a hymn through it (silence)?"

"Have you become such that ' you cannot be spoken to?"

"I am silent, [25] my father. I want to ' sing a hymn to you while I am silent."

"Then ' sing it, for I am Mind." '

"I understand Mind, Hermes, ' who cannot be interpreted, [30] because he keeps within himself. ' And I rejoice, my father, because I see ' you smiling. And the universe 59 [rejoices]. Therefore there is no ' creature that will lack ' your life. For you are the ' lord of the citizens in [5] every place. Your providence protects. ' I call you father, aeon ' of the aeons, great divine spirit. ' And by a spirit he gives ' rain upon everyone. What [10] do you say to me, my ' father, Hermes?"

"Concerning these things I ' do not say anything, my son. ' For it is right before God ' that we keep silent about what is hidden." [15]

"Trismegistus, let not ' my soul be deprived of the ' great divine vision. For ' everything is possible for you as master ' of the universe."

"Return to [20] ⟨praising⟩, my son, and sing ' while you are silent. Ask what ' you want in silence." '

When he had finished praising he ' shouted, "Father [25] Trismegistus! What shall I say? ' We have received this light. And ' I myself see this same vision ' in you. And ' I see the eighth and the souls [30] that are in it and the angels ' singing a hymn to the ninth and ' its powers. And I see ' him who has the ' power of them all, creating 60 those ⟨that are⟩ in the spirit."

"It is advantageous from [now on] ' that we keep silence in a reverent posture. ' Do not speak about the vision ' from now on. It is proper to [sing a hymn] [5] to the father until the day to quit (the) body." '

"What you sing, my ' father, I too want to sing." '

"I am singing a hymn within myself. ' While you rest yourself, be active in praise. [10] For you have found what you seek." '

"But it is proper, ' my father, that I praise because I ' am filled in my heart?"

"What is proper ' is your praise that you [15] will sing to God ' so that it might be written in this imperishable book." '

"I will offer up ' the praise in my heart, as I ' pray to the end of the universe and [20] the beginning of the beginning, to the object ' of man's quest, the ' immortal discovery, the begetter of ' light and truth, the '

sower of reason, the love of [25] immortal life. No | hidden word will be able to speak about you, | Lord. Therefore my mind | wants to sing a hymn to you | daily. I am the instrument [30] of your spirit; Mind is your | plectrum. And your counsel | plucks me. I see **61** myself! I have received power from you. | For your love has reached us." |

"Right, my son." |

"Grace! | After these things I give thanks [5] by singing a hymn to you. For I have | received life from you, when you made me wise. I | praise you. I call | your name that is hidden within me: [10] a ō ee ō ēēē ōōō iii | ōōōō ooooo ōōō | ōō uuuuuu ōō | ōōōōōōōōō | ōōōōōōōōō[15]ōō. You are the one who exists | with the spirit. I sing a hymn | to you reverently." |

"My son, | write this book for the temple at Diospolis [20] in hieroglyphic characters, | entitling it 'The Eighth | Reveals the Ninth.'" |

"I will do it, my ⟨father⟩, as | you command [25] now." |

"My ⟨son⟩, | write the language of the book on steles | of turquoise. My son, | it is proper to write this book | on steles of turquoise, [30] in hieroglyphic characters. | For Mind himself has | become overseer **62** of these. Therefore I command | that this teaching be carved | on stone, and that you place it in | my sanctuary. Eight [5] guardians guard it with[. . .] | of the Sun. The males | on the right are frog-faced, | and the females | on the left are cat-faced. [10] And put a square | milk-stone at the base of the | turquoise tablets | and write the name on the | azure stone tablet [15] in hieroglyphic characters. | My son, you will do this | when I am in Virgo, | and the sun is in the first half of the | day, and fifteen degrees have [20] passed by me." |

"My father, | everything that you say I will | do eagerly." |

"And write | an oath in the book, lest those who | read the book bring [25] the language into | abuse, and not (use it) | to oppose the acts of fate. | Rather, they should submit | to the law of God, [30] without having transgressed at all, | but in purity asking | God for wisdom and | knowledge. And he who **63** will not be begotten at the start by God | comes to be by the general | and guiding discourses. | He will not be able to read the things written [5] in this book, although his | conscience is pure within him, since he | does not do anything shameful, | nor does he consent | to it. Rather, by stages [10] he advances and enters into | the way of immortality. And | thus he enters into the | understanding of the eighth that | reveals the ninth." |

"So [15] shall I do it, my father." |

"This | is the oath: I make him who will | read this holy book swear by heaven | and earth and fire and | water and seven rulers of substance

[20] and the creating spirit in them | and the ⟨unbegotten⟩ God | and the self-begotten one | and him who has been begotten, that he will | guard the things that Hermes has said. [25] And those who keep the oath, | God will be reconciled with them | and everyone whom we have | named. | But wrath will come to each one [30] of those who violate the oath. | This is the perfect one who is, | my son."

THE PRAYER OF THANKSGIVING (VI,7)

Introduced and translated by

JAMES BRASHLER, PETER A. DIRKSE, and DOUGLAS M. PARROTT

Edited by

DOUGLAS M. PARROTT

This short, almost perfectly preserved Hermetic prayer expresses in carefully constructed liturgical language the gratitude of one who has received deifying knowledge. Although set off with decorations like those regularly used with titles in the Nag Hammadi codices, the heading, "This is the prayer that they spoke," was originally only an introductory line. Together with the concluding statement, this heading forms a narrative framework for the prayer.

The scribal note, which immediately follows *The Prayer of Thanksgiving*, shows that the prayer was contributed by the copyist, who had a collection of Hermetic materials. Presumably he thought that the prayer was an appropriate way to conclude the account of the mystical experience described in VI,6. The note suggests that after he had copied the prayer, the copyist was uncertain whether he should have done it, and was seeking in an oblique way to justify his action (rather than being bold, he was in fact restrained!). His action may have been responsible for an unusual crowding of the Coptic text in the remaining pages of the codex. The theory that the scribal note refers to VI,8 was based on the mistaken supposition that the note was written over the erased title of VI,8 after VI,8 was copied (see introduction to VI,8).

Version VI,7 is one of three versions of the Hermetic *Prayer of Thanksgiving*. The context of the prayer is different in each case. In the Greek text called Papyrus Mimaut, it is part of a long prayer embedded in a magical composition. In the Latin *Asclepius*, it forms the conclusion of the tractate. And here it is appended to another Hermetic tractate. This suggests that it was originally an independent piece of tradition.

Pr. Thanks. is especially significant for the clear evidence it presents of the existence of Hermetic cultic practices. The prayer itself reflects liturgical usage, as its balanced language attests. Moreover, the concluding statement mentions a ritual embrace or kiss (also found in VI,6 at 57,26-27) after the prayer, and a cultic meal. These references to cultic practices suggest that the primary *Sitz im Leben* of *Pr. Thanks.* was a Hermetic community dedicated to the encouragement of the visionary experience alluded to in 64,16-17 and the preservation of the mystical knowledge communicated in that experience. While it is not possible to assign a date to such communities, it is reasonable to assume that they flourished in the second and third centuries C.E. and possibly even earlier.

THE PRAYER OF THANKSGIVING

VI 63, 33-65, 7

This is the prayer that they spoke: | "We give thanks to You! Every soul [35] and heart is lifted up to You, | undisturbed name, **64** honored with the name | 'God' and praised | with the name 'Father,' | for to everyone and everything [5] (comes) the fatherly kindness and | affection and love, | and any teaching there may be that is sweet | and plain, giving | us mind, speech, [10] (and) knowledge: mind, | so that we may understand You, | speech, so that we may | expound You, knowledge, | so that we may know You. [15] We rejoice, having been illuminated | by Your knowledge. We rejoice | because You have shown us Yourself. We rejoice | because while we were in (the) body, You have made us | divine through Your knowledge. [20]

"The thanksgiving of the man who attains | to You is one thing: that we know | You. We have known You, | intellectual light. | Life of life, we have known You. [25] Womb of every creature, we have | known You. Womb pregnant with | the nature of the Father, we have known | You. Eternal permanence | of the begetting Father, thus have we [30] worshipped Your goodness. | There is one petition that we ask: | we would be | preserved in knowledge. | And there is one protection that we **65** desire: that we not stumble | in this kind of life." |

When they had said these things in the prayer, they | embraced each other and [5] they went to eat their | holy food, which has no blood | in it. |

SCRIBAL NOTE (VI, *7a*)

VI 65, 8-14

I have copied this one discourse of his. | Indeed, very many have come to me. I have not [10] copied them because I thought that they had come to you (pl.). | Also, I hesitate to copy these for | you because, perhaps they have (already) come to you, and | the matter may burden you. Since | the discourses of that one, which have come to me, are numerous ...

ASCLEPIUS 21-29 (VI,*8*)

Introduced and translated by

James Brashler, Peter A. Dirkse, and Douglas M. Parrott

The Hermetic tractate *Asclepius* was composed in Greek but exists in complete form only in a Latin translation. It was originally called *The Perfect Teaching*. VI,*8* is a Coptic translation of a large selection from the middle portion of the tractate. It differs from the Latin at many points, but is still recognizably from the same source as the Latin because of the similarity of contents and the way they are ordered. Two Greek passages from the middle section of *Asclepius* have survived, and VI,*8* is stylistically closer to them than to the rather expansive and rhetorical Latin.

VI,*8* has no title, either at the beginning or the end, which makes it unique in the codex. It has been suggested that a title might have been erased at the beginning of the tractate and replaced by the scribal note, which is found there, but close examination of the manuscript shows that to be unlikely. Since the scribal note suggests that *The Prayer of Thanksgiving* (VI,*7*) is the copyist's insertion, it is possible that VI,*8* may originally have been a continuation of VI,*6* (*Disc. 8-9*). In that event, the now lost title of VI,*6* could have served for it as well.

The tractate is in the form of a dialogue between an Hermetic initiate, Asclepius (two others, Tat and Amon, are mentioned in 72,30-31), and the mystagogue, Trismegistus (designated as Hermes in other Hermetic tractates). *Asclepius* as a whole was probably used in an instructional-cultic context (see introduction to VI,*6*). The contents are arranged in five general areas.

1) 65,15-37. The mystery experience (here undescribed) is likened to sexual intercourse, in that it requires an intimate interaction between two parties in which (according to Trismegistus' view) each receives something from the other.

2) 65,37-68,19. Discussion of the separation between the pious and the impious, with the former being distinguished by having learning and knowledge, and the latter, ignorance. Man needs learning and knowledge to restrain harmful passions and to become good and immortal. Indeed, with learning and knowledge man becomes better than the gods, since then he is both mortal and immortal.

3) 68,20-70,2. Trismegistus argues that men create gods according to human likenesses.

4) 70,3. This marks the beginning of the apocalyptic section. It seems to extend only to 74,6, in contrast to the Latin *Asclepius*, where it clearly continues through 331,11 (parallel to 74,11). Here are described the woes that will come upon Egypt and the final action of the creator god to end them and bring the universe to birth. This section was probably originally independent. There are a significant number of parallels to Egyptian conceptions, which can be traced back to the Ptolemaic period and before. But parallels are also found to Plato, Stoicism, the Sibylline Oracles, and the New Testament. Some have held that the apocalypse was originally a Jewish writing, while others suggest that it was ori-

ginally Egyptian because of the greater number and antiquity of these parallels. The two concepts need not be mutually exclusive in view of the large, ancient, and literarily active Jewish community in Egypt.

5) 74,7-78,42. Discussion of the ultimate fate of the individual. The restoration of the nature of the pious ones is founded upon the eternal will of God, which expresses itself in the design of the good universe. The plan of the universe is then described. The "heights of heaven" are controlled by God. Other areas, including the earth, are controlled by other gods. Every person must go to the city in the west (place of the dead?). The soul separates from the body and goes to "the middle of the air" to be judged by the great daimon, who determines reward or punishment.

The Latin *Asclepius* is one of a group of Hermetic tractates that stands between those Hermetic tractates that are pantheistic, and hence distinctively Hellenistic, and those that are dualistic. The tractates in this group contain a mixture of both emphases. In addition to *Asclepius* they are *Corp. Herm.* IX, X, and XII. The excerpt from *Asclepius* that is VI,8 has both pantheism and dualism. The pantheism is explicitly expressed in 75,10-11 ("He [God] is in every place, and he looks out over every place."). It can also be seen in the conviction that the universe is good (74,33-36) and that the demiurge and the earth goddess are beneficent (75,13-24), as well as in the panegyric on Egypt (70,3-9). The dualism is found in the discussion of the two natures of man (66,9-67,34), but whether this should be attributed to Gnosticism, as some have thought, or is merely an expression of the dualism common in the Graeco-Roman world generally, is not clear.

The pantheism mentioned above, with its positive evaluation of the world, has presented a problem for those who assume that Codex VI, as a collection, had its origin among Gnostics. It has been suggested that perhaps the pantheistic parts were overlooked by the collector, who was interested in the dualism. The pantheistic elements, however, could not have been deleted. It seems better to suppose that the codex may not have had its origin among Gnostics. Among its eight tractates, it contains two other Hermetic pieces (tractates *6* and *7*), a garbled selection from Plato's Republic (tractate *5*), a non-gnostic account of apostolic activity (tractate *1*), and a tractate that has no clear indication of gnostic influence (tractate *2*). Of the remaining two tractates (*3* and *4*), the first has been called questionably gnostic, and only the second seems to contain distinctively gnostic ideas. Thus, when the contents of the codex as a whole are considered, one has the impression of a miscellaneous collection of spiritual pieces without any clear ideological tendency running throughout. The one common theme may be the ultimate fate of the individual – the theme with which *Asclepius 21-29*, and therefore the codex as a whole, ends. There is probably no way to know how the codex found its way into a collection of predominantly gnostic works.

ASCLEPIUS 21-29

VI 65, 15-78, 43

"And if you (sg.) wish to see the reality of ' this mystery, then you should see the wonderful representation ' of the intercourse ' that takes place between ' the male and the female. For when [20] the semen reaches the climax, it leaps forth. ' In that moment ' the female receives the strength ' of the male; the male for his part ' receives the strength of the female, while [25] the semen does this. '

"Therefore the mystery of intercourse ' is performed in secret, ' in order that the two sexes ' might not disgrace themselves in front of many who do not experience [30] that reality. ' For each of them (the sexes) contributes its (own part in) begetting. ' For if it happens in the presence of those who do not understand the reality, ' (it is) laughable ' and unbelievable. And, moreover, [35] they are holy mysteries, ' of both words and deeds ' because not only are they not heard ' but also they are not seen.

"Therefore **66** such people (the unbelievers) are blasphemers. ' They are atheistic and impious. ' But the others are not many; ' rather, the pious who are counted are few. [5] Therefore ' wickedness remains among (the) many, ' since learning ' concerning the things which are ordained does not exist among them. ' For the knowledge of the things which are ordained [10] is truly the healing of the passions ' of the matter. Therefore learning ' is something derived from knowledge. '

"But if there is ' ignorance, and learning [15] does not exist in the soul of man, ' (then) the incurable passions persist in it (the soul). ' And additional ' evil comes with them (the passions) in the ' form of an incurable sore. [20] And the sore constantly gnaws at the soul, ' and through it the soul produces worms from ' the evil and stinks. But God ' is not the cause of ' these things, since he sent to men [25] knowledge and learning." '

"Trismegistus, ' did he send them to men ' alone?"

"Yes, Asclepius, ' he sent them to them (men) alone. [30] And it is fitting that we tell ' you why to men ' alone he granted ' knowledge and learning, ' the allotment of his good. [35]

"And now listen! God ' and the Father, even the Lord, created ' man subsequent to the gods, ' and he took him from **67** the region of matter. [Since] matter ' is involved in the creation of [man] ' of [. . .], the passions are ' in it. Therefore [5] they continually flow over his ' body, for

this living creature would not have existed ¹ in any other way except that he had taken this ¹ food, since ¹ he is mortal. It is also inevitable ¹⁰ that inopportune desires, ¹ which are harmful, dwell in him. ¹ For the gods, since ¹ they came into being out of a pure matter, ¹ do not need ¹⁵ learning and knowledge. ¹ For the immortality of the gods ¹ is learning and knowledge, ¹ since they came into being out of pure matter. ¹ It (immortality) assumed for them ²⁰ the position of knowledge and learning. ¹ By necessity he (God) ¹ set a boundary for man; he placed him ¹ in learning and knowledge. ¹

"Concerning these things (learning and knowledge), which we have mentioned ²⁵ from the beginning, he perfected them ¹ in order that by means of these things ¹ he might restrain passions and evils, ¹ according to his will. ¹ He brought his (man's) mortal existence into ³⁰ immortality; he (man) became ¹ good (and) immortal, just as ¹ I have said. For he (God) created (a) two-fold nature ¹ for him: the immortal and ¹ the mortal.

"And it ³⁵ happened this way because of the will **68** of [God] that men ¹ be better than the gods, since ¹ indeed [the] gods are ¹ immortal, but men alone ⁵ are both immortal and mortal. ¹ Therefore man has ¹ become akin to the gods, ¹ and they know the affairs ¹ of each other with certainty. The ¹⁰ gods know the things of ¹ men, and men ¹ know the things of the gods. ¹ And I am speaking about men, Asclepius, ¹ who have attained learning ¹⁵ and knowledge. ¹ But (about) those who are more vain than these, it is not fitting ¹ that we say anything base, ¹ since we are divine and are ¹ introducing holy matters. ²⁰

"Since we have entered ¹ the matter of the communion between the ¹ gods and men, know, ¹ Asclepius, that in which man ¹ can be strong! ²⁵ For just as the Father, the Lord of ¹ the universe, creates gods, ¹ in this very way man too, ¹ this mortal, earthly, living creature, ¹ the one who is not like ³⁰ God, also himself ¹ creates gods. Not only ¹ does he strengthen, but he is also strengthened. ¹ Not only is he god, but ¹ he also creates gods. Are you astonished, ³⁵ Asclepius? Are you yourself ¹ another disbeliever like the many?" **69**

"Trismegistus, [I agree with] the words (spoken) ¹ to me. [And] I believe you ¹ as you [speak]. But I have also been astonished ¹ at the discourse about [this]. And I have ⁵ decided that man is blessed, ¹ since he has enjoyed this great power." ¹

"And that which is greater than all these things, ¹ Asclepius, is worthy of admiration. ¹ Now it is clear to us ¹⁰ concerning the race of the gods, ¹ and we confess it ¹ along with everyone else, that it (the race of

the gods) has come into being ' out of a pure matter. And ' their bodies are heads only. [15] But that which men create ' is the likeness of the gods. They (the gods) are from ' the farthest part of the matter, ' and it (the object created by men) is from the outer (part) of the being ' of men. Not only [20] are they (what men create) heads but (they are) also all the other members ' of the body and according to ' their likeness. Just as ' God has willed that the inner man ' be created according to [25] his image, in the very same way ' man on earth creates gods ' according to his likeness.''

"Trismegistus ' you are not talking about idols, are you?'' '

"Asclepius, you yourself are talking [30] about idols. You see that again you yourself, ' Asclepius, are also a ' disbeliever of the discourse. You say ' about those who have soul and ' breadth, that they are idols — these who [35] bring about these great events. ' You are saying about these who give prophecies ' that they are idols — these who give **70** [men sickness and] healing ' that [. . .] them. '

"Or are you ignorant, Asclepius, ' that Egypt is (the) image [5] of heaven? Moreover, ' it is the dwelling place of heaven and all the forces ' that are in heaven. If ' it is proper for us to speak the truth, our ' land is (the) temple of the world. [10] And it is proper for you not to be ' ignorant that a time ' will come in it (our land ' when) Egyptians will seem ' to have served the divinity in [15] vain, and all their activity ' in their religion will ' be despised. For all divinity ' will leave Egypt and will ' flee upward to heaven. And Egypt [20] will be widowed; it will be abandoned by the ' gods. For foreigners ' will come into Egypt, and they will rule ' it. Egypt! Moreover, ' Egyptians will be prohibited [25] from worshipping ' God. Furthermore, they will come ' into the ultimate punishment, especially whoever ' among them is found worshipping ' (and) honoring God. [30]

"And in that day the country ' that was more pious than all countries ' will become ' impious. No longer will it be full ' of temples, but it will be full of tombs. [35] Neither will it be full of gods ' but (it will be full of) corpses. Egypt! ' Egypt will become like the ' fables. And your religious objects **71** will be [. . .] the marvelous things ' and [. . .], ' and if your words are ' stones and are wonderful. [5] And the barbarian will be ' better than you, Egyptian, ' in his religion, whether ' (he is) a Scythian, or the Hindus, or some other ' of this sort.

"And what is this that I say [10] about the Egyptian? For they (the Egyptians) will ' not abandon Egypt. For (in) the time ' (when) the gods have abandoned the land ' of Egypt and have fled upward to ' heaven, then

all Egyptians [15] will die. And Egypt will be ' made a desert by the gods
and the Egyptians. ' And as for you, River, there ' will be a day when
you will flow ' with blood more than water. And [20] dead bodies will be
' (stacked) higher than the dams. ' And he who is dead will not be
mourned ' as much as he who is alive. Indeed the latter will be ' known
as an Egyptian [25] on account of his language in ' the second period (of
time). Asclepius, ' why are you weeping? He will seem ' like (a)
foreigner in regard to ' his customs. Divine Egypt [30] will suffer evils
greater ' than these. Egypt, lover of God, ' and the dwelling place of the
gods, ' school of religion, ' will become an example of [35] impiousness.

"And in that day ' the world will not be marveled at, **72** [...] and
[immortality, ' nor] will it be worshipped ' [...] since we say that it is
' not good [...]. It has become neither [5] a single thing nor ' a vision.
But it is in danger ' of becoming a burden ' to all men. Therefore, ' it
will be despised – the beautiful world [10] of God, ' the incomparable
work, ' the energy that possesses ' goodness, the many-formed vision, '
the abundance [15] that does not envy, that is full ' of every vision. '
Darkness will be preferred to light ' and death will be preferred to ' life.
No one will gaze [20] into heaven. And the pious man ' will be counted as
insane, ' and the impious man will be honored ' as wise. The man who
is afraid ' will be considered as strong. And [25] the good man will be
punished ' like a criminal. '

"And concerning the soul, and the things ' of the soul, and the things
of immortality, ' along with the rest of what I have said [30] to you, Tat,
Asclepius, ' and Ammon, not only will they ' be considered ridiculous,
' but they will also be thought of as vanity. ' But believe [35] me (when I
say) that people of this kind will ' be endangered by the ultimate danger
' to their soul. And ' a new law will be established. **73** [...] [3] they will
[...] [5] good. [The] wicked angels ' will remain among ' men, (and) be
with them ' (and) lead them into wicked things ' recklessly, as well as into [10] atheism, wars, ' and plunderings, by teaching them ' things contrary to nature.

"In those days ' the earth will not be stable, ' and men will not sail
the sea, [15] nor will they know the stars in heaven. ' Every sacred voice
' of the word of God will ' be silenced, and the air will be diseased. '
Such is the senility of the world: [20] atheism, ' dishonor, and the disre-
gard ' of noble words.

"And when these things had happened, Asclepius, ' then the Lord,
the Father and [25] god from the only first (God), god ' the creator, when
he looked upon ' the things that happened, established his design, '

which is good, ¦ against the disorder. He took away ³⁰ error, and cut off evil. ¦ Sometimes ¦ he submerged it in a great flood, ¦ at other times he burned it in a ¦ searing fire, and at still other times ³⁵ he crushed it in wars ¦ and plagues, until he brought **74** [...] ⁵ of the work. ¦ And this is the birth of the world. ¦

"The restoration of the ¦ nature of the pious ones who are good ¦ will take place in a ¹⁰ period of time that ¦ never had a beginning. ¦ For the will of God has no ¦ beginning, even as his nature, ¦ which is his will, (has no beginning). ¹⁵ For the nature of God is will. ¦ And his will is the good." ¦

"Trismegistus, ¦ is purpose, then, will?" ¦

"Yes, Asclepius, since will ²⁰ is (included) in counsel. ¦ For ⟨he⟩ does not will what he has ¦ from deficiency. Since he is ¦ complete in every part, he wills ¦ what he (already) fully has. ²⁵ And he has every good. ¦ And what he wills, he wills. ¦ And he has the good ¦ that he wills. Therefore he has ¦ everything. And God ³⁰ wills what he wills. ¦ And the good world ¦ is an image of the Good One." ¦

"Trismegistus, ¦ is the world good?"

"Asclepius, ³⁵ it is good, as ¦ I shall teach you. For just as **75** [... ³ of soul and] life ¦ [...] of the [world ...] ⁵ come [forth] in matter, [those that are good], ¦ the change of the climate, and [the] beauty ¦ and the ripening of the fruits, and ¦ the things similar to all these. Because of this, ¦ God has control over the heights ¹⁰ of heaven. He is in every place and he looks out ¦ over every place. And (in) his place there is neither ¦ heaven nor star. And ¦ he is free from (the) body.

"Now the creator ¦ has control in the place that is ¹⁵ between the earth and heaven. He ¦ is called Zeus, that is, ¦ life. Plutonius Zeus ¦ is lord over the earth ¦ and sea. And he does not possess the nourishment ²⁰ for all mortal living creatures, ¦ for (it is) Kore who bears ¦ the fruit. These forces ¦ always are powerful in the circle ¦ of the earth, but those of others ²⁵ are always from Him-who-is. ¦

"And the lords of the earth will withdraw themselves. ¦ And they will establish ¦ themselves in a city that is in ¦ a corner of Egypt and that will be built ³⁰ toward the setting of the sun. ¦ Every man will go into it, ¦ whether they come on the sea ¦ or on the shore." ¦

"Trismegistus, ³⁵ where will these be settled now?"

"Asclepius, ¦ in the great city that is on the [Libyan] mountain **76** [... ³ it frightens ... ¦ as a] great [evil, ⁵ in] ignorance of the matter. ¦ For death occurs, [which] is ¦ the dissolution of the labors of the body ¦ and (the dissolution of) the number (of the body), when it (death)

completes ' the number of the body. [10] For the number is the union of ' the body. Now the body dies ' when it is not able to support ' the man. And this is death: ' the dissolution of the body and the destruction [15] of the sensation of the body. ' And it is not necessary to be afraid ' of this, nor because of this, but because of ' what is not known ' and is disbelieved (one is afraid).''

"But what is [20] not known ' or is disbelieved!"

"Listen, ' Asclepius! There is a great ' demon. The great God has ' appointed him to be overseer [25] or judge over the souls ' of men. And God has placed him ' in the middle of the air between the earth ' and heaven. Now, when ' the soul comes forth from (the) body, it is necessary [30] that it meet this ' daimon. Immediately he (the daimon) will surround ' this one (masc.), and he will examine him in regard to the character that he has ' developed in his life. And if ' he finds that he piously performed [35] all of his actions ' for which he came into the world, ' this (daimon) will allow him 77 [...] ' turn him [...]. ' But [if he sees ' ...] in this one [...] he brought [5] his life into [evil] deeds, ' he grasps him, as he [flees] upward ' and throws him down ' so that he is suspended between heaven and earth ' and is punished with a great punishment. [10] And he will be ' deprived of his hope and ' be in great pain.

"And that soul ' has been put neither ' on the earth nor in heaven. [15] But it has come into the open sea of the air ' of the world, the place where there is a great ' fire, and crystal water, ' and furrows of fire, ' and a great upheaval. The bodies [20] are tormented (in) various (ways). ' Sometimes they are cast ' upon raging waters; at other times ' they are cast down into the fire ' in order that it may destroy them. Now, I will not say [25] that this is the death of the soul, ' for it has been delivered from evil, ' but it is a death sentence. '

"Asclepius, it is necessary to believe ' these things and to fear them [30] in order that we might not encounter them. For ' unbelievers are impious and ' commit sin. Afterwards they will be compelled ' to believe, ' and they will not hear by word of mouth only, [35] but will experience ' the reality itself. For they kept believing that they would not endure these things. Not only 78 [...]. ' First, [Asclepius], ' all [those of the earth die ' and those who are of the] body [cease ...] [5] of evil [...] ' with these of this sort. For those who are here ' are not like those who are ' there. So with the daimons who [...] ' men, they despise [...] [10] there. Thus it is not the same. But ' truly the gods who are here ' will punish more whoever has hidden it here ' every day.'' '

"Trismegistus, what [is the] character of [15] the iniquity that is there?"

"Now you think, Asclepius, that when one takes [|] something in a temple, he is impious. [|] For that kind of a person is a thief and [|] a bandit. And this matter concerns ²⁰ gods and men. [|] But do not compare those here with those of the other place. [|] Now I want to speak [|] this discourse to you confidentially; [|] no part of it will be believed. For the souls ²⁵ that are filled with much evil will not come and go [|] in the air, but they will be put [|] in the places of the daimons, which [|] are filled with pain, (and) which are always [|] filled with blood and slaughter, and their ³⁰ food, which is weeping, mourning, [|] and groaning."

"Trismegistus, [|] who are these (daimons)?"

"Asclepius, they are the ones who [|] are called stranglers, and [|] those who roll souls down on ³⁵ the dirt, and those who [|] scourge them, and those who cast [|] into the water, and those who cast into the fire, [|] and those who bring about the pains [|] and calamities of men. For ⁴⁰ such as these are not from a [|] divine soul, nor from a [|] rational soul of man. Rather, [|] they are from the terrible evil."

THE PARAPHRASE OF SHEM (VII,*1*)

Introduced by

MICHEL ROBERGE

Translated by

FREDERIK WISSE

The first of the five tractates contained in Codex VII is entitled *The Paraphrase of Shem*. For its major part, this is an apocalypse, with the narrative frame describing the initial ascent of the seer, Shem (consistently spelled Sêem), to the top of the creation (1,5-16) and his final return to the earth (41,21-42,11). The actual revelation is provided by Derdekeas, the son of the infinite Light; it consists of a cosmogony and an anthropology (1,16-24,29), followed by a history of salvation which focuses on the account of the Flood (24,29-28,8), the destruction of Sodom (28,8-30,4), the baptism of the Savior and his ascent on the occasion of his crucifixion (30,4-40,31). The revelation concludes with an address to Shem concerning his mission on earth (40,31-41,21). To this apocalypse are added a first eschatological discourse pronounced by Derdekeas (42,11-45,31), a description of Shem's ascent to the planetary spheres at the end of his life (45,31-47,32), a second eschatological discourse of Derdekeas (47,32-48,30) and, to conclude the whole tractate, a final address to Shem (48,30-49,9).

The cosmogonic myth reported here is related to those systems which consider the universe as rooted in three principles. It opens with the description of the three great powers or roots: at the top reigns Light Infinite, called "Majesty," which is Thought filled with hearing and word; located at the bottom is Darkness, a male principle which is "wind in the waters" and possesses the Mind (*nous*) wrapped with the restless fire. Between these two powers is the Spirit, a quiet and humble light. The harmony which prevails at the beginning derives from the fact that each of those roots reigns in itself without mixing with the other two. It is important to note that the text makes no allusion to any previous action taken by Darkness to seize the Mind, nor does it mention a fall of the Mind. However, the events are essentially triggered by the will of the Majesty in an effort to save the Mind.

Suddenly Darkness stirs and the Spirit discovers the existence of the bad root. By the will of the Great Light the waters separate and Darkness comes up with his eye, the Mind. The Spirit reveals himself to Darkness and by doing so loses a part of his light to the benefit of the Mind.

The exalted Light then reveals himself through his son, Derdekeas. He appears in the likeness of the Spirit, thus initiating the salvation of the Mind and the ascent of the Spirit's light. In order to deceive Darkness, the Savior provokes the creation of the universe from water, part of which transforms into a giant Womb (also called "Nature"). The restless fire goes to the Womb. Fooled by the fire,

Darkness, on seeing the Womb, becomes unchaste, has intercourse with the Womb and ejaculates the Mind. Nature is then divided into four "clouds" or spheres, which are called Hymen, Chorion, Power and Water. On entering the Womb, the Mind collides with the Unbegotten Spirit and the "burden of the Mind" causes "astonishment" in the Spirit. This power of Astonishment diverts the burden of Mind to the effect that, clothed with the light of the Spirit, he takes resort to the cloud of Power (also called "the Middle"). The Astonishment, however, sticks to the cloud of Hymen.

The Spirit beseeches the infinite Light to have mercy on his own light. The Savior appears this time as a whirlwind to blow up the clouds: they divide, and the Mind takes shape. Derdekeas puts on his universal garment of light and prompts the ascent of the light from the cloud of Water. When the Spirit gives thanks to the infinite Light, his Astonishment produces a great power, Thought, the principle of the race of Shem, the pneumatics.

Now the Savior deposits his universal garment and puts on his trimorphic garment in order to bring to perfection the light in the three clouds of Hymen, Silence (Chorion), and the Middle. The light retained in the Middle is the part of light which was detached from Astonishment and is united with Mind. After the Flood, it is called "Faith."

The Savior descends to the cloud of the Middle, puts on a garment of fire and prostitutes himself with Nature. In its orgasm, the Womb casts off Mind in the form of a fish and gives birth to all sorts of beasts. Derdekeas puts on the garment of the Beast and prompts the Womb to produce heaven and earth and all kinds of seed. He also makes her give birth to female entities, the winds, and to male entities, the demons. The latter mate with the winds and thereby cast off the power they have, which is Mind. By the will of the Savior, Mind rules over the winds and the demons. He receives a likeness of fire, a light, a listening and a share of Logos. At the end of time, Mind will take his repose with Faith in the cloud of Hymen. The winds and the demons have intercourse for a second time and give birth to all sorts of impurity, that is, the material souls. Through the masturbation of one of the winds, barren women and sterile men are begotten. These are the psychics, who possess only a material soul and are bound to dissolve in Darkness. Finally the pneumatics come to existence, namely those who possess a particle of Mind and a thought from the light of Astonishment.

In order to detain the light of Faith and to destroy the pneumatic race, Nature plans to cause a flood, to which the Savior reacts by proclaiming the erection of a tower. Shem is saved and remains in a body so that he may have patience with Faith and pass on his revelation to postdiluvian mankind. In other words, during the time appointed to Faith, Shem and his race will live among the people who carry out the will of Nature through the observance of the law. For Nature uses the light of Faith under the form of the Law to keep to itself the noetic seed. After the flood, mankind in fact includes two classes of redeemed: the noetics, who possess a body, a soul, and a particle of Mind, and whose root is Faith, and pneumatics, who possess not only a particle of Mind but also a "thought" issued from Astonishment, and whose root is the Unbegotten Spirit.

The destruction of Sodom is also presented as an attempt by Nature to destroy the pneumatic seed. But Shem is told not to worry about his race, since thanks to his teaching they will bear the universal testimony and will repose in the place of the Unbegotten Spirit.

The Savior reveals himself for the last time when the demon (that is, John the Baptist) appears on the river in order to baptize. The baptismal rite is essentially bad because of its use of water – a primordial impure power, which in the beginning tried to detain the light of the Spirit and now tries to keep men prisoner through baptism. But by descending on the water, the Savior rescues the light of Faith and reveals to the pneumatics and the noetics the passwords which will allow them to pass without hindrance through the planetary spheres as they return to their proper root. Thanks to the "memorial" (or "universal testimony") the pneumatics ascend to the place of the Unbegotten Spirit; as for the noetics, they bear the "testimony of Faith" and ascend to Hymen, the place of Faith. This part of the tractate contains a harsh antibaptismal polemic, probably directed against the Great Church.

After his baptism, the Savior foretells his ascent at the end of his mission on earth. In its anger, Nature will try to seize him, but will only manage to crucify Soldas (that is, the terrestrial Jesus). The following allegory which narrates the beheading of Rebouel is intended to explain to the noetics the meaning of the crucifixion: it does not have the effect of purifying the water of baptism, but rather brings out the division between light and darkness. Just as Rebouel is declared blessed in her beheading, so the noetics should not hesitate to separate from the Great Church, which practises baptism, and enter the community of those who possess gnosis.

Former research has pointed out similarities between *The Paraphrase of Shem* and the tractate entitled *The Paraphrase of Seth*, which is referred to by the heresiologist Hippolytus in his report on the Sethians. But the differences between the two doctrines, especially with regard to anthropology, are too great to warrant the assumption of any direct or indirect link whatsoever between the two works. Likewise, more recent research tends not to regard *The Paraphrase of Seth* as a christianized version of *The Paraphrase of Shem*, which in that case could have been a witness of a pre-Christian Gnosticism.

THE PARAPHRASE OF SHEM

VII 1, 1-49, 9

The Paraphrase of Shem [1]

[The] paraphrase which was about [1] the unbegotten Spirit. [1]
What Derdekea⟨s⟩ revealed to me, Shem, [5] according to [1] the will of the Majesty. [1] My thought which was in my body [1] snatched me away from my race. It [1] took me up to the top of the world, [10] which is close to the light [1] that shone upon the whole area [1] there. I saw no [1] earthly likeness, but there was light. [1] And my thought separated [15] from the body of darkness as [1] though in sleep.

I heard [1] a voice saying to me, [1] Shem, since you are from [1] an un-

mixed power [20] and you are the first being upon | the earth, hear and understand | what I shall say to you first | concerning the great powers who | were in existence in the beginning, before [25] I appeared. There | was Light and Darkness | and there was Spirit between | them. Since your root | fell into forgetfulness — he who was [30] the unbegotten Spirit — I | reveal to you the truth about | the powers. The Light | was thought full of | hearing and word. They were [35] united into one form. | And the Darkness was **2** wind in waters. | He possessed the mind | wrapped in a chaotic fire. | And the Spirit between them [5] was a gentle, humble light. | These are the three | roots. They reigned each in | themselves, alone. And they covered | each other, each one with [10] its power.

But the Light, | since he possessed a great | power, knew the abasement | of the Darkness and his disorder, | namely that the root was not straight. [15] But the crookedness of the Darkness | was lack of perception, namely (the illusion that) there is no one | above him. And as long as he was able | to bear up under his evil, he was | covered with the water. And he [20] stirred. And the Spirit was frightened | by the sound. He lifted himself | up to his station. And | he saw a great, dark water. | And he was nauseated. And [25] the thought of the Spirit stared | down; he saw the infinite Light. | But he was overlooked | by the putrid root. | And by the will of the great Light [30] the dark water separated. | And the Darkness came up | wrapped in vile ignorance, | and (this was) in order that the mind | might separate from him because he prided [35] himself in it.

And when he | stirred, **3** the light of the Spirit appeared to him. | When he saw it he was astonished. | He did not know that another | Power was above him. And when he [5] saw that his likeness was | dark compared with the Spirit, he felt hurt. | And in his pain he lifted up | to the height | of the members of Darkness his mind which [10] was the eye of the bitterness of evil. | He caused his mind to take shape | in a member of the regions of the | Spirit, thinking that, by staring (down) | at his evil, he would be able [15] to equal the Spirit. But he | was not able. For he wanted to do | an impossible thing, and it did not | take place. But in order that | the mind of Darkness, which [20] is the eye of the bitterness of evil, might not be destroyed, | since he was made partially similar, | he arose and shone | with a fiery light upon | all of Hades, so that [25] the equality to the faultless Light | might become apparent. For the Spirit | made use of every form | of Darkness because he appeared | in his majesty. [30]

And the exalted, infinite Light | appeared, | for he was | very joyful.

He wished to reveal ' himself to the Spirit. And the likeness [35] of the exalted Light appeared ' to the unbegotten Spirit. **4** I appeared. [I] ' am the son of the ' incorruptible, infinite Light. ' I appeared in the likeness [5] of the Spirit, for I am the ray ' of the universal Light. ' And his appearance to me (was) ' in order that the mind ' of Darkness might not remain in Hades. [10] For the Darkness made himself like his ' mind in a part of the ' members. When I, (O) Shem, appeared ' in it (i.e. the likeness), in order that ' the Darkness might become dark to himself, [15] according to the will of the Majesty — ' in order that the Darkness might become free ' from every aspect of the power ' which he possessed — ' the mind drew the chaotic fire, with which [20] it was covered, from ' the midst of the Darkness and the water. ' And from the Darkness the water ' became a cloud. and from ' the cloud the womb took shape. [25] The chaotic fire ' which was a deviation ' went there.

And when the Darkness ' saw it (i.e. the womb) he became unchaste. ' and when he had aroused [30] the water, he rubbed the womb. ' His mind dissolved ' down to the depths of Nature. ' It mingled with the power of ' the bitterness of Darkness. And [35] her (i.e. the womb's) eye ruptured at the wickedness ' in order that she might not again bring forth ' the mind. For it was **5** a seed of Nature ' from the dark root. ' And when Nature had taken to herself ' the mind by means of the dark power, [5] every likeness took shape ' in her. And when the Darkness ' had acquired the likeness of the mind, ' it resembled the Spirit. ' For Nature rose up to expel it; [10] she was powerless against it, since ' she did not have a form from the ' Darkness. For she brought it forth in the cloud. ' And the cloud shone. ' A mind appeared in [15] it like a frightful, harmful fire. ' It (i.e. the mind) collided ' against the unbegotten Spirit ' since it possessed ' a likeness from him. In order that [20] Nature might become empty ' of the chaotic fire, ' then immediately Nature ' was divided into four parts. ' They became clouds which varied [25] in their appearance. They were called ' Hymen, Afterbirth, ' Power, (and) Water. ' And the Hymen and the Afterbirth ' and the Power were [30] chaotic fires. And ' it (i.e. the mind) was drawn from the midst ' of the Darkness and the water — since ' the mind was in the midst of Nature ' and the dark power — [35] in order that the harmful waters ' might not cling to it. **6** Because of this Nature was divided, ' according to my will, in order that ' the mind may return ' to its power which the [5] dark root, which was mixed ' with it (i.e. the mind), had taken from it. And ' he (i.e. the dark root) appeared in the womb. ' And at the division of ' Nature he separated from the dark power [10] which he possessed from '

the mind. It (i.e. the mind) went into the midst ' of the power — this was ' the middle region of Nature.

And the Spirit ' of light, when the mind [15] burdened him, was astonished. ' And the force of his Astonishment ' cast off the burden. And it (i.e. the burden) ' returned to its heat. It ' put on the light of the Spirit. [20] And when Nature moved ' away from the power of the light ' of the Spirit, the burden returned. ' And the Astonishment ⟨of the⟩ light ' cast off the burden. It stuck [25] to the cloud of the Hymen. And ' all the clouds of Darkness ' cried out, they who had separated from Hades, ' because of the alien Power. ' He is the Spirit of light who has come [30] in them. And by the will of ' the Majesty the Spirit gazed up ' at the infinite Light, ' in order that ' his light may be pitied and [35] the likeness brought up from Hades.

And ' when the Spirit had looked, I flowed **7** out — I, the son of the Majesty — ' like a wave of bright light ' and like a whirlwind of the ' immortal Spirit. And I blew from [5] the cloud of the Hymen upon the Astonishment ' of the unbegotten Spirit. It ' (i.e. the cloud) separated and cast light upon the clouds. ' These separated in order that ' the Spirit might return. Because of this the mind [10] took shape. Its repose was shattered. ' For the Hymen of Nature ' was a cloud which cannot be ' grasped; it is a great fire. ' Similarly, the Afterbirth [15] of Nature is the cloud of silence; ' it is an august fire. ' And the Power which was mixed ' with the mind, it, too, was ' a cloud of Nature which [20] was joined with the Darkness that ' had aroused Nature ' to unchastity. And the dark water ' was a frightful cloud. ' And the root [25] of Nature, which was below, ' was crooked, since it is burdensome and ' harmful. The root was ' blind with respect to the light-bondage ' which was unfathomable since [30] it had many appearances. '

And I had pity on ' the light ⟨of⟩ the Spirit which ' the mind had received. I returned ' to my position in order to pray [35] to the exalted, infinite Light **8** that ' the power of the Spirit might increase ' on the place and might be filled ' without dark defilement. And [5] reverently I said, ' "Thou art the root of the Light. ' Thy hidden form has appeared, ' O exalted, infinite ' one. May the whole power of [10] the Spirit spread and may it be filled ' with its light, O infinite Light. ' (Then) he will not be able to join ' with the unbegotten Spirit, and ' the power of the Astonishment will not be able to [15] mix with Nature. According to the will ' of the Majesty," my prayer ' was accepted.

And the voice ' of the Word was heard saying ' through the Majesty to the [20] unbegotten Spirit, "Behold, the ' power has been completed.

He who was revealed ' by me appeared in ' the Spirit. Again I shall appear. ' I am Derdekeas, the son [25] of the incorruptible, infinite Light." '

The light of ' the infinite Spirit ' came down to a feeble nature for ' a short time until [30] all the impurity of nature ' became void, and in order that ' the darkness of Nature ' might be blamed. I put on my ' garment which is the garment of the light [35] of the Majesty — which I am. ' I came in the appearance of the **9** Spirit to consider the whole light ' which was in the depths ' of the Darkness. According to the will ' of the Majesty, in order that the Spirit [5] by means of the Word might be filled with his ' light independently of the power of ' the infinite Light, ' and at my wish, the Spirit ' arose by his (own) power. [10] His greatness was granted to him ' that he might be filled with his whole light ' and depart from the whole burden ' of the Darkness. For what was behind ' was a dark fire which blew [15] (and) pressed on the Spirit. And ' the Spirit rejoiced because he was protected ' from the frightful water. But ' his light was not equal to ' the Majesty. But ⟨what⟩ he was granted [20] by the infinite Light, (he was granted it) ' in order that in all his members ' he might appear as ' a single image of light. ' And when the Spirit arose above the water, [25] his black likeness became apparent. ' And the Spirit honored ' the exalted Light: "Surely thou ' alone art the infinite one, ' because thou art above [30] every unbegotten thing, for thou hast protected ' me from the Darkness. And at thy ' wish I arose above the power ' of darkness.

And that ' nothing might be hidden from you, Shem, the thought, [35] which the Spirit from the ' greatness had contemplated, came into being, **10** since the Darkness was not able [to] ' restrain his evil. But when ' it appeared, ' the three roots became known as they [5] were from the beginning. If ' the Darkness had been able to bear ' up under his evil, the ' mind would not have separated from him, and ' another power would not have appeared. [10]

But from the time it appeared ' I was seen, the son ' of the Majesty, in order that ' the light of the Spirit might not become faint, ' and that Nature might not reign [15] over it, because it gazed at me. ' And by the will of the greatness ' my equality was revealed, that ' what is of the Power might ' become apparent. You [20] are the great Power which came into being, ' and I am the perfect Light ' which is above the Spirit ' and the Darkness, the one who puts to shame the Darkness ' for the intercourse of the impure [25] practice. For through the division ' of Nature the Majesty wished ' to be covered with ' honor up to the height of the Thought ' of the Spirit. And the Spirit received [30] rest in his power.

For the image of the Light ' is inseparable from the unbegotten Spirit.
And the lawgivers did not name ' him after all the clouds [35] of Nature,
nor is it ' possible to name them. ' For every likeness **11** into which
Nature had divided ' is a power of the ' chaotic fire which is the ' hylic
seed. The one who took to himself [5] the power of the Darkness imprisoned it ' in the midst of its members. '

And by the will of the Majesty, ' in order that the mind ' and the
whole light of the Spirit might be protected [10] from every burden and
(from) the toil of ' Nature, a voice came forth from ' the Spirit to the
cloud of the Hymen. ' And the light of the astonishment ' began to rejoice with the voice [15] which was granted to him. ' And the great Spirit
of light was ' in the cloud of the Hymen. He honored ' the infinite Light
' and the universal likeness [20] who I am, the son of ' the Majesty. It is
said: ' "Anasses Duses, thou art ' the infinite Light ' who was given by
the will [25] of the Majesty to establish ' every light of the Spirit ' upon
the place, and to separate ' the mind from the Darkness. ' For it was
not right [30] for the light of the Spirit to remain ' in Hades. For at thy
wish ' the Spirit arose to ' behold thy greatness." '

For I said these things to you, [35] Shem, that you might know **12** that
my likeness, the son of the Majesty, ' is from my ' infinite Thought,
since I ' am for him a universal likeness [5] which does not lie, (and) I am
above ' every truth and origin ' of the word. His appearance is in ' my
beautiful garment of light ' which is the voice of the immeasurable
Thought. [10] We are that ' single, sole light which came into being. ' He
appeared in another root ' in order that the power ' of the Spirit might
be raised from the [15] feeble Nature. For by the will of the ' great Light
I came forth from the ' exalted Spirit down to the cloud of ' the Hymen
without my universal ' garment.

And the Word took [20] me to himself, from the Spirit, in the first '
cloud of the Hymen of ' Nature. And I put on ' this of which the Majesty and the ' unbegotten Spirit made me worthy. [25] And the threefold
unity ' of my garment appeared ' in the cloud, by the will ' of the
Majesty, in a single form. ' And my likeness was covered [30] with the
light of my ' garment. And the cloud was disturbed, ' and it was not
able to bear my likeness. ' It shed the first power, ' the one ⟨which⟩ it
had taken from [35] the Spirit, that one which shone ' on him from the
beginning, before ' ⟨I⟩ appeared in the word ' to the Spirit. The cloud
13 would not have been able to bear both of them. ' And the light which
came forth from the cloud ' passed through the silence, until ' it came
into the middle region. And, [5] by the will of the Majesty, ' the light

mixed with him ' ⟨i.e.⟩ the Spirit which exists in the silence, ' he who had been separated from the Spirit ' of light. It was separated from the light [10] by the cloud of the silence. ' The cloud was disturbed. It was he ' who gave rest to the flame ' of fire. He humbled the dark womb ' in order that she might not reveal [15] other seed from the darkness. He ' kept them back in the middle region ' of Nature in their ' position which was in ' the cloud. They were troubled since they did [20] not know where they were. For still ' they ⟨did⟩ not possess the ' universal understanding of ' the Spirit.

And when I prayed ' to the Majesty, toward the [25] infinite Light, that ' the chaotic power ' of the Spirit might go to and fro, and ' the dark womb might be idle, ' and that my likeness might appear [30] in the cloud of the Hymen, ' as if I were wrapped in the light ' of the Spirit which went ' before me, and by the will ' of the Majesty and through [35] the prayer I came in the cloud ' in order that through my garment − ' which was from the power **14** of the Spirit − the pleroma ' of the word, might bring power to the members ' who possessed it in the Darkness. ' For because of them I appeared [5] in this insignificant place. ' For I am a helper ' of every one who has been given a name. ' For when I appeared ' in the cloud, the light [10] of the Spirit began to save itself ' from the frightful water, and (from) the clouds ' of fire which had been separated ' from dark Nature. And ' I gave them eternal honor [15] that they might not again engage ' in the impure practice.

And the light ' which was in the Hymen was disturbed ' by my power, and ' it passed through my middle region. It [20] was filled with the universal Thought. ' And through the word of ' the light of the Spirit it returned to ' its repose. It received ' form in its root and shone [25] without deficiency. And the light ' which had come forth with it from the silence ' went in the middle region ' and returned to the place. ' And the cloud shone. [30] And from it came ' an unquenchable fire. ' And the part which separated from ' the astonishment put on forgetfulness. ' It was deceived by [35] the fire of darkness. And the shock ' of its astonishment cast ' off the burden of the **15** cloud. It was evil ' since it was unclean. And ' the fire mixed with the water in ' order that the waters might become harmful. [5]

And Nature which had been disturbed ' immediately arose ' from the idle waters. ' For her ascent was shameful. ' And Nature took to herself the [10] power of fire. She became strong ' because of the light of the Spirit which ' was in Nature. Her ' likeness appeared in the water ' in the form of a frightful beast [15] with many faces, which ' is crooked

below. A light ' went down to chaos filled ' with mist and dust, in order
to ' harm Nature. [20] And the light of the Astonishment which is ' in the
middle region came to it ' after he cast off ' the burden of the Darkness.
He rejoiced ' when the Spirit arose. For he looked [25] from the clouds
down ' at the dark waters upon ' the light which was in ' the depths of
Nature.

Therefore ' I appeared that I might [30] get an opportunity to go '
down to the nether world, to the light ' of the Spirit which was burdened, ' that I might protect him from the evil ' of the burden. And
through [35] his looking down at the dark region ' the light once more **16**
came up in order that the womb might again ' come up from the water.
' She (i.e. the womb) came up by my will. ' Guilefully the eye opened.
[5] And the light ' which had appeared in the middle region ' (and) which
had separated from the Astonishment ' rested and shone upon ' her.
And the womb saw [10] things she had not seen, ' and she rejoiced joyfully in ' the light, although this was not hers – the one which ' appeared
in the middle region, in her ' wickedness, when he (i.e. the light) shone
[15] upon her. And ' the womb saw things she had not seen, ' and she was
brought down ' to the water, she was thinking that ' she had reached to
the power of light. [20] And she did not know that ' her root was made
idle by ' the likeness of the Light, and that it was to her (i.e. the root)
' that he had run.

The light was astonished, ' the one which was in [25] the middle region
and which was ' beginning and end. Therefore ' his thought gazed ' directly up at the exalted Light. ' And he called out and said, [20] "Lord,
have mercy on me, ' for my light and my effort went astray. ' For if thy
goodness does not establish ' me, I do not know ' where I am." And
when the Majesty [35] had heard him, he had mercy on him. '

And I appeared in the cloud ' of the Hymen, in the silence, **17** without my holy garment. ' With my will I honored ' my garment which has
three ' forms in the cloud of the Hymen. [5] And the light which was in
' the silence, the one from the rejoicing ' Power, contained me. ' I wore
it. And its ' two parts appeared [10] in a single form. Its ' other parts did
not appear ' on account of the fire. I became ' unable to speak in the
cloud of the Hymen, ' for its fire was frightful, [15] lifting itself up without ' humility. And in order that ' my greatness and the word ' might
appear, I placed likewise ' my other garment in the cloud of the silence.
[20] I went into the middle region ' and put on the light ' that was in it,
that was sunk in forgetfulness ' and that was separated from the Spirit
of ' astonishment, for he had cast off the burden. [25] At my wish ' noth-

ing mortal appeared | to him, but they were all immortal | things which the Spirit granted | to him. And he said in [30] the thought of the Light, ai eis | ai ou phar dou ia ei ou: | I have come in a great rest | in order that he may give rest | to my light in [35] his root, and may bring it out of **18** harmful Nature.

Then, | by the will of the Majesty, I | took off my garment of light. | I put on another garment [5] of fire which has no form, which | is from the mind of the power, | which was separated, and which was | prepared for me, according to my will, in | the middle region. For the middle region [10] covered it with a dark power | in order that I might come | and put it on. I went down | to chaos to save | the whole light from it. For without [15] the power of darkness I could not oppose | Nature. But I rested | myself upon her staring eye [20] which was a light | from the Spirit. For it had been prepared | for me as a garment and a rest | by the Spirit. Through me | he opened his eyes down to [25] Hades. He granted Nature | his voice for a time. |

And my garment of fire, according to the will | of the Majesty, went | down to what is strong, and to the [30] unclean part of Nature | which ⟨the⟩ power of darkness | was covering. And my garment | rubbed Nature in her | covering. And her unclean [35] femininity was strong. And | the wrathful womb came up **19** and made the mind dry, | resembling a fish which has | a drop of fire and | a power of fire. And when Nature [5] had cast off the mind, | she was troubled and she | wept. When she was hurt, and in | her tears, she cast off | the power of the Spirit [10] (and) remained as I. I put on | the light of the Spirit and I | rested with my garment on account of | the sight of the fish.

And in order that | the deeds of Nature might be condemned, [15] since she is blind, manifold | animals came out | of her, in accordance with the number of the | fleeting winds. All cf them came into being in | Hades searching for the light [20] of the mind which took shape. They were not | able to stand up against it. | I rejoiced over their ignorance. | They found me, | the son of the Majesty, in [25] front of the womb which has | many forms. I put | on the beast, and laid | before her a great request | that heaven and earth [30] might come into being, in order that the whole | light might rise up. | For in no other way could the power | of the Spirit be saved from bondage | except that I appear [35] to her in animal form. | Therefore she was gracious to me **20** as if I were her son. |

And on account of my request, | Nature arose since she possesses of | the power of the Spirit and the Darkness [5] and the fire. For she had

taken off ' her forms. When she had cast ' it off, she blew upon the water. ' The heaven was created. And from ' the foam of the heaven [10] the earth came into being. And at my wish it ' brought forth all kinds of food in accordance with ' the number of the beasts. And it ' brought forth dew from ' the winds on account of you (pl.) and those [15] who will be begotten the second time ' upon the earth. ' For the earth possessed ' a power of chaotic fire. ' Therefore it brought forth [20] every seed.

And when ' the heaven and the earth were created, ' my garment of fire arose in the midst ' of the cloud of Nature (and) ' shone upon the whole world [25] until Nature became ' dry. The Darkness which was ' its (i.e. the earth's) garment was cast into the ' harmful waters. ' The middle region was cleansed from the Darkness. [30] But the womb grieved because of ' what had happened. She perceived in ' her parts what was ' water like a mirror. When she ' perceived (it), she wondered [25] how it had come into being. Therefore she ' remained a widow. It also was [21] astonished (that) it was not in her. ' For still the forms ' possessed a power ' of fire and light. It (i.e. the power) remained [5] in order that it might be in Nature ' until all the powers are taken ' away from her. For just as ' the light of the Spirit was completed ' in three clouds, it is necessary [10] that also the power ' which is in Hades will be completed at the ' appointed time. For, because of the grace ' of the Majesty, I came forth to her ' from the water for the second time. [15] For my face pleased ' her. Her face also was glad. '

And I said to her, "May ' seed ' and power come forth from you [20] upon the earth." And she obeyed ' the will of the Spirit that ' she might be brought,to naught. And when ' her forms returned, they rubbed ' their tongue(s) with each other; they copulated; [25] they begot winds and ' demons and the power which ' is from the fire and ' the Darkness and the Spirit. But the form ' which remained alone cast the [30] beast from herself. ' She did not have intercourse, but ' she was the one who rubbed herself alone. ' And she brought forth a wind which ' possessed a power [35] from the fire and the Darkness ' and the Spirit.

And in order that the [22] demons also might become free from the power which they possessed ' through the impure intercourse, ' a womb was with the winds [5] resembling water. And an ' unclean penis was ' with the demons in accordance with the example ' of the Darkness, and in the way he rubbed with ' the womb from the beginning. And after [10] the forms of Nature had been ' together, they separated from ' each other. They cast off the power, ' being astonished about ' the deceit

which had happened to them. They grieved [15] with an eternal grief. They covered | themselves with their power. |

And when I had put them to shame, I arose | with my garment in the power and − | which is above the beast which is a light, [20] in order that I might make Nature | desolate. The mind which had appeared | in the Nature of Darkness, (and) which | was the eye of the heart of Darkness, | at my wish reigned over [25] the winds and the demons. And I | gave him a likeness of fire, light, | and attentiveness, and a share | of guileless word. Therefore | he was given of the greatness [30] in order to be strong in his | power, independent of the power, | independent of the light of the Spirit, and | intercourse of Darkness, in order that, at | the end of time, when **23** Nature will be destroyed, he may rest | in the honored place. | For he will be found | faithful, since he has loathed [5] the unchastity of Nature with | the Darkness. The strong power | of the mind came into being from | the mind and the unbegotten Spirit. |

But the winds, which are demons [10] from water and fire | and darkness and light, had | intercourse unto perdition. And through | this intercourse the winds received | in their womb [15] foam from the penis | of the demons. They conceived | a power in their womb. From | the breathing | the wombs of the winds girded each other [20] until the times of the birth came. | They went down to the water. | And the power was delivered, through | the breathing which moves the birth, | in the midst of the practice. And [25] every form of the birth received shape | in it. When | the times of the birth were near, | all the winds were gathered | from the water which is near the [30] earth. They gave birth to all kinds of unchastity. | And the place where | the wind alone went was permeated with | the unchastity. | Barren wives came from it [35] and sterile husbands. **24** For just as they are born, | so they bear.

Because of you (pl.), | the image of the Spirit appeared | in the earth and the water. [5] For you are like the Light. | For you possess a share | of the winds and the demons, | and a thought from the Light | of the power of the Astonishment. [10] For everything which he brought forth from | the womb upon the earth | was not a good thing for her, | but her groan and her pain, because | of the image which appeared in [15] you from the Spirit. For you are | exalted in your heart. | And it is blessedness, Shem, if [20] a part is given to someone and if he | departs from | the soul to (go) to the thought of the Light. For the soul | is a burden of the Darkness, and | those who know where the root | of the soul came from will be able | to grope after Nature also. [25] For the soul is a work of | unchastity and an (object of) scorn to the | thought of Light. For I

¹ am the one who revealed concerning ¹ all that is unbegotten. ³⁰

And in order that the sin ¹ of Nature might be filled, I made the ¹ womb, which was disturbed, pleasant − ¹ the blind wisdom − that I might ¹ be able to bring (it) to naught. And at my **25** wish, he plotted with the water ¹ of Darkness and also the Darkness, ¹ that they might wound every form ¹ of your (pl.) heart. For by ⁵ the will of the light of the ¹ Spirit they surrounded you; they bound ¹ you in Faith. And in order that ¹ his plan might become idle, ¹ he sent a demon ¹⁰ that the plan of ¹ her wickedness might be proclaimed. And he caused ¹ a flood, and he destroyed ¹ your (pl.) race, in order to ¹ take the light and to take from ¹⁵ Faith. But I proclaimed ¹ quickly by the mouth of ¹ the demon that a tower ¹ come to be up to the particle of the light, ¹ which was left in the demons and ²⁰ their race − which was ¹ water − that the demon might be protected ¹ from the turbulent chaos. ¹ And the womb planned these things ¹ according to my will in order that she might ²⁵ pour forth completely. A tower ¹ came to be through the demons. The ¹ Darkness was disturbed by his loss. ¹ He loosened the muscles of the ¹ womb. And the demon ³⁰ who was going to enter the tower was protected ¹ in order that the races might ¹ continue and might acquire coherence ¹ through him. For he possesses ¹ power from every form. ³⁵

Return henceforth, **26** O Shem, and rejoice [greatly] ¹ over your race and ¹ Faith, for without body and ¹ necessity it is protected from ⁵ every body of Darkness, bearing witness ¹ to the holy things of the greatness ¹ which was revealed to them in their ¹ thought by my will. And ¹ they shall rest in the unbegotten Spirit ¹⁰ without grief. ¹ But you, Shem, because of this, you ¹ remained in (the) body outside the cloud ¹ of light that you might remain ¹ with Faith. And Faith ¹⁵ will come to you. Her thought will be taken ¹ and given to you with a consciousness ¹ of light. And I ¹ told you these things for the benefit of your ¹ race from the cloud of light. ²⁰ And likewise what I shall say to you ¹ concerning everything, I shall reveal ¹ to you completely that ¹ you may reveal them to those who ¹ will be upon the earth the ²⁵ second time.

O Shem, the disturbance ¹ which occurred at my wish ¹ happened in order that Nature might ¹ become empty. ¹ For the wrath of the Darkness subsided. ³⁰ O Shem, the Darkness' mouth was shut. ¹ No longer does the light which ¹ shone for the world appear in it, ¹ according to my will. And when ¹ Nature had said that ³⁵ its wish was fulfilled, then every form ¹ was engulfed by the waters **27** in prideful ignorance. ¹ She (i.e. Nature) turned her ¹ dark vagina and cast from ¹ her the power of fire ⁵ which was in her from the beginning ¹ through the practice of the

Darkness. It (masc.) ' lifted itself up and shone upon ' the whole world instead of the righteous one. ' And all her forms [10] sent forth a power ' like a flame of fire up ' to heaven as a help to the ' corrupted light, which had lifted itself up. ' For they were members of the [15] chaotic fire. And she did not ' know that she had harmed herself. ' When she cast forth the power, ' the power which she possessed, ' she cast it forth from the genitals. It was the demon, [20] a deceiver, who ' stirred up the womb in every form −. '

And in her ignorance, ' as if she were doing a great ' thing, she granted the demons [25] and the winds a star each. ' For without wind and star ' nothing happens upon the earth. ' For every power is filled ' by them after they were [30] released from the Darkness and the fire ' and the power and the light. ' For in the place where their darkness and ' their fire were mixed with each other ' beasts were brought forth. And it was in the place [35] of the Darkness, and the fire, and the power **28** of the mind, and the light, ' that human beings came into existence. ' Being from the Spirit, the thought of the Light, my eye, ' exists not in every man. [5] For before the flood ' came from the winds and the ' demons, rain came to ' men. But then, in order that the power ' which is in the tower might be brought forth, [10] and might rest upon the earth ' Nature, which had been disturbed, ' wanted to harm the seed ' which will be upon the earth after ' the flood. [15] Demons were sent to them, and ' a deviation of the winds, and ' a burden of the angels, and ' a fear of the prophet, a ' condemnation of speech, that I may [20] teach you, O Shem, from ' what blindness your ' race is protected. When I have ' revealed to you all that has been spoken, ' then the righteous one will [25] shine upon the world with my garment. ' And the night and the day will ' be separated. For I shall hasten down to the ' world to take the light ' of that place, the one which [30] Faith possesses. And ' I shall appear to those who will ' acquire the thought of the light ' of the Spirit. For because of them my ' majesty appeared.

When [35] he will have appeared, O Shem, ' upon the earth, [in] the place which will be **29** called Sodom, (then) ' safeguard the insight which I ' shall give you. For those whose ' heart was pure will congregate to you, [5] because of ' the word which you will reveal. ' For when you appear ' in the world, dark Nature ' will shake against you, [10] together with the winds and a demon, ' that they may destroy ' the insight. But you, proclaim ' quickly to the Sodomites ' your universal teaching, [15] for they are your members. ' For the demon of human form ' will part from that place ' by my will, since he is ignorant. ' He

will guard this utterance. But the [20] Sodomites, according to the will of the | Majesty, will bear witness to the | universal testimony. They | will rest with a pure conscience | in the place [25] of their repose, which | is the unbegotten Spirit. | And as these things will happen, | Sodom will be burned unjustly | by a base nature. [30] For the evil will not cease | in order that your | majesty may reveal | that place.

Then **30** the demon will depart with | Faith. And then he will appear | in the four regions | of the world. And when [5] Faith appears | in the last likeness, then will | her appearance become manifest. | For the first-born is the demon | who appeared in the union [10] of Nature with many faces, | in order that Faith might | appear in him. For when he | appears in the world, | evil passions will arise, [15] and earthquakes, and | wars, and famines, and | blasphemies. For because of him the whole | world will be disturbed. | For he will seek the power [20] of Faith and Light; he will | not find it. For at that time | the demon will also | appear upon the river | to baptize with an [25] imperfect baptism, | and to trouble the world with a bondage | of water. But it is necessary | for me to appear in the members | of the thought of Faith to [30] reveal the great things of my | power. I shall separate it | from the demon who is Soldas. | And the light which | he possesses from the Spirit I shall mix [35] with my invincible garment, | as well as him whom I shall reveal **31** in the darkness for your sake | and for the sake of your race which | will be protected from the evil | Darkness.

Know, O Shem, that without [5] Elorchaios and Amoias and | Strophaias and Chelkeak | and Chelkea and Aileou, no | one will be able to pass by this wicked region. | For this is my memorial [10] that in it I have been | victorious over the wicked region. And | I have taken the light of the Spirit | from the frightful water. | For when the [15] appointed days of the | demon draw near | he who will baptize | erringly – , then I shall appear | in the baptism | of the demon to reveal [20] with the mouth of Faith | a testimony to those | who belong to her. I testify | of thee, Spark the unquenchable, | Osei, the elect of [25] the Light, the eye of heaven, and | Faith, the first and the last, | and Sophia, and Saphaia, and | Saphaina, and the righteous | Spark, and the [30] impure light. And you (sg.), east, | and west, and | north, and south, | upper air and lower air, and | all the powers and authorities, **32** you (pl.) are in Nature. | And you (sg.), Moluchtha | and Soch are from every work | and every impure effort of [5] Nature. Then I shall come | from the demon down to the water. | And whirlpools of water | and flames of fire will rise | up against me. Then I [10] shall come up from the water, having put | on the

light of Faith ' and the unquenchable fire, ' in order that through my
help ' the power of the Spirit may cross, [15] she who has been cast in the
world ' by the winds and the demons ' and the stars. And in them '
every unchastity will be filled. '

Finally, O Shem, consider [20] yourself pleasing in the thought ' of the
Light. Do not let ' your thought have dealings with ' the fire and the
body of Darkness ' which was an unclean [25] work. These things which
I teach ' you are right. '

This is the paraphrase: ' − For you did not remember ' that it is from
the firmament that [30] your race has been protected. − Elorchaios ' is
the name of the great Light, ' the place from which I have come, the
Word ' which has no equal. ' And the likeness is my honored garment.
[35] And Derderkeas is the name of his Word in **33** the voice of the Light.
And ' Strophaia is the blessed glance ' which is the Spirit. ' and it is
Chelkeach, who is my garment, [5] who has come from the Astonishment,
' who was in the cloud of the Hymen ' which appeared, as ' a trimorphic cloud. ' And Chelkea is my garment [10] which has two forms, he '
who was in the cloud of Silence. ' And Chelke is my garment which '
was given him from every region; ' it was given him in a single form [15]
from the greatness, he ' who was in the cloud of the middle region. '
and the star of the Light ' which was mentioned is my ' invincible garment which [20] I wore in Hades; ' this (i.e. the star of the Light) is the
mercy which surpasses ' the thought and the testimony ' of those who
bear witness. And ' the testimony which has been mentioned: [25] the
First and the Last, Faith, ' the Mind of the wind of darkness. And '
Sophaia and Saphaina are in ' the cloud of those who have been separated ' from the chaotic fire. [30] And the righteous Spark is ' the cloud of
light which has shone ' in your (pl.) midst. For ' in it (i.e. the cloud of
light) my garment will go ' down to chaos.

But the **34** impure light, which appeared ' in the Darkness (and)
which belongs to ' dark Nature, is a power. ' And the upper air and the
lower air, and the [5] powers and the authorities, the ' demons and the
stars, these possessed ' a particle of fire ' and a light from the Spirit. '
And Moluchthas is a wind, [10] for without it nothing is brought ' forth
upon the earth. He has ' a likeness of a serpent and ' a unicorn. His
protrusion(s) ' are manifold wings. [15] And the remainder is the womb '
which has been disturbed. You are blessed, ' Shem, for your race ' has
been protected from the dark wind which is ' many-faced. And they will
[20] bear the universal ' testimony and (bear witness) to the impure ' practice of ⟨Nature⟩. And ' they will become sublime through the '
reminder of the Light.

O Shem, [25] no one who wears the body | will be able to complete
these things. But through | remembrance he will be able to grasp | them,
in order that, when | his thought separates from the body, [30] then these
things may be revealed to him. | They have been revealed to your | race.
O Shem, it is difficult for someone | wearing a body to complete | [these
things, as] I said to you. **35** And it is a small number that will | complete
them, those who possess | the particle of the mind | and the thought of
the light of the [5] Spirit. They will keep their mind | from the impure
practice. | For many in the race of Nature | will seek the security | of the
Power. They will not find it, nor [10] will they be able to | do the will of
Faith. | For they are seed of the | universal Darkness. And those who |
find them are in much suffering. The winds [15] and the demons will hate
| them. And the bondage of the body is | severe. For where | the winds,
and the stars, | and the demons cast forth from the power [20] of the
Spirit, (there) repentance | and testimony will appear | upon them, and
mercy | will lead them to | the unbegotten Spirit. [25] And those who are
repentant | will find rest | in the consummation and Faith, | in the place
of the Hymen. | This is the Faith which will [30] fill the place which has
been | left empty. But those who do not share | in the Spirit of light and
| in Faith will | dissolve in the [Darkness], the place **36** where repentance
did not come. |

It is I who opened the eternal gates | which were shut from the begin-
ning. | To those who long for the best of [5] life, and those who are wor-
thy of the | repose, he revealed | them. I granted | perception to those
who perceive. | I disclose to them [10] all the thoughts and the teaching |
of the righteous ones. And I did not become | their enemy at all. But |
when I had endured the wrath | of the world, I was victorious. There
was not [15] one of them who knew me. | The gates of fire | and endless
smoke opened against me. | All the winds rose | up against me. The
thunderings and the [20] lightning-flashes for a time will rise | up against
me. And they will bring | their wrath upon me. | And on account of me
according to the flesh, they | will rule over them according to kind. [25]

And many who wear | erring flesh will go down | to the harmful wat-
ers through | the winds and the demons. | And they are bound by the
water. [30] And he will heal with a | futile remedy. He will lead astray, |
and he will bind the world. | And those that do the will of Nature, their
part will [. . .] **37** two times in the day of the water | and the forms of
Nature. | And it will not be granted them, when | Faith disturbs them [5]
in order to take to herself the righteous one. |

O Shem, it is necessary that | the thought be called by the Word in |

order that the bondage of the power | of the Spirit may be saved from the frightful [10] water. And it is blessedness | if it is granted someone to contemplate | the exalted one, and to | know the exalted time | and the bondage. For the water is an [15] insignificant body. And | men are not released, since | they are bound in the water, just as from | the beginning the light of the Spirit | was bound.

O Shem, they are deceived [20] by manifold | demons, thinking that through | baptism with the uncleanness | of water, that which is dark, | feeble, idle, [25] (and) disturbing, he will take away the sins. | And they do not know | that from the water to | the water there is bondage, | and error and unchastity, [30] envy, murder, adultery, | false witness, | heresies, robberies, | lusts, babblings, | wrath, bitterness, [35] great [. . .]. **38** Therefore there are many deaths | which burden their thoughts. | For I foretell | it to those who have a heart. [5] They will refrain from the impure | baptism. And those who | take heart from the light | of the Spirit will not have dealings | with the impure practice. [10] And their heart will not expire, | nor will they curse. | And the water − ⟨nor⟩ will they be given | honor. Where | the curse is, there is the deficiency. [15] And the blindness is | where the honor is. | For if they mix with the evil ones, | they become empty in the dark water. | For where the water has been [20] mentioned, there is | Nature, and the oath, and | the lie, and the loss. For only | in the unbegotten Spirit, | where the exalted Light rested, [25] has the water not | been mentioned, | nor can it be mentioned. |

For this is my appearance: | for when I have [30] completed the times | which are assigned to me upon the earth, then | I will cast from me | [my garment of fire (?)]. And **39** my unequalled garment will | come forth upon me, | and also all my garments which I | put on in all the clouds [5] which were from | the Astonishment of the Spirit. | For the air will tear my garment. | For it (i.e. my garment) will shine, and it will divide | all the clouds up to [10] the root of the Light. The repose | is the mind and my garment. | And my remaining garments, | those on the left and those on the | right, will shine [15] on the back in order that | the image of the Light may appear. | For my garments which I put | on in the three | clouds, in the last day they [20] will rest in their | root, i.e. in the unbegotten | Spirit, since they are without | fault, through the division of (the) | clouds.

Therefore I have appeared, [25] being faultless, on account of the | clouds, because they are unequal, in order that | the wickedness of Nature | might be ended. For she wished | at that time [30] to snare me. She was about to fix (to the cross) | Soldas who is the dark | flame, who

attended ' on the [. . .] of error, **40** that he might snare me. ' She took care of her faith, ' being vainglorious. '

And at that time [5] the light was about to separate ' from the Darkness, and a voice ' was heard in the world, saying, ' "Blessed is the eye which has ' seen thee, and the mind which has [10] supported thy majesty at ' my desire." It will be said by ' the exalted one, "Blessed is ' Rebouel among every race ' of men, for it is you (fem.) alone [15] who have seen." And she will listen. And ' they will behead the woman ' who has the perception, ' whom you will reveal ' upon the earth. And according to [20] my will she will bear witness, and she will ' cease from every ' vain effort of Nature ' and chaos. For the woman ' whom they will behead at that [25] time is the coherence ' of the power of the demon ' who will baptize the seed ' of darkness in severity, ' that it (i.e. the seed) may mix with unchastity. [30] He begot a woman. She was ' called Rebouel.

See, ' O Shem, how all the things I have said ' to you have been fulfilled. ' [And . . . . And the things which] you **41** lack, according to my will ' they will appear to you ' at that place upon the earth ' that you may reveal them [5] as they are. Do ' not let your thought have dealings ' with the body. For I have said these ' things to you, through the voice of the fire, ' for I entered through [10] the midst of the clouds. And I ' spoke according to the language of each one. ' This is my language which I spoke to you. ' And it will be taken from you. And ' you will speak with the voice of the world [15] upon the earth. And it will appear ' to you with that appearance ' and voice, and ' all that I have said to you. ' Henceforth proceed with Faith [20] to shine in the depths of the world. '

And I, Shem, awoke ' as if from a long sleep. ' I marveled when I received the ' power of the Light and his whole thought. [25] And I proceeded with Faith ' to shine with me. And ' the righteous one followed us with ' my invincible garment. And ' all that he had told me [30] would happen upon the earth ' happened. Nature was handed over ' to Faith, that she (i.e. Faith) might overturn ' her and that she (i.e. Nature) might stand in the Darkness. ' She brought forth a **42** turning motion while wandering ' night and day without ' receiving rest with the souls. ' These things completed her [5] deeds.

Then I rejoiced ' in the thought of the Light. ' I came forth from the Darkness and I walked ' in Faith where ' the forms of [10] Nature are, up to the top of the ' earth, to the things which are prepared.

Thy Faith ' is upon the earth the ' whole day. For all night ' and day

she surrounds [15] Nature to take to herself | the righteous one. For Nature is | burdened, and she is troubled. | For none will be able to open the forms | of the Womb except the mind [20] alone who was entrusted | with their likeness. For frightful is | their likeness of the two forms | of Nature, the one which is blind. |

But they who have [25] a free conscience | remove themselves from | the babbling of Nature. | For they will bear witness | to the universal testimony; [30] they will strip off the burden | of Darkness; they will put on | the Word of the Light; and | they will not be kept back **43** in the insignificant place. | And what they possess from | the power of the mind they | will give to Faith. They will [5] be accepted without | grief. And the chaotic | fire which they possess they | will place in the middle region of | Nature. And they will be received [10] by my garments, those which are | in the clouds. It is they | who guide their members. They | will rest in the Spirit | without suffering. And because of this the [15] appointed term of Faith appeared | upon the earth for a | short time, until | the Darkness is taken away from her, and | her testimony is revealed [20] which was revealed | by me. They who will prove | to be from her root | will strip off the | Darkness and the chaotic fire. [25] They will put on the light | of the mind and they will bear witness. | For all that I have said | must happen.

After | I cease to be upon the earth and [30] withdraw up to my rest, | a great, evil error | will come upon | the world, and many evils | in accordance with the number of the forms of **44** Nature. Evil times | will come. And when | the era of Nature is approaching | destruction, darkness will [5] come upon the earth. The number will | be small. And a demon | will come up from the power who | has a likeness of fire. | He will divide the heaven, (and) he will rest [10] in the depth of the east. | For the whole world will quake. | And the deceived world | will be thrown into confusion. Many | places will be flooded because of [15] envy of the winds and the demons | who have a name | which is senseless: Phorbea, Chloerga. | They are the ones who govern the world | with their teaching. And they lead astray [20] many hearts because of their | disorder and their unchastity. | Many places will be sprinkled | with blood. And five | races by themselves [25] will eat their | sons. But the regions of the south | will receive the Word of the Light. | But they who are from | the error of the world [30] and from the east —. | A demon will come forth | from (the) belly of the serpent. He was **45** in hiding in a desolate place. | He will perform many wonders. Many | will loathe him. A | wind will come forth from his mouth with | a female likeness. Her name will | be called

Abalphe. He will ' reign over the world from the ' east to the west.

Then ' Nature will have [10] a final opportunity. And the stars ' will cease from the sky. The mouth ' of error will be opened in order that ' the evil Darkness may become idle and ' silent. And in the last day [15] the forms of Nature ' will be destroyed with the winds and ' all their demons; they ' will become a dark lump, ' just as they were [20] from the beginning. And the ' sweet waters which were burdened ' by the demons will perish. ' For where the power ' of the Spirit has gone [25] there are my sweet ' waters. The other works ' of Nature will not be manifest. ' They will mix with the ' infinite waters of darkness. [30] And all her forms ' will cease from the middle region.

I, ' Shem, have completed these things. And ' my mind began to separate ' from the body of darkness. My **46** time was completed. And ' my mind put on the immortal ' memorial. And ' I said, "I agree with thy [5] memorial which thou hast revealed ' to me: Elorchaois, and ' thou, Amoiaiai, and thou, ' Sederkeas, and they guilelessness, ' Strophaias, and thou, Chelkeak, [10] and thou, Chelkea, and ' Chelke and Elaie, you (pl.) are ' the immortal memorial. ' I testify to thee, Spark, ' the unquenchable one, who is an eye [15] of heaven and a voice of light, ' and Sophaia, and Saphaia, ' and Saphaina, and the righteous ' Spark, and Faith, the first ' and the last, and the upper air and lower [20] air, {and thou, Chelkeak, and ' Chelke and Elaie, you (pl.) ' are the immoral memorial. ' I testify to thee, Spark, the ' unquenchable one, who is an eye of heaven [25] and a voice of light, and ' Sophaia, and Saphaia, and Saphaina, ' and the righteous Spark, ' and Faith, the First and the Last, ' and the upper air and the lower air,} and [30] all the powers and the authorities ' that are in the world. ' And you, impure light, ' and you (sg.) also, east, ' and west, and south, and [35] north, you (pl.) are the zones **47** of the inhabited world. And ' you (fem. sg.) also Moluchtha and Essoch, ' you (pl.) are the root ' of evil and every work and [5] impure effort of Nature." '

These are the things which I completed ' while bearing witness. I am Shem. ' On the day that I was to come forth ' from (the) body, when my thought [10] remained in (the) body, I awoke as if ' from a long sleep. And ' when I arose as it were from the burden ' of my body, I said, ' Just as Nature became old, [15] so is it also in the day of ' mankind. Blessed ' are they who knew, when they ' slept, in what power ' their thought rested. [20]

And when the Pleiades ' separated, I saw clouds ' which I shall pass by. ' For the cloud of the Spirit is ' like a pure beryl. [25] And the cloud

of the hymen | is like a shining | emerald. And the cloud | of silence is like a | flourishing amaranth. And [30] the cloud of the middle region is like | a pure jacinth. | And when the righteous one | appeared in Nature, | then – when Nature [35] was angry – she felt hurt, and she granted **48** to Morphaia to visit | heaven. The righteous one visits | during twelve periods | that he may visit them during one [5] period, in order that his | time may be completed | quickly, and Nature | may become idle.

Blessed are | they who guard themselves against the [10] heritage of death, which is | the burdensome water of darkness. | For it will not be possible to conquer them in a | few moments, since they hasten | to come forth from the error of the [15] world. And if they are conquered, | they will be kept back from them | and be tormented in the darkness | until the time of the consummation. | When the consummation [20] has come and Nature has been | destroyed, then their thoughts will | separate from the Darkness. Nature | has burdened them for a | short time. And they [25] will be in the ineffable | light of the unbegotten | Spirit without a form. | And thus is | the mind as I have said from [30] the first.

Henceforth, O Shem, | go in grace and continue in | faith upon the earth. For every | power of light and fire | will be completed by me **49** because of you. For without you | they will not be revealed until | you speak them openly. | When you cease to be upon the earth, they will [5] be given to the worthy ones. And apart from | this proclamation, let them speak | about you upon the earth, since they will | take the carefree and | agreeable land.

THE SECOND TREATISE OF THE GREAT SETH
(VII,*2*)

Introduced by

JOSEPH A. GIBBONS

Translated by

ROGER A. BULLARD and JOSEPH A. GIBBONS

The Second Treatise of the Great Seth is a revelation dialogue allegedly delivered by Jesus Christ to an audience of "perfect and incorruptible ones," that is, gnostic believers. Apart from the title, the name Seth never occurs in the text, though perhaps Jesus Christ is meant to be identified with Seth. The treatise presents, in a brief and simple way, the true story of the Savior's commission by the heavenly Assembly, his descent to earth, his encounter with the worldly powers and apparent crucifixion, and his return to the Pleroma. To this story of the Savior are added an exhortation to the Savior's followers and a promise of future blessedness. As the Savior says to the gnostic believers at the close of his discourse, "Rest then with me, my fellow spirits and my brothers, for ever."

There is no doubt that *The Second Treatise of the Great Seth* is a work that is both Christian and gnostic. On the one hand, Christian elements are tightly woven into the fabric of the treatise. The tractate accepts the New Testament or parts of it, and claims to be the revelation of Jesus Christ. Furthermore, the crucifixion figures prominently in the tractate; in fact, it is described in three separate scenes within the tractate. On the other hand, *The Second Treatise of the Great Seth* is also clearly gnostic: knowledge is the means of salvation. The God of this world is evil and ignorant, and can be identified with the God of the Old Testament; in addition, all his minions are mere counterfeits and laughingstocks. The interpretation of the crucifixion is that of the Gnostic Basilides as presented by the heresiologist Irenaeus: Simon of Cyrene is crucified in the place of the laughing Jesus.

The purpose for which *The Second Treatise of the Great Seth* was written is plainly polemical. The entire first part (49,10-59,18) describes the true history of Jesus Christ and emphasizes, over against orthodox Christianity, his docetic passion. The second part of the tractate (59,19-70,10) is a refutation of orthodoxy's claim to be the true church. Despite the trials and persecutions apparently instigated by the orthodox church, by those ignorant and imitative persons "who think that they are advancing the name of Christ," the gnostic believers will enjoy true brotherhood on earth, and bliss in the joy and union of eternal life.

THE SECOND TREATISE OF THE GREAT SETH

VII 49, 10-70, 12

And the perfect Majesty is at rest ' in the ' ineffable light, ' in the truth of the mother ' of all these, and all of you [15] that attain to me, ' to me alone who am perfect, because of ' the Word. For I exist with all the ' greatness of the Spirit, which is a ' friend to us and our [20] kindred alike, since I brought ' forth a word to the glory ' of our Father, through ' his goodness, as well as an ' imperishable thought; that is, the Word [25] within him − ' it is slavery that we shall die with ' Christ − and an imperishable ' and undefiled thought, an ' incomprehensible marvel, the writing [30] of the ineffable water ' which is ' the word from us. It is I who am in ' you (pl.) and you ' are in me, just as the [35] Father is in you **50** in innocence.

Let us ' gather an assembly together. ' Let us visit that creation ' of his. Let us send someone [5] forth in it, just as he visited ' ⟨the⟩Ennoias, the regions ' below. And I said these things ' to the whole multitude of the ' multitudinous assembly of the [10] rejoicing Majesty. ' The whole house of the Father of Truth rejoiced ' that I am the one who is ' from them. I produced thought ' about the Ennoias which came [15] out of the undefiled Spirit, ' about the descent upon the water, ' that is, the regions below. ' And they all had ' a single mind, since it [20] is out of one. They charged ' me since I was willing. ' I came forth to reveal ' the glory to my kindred ' and my fellow spirits. [25]

For those who were ' in the world had been prepared by the will ' of our sister Sophia − ' she who is a whore − ' because of the innocence which [30] has not been uttered. And she did not ' ask anything from ' the All, nor from the greatness ' of the Assembly, nor from the ' Pleroma. Since she was first she came forth **51** to prepare monads and ' places for the Son of Light, ' and the fellow workers ' which she took from [5] the elements below ' to build ' bodily dwellings from them. ' But, having come into being in an ' empty glory, they ended [10] in destruction in the dwellings ' in which they were, since they were ' prepared by ' Sophia. They stand ready ' to receive [15] the life-giving word of ' the ineffable Monad ' and of the greatness of the assembly ' of all those who persevere ' and those who are [20] in me.

I visited a ' bodily dwelling. I cast ' out the one who was ' in it first, and I ' went in. And [25] the whole multitude ' of the archons became troubled. ' And all the matter of the archons ' as well as all the begotten

powers of the earth ' were shaken when [30] it saw the likeness of the Image, ' since it was mixed. And I am the one who ' was in it, not resembling ' him who was in it ' first. For he was an **52** earthly man, but I, ' I am from above ' the heavens. I did not refuse ' them even to become [5] a Christ, but I did not reveal ' myself to them in the love ' which was coming forth from me. ' I revealed that I am a ' stranger to the regions [10] below.

There was a great ' disturbance in ' the whole earthly area with ' confusion and flight, as well as (in) the plan ' of the archons. And some [15] were persuaded, when they saw ' the wonders which were being accomplished by ' me. And ' all these, with the race, that came ' down, flee from him [20] who had fled from the throne ' to the Sophia of hope, ' since she had earlier given the sign ' concerning us and all the ones ' with me — those of the race [25] of Adonaios. Others ' also fled, as if ' from the Cosmocrator ' and those with them, ' since they have brought every (kind of) punishment [30] upon me. And there was a flight ' of their mind ' about what they would counsel ' concerning me, thinking ' that she (Sophia) is the whole greatness, and [35] speaking false witness, ' moreover, against the Man and the whole greatness **53** of the assembly. ' It was not possible for them to know ' who the Father of ' Truth, the Man of the [5] Greatness, is. But they who received ' the name because of contact with ' ignorance — which (is) a burning ' and a vessel — having created ' it to destroy Adam [10] whom they had made, in order to ' cover up those who are theirs ' in the same way. But they, ' the archons, those of the place of Yaldabaoth, ' reveal the realm of [15] the angels, which ' humanity was seeking ' in order that they may not know the Man of Truth. ' For Adam, ' whom they had formed, appeared to them. [20] And a fearful motion came about ' throughout their entire dwelling, lest ' the angels ' surrounding them rebel. For without those ' who were offering praise — I did [25] not really die lest ' their archangel become empty. '

And then ' a voice — of the Cosmocrator — ' came to the angels: [30] "I am God and ' there is no other beside me." But I laughed joyfully ' when I examined his empty glory. ' But he went on to [35] say, "Who **54** is man?" And the entire host ' of his angels who had ' seen Adam and his dwelling were laughing ' at his smallness. And [5] thus did their Ennoia come to be ' removed outside the Majesty ' of the heavens, i.e. the ' Man of Truth, ' whose name they saw since he is [10] in a small dwelling place, ' since they are small (and) senseless ' in their empty Ennoia, ' namely their laughter. It was ' contagion for them.

The whole greatness [15] of the Fatherhood of the ' Spirit was at rest in ' his places. And I am he ' who was with him, since I have ' an Ennoia of a single emanation [20] from the eternal ones ' and the ' undefiled and immeasurable incomprehensibilities. ' I placed the small Ennoia ' in the world, [25] having disturbed them and ' frightened the whole multitude of the ' angels and their ruler. And I ' was visiting them all ' with fire and [30] flame because of my Ennoia. And ' everything pertaining to them was brought about ' because of me. And there came about a disturbance ' and a fight around ' the Seraphim and Cherubim, [35] since their glory will fade, **55** and the confusion around ' Adonaios on both sides ' and their dwelling − to the Cosmocrator ' and him who said, [5] "Let us seize him"; others ' again, "The plan will certainly not materialize." ' For Adonaios knows me ' because of hope. ' And I was [10] in the mouths of lions. And ' the plan which they devised ' about me to release ' their Error and their senselessness − ' I did not succumb to them as [15] they had planned. But I was ' not afflicted at all. Those who were there punished ' me. And ' I did not die in reality ' but in appearance, lest [20] I be put to shame by them ' because these are my kinsfolk. I ' removed the shame from me ' and I did not become fainthearted in the face of what ' happened to me at their hands. [25] I was about to ' succumb to fear, and I ' ⟨suffered⟩ according to their sight ' and thought, in order that ' they may never find any word to speak [30] about them. For my death ' which they think happened, ' (happened) to them in their ' error and blindness, ' since they nailed their [35] man unto their death. ' For their Ennoias did not see **56** me, for they were deaf ' and blind. ' But in doing these things, they condemn ' themselves. Yes, they saw [5] me; they punished me. ' It was another, their father, ' who drank the gall and the vinegar; ' it was not I. They struck ' me with the reed; it was another, Simon, [10] who bore the cross on ' his shoulder. ' I was another upon whom they placed ' the crown of thorns. ' But I was rejoicing in the height [15] over all the wealth ' of the archons and the offspring ' of their error, of their ' empty glory. And I was ' laughing at their ignorance. [20]

And I subjected all their powers. ' For as I came ' downward no one saw me. ' For I was altering my shapes, ' changing from [25] form to form. And ' therefore, when I was at their gates ' I assumed their likeness. ' For I passed them by ' quietly, and I was viewing the [30] places, and I was not afraid ' nor ashamed, ' for I was undefiled. And I was ' speaking with them, ' mingling with ' them through those who are [35] mine, and trampling on those who **57** are harsh to them with zeal, ' and quenching the flame. ' And I was doing all these things ' because of my

desire [5] to accomplish what I desired ' by the will of the Father above. '

And the Son ' of the Majesty, who was hidden ' in the regions below, [10] we brought to the height where I ⟨was⟩ ' in all these aeons with them, ' which (height) no one has seen ' nor known, where ' the wedding of the wedding robe is, [15] the new one and ' not the old, nor does it perish. ' For it is a new and perfect bridal chamber of the ' heavens, as I ' have revealed (that) there are [20] three ways: an ' undefiled mystery in a ' spirit of this aeon, which does not ' perish, nor is it fragmentary, ' nor able to be spoken [25] of; rather, it is ' undivided, universal, ' and permanent. For the soul, the one ' from the height, will not speak ' about the error which is here, nor [30] transfer from these aeons, ' since it will be ' transferred when it becomes free and when it ' is endowed with nobility ' in the world, standing **58** before the Father without weariness ' and fear, always mixed ' with the Nous of power (and) ' of form. They will see me [5] from every side without hatred. ' For since they see me, they are being seen (and) ' are mixed with them. Since they ' did not put me to shame, they were not ' put to shame. Since they were not afraid [10] before me, they will pass by ' every gate without fear and ' will be perfected in the third ' glory.

It was ' my going to [15] the revealed height which the world did not accept, ' my third baptism in a revealed image. ' When they had fled from ' the fire of the ' seven Authorities, and [20] the sun of the powers of ' the archons set, darkness took them. ' And the world became poor ' when he was restrained with a multitude ' of fetters. They nailed him [25] to the tree, and they fixed him with ' four nails of brass. The ' veil of his temple ' he tore with his hands. It was a ' trembling which seized [30] the chaos of the earth, ' for the souls which were ' in the sleep below were released. ' And they arose. They went about ' boldly, having shed **59** zealous service of ignorance ' and unlearnedness ' beside the dead tombs, ' having put on the new man, [5] since they have come to know ' that perfect Blessed One of ' the eternal and incomprehensible Father ' and the infinite light, ' which is I, since I came to [10] my own and united ' them with myself. There is no need ' for many words, ' for our Ennoia was with their Ennoia. ' Therefore they knew what [15] I speak of, for we took counsel ' about the destruction of the ' archons. And therefore I did ' the will of the Father, who is I. '

After we went forth from our home, [20] and came down to this world, ' and came into being in the world ' in bodies, we were hated ' and persecuted, not only ' by those who are ignorant, but [25] also by those who think that ' they are advancing the name of Christ, ' since they

were unknowingly empty, | not knowing | who they are, like dumb animals. ³⁰ They | persecuted those who have been liberated | by me, since they hate them − | those who, should they shut | their mouth, would weep with a ³⁵ profitless groaning because **60** they did not fully know me. | Instead, they served two masters, | even a multitude. But you will become | victorious in everything, in ⁵ war and battles, | jealous division | and wrath. But in the | uprightness of our love we are | innocent, pure, ¹⁰ (and) good, since we have a mind | of the Father in an | ineffable mystery. |

For it was ludicrous. It is I | who bear witness that it was ludicrous, ¹⁵ since the archons do not know | that it is an | ineffable union of | undefiled truth, as exists | among the sons of light, ²⁰ of which they made an imitation, | having proclaimed | a doctrine of a dead man | and lies so as to resemble the freedom | and purity of ²⁵ the perfect assembly, | (and) ⟨joining⟩ themselves with their doctrine | to fear and slavery, | worldly cares, | and abandoned worship, ³⁰ being small (and) ignorant since they do not | contain the | nobility of the truth | for they hate the one in whom | they are, and love ³⁵ the one in whom they are not. | For they did not know the **61** Knowledge of the Greatness, | that it is from above | and (from) a fountain of truth, and that | it is not from slavery ⁵ and jealousy, | fear and love of | worldly matter. For that | which is not theirs and that which | is theirs they use ¹⁰ fearlessly and freely. | They do not desire because | they have authority, and (they have) a | law from themselves over | whatever they will wish. ¹⁵

But those who have not are poor, | that is, those who do not possess him. | And they desire him and | lead astray those, who through | them have become like those who possess ²⁰ the truth of their freedom, | just as they bought us for | servitude and constraint of | care and fear. This person is | in slavery. ²⁵ And he who is brought by | constraint of force and threat | has been guarded by | God. But the entire nobility | of the Fatherhood ³⁰ is not guarded, since he guards only him | who is from him, without | word and constraint, since he is united | with his will, he who belongs only to the | Ennoia of the Fatherhood, ³⁵ to make it perfect | and ineffable through **62** the living water, to be | with you mutually in wisdom, | not only in word | of hearing but in deed ⁵ and fulfilled word. | For the perfect ones are worthy to be established | in this way and to be | united with me, in order that they may not share | in any enmity, in ¹⁰ a good friendship. I | accomplish everything through the Good One, | for this is the union of the truth, | that they should have no adversary. | But everyone ¹⁵ who brings division − and

he will learn no wisdom at all ¹ because he brings division and ¹ is not a friend − is hostile to ¹ them all. But he who lives ²⁰ in harmony and friendship ¹ of brotherly love, ¹ naturally and not artificially, ¹ completely and ¹ not partially, this person is truly the desire ²⁵ of the Father. He is the ¹ universal one and perfect love. ¹

For Adam was a laughingstock, ¹ since he was made a counterfeit ¹ type of man ³⁰ by the Hebdomad, ¹ as if he had become stronger ¹ than I and my brothers. We ¹ are innocent with respect to him, ¹ since we have not sinned. ³⁵ And Abraham and Isaac ¹ and Jacob were a laughingstock, since they, ¹ the counterfeit fathers, were given a name ¹ by the Hebdomad, as if **63** he had become stronger than I ¹ and my brothers. We are ¹ innocent with respect to him, since we have not sinned. ¹ David was a laughingstock ⁵ in that his son was named the Son ¹ of Man, having been influenced ¹ by the Hebdomad, ¹ as if he had become stronger than I ¹ and the follow members of my race. ¹⁰ But we are innocent with respect to him; ¹ we have not sinned. Solomon was a laughingstock, ¹ since he thought that he was Christ, ¹ having become vain through ¹ the Hebdomad, as if he had become ¹⁵ stronger than I and my brothers. ¹ But we are innocent with respect to ¹ him. I have not sinned. ¹ The 12 prophets were laughingstocks, ¹ since they have come forth as imitations of ²⁰ the true prophets. They came into being ¹ as counterfeits through ¹ the Hebdomad, as if ¹ he had become stronger than I ¹ and my brothers. But we are ²⁵ innocent with respect to him, since we have not sinned. ¹ Moses, ¹ a faithful servant, was a laughingstock, ¹ having been named "the Friend," ¹ since they perversely bore witness concerning him ³⁰ who never ¹ knew me. Neither he ¹ nor those before him, from ¹ Adam to Moses and ¹ John the Baptist, ³⁵ none of them knew me nor **64** my brothers.

For they had a ¹ doctrine of angels ¹ to observe dietary laws and ¹ bitter slavery, since they never ⁵ knew truth, ¹ nor will they know it. ¹ For there is a great deception ¹ upon their soul making it impossible ¹ for them ever to find a Nous of ¹⁰ freedom in order to know ¹ him, until they come to know the Son ¹ of Man. Now concerning my Father, ¹ I am he whom the world ¹ did not know, and because of this, ¹⁵ it (the world) rose up against me and my brothers. ¹ But we are innocent with respect to ¹ him; we have not sinned. ¹

For the Archon was a laughingstock because he said, ¹ "I am God, and ²⁰ there is none greater than I. I ¹ alone am the Father, the Lord, and ¹ there is no other beside me. I ¹ am a jealous God, who ¹ brings the sins of the fathers ²⁵ upon the children for three and ¹ four genera-

tions.'' As if he had ' become stronger than I and my brothers! ' But we are innocent ' with respect to him, in that we have not sinned, [30] since we mastered his teaching. Thus ' he was in an empty glory. ' And he does not agree ' with our Father. And thus ' through our fellowship [35] we grasped his teaching, since he ' was vain in an ' empty glory. And he does ' not agree with our Father, ' for he was a laughingstock and **65** judgment and false prophecy. '

O those who do ' not see, you do not see your ' blindness, i.e. this which was [5] not known, nor ' has it ever been known, nor ' has it been known about him. ' They did not listen to firm obedience. ' Therefore they proceeded [10] in a judgment of error, ' and they raised their ' defiled and murderous hands against him ' as if they were beating the air. ' And the senseless and blind ones [15] are always senseless, ' always being slaves ' of law and ' earthly fear.

I am Christ, ' the Son of Man, the one [20] from you (pl.) who is among you. ' I am despised for your sake, in ' order that you yourselves ' may forget the difference. ' And do not become female, [25] lest you give birth to evil ' and (its) brothers: jealousy ' and division, anger ' and wrath, fear ' and a divided heart, and [30] empty, non-existent desire. ' But I am ' an ineffable mystery to you. '

Then before the ' foundation of the world, [35] when the whole multitude ' of the Assembly came together ' upon the places of the Ogdoad, **66** when they had taken counsel about a ' spiritual wedding which is in union, ' and thus he was perfected ' in the ineffable places [5] by a living word, ' the undefiled wedding was consummated ' through the Mesotes ' of Jesus, who inhabits ' them all and possesses [10] them, who abides in an ' undivided love of power. ' And surrounding him, he ' appears to him as ' a Monad of all these, [15] a thought and a father, since he is ' one. And he stands ' by them all, since he ' as a whole came forth alone. And ' he is life, since he came from the [20] Father of ineffable ' and perfect Truth, ' (the father) of those who are there, the union ' of peace and a friend ' of good things, and life [25] eternal and undefiled joy, ' in a great harmony ' of life and faith, ' through eternal life ' of fatherhood and [30] motherhood and sisterhood ' and rational wisdom. ' They had agreed with Nous, ' who stretches out (and) will stretch ' out in joyful union [35] and is trustworthy **67** and faithfully listens to ' someone. And he is in fatherhood ' and motherhood ' and rational brotherhood [5] and wisdom. And this is a ' wedding of truth, ' and a repose of incorruption, ' in a spirit of truth, ' in every mind, and a [10] perfect light in an ' unnameable mystery. ' But this is not, nor ' will it happen among

us ˈ in any region or place ¹⁵ in division and breach ˈ of peace, but (in) union ˈ and a mixture of love, all of which ˈ are perfected in the one who is. ˈ

It (fem.) also happened in the places ²⁰ under heaven for their reconciliation. ˈ Those who knew me ˈ in salvation and undividedness, ˈ and those who existed ˈ for the glory of the father ²⁵ and the truth, having been separated, ˈ blended into the one ˈ through the living word. ˈ And I am in the spirit ˈ and the truth of the ³⁰ motherhood, just as he has been there; ˈ I was among those ˈ who are united in the friendship ˈ of friends forever, ˈ who neither know ³⁵ hostility at all, ˈ nor evil, but who are united **68** by my Knowledge ˈ in word and peace ˈ which exists in perfection ˈ with everyone and in ⁵ them all. And those who ˈ assumed the form of my type will ˈ assume the form of my word. Indeed, these ˈ will come forth in light forever, ˈ and (in) friendship with each other ¹⁰ in the spirit, since they have known ˈ in every respect (and) indivisibly ˈ that what is is One. And ˈ all of these are one. And thus ˈ they will learn about the One, as (did) ¹⁵ the Assembly and those dwelling ˈ in it. For the father ˈ of all these exists, being immeasurable ˈ (and) immutable: Nous ˈ and Word and Division ²⁰ and Envy and Fire. ˈ And he is entirely one, being ˈ the All with them all in a ˈ single doctrine because all these ˈ are from a single spirit. ²⁵ O unseeing ones, why ˈ did you not know the mystery ˈ rightly? ˈ

But the archons ˈ around Yaldabaoth were disobedient because of ³⁰ the Ennoia who went down to him ˈ from her sister Sophia. ˈ They made for themselves a union ˈ with those who were with ˈ them in a mixture of **69** a fiery cloud, which ˈ was their Envy, and the rest ˈ who were brought forth by ˈ their creatures, as if ⁵ they had bruised the noble pleasure ˈ of the Assembly. ˈ And therefore they revealed ˈ a mixture of ignorance ˈ in a counterfeit ¹⁰ of fire and ˈ earth and a murderer, since ˈ they are small and untaught, ˈ without knowledge having dared ˈ these things, and not having understood ¹⁵ that light has fellowship ˈ with light, and darkness ˈ with darkness, and the ˈ corruptible with the perishable, ˈ and the imperishable with the incorruptible. ²⁰

Now these things I have presented to you (pl.) − ˈ I am Jesus Christ, the Son of ˈ Man, who is exalted above the heavens −, ˈ O perfect and incorruptible ones, ˈ because of the ²⁵ incorruptible and perfect mystery ˈ and the ineffable one. ˈ But they think that we decreed ˈ them before the foundation ˈ of the world in order that, ³⁰ when we emerge from the places ˈ of the world, we may present there ˈ the symbols of ˈ incorruption from the ˈ spiritual union unto **70** knowledge. You (pl.) do not

know ' it because the fleshly cloud ' overshadows you. ' But I alone am the friend of Sophia. [5] I have been in the bosom ' of the father from the beginning, in the place ' of the sons of the truth, and ' the Greatness. Rest then with me, ' my fellow spirits and my brothers, [10] for ever. '

Second Treatise '
of the Great Seth

APOCALYPSE OF PETER (VII,*3*)

Introduced by

JAMES BRASHLER

Translated by

JAMES BRASHLER and ROGER A. BULLARD

The *Apocalypse of Peter* is a pseudonymous Christian Gnostic writing that contains an account of a revelation seen by the apostle Peter and interpreted by Jesus the Savior. The persecution of Jesus is used as a model for understanding early Christian history in which a faithful gnostic remnant is oppressed by those "who name themselves bishop and also deacons."

This document belongs to the literary genre of the apocalypse. It is organized around three vision reports attributed to Peter. The visions are explained by the Savior, who functions as the interpreting angel commonly found in apocalyptic literature. In a series of prophecies that actually reflect past events, the early Christian church is portrayed as divided into various factions which oppose the gnostic community. The world is a hostile environment for the immortal souls (the Gnostics), who outwardly resemble the mortal souls (non-Gnostics) but inwardly differ from them by virtue of their immortal essence. Having been given knowledge of their heavenly origin, the Gnostics long for the return of the heavenly Son of Man, who will come as the eschatological judge to condemn the oppressors and vindicate the Gnostics.

The apocalyptic form of this tractate has been employed to present a gnostic understanding of Christian tradition about Jesus. The traditional material is skillfully interpreted in accordance with gnostic theology. The first visionary scene, depicting the hostile priests and people about to kill Jesus (72,4-9) is interpreted in terms of at least six groups characterized as "blind ones who have no guide." Many of these groups appear to be from the orthodox church, but some of them may be better understood as rival gnostic sects. The second scene (81,3-14) describes Peter's vision of the crucifixion of Jesus. The accompanying interpretation by Jesus makes a distinction between the external physical form and the living Jesus; the latter stands nearby laughing at his ignorant persecutors. The third visionary scene (82,4-16) corresponds to the resurrection of Jesus in orthodox tradition, but it is interpreted in gnostic terms as a reunification of the spiritual body of Jesus with the intellectual light of the heavenly pleroma.

The *Apocalypse of Peter* is significant in several respects. It contains important source material for a gnostic Christology that understands Jesus as a docetic redeemer. The view of the Gnostic community, including its relationship to Peter as its originator, is another key theme of this document. Of considerable interest are the identity of the gnostic group to which the writing is addressed, and the stage of the controversy, between emerging orthodoxy and heresy, presupposed

by the tractate. It would appear that the *Apocalypse of Peter* was written in the third century, when this distinction between orthodoxy and heresy was rather clearly drawn.

APOCALYPSE OF PETER

VII 70, 13-84, 14

Apocalypse of Peter ¦

As the Savior was sitting in [15] the temple in the three hundredth (year) of ¦ the covenant and the agreement of ¦ the tenth pillar, and ¦ being satisfied with the number ¦ of the living, incorruptible Majesty, [20] he said to me, "Peter, ¦ blessed are those ¦ above belonging to the Father ¦ who revealed life ¦ to those who are from the life, through [25] me, since I reminded (them), ¦ they who are built ¦ on what is strong, ¦ that they may hear my word ¦ and distinguish words [30] of unrighteousness and ¦ transgression of law ¦ from righteousness, as **71** being from the height of ¦ every word of this pleroma ¦ of truth, having ¦ been enlightened in good pleasure by [5] him whom the principalities sought. ¦ But they did not find ¦ him, nor was he mentioned ¦ among any generation of ¦ the prophets. He has [10] now appeared among these, ¦ in him who appeared, ¦ who is the Son of Man ¦ who is exalted above the heavens in ¦ a fear of men of like essence. [15] But you yourself, Peter, ¦ become perfect ¦ in accordance with your name with myself, ¦ the one who chose you, because ¦ from you I have established a base [20] for the remnant whom I have ¦ summoned to knowledge. ¦ Therefore be strong until the ¦ imitation of righteousness − ¦ of him who had summoned you, [25] having summoned you ¦ to know him in a way which is ¦ worth doing because of the rejection ¦ which happened to him, and the sinews ¦ of his hands and his feet, [30] and the crowning ¦ by those of the middle region, ¦ and the body of ¦ his radiance which they bring ¦ in hope of **72** service because of a reward ¦ of honor − as he was about to reprove ¦ you three times ¦ in this night."

And as he was saying [5] these things, I saw the priests ¦ and the people running up ¦ to us with stones, as if they ¦ would kill us; and I was afraid ¦ that we were going to die.'

And [10] he said to me, "Peter, I have told ¦ you many times that ¦ they are blind ones who have ¦ no guide. If you want ¦ to know their blindness, [15] put your hands upon (your) eyes − ¦ your robe − and say ¦ what you see." ¦

But when I had done it, I did not see ǀ anything. I said, "No one sees (this way)." [20]

Again he told me, ǀ "Do it again."

And there came ǀ in me fear with ǀ joy, for I saw a ǀ new light greater than the [25] light of day. Then ǀ it came down upon the Savior. ǀ And I told him about those things ǀ which I saw.

And ǀ he said to me again, "Lift up [30] your hands and ǀ listen to what **73** the priests and the people are saying."

And ǀ I listened to the priests as they sat ǀ with the scribes. The multitudes were ǀ shouting with their voice.

When he [5] heard these things from me ǀ he said to me, "Prick up your ears ǀ and listen ǀ to the things they are saying." ǀ

And I listened again. "As you sit [10] they are praising you."

And ǀ when I said these things, the Savior said, ǀ "I have told you that these (people) ǀ are blind and ǀ deaf. Now then, listen to [15] the things which they are telling you ǀ in a mystery, and ǀ guard them. Do not tell them to the ǀ sons of this age. ǀ For they shall blaspheme [20] you in these ages since they ǀ are ignorant of you, ǀ but they will praise you in knowledge. ǀ

"For many ǀ will accept our teaching in the beginning. [25] And they will turn ǀ from them again by the will ǀ of the Father of their error, ǀ because they have done what he wanted. ǀ And he will reveal them [30] in his judgment, i.e. ǀ the servants of the Word. ǀ But those who became **74** mingled with these shall become ǀ their prisoners, ǀ since they are without perception. ǀ And the guileless, good, [5] pure one they push ǀ to the worker of death, ǀ and to the kingdom of ǀ those who praise Christ ǀ in a restoration. [10] And they praise the men ǀ of the propagation of falsehood, ǀ those who will come after you. ǀ And they will cleave to the name ǀ of a dead man, thinking [15] that they will become pure. But ǀ they will become greatly defiled and they will ǀ fall into a name of error, ǀ and into the hand of an ǀ evil, cunning man and a [20] manifold dogma, and they will be ǀ ruled ǀ heretically.

"For some ǀ of them will ǀ blaspheme the truth and [25] proclaim evil teaching. And ǀ they will say evil things ǀ against each other. Some ǀ will be named: ǀ (those) who stand in (the) strength [30] of the archons, of a man ǀ and a naked woman ǀ who is manifold ǀ and subject to much ǀ suffering. And **75** those who say these things will ǀ ask about dreams. And if they ǀ say that a dream ǀ came from a demon [5] worthy of their error, then ǀ they shall be given perdition instead ǀ of incorruption.

"For evil ǀ cannot produce ǀ good fruit (cf. Lk 6:43). For [10] the place

from which each of them is ' produces that which is like itself; ' for not every soul is ' of the truth, nor ' of immortality. [15] For every soul of these ages ' has death assigned to it ' in our view, because ' it is always a slave, ' since it is created for its desires [20] and their eternal ' destruction, in which ' they are and ' from which they are. ' They (the souls) love the creatures [25] of the matter which came forth ' with them.

"But ' the immortal souls are not like these, ' O Peter. But indeed, as long as ' the hour is not yet come, (the immortal soul) [30] shall ' resemble a mortal one. ' But it shall not reveal ' its nature, that it ' alone is the **76** immortal one, and thinks about ' immortality, having faith, ' and desiring to renounce ' these things.

"For people do not gather [5] figs from thorns or from ' thorn trees, if they ' are wise, nor grapes ' from thistles (cf. Lk 6:44). ' For on the one hand, that which is [10] always becoming is in that ' from which it is, being ' from what is not good, which ' becomes destruction for it (the soul) and ' death. But that (immortal soul) which comes to be [15] in the Eternal One is in the One of ' the life and the immortality of ' the life which they resemble. '

"Therefore all that which exists ' not will dissolve into what [20] exists not. ' For deaf and ' blind ones join only with ' their own kind. '

"But others shall change [25] from evil words ' and misleading ' mysteries. Some ' who do not understand mystery ' speak of things which [30] they do not understand, ' but they will boast ' that the mystery ' of the truth is theirs ' alone. And [55] in haughtiness **77** they shall grasp at pride ' to envy the ' immortal soul which has become a pledge. ' For every authority, rule, [5] and power of the aeons ' wishes to be with ' these in the creation of ' the world, in order that those who ' are not, having been forgotten [10] by those that are, ' may praise them, ' though they have not been saved, nor have they ' been brought to the Way by them, ' always wishing [15] that they may become ' imperishable ones. ' For if the immortal soul ' receives power in an ' intellectual spirit −. But immediately [20] they join with one ' of those who misled them. '

"But many others, ' who oppose the ' truth and are the messengers [25] of error, will ' set up their error and ' their law against ' these pure thoughts of mine, ' as looking out [20] from one (perspective), thinking ' that good and evil ' are from one (source). ' They do business in **78** my word. And they will propagate ' harsh fate. ' The race of immortal ' souls will go in it [5] in vain ' until my Parousia. ' For they shall come out of them − ' and my forgiveness of ' their transgressions [10] into which they fell through ' their adversaries, ' whose ransom I got ' from the

slavery in which ' they were, to give them [15] freedom that they may create ' an imitation remnant ' in the name of a dead man, ' who is Hermas, of the ' first-born of unrighteousness, [20] in order that the light which exists ' may not be believed ' by the little ones. ' But those of this sort are the workers ' who will be cast into the outer darkness, [25] away from the sons ' of light. For neither will they ' enter, ' nor do they permit ' those who are going up to [30] their approval for ' their release.

"And still others ' of them who suffer think ' that they will perfect **79** the wisdom of the brotherhood ' which really exists, which is the ' spiritual fellowship with those ' united in communion, [5] through which ' the wedding of ' incorruptibility shall be revealed. ' The kindred race ' of the sisterhood will appear [10] as an imitation. ' These are the ones who oppress ' their brothers, saying ' to them, 'Through this ' our God has pity, [15] since salvation comes ' to us through this,' not knowing ' the punishment of those who ' are made glad by those who ' have done this thing to the little ones whom [20] they saw, (and) whom they took ' prisoner. '

"And there shall be others ' of those who are outside our ' number who name themselves [25] bishop and also ' deacons, as if they have received ' their authority from God. ' They bend themselves under the ' judgment of the leaders. [30] Those people are ' dry canals." '

But I said, "I am afraid because ' of what you have told me, that **80** indeed little (ones) are, in our view, the ' counterfeit ones, ' indeed, that there are multitudes that will mislead ' other multitudes of living ones, [5] and destroy them among ' themselves. And when they speak your name ' they will be believed." '

The Savior said, "For a time ' determined for them in [10] proportion to their error they will ' rule over the little ones. And ' after the completion of ' the error, the ' never-aging one of the immortal understanding [15] shall become young, and they (the little ones) shall rule over ' those who are their rulers. ' The root of their error ' he shall pluck out, and he shall ' put it to shame so that it shall be manifest [20] in all the impudence which it ' has assumed to itself. And ' such ones shall become ' unchangeable, O Peter.

"Come, ' therefore, let us go on with the completion [25] of the will of the ' incorruptible Father. ' For behold, those who will ' bring them judgment are coming, and they ' will put them to shame. But me [30] they cannot touch. ' And you, O Peter, shall ' stand in their midst. Do not be ' afraid because of your cowardice. **81** Their minds shall be closed, ' for the invisible one ' has opposed them."

When ' he had said those things, I saw him [5] seemingly being seized ' by them. And ' I said, "What do I see, ' O Lord, that it is you yourself ' whom they take, and that you are [10] grasping me? Or who is this one, ' glad and laughing on the tree? ' And is it another one ' whose feet and ' hands they are striking?" [15]

The Savior said to me, "He whom you saw ' on the three, glad ' and laughing, this is the ' living Jesus. But this one ' into whose hands and [20] feet they drive the nails is his fleshly part, ' which is the substitute ' being put to shame, the one ' who came into being in his likeness. ' But look at him and me." [25]

But I, when I had looked, said, ' 'Lord, no one is looking at ' you. Let us flee this ' place."

But he said to me, ' "I have told you, [30] 'Leave the blind alone!' ' And you, see how ' they do not know what they are saying. **82** For the son of ' their glory instead of my servant ' they have put to shame." '

And I saw someone about to approach [5] us resembling him, even him ' who was laughing on the tree. ' And he was ⟨filled⟩ with a ' Holy Spirit, and he is the ' Savior. And there was a great, [10] ineffable light around them, ' and the multitude ' of ineffable and ' invisible angels ' blessing them. [15] And when I looked at him, ' the one who gives praise was revealed. '

And he said to me, ' "Be strong, for you are the one to whom ' these mysteries have been given, [20] to know them through revelation, ' that he whom they crucified is ' the first-born, and the home ' of demons, and the stony vessel (?) ' in which they dwell, of Elohim, [25] of the cross ' which is under the Law. ' But he who stands near him ' is the living Savior, the first ' in him, whom they seized [30] and released, ' who stands joyfully ' looking at those who did him ' violence, while they are divided among themselves. **83** Therefore he laughs ' at their lack of perception, ' knowing that they are born blind. ' So then [5] the one susceptible to suffering shall come, since the body ' is the substitute. But what they ' released was my incorporeal ' body. But I am the intellectual ' Spirit filled with [10] radiant light. He ' whom you saw coming to ' me is our intellectual ' Pleroma, which unites ' the perfect light with [15] my Holy Spirit.

"These things, then, ' which you saw you shall present ' to those of another race ' who are not of this age. ' For there will be no honor [20] in any man ' who is not immortal, ' but only (in) those who were chosen ' from an immortal substance, ' which has shown [25] that it is able to contain him ' who gives his abundance. Therefore ' I said, 'Every one '

who has, it will be given to him, and ' he will have plenty' (Mt 25:29).
³⁰ But he who does not have, that is, ' the man of this place, who is '
completely dead, who ' is removed from the planting ' of the creation
of what is begotten, **84** whom, if one ' of the immortal essence appears,
' they think that ' they possess him — ⁵ it will be taken from him and '
be added to the one who is. You, ' therefore, be courageous and do not
' fear at all. For I shall be ' with you in order that none ¹⁰ of your
enemies may prevail over you. ' Peace be to you. Be strong!'' '

When he (Jesus) had said these things, he (Peter) came ' to himself. '

Apocalypse of Peter

THE TEACHINGS OF SILVANUS (VII,*4*)

Introduced and translated by

MALCOLM L. PEEL and JAN ZANDEE

The eclectic spirit of the second and early third centuries is clearly reflected in the fourth tractate of Codex VII, *The Teachings of Silvanus*. Its author, like other educated Christians, found it necessary both to reject erroneous pagan thought and yet, simultaneously, to appropriate the best of such thought to clarify and make cogent the Faith. The resultant text, a rare specimen of Hellenistic Christian wisdom literature, displays a remarkable synthesis of biblical and late Jewish ideas with Middle Platonic and late Stoic anthropological, ethical, and theological concepts. The synthesis has a didactic purpose: to impart the wisdom of Christ which confers the self-controlled and "quiet" life, enables one to be "pleasing to" the Divine, and, ultimately, helps one "become like God."

Unlike the other four tractates in Codex VII, *Teach. Silv.* is not gnostic and may even contain some anti-gnostic polemic. It is explicitly affirmed, for example, that all creation has been brought into being by God through his "hand," the Christ. Thus, unlike the gnostic dualists, one should never describe the Creator (demiurge!) as "ignorant," in spite of the author's pessimism regarding interpersonal relations (97,30-98,10). Moreover, instead of a docetic view of Christ, the author states that the Savior "bore affliction" for our sins, "died" as a "ransom" and gave his life for others, and put on "humanity." With respect to anthropology, while the author does espouse a tripartite view of man ("mind," "soul," and "body") similar to the gnostic, he departs sharply from their views that one is "saved by nature." Every human being, the text maintains, possesses both divine "reason" and "mind" and thus has the capacity for salvation; God wishes for all to be saved.

Perhaps what helped attract the *Teach. Silv.* to the predominantly gnostic collection of writings that constitute the Nag Hammadi library, however, was its rather austere and somewhat ascetic ethic. The text counsels keeping under control base passions, passions and unclean thoughts which are induced by the adversary, Satan. One is to have God alone as a friend, for all the world is deceitful and full of pain. Moreover, "austerity" is a type of life to be preferred, and "fornication" is to be avoided rigorously, as is "lust." Especially must one struggle with Satan, the adversary, who offers temptations in subtle disguises, and whose evil powers seek to infest one's life. Such an ascetic and almost "anchoritic" ethic could have appealed to Gnostics, as could also other concepts in the text, such as the "bridal chamber" in 94,27-29.

The literary genre of *Teach. Silv.* is clearly indebted to Jewish and Hellenistic Jewish wisdom literature; though the author is also influenced by the Cynic-Stoic diatribe and the Hellenistic hymn styles. Influence from the Jewish side, though, is exhibited in the direct quotes in *Teach. Silv.* of canonical and apocryphal (e.g., 112,37-113,7 = Wis 7:25-26) wisdom writings.

With respect to content, the first part of *Teach. Silv.* is more Hellenistic and philosophical in character. The latter part is more specifically Christian and biblical in imagery.

In the initial part (84,15-99,4) the writer's main concern is with the state of the soul. To prevent its being inhabited and overcome by base passions and irrational impulses (symbolically described as "robbers" and "wild, savage beasts," the reader is admonished to let the "mind" (*nous*) become his "guiding principle" and "reason" (*logos*) become his "teacher." The terminology and emphases clearly echo the anthropology and ethics of the late Stoa and of Middle Platonism.

In the second part of the tractate (99,6-118,7), on the other hand, emphasis is placed on the salvation of the soul made possible by the Redeemer-Revealer Christ, Son of Almighty God. At the outset, the author echoes the Platonic discussion of the "One and the many," utilizing this concept to discuss how Christ and God, like the "mind" in man's body, is present all places without being confined to a single place. Such "topological theology" both presupposes a non-dualistic cosmology in rather anti-gnostic fashion and offers an implicit refutation of the pantheistic theology of Stoicism. In conclusion, the reader is exhorted to seek Christ's inward help in illuminating "reason," in escaping the control of evil powers, in purifying one's life, and in seeking the lasting rewards of his wisdom and God's way (117,5-118,7).

As to the authorship of *Teach. Silv.*, we know of several early prominent Christians who bore the name "Silvanus." The late dates of their activity, however, and the differences of their teaching from that of our tractate seem to rule out consideration of any of them as its author. Rather, we are probably to recognize in the name "Silvanus" that common device used in Christian apocryphal literature of attributing a later, anonymous writing to a figure known by name in the New Testament canon. Such a "Silas" or "Silvanus" was a prominent member of the Jerusalem Church, cotraveller with Paul (Ac 15:22-40; 16:19-29; etc.), and possibly the amanuensis of "Peter's" named in 1 Peter 5:12. So, here is yet another Nag Hammadi tractate identified with the circle of influence emanating from Paul and Peter (cf. *Pr. Paul*, *Apoc. Paul*, *Acts Pet. 12 Apost.*, *Apoc. Pet.* and *Ep. Pet. Phil.*). As to who the author of *Teach. Silv.* actually was, however, we must state (as did Origen of the author of Hebrews) "in truth (only) God knows!"

In dating the text, we are mainly dependent on internal evidence, though dates have been found in the cartonnage used to strengthen the leather envelope that contained Codex VII. These dates point toward the third quarter of the fourth century as the probable time of the manuscript's burial near ancient Chenoboskia. Internal evidence includes the author's apparent knowledge of all major divisions of Old and New Testament canons; the stage of development of the Church's doctrine of Christ's "Descent into Hell" that was familiar to the author; the affinities of the text's "Logos" and "Wisdom" Christology to that of the Alexandrine Fathers, Clement of Alexandria and Origen; and the close parallels of the thought of the later Stoa (notably, Marcus Aurelius) and Middle Platonists (especially Albinus) with that of the author of *Teach. Silv.* Cumulatively, such evidence points toward the late second to early third century.

Many striking parallels that can be adduced to our text from Philo, *Sent. Sex-*

tus, Clement of Alexandria, Origen, and even Athanasius underscore its affinities with what has become known as Alexandrian theology. Its theology, Christology, cosmology, anthropology, and ethics all point, in their similarity, toward Alexandrian Egypt as the probable provenance.

The concluding note (118,8-9) is secondary, probably added by the copyist. It is surrounded by magical signs related to Christ's designation as "ichthys" ("fish"), an acrostic signifying "Jesus Christ, Son of God, Savior." It may well have been added by the copyist in response to the impressive Christology he has just copied in the text. For him Christ is truly the "extraordinary wonder"!

THE TEACHINGS OF SILVANUS

VII 84, 115-118, 7
118, 8-9

The Teachings of Silvanus |

Abolish every childish time of life, | acquire for yourself strength | of mind and soul, | and intensify the struggle against [20] every folly of the passions | of love and base wickedness, | and love of praise, | and fondness of contention, | and tiresome jealousy and wrath, [25] and anger and the desire | of avarice. Guard | your (pl.) camp and | weapons and spears. Arm | yourself and all the soldiers [30] which are the words, and the commanders | which are the counsels, and your **85** mind as a guiding principle.

My | son, throw every robber | out of your gates. Guard | all your gates with torches [5] which are the words, and | you will acquire through all these things a | quiet life. But he who will not guard | these things will become like a | city which is desolate since it has been [10] captured. All kinds of wild beasts have | trampled upon it, for thoughts which | are not good are evil wild beasts. | And your city | will be filled with robbers, and you [15] will not be able to acquire peace, | but only all kinds of savage wild beasts. | The Wicked One, who is | a tyrant, is lord over these. While | directing this, he (the Wicked One) is beneath the great [20] mire. The whole city | which is your soul will perish. |

Remove yourself from these things, O | wretched soul. | Bring in your guide and [25] your teacher. The mind is the guide, | but reason is the teacher. | They will bring you | out of destruction and dangers. |

Listen, my son, to my [30] advice! Do not show your back | [to] your enemies and flee, but | rather pursue them as a [strong one]. **86** Be not an animal, with men | pursuing you; but | rather, be a man, with you

pursuing ˈ the evil wild beasts, lest somehow ⁵ they become victorious over you and trample ˈ upon you as on a dead man, ˈ and you perish due to ˈ their wickedness.

O wretched ˈ man, what will you ¹⁰ do if you fall into their ˈ hands? Protect yourself ˈ lest you be delivered into the hands of your ˈ enemies. Entrust yourself to this ˈ pair of friends, reason ¹⁵ and mind, and no one ˈ will be victorious over you. May God ˈ dwell in your camp, ˈ may his Spirit protect your ˈ gates, and may the mind of divinity ²⁰ protect the walls. Let holy reason ˈ become a ˈ torch in your mind, burning ˈ the wood which is the whole of sin. ˈ

And if you do these things, O my son, ²⁵ you will be victorious over all your enemies, ˈ and they will not be able to wage war ˈ against you, neither will they be able ˈ to resist, nor will they ˈ be able to get in your way. ³⁰ For if you find these, you will despise ˈ them as deniers of truth. ˈ They will speak with you, [cajoling] ˈ you and enticing (you), not because they are [afraid] **87** of you, but because they are afraid of ˈ those who dwell within you, ˈ namely, the guardians of the divinity ˈ and the teaching.

My son, ⁵ accept the education and the teaching. ˈ Do not flee from the education and ˈ the teaching, but when you are taught, ˈ accept (it) with joy. And if ˈ you are educated in ¹⁰ any matter, do what is good. ˈ You will plait a crown of ˈ education by your guiding principle. ˈ Put on the holy teaching ˈ like a robe. Make yourself noble-minded ¹⁵ through good conduct. ˈ Obtain the austerity of ˈ good discipline. Judge ˈ yourself like a wise judge. ˈ Do not go astray from my teaching, ²⁰ and do not acquire ignorance, ˈ lest you lead your people astray. ˈ Do not flee from the divine ˈ and the teaching which are within ˈ you, for he who is teaching ²⁵ you loves you very much. ˈ For he shall bequeath to you a worthy austerity. ˈ Cast out the animal nature ˈ which is within you, ˈ and ³⁰ do not allow base thought to enter you. For . . . you ˈ know the way which I teach.

If it is good to rule over the [few], ˈ as you see it, ³⁵ [how] much better is it that you **88** rule over everyone, since you are exalted ˈ above every congregation and every people, ˈ (are) prominent in every respect, ˈ and (are) a divine reason, having ⁵ become master over every power ˈ which kills the soul.

My son, does anyone ˈ want to be a slave? ˈ Why, then, do you trouble yourself wrongly? ˈ

My son, do not ¹⁰ fear anyone except ˈ God alone, the Exalted One. ˈ Cast the deceitfulness of the Devil ˈ from you. Accept the light ˈ for

your eyes, and cast [15] the darkness from you. Live ' in Christ, and you will acquire ' a treasure in heaven. Do not become ' a sausage (made) of many things ' which are useless, and do not [20] become a guide ' in your blind ignorance. '

My son, listen to my ' teaching which is good and useful, ' and end the sleep which weighs heavily upon you. [25] Depart from the forgetfulness ' which fills you with darkness, ' since if you were unable ' to do anything, I would not have said these things ' to you. But Christ has come in order to give you [30] this gift. Why do you ' pursue the darkness when the light ' is at your disposal? Why ' do you drink stale water though ' sweet is available for you? [35] Wisdom summons [you], **89** yet you desire folly. ' Not by your own desire do you do ' these things, but it is the animal nature ' within you that does them. [5]

Wisdom summons you ' in her goodness, saying, ' "Come to me, all of you, ' O foolish ones, that you may receive a ' gift, the understanding which is [10] good and excellent. I am giving to you ' a high-priestly garment ' which is woven from every (kind of) wisdom." What else ' is evil death except ' ignorance? What else is [15] evil darkness except familiarity ' with forgetfulness! Cast your anxiety ' upon God alone. Do not become ' desirous of gold and silver ' which are profitless, but [20] clothe yourself with wisdom like ' a robe, put knowledge ' on yourself like ' a crown, and be seated upon a throne ' of perception. For these are yours, [25] and you will receive them again on high ' another time.

For a foolish man ' usually puts on folly ' like a robe, and ' like a garment of sorrow [30] he puts on shame. And ' he crowns himself with ignorance ' and takes his seat ' upon a throne of ' [nescience]. For while he is [without reason], **90** he leads only himself astray, for ' he is guided by ignorance. ' And he goes the ways ' of the desire of every passion. [5] He swims in the desires ' of life and has sunk. ' To be sure, he thinks that he finds profit ' when he does all the things ' which are without profit. The [10] wretched man who goes ' through all these things will die because ' he does not have the mind, ' the helmsman. But he is like ' a ship which the wind tosses [15] to and fro, and like ' a loose horse which has no rider. ' For this (man) ' needed the rider which is reason. ' For the wretched one went astray [20] because he did not want ' advice. He was thrown to and ' fro by these three misfortunes; ' he acquired death as ' a father, ignorance [25] as a mother, and evil counsels − ' he acquired them ' as friends and brothers. ' Therefore, foolish one, you should mourn for yourself. '

From now on, then, my son, return [30] to your divine nature. ' Cast

from [you] these evil, ' deceiving friends! ' [Accept] Christ, [this true friend], **91** as a good teacher. Cast ' from you death, which has ' become a father to you. ' For death did not exist, nor [5] will it exist at the end.

But ' since you cast from yourself ' God, the holy Father, ' the true Life, the Spring ' of Life, therefore you have [10] obtained death as a father ' and have acquired ignorance ' as a mother. They have robbed ' you of the true knowledge. '

But return, my son, to [15] your first Father, God, ' and Wisdom your mother, ' from whom you came into being ' from the very first in order that you might fight against ' all of your enemies, the Powers [20] of the Adversary.

Listen, ' my son, to my advice. ' Do not be arrogant in opposition to ' every good opinion, ' but take for yourself the side of the divinity [25] of reason. Keep the holy ' commandments of Jesus Christ, and ' you will reign over every place ' on earth and will be ' honored by the angels [30] and the archangels. ' Then you will acquire them as friends and ' fellow servants, and you will acquire ' places in [heaven ' above].

Do not bring **92** grief or trouble to the divine [which is] ' within you. But when you will care for ' it, will request of it ' that you remain pure, and will become [5] self-controlled in your soul ' and body, you will become ' a throne of wisdom and ' one belonging to God's household. He will ' give you a great light through [10] it (wisdom).

But before everything (else), ' know your birth. Know ' yourself, that is, from what substance you are, ' or from what ' race, or from what species. [15] Understand that you have come into being ' from three races: ' from the earth, from the ' formed, and from the created. ' The body has come into being from [20] the earth with an earthly substance, ' but the formed, for the sake of ' the soul, has come into being from the thought ' of the Divine. The created, however, is the mind, ' which has come into being in conformity with the image [25] of God. The divine mind ' has substance ' from the Divine, but the soul ' is that which he (God) has formed for their ' own hearts. For I think [30] that it (the soul) exists as wife of that which ' has come into being in conformity with the image, ' but matter is the substance ' of the body which has come into being from the earth. '

[If] you mix yourself, you will acquire the **93** three parts as you ' fall from virtue into ' inferiority. Live according to ' the mind. Do not think about things belonging to [5] the flesh. Acquire strength, ' for the mind is strong. ' If you fall from ' this other, you have become male-

female. ' And if you cast out of yourself the substance of the mind, [10] which is thought, ' you have cut off ' the male part and turned yourself to the female part ' alone. You have become psychic ' since you have received the substance of the [15] formed. If you cast out the smallest part of this ' so that ' you do not acquire again a ' human part − but you have accepted for ' yourself the animal thought and [20] likeness − you have become fleshly ' since you have taken on animal nature. ' For (if) it is difficult to find a psychical man, ' how much more so to find ' the Lord!

But I say that [25] God is the spiritual one. ' Man has taken shape from ' the substance of God. ' The divine soul ' shares partly in this One (God); furthermore, [30] it shares partly in the flesh. ' The base soul ' is wont to turn from side to side ' [. . .] which it imagines the truth. '

It is [good] for you, O man, **94** to turn yourself toward the human rather' than toward the animal nature − ' I mean toward the fleshly (nature). You ' will take on the likeness of the part toward which you will turn yourself. [5]

I shall say something further ' to you. Again, for what ' will you (masc. sg.) be zealous? Did you (fem. sg.) wish ' to become animal when you had come into ' this kind of nature? [10] But rather, share in ' a true nature of life. ' To be sure, animality will guide you ' into the race of the earth, ' but the rational nature will [15] guide you in rational ways. ' Turn toward the rational nature ' and cast from ' yourself the earth-begotten nature. '

O soul, persistent one, [20] be sober and shake off your ' drunkenness, which is the work of ' ignorance. If you persist ' and live in the ' body, you dwell in rusticity. [25] When you entered ' into a bodily birth, you were ' begotten. Come into being inside ' the bridal chamber! Be illuminated ' in mind!

My son, do not [30] swim in any water, ' and do not allow yourself to be defiled ' by strange kinds of knowledge. ' Certainly you know [that] **95** the schemes of the Adversary ' are not few and (that) ' the tricks which he has ' are varied? Especially has the noetic [5] man been robbed ' of the intelligence ' of the snake. For it is fitting for you ' to be in agreement with the ' intelligence of (these) two: with the [10] intelligence of the snake and with ' the innocence of the dove − ' lest he (the Adversary) come into you ' in the guise of a flatterer, ' as a true friend, saying, [15] "I advise ' good things for you." '

But you did not recognize the ' deceitfulness of this one when ' you received him as a true friend. [20] For he casts into your heart ' evil

thoughts ' as good ones, and ' hypocrisy in the guise of ' true wisdom,
²⁵ avidity in the guise ' of conservative frugality, ' love of glory ' in the
guise of that which is beautiful, ' boastfulness and ³⁰ pride in the guise
' of great austerity, and ' godlessness as ' [great] godliness. **96** For he
who says, "I have ' many gods," is godless. ' And he casts spurious
knowledge ' into your ⁵ heart in the guise of mysterious words. ' Who
' will be able to comprehend his thoughts and ' devices which are varied
since he is ' a Great Mind for those who wish ¹⁰ to accept him as king?

My ' son, how will you be able ' to comprehend the schemes of this
one or his ' soul-killing counsel? ' For his devices and the ¹⁵ schemes of
his wickedness are many. And ' think about his entrances, that is, how
' he will enter your ' soul and in what garment ' he will enter you.

Accept ²⁰ Christ, who is able ' to set you free, and who has ' taken on
the devices of that one ' so that through these he ' might destroy him by
²⁵ deceit. For this is the king whom you have ' who is forever invincible,
' against whom ' no one will be able to fight nor ' say a word. This is ³⁰
your king and your father, ' for there is no one like him. ' The divine
teacher is with [you] **97** always. He is a helper, ' and he meets you because of the good ' which is in you.

Do not put maliciousness ' in your judgment, ⁵ for every malicious
man ' harms his heart. ' For only a foolish man is wont ' to his destruction, ' but a wise man knows ¹⁰ his way.

And a foolish man ' does not guard against speaking (a) mystery. ' A
wise man, (however), ' does not blurt out every word, ' but he will be
discriminating ¹⁵ toward those who hear. Do not mention ' everything
in the presence ' of those whom you do not know. '

Have a great number of friends, ' but not counselors. ²⁰ First, examine your ' counselor, for do not ' honor anyone who flatters. ' Their
word, to be sure, is sweet as ' honey, but their heart is full ²⁵ of
hellebore. For whenever ' they think that they have become ' a reliable
friend, ' then they will deceitfully turn ' against you, and they will cast
you down ³⁰ into the mire.

Do not ' trust anyone as a friend, ' for this whole world ' has come
into being deceitfully, and ' every [man] is troubled ³⁵ [in vain]. All
things [of] **98** the world are not profitable, ' but they happen in vain. '
There is no one, not even a brother, (who is trustworthy), ' since each
one is seeking ⁵ his own advantage.

My son, do not ' have anyone as a friend. ' But if you do acquire one,
do not entrust yourself ' to him. Entrust yourself to ' God alone as
father ¹⁰ and as friend. For everyone ' proceeds deceitfully, ' while the

whole earth is full of suffering and ' pain – things in which there is no profit. ' If you wish to pass your [15] life in quiet, do not keep company ' with anyone. And if you do keep ' company with them, be as if ' you do not. Be pleasing ' to God, and you will [20] not need anyone.

Live ' with Christ, and he will save ' you. For he is the true light ' and the sun of life. ' For just as the sun which is visible [25] and makes light for the eyes of the flesh, ' so Christ ' illuminates every mind ' and the heart. For (if) a wicked man ' (who is) in the body (has) an evil death, [30] how much more so (does) ' he who has ' his mind blind. ' For every blind man [goes along ' in such a way] that he (?) is seen [just] [99] as one who does not have ' his mind sane. He does not ' delight in acquiring the light ' of Christ, which is reason. [5]

For everything which is visible ' is a copy of that which ' is hidden. For as a fire which ' burns in a place without being confined ' to it, so it is with [10] the sun which is in the sky, all of whose rays ' extend to places ' on the earth. Similarly, ' Christ has a single being, ' and [15] he gives light to every place. This ' is also the way in which he speaks of our ' mind, as if it were a lamp ' which burns and lights up the place. ' (Being) in a part of the soul, [20] it gives light to all the parts. '

Furthermore, I shall speak of what is ' more exalted than this: the mind, with respect to ' actual being, is in a place, ' which means it is in the body; [25] but with respect to thought, the mind ' is not in a place. For how can it ' be in a place when ' it contemplates every place? '

But we are able [30] to mention what is more exalted than this: ' for do not think in your heart ' that God exists ' [in a] place. If ' you localize the [Lord of] all [100] in a place, then it is fitting for you to ' say that the place is more exalted than he who ' dwells in it. For that which contains ' is more exalted than that which is contained. [5] For there is no place which is called ' incorporeal. ' For it is not right for us to say that ' God is corporeal. ' For the consequence (would be) that we (must) attribute both [10] increase and decrease to the corporeal, ' but also that he (God) who is subject to these ' will not remain imperishable. '

Now, it is not difficult to know ' the Creator of all creatures, [15] but it is impossible to comprehend ' the likeness of this One. For ' it is difficult not only for men to ' comprehend God, but it is (also) difficult ' for every divine being, (both) the angels [20] and the archangels. ' It is necessary to know ' God as he is. ' You cannot ' know God through [25] anyone except Christ ' who has ' the image of the Father, ' for this image reveals the true likeness ' in correspondence to that which is revealed. [30] A king is not usually known apart from ' an image.

Consider these things about ' God: he is in every place; ' on the other hand, he is in [no] ' place. [With respect to power], **101** to be sure, he is in every place; ' but with respect to divinity, he is in no ' place. So, then, it is ' possible to know God a [5] little. With respect to his power, ' he fills every place, but in ' the exaltation of his divinity ' nothing contains him. ' Everything is in God, [10] but God is not in anything. '

Now what is it to know God? ' God is all which is in the truth. ' But it is as impossible ' to look at Christ as [15] at the sun. God sees ' everyone; no one looks at ' him. But Christ without ' being jealous receives and gives. He ' is the Light of the Father, as he gives [20] light without being jealous. ' In this manner he gives light to every place. '

And all is Christ, ' he who has inherited all ' from the Existent One. [25] For Christ is the idea ' of incorruptibility, and [30] he is the Light which is shining undefiled. ' For the sun (shines) on every impure place, ' and yet it is not defiled. ' So it is with Christ: even if ' [he is in the] deficiency, yet [he] is without deficiency. [35] And even if [he has been begotten], **102** he is (still) unbegotten. So it is with ' Christ: if, on the one hand, he is comprehensible, ' on the other he is incomprehensible ' with respect to his actual being. [5] Christ is all. ' He who does not possess all is unable to ' know Christ.

My son, ' do not dare to say a word about ' this One, and do not confine the God of all [10] to mental images. ' For he (God) who condemns ' may not be condemned by the one who ' condemns. Indeed, it is good ' to ask and to know who [15] God is. Reason and mind ' are male names. Indeed, let him who wishes ' to know about this One ' quietly and ' reverently ask. For there is no small danger [20] in speaking about these things, since you ' know that you will be judged ' on the basis of everything that you say. '

And understand by this that he who is in ' darkness will not be able to see anything [25] unless he receives the light and recovers (his) sight ' by means of it. Examine yourself (to see) ' whether you wholly have ' the light, so that if you ' ask about these things, you may understand [30] how you will escape. ' For many are seeking in ' darkness, and they grope about, ' wishing to understand since ' there is no light for them.

My **103** son, do not allow your mind to stare ' downward, but rather let ' it look by means of the light ' at things above. [5] For the light will always come from above. ' Even if it (the mind) is upon the earth, ' let it seek to pursue the ' things above. Enlighten your ' mind with the light of heaven [10] so that you may turn to ' the light of heaven.

Do not tire ' of knocking on the door of reason, ' and do not cease '

walking in the way of [15] Christ. Walk in it so that | you may receive rest from your | labors. If you walk in another | way, there will be no | profit in it. For also those who walk [20] in the broad way | will go down at their end | to the perdition of the mire. | For the Underworld is open wide for the soul, | and the place of perdition is broad. [25] Accept Christ, | the narrow way. For he is oppressed | and bears affliction for your | sin.

O soul, persistent one, | in what ignorance you exist! [30] For who | is your guide | into the darkness? How many likenesses | did Christ take on because of you? | Although he was God, he [was found] **104** among men as a man. | He descended to the Underworld. He released | the children of death. They were | in travail, as [5] the scripture of God has said. And | he sealed up the (very) heart | of it (the Underworld). And he broke its (the Underworld's) strong bows | completely. And | when all the powers had seen [10] him, they fled so that he might | bring you, wretched one, | up from the Abyss, and might die for you | as a ransom for your sin. He saved | you from the strong hand of the Underworld. [15]

But you yourself, difficult (though it be), give to him your | fundamental assent with (even so much as) a hint | that he may take you up with | joy! Now the fundamental choice, | which is humility of heart, is the gift of Christ. [20] A contrite heart is the acceptable sacrifice. | If you humble yourself, you will be greatly exalted; | and if you exalt yourself, | you will be exceedingly humbled.

My son, [25] guard yourself against wickedness, | and do not let the Spirit of Wickedness | cast you down into the Abyss. | For he is mad and bitter. | He is terrifying, and he casts [30] everyone down into a pit | of mire.

It is a great | and good thing not to love | fornication and not even to think | of the wretched matter **105** at all, for to think of it is death. | It is not good for any man | to fall into death. | For a soul which has been found in [5] death will be without reason. | For it is better not to live than | to acquire an animal's life. | Protect yourself lest you are burned | by the fires of fornication. [10] For many who are submerged in fire are | its servants whom | you do not know as | your enemies.

O my son, strip off | the old garment of fornication, [15] and put on the | garment which is clean and shining, | that you may be beautiful in it. | But when you have this garment, | protect it well. Release yourself [20] from every bond so that you may | acquire freedom. | If you cast out of yourself | the desire whose | devices are many, you will [25] release yourself from the sins of lust. |

Listen, O soul, to my ' advice. Do not become ' a den of foxes and snakes, nor ' a hole of serpents and ³⁰ asps, nor a dwelling place ' of lions, or a place of refuge ' of basilisk-snakes. When these things ' happen to you, O soul, what ' will you do? For these are the powers **106** of the Adversary. ' Everything which is dead will come ' into you through them (the powers). ' For their food is everything which is dead ⁵ and every unclean thing. For when these ' are within you, what living thing ' will come into you? ' The living angels will detest you. ' You were ¹⁰ a temple, (but) you have made yourself a tomb. Cease ' being a tomb, and become (again) ' a temple, so that uprightness ' and divinity may remain in ' you.

Light the light within you. ¹⁵ Do not extinguish it. Certainly no one ' lights a lamp for wild beasts or ' their young. ' Raise your dead who have died, ' for they lived and have died for ²⁰ you. Give them life. ' They shall live again.

For the Tree of ' Life is Christ. He is ' Wisdom. For he is Wisdom; ' he is also the Word. He ²⁵ is the Life, the Power, ' and the Door. He is the Light, ' the Angel, and ' the Good Shepherd. Entrust yourself ' to this one who became ³⁰ all for your sake.

Knock ' on yourself as upon ' a door, and walk upon ' yourself as on a straight road. ' For if you walk on the road, ³⁵ it is impossible for you to go astray. **107** And if you knock with this one (Wisdom), you ' knock on hidden treasures. '

For since he (Christ) is Wisdom, ' he makes the foolish man wise. ⁵ It (Wisdom) is a holy kingdom ' and a shining robe. ' For it (Wisdom) is much gold ' which gives you great honor. ' The Wisdom of God ¹⁰ became a type of fool for you ' so that it might take you up, ' O foolish one, and make you a wise man. ' And the Life died ' for you when he (Christ) was powerless, ¹⁵ so that through his death ' he might give life to you who have died. '

Entrust yourself to ' reason and remove yourself from ' animalism. For ²⁰ the animal which has no ' reason is made manifest. ' For many think that they have ' reason, but if you ' look at them attentively, ²⁵ their speech is animalistic. '

Give yourself gladness from the true ' vine of Christ. ' Satisfy yourself with the true wine ' in which there is no drunkenness ³⁰ nor error. ' For it (the true wine) marks ' the end of drinking since there ' is usually in it what gives joy ' to the soul and ³⁵ the mind through the Spirit of God. **108** But first, nurture your reasoning powers ' before you drink ' of it (the true wine).

Do not pierce yourself with ' the sword of sin. Do not burn yourself, [5] O wretched one, with the fire ' of lust. Do not surrender yourself ' to barbarians like a prisoner, ' nor to ' savage beasts which want [10] to trample upon you. ' For they are as lions ' which roar very loudly. Be not ' dead lest they ' trample upon you. You shall be man! [15] It is possible for you through reasoning ' to conquer them. '

But the man who does nothing is unworthy of ' (being called) rational man. The rational man ' is he who fears God. [20] He who fears ' God does nothing insolent. ' And he who guards himself ' against doing anything insolent is one ' who keeps his guiding principle. [25] Although he is a man who exists ' on earth, he makes himself like ' God.

But he who makes himself like ' God is one who does ' nothing unworthy of God, [30] according to the statement of Paul ' who has become like ' Christ.

For who shows reverence ' for God while not wanting ' to do things which are pleasing [35] to him? For piety ' is that which is **109** from the heart, ' and piety from ' the heart (characterizes) every soul which is near to ' God.

The soul which is [5] a member of God's household is one which ' is kept pure, ' and the soul which has put on Christ ' is one which is pure. ' It is impossible for it to sin. [10] Now where Christ is, there ' sin is idle.

Let Christ ' alone enter your world, ' and let him bring to naught ' all powers which have come upon you. [15] Let him enter the temple which is ' within you so that he may cast ' out all the merchants. Let him ' dwell in the temple which is ' within you, and may you become [20] for him a priest and a Levite, ' entering in purity. '

Blessed are you, O soul, if you ' find this one in your temple. '

Blessed are you still more if you perform his [25] service.

But he who will defile ' the temple of God, that one God ' will destroy. For you lay yourself open, ' O man, if you ' cast this one out of your [30] temple. For whenever ' the enemies do not see Christ ' in you, then they will come into ' you armed in order to crush ' you.

O my son, I have given [35] you orders concerning these things many times **110** so that you would always guard your ' soul. It is not you who ' will cast him (Christ) out, but ' he will cast you out. For [5] if you flee from him, you will ' fall into great sin. ' Again, if you flee from him, you will ' become food for your enemies. ' For all base persons flee from [10] their lord, and the (man) base in virtue ' and wisdom flees from ' Christ. For every man who is ' separated (from him) falls into the claws ' of the wild beasts.

Know who Christ is, [15] and acquire him as a friend, | for this is the friend who is faithful. | He is also God and | Teacher. This one, being God, became | man for your sake. It is this one who [20] broke the iron bars | of the Underworld and the bronze bolts. | It is this one who attacked | and cast down | every haughty tyrant. It is he [25] who loosened from himself the chains | of which he had taken hold. | He brought up the poor from the | Abyss and the mourners from | the Underworld. It is he who humbled [30] the haughty powers; | he who put to shame haughtiness | through humility; he who has cast | down the strong and | the boaster through weakness; [35] he who in his contempt scorned that which is **111** considered an honor | so that | humility for God's sake might be highly exalted; | (and) he who has put on humanity. [5]

And yet, the divine Word is God, | he who bears patiently with man always. | He wished to produce | humility in the exalted. He (Christ) who has | exalted man became like [10] God, not in order that he | might bring God down to | man, but that man might become | like God.

O this | great goodness of God! [15] O Christ, King who has revealed | to men the Great Divinity, | King of every virtue and | King of life, King of ages and | Great One of the heavens, hear my words [20] and forgive me!

Furthermore, | he manifested a great zeal | for Divinity.

Where is a man (who is) wise | or powerful in intelligence, | or a man whose devices are many [25] because he knows wisdom? | Let him speak wisdom; let him utter | great boasting! | For every man has become a fool and has spoken out of | his (own) knowledge. For he (Christ) confounded the [30] counsels of guileful people, and | he prevailed over those wise in their own | understanding.

Who will be able | to discover the counsel of the | Almighty, or to speak of the [35] Divinity, or to proclaim it correctly? **112** If we have not even been able to | understand the counsels of our companions, | who will be able to comprehend the Divinity | or the divinities of [5] the heavens? If | we scarcely find things on earth, | who will search for the things of | heaven? A Great Power | and Great Glory has made the world | known.

And the Life | of Heaven wishes to renew all, | that he may cast out that which is | weak and every black form, | that everyone may shine forth in [15] heavenly garments in order to make manifest | the command of the Father (who) is exceedingly brilliant, | and that he (Christ) may | crown those wishing to contend | well. Christ, being judge of the con-

test, [20] is he who crowned every one, ' teaching every one ' to contend. This one who contended ' first received the crown, gained dominion, ' and appeared, giving light [25] to everyone. And all were ' made new through the Holy Spirit ' and the Mind.

O Lord Almighty, ' how much glory shall I give Thee? ' No one has been able [30] to glorify God adequately. ' It is Thou who hast given glory ' to Thy Word in order to save ' everyone, O Merciful God. (It is) he who ' has come from Thy mouth and has risen from [35] Thy heart, the First-born, the Wisdom, ' the Prototype, the First ' Light.

For he is light from **113** the power of God, and ' he is an emanation of the pure glory ' of the Almighty. ' He is the spotless mirror of the working [5] of God, and he is the image of his ' goodness. For he is also the Light ' of the Eternal Light. He is the eye ' which looks at the invisible ' Father, always serving [10] and forming ' by the Father's will. He ' alone was begotten by the Father's good pleasure. ' For he is an incomprehensible Word, ' and he is Wisdom [15] and Life. He gives life to and ' nourishes all living things and powers. ' Just as the ' soul gives life to all the members, ' he rules all with [20] power and gives life to them. ' For he is the beginning and ' the end of everyone, watching over ' all and encompassing them. ' He is troubled on behalf of everyone, and he rejoices [25] and also mourns. On the one hand, he mourns ' for those who have gotten as their lot the place ' of punishment; on the other, he is troubled ' about every one whom he arduously brings ' to instruction. [30] But he rejoices over everyone who ' is in purity.

Then beware, ' lest somehow you fall into the hands of the ' robbers. Do not allow sleep ' to your eyes nor [35] drowsiness to your eyelids that ' you may be saved like a gazelle ' from nets and like a **114** bird from a trap.

Fight the ' great fight as long as the fight lasts, ' while all the powers are ' staring after you — not only the holy ones, [5] but also all the powers ' of the Adversary. Woe ' to you if you are vanquished in the midst ' of every one who is watching you! ' If you fight the fight and [10] are victorious over the powers which fight against you, ' you will bring great joy to every ' holy one, and yet ' great grief to your enemies. Your ' judge helps (you) completely [15] since he wants you to be victorious.

Listen, my ' son, and do not be slow ' with your ears. Raise yourself up when you have left your old man behind ' like an eagle. Fear [20] God in all your acts, ' and glorify him through ' good work. You know that

every man who is ' not pleasing to God is the son of perdition. [25] He will go down to the Abyss ' of the Underworld.

O this patience ' of God, which bears with ' every one, which desires that ' every one who has become [30] subject to sin be saved!

But no one prevents ' him (God) from doing what he wants. ' For who is stronger than him that ' he may prevent him? To be sure, ' it is he who touches the earth, [35] causing it to tremble and also causing ' the mountains to smoke. (It is) he who has ' gathered together such a great sea **115** as in a leather bag and ' has weighed all the water on his scales. ' Only the hand of the Lord ' has created all these things. [5] For this hand of the Father is Christ, ' and it forms all. ' Through it, all has come into being ' since it became the mother of all. ' For he is always [10] Son of the Father. '

Consider these things about God Almighty ' who always exists: ' this One was not always ' King for fear that [15] he might be without a ' divine Son. For all dwell ' in God, (that is), the things which have come into being ' through the Word, who is ' the Son as the image of the Father. [20]

For God is nearby; he ' is not far off. All divine limits ' are those which belong to God's household. ' Therefore, if the divine agrees with ' you partially in anything, [25] know that all of the Divine ' agrees with you. But this ' divine is not pleased with anything ' evil. For it is this which ' teaches all men what is good. [30] This is what God has ' given to the human race ' so that for this reason every man ' might be chosen ' before all the angels [35] and the archangels. '

For God does not need ' to put any man to the test. **116** He knows all things ' before they happen, and ' he knows the hidden things of the heart. ' They are all revealed and [5] found wanting in his presence. Let ' no one ever say that God ' is ignorant. For it is not right ' to place the Creator of ' every creature in ignorance. [10] For even things which are in darkness ' are before him like (things in) the light. '

So, there is no other one hidden except ' God alone. But he is revealed ' to everyone, and yet [15] he is very hidden. He is revealed ' because God knows ' all. And if they do not wish ' to affirm it, they will be corrected by ' their heart. Now he is hidden because [20] no one perceives the things of God. ' For it is incomprehensible and ' unfathomable to know ' the counsel of God. Furthermore, ' it is difficult to comprehend him, and it is difficult [25] to find Christ. For he is the one who dwells ' in every place, and also he is ' in no place. For no one ' who wants to will be able to know ' God as he actually is, [30] nor Christ, nor

| the Spirit, nor the chorus of | angels, nor even the archangels, **117** as well as the thrones of the spirits, | and the exalted lordships, | and the Great Mind. If you do not | know [yourself], you will not be able [5] to know all of these.

Open | the door for yourself that you may know | the One who is. Knock on | yourself that the Word | may open for you. For he [10] is the Ruler of Faith and | the Sharp Sword, having become all | for everyone because he wishes | to have mercy on everyone.

My son, | prepare yourself to escape from the [15] world-rulers of darkness and of | this kind of air which is full of powers. | But if you have | Christ, you will conquer this entire world. | That which you will open [20] for yourself, you will open. | That which you will knock upon for yourself, you will | knock upon, benefiting yourself. |

Help yourself, my son, | (by) not proceeding with things in which [25] there is no profit.

My son, | first purify yourself toward the outward life | in order that you may be able | to purify the inward.

And | be not as the merchants [30] of the Word of God.

Put | all words to the test first | before you utter them. |

Do not wish to acquire honors which | are insecure, nor **118** the boastfulness which brings | you to ruin.

Accept | the wisdom of Christ (who is) patient | and mild, and guard [5] this, O my son, knowing | that God's way is always | profitable. |

****

Jesus Christ, Son of God, Savior (Ichthus), Wonder |
Extraordinary

THE THREE STELES OF SETH (VII,5)

Introduced by

James E. Goehring

Translated by

James M. Robinson

The Three Steles of Seth offers a rare view into the worship practice of a Gnostic Sethian community. These Gnostics identified their teachings with the primal revelation of God to Adam, which had passed through Seth to his descendants (*The Apocalypse of Adam*, V,5). Lost and forgotten for ages, this Sethian gnosis had been revealed anew in the latter days. The recipients of this renewed revelation understood themselves as "the living and unshakable race" (118,12-13), the true latter-day descendants of Seth (hence the modern label of Sethian Gnosticism). *The Three Steles of Seth* is presented as part of this latter-day revelation, in this case to Dositheos, the supposed Samaritan founder of Gnosticism.

The text, which shows no Christian influence, is indebted to Jewish and Neoplatonic traditions. In Genesis, Seth marks a new beginning after the tragic conflict between Cain and Abel (Gn 3:25-5:8). Appointed by God to replace Abel, he is a son in the likeness of his father Adam, as Adam is in the likeness of God. It is in his time that "men began to call upon the name of the Lord." According to the first-century Jewish historian Josephus (*Ant.* I,67-71), Seth's descendants continued to follow his godfearing ways for seven generations, after which they too fell into a life of depravity. During this time, they preserved and added to the knowledge transmitted by Adam to Seth. Forwarned of impending divine judgements by water and fire, they preserved this knowledge for future generations on two steles, one of stone to survive the flood and one of brick to survive the fire.

This legend accounts for the presentation of the present text as the content of steles attributed to Seth (cf. *Zost.* 130,1-4 and *Gos. Eg.* 68,10-23). The expansion from the original two steles in the Jewish legend to three represents the influence of Neoplatonic conceptions of the divine triad. The three steles or hymnic prayers of the present text are addressed in ascending order to the threefold nature of god: the Selfbegotten Son, the male virgin Barbelo (mother), and the Unbegotten Father.

Ecstatic trips through the heavens are well attested in Sethian Gnosticism. The Sethian tractates *Zostrianos* and *Allogenes* record such journeys by the seers for which the texts were named. These accounts, however, record what was revealed to the seer in his ascent. The invocations of the seer to the divine triad are only noted in passing, as when Zostrianos affirms, "I joined with them all and blessed the Kalyptos aeon and the virgin Barbelo and the Invisible Spirit. I became all-perfect." In *The Three Steles of Seth* these blessings or hymnic prayers are recorded in full.

Since *Allogenes* may be interpreted as another name for Seth, both tractates may commemorate the ascent of the community's primal ancestor to the divine triad. However, while *Allogenes* records for edification what was revealed to the seer, *The Three Steles of Seth* preserves the invocations of the seer as a prototype to serve the latter-day Sethian community in its liturgical reenactment of his ascent. While the hymnic prayers are set forth in the tractate as prayers of Seth, first person plural references in the text (e.g. 124,17-18) betray the use of the prayers in the worship practice of the community. The text has led Hans Martin Schenke to posit the existence of a Sethian mystery of ascension. The three subdivisions of the text thus correspond to the three stages or levels in the worshippers' ascent to the threefold nature of god, since at the conclusion of the tractate one must return from the third back down to the second and first.

Neoplatonic philosophical terminology abounds in the text, especially the Existence-Life-Mind triad in the deity. The terminology is also found in the related tractates of *Zostrianos*, *Allogenes*, and *Marsanes*, which together form a cluster of Sethian Gnostic texts with close ties to Neoplatonism. *Zostrianos* and *Allogenes* are both mentioned by Porphyry in his *Life of Plotinus* as texts refuted by Plotinus, who taught a course "Against the Gnostics" in 265-266 C.E. Thus a dating for this stage of Sethian Gnosticism and therefore for *The Three Steles of Seth* is suggested. Provenience is uncertain, though the philosophical nature of the text would be much at home in Alexandria, Egypt.

The scribal note at the end of the text (127,28-32) has been variously interpreted as applying to *The Three Steles of Seth* alone or to the codex as a whole.

THE THREE STELES OF SETH

VII 118, 10-127, 27
127, 28-32

The revelation of Dositheos ' about the three steles ' of Seth, the Father of the living ' and unshakable race, which ' he (Dositheos) saw and understood. [15] And after he had read them, he ' remembered them. And he gave them ' to the elect, just ' as they were ' inscribed there. [20]

Many times I joined in ' giving glory with the powers, and I became worthy of the ' immeasurable majesties. '

Now they (the steles) are as follows:

The First [25]
Stele of Seth.

I bless ' thee, Father Geradama(s), I, ' as thine (own) Son, ' Emma-cha Seth, whom thou didst beget ' without begetting, as a blessing [30] of our God; for I am ' thine (own) Son. And thou **119** art my mind, O my

Father. And ˈ I, I sowed and begot; ˈ [but] thou hast [seen] the majesties. ˈ Thou hast stood imperishable. I ⁵ bless thee, Father. Bless me,
ˈ Father. It is because of thee that I exist; ˈ it is because of God that
thou dost exist. Because ˈ of thee I am with ˈ that very one. Thou art
light, ¹⁰ since thou beholdest light. Thou hast ˈ revealed light. Thou art
ˈ Mirotheas; thou art my Mirotheos. ˈ I bless thee as ˈ God; I bless thy
¹⁵ divinity. Great is the ˈ good Self-begotten who ˈ stood, the God who
had already ˈ stood. Thou didst come in goodness; ˈ thou hast appeared, and thou hast ²⁰ revealed goodness. I shall utter ˈ thy name, for
thou art a first ˈ name. Thou art unbegotten. Thou ˈ hast appeared in
order that thou ˈ mightest reveal the eternal ones. ²⁵ Thou art he who is.
Therefore ˈ thou hast revealed those who really ˈ are. Thou art he who
is uttered ˈ by a voice, ˈ but by mind art thou ³⁰ glorified, thou who hast
ˈ dominion everywhere. Therefore ˈ [the] perceptible world too ˈ knows
thee because of ˈ thee and they seed. Thou art merciful. **120**

And thou art from another race, ˈ and its place is over another race.
ˈ And now thou art from another ˈ race, and its [place is] over another
⁵ race. Thou art from another ˈ race, for thou art not similar. And thou
ˈ art merciful, for thou art eternal. ˈ And thy place is over a race, ˈ for
thou hast caused all these to increase; and for the sake of ¹⁰ my seed. For
it is thou who knows ˈ it, that its place is in begetting. But they ˈ are
from other races, for ˈ they are not similar. But their place is over ˈ
other races, for their place is in ¹⁵ life. Thou art Mirotheos.

I bless his power which was ˈ given to me, who caused the ˈ male-
nesses that really are to become ˈ male three times; ²⁰ he who was divided into the pentad, the one who ˈ was given to us in triple ˈ power, the
one who was begotten without begetting, the one who ˈ came from that
which is elect; because of ²⁵ what is humble, he went ˈ forth from the
midst.

Thou art a Father ˈ through a Father, ˈ a word from a command. ˈ
We bless thee, Thrice Male, ³⁰ for thou didst unite the all ˈ through
them all, for thou hast ˈ empowered us. Thou hast arisen from ˈ one;
from one thou hast gone forth; ˈ thou hast come to one. [Thou] hast
saved, ³⁵ thou hast saved, thou hast saved us, O ˈ crown-bearer, crown-
giver! **121** We bless thee eternally. ˈ We bless thee, once we have ˈ been
saved, as the perfect individuals, ˈ perfect on account ⁵ of thee, those
who [became] perfect with thee ˈ who is complete, who completes, ˈ the
one perfect through all these, ˈ who is similar everywhere.

Thrice ˈ Male, thou hast stood. Thou hast already ¹⁰ stood. Thou
wast divided everywhere. Thou didst continue being one. And ˈ those

whom thou hast willed, thou hast saved. | But thou dost will to be saved | all who are worthy.

Thou art [15] perfect! Thou art perfect! | Thou art perfect!

The First |
Stele of Seth |

The Second Stele |
of Seth [20]

Great is the first aeon, | male virginal Barbelo, | the first glory | of the invisible Father, she | who is called [25] "perfect."

Thou (fem.) hast seen first | the one who truly pre-exists | because he is a non-being. And | from him and through | him thou hast pre-existed [30] eternally, the non-being | from one indivisible, | triple [power], thou a triple | power, [thou a] great monad | from [a] pure monad, **122** thou an elect monad, the | first [shadow] of the holy | Father, light from | light.

[We] bless thee, [5] producer (fem.) of perfection, aeon-giver (fem.). | Thou hast [seen] the eternal | ones because they are from a shadow. | And thou hast become numerable. And | thou didst find, thou didst continue being [10] one (fem.); yet becoming numerable in division, thou | art three-fold. Thou art truly | thrice, thou one (fem.) | of the one (masc.). And thou art from | a shadow of him, thou a Hidden One, [15] thou a world of understanding, | knowing those of the one, that they | are from a shadow. And these | are thine in the heart.

For | their sake thou hast empowered the eternal ones [20] in being; thou hast empowered | divinity in living; | thou hast empowered knowledge in | goodness; in | blessedness thou hast empowered the [25] shadows which pour from the one. | Thou hast empowered this (one) in knowledge; | thou hast empowered another one in creation. | Thou hast empowered him who is equal | and him who is not equal, him [30] who is similar and him who is not similar. | Thou hast empowered in begetting, and | (provided) forms in [that which] exists | to others. [. . . . | Thou hast] empowered **123** these. – He is that One Hidden | [in] the heart. – And [thou hast] come forth to | these and [from] these. Thou art divided | [among them]. And thou dost [5] become a great male [noetic] First-Appearer. |

Fatherly God, | divine child, | begetter of multiplicity according to a division | of all who really are, [10] thou (masc.) hast appeared to them all

in ' a word. And thou (masc.) dost possess ' them all without begetting ' and eternally indestructible ' on account of thee (fem.). [15]

Salvation has come to us; from ' thee is salvation. Thou art ' wisdom, thou knowledge; thou ' art truthfulness. On account of thee is ' life; from thee is life. [20] On account of thee is mind; from ' thee is mind. Thou art mind, ' thou a world of truthfulness, ' thou a triple power, thou ' threefold. Truly thou art [25] thrice, the aeon of ' aeons. It is thou only ' who sees purely the first ' eternal ones and the unbegotten ones. '

But the first divisions are as [30] thou wast divided. Unite us ' as thou hast been united. ' Teach us [those] things which thou dost see. ' Empower [us] that we may **124** be saved to eternal life. ' For [we] are [each] a shadow ' of thee as thou art ' a shadow [of that] [5] first pre-existent one. Hear ' us first. We are eternal ones. ' Hear us as the ' perfect individuals. Thou art the aeon ' of aeons, the all-perfect one [10] who is established.

Thou hast heard! ' Thou hast heard!
Thou hast saved! Thou hast saved! '
We give thanks! We bless thee always! ' We shall glorify thee! '

The Second Stele [15]
of Seth '

The Third Stele '

We rejoice! We rejoice! We rejoice! '

We have seen! We have seen! We have seen the ' really pre-existent one (masc.), [20] that he really exists, that he is the ' first eternal one.

O Unconceived, ' from thee are the eternal ones ' and the aeons, the all-perfect ones ' who are established, and the [25] perfect individuals.

We bless ' thee, non-being, existence ' which is before existences, ' first being which is before ' beings, Father of [30] divinity and life, ' creator of mind, ' giver of good, giver of ' blessedness!

We all bless ' thee, knower, in [35] a [glorifying] blessing, (thou) **125** because of whom [all these are. ' ... really, ' ...], who knows thee ' [through] thee alone. For there is no one [5] [who is] active before ' thee. Thou art an only and living [spirit]. ' And [thou] knowest one, ' for this one who belongs to thee is on every side. ' We are not able to express him. For [10] thy light shines upon us. '

Present a command to us ' to see thee, so that ' we may be saved. Knowledge of thee, it ' is the salvation of us all. Present [15] a command!

When thou dost command, ' we have been saved! Truly we have been '
saved! We have seen thee by mind! ' Thou art them all, for thou dost
save ' them all, he who [20] was not saved, nor was he ' saved through
them. ' For thou, thou hast commanded us. '

Thou art one. Thou art one, just as ' there is one (who) will say [25] to
thee: Thou art one, thou art a single living spirit. ' How shall we give '
thee a name? We do not have it. ' For thou art the existence ' of them
all. [30] Thou art the life of them ' all. Thou art the mind ' of them all. '
[For] thou [art he in whom they all] rejoice. **126**

Thou hast commanded all these ' [to be saved] through thy ' word
[...] ' glory [5] who is before him, Hidden One, blessed ' Senaon, [he
who begat] ' himself, [Asi]neu(s). ' [...]ephneu(s), Optaon, Elemaon '
the great power, Emouniar, [10] Nibareu(s), Kandephor(os), Aphredon, '
Deiphaneus, thou ' who art Armedon to me, power-begetter, ' Thalana-
theu(s), Antitheus, ' thou who existeth within [15] thyself, thou who art
before ' thyself — and after thee ' no one entered into activity.

As what shall we ' bless thee? We are ' not empowered. But we give
thanks, [20] as being humble toward thee. For thou hast ' commanded us,
as he who ' is elect, to glorify thee to the extent that ' we are able. ' We
bless thee because we were saved. [25] Always we glorify ' thee. For this
reason we shall ' glorify thee, that we may be ' saved to eternal salvation. ' We have blessed thee, for we are [30] empowered. We have been
saved, for thou ' hast willed always ' that we all do this.

We ' all did this. [...] ' not through [... 127[3] aeon. ...], ' the one
who was [5] [...], we and those ' who [...]. He who will ' remember
these and give ' glory always will ' become perfect among those who are
perfect [10] and impassable beyond ' all things. For they all bless ' these
individually and together. ' And afterwards they shall be ' silent. And
just as they [15] were ordained, they ascend. ' After the silence, they descend ' from the third. ' They bless the second; ' after these the first. [20]
The way of ascent is the way ' of descent.

Know therefore, ' as those who live, that you have ' attained. And
you taught ' yourselves the infinite things. [25] Marvel at the truth which
is within ' them, and (at) the revelation. '

The Three Steles of Seth. '

****

This book belongs to the fatherhood. '
It is the son who wrote it. [30]
Bless me, O father. I bless '
you, O father, in peace. '
Amen.

ZOSTRIANOS (VIII, *1*)

Introduced and translated by

JOHN N. SIEBER

The tractate *Zostrianos*, a heavenly journey apocalypse, is the major work in Codex VIII and one of the longest works in the Nag Hammadi library. Unfortunately Codex VIII suffered extensive damage prior to its discovery and conservation in modern times so that almost every page of *Zostrianos* is incomplete and some pages now exist only as fragments. Consequently, much of the text of the tractate is now lost. In spite of these problems *Zostrianos* offers an interesting example of how some Gnostics combined a mythological world view and a philosophical interpretation of it, based on Platonic thought.

The book opens with an account of the call of its central character, Zostrianos, to leave this world and to journey through the heavens in pursuit of saving gnosis. In antiquity this Zostrianos was linked to the lineage of the famous Persian magus Zoroaster. His call is recounted in autobiographical fashion. He was deeply depressed, ready to commit suicide in the desert, when suddenly an angel appeared to him and called him to gnosis. Leaving his physical body behind on earth, he ascended with the angel through the lower reaches of the heavenly realms. At each level he was initiated through a baptism into the gnosis revealed there.

As Zostrianos' journey continued he met a succession of angelic guides, questioned them and learned from each of them the gnosis of the various heavenly aeons through which he passed. The knowledge consisted largely in learning the names of the inhabitants of the heavenly world and sorting out the relationships between them. When his tour of the heavens was complete, Zostrianos descended once again to the physical world, where he wrote down the gnosis for the benefit of the elect, the holy seed of Seth. The tractate concludes with a brief but compelling homily in which Zostrianos exhorts his readers to abandon this oppressive world and to seek salvation through gnosis.

Zostrianos' mythological gnosis posits a high god named the thrice powerful Invisible Spirit from whom everything else has emanated. The physical earth and its inhabitants represent the lowest and most ignorant level. Between it and the Spirit lies a vast aeon system called Barbelo and understood as the "thought" of the Spirit. Barbelo herself is divided into three constituent aeons: the uppermost aeon is named Kalyptos (the hidden or veiled aeon), in the middle is located the Protophanes (the first-visible or first-appearing aeon), and at the bottom is the Autogenes (the self-generated or self-begotten aeon). Each of these aeons has its own system of constituent beings called lights, glories, angels, waters, etc.

The philosophical interests of the tractate are clear from its use of questions, categories, and terms best known to us from the Neoplatonic school of Plotinus. Zostrianos never tires of asking his angelic revealers about how this changeable world came into existence from an unchanging source, or about why there are

different kinds of souls or animals or human beings. Their answers assert that each successive layer of the universe is formed on the basis of the models in the layer above and that each layer is less perfect than its model. Of special interest is the identification of the three Barbelo aeons with the philosophical triad of existence, mind, and life. These and other references make it almost certain that this tractate is the one mentioned by Porphyry (*Vit. Plot.*, 16) as one of the spurious apocalypses in circulation in Plotinus' day and assigned by him to his pupil Amelius for refutation.

Zostrianos shares both its philosophical concern and some of its mythological world with three other tractates from the Nag Hammadi library: *The Three Steles of Seth* (VII,*5*), *Marsenes* (X,*1*) and *Allogenes (XI,3)*. There are also some mythological ties, especially with regard to the names of the Autogenes system, with some of the more Christian works such as *The Gospel of the Egyptians* (III,*2* and IV,*2*) and *The Apocryphon of John* (II,*1* et al.), and with *The Untitled Text* of the Bruce Codex.

Except for a few allusions to the New Testament and Christianity in the extant text, the author of *Zostrianos* seems to have no specific interest in things Christian. He rejects the ways of the others, his opponents, but it is not clear if they are Christians or Platonists or some other group. His use of liturgical formulas, baptisms, and magical vowel strings indicates the book may have been used by a group of Gnostics in worship or contemplative exercises, but we are unable to identify this group on the basis of the reports of Christian heresiologists.

ZOSTRIANOS

VIII 1, 1-132, 9

[...] of the [...] the words ' [...] live forever, these I ' [...] Zostrianos ' [...] and [...] and Iolaos, [5] when I was in the world for these ' like me and [those] after me, ' [the] living elect. As God lives, ' [...] the truth with truth ' and knowledge and eternal [10] light.

After I parted from the ' somatic darkness in me and ' the psychic chaos in mind ' and the feminine desire ' [...] in the darkness, I did not use it [15] again. After I found the infinite ' part of my matter, then I reproved the ' dead creation within me ' and the divine Cosmocrater ' of the perceptible (world) by preaching [20] powerfully about the All to those ' with alien parts. '

Although I tried their ways ' for a little while after ' the necessity of begetting brought me [25] to the revealed, I was never pleased with ' them, but I always ' separated myself from them ' because I came into being through ' a holy [...], yet mixed. [30] When I had set straight my sinless ' soul, then I strengthened **2** the intellectual [...] ' and I [...] ' in the [...] ' of my God [...] [5] [...] I having done [...] ' grow strong in a holy spirit ' higher than god.

It [came] ' upon me alone as I was setting myself straight, [and] ' I saw the perfect child [. . .] ¹⁰ [. . .]. With him who [. . .] ' many times and many ways [he] ' appeared to me as a ' loving father, when I was seeking the ' male father of all (who are) ¹⁵ in thought, perception, (in) ' form, race, [region . . .], ' (in) an All which ' restrains and is restrained, ' (in) a body yet without a body, ²⁰ (in) essence, matter and [those that] ' belong to all these. It is with ' them and the god of the unborn ' Kalyptos and the power [in] them all that ' existence is mixed.

(About) existence: ²⁵ how do those who exist, being from ' the aeon of those who exist, (come) from ' an invisible, undivided and ' self-begotten spirit? Are they ' three unborn images having ³⁰ an origin better than existence, ' existing prior [to] all [these], ' yet having become the [world . . .]? ' How are those opposite it and all these 3 [. . .] good, he ' and an ' excuse. What is that one's place? ' What is his origin? ⁵ How does the one from him ' exist for him and all these? How ' [does he come into existence] as a simple one, ' differing [from] himself? Does he exist as ' existence, form, and ¹⁰ blessedness? By giving strength is ' he alive with life? How ' has the existence which does not exist ' appeared from an existing power? '

I pondered these things to understand them; ¹⁵ according to the custom of my race ' I kept bringing them up to the god ' of my fathers. I kept praising ' them all, for my forefathers ' and fathers who sought found. ²⁰ As for me, I did not cease seeking ' a resting place worthy of my spirit, ' since I was not yet bound in the perceptible ' world. Then, as I was deeply ' troubled and gloomy because of the ²⁵ discouragement which encompassed me, ' I dared to act and ' to deliver myself to the wild beasts of the ' desert for a violent death.

There stood ' before me the angel of the knowledge ³⁰ of eternal light. He said to me, ' 'Zostrianos, why have you gone mad ' as if you were ignorant of the great eternals 4 who are above? [. . .] ' you [. . .] ' [. . .] say also [. . .] ' that you are now saved, [. . .] ⁵ [. . .] in eternal death, nor [. . .] ' [. . .] those whom you know ' in order to [. . .] save others, [namely] ' my father's chosen elect? [Do you] ' [suppose] that you are the father of [your race . . .] ¹⁰ or that Iolaos is your father, a [. . .] ' angel of god [. . .] ' you through holy men? ' Come and pass through each ' of these. You will return to them another [time] ¹⁵ to preach to a living [race . . .] ' and to save those who are ' worthy, and to strengthen the elect, ' because the struggle of the aeon is great ' but one's time in this world is short.'

²⁰ When he had said this [to me], ' I very quickly and very ' gladly

went up with him ' to a great light-cloud. I cast ' my body upon the earth [25] to be guarded by glories. I was ' rescued from the whole world ' and the thirteen aeons ' in it and their angelic beings. ' They did not see us, but their [30] archon was disturbed at [our] ' passage, for the light-cloud **5** [...] it is better ' than every [worldly ...] one. ' Its beauty is ineffable. ' With strength it provides light [5] [guiding] pure spirits ' as a spirit-savior ' and an intellectual word, ' [not] like those in the world ' [...] with changeable matter [10] and an upsetting word. '

Then I knew that the power ' in me was set over the darkness ' because it contained the whole light. ' I was baptized there, and [15] I received the image of the glories ' there. I became like ' one of them. I left the ' airy-[earth] and passed by the ' copies of the aeons, after [20] washing there seven times ' [in] living [water], once for each ' [of the] aeons. I did not cease until ' [I saw] all the waters. ' I ascended to the Exile [25] which really exists. I was baptized and ' [...] world. I ascended to the ' Repentance which really exists ' [and was] baptized there ' four times. I passed by the **6** sixth aeon. ' I ascended to the [...] ' I stood there after having seen light ' from the truth which really exists, from [5] its self-begotten root, and ' great angels and glories, [...] ' number.

I was baptized in the [name of] ' the divine Autogenes ' by those powers which are [upon] [10] living waters, Michar and Micheus. ' I was purified by [the] great ' Barpharanges. Then they [revealed] ' themselves to me and wrote me in glory. ' I was sealed by [15] those who are on these powers, [Michar] ' Mi[ch]eus, Seldao, Ele[nos] ' and Zogenethlos. I became ' a root-seeing angel ' and stood upon the first [20] aeon which is the fourth. ' With the souls I blessed the ' divine Autogenes and the ' forefather Geradamas, [an eye of] ' the Autogenes, the first perfect [25] [man], and Seth Emm[acha Seth], ' the son of Adamas, the [father of] ' the [immovable race ...] and the [four] ' [lights ...] ' [...] [30] Mirothea, the mother [...] ' [...] and Prophania [...] ' of the lights and De-[...] **7** [...]

I was ' [baptized] for the second time in the name ' of the divine Autogenes ' by these same powers. I [5] became an angel of the ' male race. I stood upon ' the second aeon which is the ' third, with the sons of ' Seth I blessed each of them.

[10] I was baptized for the third time ' in the name of the divine Autogenes ' by each of these powers. ' I became a holy angel. ' I stood upon the third [15] aeon which is the second. I ' blessed each of them.

I was baptized ' for the fourth time by ' [each of] these powers. I became ' [a] perfect [angel] [20] [I stood upon] the fourth aeon ' [which is the first], and ' [I blessed each of them.]

Then I sought ' [...] I said ' [...] I [25] [...] of ' [...] I ' [...] ' [...]
why [...] ' [...] with power [...] [30] about them in another way in the
reports 8 of men? Are these their ' powers? Or, are these the ones, but
' their names differ from one another? Are ' there souls different from
souls? [5] Why are people different ' from one another? What and in
what way ' are they human?'

The great ruler ' on high, Authrounios, said to me, ' 'Are you asking
about those [10] whom you have passed by? And ' about this airy-earth,
why ' it has a cosmic model? And ' about the aeon copies, how ' many
there are, and, why they are [not] in pain? [15] And, about Exile and '
Repentance and the creation of the ' [aeons] and the world which [...]
' really [...] ' you, about [...] [20] me, them [...] ' nor [...] ' you [...]
' invisible [spirit ...] ' and the [...] [25] of [...] ' [...] ' [...] ' [...] '
and [...] [30] [...] when I [...]

9 The great ruler on high, ' Authrounios, said to me, 'The ' airy-earth
came into being by a ' word, yet it is the begotten [5] and perishable ones
whom it reveals ' by its indestructibility. In regard to the coming ' of the
great judges, (they came) so as not ' to taste perception and to ' be
enclosed in creation, and when [10] they came upon it and saw through '
it the works of the world, ' they condemned its ruler to death ' because
he was a model of the world, ' a [...] and an origin of matter [15] begotten of lost darkness. '

When Sophia looked at [...] them ' she produced the darkness, as
she ' [... she] is beside the ' [... he is a] model [20] [...] of essence '
[...] form ' [...] to an image ' [...] I ' [...] the All [25] [...] ' [...] '
[...] darkness [...] ' [...] say [...] powers ' [... aeons] of [creation
...] to [30] see any of the eternal ones. 10 he saw a reflection. In relation
to ' the reflection which he saw ' in it, he created the world. ' With a
reflection of a reflection [5] he worked at producing the world, ' and then
even the reflection belonging to ' visible reality was taken from him.
But to ' Sophia a place of rest was given ' in exchange for her repentance. [10] Thus, there was in her no ' prior reflection, pure ' in itself
beforehand.

After they had ' already come into being through it, he ' used his imagination (and) produced the [15] remainder, for the image of Sophia '
was always being lost because ' her countenance was deceiving. But the
Archon ' [...] and made a body which [...] ' concerning the greater
[...] [20] down [...] ' when I saw [...] ' to the heart [...] ' [...] ' he
having [...] [25] [...] ' [...] ' [...] ' [...] ' perfect through [...] [30]
[...] ' [...] through him, as he 11 [revealed] the destruction of the

world ' by his [immutability]. It is in the ' following way that the copies of the ' aeons exist. They have not [5] obtained a single power's shape. ' It is eternal glories that they ' possess, and they dwell ' in the judgment seats of each of ' the powers.

But when [10] souls are illuminated by ' the light in them and ' (by) the model which often comes ' into being in them without ' suffering, she did not think that she saw [15] [...] and the eternal ' [...] in the blessed ' [...] each single one ' [...] each of ' [...] light [20] [... all], and she ' [...] whole, and she ' [...] and a ' [...] and she ' [...] she who [25] [...] ' [...] ' [...] ' [...] ' of repentance. [Souls] **12** are located according to the power ' they have in themselves, [...] ' lower are produced ' by the copies. [5] Those who receive a model ' of their souls are still in the ' world. They came into being ' after the departure of the aeons, ' one by one, and they are removed [10] one by one from the ' copy of Exile ' to the Exile that really ' exists, from the copy of ' Repentance to the Repentance [15] that really exists, [and from the] ' copy of Autogenes ' to [the Autogenes] that really ' exists. The remainder [...] ' the souls [...] [20] exist in a [...] ' all [...] ' of aeons [...] ' [...] ' and [...] [25] [through ...] ' the [...] ' [...] ' [...] ' [...] [30] of [...] ' these [...] **13** [blessed the] god above, ' the great aeons, the ' unborn Kalyptos, the great ' male Protophanes, the perfect [5] child who is higher than god, ' and his eye, Pigeradamas. '

I called upon the ' Child of the Child, Ephesech. He ' stood before me and said, [10] 'O angel of god, O son of the ' father, [...] the perfect man. ' Why are you calling on me and ' asking about those things which you know, ' as though you were [ignorant] of them?' And [15] I said, 'I have asked about the ' mixture [...] it is perfect and gives ' [...] there is power which ' [has ... those] in which we receive baptism ' [...] these names are [20] [different ...] and why ' [...] from one ' [...] in the ' [... from] others ' [...] men [25] [... different] ' [...] ' [...] ' [...]

14 He said, '[Zost]rianos, ' listen about these [...] ' for the first [...] ' origins are three because they have [5] appeared in a single origin [of] the ' Barbelo aeon, not like some ' origins and powers, nor ' like (one) from an origin and ' power. It is to every origin that they [10] have appeared; they have strengthened every power; ' and they appeared from that which ' is far better than themselves. These (three) are ' Existence, Blessedness ' and Life. [...] [15] [...] their companions [...] ' in a [...] ' and concerning the [...] ' having named [...] ' more than [...] [20] and [...] ' a perfect [...] ' from a [...] ' [...] ' [...] [25] [...] ' [...] ' [...] ' [...]

15 And a water of each one of ' them [...] ; therefore [...] waters are the perfect ones. ' It is the water of life that [5] belongs to Vitality in which you now ' have been baptized in the Autogenes. ' It is in the [water] of Blessedness ' which belongs to Knowledge that you ' will be baptized in the Protophanes. [10] It is the water of Existence ' [which] belongs to Divinity, ' the Kalyptos. ' Now the water of Life ' [exists in relation to ...] power; that belonging [15] to Blessedness in relation to essence; ' that belonging to [Divinity] in relation to ' [Existence ...]. But all these ' [...] authority and ' [...] those who [20] [...] water which ' [becomes pure ...] ' [...] according to ' [... when they] depart ' [...] [25] [...] ' [...] ' [...] '

[...] **16** Existence as [he] is ' in it. [He] not only [was dwelling] ' in Thought, but he also [...] ' them that it is he who is [Being] in the [5] following way. In order that this world ' might not be endless and formless, ' he placed a [...] over it; ' but in order that [he] might become ' something, the truly young crossed [10] it with what ' is his, [thus] ' Existence. It is with the [son] that ' he is located, with him that he seeks, him that ' he surrounds [...] [15] everywhere [...] ' from the truth [...] ' takes him who [...] ' exists [...] ' activity [...] [20] life [...] ' his word also [...] ' are these after [...] ' they became [...] ' [...] [25] [...] ' [...] ' [...] ' [...] '

[...] **17** and the power is with the ' Essence and Existence ' of Being, when the water exists. ' But the name in which they wash [5] is a word of the water. Then ' the first perfect water of ' the triple-power of the Autogenes ' [is] the perfect soul's ' life, for it is a word of [10] the perfect god while coming into ' being [...] ' for the Invisible Spirit ' is a fountain of them all. ' Thus, the rest are from [knowledge ...] as [15] his likeness. [But] he who knows himself ' [...] what kind and what ' [...] alive at one time ' [...] live with a ' [...] he is the [20] [...] life, in the ' [...] become ' [limitless ...] his [... his] ' [own ...] the name ' [...] [25] [...] ' [...] ' [...] **18** he really exists. It is he because he ' limits himself. They approach ' the water according to this ' single power and the likeness of order. [5]

The great male invisible Mind, ' the perfect Protophanes ' has his own water ' as you [will see] ' when you arrive at his place. This [10] is also the case with the unborn Kalyptos. ' In accordance with each one exists a ' partial entity with a first form, ' so that they might become perfect in this way; ' for the self-begotten aeons [15] are four perfect entities. [The] individuals ' of the all-perfect ones [...] ' them as perfect individuals. And ' the [...] aeon [...] ' of the Autogenes [...] [20] for all [...] '

[perfect] male [. . .] ' for the alls [. . .] ' [perfect god . . . the triple-] '
male [. . .] [25] [perfect] individual [. . .] ' in the [. . .] ' [. . .] ' [. . .] '
[. . .] [30] [. . .] ' [. . .] **19** perfect, those who exist according to ' a form,
a race, an ' All and a partial difference. ' This is also the case with the
highway of ascent which [5] is higher than perfect and Kalyptos. '

The Autogenes is the ' chief archon of his ' own aeons and angels ' as
his parts, for those [10] who are the four individuals ' belong to him; they
belong to the fifth ' aeon together. The ' fifth exists in one; the four '
[are] the fifth, part by part. [15] But these [four] are ' complete individually [because they] have a ' [. . .] it is also [. . .] with ' [the triple
male] individual ' [. . .] for he is a [. . .] of [20] [. . .] god, the ' invisible
[Protophanes] ' [. . . male] mind ' [. . .] which ' exists ' [. . .] [25] [. . .] '
[. . .] ' [. . .] ' [. . .] ' [. . .] **20** living and perfect parts. '

(About) the All and the all-perfect ' race and the one who is higher
than perfect ' and blessed. The [5] self-begotten Kalyptos ' pre-exists
because he is an origin of ' the Autogenes, a god and ' a forefather, a
cause of the ' Protophanes, a father [10] of the parts that are his. ' As a
divine father he is ' foreknown: but he is ' unknown, for he is a power
and ' a father from himself. [15] Therefore, he is [fatherless]. ' The Invisible Triple Powerful, ' First Thought [of] all [these], the ' Invisible Spirit
[. . .] ' is a [. . .] and [20] Essence which [. . .] ' and Existence [. . .] ' there
are [existences] ' the [. . .] ' blessed [. . .] [25] the [. . .] ' all these [. . .] '
the [. . .] ' [. . .] ' [. . .] [30] [. . .] **21** exist in them, [and] they [. . .] ' in
others [. . .] ' by them all ' in many places. They are in [5] every place that
he ' loves and ' desires, yet ' they are not in any place. ' They have
capacity for spirit, ' for they are incorporeal yet are better [10] than incorporeal. They are undivided with ' living thoughts and a power ' of truth
with those purer ' than these since with respect to ' him they are purer
and [15] are not like the bodies which ' are in one place. ' Above all, they
have ' necessity either in relation to the All ' or to a part. ' Therefore,
the [20] way of ascent [. . .] it is pure ' [. . .] each ' [. . .] herself and ' [. . .]
' [. . .] them [25] [. . .] ' [. . .] ' [. . .] ' [. . . above all] ' [. . .] **22** particular
aeons.

Then ' [he said], 'How then can he ' contain an ' eternal model? The
[5] general intellect shares ' when the self-begotten ' water becomes
perfect. ' It one knows him and ' all these, one is the [10] protophanic
water. If ' one joins oneself with all these, one is ' that water which
belongs to Kalyptos, ' whose image is still in the ' aeons. To understand
individually [15] all their parts, they are [. . .] , those ' of the All where '
knowledge is. They have ' [separated] from the one whom they knew

and ' (from) fellowship [20] with one another. The All and all ' these, when they [...] ' wash in the [washing of] ' [Autogenes] he [...] ' of [...] [25] [...] ' [...] ' [...] ' [...] ' [...] 23 he appears to [him], ' that is, when one knows how ' he exists for him and (how) he has ' fellowship with their companions, one has [5] washed in the washing of Protophanes. ' And if in understanding the ' origin of these, ' how they all appear from ' a single origin, how [10] all who are joined come to ' be divided, how those ' who are divided join ' again, and how the parts ' [join with] the alls and the [15] species and [kinds − if] ' one understands these things, one has washed ' in the washing of Kalyptos.

According ' to each of [the] places one has ' a portion of the [20] eternal ones [and] ascends ' [...] as he ' [...] pure and simple, ' he is always [...] ' one of the [...] [25] [always] he is pure for simpleness. ' He is filled [...] ' [in ...] Existence ' and a holy spirit. There is ' 24 nothing of his outside of him. He can ' [see] with his perfect soul those ' who belong to Autogenes; with his mind ' , those who belong to the Triple Male, and with [5] his holy spirit, those who belong to Protophanes. ' He can learn of Kalyptos ' through the powers of the spirit from whom they ' have come forth in a far better ' revelation of the Invisible [10] Spirit. And by means of thought ' which now is in silence and ' by First Thought (he learns) of the Triple ' Powerful Invisible Spirit, since there ' is then a report and power of silence which [15] is purified in a life-giving spirit. ' (It is) perfect and [...] perfect ' and all-perfect. '

Glories, therefore, which ' are set ' over these, are [life-givers] who have [20] been baptised in truth and knowledge. ' Those who are worthy are guarded, ' but those who [are] not ' from this race [...] ' and go [...] these [25] who [...] ' [...] in the fifth, he being [...] ' [...] copy ' [...] of the aeons ' [...] namely a washing [30] but if ' [he] strips off the world 25 and lays aside [knowledge], ' and (if) he is he who has no ' dwelling place and power, then ' because he follows the ways of the others, [5] he is also a sojourner, but (if) he is one ' who has committed no sin because ' knowledge was sufficient for him, he ' is not anxious when he repents, ' and then washings are appointed' [10] in these in addition.

(Concerning) (the path ...) ' to the self-begotten ones, those ' in which you have now been baptised each ' time, (a path) worthy of seeing the [perfect ...] ' individuals: it serves as knowledge [15] of the All since it came into being ' from the powers of the self-begotten ones, ' the one you acquire when you pass ' through the all-perfect aeons. ' When you receive the third [20] washing [...], you will learn ' about the [...] really [...] ' in [that] place.

About these names, ' they are as follows: because ' he is one, they [...] ²⁵ is like [...] ' while he [came into being ...] ' exists and [...] ' a word they [said ...] **26** This is a name which really exists ' together with [these] within her. ' These who exist do so in ' [...] ... resembles. ⁵ His resemblance in kind (is) within what is ' his own. He can see it, understand it ' enter it, (and) ' take a resemblance from it. Now ' (they can) speak aloud and hear sounds, but ¹⁰ they are unable to obey because they ' are perceptible and somatic. ' Therefore, just as they are able to contain ' them by containing them thus, ' so is he an image which is [...] ¹⁵ in this way, having come into existence ' in perception [by] a word which ' is better than material nature ' but lower than intellectual ' essence.

Do not be amazed about the ²⁰ differences among souls. ' When they think they are ' different and do [not resemble] ' [...] of those who [...] and ' that [...] ²⁵ aloud [...] he being lost ' [...] their [souls] ' [...] body, and that ' [... his] time, he ' [...] a desire, **27** their souls exist as [...] ' their body. As for those who are ' totally pure, there are four [...] that they ' possess; but those [in] ⁵ time are nine. Each one ' of them has its species ' and its custom. Their likenesses ' differ in being separated, and ' they stand.

Other immortal souls ¹⁰ associate with all ' these souls because of ' the Sophia who looked down; ' for there are three species of ' immortal soul: first, those who have ¹⁵ taken root upon the Exile ' because they have no ability ' to beget, (something) that only those ' who follow the ways of ' the others have, the one being a ²⁰ single species which ' [...]; being second, those who stand ' [upon the] Repentance which ' [...] sin, ' (it) being sufficient [... knowledge ...] ²⁵ being new [...] ' and he has [...] ' difference [...] they have ' sinned with the others [and] **28** they have repented with the others ' [...] from them alone, ' for [...] are species which exist in ' [...] with those who committed ⁵ all sins and repented. ' Either they are parts, or they ' desired of their own accord. ' Therefore, their other aeons are six ' according to the place which has come ¹⁰ to each (fem.) of them. The ' third (species) is that of the souls of ' the self-begotten ones because they ' have a word of the ineffable ' truth, one which exists in ¹⁵ knowledge and [power] from ' themselves alone and eternal [life]. ' They have four ' differences like the species ' of angels who exist: ²⁰ those who love the truth; ' those who hope; those who ' believe having [...]; those who are [...] ' They exist, he being [...] ²⁵ the self-begotten ones [...] ' he is the one belonging to [perfect ... life]; ' the second is [...] the ' [...]

knowledge ' [...] the fourth is [30] that one [belonging to the] immortal [souls ...]

29 The four Lights dwell ' [there] in the following way. [Armozel] is ' placed upon the first aeon. ' (He is) a promise of god, [...] of [5] truth and a joining of soul. ' Oroiael, a power (and) seer ' of truth, is set over ' the second. Daveithe, a vision ' of knowledge, is set over [10] the third. Eleleth, an eager desire ' and preparation for truth, ' is set over the fourth. ' The four exist because they ' are expressions of truth and [15] knowledge. They exist, although they ' do not belong to Protophanes but ' to the mother, for she is a thought of ' the perfect mind of the ' light, so that immortal souls [20] might receive knowledge for themselves. ' [...] at these, the Autogenes ' [...]rse[...]oas, a ' life [...] all ' he is a word [...] [25] ineffable [...] truth ' he who says [... revelation] ' concerning the [...] ' that it exists as [...] ' exists above in [...] **30** [... joined] in a yoking of it ' in light ' and thought within his ' [...].

Since Adamas, the perfect [5] man, is an eye of Autogenes, ' it is his knowledge which comprehends ' that the divine Autogenes ' is a word of the perfect mind ' of truth. The son of [10] Adam, Seth, comes to ' each of the souls. As knowledge ' he is sufficient for them. Therefore, ' [the] living [seed] came into existence ' from him. Mirothea is [...] [15] the divine Autogenes, a [...] ' from her and [...], she being a thought ' of the perfect mind because of ' that existence of hers. What is it? ' Or did she exist? [...] [20] does she exist? Therefore, ' the divine Autogenes ' is word and knowledge, and the ' knowledge [... word.] ' Therefore [...] [25] Adama[s ...] ' of the [simple ones] when she appeared ' [...] a change of [the] ' souls [...] she herself is [...] ' [...] perfect.

Concerning [30] the [perfect one ...] angelic beings **31** [...] ' [becomes then] ' [souls] ' [die ...] [5] [... the world ...] ' [...] the copies ' [...] really ' [...] which [exists] ' [...] repentance [10] [...] to this place ' [...] which exists ' [...] aeons, if ' [...] and she loves ' [...] she stands upon [15] [...] aeon ' having the Light ' [Ele]leth [...] become a ' [...] god-seer ' [But] if she hopes, then she [20] perceives. And a [...] race ' [...] she stands upon ' [...] ' [...] ' [...] ' [25] [...] ' [...] ' [...] ' [...] ' [...] ' **32** [...] she is chosen ' [...] ' [...] ' [...] light [5] Ar[mozel] '

[...] one [...] ' [bless] ' upon the [power ...] you ' stand upon [...] [10] the light which [...] ' and without measure [...] ' the aeon is great [...] ' [...] those alone [...] ' from the perfect [...] [15] that power [...] ' be able, and [...] ' be able [...] ' of his soul [...] ' perceptible [...] not with [...] [20] [... but] you are [...] ' individually [...] ' there

being nothing [...] ' him [...] ' which he [...] ²⁵ [...] ' [...] ' [...] ' [in ...] **33** and [...] ' upon every one [...] ' every [...] ' [...] formless [...] ⁵ [...] and this one ' [...] and this [model ...] ' [...] and some ' [...] eternal, nor ' [...] an all ¹⁰ [...] increasing from this ' [...] he is light ' [...] because he lacked ' [...] the perfect mind ' [...] undivided ¹⁵ [...] perfect light ' [...] and he is in ' [...] Adamas ' [... the] Autogenes ' [...] and he goes ²⁰ [...] mind ' [...] the divine Kalyptos ' [...] knowledge ' [...] but ' [...] soul ²⁵ [...] ' [...] ' [...] ' [...] ' [...] **34** [...] existence ' [...] she having ' [...] ' [...] some second ⁵ powers and [...] ' and some third [...] ' appear [...] ' which [...] ' [...] ¹⁰ soul [...] '

And the aeons [...] ' dwelling place [...] ' souls and [...] ' gods [...] ¹⁵ higher than god [...] ' of the self-begotten ones [...] ' Autogenes [...] ' first [...] ' angel [...] ²⁰ invisible [...] ' some [...] ' soul and [...] ' aeons [...] ' and to the souls [...] ²⁵ angel [...] ' [...] ' [...] ' [...] ' [...] ³⁰ [...] **35** she [...] ' eternal [...] ' times. And [...] ' [...] ⁵ and if [...] namely a soul ' [...] becomes an ' [angel ...], and [...] ' world [...] angels and ' [...] that holy one ¹⁰ [...] and aeon which ' [... Autog]enes has ' [...] them, the [...] ' [...] archon ' [...] they have ¹⁵ [...] difference which ' [...] she is not, to speak ' [...] ' [...] and ' [...] divine Autogenes ²⁰ [...] which exists' [...] hear ' [...] Autogenes ' [...] of ' [...] ²⁵ [...] ' [...] ' [...] ' [...] ' **36** [...] has ' [...] existence ' [...] life ' [...] exist, concerning [the] ⁵ [...] word [...] ' the child [...] male ' for a generation [...] ' [...] ' invisible spirit [...] ¹⁰ in the perfect [...] ' [...] ' and an origin [...] ' love and [...] ' of Barbelo [...] ¹⁵ and a [...] ' the [...] mind [...] '

These are two [...] ' thought [...] ' from the [...] ²⁰ in Barbelo [...] ' and the Kalyptos [...] ' all these [...] the ' virgin [...] ' she [appears] ²⁵ in a [...] ' and [...] ' [...] ' [...] ' [...] **37** in that one [...] power ' [...] ' [he is not] from [him, but ...] ' (is) from the power of that one ⁵ [... really ... exists], she ' [...] is his ' [...] they being first ' [...] of that one ' [...] and he is the ¹⁰ [...] he alone ' [...] give him enough ' [...] to him ' [...] all, he gives ' [...] through the ¹⁵ [...] for [because of] him some ' [...] in order that he might ' [...] and that one which ' [...] him ' [...] undivided ²⁰ [...] Barbelo ' [...] in order that he might ' [...] blessedness ' [...] ' [...] all ²⁵ [...] he comes ' [...] ' [...] ' [...] ' [...] **38** a [...] of the perfect ' [mind ...] and he ' [...] perfect spirit ' [...] perfect, he lives ⁵ forever [...] ' him, and [...] he ' exists [...] ' of the [...] ' he is [a word] from [...] ¹⁰ which is in [...]

ᐧ of them all [...] ᐧ eternal [...] ᐧ [...] in the triple-[powerful ᐧ is in the [...] [15] [...] those which [are ᐧ perfect [...] ᐧ the Protophanes [...] ᐧ mind, but [...] ᐧ pure [...] [20] and he [...] ᐧ of an image [...] ᐧ appear [...] ᐧ and the [...] ᐧ [...] [25] him [...] ᐧ [...] ᐧ [...] ᐧ [...] ᐧ [...] [30] [...] **39** [...] ᐧ [...] namely ᐧ [...] ᐧ [...] [5] [...] because of him they ᐧ [...] I mark it ᐧ [...] he is simple ᐧ [...] for he is ᐧ [...] as he exists [10] [...] as to another ᐧ [...] that is, ᐧ [...] need.

Concerning ᐧ [...] triple-male ᐧ [...] really exists of [15] [...] mind knowledge ᐧ [...] those who exist ᐧ [...] which he has ᐧ [...] really exist ᐧ [...] and a [...] [20] [...] and she ᐧ [...] second ᐧ [...] perfect which ᐧ [...] appear ᐧ [...] in him they [25] [...] Kalyptos ᐧ [...] ᐧ [...] ᐧ [...] ᐧ [... species ...] [30] [...] ᐧ [...] **40** [...] ᐧ [...] ᐧ [...] ᐧ [...] [5] second species [...] ᐧ a knowledge [...] ᐧ [Protophanes ...] ᐧ [male ...] ᐧ he has [...] [10] existence [...] ᐧ unborn, they [...] ᐧ third [...] ᐧ [... he] has [...] ᐧ knowledge and [...] [15] exist together [...] ᐧ all-perfect [...] ᐧ blessed since there is not [...] ᐧ [...] ᐧ [...] [20] god [...] ᐧ with him [...] ᐧ [...] ᐧ perfect [...] ᐧ of the [...] [25] Kalyptos [...] ᐧ [...] ᐧ [...] ᐧ [...] ᐧ [...] **41** [...] know ᐧ [...] of ᐧ [... Protophanes ...] ᐧ [...] the mind [5] [...] the powers ᐧ [...] the all ᐧ [...] and he [exists] ᐧ [...] this knowledge. ᐧ

[...] divine, the Autogenes. [10] [The] divine [Autogenes] ᐧ [...] the child ᐧ [...] triple-male, this male ᐧ [...] is [...] and a species ᐧ [...] perfect because it does not have [15] [...] in a ᐧ [...] knowledge like that one ᐧ [...] a being of the individuals ᐧ [and] a single knowledge of the ᐧ individuals [...] according to the all [20] [...] perfect. ᐧ But the male [...] mind ᐧ the Kalyptos, ᐧ [but] the [...] divine Kalyptos ᐧ [...] and a power [25] [...] of all these ᐧ [... really ...] ᐧ [...] ᐧ [...] ᐧ [...] [30] [Protophanes ...] ᐧ [...] **42** [Protophanes ...] ᐧ [...] mind ᐧ [...] ᐧ [...] [5] she who belongs to the all [...] ᐧ unborn [...] ᐧ man [...] ᐧ they [...] ᐧ with that one who [...] [10] and he who [...] ᐧ he who dwells [...] ᐧ [...] in the perceptible [world ...] ᐧ he is alive with that ᐧdead one [...] ᐧ [...] all [...] [15] obtain salvation [...] ᐧ that dead one.

And all of them ᐧ did not need salvation [...] ᐧ first, but they are safe ᐧ and exist very humbly. [20] Now (about) the man [of] those who are dead: ᐧ his soul, [his mind and ᐧ his body all [are dead]. ᐧ Sufferings [...] ᐧ fathers of [...] [25] material [...] ᐧ the fire [...] ᐧ [...] ᐧ [...] ᐧ [...] [30] [...] **43** it crosses over. And the second ᐧ man is the immortal soul ᐧ in those who are dead. ᐧ If it is anxious over itself, then [5] [when it seeks] those ᐧ things which are profitable [according to ...] each one ᐧ of them, [then it] experiences ᐧ bodily suffering. They ᐧ [...] and it [10]

[... because] it has ' an eternal god, it ' associates with daimons. '

Now concerning the man in the ' Exile; when [15] he discovers the ' truth in himself, he is far ' from the deeds of the others ' who exist [wrongly] (and) stumble. ' (Concerning) the man who repents: [20] when he renounces ' the dead and desires ' those things which are because of immortal ' mind and his immortal soul, ' first he [...] makes [25] an inquiry about it, ' not about conduct ' but about their deeds, ' for from him he [...] ' [...] and [30] [...] obtain [...] 44 and the man who can be saved ' is the one who seeks him and ' his mind and who finds each one ' of them. Oh how much power [5] he has! And the man ' who is saved is the one who has not known ' how these [...] ' exist, but he ' himself by means of [the] word [10] as it exists [...] ' received each one [...] ' in every place, having become ' simple and one, for then ' he is saved because he can [15] pass through ' all [these]. He becomes the [...] ' all these. If he ' [desires] again, then he parts ' from them all, and he [20] withdraws to himself [alone]; ' for he can become divine ' by having taken refuge in god.' '

When I heard this, ' I brought a blessing to the living [25] and unborn God ' in truth and (to) the unborn Kalyptos ' and the Protophanes, ' the invisible, male, perfect ' Mind, and the invisible [30] triple-male Child ' [and to the] divine Autogenes. 45 I said to the child of the child ' Ephesek who was with me, "Can ' your wisdom instruct me about ' the scattering of the man [5] who is saved, and (about) ' those who are mixed with him, and ' who those are who share with him, ' in order that the living elect ' might know?"

Then the [10] child of the child Ephesek ' told [me ...] openly, ' "If he withdraws ' to himself alone many ' times, and if he comes into being with reference [15] to the knowledge of the others, ' Mind and the immortal [Origin] will not ' understand. Then ' it has a shortage, [...] ' for he turns, has nothing and [20] separates from it and ' stands [...] and comes into being ' by an alien [impulse ...], ' instead of becoming one. ' Therefore, he bears many forms. [25] When he turns aside, he ' comes into being seeking those things that ' do not exist. When he ' falls down to them in thought ' and knows them in another way [30] because he is powerless, unless perhaps 46 he is enlightened, he becomes ' a product of nature. Thus ' he comes down to birth because of it ' and is speechless because of the [5] pains and infiniteness of matter. Although he possesses an ' eternal and immortal power, ' he is bound within the [movement] ' of the body. He is [made] alive [10] and is bound [always] ' within cruel, ' cutting bonds ' by every evil breath, until ' he [acts] again and begins again [15] to come to his senses.

Therefore, ' powers are appointed for their salvation, ' and each one of them is ' in the world. Within the self-begotten ' ones corresponding to each of [20] the [aeons] stand glories ' so that one who is in the [world] ' might be safe beside them. The glories ' are perfect thoughts appearing in ' powers. They do not perish because they [are] models [25] for salvation [by] which each ' one is saved. ' He receives a model (and) ' strength from each of them, and ' with the glory as a helper [30] he will thus pass out from the world ' [and the aeons . . .].

These **47** are the guardians of the immortal ' soul: Gamaliel and ' Strempsouchos, Akramas ' and Loel, and Mnesinous. [5] [This is the] immortal spirit, Yesseus- ' Mazareu[s]-Ye[s]sedekeus. ' He is [. . .] of the child ' [. . .] or, the child of the child, and ' [. . .] But Ormos [10] is [. . .] on the living seed ' and Kam[. . .]el is the spirit-giving. ' There stand before [them] ' Seisauel and Audael and Abrasax, ' the myriads-Phaleris, Phalses, [15] [and] Eurios, the guardians of ' [the] glory-Stetheus, ' Theo[pe]mptos, Eurumeneus ' and Olsen. Their assistants in ' everything are Ba[. . .]mos, [20] [.]son, Eir[.]n, Lalameus, ' Eidomeneus and Authrounios. ' The judges are Sumphthar, ' Eukrebos and Keilar. ' The inheritor is Samblo. [25] The angels who guide ' the clouds are the clouds Sappho ' and Thouro.''

When he had said ' these things, he told me about all of those ' in the self-begotten [30] aeons. They were all **48** eternal Lights, perfect ' because they were perfected individually. ' I saw corresponding to each one of ' the aeons a living earth, a [5] living water, [air made] ' of light and a fire [that] ' cannot burn, because all of [them . . .] are ' simple and immutable, ' simple and [10] eternal [living beings], ' having [. . .] of ' many kinds, trees ' of many kinds that do not ' perish, [also] tares [15] of this sort and all of these: ' imperishable fruit, ' living men and every species, ' immortal souls, ' every form and [20] species of mind, ' true gods, ' angels existing in ' great glory, an ' indissoluable body, [25] an unborn birth and ' an immovable perception. ' Also there was the one who ' suffers, although he is unable to suffer, ' for he was a power of a power.

49 [. . .] ' [. . .] change ' [. . .] indissoluable ' [. . .] these [5] [. . .] all ' [. . .] they are [. . .] they ' [. . . through all] of them ' [. . . exist] in ' [. . . exist] [10] [. . .] come into being ' [. . .] (lines 12ff do not survive) **50** of [. . .] ' [simple . . .] ' perfect [. . .] ' eternal [. . .] [5] aeons [. . .] ' and the [. . .] ' receive power [. . .] ' and their [. . .] ' in a [. . .] [10] for [. . .] ' [. . .] not [. . .] (lines 12ff do not survive)

51 [. . .] in ' [. . .]thorso[. . .]s ' [. . .] silence ' [. . .] he is [. . .] [5] [. . .]

he is god ' [...] we were blessing ' [...] Geradama[s] ' [... mother] of
[...] ' [...] she is the glory [10] [...] our ' [...] mother ' [...] and
Pleistha ' [the mother] of the angels with ' [the son] of Adam, Se[th] [15]
[Emma]cha Seth, the father of ' [the] immovable [race ...] and [...] '
[the] four Lights, Arm[mosel], ' [Oroia]el, Daveithe, Eleleth. ' [Each of
these] we blessed by name. [20] [We] saw the self-controlled ' [glory], the
triple [...] ' triple-male ' [...] majesty, as we said ' "You are one, you
are [25] [one], you are one, child **52** of [the child] ' Yato[...] ' exist [...]
' [...] [5] [... you are] ' one, you [...] ' Semelel [...] ' Telmachae[...]
' omothem[...] [10] male [...] ' [...] he begets [... the] ' self-controlled
[glory ...] ' can desire him whom [...] ' all-perfect [...] [15] all. Akron
[...] ' the triple-male, a a [...] ' o o o o o b + i r e i s e [...] ' you are
spirit from ' spirit; you are light [20] from light; you are [silence ...] '
from silence; [you are] ' thought from thought, ' the son of [god] ' the
god, seven ... [...] [25] ... let us speak [...] **53** [...] ' [...] ' [...] '
[...] word [5] [...] the [...] ' [...] and the [...] ' [...] ' [...] not a
time ' [...] invisible [10] Barbelo ' [...] the ' [...] the triple-male '
Prones, and she who belongs to ' all the glories, Youel.

[15] [When I was] baptized the fifth ' [time] in the name of the '
Autogenes by ' each of these powers, I ' became divine. [20] [I] stood
upon the fifth ' aeon, a preparation of ' all [these], (and) saw all those
' belonging to the Autogenes ' who really exist. [25] I was baptized five **54**
times [...] ' and [...] ' of the [...] ' zareu[s] [5] from [...] ' that [...]
' perfect [...] ' and the great [...] ' glory, she who belongs to [...] [10]
[...] ' god, the [...] ' appear [...] ' perfect which is doubled [...] '
she who belongs to all the species [...] [15] male, the self-controlled '
glory, the mother [...] ' [the] glories, Youel, and the ' [four] Lights of
[the] ' [great] Protophanes, [20] Mind, Selmen, [and those] ' with him,
the ' god-[revealers] Zach[thos] ' and Yachthos, Sethe[us] ' and An-
tiphan[te]s, [Sel-] [25] dao and Ele[n]nos [...] **55** [...] ' [...] go ' [...]
the ' [...] their [5] [...] likeness ' [... exist] as ' [...] of the ' [...], for
[...] see [...] ' [...] aeon [10] [...] more ' [...] Light ' [...] more
glories ' [...] the following are in accordance with ' [each one] of the
aeons: a [15] living [earth] and a ' [living] water, and air made of ' light
and a blazing ' fire which cannot ' [burn], and living beings and [20] trees
and souls ' [and] minds and men ' [and] all those who are ' [with them],
but (there are) no gods ' [or] powers or [25] angels, for all these **56** are
[...] ' and [...] ' and [...] ' exist [...] [5] all [...] ' all [...] ' [...] all
[...] ' [...] they being [...] ' and they being [...]

[10] [...] and [...] ' [and] those [...] ' him, the Autogenes. [I] '

received a likeness from [all] these. ' The aeons [of the] Autogenes [15] opened (and) a [great Light] ' came forth [...] ' from the aeons of the [triple-] ' male, and they [glorified] ' them. The four [20] aeons were desiring ' within a [...] aeon ' the [...] pattern [...] ' single one existing [...] ' Then E[phesek], the [25] child of the child [...] 57 [...] ' [...] ' [...] ' [...] [5] [... Yesseus] Maza ' [reus Yessede]keus [...] ' [...] of ' [... seal ...] upon him ' [...] and Gabriel [10] [...] ' [...] seal ' [...] four races '

There came before me she who belongs to ' [the glories], the male and [15] [virginal ...] Yoel. ' [I] deliberated about the crowns, ' (and) she said to me, "Why ' [has] your spirit deliberated ' [about] the crowns and the [20] [seals] on them ' [...] are the crowns which strengthen ' every [spirit ...] and every soul, ' and [the] seals which are ' [upon] the triple races and [25] [...] the invisible spirit 58 are [...] ' [...] ' [...] ' [...] [5] and [...] ' [virgin ...] ' [...] and [...] ' [...] seek [...] ' [...] in the [...] [10] [in] them [...] ' [...] and [...] ' [...] he [strengthened] ' and the seals [...] ' race are those belonging to the Autogenes [15] and the Protophanes ' and the Kalyptos.

The [Invisible] ' Spirit [is] a psychic ' and intellectual power, ' a knower and [20] a fore-knower. Therefore ' he is with [Gabriel] ' the spirit-giver [so that] ' when he gives a ' holy spirit he might [25] seal him with the crown and crown him, ' [having] gods [...] 59 [...] ' [...] the ' [...] ' [...] [5] [...] the ' [...] ' [...] ' [...] spirit ' [...] to one (fem.) [10] [...] ' [...] they exist ' [...] and they were ' not [in] them in order that they might ' [become] simple [15] and [might] not be doubled ' [according to] any pattern. ' [These] then are the ' simple, perfect individuals. ' [...] and all these [20] [...] of the aeons ' [...] him, all these ' [...] who exist in a place ' [...] all-perfect it required a great ' [...] to see them, [25] for [...] 60 [...] ' [...] ' [...] ' perfect [...] [5] [...] ' [...] ' [...] every [...] ' exist [...] ' he is [...] [10] [hear] him [...] ' [...] and [...] ' in thought [...] ' a first thought [...] ' since [...] is in a power [15] she is perfect [...] ' it is fitting for you to [...] ' about everything, and [...] ' those to whom you will listen ' through a thought [20] of those higher than perfect ' and also those whom you will [know] ' in a soul [of] ' the perfect ones." '

[When] she has said this, she [baptized me] 61 [...] ' [...] ' [...] ' [...] [5] [...] ' [...] ' [...] the first ' [... and] I received power ' [...] [10] [... I] received the form ' [...] received [...] ' [...] existing upon my ' [...] receive a holy spirit ' [I] came into being [really] existing. [15] Then, she brought me ' into the great [aeon] ' where the perfect ' triple-

male (is). ' I saw [20] the invisible child ' within an invisible ' Light. Then ' [she] baptized me again in **62** [...] ' [...] ' [...] ' [...] [5] [...] her [...] ' [...] ' [and] I [...] ' I was able to [...] ' [...] the great one [...] [10] and perfect [...] '

Yoel who belongs to all [the glories] ' said to me, ' "You have [received] all the [baptisms] ' in which it is fitting to [be] baptized, [15] and you have become [perfect] ' [...] the hearing of [...] ' all. Now [call] again ' upon Salamex and [...] ' and the all-perfect Ar[...] [20] the Lights of the [aeon] ' Barbelo and the immeasurable ' knowledge. They ' will reveal **63** [...] ' [...] invisible ' [...] ' [...] [5] [...] ' [...] which [...] ' [... virgin] Barbelo ' [and] the Invisible ' [triple] powerful Spirit."

[When] [10] Youel who belongs to all the glories ' [had said this] to me, she ' [put me down] and went and stood ' before the Protophanes. ' Then, I was [15] [...] over my spirit, ' [while] praying fervently to the great ' Lights in ' thought. I began calling ' upon Salamex and Se- [20] [...]en and the all-perfect ' [...]e. I saw ' glories which are ' greater than powers, ' [and] they annointed me. I was able **64** [...] ' in my [...] ' and [...] ' [...]

[5] [...] ' she covered [...] ' all [...] ' Salamex [and] ' those [who] have revealed [10] everything [to me] saying, ' "Zostrianos, [learn] ' of those things ' about which you asked. ' [...] ' and [he is] a single one [who] [15] exists before [all] these ' who really exist [in the] ' immeasurable and undivided ' Spirit [...] ' [...] the All which [exists] [20] in him and the [...] ' [...] and that one which [...] ' after him. It is he alone ' who crosses it [...]

65[...] ' [...] ' [...] ' [...] [5] [...] all these ' [...] he is [...] ' [...] first [...] ' [... of] thought ' [...] of every power [10] [... downward] ' [...] he is established ' [...] stand, he [passes] ' into the pathway to a place ' [...] and infinite. [15] He is far higher than ' every unattainable one, yet he gives ' [...] greater than any body ' (and) is purer than every unembodied one, ' entering every [20] thought and every body ' [because he] is more powerful than everything, every race and species, ' as their All. **66** [...] exist ' [...] ' [...] ' [...] [5] [...] ' to a partial [...] ' [...] part [...] ' [exist] in a [...] ' know her [...] [10] [... he is] from him ' [...] which really exists, ' who (is) from ' the Spirit who [really] exists, ' the one alone [...] [15] for they are powers of ' [...] Existence [...] ' and Life and ' Blessedness.

In ' Existence he exists [as] [20] a simple head, ' his [word] and species. ' Let the one who will find ' him come into existence. ' Existing in [25]

Life, he is alive [. . .] **67** [. . .] ' [. . .] ' [he having] knowledge ' [. . .] know all these [5] [. . .] him alone ' [. . .] for god [. . .] ' unless [. . .] ' [. . .] alone, and he [. . .] ' [. . .] in him [. . .] [10] [. . .] the single [. . .] ' [. . .] for he exists as [. . .] ' [in] that which is his, which ' [exists] as a form of a form, ' [. . .] unity of the [15] [. . .]. He exists as [the] ' [. . .] since he is in ' [the] mind. He is within ' it, not coming forth to any ' place because he is a single [20] perfect, simple spirit. ' [Because] it is his place and ' [. . .], it is within him and the All ' that he comes into being. ' It is he who exists, he who **68** [. . .] ' [. . .] and a [. . .] ' and a [protector] ' in him.

Life [. . .] [5] and activity of the ' insubstantial [. . .] the [. . .] ' which exists in him ' [exists] in him [. . .] ' exists because of [him . . .] [10] blessed and a [. . .] ' perfect, and [. . .] ' which exist in [. . .] ' which really exists. ' The form of the activity [15] which exists is blessed. ' By receiving Existence, ' he receives power, the [. . .] ' a perfection [. . .] ' separate forever. Then [20] he exists as a perfect one. Therefore, ' he exists as a perfect one ' because he is undivided ' with his own region, ' for nothing exists [25] before him except ' the [perfect] unity.

(Pages 69-72 are blank; they may have been numbered.)

73 existence [. . .] ' [. . .] she is salvation [. . .] ' [all . . .] and he [. . .] ' [. . .] be able, nor does he [. . .] [5] [. . .] him, if he ' [. . .] him to him, all these [. . .] ' [. . .] for he [who] ' [. . .] in existence ' [. . .] this one, he totally [10] [exists] as Life, and in ' Blessedness he has knowledge. ' If he apprehends the ' [glories], he is perfect; ' but if he apprehends [15] [two] or one, he is drunk, ' as he has received ' [from] him. It is because of [him] ' that there exist those with souls ' and those without souls; [20] because of him (exist) those who will be saved; ' because of him (exist) those who will ' [perish] since they have not [received] ' from him; because of ' [him] (exists) matter and [25] bodies; because of him (exist) non- **74** [. . .] ' [because of] him [. . .] ' every [. . .] because of [. . .] ' [. . .] this one [. . .] who [pre-] [5] exists and he [. . .] ' [. . .] a [simple] head, ' [a] single spirit [. . .] ' he is [. . .], and [. . .] ' existence, form, [. . .] [10] [. . .] of him.

It is [in accordance with] ' Activity, that is [. . .] Life, ' and in accordance with perfection, ' that is intellectual ' power, that she is a [. . .] Light. [15] It is at one time that the three stand, ' at one time they move. ' It is in every place yet ' not in any place that the ineffable ' unnameable one [. . .] [20] and produces ' them all. [. . .] ' exist from him[. . .] ' resting in him [. . .] ' in her perfection [25] he has not received from [every] form **75** because of him ' [. . .] ' [. . .] ' [. . .] anything

[...] [5] [...] ' [...] ' [...] in existence ' [...] dwell in the ' [...] of life. But in [10] perfection and ' [knowledge] (is) Blessedness. '

All [these] dwell ' [in the] indivisibility of ' [the] Spirit. Because of [15] knowledge [...] is ' [divinity] and [...] ' and blessedness ' and life and ' knowledge and goodness [20] and unity ' and singleness. ' In short, all these (are) the ' purity of barrenness ' [...] pre-exists him [25] [...] all these and the **76** [...] his [...] ' [...] in [...] ' [...] ' [...] [5] [...] ' [...] ' aeon, a [...] ' in a [...] ' barrenness, he [...] [10] he always [...] ' him when he saw him [...] ' It is because he [is] one that he is ' simple. Because he is ' Blessedness in [15] perfection [...] one, ' perfect and [blessed]. ' It is because she was in need of his [...] ' that she was in need of this from him, ' because he followed [her] [20] with knowledge. ' It is outside of him that ' his knowledge dwells; ' it dwells with the one who ' examines himself, [25] a reflection and a [...] **77** [...] be in need of [...] ' [...] ' [...] simple ' [...] [5] [...] and ' [...] he [...] ' [...] this, she [...] ' [...] the pleroma ' [...] which she did not desire [10] for herself.

She has ' [...] him outside of the ' [perfection], she has divided, ' for she is [the] all-perfection ' [of] perfection, [15] existing as thought. ' With respect to him ' [she] is a begetting which follows ' him, and as one from ' his ineffable power [20] she has ' a first power and ' the first barreness ' after him, ' because with respect to all the [25] rest a first aeon **78** [...] ' [...] ' [...] ' [all ...] [5] [...] ' [...] of the [...] ' [...] and him [...] ' know him, he really ' exists as an aeon [...] [10] and in Activity [...] ' power and a [...] ' she did not begin [...] ' time, but she [appeared] ' from eternity, [15] having stood before ' him in eternity. ' She was darkened by the ' majesty of his [...] ' She stood [20] looking at him and rejoicing ' because she was filled with his ' kindness, [...] ' but when she had [...] **79** [...] ' [...] ' [...] ' [...] [5] [...] ' [...] she [...] ' [...] first existence ' [...] insubstantial and ' that [....] [10] It is [from] the undivided one ' that [it] moves toward Existence ' in activity and [intellectual] ' perfection and intellectual life, ' which was [15] Blessedness and ' Divinity.

The [whole] Spirit, ' perfect, simple ' and invisible, ' has become singleness [20] in Existence and ' activity and a ' simple triple-[power], ' an invisible spirit, an ' image of that which [25] really exists, the one **80** [...] ' [...] ' [...] ' [...] [5] [...] ' of the really [existing] one [...] ' [he] exists in a [...] ' she being an image [...] ' in a turning [...] [10] power to join with his [...] ' she having seen the [...] ' which existed [...] ' all-perfection [...] ' that one, because he [...] [15] pre-exist and

[...] ' rest upon all these, he [...] ' pre-exist being known ' as triple-powerful.

The ' Invisible Spirit has not [20] ever [been] ignorant. He always ' knew, but he was always ' perfection [and] ' blessedness [....] **81** She became ignorant [...] ' and she [...] ' body and [...] ' promise [...] [5] light [...] ' [...] she exists [...] ' [...] in order that ' she might not come forth anymore ' nor come into existence apart [10] from perfection. She ' knew herself and him. ' Having made herself stand, ' she was at rest ' because of him, [15] since she was ' [from] him who really exists, ' {she was from him who ' really exists} and all ' those. (Thus), she knows herself [20] and him who pre-exists. '

By following him ' they came into being existing {they ' came into being existing} and ' appearing through those **82** [who pre-]exist. And ' [...] through the ' [...] they having appeared ' [...] two [5] [...] they appeared ' [... the one] who ' knows him beforehand, as ' an eternal space, ' since he had become [10] his second knowledge, ' once again the knowledge of ' his knowledge, the unborn ' Kalyptos. [They] ' stood upon him [15] who really exists, ' for she knew about him, ' in order that those who follow ' her might come into being having ' a place and that [20] those who come forth (from her) ' might not be before her but ' might become holy ' (and) simple. She is the ' comprehension of god **83** who pre-[exists. She] ' rested [...] ' to the simple [...] ' salvation [5] salvation [...] ' [...] he [...] ' [...] light which was fore- ' [known]. She was called ' Barbelo because (of her being) [10] thought; the triple [race] ' (which is) male, virginal ' (and) perfect and her ' knowledge through which she came ' into being in order that they might not [15] [...] her down and that ' she might not come forth anymore ' through those ' in her and those who follow ' her. Rather, she is [20] simple in order that she might ' be able to know the god ' who pre-exists because ' she came into being as a good (product) ' of him since she [25] [...] **84** [...] barrenness ' [...] third ' [...] two ' [...] of this way [...] [5] [...] and male [...] ' [...] ' [...] and the ' [...] barrenness [...] ' [...] she is a second [...] [10] she stood [...] ' first of the reality [which] ' really exists [...] ' [...] the blessedness [...] ' of the Invisible [Spirit], [15] the knowledge [...] the first ' existence in the ' simplicity of the ' Invisible Spirit ' in the unity. It is in [20] that pure singleness that ' he is similar and [...] ' species. And he who [...] ' exist [...] **85** [...] ' [...] ' [...] ' [...] [5] [...] ' [...] ' [...] and knows ' [...] and the ' [...] and the [perfection] [10] and [...] produces and ' [...] the first Kalyptos ' [...] them all, ' existence and activity, ' divinity, race [15] and species.

But are powers ' one? In what way ' (is it) that he is one, that is, ' not a partial one, but ' (one of) those of the All? What [20] is the unity which is unity? ' Is he from ' [. . .] activity [. . .] life ' and [. . .] of ' [. . .]. And [. . .] **86** [. . .] ' [. . .] ' [. . .] ' [. . .] [5] [. . .] ' [. . .] ' [. . .] ' power [. . .] ' as [. . .]

[10] [. . .] perceptible [. . .] ' [. . .] all-perfect [. . .] ' [. . .] she having spoken, [. . .] ' "You are great, Aphr[edon].' You are perfect, Neph[redon]." [15] To his existence she says, ' "You are great, Deipha[. . .]. ' She [is] his activity and life ' and divinity. ' You are great, Harmedon [. . .], [20] who belongs to all the glories, Epiph[a- ' and his blessedness and ' the perfection [of] the ' singleness [. . .] ' all [. . .]" **87** [. . .] ' [. . .] ' [. . .] ' [. . .] [5] [. . .] ' [. . .] ' [. . .] forever ' [. . .] intellectual ' [. . .perfect] [10] [the virgin Barb]elo ' through the simplicity ' of the blessedness ' of the triple powerful ' Invisible Spirit. She [15] who has known him ' has known herself. And he, being ' one everywhere, being ' undivided, having ' [. . .] has [. . .] and she has known [20] [herself as] his activity ' [. . .] and he has known ' [. . .] knowledge ' [. . .] within **88** [. . .] ' [. . .] ' [. . .] ' [. . .] [5] [. . .] ' [. . .] ' [. . .] ' [. . .] ' bless [. . .] [10] [. . .] Be[ritheus, Erignaor], ' Or[imeni]os, Ar[amen], ' Alphl[ege]s, Elilio[upheus], ' Lalamenu[s], Noetheus [. . .] ' great is your name [. . .] [15] it is strong. He who knows (it) ' knows everything. You are ' one, you are one, Siou, E[. . .], ' Aphredon, you are the [aeon] ' of the aeons of the [20] perfect great one, the first ' Kalyptos of the [. . .] ' activity, and [. . .] ' he is [. . .] ' his image [. . .] [25] of his, he [. . .]

89 [. . .] ' [. . .] ' [. . .] ' [. . .] [5] [. . .] ' [. . .] ' [. . .] ' [. . .] ' [. . . existence] [10] [. . .] and he ' [. . .] ' [. . .] ' [. . .] in ' [. . . the glory] [15] [. . .] glories ' [. . .] a ' [. . .] in ' [. . .] ' [. . .] [20] [. . .] ' [. . .] aeon ' [. . .] ' [. . .] ' [. . .] **90** [. . .] ' [. . .] ' [. . .] ' [. . .] [5] [. . .] ' [. . .] ' [. . .] ' [. . .] ' exist [. . .] [10] [. . .] ' [. . .] ' [and ' [. . .] ' [. . .] [15] [. . .] ' [blessed . . .] ' [. . .] ' [perfect . . .] ' [. . .] [20] [. . .] ' [. . .] ' [. . .] ' [. . .] ' [. . .] [25] [. . .] **91** [. . .] ' [. . .] ' [. . .] ' [. . .] [5] [. . .] ' [. . .] ' [. . .] ' [. . .] ' [. . .] god [10] [. . .] ' [. . .] ' [. . .] ' [. . .] first ' [. . .] and powers [15] [. . . all-perfect] ' they are [. . .] ' of all these and a ' cause of [them] all, a ' [. . .] Barbelo ' [. . .] [20] [. . .] him and ' [. . .] all these ' [. . .] he not having ' [. . .] and his ' [. . .] become [25] [. . .] but **92** [. . .] ' [. . .] ' [. . .] ' [. . .] [5] [. . .] ' [. . .] ' [. . .] ' [. . .] ' [. . .] [10] of [. . .] ' [. . .] ' [and . . .] ' [. . .] ' [. . .] [15] and a [. . .] ' in a [. . .] ' according to the [thought] which ' really [exists . . .] which exists as [. . .] ' name [. . .] [20] [. . .] ' Kalyptos [. . .] ' the [. . .] ' triple [. . .] ' [. . .] [25] but [. . .] **93** name him.

All these come, ' as it were, ' from him who is pure. ' If you give

glory [5] because of him, and if you ' [. . .] existence ' [. . .] his ' [. . .] a
' [. . .] simple [10] [. . .] ' [. . .] ' [. . .] he will ' [. . .] ' [. . .] that one [15]
[. . . know] him ' [. . .] ' [. . .] perfect ' he being [. . . perfect] ' and [. . .]
[20] [. . .] perfect ' [. . .] ' [. . .] his ' [. . .] ' [. . .] him [25] [. . .] to the ' [. . .]
94 he was not able to see her. ' Therefore, it is impossible to receive '
him in this way in ' majestic purity [5] as a perfect head of ' [him who] is
in [. . .] ' [. . .] which ' [. . . know] him ' concerning [. . .] say [10] it [. . .]
' [. . .] ' [. . .] ' which [. . .] ' [. . .] [15] [. . .] ' which [. . .] for ' [. . .] ' [. . .
exist] together ' [. . .] and [. . .] [20] [. . .] ' [. . .] ' [. . .] ' [. . .] ' [. . .] [25]
nor [. . .] **95** differences between these and ' angels, and differences '
between these and men, ' and differences between [5] these and existence.
' And [. . .] ' [. . .] ' [. . .] and [perception] ' [. . .] [10] [. . .] ' [. . .] really
' [. . .] ' for [. . .] the [perceptible] ' world [. . .] like [15] [. . .] ' existence
[. . .] ' for [. . .] ' and [. . .] ' [. . .] (lines 20ff do not survive) **96** will approach him in knowledge. ' He receives power, but he who is ' far from
him is humbled.'' '

And I said, ''Why [5] then have the judges come ' into being? What
[. . .] is the [suffering] of ' the [. . .] for ' [. . .] ' and [. . .] [10] [. . .] '
[. . .] ' but [. . .] ' [. . .] ' through [. . .] who [. . .] [15] suffering [. . .]
through [. . .] ' the [. . .] ' [. . .] exists ' [. . .] she ' dwells [. . .] [20] [. . .]
' [. . .] (lines 22ff, ca. 4 lines, do not survive) **97** male, since she is
knowledge [of] ' the triple powerful invisible ' great Spirit, the image of
' [the first] Kalyptos, the [5] [blessedness] in the ' [invisible] Spirit, [. . .]
the ' [. . .] ' [. . .] for ' [. . .] he knows [10] [. . .] ' [. . .] ' [. . .] ' [. . .] fill
' [. . .] she [15] appears [. . .] ' knowledge [. . .] she ' stands [. . .] ' [. . .]
' [. . .] [20] [. . .] (lines 21ff, ca. 6 lines, do not survive) **98** [. . .] a perfect
unity of ' a complete unity, and ' when she divided the All [. . .] ' from
the All [. . .] [5] existence and [. . .] ' [. . .] the thoughts [. . .] ' [. . .] '
[. . .] ' [perception] [10] [. . .] ' [. . .] ' [. . .] ' [. . .] ' [. . .] [15] [. . .] ' [. . .]
' [. . .] ' [. . .] ' [. . .] [20] [. . .] ' [. . .] (lines 22ff, ca. 5 lines, do not survive) **99** [. . .] ' [existence . . .] ' [. . .] in [. . .] which ' [. . .] [5] knowledge
' [. . .] ' [. . .] ' [. . .] ' [. . .] she blesses [10] [. . .] ' [. . .] ' [. . .] ' [. . .] '
[. . .] which [15] [. . .] ' [. . .] and ' [. . .] ' [. . .] ' [. . .] [20] [. . .] (lines 21ff,
ca. 6 lines, do not survive)

100 [. . .] ' [. . .] ' [. . .] ' [. . .] [5] [. . .] ' Arm[ozel ' [. . .] ' [. . .] ' is the
[. . .] [10] [through . . .] ' power [. . .] ' [. . .] ' [. . .] ' [. . .] [15] which [. . .]
' [. . .] ' [. . .] ' [. . .] ' [. . .] [20] [. . .] ' [. . .] (lines 22ff, ca. 4 lines, do not
survive) **101** [. . .] invisible [. . .] ' [. . .] that one [. . .] ' [. . . this] is the
[. . .] ' [. . .] [5] [. . .] ' form ' [. . .] ' [. . .] ' [. . .] of a ' [. . .] [10] [. . .] ' [. . .]
' [. . .] Kalyptos ' [. . .] undivided ' [. . .] [15] [. . .] ' [. . .] ' [. . .] ' [. . .]

' [...] (lines 20ff, ca. 4 lines, do not survive) **102** [...] which exist [...]
' [...] the [...] ' [...] ' and [...] ⁵ [...] ' [...] ' [...] ' [...] ' he [...]
¹⁰ [...] ' [...] ' [...] ' and [...] ' those [...] ¹⁵ a [...] ' [...] ' [...]
' [...] ' some [...] ²⁰ [...] ' [...] (lines 22ff, ca. 4 lines, do not survive) **103** [...] origin [...] ' [which] really exists [...] ' [...] exist [...
essence] ' [...] in ⁵ [... this] is ' [...] the ' [...] ' [...] ' [...] ¹⁰ [...]
' [...] ' [...] they ' [...]not ' [...] ¹⁵ [...] this ' [...] ' [...] ' [...] '
[...] (lines 20ff, ca. 6 lines, do not survive)

104 [...] she appears ' [...] of those who [...] ' [...] of the [...] '
and [...] ⁵ this [...] ' the [...] ' [...] ' see [...] ' [...] ¹⁰ [...] ' [...]
' [...] ' [...] ' he [...] ¹⁵ really [...] ' [...] ' that [...] ' and [...] '
[...] ²⁰ [...] ' [...] ' [...] ' [...] (lines 24ff, ca. 4 lines, do not survive)
105 are those who [stand ...] ' the aeon of [...] ' come up to [...] '
[...] which ⁵ exist in [...] he ' on the one hand [...] ' [...] he ' [...]
one ' [...] an origin ¹⁰[...] ' [...] and ' [...] he ' [...] matter ' [...]
single ¹⁵ [...] ' [... exist] ' [...] ' [...] ' [...] which ²⁰ [...] and '
[...] (lines 22ff, ca. 4 lines, do not survive) **106** [...] and he exists '
[...] he is [...] and ' [...] mark of a [...] ' [...] an ⁵ [...] nor of
[...] ' [...] he [...] ' which [...] ' [...] ' [...] ¹⁰ and [...] ' [...] '
number [...] ' live [...] ' according to [...] ¹⁵ which [...] ' [...] '
[...] ' [...] ' [...] ²⁰ which [...] ' [...] ' [...] (lines 23ff, ca. 4 lines,
do not survive) **107** them [...] ' [...] and [...] ' existence [...] ' [...]
and the [...] exist ⁵ as [...] ' reflection [...] first ' [...] ' [...] first '
[...] of the ¹⁰ [...] ' [...] ' [...] he ' [...] ' [...] ¹⁵ [...] ' [...] ' [...]
' [...] ' [...] ²⁰ [...] ' [...] (lines 22ff, ca. 6 lines, do not survive) **108**
[...] not, they giving [...] ' [...] he who exists [...] ' [...] all and ' he
[...] a multitude ⁵ [...] creation ' [...] ' and [...] ' [...] ' [...] ¹⁰ the
[...] ' [...] ' in the [...] ' these [...] ' the [...] ¹⁵ of [...] ' alive [...]
' [...] ' [...] ' [...] ²⁰ [...] ' in [...] ' [...]

(Pages 109-112 do not survive)

113 and angels and ' daimons and minds and ' souls and living beings
and ' trees and bodies and ⁵ those which are before them: those ' of the
simple elements ' of simple origins, and ' those which are in ' [...] and
unmixed confusion, air ¹⁰ [and] water and earth ' and number and yoking ' and movement and [...] ' and order and breath and ' all the rest.
They are ¹⁵ fourth powers which are ' [in] the fourth aeon, those '
which] are in the [...] and ' [...] perfect of [...] powers ' [...] powers
[...] of ²⁰ [...] of ' [...] angels ' [of the] angels, souls ' [of the] souls,
living beings ' [of the] living beings, trees [of] ²⁵ [the trees ...] ' [...]
and [...] ' [...] ' [...] **114** his own.

There are those ' who are as begotten, and ' those who are in an unborn ' begetting, and there are those [5] who are holy and eternal, ' and
the immutable ones ' in death and ' destruction in indestructibility; '
and there are those who are as [10] All; there are those [who are] ' races
and those who are [in] ' a world and order; there are ' those in [in-
destructibility], ' and there are the first [who stand] [15] and the second
[in] ' all of them. [All] those [who] ' are from them and [those who] '
are [in] them, and [from] ' these who [follow] them [...] [20] [...] ' these
[...] ' and [the] fourth aeons ' stood [...] ' [...] they existing [...] [25]
[...] ' [...] **115** in them, he being scattered abroad. ' They are not
crowded against one another, ' but to the contrary they are alive, ' existing in themselves and [5] agreeing with one another, as ' they are from
a single ' origin. They are reconciled ' because they are all ' in a single
aeon of Kalyptos, [10] [...] being divided in power, ' for they exist in accord with each ' of the aeons, standing in ' relationship to the one which
has reached them. '

But Kalyptos is [a] single aeon; [15] [he] has four different ' aeons. In
accord with ' each of the aeons ' they have powers, not ' like first and
second (powers), [20] for all these [are] ' eternities, [but] they are different
' [...] and order and glory ' [...] which exists ' [in ...] four aeons and
[25] [...] who pre-exists ' [...] god [...] ' [...] they are [...] ' [...]

116 All of them exist ' in one, dwelling together ' and perfected individually ' in fellowship and [5] filled with the aeon which ' really exists.
There are ' those among them (who stand) ' as dwelling in essence ' and
those (who stand) as essence [10] in conduct or [suffering] because ' they
are in a second, for ' the unengenderedness of the ungenerated ' one
who really exists ' is among them. When the ungenerated [15] have come
into being, their power ' stands; there is an ' incorporeal essence with
[an] ' imperishable [body]. The ' [immutable one] is [there] [20] who [real-
ly] exists. ' Because it transforms [through] ' change, the [...] in
destructible fire ' stands with [all] ' [these ...] [25] [...] one [...] **117** he
stands. It is there that ' all living beings dwell, ' existing individually
(yet) all ' joined together. The knowledge [5] of the knowledge is there '
together with a setting up of ignorance. ' Chaos is there ' and a perfect
place ' for all of them, and they are strange. [10] True Light (is there), '
also enlightened darkness together with the one ' who does not really
exist − ' [he] does not really exist. ' [...] the non-being who does [15] not
exist at all. But it is he, the ' Good, from whom derives ' the good and
what is pleasant ' and the divine; (it is he) from ' [whom] comes God
and he who [20] [...], he who is great. ' For [...] in part ' [...] form and

God ' that [. . .] and the one [. . .] ' [. . .] a god [. . .] [25] [. . .] all these
[. . .] ' [. . .] darkness [. . .] ' [. . .] **118** and a race. He has ' not mixed
with anything, but he remains ' alone in himself and ' rests himself on
his [5] limitless limit. ' He is [the] God of those who ' really exist, a seer
' and a revealer of God. '

When she had strengthened him who [knew her], [10] the aeon Barbelo,
the ' knowledge of the Invisible Triple ' Powerful Perfect Spirit, in
order to [. . .] ' her, said, "He [. . .] ' a life. I am alive in [. . .] [15] You,
the One, are alive. He is alive, [he] ' who is three. It is you who are [the]
' three who are three [doubled . . .] ' e e e. The first of seven [. . .] ' the
third [. . .] [20] the second [. . .] ' e e e e a a a a a a a a [. . .] ' [. . .] two, but
he [four . . .] ' [. . .] knowledge [. . .] ' [. . .]

[25] [. . .] **119** a part? What kind of mind, and ' what kind of wisdom?
What kind of understanding, ' what kind of teaching? His ' Lights are
named (as follows): the first [5] [is Arme]don and she who is with him, '
[. . .]; the second is ' Diphane [. . . and] she who is with him, Dei- ' ph[a
. . .]; the third is ' [Malsed]on and she who is with him [10] [. . .]; the
fourth is ' [. . .]s and she who is with him, Olmis. '

Kalyptos exists having ' [. . .] with his Form. ' He is invisible to all [15]
these so that they all might be ' strengthened by him [. . .] ' [. . .] he exists in ' [. . .] all-perfect because ' [he has] four existing [20] [. . .] ' [. . .]
nor according to a ' [. . .] alone ' [. . . B]arbelo [. . .] ' [. . .] [25] [. . .] **120**
know him and the one who is set ' over a second. The first ' of the aeons
is Harmedon, ' the father-glory. The second [5] Light (is) one whom [he
does] not [know], ' but all the [individuals], ' wisdom [. . .] exist ' in the
fourth aeon ' who has revealed [himself] [10] and all the glories. [The
third] ' Light (is) he [. . .] ' not him, as the word of all ' [the forms] and
that other ' [glory], understanding, [who is] [15] in the third [aeon]. '
There are four in ' Malsedon and [. . .] ' nios. The fourth ' Light is the
one who [. . .] [20] of all the forms ' existing [. . .] ' a teaching and glory
[. . .] ' and the truth of the [four aeons], ' Olmis, [. . .] and the [. . .] [25]
[. . .] ' [. . .] **121** fifth.

The first (is the one) ' who is the second, that is, it is ' the all-perfect
Kalyptos, ' for the four Lights [5] exist. It is Kalyptos who has ' divided
again, and they exist together. ' All who know those who ' exist as
glories ' are perfect. This one [10] [. . .] knows everything about ' them all
is all-perfect. ' From him is every ' power, every one and ' their entire
aeon, because they all [15] come to him and ' they all come from him, '
the power of them ' all (and) the origin of them all. ' When he learned
[20] [of them], he became a ' [. . .] aeon and a ' ingenerateness. ' [. . .]

other aeons ' [in ...] a [...] [25] [...] ' [...] **122** become a Barbelo, he ' becomes a first aeon ' because of the eternity of the ' Invisible Spirit, the second [5] ingenerateness.

These are all ' the glories: the limitless ' Aphredons, [...] the ' ineffables, the revealers, ' all the [...] immutables, [10] the glory-revealers, ' the twice-revealed ' Marsedons, the limitless Solmises, ' the self-revealers ' who are [full] [15] of glory, those who [wait for] ' glory, the blessers, the M[arse-] ' dons, the Kalyptoi who [...] ' the limits [...] ' upon the limits [...] [20] those who exist [...] ' [...] ' [...] ' [...] (Lines 24ff, 1 or 2, do not survive) **123** ten thousand glories ' in them.

Therefore, he is ' a perfect glory so that whenever ' he can join (another) and [5] prevail, he exists as perfect. ' Thus, even if he enters ' into a body and a death (coming) from ' matter, they do not ' receive greater honor because of [10] their all-perfectness from whom ' came all these, being perfect, together with ' those who are with him. Indeed, each ' of the aeons has ' ten thousand aeons [15] in himself, so that by existing together ' he may become a perfect ' aeon.

He exists in the ' [Blessedness] of the Triple ' [Powerful] Perfect Invisible [20] [Spirit ...] silence ' [...] who became first ' [...] and the knowledge ' [...] ' [...] [25] [...] **124** whole, a silence of the second ' knowledge, the first thought ' in the will of the Triple ' Powerful, because he commanded it [5] to know him, so that he might become ' all-perfect and perfect ' in himself. By simplicity ' and blessedness he is ' known. [I received] [10] goodness through that ' follower of the Barbelo aeon ' who gives being to himself. ' [...] is not the power, but she is the one who ' belongs to him.

The aeons which really [15] exist do so in silence. ' Existence was inactivity, ' and knowledge of the self-established ' Kalyptos was ineffable. ' Having come [from the] [20] fourth, the [...] ' thought, the Proto[phanes], ' as (the) Perfect Male [Mind] ' [...] ' [...] **125** he is his image, equal to ' him in power and glory but ' with respect to order higher than ' him, (yet not higher) in aeon. [5] Like him he has all ' these (parts) living (and) dwelling together ' in one. Together with the aeon ' in the aeons he has ' a fourfold difference [10] with all the rest who ' are there.

But ' Kalyptos really exists, ' and with him is located she who belongs to ' all the glories, Youel, the male [15] virgin glory, through ' whom are seen the ' all-perfect ones. Those ' who stand before him are the triple ' [...] child, the triple [20] [...], the Autogenes ' [...] He has ' [...] in one ' [... the one] again who prevails over the ' [...] existing in [...] [25] **126** of ten thousand-fold.

The ˡ first aeon ˡ in him, from whom is ˡ the first Light, (is) Solmis [5] and the god revealer, ˡ since he is infinite according to the ˡ type in the Kalyptos aeon ˡ and Doxomedon. ˡ The second aeon (is) Akremon [10] the ineffable together with ˡ the second Light ˡ Zachthos and Yachtos. The ˡ third aeon is ˡ Ambrosios the virgin together with [15] the third Light ˡ Setheus and Antiphantes. ˡ The fourth aeon ˡ is the blesser [. . .] ˡ race with [the] [20] fourth Light [Seldao] ˡ and Elenos.

The [. . .] ˡ him [. . .] ˡ [. . .] Arm[edon ˡ [. . .] **127** phoe zoe zeoe ze[. . .] zosi ˡ zosi zao zeooo zesen zes- ˡ en — the individuals and the four ˡ who are eight-fold are alive. [5] eoooo eaeo — you who are before ˡ them, and you who are in them ˡ all. They are within ˡ the perfect male Armedon ˡ Protophanes [10] of all those who dwell together. ˡ Since all the individuals were ˡ existing as perfect ones, ˡ the Activity of all the ˡ individuals appeared again [15] as the divine Autogenes.

He ˡ stands within an ˡ aeon because there are within him ˡ four dif- ferent ˡ self-begotten aeons. The [20] first aeon in him ˡ as the first Light ˡ (is) [Harmoze]l-Orneos-Euthrou- ˡ nios. [He] was called ˡ [. . .] [25] [. . . The] second [aeon as] ˡ [the second Light is] ˡ [Oraiael . . .]- udas[. . .]os, Ap[. . .] **128** Arros[. . .]. The third (aeon) ˡ of the third Light (is) ˡ Daveithe-Laraneus- ˡ Epiphanios-Eideos. The fourth [5] (aeon) as the fourth Light ˡ (is) Eleleth-Kodere- ˡ Epiphanios- Allogenios. But as ˡ for all the rest who are in ˡ matter, they were all left (there). [10] It was because of knowledge of ˡ greatness, audacity and power that ˡ they came into existence and ˡ comforted themselves. Because they did not ˡ know God, they shall pass away. [15] Behold, Zostrianos, you have heard ˡ all these things of the gods ˡ are ignorant and (which) seem ˡ infinite to angels.'' ˡ

I took courage and said, [20] "I am [still] wondering about the Triple ˡ Powerful Invisible Perfect Spirit: ˡ how he exists for himself, [how he causes] ˡ everything [. . .] who ˡ really exist [. . .] [25] what is the [. . .] ˡ [. . .] and [. . .] ˡ [. . .] of [. . .] **129** very [. . .] they set [me] down (and) left. ˡ

Apophantes and Aphropais, ˡ the Virgin-light, came before me ˡ and brought me into Protophanes, [5] (the) great male perfect ˡ Mind. I saw all of them ˡ as they exist ˡ in one. I joined ˡ with them all (and) blessed the [10] Kalyptos aeon, the ˡ virgin Barbelo and the Invisible ˡ Spirit. I became all-perfect ˡ and received power. I was written ˡ in glory and sealed. [15] I received there ˡ a perfect crown. I came ˡ forth to the perfect individuals, ˡ and all of them were questioning ˡ me. They were listening to the [20] loftiness of my knowledge. They ˡ were rejoicing and ˡ receiv-

ing power. When I again ' came down to the aeons of ' Autogenes, I received a true [25] image, pure (yet) suitable for ' the perceptible (world).

I came ' down to the aeon copies ' and came down here **130** to the airy-earth. I wrote ' three tablets (and) left them ' as knowledge for those who would ' come after me, the living elect. [5] Then I came down to the perceptible ' world and put on ' my image. Because it was ignorant, ' I strengthened it (and) went about ' preaching the truth to everyone. [10] Neither the angelic beings of ' the world nor the archons ' saw me, for I negated a multitude ' of [judgments] which brought me near death. '

But an erring multitude [15] I awakened saying, ' "Know those who are alive and the holy ' seed of Seth. Do not [show] ' disobedience to me. [Awaken] ' your divine part to God, and [20] as for your sinless elect soul, ' strengthen it. Behold ' death here and ' seek the immutable ' ingenerateness, the [Father] of [25] everything. He invites you, ' while they reprove you. Although they ill-treat **131** you, he will not abandon you. '

Do not baptize yourselves with death ' nor entrust yourselves to those ' who are inferior to you instead of to [5] those who are better. Flee from the madness ' and the bondage of femaleness ' and choose for yourselves the salvation ' of maleness. You have ' not come to suffer; rather, you have [10] come to escape your bondage.

Release ' yourselves, and that which has bound ' you will be dissolved. Save ' yourselves so that your soul ' may be saved. The kind Father [15] has sent you the Savior ' and given you strength. Why ' are you hesitating? Seek when you are ' sought; when you are invited, ' listen, for time is [20] short.

Do not be led ' astray. The aeon of the ' aeons of the living ones is great, ' yet (so also is) the [punishment] ' of those who are unconvinced. [25] Many bonds and chastisers ' surround you. **132** Flee quickly ' before death reaches you. ' Look at the Light. Flee ' the Darkness. Do not be led [5] astray to your destruction. '

Zostrianos '
Oracles of Truth of ' Zostrianos '
God of Truth '
Teachings of Zoroaster

THE LETTER OF PETER TO PHILIP (VIII,*2*)

Introduced by

MARVIN W. MEYER

Translated by

FREDERIK WISSE

The Letter of Peter to Philip fills most of the concluding nine pages of Codex
VIII. Situated immediately after the tractate *Zostrianos*, *The Letter of Peter to
Philip* opens with a superscribed title (132,10-11) derived from the letter which
forms the first part of the tractate. Like several other tractates in the Nag Hammadi library (*Ap. Jas.*, *Treat. Res.*, *Eugnostos*), *The Letter of Peter to Philip* is
presented, in part, as a letter. Besides these letters in the Nag Hammadi library,
other letters were also in use among the Gnostics (for example, Ptolemy's *Letter
to Flora*, and letters of Valentinus, Monoimus the Arabian, and perhaps Mar-
cion). Furthermore, just as a magnificent epistolary tradition developed around
Paul and the Pauline school, so also a more modest collection of letters came to
be ascribed to Peter. These Petrine or pseudo-Petrine letters include, in addition
to *The Letter of Peter to Philip*, the catholic letters of Peter in the New Testament, the *Epistula Petri* ("Epistle of Peter") at the opening of the Pseudo-
Clementines, and perhaps another letter of Peter known only from a brief quota-
tion in Optatus of Milevis. Of these letters the pseudo-Clementine *Epistula Petri*
is of special interest, since it shares a number of features with *The Letter of Peter
to Philip*. Not only is it prefixed to a collection of materials relating to Peter; it
also seeks to attest the authority of Peter, and as it concludes, the *Contestatio*
begins by referring to the recipient – James the Just – reading and responding
to the letter in a manner like that of Philip in the *Letter of Peter to Philip*
133,8-11. *The Letter of Peter to Philip*, however, is not to be identified with any
of these letters attributed to Peter and must represent a newly discovered work
in the Petrine corpus.

In its present form *The Letter of Peter to Philip* is clearly a Christian Gnostic
tractate. Taken as a whole, the tractate is to be seen as a part of the Petrine tradition: Peter is the leader, the spokesman, the preacher among the apostles, and
he may very well be described as having his own disciples (139,10). The only other
apostle mentioned by name is Philip, who is submissive to the authority of Peter
and whose place in the tractate seems intended to highlight the pre-eminent
authority of Peter. With their leader, Peter, the apostles gather at Olivet and are
taught by the risen Savior; upon returning to Jerusalem, they teach in the temple
and perform healings; and eventually they go forth to preach, filled with holy
spirit. In other words, not only the place of Peter but also the scenario of the narrative would suggest that *The Letter of Peter to Philip* shares important features
with part of the first (Petrine) section of the Acts of the Apostles (chapters 1-12).

That the author of *The Letter of Peter to Philip* makes use of Christian traditions cannot be doubted. In particular, numerous parallels between this tractate and the first half of the Acts may be noted, including scenes, themes, and terms which are similar to these two documents. Even the genre of literature they represent — a narrative on Peter and the apostles within which are included revelatory, liturgical, and edificatory materials — is similar, although in the case of *The Letter of Peter to Philip* the narrative has been prefixed with a letter of Peter. Furthermore, the author of *The Letter of Peter to Philip* is familiar with other Christian traditions besides Lukan materials. The Savior's second revelatory answer (136,16-137,4) resembles the Johannine Logos hymn (Jn 1:1-18), but the similarities must not be overdrawn. Again, the traditional kerygmatic formulae in the credo of the sermon (139,15-21) show affinities with similar formulae to be found throughout early Christian literature (the parallels in John 19 are particularly close to the credo in *The Letter of Peter to Philip*), and the little "Pentecost" of *The Letter of Peter to Philip* (140,1[?]-13) shares features with the Johannine "Pentecost" account (20:19-23). Moreover, the author of this tractate also mentions previous revelatory utterances of the Savior (135,5-6; 138,2-3, 22-24; 139,11-12), utterances frequently said to have been given while Jesus was embodied. Presumably these revelations of the embodied Savior could refer to such teachings as are presented in the canonical gospels, and the "four words" of 140,25 could have been understood as the four gospels to be sent to the four directions. (Hans-Gebhard Bethge suggests that originally the text of 140,25 may have read "the four directions," which eventually could have been modified to read "four words.") Hence, it is clear that the author of *The Letter of Peter to Philip* is conversant with early Christian materials and desires to establish continuity with these earlier traditions.

Gnostic emphases are clearly visible in the narrative framework of *The Letter of Peter to Philip*. In particular this observation applies to the gnostic "dialogue," the revelatory discourse of the Savior uttered in answer to the questions of the apostles. The first four revelatory answers (135,8-137,13) are at most marginally Christian, though they have been taken over and legitimated as revelations of the risen Lord. The first answer (135,8-136,15), which provides an abbreviated version of the myth of the mother, illustrates no overtly Christian features at all. It reflects a rather simple version of the myth, and is similar to the Sophia myth of *The Apocryphon of John* and the Barbelognostics of Irenaeus (*Haer.* 1.29.1-4) in terminology and general presentation. This set of four revelatory answers furnishes a gnostic perspective on the fall into deficiency and the attainment of fullness, and the imprisonment and the struggle of Gnostics in the world. To this set of answers has been appended an additional question and answer (137,13-138,3) which utilizes different terms and focuses upon the life and mission of the apostles. Gnostic in perspective like the other answers, this additional answer does show Christian concerns, and illustrates a dominant interest of *The Letter of Peter to Philip*, the suffering of the believer.

In addition to the questions and answers in the gnostic dialogue, other materials similarly used in the tractate may also show gnostic proclivities. The two prayers of the gathered apostles (133,17-134,9) contain traditional terms and themes commonly found in early Christian prayers, but also proclaim a luminosity and glory which make them especially appropriate as the prayers of Gnostic

Christians. Likewise, the description of the resurrected Christ as a light and a voice (134,9-14; 135,3-4; 137,17-19; 138,11-13,21-22) represents a primitive way of depicting the appearances of the risen Lord (Mk 9:2-8 par.; 2 P 1:16-19; Ac 9:1-9; 22:4-11; 26:9-18; 1 Co 15; Rv 1:12-16), but among Gnostic Christians such theophanic descriptions were particularly appreciated.

In the brief sermon of Peter (139,9-140,1[?]) gnostic tendencies are even more clearly seen. To be sure, a traditional Christian credo constitutes the first part of the sermon (139,15-21), and traditional terms are applied to Jesus ("the Lord Jesus," "the Son," "the author of our life"), but the credo is interpreted according to the Gnostic Christian theology of the author of *The Letter of Peter to Philip*. From the time of his incarnation Jesus suffered, but he suffered as one who is "a stranger to this suffering" (139,21-22). A Christological tension remains as the sermon stresses both the reality of Jesus' sufferings and the glory of his divinity. In contrast to the suffering illuminator Jesus, the sermon continues, the followers of Jesus suffer because of "the transgression of the mother" (139,23). This phrase is reminiscent of references to the fall of mother Eve, and refers, for the Gnostic Christian author, to the mother often named Sophia in other versions of the myth. She is also called "the mother" at 135,12, and her tragic fall is seen as the source of human sufferings. Hence, this reference to "the transgression of the mother" may provide another point of contact between the figures of Eve and Sophia in gnostic literature.

It is possible, then, to suggest a general outline for the literary history of *The Letter of Peter to Philip*. On the basis of the parallels with *The Apocryphon of John* and Irenaeus, we suggest that *The Letter of Peter to Philip* was written around the end of the second century C.E. or into the third. The author of the text presumably wrote in Greek: such may be intimated by the presence of Greek loan words and Greek idioms. The author apparently was a Christian Gnostic who was well versed in the Christian tradition, and who used and interpreted that tradition in a Christian Gnostic fashion. A gnostic dialogue has been constructed, though it is less a true dialogue than a revelatory discourse of Christ in answer to questions raised by the apostles. Within this dialogue are included gnostic materials which are non-Christian or only marginally Christian; these materials have been adopted as revelatory disclosures of the risen Christ. On the basis of the Christian and gnostic traditions with which the author was familiar, the author compiled a narrative document with a revelatory focus. The letter itself was added at the beginning of this narrative in order to stress the authoritative place of Peter, and *The Letter of Peter to Philip* subsequently received its present title. Finally, the Greek tractate was translated into Coptic, and found its way into Codex VIII of the Nag Hammadi library.

According to the reports of James M. Robinson and Stephen Emmel, another Coptic text of *The Letter of Peter to Philip* is to be found in a papyrus codex which, at the present time, is neither published nor available for study.

THE LETTER OF PETER TO PHILIP

VIII 132, 10 — 140, 27

The letter of Peter Which He [
Sent to Philip [

"Peter the apostle of Jesus [Christ, to Philip our beloved [brother and our fellow apostle [15] and (to) the brethren who are with you: greetings! [Now I want you to know, our brother [that] [we received orders from [our Lord and the Savior of [the whole world that [we] should come [together] [20] to give instruction and [preach in the salvation [which was promised us by **133** our Lord Jesus Christ. But as for you, [you were separate from us, and [you did not desire us to come together [and to know how we should organize [5] ourselves in order that we might tell the good news. [Therefore would it be agreeable to you, our brother, to [come according to the orders of our [God Jesus?"

When Philip had received these, [and when he had read [10] them, he went to Peter [rejoicing with gladness. [Then Peter gathered [the others also. They went upon [the mountain which is called [15] "the (mount) olives," the place where they used [to gather with the blessed [Christ when he was in the body.

Then, [when the apostles [had come together, and had thrown themselves upon [20] their knees, they prayed thus [saying, "Father, Father, [Father of the light, who [possesses the incorruptions, [hear us just as [thou hast] [25] [taken pleasure] in thy holy [child Jesus Christ. For he [became for us an illuminator **134** in the darkness. Yea hear us." [

And they prayed again another time [saying, "Son [of life, Son of [5] immortality who is in [the light, Son, Christ of [immortality, our Redeemer, [give us power, for they [seek to kill us."

Then [10] a great light appeared [so that the mountain shone [from the sight of him who had [appeared. And a voice called [out to them saying, [15] "Listen to my words that I may speak [to you. Why are you asking [me? I am Jesus Christ who [am with you forever."

Then [the apostles answered [20] and said, "Lord, [we would like to know the deficiency [of the aeons and their pleroma." [And: "How are [we detained in this dwelling place?" [25] Further: "How did we come to this place?" And: "In what [manner shall we depart?" Again: "How do we have **135** [the] authority of boldness?" [[And]: "Why do the powers fight against us?" [

Then a voice came to them out | of the light saying, [5] "It is you yourselves who are witnesses | that I spoke all these things to you. | But because of your unbelief | I shall speak again. First | of all concerning [the deficiency] of the aeons, this [10] [is] the deficiency, when the disobedience | and the foolishness | of the mother appeared | without the commandment of the majesty | of the Father. She wanted [15] to raise up aeons. And when she | spoke, the Arrogant One followed. | And when she left behind a | part, the Arrogant One | laid hold of it, and it became a [20] deficiency. This is the deficiency | of the aeons. Now when the Arrogant One | had taken a part, he sowed it. | And he placed powers over | it and authorities. [25] And [he] enclosed it in the aeons | which are dead. And all the | powers of the world rejoiced | that they had been begotten. **136** But they do not know the | pre-existent [Father], since they are | strangers to him. But this is the one to whom | they gave power and whom they served [5] by praising him. But he, the Arrogant One, | became proud on account of | the praise of the powers. He became | an envier and he wanted to | make an image in the place [of an image] [10] and a form in the place of a form. | And he commissioned the powers within | his authority to mold | mortal bodies. And they came | to be from a misrepresentation, from [15] the semblance which had emerged. |

Next concerning the pleroma: I am the one who | was sent down in the body | because of the seed which had fallen away. | And I came down into their mortal mold. [20] But they did not | recognize me; they were thinking of me that I | was a mortal man. And I | spoke with him who belongs to me, and he | harkened to me just as you too [25] who harkened today. | And I gave him authority in order that | he might enter into the inheritance | of his fatherhood. And I took **137** [. . .] they were filled | [. . .] in his salvation. And since | he was a deficiency, for this reason he | became a pleroma.

It is because of this [5] that you are being detained, because you | belong to me. When you strip off | from yourselves what is corrupted, then | you will become illuminators | in the midst of mortal men. [10]

And this (is the reason) that you will fight against the powers, | because [they] do not have rest like | you, since they do not wish | that you be saved."

Then the apostles | worshipped again saying, [15] "Lord, tell us: In what | way shall we fight against the archons, since | [the] archons are above us?"

Then | [a] voice called out to them from | the appearance saying, [20]

"Now you will fight ' against them in this way, for the archons are ' fighting against the inner man. And you ' are to fight against them in this way: Come ' together and teach in the world [25] the salvation with a promise. And ' you, gird yourselves with the power ' of my Father, and let ' your prayer be known. And he, the ' Father, will help you as he has [30] helped you be sending me. **138** Be not afraid, [I am with you forever,] ' as I previously [said to] ' you when I was in the body." Then ' there came lighting and [5] thunder from heaven, and ' what appeared to them in that place was taken ' up to heaven.

Then ' the apostles gave thanks to ' the Lord with every blessing. And [10] they returned to Jerusalem. ' And while coming up they spoke with ' each other on the road concerning the light ' which had come. And a remark was made ' concerning the Lord. It was [15] said, "If he, our Lord, ' suffered, then how much (must) we (suffer)?" '

Peter answered saying, ' "He suffered on [our] behalf, ' and it is necessary for us too [20] to suffer because of our smallness." ' Then a voice came to them ' saying, "I have told you ' many times: It is necessary for you ' to suffer. It is [25] necessary that they bring you to synagogues ' and governors, ' so that you will suffer. But he ' who does not suffer and does not **139** [...] ' [... the] Father ' [...] in order that he may ' [...]."

And the apostles [5] rejoiced [greatly] and came up ' to Jerusalem. And they came up to the temple and gave ' instruction in salvation in the name of ' [the] Lord Jesus Christ. And they healed ' [a] multitude.

And Peter opened his mouth, [10] he said to his (fellow) disciples, ' "[Did] our Lord Jesus, when he was in the body, ' show us everything? For he ' came down. My brothers, listen to my voice." ' And he was filled with a holy spirit. [15] He spoke thus: "Our illuminator, Jesus, ' [came] down and was crucified. And he bore ' a crown of thorns. And he put on ' a purple garment. And he was ' [crucified] on a tree and he was buried in [20] a tomb. And he rose from the ' dead. My brothers, Jesus is a stranger ' to this suffering. But we are ' the ones who have suffered through the transgression of the mother. ' And because of this, he did everything [25] like us. ' For the Lord Jesus, the Son of the immeasurable glory of the ' Father, he is the author ' of our life. My brothers, let ' us therefore not obey these lawless ones [30] and walk in **140** [... Then] ' Peter [gathered together the others also] ' saying, ["O, Lord Jesus] ' Christ, author [of our] rest, [5] give us a spirit of understanding ' in order that we also may ' perform wonders."

Then Peter ' and the other apostles saw [him] ' and they were filled

with a holy spirit. [10] And each one ' performed healings. And they parted ' in order to preach the Lord ' Jesus. And they came together ' and greeted each other [15] saying, "Amen."

Then ' Jesus appeared saying ' to them, "Peace to you [all] and ' everyone who believes in ' my name. And when you depart, [20] joy be to you and ' grace and power. And be not ' afraid; behold, I am with you ' forever."

Then the apostles ' parted from each other [25] into four words in order to ' preach. And they went ' by a power of Jesus, in peace.

MELCHIZEDEK (IX,*1*)

Introduced by

BIRGER A. PEARSON

Translated by

SØREN GIVERSEN and BIRGER A. PEARSON

This tractate is the only writing of the Nag Hammadi corpus that features, or even names, the mysterious "priest of God Most High" encountered by the patriarch Abraham, according to Genesis 14:18 (cf. Ps 110:4). Its title is partially preserved on one of the fragments making up page 1 of Codex IX. Unfortunately, this codex is in a rather bad state of preservation. Only 19 lines of text (out of approximately 745) from the tractate *Melchizedek* are completely preserved, and less than 50 percent of the total text is recoverable even by means of conjectural restoration. Thus, since there is no other extant copy of this tractate, only a very imperfect picture of its content is possible to attain, and what has been preserved is susceptible to more than one interpretation. The following account must be read with these caveats in mind.

In terms of literary genre, this tractate is an apocalypse, specifically an "apocalypse of Melchizedek." It contains revelations putatively given by heavenly intermediaries to Melchizedek, who communicates the revelations to a privileged few. Readers are implicitly invited to see themselves as sharing in these special revelations, as members of these privileged few.

The tractate consists of three main parts:

I. 1,1(?)-14,5: The tractate apparently opens with a brief vocative address by Melchizedek to Jesus Christ, but there quickly follows a third revelation addressed to Mechizedek by a heavenly informant whose name has been restored as "Gamaliel" (5,18). An important feature of this revelation, addressed to the "priest of God Most High" (12,10-11; cf. Gn 14:18), is a prophecy of the ministry, death, and resurrection of the Savior, Jesus Christ. It also contains a remarkable passage which predicts the coming of (docetic) heretics who will deny the physical reality of Jesus' incarnation, death, and resurrection (5,1-11). Melchizedek himself plays a role in this revelation, for a future high-priestly office is prophesied for him (esp. 5,11-17). A prophecy of the final triumph over death concludes this first revelation (14,8-9).

II. 14,15-18,11 (?): Melchizedek then arises with joy, and undertakes several ritual actions which may also provide for us some insights into the cultic life of the community for which the writing as a whole is intended: prayers of thanksgiving, baptism, reception of the priestly name, and a presentation of spiritual offerings. This liturgical section also includes a lengthy set of invocations, each beginning "Holy are you," addressed to members of the heavenly world (16,16-18,7; cf. 5,27-6,10). What is of special interest here is that most of the

names of these divine beings are names that appear in such gnostic texts as *The Apocryphon of John* and other tractates associated with Sethian Gnosticism. These names include Barbelo, Harmozel, Oroiael, Daveithe, Eleleth, and others.

III. 18,11(?)-27,10: A second set of revelations transports Melchizedek into the future, again centering on the crucifixion and resurrection of Jesus Christ. But this time — if our reconstruction of the fragmentary text is correct — Melchizedek is given to understand that the spiritual triumph of Christ over his enemies will be that of Melchizedek himself!

Our tractate thus presents a number of challenging features of special interest to the historian of religions; it is indeed a mélange of traditions of Jewish, Christian, and Gnostic stamp. Its presentation of the figure of Melchizedek is a case in point: he is not only the ancient "priest of God Most High" known to us from the Bible, but he also returns as an eschatological "high-priest" and "holy warrior." Such Jewish apocalyptic material as the Melchizedek fragments from Qumran (11QMelch) and *2* (Slavonic) *Enoch* shed considerable light on these features.

In this tractate, Melchizedek's appearance in the endtime is tied to the career of Jesus Christ: his incarnation, death, and resurrection. In other words, Jesus Christ *is* Melchizedek! Such an idea can be understood as rooted in an interpretation of Hebrews 7:3. Moreover, the idea that Melchizedek is the "Son of God" (i.e., identical to Jesus Christ) gained currency in some early Christian circles, particularly in Egypt.

Can anything be determined about the religious community for which our tractate was composed? The fourth-century bishop of Salamis in Cyprus, St. Epiphanius, gives us an account of a Christian sect whose members referred to themselves as "Melchizedekians" (*Haer.* 55). A comparison of Epiphanius' account with *Melchizedek* reveals enough features in common to suggest that the latter may have originated in a group of "Melchizedekians," features such as the glorification of the priesthood of Melchizedek and a Christology that insisted on the true humanity of Christ. (The Melchizedekians were not Gnostics.)

But what of the gnostic features clearly discernible in the text? These include the divine names from gnostic mythology already mentioned, a fragment of a theogonic myth (9,1-10), a gnostic interpretation of the paradise story (9,28-10,11), and a reference to the "children of Seth" (5,20). One possible explanation of these features is that an earlier form of the text has undergone a process of gnostic editing: the latest redactor was a Gnostic who identified Melchizedek-Christ with the gnostic savior Seth and who interpolated into the text the various gnostic features that are now found in it. The final form of *Melchizedek* is thus a product of Sethian Gnosticism. Other explanations are, of course, possible.

The tractate *Melchizedek* was written originally in Greek, probably in Egypt. A third-century date is likely, though it could be earlier (or later).

MELCHIZEDEK

IX 1, 1-27, 10

Melchizedek |

Jesus Christ, the Son [of God | ...] from [...] ^{5} the aeons that. I [might tell] | all of the aeons, and in (the case of) | each one of the aeons [that I might tell | the] nature of the aeon, what | it is, and that I might put on | friendship and goodness | as a garment, O brother [...] and [...] ^{19} their end [...]. | And he will [reveal | to them] the truth [...] in [...] ^{25} proverb(s) [... 2 at first] in parables | [and riddles ...] proclaim ^{5} them. Death will [tremble] | and be angry, not only | he himself, but also his [fellow] | world-ruling archons [and] | the principalities and the authorities, the ^{10} female gods and the male gods | together with the archangels. And [...] ^{16} all of them [... | the] world-rulers [...] | all of them, and all the | [...], and all the [...]. ^{20}

They will say [... concerning] | him, and concerning [...] | and [...] ^{25} they will [...] | hidden [mysteries ...] 3^3 out of | [...] the All. They will ^{5} [...] this the [lawyers] | will [bury] him quickly. | [They will] call him, | "impious man, lawless | [(and) impure]." And [on] the ^{10} [third] day he [will rise | from the] dead [... 4^4 holy disciples. And] | the Savior [will reveal] to them [the world] | that gives life to the [All.] |

[But] those in the heavens spoke [many] | words, together with | those on the earth [and those] ^{10} under the earth. [...]. 5

[Which] will happen in his name. | [Furthermore], they will say of him that he is | unbegotten though he has been begotten, (that) he does | not eat even though he eats, (that) he does not drink ^{5} even though he drinks, (that) he is uncircumcised | though he has been circumcised, (that) he is unfleshly | though he has come in flesh, (that) he did not | come to suffering ⟨though⟩ he came to suffering, | (that) he did not rise from the dead ^{10} ⟨though⟩ he arose from [the] | dead.

[But] all the [tribes and] | all [the peoples] will speak [the truth], | who are receiving from [you] | yourself, O [Melchizedek], ^{15} Holy One, [High-Priest], | the perfect hope [and] | the [gifts of] life. [I am | Gamaliel] who was [sent] | to [...] the congregation of [the ^{20} children] of Seth, who are above | [thousands of] thousands and [myriads] | of myriads [of the] aeons [...] | essence of the [aeons | a] ba [...] aiai ababa. O ^{25} divine [...] of the [... | nature ... | O Mother] of the aeons, [Barbelo, | O first-]born of the aeons, 6 splendid Doxomedon,

Dom[. . .] ' O glorious one, Jesus Christ, ' O chief commanders of the luminaries, you [powers] ' Armozel, Oroiael, Daveithe, [5] Eleleth, and you man-of-light, ' immortal Aeon Pigeradamas, ' and you good god of the ' beneficent worlds, Mirocheirothetou, ' through Jesus Christ, the Son [10] of God. This is the one whom I proclaim, ' inasmuch as there has [visited ' the One who] truly exists ' [among those who] exist [. . . ' do(es)] not [exist], Abel Baruch – [15] [that] you (sg.) [might be given] the knowledge [of the truth ' . . .] that he is [from ' the] race of the High-priest ' [which is] above [thousands of thousands] and ' [myriads] of myriads of the aeons. The [20] adverse [spirits are] ' ignorant of him and (of) their (own) ' destruction. Not only (that, but) I have come to ' [reveal] to you [the] truth ' [which is] within the [brethren.] He included [25] himself [in the] living ' [offering] together with your [offspring.] He ' [offered] them up as an [offering to ' the] All. [For it is not] cattle ' [that] you will offer up [for sin(s)] **7** of unbelief [and for] ' the ignorances [and all the] wicked ' [deeds] which they [will do . . .]. ' And they do [not] reach ' [the] Father of the All [. . .] ' the faith [. . .] [27] to receive [baptism . . .] ' waters [. . .]. **8** For [the waters] which are above ' [. . .] that receive baptism ' [. . .]. But receive [that baptism ' which is] with the water which [. . .] [5] while he is coming [. . . [9] baptism] as they [. . .] [28] pray for the [offspring of the] **9** archons and [all] the angels, together with ' [the] seed ⟨which⟩ flowed [forth from ' the Father] of the All [. . . ' the] entire [. . .] from [. . . [5] there were] engendered the [gods and the angels] ' and the men [. . .] ' out of the [seed] ' all of [the ' natures], those in [the heavens and] ' those upon the earth and [those] [10] under [the earth . . .] [25] nature of the females [. . .] ' among those that are in the [. . .] ' they were bound with [. . .] [But this] is [not] (the) true Adam **10** [nor] (the) true Eve.

[For ' when they ate] of the tree [of ' knowledge] they trampled [the ' Cherubim] and the Seraphim [5] [with the flaming sword]. They [. . .] ' which was Adam's ' [. . . the] world-rulers and ' [. . .] them out ' [. . .] after they had brought forth [10] [. . .] offspring of the archons and ' [their worldly things], these belonging to [. . .] [25] light [. . .]. ' And the females and the [males,] ' those who exist with [. . . ' hidden] from every nature, [and they will ' renounce] the archons [. . . **11** who] receive from him the [. . .]. ' For [they] are worthy of [. . . ' immortal], and [great . . .] ' and [great [. . . [5] and] great [. . .] ' sons of [men . . . ' disciples . . . ' image] and [. . .] ' from the [light [10] . . .] which is holy. ' For [. . .] from the ' [beginning . . .] a seed [. . .]. **12**

But I will be silent ' [. . .] for we [are ' the brethren who] came down

from ¹ [the] living [...]. They will [...] ⁵ upon the [...] ⁷ of Adam ¹
[... Abel], Enoch, [Noah ... ¹⁰ you], Melchizedek, [the Priest] ¹ of
God [Most High ...] ¹ those who [...] ¹ women [...].

[...] **13** these two who have been chosen will ¹ [at] no time nor ¹ [in]
any place will they be convicted, ¹ whenever they have been begotten, ⁵
[by] their enemies, by their friends, ¹ [nor by strangers nor their ¹ [own]
kin, (nor) by the [impious] ¹ nor the pious ¹ [All of] the adverse natures
will ¹⁰ [...] them, whether ¹ [those that] are manifest, or those that ¹
[are] not [manifest], together with those ¹ [that dwell] in the heavens
and those that are ¹ [upon] the earth and those that are under ¹⁵ the
earth. They will make [war ...] ¹ every one. ¹ For [...] whether in the
[...] ²¹ many [...]. ²⁵ And these in the [...] ¹ every [one] will [...]. ¹
These will [...] ¹ with every blow [...] **14** weaknesses. These will be ¹
confined in other forms [and ¹ will] be punished. [These] ¹ the Savior
will take them [away ¹ and] they will overcome everything, [not with] ¹
their mouths and words ¹ but by means of the [...] ¹ which will be done
for [them. He will] ¹ destroy Death.

[These things] ¹⁰ which I was commanded ¹ to reveal, these things ¹
reveal [as I (have done)]. ¹ But that which is hidden do not reveal ¹ [to]
anyone, unless [it is revealed] ¹⁵ to you (to do so)."

And [immediately ¹ I] arose, [I, Melchizedek], ¹ and I began to [...]
¹ God [...] ¹ that I should [rejoice ...] ²¹ while he [is acting ...] ¹ living
[... ¹ I said], "I [... ²⁶ and I] will not cease, from [now on ¹ for ever],
O Father of the [All, ¹ because] you have had pity on me, and **15** [you
have sent the] angel of light ¹ [...] from your [aeons ¹ ... to] reveal
[...] ¹ when he came he ⁵ [caused] me [to be raised up] from ignorance
¹ and (from) the fructification ¹ of death to life. For ¹ I have a name, ¹
I am Melchizedek, the Priest ¹⁰ of [God] Most High; I ¹ [know] that it
is I who am truly ¹ [the image of] the true High-Priest ¹ [of] God Most
High, and ¹ [...] the world. For it ¹⁵ is not [a] small [thing that] ¹ God
[...] with [...] ¹ while he [...]. ¹ And [... the angels that ¹ dwell upon
the] earth [...] ²² is the [sacrifice of [...] ¹ whom Death deceived. ¹
When he [died] he bound them ²⁵ with the natures which are [leading
them astray]. ¹ Yet he offered up **16** offerings [...] ¹ cattle [...] ¹ I gave
them to [Death ¹ and the angels] and the [...] ⁵ demons [...] ¹ living
offering [...] ¹ I have offered up myself to you as an offering, together
with those that are mine, to ¹ you yourself, (O) Father of the All, and ¹⁰
those whom you love, who have come forth ¹ from you who are holy
(and) [living]. And ⟨according to⟩ ¹ the [perfect] laws I shall pronounce
¹ my name as I receive baptism [now] ¹ (and) for ever, (as a name)

among the living (and) [15] holy [names], and (now) in the [waters], Amen.

[Holy are you], ' Holy are [you], Holy are you, O [Father ' of the All], who truly exist [...] ' do(es) not exist, [Abel Baruch [20] ...] for ever and ever, [Amen]. ' Holy are [you, Holy are you], Holy are [you, ' ...] before [... ' for ever and] ever, ' [Amen]. Holy are [you], Holy are [you, [25] Holy are you, Mother of the] aeon(s), ' Barbelo, ' for ever and ever, [Amen. ' Holy are you], Holy are you, Holy are you, ' [First]-born of the aeons, [30] Doxomedon. [... 17 for ever] and ever, Amen. ' [Holy are you, Holy are you], Holy are you. [... [5] for ever and ever], Amen. ' [Holy are you, Holy are you], Holy are you. [...] [8] [first] aeon, ' [Harmozel, for] ever and ever, [10] [Amen. Holy are you], Holy are you, ' [Holy are you], commander, luminary ' [of the aeons], Oriael, for ' [ever and ever], Amen. Holy are you, ' [Holy are you, Holy are you], commander [15] [of the aeons], man-of-light, ' [Daveithe], for ever ' [and ever, Amen]. Holy are you, ' [Holy are you, Holy are you, commander-in-chief Eleleth, ... [20] the] aeons [... for [25] ever and ever], Amen. ' [Holy are you], Holy are [you], Holy are you, ' good [god of] 18 the [beneficent] words, ... ' Mirocheirothetou, [for] ' ever and ever, [Amen. ' Holy are] you, [Holy are you, Holy are you], [5] Commander-in-chief [of the] ' All, Jesus Christ, [for ever and ever], ' Amen.

[...]. [9] Blessed [...] ' confession. [And ...] ' confess him [...] ' now [...] ' then it becomes [...] ' fear [and ...] [15] fear and [...] ' disturb [...] ' surrounding [them ...] ' in the place [which has a] ' great darkness [in it [20] and] many [...] ' appear [...] ' there [... appear ...] 19 And ' [...] they were clothed with ' [...] all and [...] [10] disturbances. They gave ' [...] their words ' [...] and they said to me, ' [... Melchizedek, ' Priest] of God [Most High ... they] spoke as though [... ' their] mouths [...] ' in the All [...] [24] lead astray [...] 20 with his [...] ' worship [and ...] ' faith [and ...] ' his prayers, And [...] [6] those that [are his ...] ' first [...]. [10] They did not care that [the ' priesthood] which you perform, [which] ' is from [... [14] in the] counsels of [...] ' Satan [...] ' the sacrifice ' [...] his doctrines [...] [20] of this aeon [... [25] which] exist(s) [in ...] ' lead(s) [astray ...] 21 and some [...] [4] he gave them to [... [6] and] thirteen [...] 22 throw [him ... ' in order that] you might [... [4] for] immediately [... ' by means of ... ' on the ground]. The [... (p. 23 almost completely missing) [24][2] which is above ...] 25 me. And ' [...] you (pl.) struck me, ' [...] you threw me, ' [...] corpse. And [5] [you crucified me] from the third hour ' [of the Sabbath-eve] until ' [the ninth hour]. And after ' [these things

I arose] from the ' [dead. . . .] came out of ^{10} [. . .] into me. [. . .] ' my eyes [saw . . . ^{12} they did not] find anyone [. . .] **26** greeted [me . . .]. ' They said to me, "Be [strong, O Melchizedek], ' great [High-priest] ' of God [Most High, for the archons], ' who [are] your [enemies], ' made war; you have [prevailed over them, and] ' they did not prevail over you, [and you] ' endured, and [you] ' destroyed your enemies [. . .] ^{10} of their [. . .] ' will rest, in any [. . .] ' which is living (and) holy [. . . ' those that] exalted themselves against him in [. . .] ' flesh.

[. . . **27** with] the offerings, working on that ' which is good, fasting ' with fasts.

These revelations ' do not reveal to anyone ^{5} in the flesh, since they are incorporeal, ' unless it is revealed to you (to do so)." '

When the brethren who belong to the ' generations of life had said these things, they ' were taken up to (the regions) above ^{10} all the heavens. Amen.

THE THOUGHT OF NOREA (IX,2)

Introduced by

BIRGER A. PEARSON

Translated by

SØREN GIVERSEN and BIRGER A. PEARSON

Comprising only 52 lines of text, this tractate is one of the shortest of the Nag Hammadi corpus. The pages of the manuscript on which it is found are damaged, but they preserve enough text to allow for the restoration of almost the entire tractate. The Coptic text, however, is manifestly corrupt at points, and textual emendation has been deemed necessary here and there (indicated in the translation with pointed brackets).

The tractate bears no title in the manuscript. The one used in this edition is a phrase found in the text itself, at the end of the tractate (29,3). Another title is in use in German scholarship: "Ode on Norea," a designation that also defines the literary genre of this writing: an ode or hymn.

The hymnic features evident in the text include *parallelismus membrorum*, repetition, and a balanced structure, characteristics of Semitic poetry. *Norea* does not, however, satisfy the requirements of Greek poetry, for no traditional Greek meter can be ascribed to the original Greek text of which this Coptic version is a translation.

The tractate has a clear fourfold structure:

I. 27,11-20: The tractate begins with an invocation addressed to a divine triad consisting of Father, Mother, and Son, the basic primal triad found in Sethian Gnosticism. The incomprehensible Father is a primal Mind, here also called Adamas (28,30; 27,26), whose Thought (*ennoia*) is a primal spiritual Mother. Their son is Mind (*nous*), also called Logos (27,18) and Autogenes (28,6).

II. 27,21-28,12: The invocation is expressly attributed to Norea: "It is Norea who [cries out] to them" (27,21-22). Her cry for deliverance results in her restoration to the divine world, her proper place (=the Pleroma), 27,23; 28,22).

III. 28,12-23: While remaining in the pleroma, Norea also has a saving role to play in propagating "words of Life" (28,13-14).

IV. 28,24-29,5: Norea's own salvation is aided by the intercession of the "four holy helpers" (28,27-28), figures who are easily identifiable as the four "luminaries" of Sethian Gnosticism: Harmozel, Oroiael, Daveithe, and Eleleth (cf., e.g., *Melch*. IX 6,3-5). Her "thought" (29,3) is the gnosis that brings about for all of her spiritual progeny ultimate reintegration into the godhead. Thus, in saving others, Norea saves herself.

From what has already been said, there can be no doubt that *Norea* is a gnostic text in the full technical sense of that term. It has justifiably been included among those gnostic texts which are classified as Sethian, in the sense that they share es-

sential features of a discrete gnostic system conveniently labeled as Sethian. (Hans-Martin Schenke is the foremost proponent of this classification, which applies to the following texts of the Nag Hammadi corpus: *Ap. John, Hyp. Arch., Gos. Eg., Apoc. Adam, Steles Seth, Zost., Norea, Marsanes, Allogenes,* and *Trim. Prot.*) The Sethian system includes the following essential elements: 1) the gnostic triad of Father, Mother, and Son; 2) the four "luminaries" subordinate to the Son; and 3) the figure of Seth and/or his feminine counterpart, Norea. All of these elements are found in our tractate.

There are no clear indications of Christian influence in this tractate, and such Jewish influence as can be found in it belongs to its prehistory, i.e., the earlier formulations of the Sethian system which is reflected in it.

The most interesting feature of *Norea* is the savior figure depicted in it, Norea. This figure occurs in a wide range of gnostic literature, Sethian and non-Sethian, with considerable variation in the spelling of her name: Norea, Orea, Noraia, Oraia, Horaia, Nora, Noria, Nuraita, and Nhuraita. She is represented in the literature as the daughter of Adam and Eve, sister-wife of Seth, or as the wife of Noah or Shem. She is sometimes portrayed as the intended victim of rape by the wicked archons, as in *The Hypostasis of the Archons* (II,*4*), a text which stands in close relationship with *Norea*. Comparative analysis of the gnostic texts, together with certain traditions from Jewish *aggadah* featuring a Cainite woman called Naamah (cf. Gn 4:22), shows that Norea is a gnostic derivative of the figure of Naamah. The original spelling of her name in Greek is *Horaia*, the semantic equivalent of Hebrew *Na'amah* ("pleasing, lovely").

Norea thus has a previous career in Jewish legend as a naughty girl, Naamah, cavorting with the fallen "sons of God" (Gn 6:2). A completely opposite picture of Norea is presented in *Hyp. Arch.*, according to which she is an undefiled virgin and a spiritual helper to (gnostic) humankind (II 91,34-92,2; cf. Gn 2:18). It is this picture of Norea that is reflected in our tractate as well. Indeed, in *Norea*, the saving role of Seth has disappeared completely; it is Norea who is the gnostic "saved savior." As such she can be regarded as a symbolic equivalent of Sophia ("wisdom") as well as a symbol of the gnostic soul in need of redemption and reintegration into the godhead.

It is not possible to come to any definite conclusion as to the tractate's provenance, but Syria or Egypt are the most likely possibilities. A date in the late second, or early third, century is plausible. We have no information on the question of its authorship, but *Norea* is one of the Nag Hammadi tractates that could easily have been written by a gnostic woman.

THE THOUGHT OF NOREA

IX 27, 11-29, 5

Father of All, [Ennoia] | of the Light | [dwelling in the heights | above the (regions) below, [15] Light dwelling [in | the] heights, Voice of | Truth, upright Nous, | untouchable Logos, | and [ineffable] Voice, [20] [incomprehensible] Father! |

It is Norea who [cries out] ' to them. They [heard], ' (and) they received her into her place ' forever. They gave it [25] to her in the Father of Nous, ' Adamas, as well as the voice ' of the Holy Ones, **28** in order that she might rest ' in the ineffable Epinoia, ' in order that ⟨she⟩ might inherit ' the first mind [5] which ⟨she⟩ had received, and that ⟨she⟩ might rest ' in the divine Autogenes, ' and that she (too) might generate ' herself, just as [she] also has ' inherited the [living] Logos, [10] and that she might be joined to ' all of the Imperishable Ones, and [speak] ' with the mind of the Father.

And ' [she began] to speak with words of ' [Life], and ⟨she⟩ remained in the [15] [presence] of the Exalted One, [possessing ' that] which she had received before ' the world came into being. ' [She has] the [great ' mind] of the Invisible One, [and [20] she gives] glory to ⟨her⟩ Father, [and ' she] dwells within those who [...] ' within the Pleroma, ' [and] she beholds the Pleroma. '

There will be days when she will [25] [behold] the Pleroma, and ' she will not be in deficiency, ' for she has the four ' holy helpers who intercede ' on her behalf with the Father of [30] the All, Adamas. He it is **29** who is within all of the Adams, ' possessing the ' thought of Norea who speaks ' concerning the two names which create [5] a single name.

THE TESTIMONY OF TRUTH (IX,*3*)

Introduced by

BIRGER A. PEARSON

Translated by

SØREN GIVERSEN and BIRGER A. PEARSON

This tractate is unfortunately poorly preserved, owing to the fragmentary condition of the manuscript. Almost half of the text is lost. Even so, enough material is extant or recoverable to enable us to gain a rather good picture of the tractate's content.

It is possible that a title was originally appended to the tractate at the end (as is the case with 21 of the other tractates in the Nag Hammadi corpus); if so, it would have been part of the last inscribed folio of the codex, which is now lost (pp. 75-76). The title now in universal use has been editorially assigned on the basis of content ("word of truth," 31,8; "true testimony," 45,1), and underscores the author's concern to establish "true" faith and praxis while also exposing the false claims of "heretical" opponents.

Indeed, one of the most interesting features of this tractate is that we see in it the other side of the theological arguments we know so well from the ecclesiastical heresiologists. The author is a Christian Gnostic polemicist, with a strict encratic world view and lifestyle. His chief opponents are catholic Christians of the ecclesiastical establishment. Surprisingly, our gnostic author does not spare fellow Gnostics similar polemical treatment, i.e., Gnostics whose lifestyle and ritual practice differ from his own.

The tractate consists of two main parts. The first is a well-constructed homily on truth versus falsehood, addressed to fellow members of a Christian Gnostic community (29,6-45,6). Its purpose is to bolster the convictions of the author's fellow Gnostics and to warn them against the errors of (catholic) Christian opponents. The second part (45,6-end) consists of miscellaneous additions, including elaborations of themes already sounded in the homily itself. It is in this section that the polemics against other Gnostics occur.

I. The homily opens with an exordium in which the author appeals to those endowed with spiritual hearing. An attack is then launched against the Law, which for the author is summed up in the command to procreate. The polemics continue with attacks on those who espouse martyrdom in the belief that there will be a "carnal resurrection" (31,22-38,27). Sexual "defilement" (39,5), i.e., marriage and procreation, is vigoriously criticized (38,27-41,4), with Jesus' virgin birth used as a sign that Christians should lead a virginal life (40,5-7). The capstone of the homily as a description of the career of the archetypical Gnostic: his renunciation of the world and his reintegration into the realm of imperishability (41,4-44,30). A peroration sums up the "true testimony": self-knowledge is knowledge of God and leads to the "crown unfading" (44,30-45,6).

II. The appended miscellanea occur in a portion of Codex IX which has sustained considerable damage and loss. It is nevertheless clear that the polemical tone sounded in the homily consists of a gnostic midrash on the serpent of Genesis 3 (45,23-49,10). It retells the paradise story in such a way as to portray the serpent as the revealer of life and knowledge, and God (the Creator) as a malevolent and ignorant demon. This material is probably based on a previously existing source, to which the author of *Testim. Truth* has added some editorial touches, including an allegorical interpretation of the serpent as a symbol of Christ (49,7).

Another interesting section, unfortunately very fragmentary, consists of polemics against the tenets of such other Gnostics as Valentinus (56,2-5), Basilides and his son Isidore (57,6-8), and the Simonians (58,2-3). It is presumably on the basis of their ethical and ritual practices that those teachers and groups are regarded by the author of *Testim. Truth* as heretics. For example, the Valentinians are criticized for their use of the sacrament of baptism (55,7-9); water baptism is consistently condemned in *Testim. Truth* (69,7-24; cf. 30,18-30). The Simonians are criticized for marrying and begetting children (58,2-4), a criticism that would extend to the Valentinians and Basilidians as well.

In short, from beginning to end, our tractate is filled with the polemics of a teacher who earnestly believed that his version of Christian faith and praxis was the only true one, a pamphleteer whose hatred of "heresy" was the match of that of an Irenaeus, a Hippolytus, or a Tertullian. Indeed, our author can be regarded as a mirror-image of the great heresiologists of the Church, representing the other side of the argument.

Who was this man? From what can be gathered from the tractate itself, he was probably an Alexandrian whose Gnostic Christianity was heavily influenced by other Alexandrian gnostic traditions, especially Valentinianism. Yet he rejected certain features of Valentinian doctrine and practice. As it happens, Clement of Alexandria has provided us with information about a gnostic teacher who fits the situation of our author very well: Julius Cassianus. This man had "departed from the school of Valentinus" (*Strom.* III.93) and espoused a strict encratism, condemning marriage and sexual intercourse. Julius Cassianus, of all the heretics known to us by name from ancient sources, is the most likely candidate for the authorship of *Testim. Truth*.

Even if Julius Cassianus is not its author, *Testim. Truth* is most plausibly to be situated in Alexandria and dated to the end of the second century or the beginning of the third.

THE TESTIMONY OF TRUTH

IX 29, 6-74, 30

I will speak to those who know | to hear not with the ears | of the body but with the ears | of the mind. For many have sought [10] after the truth and have not | been able to find it; because there has taken hold

of them [the] ' old leaven of the Pharisees ' and the scribes [of] [15] the Law. And the leaven is [the] ' errant desire of ' the angels and the demons ' and the stars. As for the Pharisees ' and the scribes , it is they [20] who belong to the archons who ' have authority [over them]. '

For no one who is under ' the Law will be able to look ' up to the truth for they will not be [25] able to serve two masters. ' For the defilement of the Law ' is manifest; [30] but undefilement belongs to the ' light. The Law commands ' (one) to take a husband (or) to take a wife, and ' to beget, to multiply like the sand [5] of the sea. But passion which ' is a delight to them constrains ' the souls of those who are begotten ' in this place, those who defile ' and those who are defiled, [10] in order that the Law might ' be fulfilled through them. And ' they show that they are assisting ' the world; and they ' [turn] away from the light, [15] who are unable ' [to pass by] the archon of [darkness] ' until they pay the last [penny]. '

But the Son of Man ' [came] forth from Imperishability, [20] [being] alien to defilement. He came ' [to the] world by the Jordan ' river, and immediately the Jordan ' [turned] back. ' And John bore witness to the [25] [descent] of Jesus. For it is he ' who saw the [power] ' which came down upon ' the Jordan river; for he knew ' that the dominion of [30] carnal procreation had come to an end. The Jordan ' river is the power ' of the body, that is, the senses [31] of pleasures. The water ' of the Jordan is the desire ' for sexual intercourse. John ' is the archon of [5] the womb.

And this is what the ' Son of Man reveals to us: ' It is fitting for you (pl.) ' to receive the word of truth. If ' one will receive it [10] perfectly, − . But as for one who is [in] ' ignorance, it is difficult for him ' to diminish his works of [darkness] ' which he has done. Those who have [known] ' Imperishability, [however], [15] have been able to struggle against [passions ...] [17] I have said [to ' you], "Do not build [nor] ' gather for yourselves in the [place] [20] where the brigands break open, ' but bring forth fruit ' to the Father."

The foolish − thinking [in] ' their heart [that] ' if they confess, "We [25] are Christians," in ' word only (but) not with power, while ' giving themselves over to ' ignorance, to a ' human death, [30] not knowing where they are going [32] nor who ' Christ is, thinking that they ' will live, when they are (really) in error − ' Hasten towards the principalities [5] and the authorities. They fall ' into their clutches because of the ' ignorance that is in ' them. For (if) only ' words which bear testimony [10] were effecting salvation, the whole world ' would endure this thing ' [and] would be saved. ' [But it is in this way that they '

[drew] error to themselves. [... [18] they do] not [know] that they [will destroy] ' themselves. If the [Father [20] were to] desire a [human] sacrifice, ' he would become [vainglorious]. '

For the Son of ' [Man] clothed himself with their ' first-fruits; he went down to [25] Hades and performed many mighty works. ' He raised the dead ' therein; and the ' world-rulers of darkness became envious [33] of him, for they did not find ' sin in him. But ' he also destroyed their works ' from among men, so that [5] the lame, the blind, ' the paralytic, the dumb, (and) the ' demon-possessed were granted ' healing. And he walked ' upon the waters of the sea. [10] For this reason he [destroyed] ' his flesh from [...] ' which he [...]. And he [became ' ...] salvation [... ' his death ... [19] everyone ...] [20] how many [they are! They are] ' blind [guides, like the disciples]. ' They boarded [the ship, (and) at about thirty] ' stades, they [saw Jesus ' walking] on the [sea. These] [25] are [empty] martyrs, ' since they bear witness only [to] ' themselves. And yet they are ' sick, and they are not able to raise [34] themselves.

But when they are ' "perfected" with a (martyr's) death, this ' is the thought that they have ' within them: "If we [5] deliver ourselves over to death ' for the sake of the Name we will be saved." These matters ' are not settled in this way. But ' through the agency of the wandering ' stars they say [10] that they have "completed" their [futile] ' "course," and [...] ' say, [...]. ' But these [...] ' they have [delivered [15] themselves ...]. [23] But they resemble ' [...] them. They do not have [25] the word which gives ' [life].

[And] some say, ' "On the last day ' [we will] certainly arise [35] [in the] resurrection." But they do not ' [know what] they are saying, ' for the last day ' [is when] those belonging to Christ [5] [... the] earth which ' is [...]. when the [time] ' was fulfilled, he destroyed ' [their archon] of ' [darkness ...] soul(s) [... [20] he ' stood ...] ' they asked [what they have been] ' bound with, [and how they] ' might properly [release themselves]. [25] And [they came to know] ' themselves, [(as to) who they are], ' or rather, where they are [now], ' and what is the [place [36] in] which they will rest ' from their senselessness, [arriving] ' at knowledge. [These] ' Christ will transfer to [the heights] [5] since they have [renounced] ' foolishness, (and have) advanced ' to knowledge. ' And those who [have ' knowledge ...] [21] the great ' [... the resurrection ' ... he has come to] know ' [the Son of Man], that [25] [is, he has come to] know [himself. ' This] is the perfect life, ' [that] man know ' [himself] by means of the All. '

[Do not] expect, therefore, [30] [the] carnal resurrection, [37] which [is]

destruction, [and they are not ' stripped] of [it (the flesh) who] ' err in [expecting] ' a [resurrection] [5] that is empty. [They do] not [know] ' the power [of God], ' nor do they [understand the interpretation] ' of the scriptures [on account of their] ' double-mindedness. [The [10] mystery] which [the Son of Man ' spoke about ...] ' in order that [...] ' destroy [...] [16] man who [... book] ' which is written [...] ' for [they] have [... [20] blessed ...] ' within [them, and they] ' dwell before [God under the ' light yoke. Those who do not] ' have [the life-giving word] [25] in their [heart will die]; ' and in [their] thought ' they have become manifest to [the Son] ' of Man, according to [the manner of their] ' activity and their [error ...] [38] of this sort. They ' [...] as he divides the ' [...] and they [do not] understand ' [that the Son] of Man [5] is coming from him. '

But [when they have come] up to ' [...] sacrifice, they die ' [in a] human [way], and they ' [deliver] themselves [...] [12] a death [...] [16] those who ' [...] they are many ' [...] each ' [one ...] pervert [20] [...] gain ' [... their] mind. ' [Those who receive him] to themselves ' [with uprightness] and ' [power] and every knowledge [25] [are the ones whom] he will transfer ' [to the] heights, unto ' [life] eternal.

[But] those who receive ' [him] to themselves with ' [ignorance], the pleasures [39] which are defiled prevail over [them]. ' It is those people who used to [say], ' "God created [members] ' for our use, for us to [grow in] [5] defilement, in order that [we might] ' enjoy [ourselves]." ' And they cause [God to] ' participate with them [in] ' deeds of this [sort; and] [10] they are [not] steadfast [upon] ' the earth. [Nor will they reach] ' heaven, [but ...] ' place will [...] ' four [...] [18] unquenchable [... [22] word ...] ' upon [the Jordan river] ' when he came [to John at] [25] the time he [was baptized]. ' The [Holy] Spirit [came] ' down upon him [as a] ' dove [...] ' accept for ourselves that [he] was born [30] of a virgin [and] ' he took flesh; he [... [40] having] received power. ' [Were we also begotten from ' [a] virginal state ' [or] conceived by the word? [5] [Rather, we have been born] again by ' [the word]. Let us therefore strengthen ' [ourselves] as virgins in the ' [...].

The males dwell ' [...] the virgin [10] by means of ' [...] in the word ' [...]. But the word of ' [...] and spirit [...] [18] is the Father ' [...] for the man [... [21] like Isaiah, who was sawed ' with a saw, (and)] he became two. ' [So also the Son of Man ' divides] us by [25] [the word of the] cross. It ' [divides the day from] the night and ' [the light from the] darkness and the corruptible ' [from] incorruptibility, and it ' [divides] the males from the females. [30] But [Isaiah] is the type [41] of the body. The

saw ' is the word of the Son of ' Man which separates us from the ' error of the angels.

No one [5] knows the God of truth ' except solely the man who ' will forsake all of the ' things of the world, having renounced ' the whole place, (and) having [10] grasped the fringe of his garment. ' He has set himself up as a [power]; ' he has subdued desire in every [way] ' within himself. He has [...] ' and he has turned to him [...] [15] having also examined [...] ' in becoming [... ' the] mind. And [he ... from] ' his soul [...] ' there [...] [20] he has [...] [22] in what way [...] ' the flesh which [...] ' in what way [...] [25] out of it, and ' how many [powers does he have]? ' And who is the one who has bound him? ' And who is the one who will loose him? And what ' is the light? And what is the darkness? [30] And who is the one who has created [the earth]? ' And who is God? [And who] [42] are the angels? And what is soul? ' And what is spirit? And where is ' the voice? And who is the one who speaks? And who ' is the one who hears? Who is the one who gives pain? [5] And who is the one who suffers? And who ' is it who has begotten the corruptible flesh? ' And what is the governance? ' And why are some ' lame, and some [10] [blind], and some ' [...], and some ' [...], and some ' rich, [and] some ' poor? And why [15] are [some powerless, ' some] brigands? [...] [21] he having ' [...] as he again ' [...] fighting ' against ' [thoughts] of the archons [25] and the powers and the demons, ' not giving them a place ' in which to rest. ' [But] he struggled against their passions ' [...] he condemned [43] their error. He cleansed his ' soul from the transgressions ' which he had committed with an alien hand. ' He stood up, being upright within [5] himself, because he exists in ' everyone, and because he has ' death and life ' within himself, and he exists ' in the midst of both of them. [10] And when he had received the power ' he turned towards the parts of the right, ' and he entered into the truth, ' having forsaken all things pertaining to the left, ' having been filled with wisdom, [15] with counsel, with understanding ' and with insight, and an ' eternal power. [And] ' he broke open his bonds. [Those who had] ' formed the whole place [20] [he] condemned. [But they ' did not] find [...] hidden ' within him.

[And he gave command] ' to himself; he [began to] ' know [himself and] [25] to speak with his [mind], which ' is the father of the truth, concerning the unbegotten ' aeons, and concerning ' the virgin who brought forth ' the light. And he thinks [30] about the power which ' flowed over the [whole] place, [44] and which takes hold of him. And ' he is a disciple of his mind ' which is male. He began ' to keep silent

within [5] himself until the day when | he should become worthy to be received | above. He rejects for himself | loquacity and | disputations, and he endures [10] the whole place; and he bears up | under them, and he endures | all of the evil things. | And he is patient | with every one; he makes himself equal [15] to every one, and he also separates | himself from them. And that which someone | [wants, he brings] to him, | [in order that] he might become perfect | [(and) holy]. When the [... [20] he] | grasped [him], having bound him | upon [...] and he was filled | [with wisdom. He] bore witness to the truth | [...] the power, and he went [25] [into] Imperishability, the place | whence he [came] forth, having left | the world which has | the appearance of the [night, | and] those that whirl the [30] [stars in] it.

This, therefore, is **45** the true testimony: When | man comes to know himself | and God who is over the truth, | he will be saved, and he [5] will crown himself with the crown | unfading.

John | was begotten by the World through | a woman, Elizabeth; | and Christ was begotten by [10] the world through a virgin, | Mary. What is (the meaning of) this mystery? | John was | begotten by means of a womb | worn with age, but Christ [15] passed through a virgin's womb. | When she had conceived she gave birth to | the Savior. Furthermore she | was found to be a virgin again. | Why, then, do you (pl.) [err] [20] and not seek after these mysteries | which were prefigured | for our sake? |

It is written in the Law concerning this, | when God gave a command [25] to Adam, "From every [tree] | you may eat, [but] from | the tree which is in the midst of | Paradise do not eat, | for on the day that you eat [30] from it you will surely | die." But the serpent was wiser **46** than all the animals that | were in Paradise, and | he persuaded Eve, saying, | "On the day when you eat [5] from the tree which is in the midst | of Paradise | the eyes of your mind will be opened." | And Eve obeyed, | and she stretched forth her hand; [10] she took from the tree and | ate; she also gave to her husband with | her. And immediately they knew | that they were naked, | and they took some fig leaves [15] (and) put them on as girdles. |

But [God] came at the time of | [evening] walking in the midst | [of] Paradise. When | Adam saw him he hid himself. [20] And he said, "Adam, where are you?" | He answered (and) said, | "[I] have come under the fig tree." And at that very moment | God [knew] that he had [25] eaten from the tree of | which he had commanded him, "Do not | eat of it." And | he said to him, "Who is it **47** who has instructed you?" And Adam answered, | "The woman whom you have | given me." And

the woman said, | "It is the serpent who instructed me." [5] And he curs-
ed the serpent, and | called him "devil." | And he said, "Behold, Adam
has | become like one of us, | knowing evil and [10] good." Then he said,
"Let us | cast him out of Paradise | lest he take from the tree | of life
and eat and live for | ever."

But of what sort is [15] this God? First [he] | maliciously refused Adam
from | eating of the tree of knowledge. | And secondly | he said,
"Adam, where are you?" [20] God does not have | foreknowledge;
(otherwise), would he not know from the | beginning? [And] afterwards
| he said, "Let us cast him [out] [25] of this place, lest he | eat of the tree
of | life and live for ever." | Surely he has shown | himself to be a mali-
cious [30] grudger. And **48** what kind of a God is this? | For great is the
blindness | of those who read, and they did not | know him. And he
said, "I am [5] the jealous God; I will bring | the sins of the fathers upon
| the children until three (and) four generations." | And he said, "I will
make | their heart thick, and I will [10] cause their mind to become blind,
that | they might not know nor | comprehend the things that | are said."
But these things he has | said to those who believe in him [15] [and] serve
him!

And | [in one] place Moses writes, | "[He] made the devil a serpent |
⟨for⟩ [those] whom he has in his generation." | Also in the book which
is [20] called "Exodus," | it is written thus (cf. 7:8-12): "He contended
against the | [magicians], when the place was full | [of serpents] ac-
cording to their [wickedness; and | the rod] which was in the hand of
Moses [25] became a serpent, (and) it swallowed | the serpents of the ma-
gicians."

Again | it is written (Nm 21:9), "He made a serpent of | bronze (and)
hung it upon a pole **49** [. . .] which [. . .] [3] for the [one who will gaze]
upon | [this] bronze [serpent], none [5] [will destroy] him, and the one
who will | [believe in] this bronze serpent | [will be saved]."

For this is Christ; | [those who] believed in him | [have received life].
Those who did not believe [10] [will die].

What, then, is this | [faith? They] do not [serve . . . [28] and you (pl.)
. . .] | we [. . . **50** and] you [do not understand Christ | spiritually when
you say], | "We [believe] in Christ." For [this] | is the [way] Moses
[writes] [5] in every book. The [book of | the] generation of Adam [is
written for those] | who are in the [generation] of [the Law]. | They
follow the Law [and] | they obey it, [and . . .] [11] together with the [. . .].
(pp. 51-54 almost completely missing)

[. . . , ". . . **55** the] Ogdoad, which is the | eighth, and that we might

receive ¦ that [place] of salvation." ¦ [But they] know not what salvation is, [5] but they enter into ¦ [misfortune] and into a ¦ [. . .] in death, in the ¦ [waters]. This [is] the baptism ¦ [of death which they observe . . .] [16] come to death ¦ [. . . and] this is ¦ [. . .] according to [. . .] **56** he completed the course [of] ¦ Valentinus. He himself ¦ speaks about the Ogdoad, ¦ and his disciples resemble [the] [5] disciples of Valentinus. ¦ They on their part, moreover, [. . .] ¦ leave the good, [but] they ¦ have [worship of] ¦ the idols [. . .] [18] he has spoken [many words, and he has] ¦ written many [books . . .] [20] words [. . . **57** they are] manifest from ¦ [the] confusion in which they are, ¦ [in the] deceit of the world. ¦ For [they] go to that place [5] together with their knowledge ¦ [which is] vain.

Isidore also, ¦ [his son], resembled ¦ [Basilides]. He also ¦ [. . .] many, and [he [10] . . .] but he did not [. . .] ¦ this [. . .] ¦ other disciple(s) ¦ [. . .] blind [. . . ¦ but he] gave them [15] [. . . pleasures . . .] **58** they do [not] agree [with] ¦ each other. For the [Simonians] ¦ take [wives] ¦ (and) beget children; but the [. . .] [5] abstain ¦ from their [. . .] nature ¦ [. . .] a [passion . . .] ¦ the drops [of . . .] ¦ anoint [them . . .] [11] which we [. . . they ¦ agree] with [each other . . .] ¦ him [. . .] they [. . .] **59** judgment(s) ¦ [. . .] these, on account of the ¦ [. . .] them ¦ [. . .] the heretics [5] [. . .] schism(s) [. . .] ¦ and the males ¦ [. . .] are men ¦ [. . .] will belong ¦ [to the world-rulers] of darkness [. . .] [11] of [the world . . .] [13] they have ¦ [. . .] the [archons [15] . . . power(s) . . .] [17] judge [them ¦ . . .]. But [the . . .] ¦ word(s) of [. . .] **60** speak, while they [. . .] ¦ become [. . .] ¦ in a fire [unquenchable . . .] ¦ they are punished.

[But these] [5] who are [from the generation] ¦ of the Son of [Man have revealed] ¦ to the [. . . in] all of [the ¦ affairs . . .]. [11] But [it is difficult] to [. . .] ¦ to find [one . . .] ¦ and [two . . .]. [16] For the [Savior said to his] ¦ disciples, [. . .] ¦ one in [. . . **61** and] he has ¦ [. . .] wisdom as well as ¦ [counsel and] understanding and ¦ [intelligence] and knowledge [5] [and power] and truth. ¦ [And he has] some ¦ [. . .] from above ¦ [. . .] the place where ¦ [the Son of Man . . .] [12] power [. . .] ¦ guard against [. . .] **62** he knows [. . .] ¦ understands [. . .] [4] worthy of him [. . .] ¦ true [. . .] ¦ alien [. . .]. ¦ But [. . .], together with [. . .] ¦ evil, in [. . .] [11] he received [baptism . . .] ¦ and those that [. . . (pp. 63-64 missing) **65** in] a dream ¦ [. . .] silver [. . .]. ¦ But [. . .] becomes [wealthy ¦ . . .] among the [authorities . . .]. [6] But [the] sixtieth ¦ [. . .] thus ¦ [. . .] world ¦ [. . .] they [10] [. . .] gold [. . . [29] they] think, [. . .] [31] we have been released from **66** the flesh. [. . .] [3] not turn him to [. . .] ¦ Jesus [. . . [6] the] beginning [. . .] ¦ a son [. . .] [9] out of [. . . which ¦ is] the pattern [. . . ¦ light of . . .] [28] to find from [. . .] ¦ defilement which [. . . [31] they] do not blaspheme

[... **67** them] not, neither is there any [pleasure] ' nor desire, nor ' [can they] control them. It is fitting ' that they should become undefiled, [5] in order that they might ' [show] to every [one] that they ' [are from] the [generation of the] Son of Man, ' since it is about [them] that the Savior bore ' witness.

But [those who are] from [10] the seed [of Adam] are manifest ' by their [deeds which are] their [work]. ' They have not ceased [from desire which is ' wicked ...]. ' But some [15] [...] the dogs ' [...] the angels ' for [...] which they beget ' [...] will come [...] with their [...] [28] move as they ' [... on] the day when they will beget [30] [children]. Not only that, but they ' have intercourse while they are giving suck. **68**

But others are caught up in the death of [...]. ' They are [pulled] ' ⟨every⟩ which way, (and) they are gratified ' by unrighteous Mammon. [5] They lend money [at interest]; they [waste time]; ' and they do not work. But he who is ' [father] of [Mammon is (also)] ' (the) father of sexual intercourse.

But he who ' is able to renounce them [10] shows [that] he is [from] the generation ' of the [Son of Man], (and) has ' power to accuse [them. ' ... he] ' restrains [...] [15] part(s) in a [...] ' in wickedness [and he makes] the ' outer like the [inner. He resembles] an ' angel which [... [20] power ...] ' said them. But the one [...]. [27] And having withdrawn [...] he became ' silent, having ceased from loquacity ' and disputations. **69** But he [who has] found the [life-giving word ' and he who] has come to know [the Father of Truth ' has come to rest]; he has ceased [seeking], having ' [found]. And when he found he became [silent]. [5] But few are the things he used to say to those that ' [...] with their intellectual mind the ' [...].

There are some who, upon entering ' the faith, receive a baptism ' on the ground that they have [it] as a hope [10] of salvation, which they call ' "the [seal,"] not [knowing] ' that the [fathers of] the world are ' manifest that [place. But] ' he himself [knows that] he is sealed. [15] For [the Son] of [Man] ' did not baptize any of his ' disciples. But [... if those who] are baptized ' were headed for life, ' the world would become [20] empty. And the fathers of ' baptism were defiled. '

But the baptism of truth is ' something else; it is by renunciation of [the] ' world that it is found. [But those who] [25] say [only] with the tongue [that ' they] are renouncing it [are lying], ' and they are coming to [the place] ' of fear. Moreover they are humbled ' within it. Just as those to whom it was given, [30] to have been condemned, ' [they shall] get something!

They are ' wicked in their behavior! Some ' of them fall away **70** [to the worship of] idols. [Others] ' have ' [demons] dwelling with them [as did] ' David the king. He is the one who ⁵ laid the foundation of Jerusalem; and his son ' Solomon, whom he begat ' in [adultery], is the one who ' built Jerusalem by means of the demons, ' because he received [power]. When he ¹⁰ [had finished building, he imprisoned] the demons ' [in the temple]. He [placed them] into seven ' [waterpots. They remained] a long [time ' in] the [waterpots], abandoned ' [there]. When the Romans [went] ¹⁵ up to [Jerusalem] they discovered ' [the] waterpots, [and immediately] ' the [demons] ran ' out of the waterpots as those who ' escape from prison. And ²⁰ the waterpots [remained] pure (thereafter). ' [And] since those days, [they dwell] with men who are ' [in] ignorance, and ' [they have remained upon] the earth.

Who, then, is ²⁵ [David]? And who is Solomon? ' [And] what is the foundation? And what is the ' wall which surrounds Jerusalem? And who ' are the demons? And what are the ' waterpots? And who are ³⁰ the Romans? But these [are mysteries ...] **71** ¹² victorious over [... the Son] ' of Man [... ¹⁴ undefiled ...] ¹⁸ and he [...] ' when he [...]. ²⁰ For [...] is a great [...] ²² to this nature [...] ²⁴ those that [...] ' all in [a ...] blessed ' and they [... like a] ' salamander. [It] goes into ' the flaming fire which burns ' exceedingly; it slithers into the [furnace ... **72** ¹⁴ the] furnace [...] ¹⁶ the boundaries ' [...] that they might see ' [...] and the power ' [...] sacrifice. Great is the sacrifice [... ²² but] in a ' [...] aside ' [...]. And ²⁵ [the Son] of Man [...] ' and [he has become] manifest through ' the bubbling fountain of [immortality. **73** ...] ' he is pure, ' [and he] is [...]. A free man ' [is not] envious. He is set apart from ⁵ everyone, from [every audacity and] envy ' the [power of] which is great [...] is (a) ' disciple [...] ' pattern of law [...] ' these [...] ¹⁰ only [...] ¹³ they placed ' him under a[...] ¹⁵ a teaching [...] ¹⁷ his teaching, saying, "[Even if] an [angel] ' comes from heaven, and preaches ²⁰ to you beyond that which we preached ' to you, may he be ' anathema," (cf. Ga 1:8) not letting the [...] ' of the soul which [...] ' freedom [...]. ²⁵ For they are still immature [...] ' they are not able to [keep] ' this law which works ' by means of these heresies — ' though it is not they, but the powers ³⁰ of Sabaoth — by means **74** of the [...] ' the doctrines [...] ' as they have been jealous of some [... ' law(s)] in Christ. Those who will [...] ⁵ power [...] they reach the [...] ' the [twelve] ' judge [...] them ' [...] the fountain of ' [immortality ...] ¹³ in order that [... ¹⁷ good ...] ' the whole place. ' [...] there the enemies. ²⁰ He baptized himself, and the ' [...] he became divine; he flew

[|] [up], (and) they did not grasp him. [|] [...] there the [enemies [|] ...] since it was not possible ²⁵ [for them to bring him] down again. [|] If every [...] grasps him [|] [with] ignorance, attending [|] to those who teach in the corners [|] by means of carved things and [|] artful tricks, they will not be able [...].

MARSANES (X,*1*)

Introduced and translated by

BIRGER A. PEARSON

Codex X is extant only in fragments representing considerably less than half of its original content. Codices X and XII are the two Nag Hammadi manuscripts which have suffered the most loss. But, unlike Codex XII, the fragments of Codex X represent literature that is previously unknown; that is to say, there does not exist any other extant copy of the tractate(s) contained in it. We do not even know how large Codex X originally was, for the 68 inscribed pages to which the extant fragments are assigned represent an absolute minimum; the original codex could very easily have consisted of over 90 inscribed pages.

We do not know for sure that Codex X contained only one tractate, though what can be determined of the content of the extant fragments suggests that this is the case. Letter-traces of a tractate title, with decorations, occur on a small fragment of the last inscribed page (68). The proper name "Marsanes" has been restored from these letter-traces; hence the title *Marsanes*.

Marsanes is the name of a gnostic prophet known from two other sources: the untitled tractate found in the Bruce Codex names Marsanes and Nikotheos as "perfect men" who had seen visions of a divine being called "the triple-powered one," an emanation of the supreme Father (Cod. Bruc. *Untitled*, ch. 7). Epiphanius of Salamis mentions among the prophets honored by the "Archontic" Gnostics "a certain Martiades and Marsianos, who had been snatched up into the heavens and had come down after three days" (*Haer*. 40.7.6). ("Marsianos" is simply a Greek variant of "Marsanes.") It is quite possible that the author of the Bruce Codex tractate had access to *Marsanes*, and our tractate may also have circulated among the "Archontics" discussed by Epiphanius.

In terms of genre, our tractate is an apocalypse, specifically an "apocalypse of Marsanes." "Marsanes" may be a name adopted by the gnostic author (*mar* means "master" in Syriac). Alternatively, an anonymous author is attributing his writing to a well-known gnostic prophet. In either case, the text contains purported revelations and reports of visionary experiences. There are also passages of a paraenetic character with which the author exhorts and encourages his readers. The text is addressed to members of a gnostic community who have already been initiated (see e.g., 2,19-21; 3,4-9).

The third-century Neoplatonist philosopher, Porphyry, in a biography of his great teacher, Plotinus, refers to certain "sectarians who had abandoned the ancient philosophy" (i.e. Platonism). These sectarians were Gnostics, with whom members of Plotinus' school had come in contact. Porphyry reports that these people "produced apocalypses of Zoroaster and Zostrianos and Nikotheos and Allogenes and Messos and others of this sort" (*Vit. Plot.* 16). Two of the apocalypses referred to by Porphyry are now available to us in Coptic versions in the Nag Hammadi corpus: *Zostrianos* (VIII,*1*) and *Allogenes* (XI,*3*). *Marsanes*, in terms of its content, is very closely related to these two tractates.

Too much of our tractate is now lost to allow us to give a full account of its content, or even to outline its structure. The first ten pages are relatively intact, however. This part of the tractate contains material relating to a gnostic ascent experience, and includes a discussion of the various levels of reality, symbolically referred to as "seals." These levels range from the "worldly" and "material," characterized by corporeal existence (2,16-21), to the realms of the invisible Three-Powered One, the Non-being Spirit, and the unknown Silent One (4,12-23).

The next-best preserved section is from the middle of the codex (pp. 24-42), and contains material on the mystical meaning of the letters of the alphabet and their relation both to the human soul and to the names of the gods and angels of the zodiacal realm and the other spheres of the heavens.

The material at the end of the codex is extremely fragmentary, but there are indications of visionary experiences and a reference to heavenly intermediaries who "spoke like the angels" (63,4). One of these is mentioned by name: Gamaliel (64,19), an angel who appears in a number of Sethian Gnostic sources, including *Melchizedek* (IX,*1*:5,18). This part of the tractate also includes references to a kind of baptismal ceremony (55,20; 66,1-5). The tractate ends with a word of encouragement to "those who will know [him]" (68,17, probably referring to the supreme Father; cf. 1,11-25).

Marsanes has been classified as a Sethian writing, on the basis of features in it which relate to the Sethian Gnostic system (as delineated especially by Hans-Martin Schenke). Seth is nowhere mentioned in the extant fragments, but the revelatory role assigned to Marsanes in this tractate makes it possible for us to see in him an avatar of Seth the savior.

There are no hints in our tractate of any Christian elements or influences, and such items of Jewish origin as are reflected must be assigned to its prehistory, i.e., to the Sethian Gnostic system lying behind the text.

Marsanes is one of the Sethian Gnostic tractates in the Nag Hammadi corpus that have been profoundly influenced by Platonist philosophy. The others are *The Three Steles of Seth* (VII,*5*), *Zostrianos* (VIII,*1*), and *Allogenes* (XI,*3*). In fact, both in terms of its metaphysics and its ritual references, *Marsanes* represents a kind of Platonism which coheres well with that of the Syrian Neoplatonist philosopher, Iamblichus of Chalcis (ca. 250-325 C.E.). For *Marsanes*, as for Iamblichus, matter is not evil; indeed, it is capable of salvation (see esp. 5,14-26). Here we see a definite attenuation of the radical dualism characteristic of earlier gnostic texts. For *Marsanes*, as for Iamblichus, the descent of the soul into matter is not regarded as a fall but as a demiurgic function, a doctrine based on Plato's discussion of the soul and its descent in the *Timaeus* (41a-42b). In *Marsanes*, the descent of a figure called "the Self-begotten One" (Autogenes) represents symbolically the descending soul in its demiurgic function (5,27-6,16). Similar ideas are expressed in Iamblichus' famous treatise, *On the Mysteries of Egypt* (*De mysteriis* VIII.3).

In terms of its ritual allusions, *Marsanes* is comparable to that variety of late Platonism in which theurgy was cultivated. Theurgy (*theourgia*: "the works [*erga*] of the gods [*theoi*]") is religious ritual whose chief aim is to assist the human soul in its reascent. The *Chaldaean Oracles*, a second-century collection

of revelatory poetry, is the classic authority for theurgy, but Iamblichus is probably the greatest exponent and theorist of theurgy among the philosophers. Study
of his great work on religious ritual (*De mysteriis*, referred to above) opens up
some interesting possibilities for understanding the enigmatic ritual allusions in
Marsanes. One can thus view *Marsanes* as a text in which gnostic theurgy plays
a crucial role.

Examples of *Marsanes'* preoccupation with ritual include the material on the
"thirteen seals" (2,12-4,23), which is probably related to a gnostic ritual of ascent. (Cf. *Steles Seth*, which contains prayers and invocations used in such a
ritual.) The material on the letters of the alphabet and the nomenclature of the
gods and the angels (pp. 19-40) also is related to the ascent ritual, and probably
involves ritual chant and special instructions expected to assist the soul in its ascent. An enigmatic reference to "wax images" and "emerald likenesses" (35,1-3)
reminds us of Iamblichus' discussion of the use of stones, plants, etc., in theurgic
ritual (*De mysteriis* V.23). Even the baptismal references already mentioned
(55,20; 66,1-5) could be understood in association with an ascent ritual. (This is
probably the case with the references to baptism in *Zostrianos*; see e.g., VIII
5,14-7,22.)

The tractate *Marsanes* was probably written sometime in the third century.
There are strong indications of a Syrian background for its gnostic author, but
this person could have been active in any number of places in the Mediterranean
world, such as Rome or Egypt, though Syria is probably the best guess. From
there the original Greek version would have been brought to Egypt and translated
into Coptic.

MARSANES

X 1, 1-68, 18

[...] [11] and a [reward]. They [came to know]; they | found him with
a pure heart, | (and) they are not afflicted by him | with evils. Those
who have received [15] you (pl.) will be given their | choice reward for |
endurance, and he will | ward off [the] | evils from them. [But] let none
[20] of us be distressed [and] | think [in] his | heart that the great | Father
[...]. | For he looks upon the All [and] [25] takes care of them all. | And
[he] has shown to them | his [...]. | Those that [...] **2** [11] at first. |

But as for the thirteenth | seal, I have established it, | together with
[the] summit of [15] knowledge and the certainty | of rest. The first | [and
the] second and the | [third] are the worldly | and the material. I have [20]
[informed] you concerning these, that you should | [...] your bodies.
And | [a] sense-perceptible [power] | will [...] those who will rest, | and
they will be kept [25] [from] passion and division | [of the] union.

The fourth | [and the] fifth which are above, | [these] you have come

to know ' [... divine]. **3** He exists after the [...] ' and the nature of the [...] ' that is, the one who [...] ' three. And [I have [5] informed] you of [...] ' in the three [...] ' by these [two. I have ' informed] you concerning [it, that it] ' is incorporeal [...] [11] and after [...] ' within [...] ' every [...] which [...] ' your [...]. The [fifth, [15] concerning the] conversion [of] ' those that are within me, and ' concerning those who dwell in that place. '

But the sixth, ' concerning the self-begotten ones, [20] concerning the incorporeal being ' which exists partially, ' together with those who exist in ' the truth of the All [...] ' for understanding and [25] assurance. And the [seventh], ' concerning the self-begotten power, ' which [is the] ' third [perfect ...] **4** fourth, concerning salvation ' [and] wisdom. And the eighth, ' concerning the mind which is ' [male, which] appeared [5] [in the beginning], and (concerning) the being ' [which is incorporeal] and the ' [intelligible] world. The ninth, ' [...] of the power ' [which] appeared [in the [10] beginning. The] tenth, [concerning ' Barbelo, the] virgin [...] ' of the Aeon. ' [The eleventh] and [the ' twelfth] speak of the [15] Invisible One who possesses ' three powers ' and the Spirit which does not ' have being, belonging to ' the first Unbegotten (fem.). The [20] thirteenth speaks concerning ' [the] Silent One who was not ' [known], and the primacy of ' [the one who] was not distinguished. '

For I am he who has [25] [understood] that which truly exists, ' [whether] partially or ' [wholly], according to difference ' [and sameness], that they exist from the ' [beginning in the] entire place which is **5** eternal, ⟨i.e.⟩ all those that have come into ' existence whether without being ' or with being, those who are ' unbegotten, and the divine aeons [5] together with the angels, and the ' souls which are without guile, ' and the soul-[garments], ' the likenesses of [the] ' simple ones. And [afterwards they] [10] have been mixed with [...] ' them. But still [... the] ' entire being [... which] ' imitates the [incorporeal being] ' and the unsubstantial (fem.). [Finally] [15] the entire defilement [was saved] ' together with the immortality of ' the former (fem.). I have deliberated ' and have attained to the boundary of the sense-perceptible ' world, ⟨I have come to know⟩ part by part [20] the entire place ' of the incorporeal being, and ' ⟨I⟩ have come to know the intelligible world. ' ⟨I have come to know⟩, when ⟨I⟩ was deliberating ' whether in every respect the sense-perceptible [25] world is [worthy] ' of being saved entirely.

[For] ' I have not ceased speaking [of the] ' Self-begotten One, O [...] ' became [...] **6** part by part the entire place. ' He descended; again he descended ' ⟨from⟩ the Unbegotten One ' who does not have

being, who [5] is the Spirit. That one who exists ' before all of them reaches ' [to the divine] Self-engendered One. ' The one having ' [being] searches [10] [...] and he exists ' [... and] he is like ' [...] and from ' [...] dividing ' [...] I became [15] [...] for many, as it is manifest ' that he saved a multitude. '

But after all of these things ' I am seeking the kingdom ' of the Three-Powered One, [20] which has no beginning. Whence ' did he appear and ' act to fill the ' entire place with his power? And ' in what way did the unbegotten ones [25] come into existence, since they were not begotten? And ' what are [the] differences among the [aeons? ' And] as for those who are unbegotten, ' how many [are they]? And in what respect ' [do they differ] from each other? **7**

When I had inquired about these things ' I perceived that he had worked ' from silence. He exists ' from the beginning among those that [5] truly exist, that belong to the One who ' exists. There is another, existing ' from the beginning, belonging to the One who ' works within the Silent One. ' And the silence [...] [10] him works. ' For as much as this one [...] ' that one [works from] ' the [silence which belongs to the] ' Unbegotten One among [the aeons, and from] [15] the beginning he does not have [being]. ' But the energy of ' that One ⟨is⟩ the Three-Powered One, ' the One unbegotten [before] ' the Aeon, not having [being]. [20] And it is possible to behold the supremacy of the ' silence of the Silent One, ' i.e. the supremacy ' of the energy of the ' Three-Powered. And the One who [25] exists, who is silent, [who is] ' above the [heaven ...], ' revealed [the ' Three-Powered, First]-Perfect ' One.

[When he ...] **8** to the powers, they rejoiced. ' Those that are within me were perfected ' together with all the ' rest. And they all blessed [5] the Three-Powered, ' one by one, who ' is [the] First-Perfect One, ' [blessing] him in purity, [everywhere] ' praising the Lord [10] [who exists] before the All, ' [... the] Three-Powered. ' [...] their worship ' [...] myself, ' [and I will still go on [15] inquiring] how they had ' become silent. I will understand a ' power which I hold ' in honor.

The third ' power of the Three-Powered, [20] when it (fem.) had perceived him, ' said to me, "Be silent ' in order that you might know; run, ' and come before me. But ' know that this One was [25] [silent], and obtain understanding." ' For [the power] is attending ' [to me, leading] me into ' [the Aeon which] is Barbelo, ' [the] male [Virgin]. **9**

For this reason the ' Virgin became male, ' because she had been divided from the male. The ' Knowledge stood outside of him, [5] because it belongs to him. ' And she who exists, she who sought, ' possesses (it),

just as ' the Three-Powered One possesses. ' She withdrew [10] from them, from [these] two [powers], ' since she exists [outside of] ' the Great One, as she [...] ' who is above [...] ' who is silent, [who has] [15] this [commandment] ' to be silent. His knowledge ' and his hyposta- sis ' and his activity ' are those things of which the power [20] of the Three-Powered spoke, ⟨saying⟩, ' We all have ' withdrawn to our- selves. We have [become] ' silent, [and] ' when we came to know [him, that is], [25] the Three-Powered, [we] ' bowed down; we [...; we] ' blessed him [...] ' upon us." [...]. '

[... the] invisible [Spirit] **10** ran up ' to his place. The whole place ' was revealed; the whole place unfolded ' ⟨until⟩ he reached the upper region. [5] Again he departed; he caused the ' whole place to be illuminat- ed, and the whole ' place was illuminated. And [you] (pl.) have been given ' the third part of ' [the spirit] of the power of the One [10] [who possesses] the three ' [powers]. Blessed is [...]. He said, "O [you ' who dwell in these] places, it is necessary ' [for you to know] those that are higher [15] than these, and tell them to the ' powers. For you (sg.) will be- come ' [elect] with the elect ones ' [in the last] times, ' [as] the invisible Spirit [20] [runs] up above. And you ' [yourselves], run with him ' [up above], since you have ' [the] great crown which ' [...].

But on the day [25] [...] will beckon ' [...] run up above ' [...] and the sense-perceptible ' [...] visible ' [...] and they [...] (pp. 11-12 missing) **13** [15] the perception. He is for ' ever, not having being, ' in the One who is, who is silent, ' the One who is from the beginning, ' [who] does [not] have being [20] [...] part of [...] ' indivisible. The [...] ' con- sider a [... [24] ninth ...] **14** [15] I [was dwelling] ' among the aeons which have ' been begotten. As I was permitted, [I] have ' come to be among those that were not [begotten]. ' But I was dwelling] ' among the aeons which have ' been begotten. As I was permitted, [I] have ' come to be among those that were not [begotten]. ' But I was dwelling in the [great] [20] Aeon, as I [...]. ' And [... ' the] three powers [...] ' the One who [possesses] ' the [three] powers. The [three [25] powers ... **15** the] Silent One and the ' Three-Powered One [... ' the] one that does not have breath. ' We took our stand [...] [5] in the [...] [13] we entered [...] ' breath [... **16** who] does not have breath, ' [and he] exists in a [... ' completely]. And I saw ' [...] him to the great (fem.) [5] [...] they knew [him ...] [12] limit [...] ' and [I ...] ' alone [...] **17** is active ' [...] why, [again], (does) knowledge ' [...] ignorant, and [...] ' he runs the risk [5] [...] that he become [... [9] on account of ...]. [15] Those ' [...]. But it is necessary that a ' [...] does not have form ' [...] to this one

| [...] exists before [20] [...] the thought | [... from] the beginning | [...] the one that [...] **18** these [...] | look(ed) at [...] in nine [... the] | cosmic hebdomad [...] | in a day of [...] [5] for ever [...] [14] and [... after] | many [years ...] | when I saw the [Father I came to] | know him, and [...] | many [...] | partial [...] [20] for ever [...] | the material ones [...] | worldly [...] | above [...] | in addition [...] **19** [13] he [...] [15] out of [...] | into those that [...] | them into [...] | name | [them. And] (as for) their nomenclature, [20] [bear] witness yourselves | [that you are] inferior to [their | ...] and their [hypostasis]. |

But [in addition, when ...] **20**[14] hidden [... | the] third | [power]. The blessed Authority (fem.) | said [...] | among these and [...] | i.e. she who [does not have ...]. [20] For there is not glory [...] | nor even the one who [...]. | For indeed the one who [...]. [24] For [...] **21**[14] and the [signs of the Zodiac ...] | and the [...] | and [...] | which do not have [...] | acquire for [... | revolution ...]. [20] But [the] soul(s) [...] | there [...] | body(s) of this | [...] soul(s) of heaven [...] | around [...] [25] shape [...] | which is [...] **22**[15] those that [...] | there [... [19] all the likenesses ...] | them [...] | all the forms [...] | shape(s), so that [they ... | and] become [...] | themselves [...] [25] and the [...] | the animals [...] | and the [...] (pp. 23-24 missing) **25** there.

But their | powers, which are the angels, | are in the form of | beasts and animals. [5] Some among them are | [polymorphous], and contrary to | [nature] they have | for their names which [...]. | They are [divided] and [...] [10] according to the [... | and ...] in [form ...]. | But these that are | [aspects] of sound according to the third | originate from being. [15] And concerning these, all of | these (remarks) are sufficient, | since we have (already) spoken about them.

For [this] | division takes place | again in these regions in [the manner] [20] we have mentioned from the [beginning]. | However the soul, on the | other hand, [has] | different shape⟨s⟩. | The shape of the soul exists [in [25] this] form, | i.e. (the soul) that came into | existence of its own accord. The shape | is [the second] **26** spherical part | while the first allows [it], | eēiou, the self-begotten soul, | aeēiouō. [5] [The] second schema, | eēiou, ... by those [having] | two sounds (diphthongs), the first being | placed after them [...] [12] the light.

[Control] | yourselves, receive [the] | imperishable seed, [15] bear fruit, and | do not become | attached to your possessions. |

But know that the oxytones | exist among the vowels [20] and the | diphthongs which are | next to them. But the [short] | are inferior, and the [...] | are [...] [25] by them. Those that [...] | since they are inter-

mediate ' [...]. The sounds of ' [the semivowels] are **27** superior to the voiceless (consonants). ' And those that are double are superior ' to the semivowels which ' do not change. But the aspirates [5] are better than the inaspirates (of) ' the voiceless (consonants). ' And those that are intermediate will [accept] ' their combination in which they are; ' they are ignorant [of] [10] the things that are good. They (the vowels) ' are combined with the [intermediates] ' which are less. [Form] by [form], ' ⟨they constitute⟩ the nomenclature of the [gods] ' and the angels, [not] because [15] they are mixed with each other ' according to every form, but ' only (because) they have ' a good function. ' It did not happen [20] that ⟨their⟩ will was revealed. '

Do not keep on [sinning], ' and do not dare to ' make use of sin.

But [I] ' am speaking to you (sg.) [concerning the ' three ... shapes] ' of the soul. [The] ' third [shape of the soul] ' is [...] **28** is a spherical one, put ' after it, from the ' simple vowels: ' eee, iii, ooo, uuu, ōōō. [5] The diphthongs were ' as follows: ai, au, ' ei, eu, ēu, ou, ōu, oi, ēi, ' ui, ōi, auei, euēu, oiou, ' ggg, ggg, ggg, aiau, [10] [eieu], ēu, oiou, ōu, ggg, ' [ggg], aueieu, oiou, ēu, ' three times for a male soul. ' The third ' shape is spherical. [15] The second shape, being ' put after it, has ' two sounds. The male soul's ' third shape ' (consists) of the [20] simple vowels: ' aaa, eee, ēēē, iii, ooo, ' uuu, ōōō, ōōō, ōōō. ' [And] this shape is different ' [from] the first, but [25] [they resemble] each other ' [and they] make some ' [ordinary sounds] of ' [this sort: aeē]oō. And **29** from these (are made) the diphthongs. '

So also the ' fourth and the fifth. ' With regard to them, they were not allowed to [5] reveal the whole topic, ' but only those things that are apparent. ' You (pl.) were taught ' about them, that you should perceive them ' in order that they, too, might [10] all seek and find [who] ' they are, either ' by themselves alone [...] ' or by each other, ' or to reveal [destinies] [15] that have been determined from the beginning, ' either with reference to themselves alone [or] ' with reference to one another, just as [they] ' exist with each other [in] ' sound, whether partially [20] or formally.

[They are] ' commanded [to] ' submit or their ' [part] is generated and ' formal. Either (they are commanded) by [the [25] long] (vowels) or [by] ' those of [dual time value, or] ' by [the short (vowels)] ' which are small [...] **30** or the oxytones or the ' intermediates or the barytones. '

And ⟨the⟩ consonants ' exist with the vowels, [5] and individually ' they are commanded, ' and they submit. ' They constitute the nomenclature ' [of] the angels. And [10] [the] consonants are ' self-existent, '

[and] as they are changed ' ⟨they⟩ submit ' to the hidden [15] gods by means of ' beat and ' pitch and ' silence and impulse. ' [They] summon the semivowels, [20] all of which ' submit to them with ' one [accord]; since it is only ' the [unchanging] double (consonants) ' that coexist with the semivowels. [25]

But the aspirates ' [and the inaspirates] and the ' [intermediates] constitute ' [the voiceless (consonants). Again ' . . . they] are combined ' [with each other, and] they are separate **31** from one another. They are ' commanded, and they submit, ' and they constitute an ' ignorant nomenclature. [5] And they become one or ' two or three or [four] ' or five or six up to ' seven having a ' [simple] sound, ⟨together with⟩ these which [have] ' two [sounds], . . . the place [of the ' seventeen consonants. Among] ' the first names [some] are ' less. And ' since [these] do not have being, [15] either [they] are an aspect [of] ' being [or] they divide ' the nature [of] the mind ' which [is masculine] (and) which is [intermediate]. '

And you (sg.) [put] in [20] those that resemble each other [with] ' the vowels [and] ' the consonants. Some ' are: bagadazatha, ' begedezethe, [bēgēdē][25]zēthē, [bigidizithi, bogo] ' dozotho, [buguduzuthu], ' bōgōdōzōthō. [And] ' the rest [. . .] ' ba[bebēbibobubō]. **32** But the rest are ' different: abebēbi'bob, in order that you (sg.) might [collect] ' them, and be separated from the [5] angels.

And there ' will be some effects. ' The first (fem.), ' which is good, is from ' [the] triad. It [. . .] [10] has need of [. . .] [12] their shapes. ⟨The⟩ dyad ' and the monad ' do not resemble anything, but [15] they are first to exist. ' The dyad, being divided, ' is divided [from the] monad, [and ' it] belongs to the hypostasis. ' But the tetrad received (the) [elements], [20] and the pentad ' received concord, and the ' [hexad] was perfected by ' itself. The ' [hebdomad] received beauty, [25] [and the] ogdoad ' [received . . .] ' ready [. . .] [29] greatly. **33** And the [decad revealed] ' the whole place. ' But the eleven and the ' [twelve] have traversed [5] [. . .] not having [. . .] ' it [is higher . . .] ' seven [. . . [15] name(s) . . .] [17] promise that [. . .] ' begin [to separate] ' them by means of [20] a mark [and] ' a point, the [one which ' quarrels] from the one which is [an enemy]. '

Thus [. . .] ' of being [. . .] [26] the [letters . . .] ' in [a **34** holy] or according to a [bond] ' existing separately. ' [And] ⟨they⟩ exist with each ' [other] in generation or [in [5] birth. And] according to [. . .] ' generation] they do not have ' [. . .] these [. . .] [18] one [. . .] speaking ' [the] riddle.

Because within [20] [the] sense-perceptible world ' there exists the tem-

ple [which measures] seven hundred [cubits], and a river which [. . .] within [25] [. . . for] ever, they [. . .] three [. . .] to the four [. . .] seals [. . .] clouds [35] [and the] waters, and the [forms of the] wax images, [and] some emerald likenesses.

For the rest, I will [5] [teach you (sg.)] about them. This is [the] generation of the names. That (fem.) which [was not] generated [. . . from the] beginning [. . .] [15] with regard to [. . .] [18] time(s), when [confined], when spread out, when [diminished]. [20] But there exists the gentle [word], and there exists another word which [approaches] being [. . .] in this [manner . . .]. [26] And he [. . .] the difference [. . .] and the [. . .] [36] the all and a [. . .] the [undivided] beings and the power [. . .] having [a] [5] share in [the joy] separately and [. . .] whether [. . .] [15] power [. . . he] exists [in] every place [. . .] them always. [He] dwells with the corporeal [20] and the incorporeal ones.

This is the word of the hypostases that one should [. . .] in this way. If [. . .] with their [25] [. . .] helping [those who stir up] the [. . .] manifest [. . .] if one [37] knows him, he will [call] upon him.

But there are words, some of which are [two [5] but others] existing [separately . . . [13] and] they [. . .] [15] or those which [. . .] [17] or according to [those that] have duration. And [these] either are separate from [them] [20] or they are joined to one another, or with themselves, either [the] diphthongs, or the simple [vowels], or every [. . .] or [. . .] [25] or [. . . exist] just as [. . . exist . . .] the [consonants . . .] [38] they exist individually until they are divided and doubled. Some have the power [5] [. . .] according to the [letters that are consonants . . .] [12] become [. . .] [15] by themselves [. . .] and three (times) [for the] vowels, and twice [for] the consonants, [20] [and] once for the entire place, and with ignorance for [those which] are subject to change [. . . which] became [25] [. . .] together with the [entire place . . .] finally.

And [. . .] they all [. . . they] are [39] hidden, but they were pronounced openly. They did not stop without being revealed, nor did they stop without [5] naming the angels. The vowels [join] the [consonants, whether] without [or] within, [10] [. . .] they said [. . . teach you (sg.) . . .] again [for ever. They were counted] four times, (and) they were [engendered] [15] three times, and they became [. . .]. [18]

For these reasons we have acquired sufficiency; for it is fitting that [20] each one acquire power for himself to bear fruit, and that we never cast aspersions [on] the mysteries [25] [. . .] the [. . .].

For [. . .] which [is . . . the] souls [. . .] the] signs of the Zodiac [. . .] [40] a new hypostasis.

And the reward which will ' be provided for such a one ' is salvation.
[5] But the opposite will ' happen there to the one ' who commits sin.
[The one who commits] sin ' by himself [...] will be ' [in a ... in a ...]
[12] in order that ' before you (sg.) examine ' the one who ⟨...⟩, one [15]
might [tell] another ' [about an] exalted power ' and a divine knowledge
' and a might which ' cannot be resisted. [20] But you shall examine ' who
is worthy that he should ' reveal them, knowing ' that [those] who commit sin [...] ' down to [...] [25] as they [... ' the Father ...] **41** that
which is fitting. Do not desire ' to give power to the sense-perceptible
world. ' Are you (pl.) not attending to me, ' who have received salvation [5] from the intelligible world? ' But (as for) these ⟨words⟩ –
watch yourselves – ' do not [...] them as a(n) ' [... [12] understand ...]
and he takes [... ' the rest], ' I [will speak of] them. The [perfection [15]
...] in order that ' it might increase [...] who commit sin [...] [18] the
embodied souls did not understand ' them. Those that are upon [20] the
earth as well as those outside of ' the body, those in heaven, are ' more
than the angels. The place ' which we [talked] about in ' [every]
discourse, these [...] [25] stars [...] [27] book(s) [...] ' whether already
[...] ' into the [...] [30] blessed is [...] **42** whether he is gazing at the '
two or he is gazing at ' the seven planets ' or at the twelve [5] signs of the
Zodiac or at ' the thirty-[six] Decans [...] [12] are [... ' these reach up]
' to [...] [16] and ' [these] numbers, whether [those in heaven] ' or those
upon the earth, ' together with those that are under the [earth], [20] according to the relationships and ' the divisions among ' these, and in the
rest ' [...] parts ' [according to kind and] according to ' [species ... [27]
they] will [submit ' since] she has power ' [...] above [30] [... they exist]
apart [...] **43**[6] every [...] [20] body(s) [... ' a] place [... divine Barbelo
...] **44**[4] reveal them [...] ' in this [manner ...] ' this [... [20] intelligible
angels], as she [...] ' intelligible [... ' above ...] ' save(d) from [...]
[27] them [...] **45**[3] world [...] ' and [... [6] world ...] [21] they came [...]
[24] those who [...] **46**[5] is [...] ' like [...] [20] the voice of ' [...] name(s)
[and ... [23] for] ever [... ' name(s) ' ...]. (pp. 47-54 missing)

[...] **55**[17] (after) I was silent, [I said], ' "Tell [me, ...] ' what is the
[power ...] [20] will wash [... ' entire generation ...] **56**[17] greatly, the '
[...] much ' [...] he is [...], and [20] [...] all [...] ' in the [... **57**[18]
knowledge ...] [20] persevere [...] ' the great [...] ' for I [became ...]
58[20] bone(s) of the ' [...] in the [worldly ... (pp. 59-60 missing) **61**
which is] under [...] your daughters [...] [3] for just as ' [... the] kingdom of [...]. [5] But this one [...] [12] every [...] **62** in the one who [...]
' not. [And ...]. '

For it is [...] who [... ' you (pl.) did not] know the [...] ⁵ for the [... ¹⁰ partially ...] **63** in ' [...] remainder ' down [... the] earth. And they ' [spoke] like the angels ⁵ [...] he was like the ' wild [animals].

And he said, [... ⁸ for] ever [...] ¹⁷ from [...] ' the number [...] ' I saw [...] ²¹ and his [...] a [voice ...] ' and [...] his **64** I [...] ' because I [saw] all of [the lights] ' around [me, blazing ' with] fire. [And ...] ⁵ me in their midst [...] ¹⁶ angel(s) [who ...] ' beside me. [And ...] ' the [one ...] ' Gamaliel, ²⁰ [the one] who is in command of [the spirits] which [...] **65** the angels ' [...] which receive ' [all of them ...] ' with those whom they [... ⁵ and] he [took] me ' [... he finished ... ¹⁰ her] members [...] ¹⁴ the [invisible ... ¹⁷ judgment ...] ' thrown ' [...] every [... which is placed ... ²¹ fountain] of ' [immortality ...] living ' [...] the two ' [... silent ²⁵ ... god(s)] **66** wash it (fem.) from [... ' of God ...] ' the one whom they [sealed] ' has been adorned [with the ⁵ seal of] heaven. [...] ¹¹ to his [...] ' great [...]. ¹⁷

And I [saw ... ¹⁹ unmixed ...] ' those who [...] **67** they will become ' [...] of God ' [...] a woman ' [...] while she is in [travail ⁵ ...] when she gives birth, [...] ¹⁰ with [...] ¹² all of [...] ' thing ' [...] men [...] and ¹⁵ [...] women [and men ' of this kind ... ' no one] ⟨of⟩ those [that are upon the] earth ' [knew] that [...] ' every [...] them, ²⁰ [and they will] take pity on these, [together with the] ' home-[born], for these will [pay ' ...] God [...] ²⁴ aeon(s) [...] **68** with those who will [...] ' who have [...] ' God [...] ' from the [beginning ...] ⁵ in [the ...] ' fear [... ⁸ name(s) ... ¹² mysteries] ' in [...] ' God [...] ¹⁶ manifest [...] ' those who will know [him]. '

[M]arsanes

THE INTERPRETATION OF KNOWLEDGE (XI,*1*)

Introduced by

ELAINE H. PAGELS

Translated by

JOHN D. TURNER

The Interpretation of Knowledge offers a unique opportunity to see how a gnostic teacher uses New Testament writings and applies them to the church. Features of style and structure suggest that the text presents a homily intended for delivery in a service of worship. The structure of the discussion follows a common pattern of worship, in which readings from the gospel are followed by readings from the apostle (that is, from Paul). Correspondingly, an early section of *The Interpretation of Knowledge* (9,21-14,15) uses passages known from Matthew to interpret the Savior's teaching and his passion; the following section (14,15-21,34) uses texts from 1 Corinthians and probably Romans, Colossians, Ephesians, and Philippians to interpret the church as the "body of Christ."

The author is concerned to address a community that is torn by jealousy and hatred over the issue of spiritual gifts. Some members refuse to share their spiritual gifts with one another; others envy those who have received such gifts as prophecy and public speaking and so stand out in the congregation. Some despise others whom they consider ignorant (that is, lacking *gnosis*); the rest feel slighted and resentful.

The author's concern throughout *The Interpretation of Knowledge* is to rectify this divisive situation. Having recalled how the Savior taught the oneness of the Father (9,28-29), and, further, how the "great Son" voluntarily accepted humiliation for the sake of his "small brothers" (14,28-29), he now applies the lessons of unity and of humility to the church. First he recalls how the church received redemption; the Savior abolished the "old bond of debt" which enslaved those "condemned in Adam" (14,34-36; cf. Cl 2:14) and proclaimed in its place the "edict of the Father" (14,29-31), offering forgiveness of sins and release from death (14,36-38). From 13,20 through 21,35 the author takes up Paul's metaphor of the body and its members (cf. Ro 12:4-8; 1 Co 12:12-31) and combines it with the images of Christ as the Head of the body, the church (cf. Cl 1:18; 2:19; Ep 4:15-16) in order to remind the members that they all share in the "same body" and the "same Head." Despite the diversity of gifts (cf. 1 Co 12:4), each member shares in the same grace (16,18-24; cf. Ro 12:6); the same power which inspires the speaker enables the listener to understand what he says (16,31-38). Those who receive lesser gifts are not to complain, but to rejoice that they also share in the body (18,28-38; 1 Co 12:14-26). Those who receive greater gifts, such as knowledge (*gnosis*; cf. 1 Co 12:8) are not to despise others as inferior or ignorant (17,25-26). On the contrary, "you are ignorant when you hate

them" (17,27), for those who show hatred and jealousy toward others demonstrate by their attitude that they still resemble the jealous and ignorant demiurge. These attitudes betray their ignorance of God (15,30-33), the true Father, and of his Son.

Amplifying Paul's image of the church as a spiritual organism, the author takes up the metaphor of the plant with roots, branches, and fruits, "the roots have a connection with one another, and their fruits are undivided" (19,31-33). As the roots exist for the sake of the fruits and for another, "let us become like the roots, since we are equal" (19,36-37). The text concludes with warnings of persecution (20,20-38) and the exhortation to overcome sin; those who do overcome it shall receive a "crown of victory, even as our Head was glorified by the Father" (21,30-34).

The author, who identifies himself as a member of the church, shares scriptural texts and terms familiar to us from early Christian orthodoxy, while using Valentinian theology to interpret these to his audience. This teacher envisions the church he addresses as including both psychic and pneumatic Christians; he may have addressed this homily to both, or specifically to the small circle of the elect. This text offers a significant primary source for understanding how some Gnostic Christians − and specifically certain Valentinian Christians − understand the church in the light of Jesus' teaching and of Paul's letters.

THE INTERPRETATION OF KNOWLEDGE

XI 1, 1-21, 35

[... [14] they came to] believe by means of [signs ¦ and] wonders [and fabrications. ¦ The likeness] that came to be through [them ¦ followed] him, but through ¦ [reproaches] and humiliations [before they received ¦ the apprehension] of a vision [they fled [20] without having] heard [that the Christ] ¦ had been crucified. ¦ [But our] generation is fleeing since it does not yet ¦ [even believe that the Christ ¦ is alive. In order] that our faith [25] [may be] holy (and) pure, ¦ [not relying upon] itself actively, but ¦ [maintaining] itself planted in ¦ [him, do not] say: "Whence ¦ [is the] patience to measure faith?", [30] for each one is persuaded ¦ [by the things] he believes. If ¦ he disbelieves them, then [he] would be unable ¦ [to be persuaded]. But it is a great thing ¦ for a man who has [35] faith, since he is [not] in unbelief, ¦ which is the [world].

[Now] the world ¦ [is the place of] unfaith [and ¦ the place of death]. And death [exists as **2** ... [15] likeness and] they will [not believe]. ¦ A holy thing is the faith [to see ¦ the likeness]. The opposite is [unfaith ¦ in the likeness]. The things that he will grant [them ¦ will support] them. It was impossible [for them [20] to attain] to the imperishability [...] ¦ will [become ...] ¦ loosen [... [24] those who] were sent [...]. ¦ For [he who] is distressed [will not believe]. ' He [is unable] to bring a [great ' church] since it is gathered out of [a small ' gathering].

He became an [emanation of] ' the trace. For also they say [about] [30] a likeness that it is apprehended [by means of ' his trace]. The structure [apprehends by means of ' the] likeness, but God [apprehends ' by means of] his members. [He knew ' them] before they were begotten, [and they [35] will know] him. And the one who [begot ' each] one from [the first will ' indwell] them. He will [rule over them]. ' For it is [necessary] for [each one 3 . . . [26] The] Savior [removed himself] since it is [fitting]. ' Indeed, [not ignorant] but [carnal ' is the] word who [took him] as a husband. ' And it is [he] who exists [as an image], since [30] [that one (masc.)] also [exists], as well as that one (fem.) ' [who brought] us forth. [And she caused] him to know ' [that] she is [the] Womb. This [is a] marvel of hers ' [that she] causes us to transcend [patience. ' But this is] the marvel: he [loves [35] the one who] was first to [permit] a virgin ' [. . .]. It is fitting to [. . .] her ' [. . .] unto death ' [. . . desire] to practice 4 [. . .]. [24] Therefore ' [she yielded] to him in [her path]. ' He was [first to fix] our eye [upon this] ' virgin [who is fixed] to the [cross] ' that is in those [places. And] we see [that ' it is] her water [which] the supreme authority [granted] [30] to the one [in whom] there is [a sign. This ' is that] water of [immortality which] ' the great [powers] will grant to [him while he is] ' below [in the likeness] of [her young son. ' She did not stop] on his account. She [. . .] [35] the [. . .] he became [. . .] ' in the [. . .] word that [appears] ' to the . . .] word that [appears] ' to the [. . .]. ' He [did not . . . 5 . . .] [14] in [. . .] ' through [. . .] ' come from those places. [Some fell] ' in the path. Others [fell in the rocks]. ' Yet still others he [sowed in the thorns]. ' And still others [he gave to drink ' . . .] [21] and the shadow. Behold [. . .] ' he [. . . . [25] And] this [is the eternal reality] ' before the souls come forth from ' [those who] are being killed.

But he was ' being pursued in that place ' by the trace produced by [30] the Savior. And he was crucified ' and he died — not his own [death, ' for] he did [not at all] deserve to die ' [because ' of] the church of mortals. [And he was ' nailed] so that [they] might keep [35] him in the church. [He answered] her ' [with] humiliations, since [in this] way he had [borne] the suffering ' which he had [suffered]. ' For Jesus is for us a [likeness] on account of 6 [. . .] [15] this [. . . ' the] entire [structure] and ' [. . . the great] bitterness of the [world ' . . .] us with the ' [. . .] by thieves [20] [. . .] the [slaves ' . . . down] to Jericho ' [. . .] they [received ' . . .]. For [. . . [25] down] to [those who] will wait ' while the entire defect restrains [them] ' until the [final] reality that is ' [their] portion, since he [brought] us down, ' having bound us in nets of flesh. [30] Since the body is [a] ' temporary dwelling which ' the rulers and [authorities] have as [an] abode, ' the man within, [after being] ' imprisoned in the fabrication, [fell] [35] into [suffering. And] having compelled [him] ' to [serve them,] they constrained him to ' serve [the] energies. They split ' the Church so as to inherit 7 [...] [10] power to [...] ' and [...] ' and [...] ' having [touched ...] ' before [...] [17] it is [the] beauty that will [...] ' wanted to [... and] ' to be with [...] [20] fighting with [one another ...] ' like others [...] ' virgin [...] ' to destroy [...] ' wound [...] [26] but she [... she likens] ' herself to the [...] ' her since they had struck [...] ' imperishable. This [...] [30] that he remain [...] ' virgin. The [...] ' her beauty [...] ' faithfulness [...] ' and therefore [...] [35] her. He hastened [...] ' he did not put up with [...] ' they despise [...]. ' For when the Mother had [8 ... [6] the] Mother [...] [8] her enemy ' [... the] teaching [... of] [11] the force [...] [15] nature [...] ' behold a maiden ' [...] he is unable ' [...] first ' [... the] opposite [...]. [20] But how has he ' [...] maiden ' [...] he was not able ' [...] he [became ' ...] killed [him [25] ...] alive ' [...] he reckoned her [...] ' better than life ' [...] since he knows that if ' [...] world created [him [30] ...] him to raise ' [him ...] up from ' [...] upon the regions [... ' those] whom they rule [...]. But [...] emitted him [35] [...] he dwells in him ' [...] the Father of the All ' [...] be more to her [...] ' him. He [9 ...] [9] like [...] ' into [...] he [has] ' them [...] ' them [...] each [one will be] ' worthy [...] take him and [... [15] the] teacher should hide himself [as if ' he were] a god [who] would embrace [his works] ' and destroy them. For [he] also ' spoke with the Church [and] he [made himself] ' her teacher of immortality, and [destroyed] [20] the arrogant [teacher] by [teaching] ' her to [die].

[And this teacher made a ' living] school, for [that teacher has] ' another school: while [it teaches us about] ' the [dead] writings, he, on the other hand, was causing us to [remove ourselves] [25] from the [surfeit] of the world; ' we were being taught about our death ' through them.

Now this is his teaching: ' Do not call to a father upon ' the earth. Your Father, who is in heaven, is one. [30] You are the light of ' the world. They are my brothers and my fellow ' companions who do the will ' of [the] Father. For what use is it if you ' gain the world and you forfeit your [35] soul? For when we were in the dark ' we used to call many "father," since we were ' ignorant of the true Father. And ' this is the great conception of [all] the sins 10 [...] [9] pleasure. We are like

' [...] him to [...] ' soul [...] men who [...] ' the [dwelling] place. '

[What] now is the [faith laid down] ' by the master who [released] him [from the great] [15] ignorance [and] the [darkness of the ignorant eye?] ' He reminded him of the good things ' [of his Father] and the race. For he said ' [to him], "Now the world is not yours; ' [may you not esteem] the form that is in it [as] advantageous; [20] [rather (it is) disadvantageous] and a [punishment]." Receive ' now the [teaching of the one who was] reproached — ' an advantage and [a profit] for the soul — ' [and] receive [his shape. It is the] shape ' [that] exists in the presence [of the Father], the word [25] and the height, that let you know him ' before you have been led astray while in (the) flesh ' of condemnation. Likewise I became very small ' so that through my humility I ' might take you up to the great height, whence [30] you had fallen. You were taken ' to this pit. If now you believe ' in me, it is I who shall take you ' above through this shape that you see. ' It is I who shall bear you upon my shoulders. Enter [35] through the rib whence you came ' and hide yourself from the beasts. ' The burden that you bear ' now [is] not yours. Whenever [you (fem.)] go 11 [...] [15] from his glory [...] ' from the first. ' From [being counted] with the female, ' sleep [brought labor] and the [sabbath] ' which [is the] world. [20] For from [being counted] with the Father, ' sleep brought [the sabbath] and [the exodus] ' from the [world of the beasts]. ' For the [world] is from ⟨the⟩ [beasts] ' and it is a [beast]. Therefore [he] [25] that is lost [has been reckoned to the] crafty one, and [that one] ' is from [the beasts] that came forth. They put upon [him a] garment of condemnation, ' for the female [had no] other ' garment [for clothing] her seed [30] except the one she first brought ' on the sabbath. For no beast ' exists in [the] Aeon. For the Father does not ' keep the sabbath but actuates the Son, ' and through the Son he continued [35] to provide himself with the Aeons. The Father has ' living rational elements ' from which he puts on ' my [members] as garments. The man 12 [... [12] this] ' is the name. The [... he] ' emitted [himself and] he [15] emitted the [reproached one. The one ' who] was reproached changed (his) name ' and, [along with that which would be] like the reproach ' he [appeared] as flesh. And ' [the humiliated one has no] equipment. He has [no] need [20] of the [glory that] is [not his]; he has ' his own [glory] with the ' [name], which is the [Son]. Now he came that we might ' become glorious [through the] humiliated one ' [that] dwells in the [places of humiliation. [25] And through [him] who was reproached ' we receive the [forgiveness] of sins. ' And through the one [who] was reproached ' and the one who [was redeemed] we receive ' grace.

But who [is it] that redeemed [30] the one who was reproached? It is [the] emanation ' of the name. For just as the flesh has need ' of a name, so also is [the] flesh an Aeon ' that Wisdom has emitted. It ' received the majesty that is descending, [35] so that the Aeon might enter ' the one who was reproached, that we might escape ' the disgrace of the carcass and be regenerated ' in the flesh [and] blood of **13** [...] [9] destiny. He [...] ' and the Aeons [... ' they] accepted the Son [although he was] ' a complete mystery [... ' each one] of his [members ...] ' grace. [When [15] he cried out, he] was separated ' from the Church like [portions of] ' the darkness from the Mother, while his [feet] ' provided him traces, and [these] ' scorched the path of [the] ascent [20] to the Father.

But [what is the way and manner (in) which] ' it (fem.) became [their Head]? Well, it (fem.) made the [dwelling place to bring forth] ' the light [to those] who dwell within ' him so that [they might] see the [ascending] Church. [25] For the Head drew ' itself up from the pit; it ' was bent over the cross and [it] ' looked down to Tartaros so that ' those below might look above. [30] Hence, for example, when someone ' looks at [someone], then the face of the one ' who looked down looks up; ' so also once the Head looked ' from the [height] to its members, our [35] members [went] above, where the Head ' was. And it, the cross, ' was [undergoing] nailing for the members, ' and solely that they might be able **14** [...] [8] have [...] ' because they were [like ...] [10] slave. The consummation [is ' thus: He whom] she indicated ' [will be completed] by the [one who] indicated. ' And the seeds [that remain will endure] ' until the All is separated [and takes] [15] shape.

And thus the decree ' will be fulfilled, for just as the woman ' who is honored until death ' [has] the advantage of time, ' [so too will it] give birth. And this offspring [20] [will] receive [the body] appointed for it ' [and] it [will become perfect]. He has ' a generous [nature since] the Son of ' God dwells in [him]. And whenever ' he acquires the All, whatever [25] he possesses will ⟨be dissolved⟩ in the ' fire because it greatly despised and ' outraged the Father. '

Moreover, when the great Son was sent ' after his small brothers, he spread [30] abroad the edict of the Father and proclaimed ' it, opposing the All. And he ' removed the old bond of debt, the one of ' condemnation. And this [is the] edict ' that was: Those who made themselves [35] enslaved have become condemned ' in Adam. They have been [brought] from ' death, received forgiveness for their ' sins and been redeemed by **15** [...] [10] since we are worthy [...] ' and [...] ' but I say [...] [14] and these [...]. ' For [...] is worthy to [...] ' God. And the Father [...

the] ' Christ removed himself [from] ' all these, since he loves [his members] ' with all his heart. [One who is jealous sets] [20] his members against [one another. If] ' he is [not] jealous, [he will not] be removed from (the) [other members and the] ' good which [he] sees. [By having a] ' brother [who] regards us [as he] [25] also is, one glorifies the [one who gives us] ' grace. Moreover, it is fitting for [each] ' of us to [enjoy] the gift ' that he has received from [God, and] ' that we not be jealous, since we know that [30] he who is jealous is an obstacle in his (own) [path], ' since he destroys only himself ' with the gift and he is ignorant ' of God. He ought to rejoice [and] ' be glad and partake of grace and [35] bounty. Does someone have a ' prophetic gift? Share it without ' hesitation. Neither approach ' your brother jealously nor 16 [...] [9] chosen as they [...] ' empty as they [escape ...] ' fallen from their [...] ' are ignorant that ' [... in this way they] have ' [...] them in [15] [...] in order that they may ' [reflect] perforce upon the things that you want ' [them to think] about when [they ' think about] you. [Now] your brother ' [also has his] grace: [20] [Do not] belittle yourself, but ' [rejoice and give] thanks spiritually ' [and] pray for that ' [one in order that] you might share the grace ' [that dwells] within him. So do not consider [him [25] foreign] to you, rather, (as) one ' who is yours, whom each ' [of] your ⟨fellow⟩ members received. ' By [loving] the Head who possesses them, ' you also possess the one from whom it is that [30] these outpourings of gifts exist ' among your brethren.

But is someone ' making progress in the Word? Do not ' be hindered by this; do not say: ' "Why does he speak [35] while I do not?", for what he ' says is (also) yours, ' and that which discerns the Word and ' that which speaks is the same power. The [Word 17 ... [14] eye] or a [hand only, although they are] ' a [single] body. [Those who belong to us] ' all serve [the Head] together. ' And] each one [of the members reckons] ' it as a member.

[They can] not ' all become [entirely a foot] [20] or entirely an eye [or entirely a hand since] ' these members will not [live alone]; ' rather they are dead. We [know that they are being put to ' death. So] why [do you love] ' the members that are still dead, [instead of those that] [25] live? How do you know [that someone] ' is ignorant of the [brethren]? ' For [you] are ignorant when you [hate them] ' and are jealous of them, since [you will not receive] ' the grace that dwells within [them], [30] being unwilling to reconcile them to [the] ' bounty of the Head. You ought to [give] ' thanks for our members and [ask] ' that you too might be granted ' [the] grace that has been given to them. [35] For the Word is rich, '

generous, and kind. Here he ' gives away gifts to ' his men without jealousy according to **18** [... [12] appeared ' in each] of the members ' [...]
himself [15] [...] since they do not fight ' [at all with one another] on account of [their] difference(s). ' [Rather] by laboring with ' [one another
they will] work with one another, ' [and if] one of them [20] [suffers, they
will] suffer with him, and ' [when each one] is saved, they are saved '
[together].

Moreover, [if they] would wait for ' [the exodus] from the (earthly)
harmony, they will ' [come to the Aeon]. If they are fit to share [25] [in]
the (true) harmony, how much the more ' [those who] derive from the
[single] unity? ' They ought to be reconciled with one ' another. Do not
accuse your Head ' because it has not appointed you as an eye but rather as [30] a finger. And do not ' [be] jealous of that which has been put in
the ' class of an eye or a hand or a foot, ' but be thankful that you do
not exist ' outside the body. On the contrary, you have [35] the same
Head on ' whose account the eye exists as well as the hand ' and the
foot and the rest of the ' parts. Why do you despise **19** the one that is
appointed as [...] ' it desired to [...] ' you slandered [...] ' does not
embrace [...] [5] unmixed [body ...] ' chosen [...] [12] dissolve [...] ' of
the Aeon [...] ' descent [...] [15] however [plucked] ' us from ⟨the⟩
[Aeons that exist in] ' that place. [Some] ' exist in the [visible] Church
– ' those who exist in the [Church] [20] of men – and [unanimously]
they proclaim [to one another] the Pleroma of [their aeon]. ' And some
exist [for death in] ' the Church on whose behalf [they] [25] go – she for
whom they are [death] – ' while others are for life. Therefore ' they
[are] lovers of abundant life. And ' each of the rest [endures] ' by his
own root. [30] He puts forth fruit ' that is like him, since the roots [have]
' a connection with one ' another and their fruits are undivided, ' the
best of each. [35] They possess them, existing for them ' and for one another. So let us become ' like the roots since we are equal **20** [...] ' that
Aeon [...] ' those who are not ours ' [...] above the [...] [5] grasp him
[...] [13] since ' [...] your soul. He will [...] [15] we gave you to him
[...]. ' If you purify ' [it, it abides in] me. If you enclose ' [it, it belongs
to the] Devil. ' [Even] if you [kill] his forces that [20] [are active, it will]
be with you. For if ' [the soul] is dead, still ' it [was enacted upon] (by)
the rulers and ' [authorities].

What, now, do you think ' [of] as spirit? Or [25] [why] do they
persecute men of ' [this] sort to death? Are ' they not satisfied to be
with the soul ' and (so) seek it? ' For every place is [excluded] from
them by [30] [the] men of God so long as they ' exist in flesh. And when

they ' cannot see them, since they (the men of God) live by ' the spirit, ' they tear apart what appears [35] as if thus they can ' find them. But what is the profit for them? ' They are senselessly mad! They rend ' their surroundings! They dig the earth! 21 [...] [3] him [...] ' hid [...] [5] exists [...] ' purify [...] [16] however [...] ' after God [...] ' seize us [...] [20] but we walk [...]. ' For if the sins [are many, how much] ' the more now is the [jealousy of the Church] ' of the Savior. For [each one] ' was capable of [both (types)] [25] of transgression, [namely that of an adept] ' and (that of) an ordinary person. It is [still] a ' single [ability] that they possess. And ' as for us, we are adepts [at] ' the Word. If we sin against [it], [30] we sin more than Gentiles. ' But if we surmount every sin, ' we shall receive the crown of ' victory, even as our Head was ' glorified by the Father. [35]

The Interpretation of Knowledge

A VALENTINIAN EXPOSITION (XI,2),

with

ON THE ANOINTING, ON BAPTISM A AND B,

and

ON THE EUCHARIST A AND B

Introduced by

ELAINE H. PAGELS

Translated by

JOHN D. TURNER

A Valentinian Exposition expounds the origin of the creation and the process of redemption in terms of Valentinian theology, specifically in terms of the myth of Sophia. The tractate thus offers the only original Valentinian account of that myth: *The Tripartite Tractate* (I,5) recounts another version that features the Logos instead of Sophia.

The author begins by promising to reveal "my mystery," and follows the account with baptismal and eucharistic prayers and benedictions. This suggests that *A Valentinian Exposition* offers a kind of secret catechism for candidates being initiated into gnosis. Following the revelation of the mystery, the candidate is invited to participate in anointing, baptism, and the eucharist, as Gnostic Christians understand these sacraments.

Besides relating the Sophia myth and referring to sacramental rituals, *A Valentinian Exposition* has a third remarkable feature: it gives firsthand evidence of theological controversies among different groups of Valentinian theologians. The heresiologists attest that gnostic teachers disagree among themselves on the interpretation of fundamental doctrines; thus *A Valentinian Exposition* demonstrates the truth of Tertullian's statement that Valentinian Christians "disagree on many specific issues, even with their own founders" (*Praescr.* 42). Irenaeus, Hippolytus, and others mention several such issues involving the story of Sophia: the interpretation of the primordial source (in what sense is it monadic or dyadic), of Limit (what are his functions) and the passion of Sophia (what motivated it). While the church fathers sketch out various positions taken on these issues, the author of *A Valentinian Exposition* engages each issue, challenging certain views and advocating others.

Valentinian theologians disagreed, first of all, on the question of whether the primordial root of all is a monad or a dyad. According to Irenaeus, Valentinus himself and the followers of his student Ptolemy said that the primal source is a dyad consisting of the Father of the All and his feminine counterpart, Silence, the Mother of all things (*Haer*. 1.11.1). But this author insists, on the contrary, that the Father is one, singular, a monad; and that the Silence, far from being the Father's dyadic syzygy, was merely the state of tranquility in which the Father reposed in his original solitude.

Second, this author discusses the function of Limit: he himself maintains that Limit possesses four powers, while other Valentinians attribute to Limit only two of those four powers. As this author interprets the story, Limit first separated Sophia's passion from the pleroma, and so protected and confirmed the aeons against the violation her transgression incurred. Yet Limit also restrained Sophia from being absorbed into the Father, and, finally, he separated her passions from her and confirmed her as well.

A third issue of controversy among Valentinian theologians concerned the interpretation of Sophia's suffering. According to Irenaeus' account, some Valentinians said that Sophia, in transgressing her role in the pleroma, only expressed the involuntary longing of all the aeons for closer communion with the Father (*Haer*. 1.2.2); others said that she willfully and audaciously attempted to rise above the condition of interdependence she shared in common with all the other aeons, and dared to imitate the Father himself (*Haer*. 1.2.3). The author of *A Valentinian Exposition* apparently takes a position closer to the latter view, which indicates that Sophia willfully violated the pleromic harmony, and later repented of this as she turned back to the Father.

This text goes on to describe how Sophia, after suffering in isolation, repented and received Christ, who descended to become her divine counterpart. Their divine reunion demonstrates the Father's will that "nothing . . . happen in the pleroma apart from a syzygy" (i.e., that all beings except himself be interdependent); and shows how all things "will come to be in unity and reconciliation."

Finally, this text offers what appear to be liturgical fragments of a Valentinian celebration of baptism and the eucharist: in this respect, as in others mentioned above, the text offers a unique and valuable opportunity to investigate various forms of Valentinian thought and ritual practice.

A VALENTINIAN EXPOSITION

XI 22, 1-39, 39

[. . .] | enter [. . .] | the abundance | [. . .] [5] those who [. . . [16] I will speak] my mystery | [to those who are] mine and | [to those who will be mine]. Moreover it is these who | [have known him who] is, the Father, that [20] [is, the Root] of the All, the | [Ineffable One | who] dwells in the Monad. | [He dwells alone] in silence, | [and silence is] tranquility since, after all, | [he was] a Monad and no one [25] [was] before him. He dwells | [in the Dyad] and in the Pair, and his | Pair is Silence. And he possessed | the All dwelling within | him. And as for Intention and [30] Persistence, Love and Permanence, | they are indeed unbegotten.

God ' came forth: the Son, Mind of the All, ' that is, it is from the Root ' of the All that even his Thought stems, [35] since he had this one (the Son) in ' Mind. For on behalf of the All he received ' an alien Thought ' since there was nothing before him. From ' that place it is he who moved 23 [... [18] a] gushing [spring]. ' Now this [is the] Root [of the All] [20] and Monad without any [one] ' before him. Now the second [spring] ' exists in Silence and [speaks] ' with him alone. And the [Fourth] ' accordingly is he [who] [25] restricted himself [in the] ' Fourth: while dwelling in the ' Three-hundred-sixtieth, he first brought ' himself (forth), and in the Second [he] revealed ' his will [and] [30] in the Fourth he spread ' himself [out].

While these things are ' due to the Root of the All, let us for our part ' [enter] his revelation ' and his goodness and his [35] descent and the All, that ' is, the Son, the Father of the All, and ' the Mind of the Spirit; ' for he was possessing this one before 24 [...]. [18] He [is] a [spring]. ' He is [one] who appears [20] [in Silence], and [he is] Mind of the All ' dwelling secondarily with ' [Life]. For he is the projector ' [of] the All and the [very] hypostasis ' of the Father, that is, [he is] the [Thought] [25] and his descent below.

When he willed, ' the First Father revealed himself ' in him. Since, after all, because ' [of him] the revelation is available to the [30] All, I for my part call the All ' "the desire of the All." And he took ' such a thought concerning the All – ' I for my part call the thought "Monogenes." ' For now God has brought [35] Truth, the one who glorifies the Root of the ' All. Thus it is he who ' revealed himself in Monogenes, ' and in him ' he revealed the Ineffable One 25 [...] [18] the Truth. [They] ' saw him [dwelling] in the Monad [and] [20] in the Dyad [and] in the Tetrad. [He] ' first brought forth [Monogenes ' and Limit]. And Limit [is the ' separator] of the All [and the confirmation ' of the All], since they are [...] [25] the hundred [...]. ' He is the [Mind ...] [30] the Son. [He is] completely [ineffable] ' to the All, and he is the confirmation ' and [the] hypostasis of the All, the [silent veil], ' the [true] High Priest, ' [the one who has] [35] the authority to enter ' the Holies of Holies, revealing ' the glory of ' the Aeons and bringing forth the ' abundance to ⟨fragrance⟩. The East 26 [... [18] that is] in [him. He is the one who ' revealed himself as] the [20] primal [sanctuary] and [the] treasury of ' [the All]. And [he] encompassed the All, ' [he] who is higher [than the] All. These for their part ' [sent] Christ [forth to ' establish her] just as [they] were established [before [25] her] descent. [And they say ' concerning] him: [... [29] He is not manifest, but ' invisible] to [those remaining within Limit]. '

And he possesses four ' powers: a separator [and a] ' confirmer, a form-provider [and a ' substance-producer]. Surely [we alone] [35] would discern ' their presences and the time ' and the places which [the] ' likenesses have confirmed because they have 27 [. . .] [18] from these [places ' . . .] the love [. . .] [20] is emanated [. . . ' the] entire Pleroma [. . .]. ' The persistence [endures] ' always, and [. . .] ' for also [. . .] [25] the time [. . .] ' more [. . . [29] that is], the proof of his [great ' love].

So why a ' [separator] and a confirmer ' and a substance-producer and a ' form-provider as others have ' [said]? For [they] say concerning [35] [Limit] that he has two powers, [a] ⟨separator⟩ and ' [a confirmer], since it separates ' [Depth] from the Aeons, in order that 28 [. . .] [18] These, then [. . .] [20] of [Depth . . .]. ' For [. . . is] the form [. . .] ' the Father of the [Truth . . . ' say] that Christ [. . .] ' the Spirit [. . .] [25] Monogenes [. . .] ' has [. . .]. [29]

[It is a great and] ' necessary thing for us to [seek with] ' more diligence and [perseverance] ' after the scriptures and [those who] ' proclaim the concepts. For about [this] ' the ancients say, [35] "[They] were proclaimed ' by God." So [let us] ' know his unfathomable ' richness! [he wanted 29 . . . [18] servitude . . .] [20] he [did not] become ' [. . .] of their life ' [. . . they look] steadfastly ' [at their book] of knowledge ' and [they regard [25] one another's appearance].

[That] Tetrad ' [projected the Tetrad ' which is the one consisting of] Word and [Life ' and Man and] Church. ' [Now the Uncreated One] projected [30] Word and Life. Word ' is [for] the glory of the Ineffable One ' while Life is for the glory of ' [Silence], and Man is for his ' own glory while Church [35] is [for] the glory of Truth. This, then, ' is the [Tetrad] begotten ' according to [the likeness] of the Uncreated (Tetrad). ' And [the] Tetrad is begotten 30 [. . . [16] the Decad (i.e., ten)] ' from [Word and Life] ' and the Dodecad (i.e., twelve) from Man], and [Church became a] [20] Triacontad (i.e., thirty). [Moreover], it is the one [from the Triacontad] ' of the [Aeons who bear fruit] ' from [the Triacontad]. ' [They] enter [jointly ' but they] come forth [singly, [25] fleeing from] the Aeons [and the Uncontainable Ones. ' And] the Uncontainable Ones, [once they had] ' looked [at him, glorified Mind] ' since [he is an Uncontainable One that exists] ' in the [Pleroma].

[But [30] the Decad] from ' Word and Life brought forth ' decads so as to make the Pleroma ' become a hundred, and ' the Dodecad from Man [35] and Church [brought] forth and [made] ' the Triacontad so as to make [the three] hundred ' sixty become the Pleroma of the ' year. And the year of the Lord 31 [. . . [18] perfect . . .] ' perfect [. . .] [20] according to [... [22] Limit] and ' [...] Limit [... [27] the] greatness ' which [...] the ' [goodness ...] him. Life [30] [...] suffer ' [...] by ' the face [...] in the presence of ' the [Pleroma ...] which he wanted ' [.... And] he wanted [35] to [leave] the Thirtieth – ' being [a syzygy] of Man and ' Church, that is, Sophia – to surpass [the Triacontad and] bring the Pleroma 32 [...] [16] his [...] ' but [... and] ' she [...] [22] the [All ...] [28] but [...] ' who [...] the All [...]. [32] He made [...] the thoughts ' and [... the] Pleroma ' through the Word [...] his [35] flesh. These, then, [are the Aeons that] are like ' them. After the [Word] entered ' it, just as [I] said before, ' also [the one who comes to be] with ' the Uncontainable One [brought] forth 33 [...] [11] before they ' [...] forth [...] ' hide him from ' [...] the syzygy and [15] [...] the movement and ' [...] project the ' Christ [...] and the seeds ' [...] of the cross ' since [... the imprints] of the nail [20] wound [...] perfection. ' [Since it is] a perfect form ' [that should] ascend into ' [the Pleroma], he did not [at all] want ' [to] consent to the suffering, [25] [but he was] detained ' [...] him by Limit, ' that is, by the syzygy, ' since her correction will ' not occur through anyone except [30] her own Son, ' whose alone is the fullness ' of divinity. He willed ' within himself bodily ' to leave the powers and he descended. [35] And these things (passions) Sophia suffered ' after her son ascended from ' her, [for] she knew ' that she dwelt in a 34 [... [10] in unity] ' and [restoration. They were] ' stopped [...] ' the brethren [...] ' these. A [...] did not [...] [15] I became [...]. ' Who indeed [are] they? [The ...], on the one hand, ' stopped her [...], on the other hand, [...] ' with the [...] ' her. These [moreover are those who were] looking at me, [20] these who [... these] ' who considered [...] the ' [death]. They were stopped [...] her ' and she repented [and she] ' besought the Father of the [truth], saying, [25] "Granted that I have [renounced] ' my consort. Therefore [I am] ' beyond confirmation as well. I deserve ' the things (passions) I suffer. ' I used to dwell in the Pleroma [30] putting forth the Aeons and ' bearing fruit with my consort." ' And she knew what she was ' and what had become of ' her.

So they both suffered; [35] they said she laughs since she remained ' alone and imitated the Uncontainable ' One, while he said she [laughs] since ' she cut herself off from her consort. 35 [...] [10] Indeed [Jesus and] Sophia ' revealed [the creature]. Since, after all, ' the seeds [of] Sophia are ' incomplete [and] formless, ' Jesus [contrived] a creature of this [15] [sort] and made it of the ' seeds while Sophia worked with ' him. [For] since they are seeds ' and [without form], he descended ' [and brought] forth that [20] pleroma [of aeons] which are in that ' place, [since even the uncreated ones of] ' those [Aeons are of] the pattern of the [Pleroma] ' and the [uncontainable] Father. ' The Uncreated One [25] [brought forth the pattern] of the uncreated, ' for it is from the uncreated ' that the Father brings forth ' into form. But the creature ' is a shadow of pre-existing [30] things. Moreover, this Jesus created ' the creature, and he worked ' from the passions ' surrounding the seeds. And he ' separated them from one another, [35] and the better passions he introduced ' into the spirit and the worse ones ' into the carnal.

Now ' first among [all] those passions 36 [...] [9] nor [...] ' him, [since, after all], Pronoia ' caused [the] correction to ' project shadows and ' images of [those who] exist [from] the ' first and [those who] are [and] [15] those who shall be. This, [then, is] the ' dispensation of believing ' in Jesus for the sake of [him who] inscribed ' the All with [likenesses and] ' images [and shadows]. [20]

After Jesus brought [forth further] ' he brought [forth] for ' the All those of the Pleroma ' and of the syzygy, that [is, the] ' angels. For simultaneously with the [25] [agreement] of the Pleroma ' her consort projected ' the angels, since he abides in ' the will of the Father. For this ' is the will of the Father: [30] not to allow anything to happen in the ' Pleroma apart from a syzygy. ' Again, the will of the Father is: ' always produce ' and bear fruit. That she should suffer, [35] then, was not the will ' of the Father, for she dwells ' in herself alone without ' her consort. Let us 37 [...] [9] another one [...] ' the Second [...] ' the son of another [...] ' is the Tetrad of the world. [And] ' that Tetrad put forth [fruit] ' as if the Pleroma [of the world were] [15] a Hebdomad. ' And [it] entered [images] ' and [likenesses and angels] ' and [archangels, divinities] ' and [ministers]. [20]

When all [these things were brought to pass ' by] Pronoia [...] ' of Jesus who [...] ' the seeds [...] ' of Monogenes [...]. [25] Indeed they are [spiritual] ' and carnal, ' the heavenly and the ' earthly. He made them ' a place of this sort and [30] a school of this sort for ' doctrine and for form. '

Moreover this Demiurge ' began to create a ' man according to his image on the one hand [35] and on the other according to the likeness of those who ' exist from the first. It was this sort of ' dwelling place that she used ' for the seeds, namely 38 [... [10] separate ' ...] God. When they ' [...] in behalf of man, ' [since] indeed [the Devil] is one ' [of] the divine beings. He removed himself [15] and seized the entire [plaza] ' of the gates and he ' [expelled] his [own] root ' from [that] place ' [in the body] and [20] [carcasses of flesh], for [he is enveloped] by ' [the man] of

God. And [Adam ' sowed] him. Therefore [he acquired] ' sons who [angered ' one another. And] Cain [killed] [25] Abel his brother, for [the Demiurge] ' breathed into [them] ' his spirit. And there [took place] ' the struggle with the apostasy ' of the angels and mankind, [30] those of the right with those of the left, ' those in heaven with those on earth ' the spirits with the carnal, ' and the Devil against God. ' Therefore the angels lusted [35] after the daughters of men ' and came down to flesh so that ' God would cause a flood. ' And he almost ' regretted that he had created the world 39 [. . . [10] the consort] ' and [Sophia and her Son] ' and the angels [and the seeds]. ' But the syzygy is the [complete one] ' and Sophia and Jesus and [the angels] [15] and the seeds are [images ' of] the Pleroma. Moreover the Demiurge ' [cast a shadow over] ' the syzygy and [the] Pleroma, ' and Jesus and [Sophia] and the [angels] [20] and the seeds. [The complete one ' glorifies] Sophia; the image ' [glorifies] Truth. [And] the glory [of ' the seeds] and Jesus [are] those of [Silence ' and] Monogenes. [And] [25] the [angels] of the males and [the ' seminal ones] of the females ' [are] all Pleromas. ' Moreover whenever Sophia [receives] ' her consort and Jesus [30] receives the Christ and the seeds ' and the angels, then [the] ' Pleroma will receive Sophia ' joyfully, and the All will ' come to be in unity and [35] reconciliation. For by this ' the Aeons have been increased; ' for they knew that ' should they change, they are ' without change.

ON THE ANOINTING

XI 40, 1-29

[. . .] [9] according to [. . .] [10] the type of [. . .] ' see him. It is fitting for ' [you at this time] to send thy Son ' [Jesus] Christ and anoint ' us so that we might be able [15] to trample [upon] the ' [snakes] and [the heads] of the scorpions ' and [all] the power of the Devil ' since he is the shepherd of [the ' seed]. Through him we [have [20] known] thee. And we [glorify] thee: ' [Glory] be to thee, the Father in the [Son, the ' Father] in the Son, the Father [in the] ' holy [Church and in the] ' holy [angels]! From [25] now on he abides [forever ' in] the perpetuity of the Aeons, ' forever until the [untraceable] Aeons ' of the Aeons. ' Amen.

ON BAPTISM A

XI 40, 30-41, 38

[This] is the fullness of the summary ' of knowledge which (summary) ' was revealed to us by ' our Lord Jesus Christ, ' the Monogenes. These are the [35] sure and necessary (items) ' so that we may walk ' in them. But they are ' those of the first baptism **41** [.... [10] The first] ' baptism [is the forgiveness] ' of sins [...] ' ⟨who⟩ said, [...] ' you to the [...] [15] your sins the [... is] ' a pattern of the [...] ' of the Christ [which ' is the] equal of the [... within] ' him. [...]. [20] For the [...] of Jesus [...]. ' Moreover, the first [baptism] ' is the forgiveness [of ' sins. We] are brought [from ' those] by [it [25] into] those of the right, [that ' is], into the [imperishability ' which is] the Jo[rdan. ' But] that place is [of] ' the world. So we have [been sent] ' out [of the world] ' into the Aeon. For [the] ' interpretation of John ' is the Aeon, while the interpretation ' of that which [is] the Jord[an] [35] is the descent which is [the upward progression], ' that [is, our exodus] ' from the world [into] ' the Aeon.

ON BAPTISM B

XI 42, 1-43, 19

[... [10] from the] world ' [into the Jordan] and from ' [the blindness] of the world ' [into the sight of] God, from ' [the carnal] into the spiritual, [15] [from] the physical ' [into the] angelic, from ' [the created] into the Pleroma, ' [from] the world ' [into the Aeon], from the [20] [servitudes] into sonship, ' [from] entanglements [into ' one another], from [the desert ' into] our village, from [the cold ' into] the hot, [from [25] ...] into a [...] ' and we [...] ' into the [... ' thus] we were brought [from] ' seminal [bodies into [30] bodies] with a perfect form. ' [Indeed] I entered by way of example ' [the remnant] for which the Christ ' [rescued] us in the ' [fellowship] of his Spirit. And [35] [he brought] us forth who are ' [in him, and] from now on the souls ' [will become] perfect spirits. '

Now [the things] granted to us ' [by the first] baptism **43** [... [15] invisible ... ' which] is his, since [... [18] speak] about ...].

ON THE EUCHARIST A

XI 43, 20-38

[We give] thanks [to you and we ' celebrate the eucharist], O Father, [remembering ' for the sake of] thy Son [Jesus Christ ' that they] come forth [...] ' invisible [...] [26] thy [Son ...] ' his [love ...] [30] to [knowledge ' ...] they are doing thy will ' [through the] name of Jesus Christ ' [and] will do thy will ' [now and] always. They are complete [35] [in] every spiritual gift and [every] ' purity. [Glory] be to thee through thy Son ' [and] thy offspring Jesus Christ ' [from now] forever. Amen.

ON THE EUCHARIST B

XI 44, 1-37

[...] [14] in the ' [...] ' the [word] of the [... ' the] holy one it is [...] [19] food and ' [drink ...] Son, since you [...] ' food of the [...] ' to us the [...] ' in the [life ...] [26] he does [not boast ' ...] that is [...] ' Church [...] ' you are pure [...] [31] thou art the Lord. [Whenever] ' you die purely, [you] ' will be pure so as to have him [...] ' everyone who will [guide] [35] him to food and [drink]. ' Glory be to thee forever. ' Amen.

ALLOGENES (XI,*3*)

Introduced by

ANTOINETTE CLARK WIRE

Translated by

JOHN D. TURNER and ORVAL S. WINTERMUTE

The tractate *Allogenes* is a revelation discourse in which a certain Allogenes receives divine auditions and visions and records them for his "son" Messos. The fictive nature of this repeated address of Allogenes to Messos is indicated by the name Allogenes, which means "stranger," "one of another race," and often in this period designates Seth or a representative of the Sethian spiritual race. The reader is thus encouraged to identify with Messos and learn from Allogenes how to overcome the fear and ignorance Allogenes initially feels, how to meditate on each step of revealed knowledge, and ultimately how to ascend into full realization of one's spiritual self within the divine.

Although *Allogenes* presents itself as a single revelation discourse, it can be divided into two parts. Part One (45,1-57,23) highlights five revelations of the female diety Youel to Allogenes. Her revelations are complex mythological descriptions of the divine powers, particularly the aeon of Barbelo. Part Two (57,24-69,19) describes in more philosophical language the ascent of Allogenes as a progressive revelation by the heavenly luminaries. Its final stage, the "primary revelation of the Unknown One," reveals the transcendent God as invisible, unfathomable, incomprehensible, "the spiritual, invisible Triple Power" which is "the best of the best" and exists, paradoxically, as "the nonbeing Existence."

The differences between these two parts of *Allogenes* can be explained in terms of different sources being used or in terms of the one writer's purpose. Source theories try to determine where certain traditions come from and how they have already developed. The Barbelo mythology of Part One is found also in *The Apocryphon of John* (BG 8502,*2*; NHC II,*1*; III,*1*; IV,*1*) where it is associated with an account of how Sophia brought deficiency into the universe. *Allogenes*' Barbelo Gnosticism, like that of *Zostrianos* (VIII,*1*) and *The Three Steles of Seth* (VII,*5*), is not interested in how evil began but in positive revelation of divine reality. Part Two of *Allogenes* also parallels *The Apocryphon of John* to the extent of a full-page description of the transcendent God in terms of what God is not. But again it departs from this tradition in the same direction as do *Zostrianos* and *The Three Steles of Seth* by presenting this knowledge as an ascent ritual in a way parallel to Hermetic Gnosticism (*Corp. Herm.* I,24-26 and NHC VI,*6*). Apparently the author has taken both Barbelo Gnosticism and philosophical monism from the same general tradition as *The Apocryphon of John* and put them in sequence with certain linking passages for a single purpose.

Assuming that the reader has already been released from evil, the writer in the persona of Allogenes leads on up the heavenly path, praising the divine, into the blessing of knowledge, the vitality of life and finally the existence that is nonexistence. The ascent rituals of Hermetism refer occasionally to community life, and *The Three Steles of Seth* uses the first person plural to praise God at each ascent level. But here the instructions are spoken to a single person who is reading and could be meant as self-help in an individual's search for God.

This tractate has attracted wide interest because the Neoplatonist Porphyry said that Plotinus attacked certain Gnostics who "produced revelations by Zoroaster and Zostrianos and Nicotheos and Allogenes and Messos and other such people" (*Vit. Plot.* 16). If this quote does indeed refer to this book named *Allogenes*, and to documents close to it (*Zostrianos* VIII,*1* bears a coded subtitle, "Words of Zoroaster") as many are proposing, it suggests a somewhat different relation of the Gnostics to later Platonism than is commonly assumed. Not only did Gnostics clearly borrow many philosophical themes from Platonism, but Platonists and Neoplatonists were being forced to deal with Gnostic schools as rivals to their own. And though Plotinus in his own tractate against the Gnostics does his best to ridicule their dualism, cult, and jargon, it is clearly the monistic Gnostics of the *Allogenes* sort who challenge him most. It is they who attribute to revelation the truths he is convinced that they have derived from Plato; it is they who believe that through self-knowledge they become superior to the heavenly bodies (*Enn.* II. 9.5-11). The question that remains is whether the Gnostics may not have had a reverse influence on Neoplatonism, specifically whether these gnostic texts could be the source of a certain existence-life-thought triad which is not attested in Neoplatonism before Proclus in the fifth century (*Theol.* 101-03).

An Alexandrian origin of the original Greek text of *Allogenes* not long after 300 C.E. would allow time for its Greek circulation and its Coptic translation before it was placed in the Nag Hammadi library early in the next century.

ALLOGENES

XI 45, 1-69, 20

[. . .] [6] since they are ' [perfect individuals and dwell] ' all [together, joined with] the ' [mind], the guardian [which I provided, [10] who] taught you (sg.). [And] it is [the power that ' exists] within you that often [extended itself ' as word] ' from the Triple-Powered One, [that One ' of] all [those] who [truly] exist [15] with the [Immeasurable One], the ' eternal [Light of] the Knowledge ' that appeared, the ' male virginal [Youth, ' the first] of the Aeons from [20] [a] unique triple-[powered Aeon], ' [the] Triple-Powered One who ' [truly exists], for when [he was stilled, ' ⟨he⟩ was extended] and ' [when he was extended], he became [complete [25] and] he received [power] from ' all of

[them]. He knows [himself ' and the perfect] Invisible [Spirit]. ' And he [came to be ' in an] Aeon who knows [30] [that] she knows That One. ' [And] she became Kalyptos ' [who] acted in those whom she ' knows. ' He is a perfect, [35] invisible, noetic ' Protophanes-Harmedon. [And] empowering ' the individuals, she is a Triple-Male. ' And being individually **46** [. . . [6] Individual on the one hand, they are together] ' on the other hand, [since she] is an existence of [theirs], and she [sees] ' them all [also] truly ⟨existing⟩. [10] [She] contains the ' divine Autogenes.

"When she [knew] ' her [Existence] ' and when she stood, [she brought] ' This One (masc.), since he saw them [all] [15] existing individually as [he] ' is. And [when they] ' become as he is, [they shall] ' see the divine Triple-Male, ' the power that is [higher than] [20] God. [He is] the [Thought] ' of all these who [exist] ' together. If he [ponders them, ' he] ponders [the] ' great male [. . .] [25] noetic Protophanes, the [procession ' of] these. When [he] ' sees it, [he sees ' also those who truly exist] ' and the procession [of those who are] [30] together. And when he [has seen ' these], he has seen the [Kalyptos]. ' And if he [sees] ' one of the hidden ones, [he] ' sees the Aeon of Barbelo. And as for [the] [35] unbegotten offspring of [That One], ' if one [sees] ' how he [lives **47** . . . [5] you have heard about the ' abundance of] each one ' of them [certainly].

[But] concerning ' the invisible, spiritual ' Triple-Powered One, hear! [He exists] as an [10] Invisible One who is incomprehensible ' to them all. He ' contains them all within [himself], ' for [they] all exist because of ' [him]. He is perfect, and he is [15] [greater] than perfect, and he is ' blessed. [He is] always [One] ' and [he] exists ' [in] them all, being ineffable, ' unnameable, [20] [being One] who exists through ' [them all] – he whom, ' [should] one discern ' [him, one would not desire] anything that ' [exists] before him among those [25] [that possess] existence, ' for [he is] the [source ' from which they were all emitted. ' He is prior to ' perfection. He was prior [30] to every] divinity, ' [and] he is prior [to] ' every blessedness since he ' provides for every power. And ' he ⟨is⟩ a nonsubstantial substance, [35] since he is a God over whom there is no ' divinity, the ' transcending of whose ' greatness and ⟨beauty⟩ **48** [. . . [6] power. It is not impossible for them] ' to receive a [revelation of] these things ' if [they] come together. ' Since it is impossible for [10] the [individuals] to comprehend the Universal One ' [situated in the] place that is higher than perfect, ' they apprehend by means of ' a First [Thought] – ' (it is) not as Being (alone), [but] [15] it is along with the ' latency of Existence that he confers Being. He [provides] ' everything for [himself] since it is ' he who shall come to be when he ' recognizes himself]. And he is [One] [20] who subsists as a [cause]' and source [of Being] and [an] ' immaterial [material and an] ' innumerable [number and a formless] ' form and a [shapeless] [25] shape and [a powerlessness and ' a power and an insubstantial ' substance and a motionless motion and an inactive ' activity. [Yet he is [30] a] provider of [provisions ' and] a divinity [of] ' divinity – but whenever ' they apprehend, they participate ' the first Vitality and [35] an undivided activity, ' an hypostasis of the First One ' from the One who truly exists. ' And a second **49** activity [...] ' however, is the [...]. [5] He is endowed with ' blessedness] and ' goodness, because [when he is] ' recognized [as the] traverser ' of the boundlessness of the [10] Invisible Spirit [that ' subsists] in him, it (the boundlessness) turns him to [it (the Invisible Spirit) ' in] order that it might know what is ' within him and ' how he exists. And [15] he was becoming salvation for ' every one by being a ' point of departure for those who truly exist, ' for through him ' his knowledge endured, [20] since he is the one who knows what ' he is. But they brought forth nothing ' beyond themselves, neither ' power nor rank nor ' glory nor aeon, [25] for they are all ' eternal. He is Vitality and ' Mentality and That-Which-Is. ' For then That'-Which-Is constantly possesses its [30] Vitality and Mentality, ' and {Life has} ' Vitality possesses ' {non}-Being and ' Mentality. Mentality [35] possesses Life and That-Which-Is. ' And the three are one, ' although individually they are three.

Now after ' I heard these things, my son **50** [Messos, I was] afraid, and ' [I turned toward the] multitude ' [...] thought [... [6] gives] power to [those who] are capable of knowing ' these things [by] a revelation ' that is much [greater]. And I ' was capable], although flesh was [10] upon [me. I] heard from you about these things ' and about the doctrine ' that is in them since the thought ' which is in me distinguished [the things that are] ' beyond measure as well as the unknowables. [15] Therefore I fear that ' my doctrine may have become ' something beyond what is fitting.

And ' then, my ' son Messos, the all-glorious One, [20] Youel, spoke to me again. She made a revelation ' to me and said, "No ' one is able to hear [these things] ' except the great powers alone, ' O Allogenes. [25] A great power was put upon you, which ' the Father ' of the All, the Eternal, put upon you ' before you came to this place, in order that ' those things that are difficult to distinguish [30] you might distinguish and those things ' that are unknown to ' the multitude you might know, ' and that you might escape (in safety) ' to the One who is yours, who [35] was first to save and ' who does not need to be saved. **51** [. . . ⁶ to] you [a] ' form [and a revelation of] ' the invisible, spiritual Triple-Powered One ' outside of which [dwells] ¹⁰ an undivided, incorporeal, ' [eternal] knowledge. '

"As with all the Aeons, ' the Aeon of Barbelo exists, ' also endowed with the types ¹⁵ and forms of those who truly ' exist, the image of ' Kalyptos. And endowed ' with the intellectual Word of ' these, he bears the ²⁰ noetic male Protophanes like ' an image, and he acts ' within the individuals either with ' craft or with skill ' or with partial instinct. ²⁵ He is endowed with the ' divine Autogenes like ' an image, and he knows ' each one of these. He ' acts separately and ³⁰ individually, continuing to rectify ' the failures ' from nature. He is endowed with ' the divine Triple-Male ' as salvation for them all ³⁵ (and) in cooperation with the Invisible Spirit. ' He is a word from a ' counsel, ⟨he⟩ is the perfect Youth. ' And this hypostatis is a **52** [. . .].

[. . . ⁷ my soul went slack] and ' I fled [and was] very disturbed. ' And [I] turned to myself ¹⁰ [and] saw the light ' that [surrounded] me and the ' Good that was in me, I became divine. '

And ' the all-glorious One, Youel, anointed me again ¹⁵ and she gave power to me. She said, "Since ' your instruction has become complete ' and you have known the Good that is within you, ' hear concerning ' the Triple-Powered One those things that you will ²⁰ guard in great ' silence and great mystery, ' because they are not spoken to ' anyone except those who are worthy, ' those who are able ²⁵ to hear; nor is it fitting ' to speak to an ' uninstructed generation concerning ' the Universal One that is higher than perfect. ' But you have ⟨these⟩ because of ³⁰ the Triple-Powered One, the One who exists ' in blessedness ' and goodness, the One ' who is responsible for all these. '

"There exists within him ³⁵ much greatness. ' Inasmuch as he is One in a **53** [. . .] ⁶ of the [First Thought, which] ' does not fall away [from those who dwell] ' in comprehension [and knowledge] ' and [understanding. And] ¹⁰ That One moved motionlessly ' in that which ' governs, lest he sink ' into the boundless by means of ' another activity of ¹⁵ Mentality. And he entered ' into himself and he appeared, ' being all-encompassing, ' the Universal One that is higher than perfect. '

"Indeed it is not through me ²⁰ that he is to such a degree anterior to knowledge. ' Whereas there is no possibility for complete ' comprehension, he is (nevertheless) known. ' And this is so because of the ' third silence of Mentality ²⁵ and the second ' undivided activity which appeared ' in the First Thought, ' that is, the Aeon of Barbelo, ' together

with the Indivisible One of [30] the divisible likenesses and the Triple- |
Powered One and the non-substantial Existence." |

⟨And⟩ the power | appeared by means of an activity | that is at rest
[35] and silent, although it uttered | a sound thus: zza | zza zza. But when
she heard | the power and she was filled **54** [. . .] [6] thou art | [. . .]
Solmis! | [. . .] according to the Vitality, | [that is thine, and] the first
activity [10] which derives from | divinity: Thou art great, | Armedon!
Thou art perfect, | Epiphaneus!

"And according to | that activity of thine, the second power [15] and
the Mentality | which derives from blessedness: | Autoer, Beritheus, |
Erigenaor, Orimenios, Aramen, | Alphleges, Elelioupheus, [20] Lala-
meus, Yetheus, Noetheus! | Thou art great! He who knows [thee] |
knows the Universal One! Thou art One, | thou art One, He who is
good, Aphredon! | Thou art the Aeon of [25] Aeons, He who is perpet-
ually!" |

Then she praised | the Universal One, saying, | "Lalameus, Noethe-
us, Senaon, | Asine[us, . . .]riphanios, [30] Mellephaneus, Elemaoni, |
Smoun, Optaon, He Who | Is! Thou art He Who Is, | the Aeon of
Aeons, the | Unbegotten, who art higher than the unbegotten (ones), [35]
Yatomenos, thou alone | for whom all the unborn ones were begotten,
| the Unnameable One! **55** [. . .] [11] knowledge." |

[Now after I] heard these things, I | [saw the glories of the perfect] in-
dividuals | [and] the all-perfect ones [15] [who exist] together, and the |
[all-perfect ones who] are before the perfect | ones.

[Again the greatly] glorious One, | Youel, said to me, | "[O Allo-
genes], in an [20] [unknowing knowledge] you know that the | [Triple-
Powered One] exists before | [the glories]. They do not exist | [among
those who exist]. They do not exist | [together] with those who exist [25]
[nor (with) those who] truly exist. | [Rather all these] exist | [as divinity]
and | [blessedness and] existence, | [and as] nonsubstantiality and [30]
non-being [existence]." |

[And then I] prayed that | [the revelation] might occur to me. | [And
then | the all-[glorious One], Youel, said to me, [35] "[O Allogenes], of
course, | [the Triple-] Male | [is something beyond] substance. | Yet
[were he insubstantial **56** . . .] [10] those who exist [in association] | with
the [generation of those] | who [truly] exist. | [The self-begotten ones
exist] | with the [Triple-Male]. [15]

"If you [seek with a | perfect] seeking, [then] | you shall know [the
Good that is] | in you; then [you will know yourself] | as well, (as) one
who [derives from] [20] the God [who truly pre-exists]. | [For] after [a

hundred] ' years there shall [come to you] ' a revelation [of That One]
' by means of [Salamex] ²⁵ and Semen [and ... the] ' Luminaries [of
the Aeon of] ' Barbelo. And [that beyond what] ' is fitting for you, [you
shall not know] ' at first, so as not [to forfeit your] ³⁰ kind. [And if so],
' then when [you receive] ' a conception [of That One, then ' you] are
filled [with] ' the word [to completion]. ³⁵ Then [you become divine] '
and [you become perfect. You receive] ' them [...] 57⁵ the seeking
[...] ' the Existence [...] ' if it [apprehends] ' anything, it is [appre-
hended by] ' that one and by ¹⁰ the very one who is comprehended. '
And then he ' becomes greater ' who comprehends and knows than ' he
who is comprehended and ¹⁵ known. But if ' he descends to his nature,
' he is less, for the ' incorporeal natures have not associated with ' any
magnitude; having ²⁰ this power, they are everywhere ' and they are nowhere, ' since they are greater than every magnitude, ' and less than
every exiguity." '

Now after ²⁵ the all-glorious One, Youel, said these things, ' she separated from me and left ' me. But I did not despair ' of the words that
I heard. ' I prepared myself ³⁰ therein and I deliberated ' with myself
for a hundred years. ' And I rejoiced exceedingly, ' since I was in a
great ' light and a blessed path ³⁵ because those whom I was ' worthy to
see as well ' as those whom I was worthy to hear ' (are) those whom it
is fitting ' that the great powers alone 58 [...] ⁶ of [God]. '

[When ' the completion of] the one hundred years [drew nigh, ' it
brought] me a blessedness ¹⁰ of the eternal hope ' full of auspiciousness.
' I saw the good divine Autogenes; ' and the Savior ' who is the ¹⁵
youthful, perfect Triple-Male Child; and his ' goodness, the ' noetic
perfect Protophanes-Harmedon; ' and the blessedness ' of the Kalyptos; and the ²⁰ primary origin of the blessedness, ' the Aeon of Barbelo
' full of divinity; ' and the primary origin of ' the one without origin,
the ²⁵ spiritual, invisible Triple-Powered ' One, the Universal One that
' is higher than perfect.

When ⟨I⟩ was taken by the ' eternal Light out of ' the garment that
was upon ³⁰ me, and taken up to ' a holy place whose ' likeness can not
be ' revealed in the world, ' then by means of a ³⁵ great blessedness I '
saw all those about whom I had ' heard. And I ' praised all of them and
I 59 [stood] upon my knowledge and [I ' inclined to] the knowledge [of]
' the Universals, the Aeon of Barbelo. '

And I saw [holy] powers ⁵ by means of the [Luminaries] ' of the
virginal male Barbelo ' [telling me ' that] I would be able to test what '
happens in the world: "O ¹⁰ Allogenes, behold your blessedness ' how

it silently abides, ' by which you know ' your proper self and, ' seeking yourself, withdraw to the Vitality [15] that you will ' see moving. And although it is ' impossible for you to stand, fear ' nothing; but if you ' wish to stand, withdraw [20] to the Existence, and you will ' find it standing and ' at rest after the likeness of the One ' who is truly at rest ' and embraces all these [25] silently and ' inactively. And when you receive ' a revelation of him by ' means of a primary revelation ' of the Unknown One – [30] the One whom if you should ' know him, be ignorant ' of him – and you become ' afraid in that place, ' withdraw to the rear because of the [35] activities. And when you become ' perfect in that place, ' still yourself. And ' in accordance with the pattern that indwells ' you, know likewise **60** [that] it is this way in [all such (matters)] ' after this (very) pattern. And ' [do not] further dissipate, [so that] ' you may be able to stand, [5] and do not desire to [be active] ' lest you fall [in any way] ' from the inactivity in [you] ' of the Unknown One. Do not ' [know] him, for it is impossible; [10] but if by means of an ' enlightened thought you should know ' him, be ignorant of him." '

Now I was listening to these things as ' those ones spoke them. There [15] was within me a stillness ' of silence, and I heard the ' Blessedness ' whereby I knew ⟨my⟩ proper self. '

And I withdrew to the [20] Vitality as I sought ⟨myself⟩, and ' I joined into it, ' and I stood, ' not firmly but ' silently. And I saw [25] an eternal, intellectual, undivided motion ' that pertains to all the ' formless powers, (which is] unlimited ' by limitation.

And when ' I wanted to stand firmly, [30] I withdrew to ' the Existence, which I found ' standing and at rest ' like an image and ' likeness of what is conferred upon [35] me by a revelation ' of the Indivisible One and the One who ' is at rest. I was filled ' with revelation by means ' of a primary revelation **61** of the Unknowable One. [As though] ' I were ignorant of him, I [knew] ' him and I received power [by] ' him. Having been permanently strengthened [5] I knew the One who ' exists in me and the Triple-Powered One ' and the revelation of ' his uncontainableness. [And] ' by means of a primary [10] revelation of the First One (who is) unknowable ' to them all, the God ' who is beyond perfection, I ' saw him and the Triple-Powered One that exists ' in them all. I was seeking [15] the ineffable ' and Unknowable God – ' whom if one should ' know him, he would be absolutely ' ignorant of him – the Mediator of [20] the Triple-Powered One who subsists in ' stillness and silence and is ' unknowable.

And when I was confirmed ' in these matters, ' the powers of the

Luminaries said to me, [25] "Cease hindering the inactivity that exists in you by seeking incomprehensible matters; rather hear about him in so far as it is [30] possible by means of a primary revelation and a revelation.

"Now he is something insofar as he exists in that he either exists and will become, [35] or acts or knows, although he lives without Mind or Life or Existence or Non-Existence, incomprehensibly. **62** And he is something along with his proper being. He is not left over in some way, as if he yields [5] something that is assayed or purified [or that] receives or gives. And he is not diminished in any way, [whether] by his own desire or whether he gives or receives through [10] another. Neither does [he] have any desire of himself nor from another; it does not affect him. Rather neither does he give [15] anything by himself lest he become diminished in another respect; nor for this reason does he need. Mind, or Life, or [20] indeed anything at all. He is superior to the Universals in his privation and unknowability, that is, the non-being existence, since he is endowed with [25] silence and stillness lest he be diminished by those who are not diminished.

"He is neither divinity nor blessedness [30] nor perfection. Rather it (this triad) is an unknowable entity of him, not that which is proper to him; rather he is another one superior to the blessedness and [35] the divinity and perfection. For he is not perfect but he is another thing **63** that is superior. He is neither boundless, nor is he bounded by another. Rather he is something [superior]. [5] He is not corporeal. He is not incorporeal. He is not great. [He is not] small. He is not a number. He is not a [creature]. Nor is he something [10] that exists, that one can know. But he is something else of himself that is superior, which one cannot know.

"He is primary revelation [15] and knowledge of himself, as it is he alone who knows himself. Since he is not one of those that exist but is another thing, he is superior to (all) superlatives [20] even in comparison to (both) what is (properly) his and not his. He neither participates in age nor does he participate in time. He does not receive anything from anything [25] else. He is not diminishable, nor does he diminish anything, nor is he undiminishable. But he is self-comprehending, as something [30] so unknowable that he exceeds those who excel in unknowability.

"He is endowed with blessedness and perfection [35] and silence — not ⟨the blessedness⟩ nor the perfection — and stillness. Rather it (these attributes) is an entity of him that exists, which one cannot **64**

[know], and which is at rest. ' Rather they are entities ' of him unknowable to them ' all.

"And he is much higher in [5] beauty than all those ' [that] are good, and he is thus ' unknowable to all of them ' in every respect. And ' through them all he is [10] in them all, not ' only as the unknowable knowledge ' that is proper to him. And ' he is united with the ' ignorance that sees him. Whether ⟨one sees⟩ [15] in what way he is unknowable, ' or sees ' him as he is ' in every respect, or ' would say that [20] he is something like ' knowledge, he has sinned against him, ' being liable to judgment because he did not ' know God. He will not ' be judged by [25] That One who ' is neither concerned for anything nor ' has any desire, ' but it (judgment) ⟨is⟩ from ' himself because he did not find the origin [30] that truly exists. He was blind ' apart from the eye ' of revelation that is at rest, ' the (one) that is activated, ' the (one) from the Triple- [35] Power of the First Thought ' of the Invisible Spirit. ' This one thus exists from 65 [. . .] [16] something [. . . set firmly on the . . . a] ' beauty and a [first emergence] ' of stillness and silence [20] and tranquility and ' unfathomable greatness. When he appeared, ' he did not need ' time nor ⟨did he partake⟩ of eternity. ' Rather of [25] himself he is unfathomably ' unfathomable. He does not activate ' himself so as to become ' still. He is not an ' existence lest he [30] be in want. Spatially he is corporeal, ' while properly he is incorporeal. ' He has ' non-being existence. ' He exists for all of them unto himself [35] without any desire. ' But he is a greater summit ' of greatness. And he is ' higher than his stillness in order that 66 [. . . [16] he] saw [them] ' and [empowered them all], although they do not ' concern [themselves] with That One at ' all, nor, if one should [20] receive from him, does he receive power. ' Nothing activates him in accordance with ' the Unity that is at rest. ' For he is unknowable; ' he is an airless place of [25] the boundlessness. Since ' he is boundless and powerless ' and nonexistent, he was not giving ' Being. Rather he contains ' all of these in himself, being at rest [30] (and) standing out of ' the one who stands ' continually, since there had appeared ' an Eternal Life, the ' Invisible and Triple-Powered Spirit [35] which is in all of these ' who exist. And it surrounds ' them all, being higher than ' them all. A shadow 67 [. . .] [17] he [was filled with power. And ' he] stood [before them], ' empowering them all, and he filled [20] them all."

And ' concerning all of these (things) you have heard ' certainly. And do not ' seek anything more, ' but go. [25] We do not know whether ' the Unknowable One has ' angels or ' gods, or whether the One who is at rest ' was containing [30] anything within himself except ' the stillness, which is he, ' lest he be diminished. ' It is not fitting to ' spend more [35] time seeking. It was ' appropriate that you (pl.) ⟨alone⟩ know ' and that they speak ' with another one. But you will receive them **68** [... [6] and he said to me], "Write down ' [the things that I] shall [tell] you and ' of which I shall remind you for the sake of ' those who will be worthy [20] after you. And you will leave ' this book upon a mountain ' and you will adjure the guardian: ' 'Come Dreadful One.'" '

And after he said these (things), he separated [25] from me. But I was full ' of joy, and I wrote ' this book which was appointed ' for me, my son Messos, in order ' that I might disclose to you the (things) [30] that were proclaimed before me in ' my presence. And at first I received ' them in great silence and ' I stood by myself, preparing ' myself. These are the things that [35] were disclosed to me, O my son **69** [Messos ... [14] proclaim ' them, O my] ' son [Messos, as the] ' seal [for] all [the ' books of] ' Allogenes. [20]

Allogenes

HYPSIPHRONE (XI,*4*)

Introduced and translated by

JOHN D. TURNER

Hypsiphrone, which means "high-minded one" or perhaps "she of exalted thought," is the fourth and last treatise of Codex XI of the Coptic library from Nag Hammadi. It presently consists of four large and two small fragments containing the lower portions of the inner and outer margins of two papyrus leaves, which must have originally contained the entirety of this short treatise. It is written in the same script as the much longer and better preserved treatise of that Codex, *Allogenes*, although there is no discernible further relationship beyond these two treatises. *Hypsiphrone* is written in an apparently standard Sahidic Coptic dialect, unlike the other treatises of Codex XI. It bears the superscript title "Hypsiph[rone]," the remainder of the title being restored from other occurrences within the treatise; since the conclusion of the treatise is not extant, it may or may not have borne a subscript title.

Apart from the poor condition of the treatise, even its cryptic title affords little insight into its content. The *incipit* "The book (or scroll) [concerning the things] that were seen [by] Hypsiphrone being [revealed] in the place of [her] virginity" adds little more. Although there is mentioned a plurality of persons speaking with one another, the treatise does not appear to be a dialogue. Instead, the whole is presented as a speech of Hypsiphrone who reports the receipt of certain revelations during her descent from the "place of her virginity" into the world. The only figure mentioned by Hypsiphrone is one Phainops, "he of the gleaming eye," who apparently presides over a fount of blood into which he breathes, and which seems to produce a fiery effect.

One may conjecture that Hypsiphrone represents some form of the personified thought of a high deity who leaves her dwelling in the transcendental realm, where there are no distinctions of gender, to descend to the earthly realm at the time of the creation of humankind. There she encounters Phainops, probably in the act of creating humankind, who apparently produces "a [man in the likeness] of blood" from his fiery fount of blood.

In spite of the paucity of text, what remains seems to have some affinity with the group of gnostic texts generally designated as Sethian. To judge from the name Hypsiphrone, one may have to do here with the Sethian figure of Eleleth, called Phronesis in *Hyp. Arch.* (93,8-97,21), one of the traditional Sethian Four Illuminators, whose name might be derived from Aramaic '*illith*, "the tall one," which could be rendered by Greek *hypsiphrone*.

The fount of blood may refer to the heavenly Adamas or heavenly archetype of Adam, described in *Orig. World* (108,2-31) as the "enlightened bloody one" (based on the Hebrew pun on *'adam*, "man," and *dam*, "blood"). In this case, Hypsiphrone would be the Illuminator Eleleth, who in some Sethian texts is regarded as the abode of Sophia and certain "repentant souls" and in others

(*Trim. Prot.*, *Gos. Eg.*) is held responsible for the act usually ascribed to Sophia: that of producing the demiurge Yaldabaoth. Eleleth/Hypsiphrone would also be responsible for the projection below of Adamas, the image of God after whom the earthly Adam is modeled. In any case, Hypsiphrone is certainly a figure similar to that of the descending and restored Sophia. Phainops, "radiant-faced one," might then be a name for either the enlightened archetypal Adamas, or, since he seems to be distinguished from the "fount of blood," for the fiery angel Sabbaoth, the brother of the evil demiurge produced by the breath of Zoe, Pistis Sophia's daughter, in an effort to imprison the demiurge (*Hyp. Arch.* 95,5-96,4). Thus, although it bears no trace of the traditional Sethian names for these figures, *Hypsiphrone* may in fact be very closely related to the other Sethian texts.

HYPSIPHRONE

XI 69, 21-72, 33

Hypsiphrone |

The book [concerning the things] that were | seen [by] Hypsiphrone | being [revealed] in [25] the place of [her] virginity. | [And she listens] to | her brethren [...] Phainops | and [...] and | they speak [with one another] [30] in a [mystery].

Now I | [was first by individual] ranking [...] 70[14] I came [forth [15] to the place] of my [virginity] | and I went down | to the [world. Then I] was told | [about] them (by) those who abide | in [the place] of my [virginity]. [20]

And I went | down [to the world] and they said | to [me, "Again] Hypsiphrone | [has withdrawn] outside | the [place of her] virginity." [25] Then the one [who] heard, | Phainops, [who breathes] into | [her fount of] blood, spread [out] | for her.

[And] he said, | ["I am Phainops ...] 71[18] err [...] [20] desire [... the number] | of just the [human] remnants | or that I may see a [man, the blood-likeness | or ...] [25] of a [... fire] and a [... in] his | hands.

Then [as for me, I said | to] him, ["Phainops] has not [come] upon | me; he [has not] [30] gone astray. [... see] a | man [...] him [...] 72[18] For [...] which he | said [...] Phainops [20] this [...].

I saw him | and [he said] to me, "Hypsiphrone, | [why do you dwell] outside me? | [Follow me] and I will | tell [you about them]." So I [25] followed [him], for [I] was | in [great] fear. And | he [told me] about a fount of [blood] | that is [revealed by] setting afire | [...] he said [...].

THE SENTENCES OF SEXTUS (XII,*1*)

Introduced and translated by

FREDERIK WISSE

Before the discovery of the fragments of the Coptic version in Nag Hammadi Codex XII, *The Sentences of Sextus* were known through Latin, Syriac, Armenian, and Georgian translations, as well as through two manuscripts in the original Greek. Apart from some patristic quotations, the Coptic version is by far the oldest witness to this collection of wisdom sayings. It appears to be a faithful and consistent translation from the Greek, and it stands closer to the critical text provided by Henry Chadwick (*The Sentences of Sextus; A Contribution to the History of Early Christian Ethics*, Texts and Studies 5, Cambridge: The University Press, 1959) than the two Greek witnesses and the other versions. As such it is of considerable value for the study of the text and of the character of the document.

Of the approximately thirty-nine original pages of the tractate, ten survive. This assumes that the Coptic version did not contain more than the 451 sentences included in the Latin translation of Rufinus. The numeration of the sentences follows Chadwick's edition.

Though most of the sentences are of non-Christian origin, they enjoyed considerable popularity in Christian circles. Their presence among the Nag Hammadi tractates is not surprising. They share an ascetic outlook with many other writings in the collection. Indeed, the overwhelmingly ascetic tone of the entire Nag Hammadi library may indicate that the compilers and users of these books were part of the early monastic movement in Egypt. For a discussion of the moral teaching of Sextus, the reader is referred to Chadwick's edition.

THE SENTENCES OF SEXTUS

XII 15, 1-16, 28; 27, 1-34, 28

(157) is [a sign] of ignorance. |

(158/159) [Love] the truth, and the lie | [use] like poison. |

(160) [May] the right time precede your words. 5

(161/162) [Speak] when it is not proper | [to be silent], but [speak concerning] the things you know | (only) then [when] it is fitting. |

(163a) [The] untimely [word | is characteristic] of an evil mind. 10

(163b) [When it is] proper to act, do not | [use a] word.

(164a) Do not wish | [to speak] first in the midst of | [a crowd].

(164b) [While it is] a skill | [to speak], it is also [a] skill 15 [to be silent].

(165a) It is [better] for you to be defeated ' [while speaking the truth], than to be victorious ' [through deceit].

(165b) [He] who is victorious through ' [deceit] is [defeated] by the truth. '

(165c) [Untrue words] are [20] [characteristic of] evil persons.

(165d) [There has to be] a great [crisis ' before] the lie [is necessary]. '

(165e) [When there is] someone, while you speak ' [the truth], even if ' [you lie there is no sin].

(165f) Do not deceive [25] [anyone, especially] him who needs ' [advice].

(165g) [If you speak] after ' [many (others) you will see better] what is profitable. '

(166) [Faithful] is he who is first with ' all [good works]. **16**

(167) Wisdom leads [the soul] ' to the place of [God].

(168) [There is no] ' kinsman of the [truth except] ' wisdom.

(169) [It is not] possible for a [believing] [5] nature to [become fond of] ' lying.

(170) A fearful [and slavish] nature ' will [not] be able to partake in ' faith.

(171a) When you are [faithful, what] ' it is fitting to say [is not of greater value than] [10] the hearing.

(171b) When you [are] ' with believing persons, desire [to listen rather than] ' to speak.

(172) A pleasure-[loving] man ' is useless [in everything]. '

(173) When there is no [(accounting of) sin, do not speak] [15] in anything (which is) from [God].

(174) [The] sins ' of those who are [ignorant are] ' the shame of those who have [taught them]. '

(175) Those on account of whom [the name of God] is blasphemed ' [are dead] [20] before God.

(176) [A wise man ' is] a doer of good works after ' God.

(177) [May your life] ' confirm [your words before those who] ' hear.

(178) What it is [not right to do], [25] do not even consider [doing it].

(179) [What you do not] ' want to [happen to you, do not do it] ' yourself [either].

(180) [What] ' it [is] shameful [to do, is also] (pp. 17-26 are missing) **27**

(307/308) He is [a wise man who commends ' God] to men, ' [and God] thinks more highly of ' the wise man than his own [works]. [5]

(309) [After] God, no one is as free ' as the wise man. '

(310) [Everything] God possesses ' the wise man has also.

(311/312) The ' wise man shares in the [10] [kingdom] of God; an evil man ' does not want the foreknowledge ' of God to come to pass.

(313) An evil soul ' flees from God. '

(314) Everything bad [15] is the enemy of God.

(315) What thinks ' in you, say with your mind ' that it is man.

(316) Where ' your thought is, ' there is your [20] goodness.

(317) Do not seek goodness ' in flesh.

(318) He who does [not] harm ' the soul neither does (so) to ' man.

(319) After God, ' honor a [wise] man, [25] [since he] is the servant ' [of God].

(320) [To make] the body of your ' [soul] a burden ' is [pride], but to be able to ' [restrain] it **28** [gently] when [it is necessary ' is] blessedness.

(321) [Do not become] ' guilty [of] your own death. ' Do not be [angry at him] who will take you [out of] [5] (the) body and kill you. '

(322) If someone brings [the wise man] ' out of the body wickedly, ' he rather [does what is] ' good for him, [for] he has been released [10] from bonds.

(323) The fear of [death] ' grieves man because of ' the ignorance of the soul.

(324) ⟨It were better⟩ ' for you had [the] man-killing sword ' not come into being; but when it comes, [15] say with your mind that it does ' not exist.

(325/326a) Someone who says, "I ' believe," even if he spends a long ' time pretending, ' he will not prevail, but he will [20] fall; as ' your heart is, (so) will be ' your life.

(326b) A godly heart ' produces a blessed life. '

(327) He who will plot [25] evil against another, [he is] ' the first [. . .]. '

(328) [Let not] an ungrateful man ' cause you to cease to do [good]. **29**

(329) [Do not say with] your mind that [these ' things] which were asked, (and) ' [you] gave immediately, are more valuable than ' [the] receiver.

(330) You will use [5] [great] property, if you give to the ' [needy] willingly. '

(331) Persuade a senseless brother ' [not to] be senseless; if he is mad, ' protect him.

(332/334) Strive eagerly [10] to be victorious over every man in ' prudence; maintain self-sufficiency. '

(333) You cannot receive understanding unless ' you know first that you possess ⟨it⟩. ' In everything there is again this sentence.

(335) The [15] members of the body are a burden to those who do not use them.

(336) It is better to serve others than to make others serve you.

(337) He whom God [20] will not bring out of (the) body, let him not burden himself.

(338) Not only do not hold an opinion which does not benefit the needy, [but also do not] listen to it.

(339) He who gives [25] [something without] respect commits an outrage. [...].

(340) If you take on the [guardianship of] orphans, you will be [the] father of many children (and) you will be **30** beloved of God.

(341) He [whom you serve] because of [honor, you have] served for a wage.

(342) If you [have given] that which honors you ... , [you have] [5] given not to man, but [you have given] for your own pleasure.

(343/344) Do not [provoke] the anger of a mob. [Know, then], what is fitting for the fortunate man to [do].

(345) It is better to die [than] [10] to darken the soul because of [the] immoderation of the belly.

(346) Say with [your] mind that the body [is] the garment of your soul; keep it, therefore, pure since it is innocent.

(347) Whatever the soul [15] will do while it is in (the) body, it has as witnesses when it goes into judgment.

(348/349) Unclean demons do lay claim to a polluted soul; a faithful (and) [20] good soul evil demons will not be able to hinder in the way of God.

(350) Do not give the word of God to everyone.

(351) For [those who] are corrupted by [glory] [25] it is not assuring to [hear] about God.

(352/353) It is not a small [danger] for us to [speak the] truth about God; [do not say **31** anything about] God before [you have] learned from [God].

(354/356) [Do not] speak with a godless person [about] God; if you are polluted [5] [on account of] impure works, [do not] speak about God.

(357) [The] true [word] about God is [the] word of God.

(355) Speak concerning the word about God [10] as if you were saying it in the presence of God.

(358) If first your mind is persuaded that you have been god-loving, then speak to whomever you wish about God. [15]

(359) May your pious works ' precede every word about ' God.

(360) Do not wish to speak ' with a crowd about ' God.

(361) Be (more) sparing with a word about [20] God (than) about a soul.

(362) It ' is better to dispose of a soul than to discard ' at random a word about ' God.

(363a) You conceive the body ' of the god-loving man, but you will not be able to [25] rule over his speech.

(363b) The lion also ' rules over the body of ' [the wise man]; also the tyrant rules ' [over it] alone.

(364) If a tyrant **32** threatens you, [then, especially], ' remember God.

(365) [He who speaks] ' the word of God [to those for whom] ' it is not lawful, he is [the betrayer] [5] of God.

(366) It is better [for] ' you to be silent about the word of [God] ' than to speak recklessly. '

(367/368) He who speaks lies about ' God is lying to [10] God; a man who does not have ' anything truthful to say about [God] ' is abandoned by God.

(369) [It is not] ' possible for you to know God when you ' do not worship him.

(370) A man who [15] does evil to someone will not be able to worship ' God.

(371) The love of man ' is the beginning of godliness. '

(372) He who takes care of men while ' praying for all of them − this is [20] the truth of God.

(373/374) It is God's business ' to save whom he wants; ' on the other hand, it is the business of the pious man ' to beseech God to save ' everyone.

(375) When you [25] pray for something and it happens ' to you through God, then ' say with your mind that [you have **33** ...]. '

(376a) [A man who] is worthy of God, ' [he] is God among ' [men], and [he is] the son of God. [5]

(376b) Both the great one exists ' and he who is next ' to the great one exists.

(377/378) It is better for ' man to be without anything ' than to have many things [10] while not giving to the needy; so also you, ' if you pray to God, ' he will not give to you.

(379) If you, from your ' whole heart, give your bread to ' the hungry, the gift is small, [15] but the willingness is great ' with God.

(380) He who thinks ' that no one is in the presence of ' God, he is not humble towards God. '

(381) He who makes his mind like unto [20] God as far as he is able, he
| is the one who honors God greatly. |

(382) God does not need anything, | but he rejoices over those who
give to the | needy.

(383) The faithful do not speak many [25] words, but their works are nu-
merous. |

(384) It is a faithful person fond of learning | who is the worker of
the truth. **34**

(385) [Adjust ... the] calamities | in order that [...].

(386) [If you] | do not do evil to anyone, you will not be afraid | of
anyone.

(387) The tyrant will [5] not be able to take away happiness. |

(388) What it is right to do, do it | willingly.

(389a) What it is not right to do, | do not do it in any way.

(389b) Promise | everything rather than [10] to say, "I am wise." |

(390) What you do well, say | with your mind that it [is] God | who
does it.

(391) No man | who ⟨looks⟩ down upon the earth [15] and upon tables
is wise. |

(392) The philosopher who is an | outer body, he is not the one | to
whom it is fitting to pay respect, but (the) | philosopher according to
the inner [20] man.

(393) Guard yourself from lying: there is | he who deceives and there
is he who is | deceived.

(394/395) Know who God is, | and know who is the one who | thinks
in you; a good man [25] is the good work | of God.

(396) They are miserable | because of whom the [word] is blas-
phemed. |

(397) Death will [not] be able to destroy (pp. 35-end are missing).

FRAGMENTS (XII,3)

Introduced and translated by

FREDERIK WISSE

It is uncertain whether the two fragments presented here in translation come from the same tractate. With no title and only one substantial fragment surviving, the character of the tractate remains obscure. It seems to present ethical teaching within a religious context. The first person singular and plural are used, and the speaker refers to "my Father," which suggests that he may be Jesus. The speaker contrasts himself and his followers with others, referred to in the third person plural, who live in wickedness and do evil deeds. Nothing in the fragments suggests that the tractate was gnostic. There is no reason to doubt that the Coptic represents a translation from the Greek.

FRAGMENTS

XII 1A, 6-29
1B, 6-29
2A, 24-29
2B, 24-29

(Fragment 1A) [...] [10] us as it is | [fitting. ...] each other, but | [...] a crowd to receive | [...] they speak ill | [...] live by wickedness [15] [...] the [...] | work evil things to | [...] the good things, and they | [...] do their own things | [...] strangers. There are [20] [...] do their own things | [...] works which [... | we] ourselves do [... | works] of those [...] | evil works [...] [25] that which we shall [... | the] works which [...] | that which [...] | every one [...]

(Fragment 1B) [...]. [9] For I speak the [...] | know [God ...] | gave their [...] | error. But [...] | they are worthy of the [...] | into God [...]. [15] And already they have [...] | the ignorance [...] | the righteousness [...] | these were worthy [of ...]. | He [...] [20] my Father who is [...] | not to them a father [...] | I think that [...] | this which the [...] | I give again to the [...] [25] they forgive [...] | spoke it [...] | it [...]

(Fragment 2A) [. . .] [26] philosopher [. . .] | they are not able to [. . .] | philosopher | [. . .] world [. . .]

(Fragment 2B) [. . .] [27] her [. . .] | begot him [. . .] | think that [. . .]

TRIMORPHIC PROTENNOIA (XIII,*1*)

Introduced and translated by

JOHN D. TURNER

Trimorphic Protennoia ("The Three-formed [Divine] First Thought") is, in its form, a Barbeloite treatise which has undergone both Sethian and Christian revisions. It is roughly contemporaneous with *The Apocryphon of John* (mid-second century C.E.), which it resembles in certain interesting ways, and is distinguished by a number of striking parallels to the Fourth Gospel and especially its prologue.

The underlying basis of *Trimorphic Protennoia* can be seen in the series consistent "I am" self-predicatory aretalogies, in which Protennoia recites her divine identity and role in the creation and salvation of the world. These are structured into an introductory aretalogy (35,1-32) identifying Protennoia as the divine First Thought followed by three similar aretalogies in the same style, the second and third of which form separately titled subtractates in the *Trimorphic Protennoia*: First, Protennoia is the Voice of the First Thought who descends first as light into darkness to give shape to her fallen members (35,32-36,27; 40,29-41,1). Second, Protennoia is the Speech of the Thought who descends to empower her fallen members by giving them spirit or breadth (42,4-27; 45,2-12; 45,21-46,3). Third, Protennoia is the Word or Logos of the Thought who descends in the likeness of the powers, assumes a human appearance, introduces the illuminatory baptismal rite of the Five Seals and restores her members into the light (46,5-6; 47,5-22; 49,15-22; 50,9-12,18-20).

One cannot fail to notice here a striking resemblance, not only to the language and structure of the Johannine prologue's narration of the descents of the Logos, but also to the similar first-person aretalogy on the three descents of Pronoia found at the end of the longer version of the *Apocryphon of John* (II,*1*:30,11-31,25), with which the *Trimorphic Protennoia* may even be genetically related.

The underlying tripartite aretalogy has been expanded by means of six narrative doctrinal insertions (36,27-40,29; 41,1-42,2; 42,27-45,2; 46,7-47,5; 47,22-49,15; 49,22-50,9). Three of these insertions, whose third-person expository prose breaks the otherwise smooth flow of Protennoia's self-referential speech, are designated as "mysteries" which Protennoia is said to have communicated to the sons of the light.

Essentially, the scheme of the divine First Thought's triple descent into this world is a derivative of speculation at home in the Hellenistic Jewish wisdom schools responsible for the personification of the figure of the divine wisdom and the development of the myth concerning her role in the creation of the world and in the subsequent enlightenment of mankind as it is found especially in 1 Enoch 42, Sirach 24, Wisdom 7-8, and in Philo. It seems that Sophia's two unsuccessful descents in 1 Enoch 42 and her successful one in Sirach 24 were combined into a total of three descents into the lower world, two resulting in partial liberation, and the third resulting in the final awakening and salvation of those who received her. This is the same pattern that underlies the Johannine prologue, which, though not a Barbeloite composition, was likely also a product of a similar form of wisdom speculation. The unique contribution of the Barbeloites seems to have been the interpretation of the three revelatory descents: first, in terms of a primal divine triad of Father, Mother and Son, second in terms of a theory of progressive revelation in which each successive appearance of the revealer is characterized by an increasing degree of articulateness and finality (Voice, Speech, and Word) and third, the association of the final descent with a Logos figure who confers final enlightenment in the form of transcendentalized baptismal rite called the Five Seals.

It is clear that the *Trimorphic Protennoia* has been secondarily Christianized. Three glosses identifying the Autogenes Son as the Christ in the first subtractate (37,[31]; 38,22; 39,6-7) probably derive from the traditional Barbeloite theogonical material common to *The Apocryphon of John* and Irenaeus, *Haer*. 1.29, upon which the author drew for the first narrative insertion. These Christian glosses would have been suggested by an equation between the Christian designation of Christ as *monogenes* and what seems to be a pre-Christian designation for the third member of the Barbeloite Father-Mother-Son triad, namely the Self-Begotten (*autogenes*) Son.

The third subtractate narrates the incognito descent of Protennoia as the Word disguised in the form of the sovereignties, powers, and angels, culminating in the final revelation of herself in the human form of her members below, but it seems to have been supplemented by an alien and tendentious Christological interpretation. In the third subtractate, traditional Christological titles such as Christ, Beloved, Son of God (i.e., "Son of the Archigenetor") and Son of Man are polemically interpreted in a consciously docetic fashion so as to suggest that these titles were inappropriately applied to the human Jesus by the apostolic church. By implication, the apostolic Jesus is shown actually to be the Christ of the evil archons; the apostolic beloved is actually the Beloved of the archons; the apostolic Son of God is the Son of the ignorant world creator; and the apostolic Son of Man is only a human being among the sons of men.

It is interesting that most of these reinterpretations of the Christology of the apostolic church in the *Trimorphic Protennoia* seem to depend on key passages from the Gospel of John to score their point in any acute fashion. It seems that the key to the relationship between these two texts lies in the recognition that *Trimorphic Protennoia* has undergone at least three stages of composition. First, there was the original triad of the aretalogical self-predications of Protennoia as Voice, Speech, and Word that were probably built up out of the Jewish wisdom tradition and maybe out of *The Apocryphon of John*'s similar Pronoia aretalogy itself sometime during the first century C.E.; there is little here that seems specifically gnostic or Christian or Sethian or Barbeloite. Second, this was supplemented, whether by the same or by a different author, by various narrative doctrinal passages based upon traditional Barbeloite theogonical materials similar to those of *The Apocryphon of John* and Irenaeus, *Haer*. 1.29. After circulation as a mildly Christian Barbeloite text in this form, the third and last stage of composition seems to have involved a deliberately polemical incorporation of

Christian, specifically Johannine Christian, materials into the aretalogical portion of the third subtractate. One might assign the third compositional stage of *Trimorphic Protennoia* to the period of struggle over the interpretation of the Christology of the Fourth Gospel witnessed by the New Testament letters of John, perhaps the first quarter or half of the second century.

TRIMORPHIC PROTENNOIA

XIII 35, 1-50, 24

[I] am [Protennoia, the] Thought that ' [dwells] in [the Light. I] am the movement ' that dwells in the [All, she in whom the] All takes ' its stand, [the first]-born⁵ among those who [came to be, she who exists] before ' the All. [She (Protennoia) is called] by three names, although she ' dwells alone, [since she is perfect]. I am ' invisible within the Thought of the Invisible ' One. I am revealed in the immeasurable, ¹⁰ ineffable (things). I am incomprehensible, ' dwelling in the incomprehensible. I ' move in every creature.

I am the life ' of my Epinoia that dwells within ' every Power and every eternal movement ¹⁵ and (in) invisible Lights and ' within the Archons and Angels and ' Demons and every soul dwelling ' in [Tartaros] and (in) every material soul. ' I dwell in those who came to be. I move in ²⁰ everyone and I delve into them all. ' I walk uprightly, and those who ' sleep I [awaken]. And I ' am the sight of those who dwell in sleep. '

I am the Invisible One within the All. ²⁵ It is I who counsel those who are hidden, since I know ' the All that exists in it. ' I am numberless beyond everyone. I ' am immeasurable, ineffable, yet ' whenever I [wish, I shall] reveal myself ³⁰ of my own accord. I [am the head of] the All. I exist ' before the [All, and] I am the All, ' since I [exist in] everyone.

I am a Voice ' [speaking softly]. I exist ' [from the first. I dwell] within the Silence ³⁵ [that surrounds every one] of them. **36** And [it is] the [hidden Voice] that [dwells within] ' me, [within the] incomprehensible, ' immeasurable [Thought, within the] immeasurable Silence. '

I [descended to the] midst of the underworld⁵ and I shone [down upon the] darkness. It is I who ' poured forth the [water]. It is I who am hidden within ' [radiant] waters. I am the one who ' gradually put forth the All by my ' Thought. It is I who am laden with the Voice. It ¹⁰ is through me that Gnosis comes forth. [I] ' dwell in the ineffable and ' unknowable ones. I am perception and knowledge, ' uttering a Voice by means of ' thought. [I] am the real Voice. ¹⁵ I cry out in everyone, and they recognize ' it (the voice], since a seed indwells [them]. ' I am the Thought of the Father and through ' me proceeded [the] Voice, ' that is, the knowledge of the everlasting things. I [20] exist as Thought for the [All] — being joined ' to the unknowable and incomprehensible Thought — ' I revealed myself — yes, I — among ' all those who recognize me. For it is I ' who am joined with everyone by virtue of [25] the hidden Thought and an exalted ⟨Voice⟩, even a Voice from ' the invisible Thought. And it is immeasurable, ' since it dwells in the Immeasurable One. It is a mystery; ' it is [unrestrainable] [30] by [the Incomprehensible One]. It is invisible ' [to all those who are] visible ' in the All. [It is a Light] dwelling in ' Light.

It is we [also who] alone [have separated] ' [from the] visible [world] [35] since we [are saved by the] ' hidden [wisdom by means of the] [37] ineffable, immeasurable [Voice]. And he who is ' hidden within us pays the tributes of his fruit ' to the Water of Life.

Then ' the Son who is perfect in every respect — that is, [5] the Word who originated through that ' Voice; who proceeded from the height; who ' has within him the Name; who is ' a Light — he (the Son) revealed the everlasting things and ' all the unknowns were known. [10] And those things difficult to interpret ' and secret, he revealed, and ' as for those who dwell in Silence with the First ' Thought, he preached to them. And ' he revealed himself to those who dwell in darkness, and [15] he showed himself to those who dwell in the abyss, ' and to those who dwell in the hidden treasuries he told ' ineffable mysteries, ' and he taught unrepeatable doctrines ' to all those who became Sons of [20] the Light.

Now the Voice that originated ' from my Thought exists as three ' permanences: the Father, the Mother, the Son. Existing ' perceptibly as Speech, it (Voice) has ' within it a Word endowed with [25] every ⟨glory⟩, and it has ' three masculinities, three powers, ' and three names. They exist in the ' manner of Three □ □ □ — which are quadrangels — ' secretly within a silence [30] of the Ineffable One.

[It is he] alone who came to be, ' that [is, the Christ. And] as for me I anointed him ' as the glory [of the] Invisible [Spirit] with ' [goodness]. Now [the Three] I established ' [alone in] eternal [glory] over [35] [the Aeons in the] Living [Water], that ' [is, the glory that surrounds him] [38] who first came forth to the Light ' of those exalted Aeons, and it is in glorious ' Light that he firmly perseveres. And [he] ' stood in his own Light [5] that surrounds him, that is, the Eye of the Light ' that gloriously shines on me. ' He perpetuated the Father of all ⟨the⟩ Aeons, who am

I, | the Thought of the Father, Protennoia, | that is, Barbelo, the [perfect] Glory [10] and the [immeasurable] Invisible One who is hidden. | I am the Image of the Invisible Spirit | and it is through me that the All took shape, | and (I am) the Mother (as well as) the Light which she appointed | as Virgin, she who is called [15] Meirothea, the incomprehensible Womb, the | unrestrainable and immeasurable Voice.

Then | the Perfect Son revealed himself to his | Aeons who originated through him, | and he revealed them and glorified them and [20] gave them thrones and stood in | the glory with which he glorified himself. | They blessed the Perfect Son, the Christ, the | only-begotten God. And they gave glory, saying, "He is! He is! The Son [25] of God! The Son of God! It is he who | is! The Aeon of Aeons beholding the | Aeons which he begot! For thou hast | begotten by thine own desire! Therefore [we] | glorify thee: ma mō ō ō ō eia ei on ei! The [Aeon] [30] of [Aeons! The] Aeon which he gave!"

Then, | moreover, the [God who was begotten] gave them (the Aeons) | a power of [life on which they might rely] and [he] | established [them. The] first | Aeon, he established [over the first]: Armedon, [35] Nousa[nios, Armozel; the] second | he established [over the second Aeon]: **39** Phaionios, Ainios, Oroiael; the third | over the third Aeon: Mellephaneus, | Loios, Daveithai; the fourth | over the fourth: Mousanios, Amethes, [5] Eleleth. Now those Aeons were begotten | by the God who was begotten − the | Christ − and these Aeons received | as well as gave glory. They were the first to appear, | exalted in their thought, and each [10] Aeon gave myriads of glories within | great untraceable lights and | they all together blessed the Perfect | Son, the God who was begotten.

Then there | came forth a word from the great [15] Light Eleleth and said, "I | am King! Who belongs to Chaos and who | belongs to the underworld?" And at that instant his Light | appeared radiant, endowed | with the Epinoia. The Powers of the Powers [20] did not entreat him and likewise immediately | there appeared the great Demon | who rules over the lowest part of the underworld | and Chaos. He has neither form | nor perfection, but on the contrary possesses [25] the form of the glory of those | begotten in the darkness. Now he is called | "Saklas," that is, "Samael," "Yaltabaoth," | he who had taken power; who had snatched | it away from the innocent one (Sophia); who had earlier overpowered [30] her who is the Light's Epinoia (Sophia) | who had descended, her from | whom he (Yaltabaoth) had come forth originally.

Now when the ' Epinoia of the [Light] realized ' that [he (Yalta-baoth)] had begged him (the Light), ' for another [order, even though he was lower] than she, she said, [35] "Grant [me another order so that] you may become for me ' [a dwelling place lest I dwell] in disorder ' [forever." And the order of the] entire house of **40** glory [was agreed] upon her ' word. A blessing was brought for ' her and the higher order released it ' to her.

And the great Demon [5] began to produce ' aeons in the likeness of the real Aeons, ' except that he produced them out of his own power. '

Then I too revealed ' my Voice secretly, [10] saying, "Cease! Desist, ' (you) who tread on matter; for behold ' I am coming down to the world ' of mortals for the sake of my portion that was in ' that place from the time when [15] the innocent Sophia was conquered, she who ' descended, so that I might thwart ' their aim which the one revealed ' by her appoints." ' And all were disturbed, [20] each one who dwells ' in the house of the ignorant light, ' and the abyss trembled. And ' the Archigenetor of ignorance ' reigned over Chaos and the underworld and [25] produced a man in my likeness. But he neither ' knew that that one would become ' for him a sentence of dissolution nor ' does he recognize the power in ' him.

But now I have come down [30] and reached down to Chaos. And ' I was [with] my own who ' were in that place. [I am hidden] within ' them, empowering [them and] giving ' them shape. And [from the first day] until [35] the day [when I will grant mighty power] ' to those who [are mine, I will reveal myself to] ' those who have [heard my mysteries], **41** that is, the [Sons] of [the] Light.

I ' am their Father and I shall tell you a ' mystery, ineffable and indivulgeable ' by [any] mouth: Every bond [5] I loosed from you, and the ' chains of the Demons of the underworld, I broke, ' these things which are bound on my members, restraining them. And ' the high walls of darkness I overthrew, ' and the secure gates of [10] those pitiless ones I broke, and I smashed ' their bars. And the evil Force and ' the one who beats you, and the one who hinders ' you, and the Tyrant, and the Adversary, ' and the one who is King, and the present Enemy, [15] indeed all these I explained to those ' who are mine, who are the Sons of the light, ' in order that they might nullify them all ' and be saved from all those bonds ' and enter into the place where they were at [20] first.

I am the first one who descended ' on account of my portion which remains, that is, ' the Spirit that (now) dwells in the soul, (but) which originated ' from the Water of Life and out ' of the immersion of the mysteries, and I spoke, ²⁵ I together with the Archons and Authorities. ' For I had gone down below their ' language and I spoke my mysteries to ' my own – a hidden mystery – and ' the bonds and eternal oblivion were nullified. ³⁰ And I bore fruit in them, that ' is, the Thought of the unchanging Aeon, and ' my house, and their [Father]. And I went ' down [to those who were mine] from the first and ' I [reached them and broke] the first strands ³⁵ that [enslaved them. Then] ' everyone [of those] within me shone, and **42** I prepared [a pattern] for those ineffable Lights that are ' within me. Amen. '

The Discourse of Protennoia: [One] '

I am the Voice that appeared through ⁵ my Thought, for I am "He who is syzygetic," ' since I am called "the Thought of the Invisible One." ' Since I am called "the unchanging Speech," ' I am called "She who is syzygetic."

I am a single ' one (fem.) since I am undefiled. I am the Mother [of] ¹⁰ the Voice, speaking in many ways, completing ' the All. It is in me that knowledge dwells, ' the knowledge of ⟨things⟩ everlasting. It is I [who] ' speak within every creature and I was known ' by the All. It is I who lift up ¹⁵ the Speech of the Voice to the ears of those who ' have known me, that is, the Sons of the Light. '

Now I have come the second time in the likeness ' of a female and have spoken with them. And ' I shall tell them of the coming end of the Aeon ²⁰ and teach them of the beginning of the Aeon ' to come, the one without change, ' the one in which our appearance will be changed. ' We shall be purified within those Aeons from which I ' revealed myself in the Thought ²⁵ of the likeness of my masculinity. I settled ' among those who are worthy in the Thought of my ' changeless Aeon.

For I shall tell you a ' mystery [of] this particular Aeon and ' tell you about the forces that are in it. ³⁰ The birth beckons: [hour] begets ' hour, [day begets day]. The months ' made known the [month. Time] has [gone round] ' succeeding [time]. This particular Aeon **43** was completed in [this] fashion, and it was estimated, and ' it (was) short, for it was a finger that released a ' finger and a joint that was separated from ' a joint. Then when the great Authorities knew ⁵ that the time of fulfillment had appeared – ' just as in the pangs of the parturient it (the time) had drawn near, ' so also had ' the destruction approached – all together the elements ' trembled, and the foundations of the underworld and the ceilings ¹⁰ of Chaos shook and a great fire shone ' within

their midst, and the rocks and the earth ' were shaken like a reed shaken
by the wind. ' And the lots of Fate and those who apportion ' the
domiciles were greatly disturbed over [15] a great thunder. And the thrones
of ' the Powers were disturbed since they were overturned, and their '
King was afraid. And those who pursue Fate ' paid their allotment of
visits to the path, and ' they said to the Powers, "What is this disturbance [20] and this shaking that has come upon us through ' a Voice
⟨belonging⟩ to the exalted Speech? ' And our entire habitation has
been shaken, and the entire ' circuit of our path of ascent has met with
' destruction, and the path upon which we go, [25] which takes us up to
the Archigenetor ' of our birth, has ceased to be established for us." '
Then the Powers answered, saying, ' "We too are at a loss about ' it
since we did not know what was responsible for it. But [30] arise, let us go
up to the Archigenetor ' and ask him." And the ' Powers all gathered
and went up to the Archigenetor. ' [They said to] him, "Where is your
boasting ' in which [you boast]? [35] Did we not [hear you say], 'I ' am
God [and I am] your Father **44** and it is I who [begot] you and there is
no [other] ' beside me'? Now behold, there has appeared ' [a] Voice belonging to that invisible Speech ' of [the Aeon] (and) which we know
not. And [5] we ourselves did not recognize to whom we ' belong, for that
Voice which we listened to ' is foreign to us, and we do not recognize '
it; we did not know whence it was. It came ' and put fear in our midst
and weakening [10] in the members of our arms. So now let ' us weep and
mourn most bitterly! ' As for the future, let us make our entire flight '
before we are imprisoned perforce and ' taken down to the bosom of
the underworld. For already [15] the slackening of our bondage has approached, ' and the times are cut short and the days have shortened '
and our time has been fulfilled, and the weeping ' of our destruction
has approached us so that ' we may be taken to the place we recognize.
[20] For as for our tree from which we grew, a fruit ' of ignorance is what
it has; and ' also its leaves, it is death that dwells in them, ' and darkness dwells under the shadow of its ' boughs. And it was in deceit [25] and
lust that we harvested it, this (tree) through ' which ignorant Chaos became for us a dwelling place. ' For behold, even he, the Archigenetor '
of our birth, about whom we boast, ' even he did not know this
Speech."

So now, [30] O Sons of the Thought, listen to me, to the Speech ' of the
Mother of your mercy, for you have ' become worthy of the mystery
hidden from (the beginning of) ' the Aeons, so that [you might receive]
it. And the consummation ' of this [particular] Aeon [and] of the evil

life [35] [has approached and there dawns **45** the] beginning of the [Aeon to come] which [has ' no change forever].

I am ' androgynous. [I am Mother (and) I am] Father since [I ' copulate] with myself. I [copulated] with myself [5] [and with those who love] me, [and] ' it is through me alone that the All [stands firm]. I am the Womb ' [that gives shape] to the All by giving birth to the Light that ' [shines in] splendor. I am the Aeon to [come. ' I am] the fulfillment of the All, that is, Me[iroth]ea, [10] the glory of the Mother. I cast [voiced] Speech ' into the ears of those who know ' me.

And I am inviting you into the exalted, perfect Light. ' Moreover (as for) this (Light), when you enter ' it you will be glorified by those [who] [15] give glory, and those who enthrone will ' enthrone you. You will accept robes from ' those who give robes and the Baptists ' will baptize you and you will become ' gloriously glorious, the way you first were [20] when you were ⟨Light⟩. '

And I hid myself in everyone and revealed [myself] ' within them, and every mind seeking ' me longed for me, for it is I ' who gave shape to the All when it had no form. [25] And I transformed their forms ' into (other) forms until the time when a form ' will be given to the All. It is through me that the Voice ' originated and it is I who put the breath ' within my own. And I cast into [30] them the eternally holy Spirit and ' I ascended and entered my Light. ' [I went up] upon my branch and ' sat [there among the] Sons of the [holy] Light. ' And [I withdrew] to their dwelling place **46** which [...] [3] become [glorious .... Amen]. '

[On Fate: Two] [5]

I am [the Word] who dwells [in the] ineffable [Voice]. ' I dwell in undefiled [Light] ' and a Thought [revealed itself] ' perceptibly through [the great] ' Speech of the Mother, although it is a male offspring [that supports me] [10] as my foundation. And it (the Speech) exists from the beginning ' in the foundations of the All.

But there is a Light [that] ' dwells hidden in Silence and it was first to [come] ' forth. Whereas she (the Mother) alone exists as Silence, ' I alone am the Word, ineffable, [15] unpolluted, immeasurable, inconceivable. ' It (the Word) is a hidden Light, bearing a Fruit of ' Life, pouring forth a Living Water from ' the invisible, unpolluted, immeasurable ' Spring, that is, the unreproducible Voice of the glory [20] of the Mother, the glory of the offspring ' of God; a male Virgin by ' virtue of a hidden Intellect, that is, ' the Silence hidden from the All, being unreproducible, ' an immeasurable Light, the source of the All, [25] the Root of the entire Aeon. It is the Foundation that supports ' every movement of the Aeons that ' belong to the mighty Glory. It is the Foundation of every foundation. ' It is the Breath of the Powers. It is the Eye of the ' Three Permanences, which exist as Voice [30] by virtue of Thought. And it is a Word ' by virtue of Speech; it was sent ' to illumine those who dwell in the [darkness]. '

Now behold [I will reveal] ' to you [my mysteries] since [35] you are my fellow [brethren, and you shall] know ' them all [...]. **47**[5] I [told all of them about ' my mysteries] that exist in [the ' incomprehensible], inexpressible [Aeons]. I taught [them the mysteries] ' through the [Voice that ' exists] within a perfect Intellect [and [10] I] became a foundation for the All, and [I ' empowered] them.

The second time I came in the [Speech] ' of my Voice. I gave shape to those who [took] shape ' until their consummation.

The third ' time I revealed myself to them [in] [15] their tents as Word and I ' revealed myself in the likeness of their shape. And ' I wore everyone's garment and ' I hid myself within them, and [they] did not ' know the one who empowers me. For I dwell within [20] all the Sovereignties and Powers and within ' the Angels and in every movement [that] exists ' in all matter. And I hid myself within ' them until I revealed myself to my [brethren]. ' And none of them (the Powers) knew me, [although] [25] it is I who work in them. Rather [they thought] ' that the All was created [by them] ' since they are ignorant, not knowing [their] ' root, the place in which they grew.

[I] ' am the Light that illumines the All. I [30] am the Light that rejoices [in my] ' brethren, for I came down to the world [of] ' mortals on account of the Spirit that remains [in] ' that which [descended] (and) came forth [from] the ' innocent Sophia. [I came] and I delivered [35] [...] and I [went] to **48** [...] [6] which he had [formerly and ' I gave to him] from the Water [of Life, which ' strips] him of the Chaos [that is ' in the] uttermost [darkness] that exists [inside] [10] the entire [abyss], that is, the thought of [the corporeal] ' and the psychic. All these I ' put on. And I stripped him of it ' and I put upon him a shining Light, that ' is, the knowledge of the Thought of the Fatherhood. [15]

And I delivered him to those who give robes − ' Yammon, Elasso, Amenai − and they [covered] ' him with a robe from the robes of the Light; ' and I delivered him to the Baptists and they ' baptized him − Micheus, Michar, [20] Mn[e]sinous − and they immersed him in the spring of the [Water] ' of Life. And I delivered him to those who ' enthrone −

Bariel, Nouthan, Sabenai − and ' they enthroned him from the throne of glory. ' And I delivered him to those who glorify − [25] Ariom, Elien, Phariel − and they glorified ' him with the glory of the Fatherhood. And ' those who snatch away snatched away − Kamaliel. ' [...]anen, Samblo, the servants of ⟨the⟩ great ' holy Luminaries − and they took him into [30] the light-[place] of his Fatherhood. And ' [he received] the Five Seals from ' [the Light] of the Mother, Protennoia, and ' it was [granted] him [to] partake of [the mystery] of ' knowledge, and [he became a Light] in [35] Light.

So, now, [.... **49**[6] I was] dwelling in them [in the form ' of each] one. [The Archons] thought ' [that I] was their Christ. Indeed I [dwell ' in] everyone. Indeed within those in whom [I revealed [10] myself] as Light [I eluded] ' the Archons. I am their beloved, [for] ' in that place I clothed myself [as] ' the Son of the Archigenetor, and I was like ' him until the end of his decree, which is [15] the ignorance of Chaos. And among the ' Angels I revealed myself in their likeness, ' and among the Powers as if I were one ' of them, but among the Sons of Man as if ' I were a Son of Man, even though I am [20] Father of everyone.

I hid myself within them ' all until I revealed myself among my members, ' which are mine, and I taught them about the ineffable ' ordinances, and (about) the brethren. But they are inexpressible ' to every Sovereignty and every ruling [25] Power except to the Sons of the Light ' alone, that is, the ordinances of the Father. These are ' the glories that are higher than every glory, that is, [the Five] ' Seals complete by virtue of Intellect. He ' who possesses the Five Seals of these [30] particular names has stripped off ⟨the⟩ garments ' of ignorance and put on ' a shining Light. And nothing ' will appear to him that belongs to the Powers ' of the Archons. Within those of this sort [35] darkness will dissolve and [ignorance] will die. ' And the thought of the creature ' which [is scattered will] present a single appearance ' and [dark Chaos] will dissolve and **50** [...] [3] and the [...] ' incomprehensible [...] [5] within the [...] ' until I reveal myself [to all my fellow ' brethren] and until I gather [together] ' all [my fellow] brethren within my [eternal ' kingdom]. And I proclaimed to them the ineffable [Five [10] Seals in order that ' I might] abide in them and they also ' might abide in me.

As for me, I put on ' Jesus. I bore him from the cursed ' wood, and established him in the dwelling places [15] of his Father. And those who watch over ' their dwelling places did not recognize me. ' For I, I am unrestrainable together with my ' Seed, and my Seed, which is mine, I shall [place] ' into the Holy Light within an [20] incomprehensible Silence. Amen. '

The Discourse of the Appearance: Three

Trimorphic Protennoia, in three parts [1]

A Sacred Scripture written by the Father [1]
with perfect Knowledge

THE GOSPEL OF MARY (BG 8502,*1*)

Introduced by

KAREN L. KING

Translated by

GEORGE W. MACRAE and R. MCL. WILSON

Edited by

DOUGLAS M. PARROTT

The extant text of *The Gospel of Mary* can easily be divided into two parts. The first section (7,1-9,24) describes the dialogue between the (risen) Savior and the disciples. He answers their questions concerning matter and sin. Relying on an exegesis of Romans 7, as Anne Pasquier has shown, the Savior argues, in effect, that sin is not a moral category, but a cosmological one; it is due to the improper mixing of the material and the spiritual. In the end all things will be resolved into their proper root. After finishing his discourse, the Savior gives them a final greeting, admonishes them to beware of any who may try to lead them astray and commissions them to go and preach the gospel of the kingdom. After he departs, however, the disciples are grieved and in considerable doubt and consternation. Mary Magdalene comforts them and turns their hearts toward the Good and a consideration of the Savior's words.

The second section of the text (10,1-23; 15,1-19,2) contains a description by Mary of special revelation given to her by the Savior. At Peter's request, she tells the disciples about things that were hidden from them. The basis for her knowledge is a vision of the Lord and a private dialogue with him. Unfortunately four pages of the text are missing here so that only the beginning and end of Mary's revelation are extant.

The revelation is in the form of a dialogue. The first question Mary asks the Savior is how one sees a vision. The Savior replies that the soul sees through the mind which is between the soul and the spirit. At this point the text breaks off. When the text resumes at 15,1, Mary is in the midst of describing the Savior's revelation concerning the rise of the soul past the four powers. The four powers are most probably to be identified as essential expressions of the four material elements. The enlightened soul, now free of their bonds, rises past the four powers, overpowering them with her gnosis, and attains eternal, silent rest.

After Mary finishes recounting her vision to the disciples, Andrew and then Peter challenge her on two grounds. First of all, Andrew says, these teachings are strange. Secondly, Peter questions, would the Savior really have told such things to a woman and kept them from the male disciples. Levi admonishes Peter for contending with the woman as against the adversaries and acknowledges that the Savior loved her more than the other disciples. He entreats them to be ashamed, to put on the perfect man, and to go forth and preach as the Savior had instructed them to do. They immediately go forth to preach and the text ends.

The confrontation of Mary with Peter, a scenario also found in *The Gospel of Thomas*, *Pistis Sophia*, and *The Gospel of the Egyptians*, reflects some of the tensions in second-century Christianity. Peter and Andrew represent orthodox positions that deny the validity of esoteric revelation and reject the authority of women to teach. *The Gospel of Mary* attacks both of these positions head-on through its portrayal of Mary Magdalene. She is the Savior's beloved, possessed of knowledge and teaching superior to that of the public apostolic tradition. Her superiority is based on vision and private revelation and is demonstrated in her capacity to strengthen the wavering disciples and turn them toward the Good.

The text belongs to the genre of the gnostic dialogue. It has, however, also been classified as an apocalypse due to several characteristics it shares with other texts of that genre: revelation dialogue, vision, an abbreviated cosmogony, a description of otherworldly regions and the rise of the soul (though there is no heavenly journey as such), final instructions, and a short narrative conclusion. The difficulty in determining genre is due in part to the fact that the text has undergone secondary redaction. Most scholars agree that the two parts of the text described above were originally separate pieces (oral or written) that were artificially combined to form the present whole. The role of Mary at the end of the first section and the altercation among the disciples at the end provide the narrative connection.

The Gospel of Mary was originally written in Greek some time in the second century. Unfortunately the two extant copies of *The Gospel of Mary* are extremely fragmentary. The earliest text comprises only a single, fragmentary leaf written in Greek, dated to the early third century (P. Rylands III 463 [22:16,1-19,4]). A longer portion of the text is extant in an early fifth-century Coptic codex (P. Berolinensis 8502,*1*), though considerable portions of the text are missing too. Of eighteen pages, only eight are extant (7-10 and 15-19,5). Though the text of the Greek fragment varies considerably from the Coptic version, it parallels the Coptic pages 17,5-21 and 18,5-19,5 and hence does not provide any new material.

THE GOSPEL OF MARY

BG 7, 1-19, 5

[...] (pp. 1-6 missing) will matter then | be [destroyed] or not?" The Savior said, | "All natures, all formations, all creatures | exist in and with one another, [5] and they will be resolved again into | their own roots. For the | nature of matter is resolved into the (roots) of | its nature alone. He who has | ears to hear, let him hear." [10]

Peter said to him, "Since you have | explained everything to us, tell us this also: ' What is the sin of the world?'' ' The Savior said, '' There is no sin, ' but it is you who make sin when [15] you do the things that are like the nature of ' adultery, which is called 'sin.' ' That is why the Good came ' into your midst, to the (essence) of every nature, ' in order to restore it [20] to its root.'' Then he continued and ' said, "That is why you ' [become sick] and die, for [. . .] **8** of the one who [. . . He who] ' understands, let him understand. [Matter gave birth to] a ' passion that has no equal, ' which proceeded from (something) contrary to nature. [5] Then there arise a disturbance in ' the whole body. That is why I said to ' you, 'Be of good courage,' ' and if you are discouraged ' (be) encouraged in the presence of the different forms [10] of nature. He who has ears ' to hear, let him hear.'' '

When the blessed one had said this, he ' greeted them all, saying, ' "Peace be with you. Receive [15] my peace to yourselves. Beware that no one ' lead you astray, saying, ' 'Lo here!' or 'Lo ' there!' For the Son of Man ' is within you. Follow [20] after him ! Those who seek him will ' find him. Go then and preach ' the gospel of the kingdom. Do not **9** lay down any rules beyond what ' I appointed for you, and do not give ' a law like the lawgiver lest ' you be constrained by it." [5] When he had said this, he departed.

But they ' were grieved. They wept greatly, ' saying, "How shall we go ' to the gentiles and preach ' the gospel of the kingdom of the Son [10] of Man? If they did ' not spare him, how will ' they spare us?" Then Mary ' stood up, greeted them all, ' and said to her brethren, "Do not weep [15] and do not grieve nor be ' irresolute, for his grace will be ' entirely with you and will protect ' you. But rather let us ' praise his greatness, for he has [20] prepared us and made us into men." When ' Mary said this, she turned their hearts ' to the Good, and they began ' to discuss the words ' of the [Savior]. **10**

Peter said to Mary, "Sister, ' we know that the Savior loved you ' more than the rest of women. ' Tell us the words of the Savior which you [5] remember – which you know ' (but) we do not, nor have we heard them." ' Mary answered and said, ' "What is hidden from you I will proclaim to you." ' And she began to speak to them [10] these words: "I," she said, "I ' saw the Lord in a vision and I ' said to him, 'Lord, I saw you ' today in a vision.' He answered and ' said to me, 'Blessed are you, that you did not waver [15] at the sight of me. For where the mind ' is, there is the treasure.' I said ' to him, 'Lord, now does he who sees the ' vision see it ⟨through⟩ the soul ⟨or⟩ through ' the spirit?' The Savior answered and [20] said. 'He does not see through the soul' nor through the spirit, but the mind which [is] ' between the two — that is [what] ' sees the vision and it is [. . .].' (pp. 11-14 missing)

"[. . .] 15 it. And desire that, ' 'I did not see you descending, ' but now I see you ascending. ' Why do you lie, since you belong to 5 me?' The soul answered and ' said, 'I saw you. You did not see me ' nor recognize me. I served ' you as a garment, and you did not know me.' ' When it had said this, it went away rejoicing 10 greatly.

"Again it came to the ' third power, which is ' called ignorance. [It (the power)] ' questioned the soul saying, ' 'Where are you going? In 15 wickedness are you bound. ' But you are bound; do not judge!' And ' the soul said, 'why do you judge ' me although I have not judged? I was bound ' though I have not bound. I was not 20 recognized. But I have recognized that ' the All is being dissolved, both the ' earthly (things) 16 and the heavenly.'

When the soul ' had overcome the third power, ' it went upwards and saw ' the fourth power, (which) took 5 seven forms. The first form ' is darkness, the second ' desire, the third ' ignorance, the fourth is the excitement of ' death, the fifth is the kingdom of the flesh, 10 the sixth is the foolish wisdom ' of flesh, the seventh is the ' wrathful wisdom. These are the seven ' [powers] of wrath. They ask ' the soul, 'Whence do you come, 15 slayer of men, or where are you going, ' conqueror of space?' The soul answered ' and said, 'What binds ' me has been slain, and what surrounds ' me has been overcome, and my desire 20 has been ended, and ignorance ' has died. In a [world] I was released 17 from a world, [and] in a ' type from a heavenly type, ' and (from) the fetter of oblivion which ' is transient. From this time on 5 will I attain to the rest of the ' time, of the season, of the aeon, in ' silence.'''

When Mary had said ' this, she fell silent, since it was to this point that the Savior ' had spoken with her. 10 But Andrew answered and said ' to the brethren, "Say what you (wish to) say ' about what she has said. ' I at least do not believe that ' the Savior said this. For certainly these teachings 15 are strange ideas." ' Peter answered and spoke concerning ' these same things. He ' questioned them about the Savior: "Did he really ' speak with a woman without our 20 knowledge (and) not openly? Are we to ' turn about and all listen ' to her? Did he prefer her to us?" 18

Then Mary wept and said to ' Peter, "My brother Peter, what do you ' think? Do you think that I ' thought this up myself in my 5 heart, or that I am lying about the Savior?" ' Levi answered and said to Peter, ' "Peter, you have always been ' hot-tempered. Now I see you ' contend-

ing against the woman like [10] the adversaries. But if the | Savior made her worthy, who are you | indeed to reject her? Surely | the Savior knows her | very well. That is why he loved her more [15] than us. Rather let us be ashamed and | put on the perfect man | and acquire him for ourselves | as he | commanded us, and preach | the gospel, not laying down [20] any other rule or other law | beyond what the Savior said." When **19** [. . .] and they began to | go forth [to] proclaim and to preach.
|

[The] Gospel |
according to [5]
Mary

THE ACT OF PETER (BG 8502,*4*)

Introduced by

Douglas M. Parrott

Translated by

James Brashler and Douglas M. Parrott

The Act of Peter is a narrative about how the virginity of Peter's daughter was preserved and the soul of one Ptolemy saved, by divine intervention exercised through Peter. The setting of *Act Pet.* is a Sunday (the place is not mentioned; cf. discussion below), when, it appears, it was customary for Peter to conduct his healing ministry. A challenge by one of the bystanders leads Peter to employ the power of God to heal his daughter of paralysis, which healing he immediately reverses (128,7-131,9). Peter's narrative, which constitutes most of the remainder of *Act Pet.*, begins with an explanation of how his daughter came to be paralyzed. When she had grown to sexual maturity, the girl was so attractive that a rich man named Ptolemy burned with desire to marry her. Her mother refused permission, whereupon Ptolemy abducted her. If the operative law was Jewish, Ptolemy's purpose may well have been to force the girl's parents to allow him to marry her (see Dt 22:28-29). Peter's prayers caused her to be paralyzed before Ptolemy could have intercourse with her, and hence her virginity was preserved (131,12-135,17). Ptolemy went blind with grief, but a vision spared him from suicide, revealed his guilt, and sent him to Peter, where his sight was restored and his soul was made to see also (135,17-138,10). Thereafter he lived an exemplary life and gave Peter and his daughter a parcel of land when he died. This Peter sold and gave the proceeds to the poor (138,12-139,17). Peter draws the moral that God cares for his own, and the whole account ends with Peter distributing bread to the crowd and retiring to his home.

Although the physical setting is not mentioned in the text, it is reasonable to think of Jerusalem, since Peter's home is spoken of (141,6), where he lives with his wife and daughter (135,1-6). Another possibility is Rome, but there is a tradition in *The Acts of Peter*, mentioned below, that he goes alone to Rome. In addition, as noted above, the operative law appears to be Jewish.

The Act of Peter probably was part of the otherwise lost beginning third of a collection of apocryphal narratives known as *The Acts of Peter*. There is extensive conceptual and literary agreement between *The Act of Peter* and the remaining *Acts of Peter*. Whether there is a close enough relationship between *The Act of Peter* and the Nag Hammadi *Acts of Peter and the Twelve Apostles* (VI,*1*) to make it likely that the latter was also part of *The Acts of Peter* remains to be seen.

Conceptually, the emphasis of *The Act of Peter* is moderately encratite. Marriage itself is not denounced (note that Peter was married and still living with his wife). What is denounced is Ptolemy's lust, which leads him to attempt to deprive a Christian maiden of her virginity by force (137,1-11). Thus, the encratism in this tractate consists in its advocacy of rigorous sexual self-control, which was a view common among Christians in the second century. There is no doubt, however, that the lack of any statement about the meaning of the narrative would have allowed it to be interpreted in a more extreme sense.

It has been suggested that the reason for the inclusion of *The Act of Peter* in a codex containing three explicitly gnostic tractates is that the scribe needed to fill up the pages after copying the first three tractates, and thus he was attracted to *The Act of Peter* by its appropriate length and the encratite tendencies in it. Considering the large amount of explicitly gnostic writing available, one wonders why he chose a work only marginally related. The editor might have been influenced by the immediately preceding tractate, *The Sophia of Jesus Christ*, which has in its conclusion, when Christ disappears from the disciples, the statement that they "began to preach the Gospel of God, the eternal Father" (129,5-9). He might have thought that an account of apostolic activity would be appropriate. But since many similar accounts would also have been circulating, there may be a further reason for the choice of this particular tractate.

The Act of Peter may have been chosen because of the rich possibilities for allegorization that it would have presented to Gnostics. Ptolemy could have represented the soul, whose attraction to the things of the world (represented by the beauty of Peter's daughter) leads to ignorance (represented by grief and blindness), and would have led to death except for the coming of the light of true knowledge (in *Act Pet.*, the vision of light and the voice of Christ [136,17-137,17]), which removes blindness (138,7-10). The paralysis of the daughter could have represented the power of divine knowledge over the powers of this world; and, of course, the daughter could also have been seen as a type of the fallen Sophia. (For related gnostic views in BG, cf. *Soph. Jes. Chr.* [BG,*3*] 103,10-106,9; 117,13-126,16). It may thus have been the deeper meanings seen in this text that attracted the gnostic compiler to it and led him to use it in the codex.

Act Pt. are dated toward the end of the second century. Hence *Act Pet.* would have been extant by that time, although it might well have had an earlier, independent existence.

THE ACT OF PETER

BG 128, 1-141, 7

Now on the first (day) of the week, | which is the Lord's day, | a crowd gathered and | brought to Peter [5] many who were | sick, in order that he might | heal them. And a person | from the crowd made bold | to say to Peter, [10] "Peter, behold, in | our presence you have caused many | blind to see, and you have | caused the deaf to hear, | and you have caused the lame to [15] walk. And you have helped | the weak and have given them | strength. But your | virgin daughter, who | has grown up to be beautiful and who has **129** believed in the name of God, ' why have you not helped her? ' For behold, one ' side of her is completely paralyzed and she lies [5] crippled there in the corner. ' Those whom you have healed are seen (about us); ' but your daughter ' you have neglected.''

Then Peter ' smiled and said to him, [10] ''My son, it is apparent to ' God alone why ' her body is not healthy. ' Know, then, that ' God was not weak or [15] unable to give ' his gift to my daughter. ' But so that your soul ' may be persuaded and those who are ' here may have more faith — .'' **130** Then he looked at ' his daughter and said to her, ' ''Arise from your place! Let ' nobody help you except Jesus [5] alone, and walk restored in ' the presence of all these (people)! ' Come to ' me!'' And she arose ' and went over to him. [10] The crowd rejoiced on account of ' what happened. ' Peter said to them, ''Behold, ' your hearts have been persuaded ' that God is not powerless [15] regarding anything ' we ask of him.'' Then ' they rejoiced even more and praised ' God.

Peter said **131** to his daughter, ' ''Go to your place, sit down, ' and become an invalid ' again. For this [5] is beneficial for you and me.'' ' The girl went back again, ' sat down in her ' place, and became again as she ' was before. The whole crowd [10] wept and begged Peter ' to make her healthy. ' Peter said to them, ' ''As the Lord lives, this ' is beneficial for her and me. [15] For on the day she was born ' to me I saw a vision and ' the Lord said ' to me, 'Peter, there has been born ' to you today a great **132** trial. For this (daughter) ' will wound many ' souls if her body ' remains healthy.' [5] But I ' thought the vision ' was mocking me.

''When ' the girl became ten ' years old, many were [10] tempted by ' her. And a man rich ' in property, Ptolemy, ' after he had seen the ' girl bathing [15] with her mother, sent ' for her so that he might take her for his ' wife. Her mother was not ' persuaded. He sent for her many ' times. He could not cease [. . .]. (pp. 133-34 are lost. The sense of these pages can be recovered from the context with the aid of a brief notice by Augustine in his treatise against Adimantus, in which he refers to an apocryphal work ''about the daughter of Peter himself who became paralysed through the prayers of her father.'' It appears, then, that Ptolemy, in his passionate desire, abducted the girl and was about to have intercourse with her by force when she was suddenly paralysed by a divine act that had been sought by Peter in prayer.) **134** [19]

''[The men-servants of] **135** Ptolemy [returned] the girl, ' and put her down ' before the house, and departed. ' And when I and her mother realized it, [5] we went down ' and found the girl ' with one whole side of her body, ' from her toes to her ' head, paralyzed and withered. [10] We picked her up, praising the ' Lord who had ' saved his servant from defilement, ' [and] pollution, and [destruction]. ' This is the cause of [15] [the fact] that the girl ' [remains] thus to this ' day.

"Now then, it is ' fitting for you to know ' the (subsequent) deeds of Ptolemy. **136** He was smitten ' in his heart and grieved ' night and ' day on account of what [5] happened to him. And ' because of (the) many tears he ' shed he became ' blind. He intended ' to go and [10] hang himself. And behold ' in the ninth hour ' of that day, ' and when he was alone ' in his bedroom, [he] [15] saw a great light ' shining in the whole house, ' and heard ' a voice saying **137** to him, 'Ptolemy, ' God did not ' give his vessels for ' corruption and pollution. [5] But it was necessary ' for you, since you believed ' in me, that you not defile ' my virgin, whom ' you should have recognized as your sister, [10] since I have become ' one Spirit for you both. ' But arise ' and go quickly to ' the house of Peter the [15] apostle and you will see ' my glory. He will explain ' the matter to you.'

"And Ptolemy ' did not hesitate. He ' commanded his men-servants **138** to lead him ' and to bring him to me. ' And when he had come ' to me he narrated everything that [5] had happened to him ' in the power of Jesus ' Christ our Lord. Then he ' saw with the eyes ' of his flesh and the [10] eyes of his soul. And ' many hoped ' in Christ. He did ' good things for them ' and he gave them [15] the gift of God. '

Afterwards Ptolemy ' died. ' He departed from life and ' went to his Lord. **139** And [when he made] his ' will, he wrote in a ' piece of land in the name of my ' daughter, since because of her [5] he believed in God ' and was saved. I myself ' took care of the administration ' entrusted to me most carefully. ' I sold [10] the land. And ' God alone ' knows, neither I, nor ' my daughter, {I sold the land} ' kept anything [15] back from the price of the land. ' But I sent the ' entire sum of money to the poor. '

"Know, then, O servant of ' Christ Jesus, that God **140** [watches over those who] ' are his and he prepares ' what is good for ' each one. But we [5] think that ' God has forgotten us. ' Now then, brothers, let ' us be penitent and ' watchful, and pray. [10] And the goodness ' of God will look ' down upon us — and we ' wait for it." And ' {all} other teachings [15] Peter spoke in the ' presence of them all. ' Praising the name **141** of the Lord Christ, ' he gave them all ' bread. ' When he had distributed it, ' he [5] arose and went ' into his house. '

The Act of Peter

Afterword

THE MODERN RELEVANCE OF GNOSTICISM

by

R̲ichard S̲mith

"The Gnostics," Edward Gibbon informed the late eighteenth century, "were distinguished as the most polite, the most learned, and the
most wealthy of the Christian name." Why would Gibbon have told such
a mischievous lie? There is nothing in the primary sources available to
him on which to base his claim. Gibbon, nevertheless, in that notorious
fifteenth chapter of the *Decline and Fall of the Roman Empire*, avoids
the old hostilities. In his witty, malicious — today we might add revisionist — style, Gibbon portrays the Gnostics with such impartiality that his
chapter becomes, if not an advertisement for heresy, then at least a
subversion of orthodoxy. His catty remarks on the early Christian
church were later bowdlerized, yet the most unkind words he has for the
Gnostics is to describe their "vain science" as "sublime but obscure."
Hardly the rascals of tradition, we can imagine Gibbon's Gnostics grac-
ing one of Mme Geoffrin's salons.

Other *philosophes* might have welcomed their presence as well, for, as
part of the Enlightenment attack on Christianity, the ancient dualist
heretics of the early church found their cause promoted. The method, or
perhaps the battle order (Gibbon's *Memoirs* speak of shooting the shaft
and sounding the alarm), was revealed by Gibbon when he fondly praised
that patron saint of the Enlightenment, Pierre Bayle. Bayle "balances
the false religions in his sceptical scales, til the opposite quantities an-
nihilate each other." Bayle's *Historical and Critical Dictionary* had no
entry on Gnostics or Gnosticism (a brand new word in his day), but gathered all of the old dualists together under the heading of Manichaeans.
The Manichaean movement had been the final flourish of Gnosticism,
and had survived through various geographical wanderings until its flare
up in southern France in the Middle Ages when it was eliminated by a
crusade. Until the eighteenth century revived an interest in the older sects
now called gnostic, the term Manichaean was used for all dualist heresies.

For Voltaire, another of Bayle's devotees, the catchword was also Manichaean. *Candide* depicts the adventures of a few silly optimists in a wicked world; a world in which Christian priests are among the most villainous troublemakers. Peter Gay has even described the book as "a declaration of war on Christianity." Yet in the midst of all the chaos Voltaire includes one sympathetic character; a wandering scholar named Martin who introduces himself to Candide as "a Manichaean." When Candide protests that there are no more Manichaeans in the world, Martin simply says, "I cannot think any other way. I think that God has abandoned this globe, or rather this globule, to some maleficent being." The events of the novel confirm Martin's assessment. Bayle had said that the gnostic belief in several eternal beings, some good, some bad, in perpetual conflict, "is not so unlikely" to "men who think and reason." Voltaire says, in his own *Philosophical Dictionary* discussing the Gnostics and Manichaeans, "to have imagined two all-powerful beings fighting each other" is not a "trivial" notion. He slyly describes Basilides' myth of "the creation of the world by god's lowest angels, and that these, not being skillful, arranged matters as we see them." In his story, *Plato's Dream*, Voltaire tells a nightmarish version of creation by an incompetent genie called Demogorgon. Dualist stories seem to have appealed to Voltaire's own sense of conflict. There is in his writings, as Roland Barthes puts it, "a kind of Manichaean struggle between stupidity and intelligence." Or, as David Hume summed up the opposition in one breath, "Stupidity, Christianity, and Ignorance."

The Enlightenment writers created a sympathetic picture of the Gnostics because heterodoxy suited their anti-orthodoxy. They emphasized the dualist critique of the world, but ignored the dualist promise of transcendent escape. The *philosophes* thus created a version of the Gnostics that was, like themselves, secular. It is because we are still the heirs of that secular agenda that an assessment of any modern relevance of Gnosticism properly begins in the eighteenth century. There was, certainly, an interest in unorthodox, esoteric, and even occult matters in earlier centuries. In the Renaissance, for example, there was something of the spirit of exploration and conquest in such studies. Disparate traditions, hermetic and cabalistic, were appropriated and harmonized with Christianity. Ficino, Agrippa, Dee, and Bruno all considered themselves Christians. They were not at all, moreover, interested in the ancient Gnostics. The eighteenth-century *philosophes* regarded Gnosticism as a counter-tradition and wielded it as a weapon in their outflanking tactics to overthrow the received tradition.

THE NAG HAMMADI LIBRARY IN ENGLISH

That the "candid but rational inquiry" (the words with which Gibbon opens his chapter on Christianity) was often a relativist pose was mostly lost on following generations. The irony was ignored and Reason itself was regarded as absolutist and a threat to the human imagination. William Blake named the enemy in his poem *Milton*:

> ... this Newtonian Phantasm
> This Voltaire & Rousseau: this Hume & Gibbon
> ... the Reasoning Power in Man
> This is a false Body: an Incrustation over my Immortal Spirit; a Selfhood,
>   which must be put off & annihilated alway ...
> I come in Self-annihilation & the grandeur of Inspiration
> To cast off Rational Demonstration by Faith in the Saviour
> To cast off the rotten rags of Memory by Inspiration
> To cast off Bacon, Locke & Newton from Albion's covering
> To take off his filthy garments, & clothe him with Imagination

This is a new use of dualist language. For Blake, salvation was the free expression of his own visionary imagination. Only a few months before his death, he wrote to a friend that he was "very near the gates of death ... but not in spirit and life, not in the real man, the imagination, which liveth for ever. In that I am stronger and stronger, as this foolish body decays." Throughout his life, Blake expressed this vision in poetic myths with a strong gnostic character. The evil demiurge of these poems he calls Urizen, a polysemous figure who suggests so much more than the creator of the physical world, Jehovah. He is also, as "prince of Light," Satan and the "Enlightenment" as his name (your Reason) signifies. He is evil for Blake because his creation limits (Horizen, his name implies, too) and his primary symbol is "the golden compasses." Like the bearded figure in Blake's famous print "The Ancient of Days," Urizen leans out of eternity and reaches down into the dark void with his compasses to measure, to divide, and to imprison. In *The Four Zoas* Blake describes the creation in images that echo and parody, like some gnostic texts, both Genesis and Plato's *Timaeus*:

> ... First the Architect divine his plan
> Unfolds, The wondrous scaffold reard all round the infinite
> Quadrangular the building rose the heavens squared by a line ...
> A wondrous golden Building; many a window many a door
> And many a division let in & out into the vast unknown
> Cubed in window square immoveable, within its walls & cielings
> The heavens were closed and spirits mournd their bondage night and day

When he finishes his creation Urizen, like Yaldabaoth, claims, "Am I not God. Who is Equal to me."

> Then he began to sow the seed he girded round his loins
> With a bright girdle & his skirt filld with immortal souls
> Howling & Wailing fly the souls from Urizen's strong hand

This evil creator depicted by Blake in his later poems helps remove some of the ambiguity from the question he had posed in "The Tyger": "What immortal hand or eye, / Dare frame thy fearful symmetry?" Where William Blake read or heard about the Gnostics is not exactly clear, but some of his views certainly echo them consciously. With the Gnostics he separates the true God from nature, and regards the creator of the natural universe as evil. Crabb Robinson, a friend of Wordsworth, talked with Blake and kept a diary. Discussing Wordsworth's "eloquent descriptions of Nature," Blake told Robinson that Wordsworth didn't believe in God, "For Nature is the work of the Devil." When Robinson pointed out the creation of the earth by God in Genesis, Blake "repeated the doctrine of the Gnostics with sufficient consistency" that his interviewer was silenced.

Harold Bloom, a contemporary interpreter of the Romantic tradition, compares Blake's Tyger with Melville's Moby Dick. Both beasts represent nature, and "nature is death." Nature "painted like a harlot," Melville wrote, "God's great, unflattering laureate, Nature." The material universe is, for Ahab, "but a mask," a cosmetic behind which lies death, like a white shroud, like the albino whale. In a short poem he called "Fragments of a Lost Gnostic Poem," Melville wrote "Matter in end will never abate / His ancient brutal claim." Two years before the publication of *Moby Dick*, Herman Melville purchased a copy of Piere Bayle's old *Dictionary*. What he read there (and elsewhere) found its way into the novel, and whether Ahab shakes his angry harpoon at a monstrous creature or a malicious gnostic creator is not distinct. "An inscrutable malice," Ahab says, "is chiefly what I hate; and be the white whale agent, or be the white whale principal, I will wreak that hate upon him. Talk not to me of blasphemy, man." Ishmael, attempting to explain this fury, compares Ahab's feelings to those of a sect of ancient Gnostics. These were the Ophites, a group that today's scholarship calls the Sethians, associated with several of our Nag Hammadi texts. Ahab, says Ishmael, deliriously transferred the idea of "that intangible malignity which has been from the beginning . . . which the ancient Ophites of the east reverenced . . . to the abhorred white whale." In the final pages of the book Ahab flings an accusation at the creator that conjures Yaldabaoth's ignorance of his own mother.

> Thou knowest not how came ye, hence callest thyself unbegotten: certainly
> knowest not thy beginning, hence callest thyself unbegun. I know that of
> me, which thou knowest not of thyself, oh, thou omnipotent. There is some
> unsuffusing thing beyond thee, thou clear spirit, to whom all thy eternity
> is but time, all thy creativeness mechanical.

In these passages from Blake and Melville, the physical world is a barrier.
Romantic writers regard that barrier with feelings from discomfort to
open hostility. The present collection of texts from Nag Hammadi shows
us that what we call Gnosticism can range between a hierarchical monism
to strict dualism. In a similar manner texts from the Romantic tradition
depict, with varying degrees of conflict, a drama of separation and reintegration. The "fall into Division," Blake wrote, "and Resurrection to
Unity." Salvation consists in what Harold Bloom describes as "the post-
Enlightenment passion for Genius and the Sublime." "The power of the
mind," as Coleridge had put it, "over the universe of death." Scholars
have found examples of "Gnosticism" in the writings of Baudelaire,
Rimbaud, the early Flaubert (in *The Temptation of Saint Antony*, a
book much inspired by his reading of Pierre Bayle), the French Symbolists, the German Idealists, the American Transcendentalists, Carlyle,
and so on. "Indeed," writes Bloom, "it could be argued that a form of
Gnosticism is endemic in Romantic tradition." His primary example of
this gnostic tendency is W.B. Yeats. Yeat's lyrics internalize the dualism
and dramatize a conflict between various aspects of the self. In such
poems as "A Dialogue of Self and Soul," the two speakers, Bloom
argues, "are precisely the *pneuma* and the *psyche* of Gnostic formulation. The place of the Gnostic alien or transmundane true God in Yeats
is taken by the imagination, which in Yeats is closer to Gnostic
transcendence than it is to the Romantic Sublime."

> If but imagination scorn the earth
> And intellect is wandering
> To this and that and t'other thing,
> Deliver from the crime of death and birth.

This internalized antithetical conflict is more boldly stated in "Sailing
to Byzantium":

> Consume my heart away; sick with desire
> And fastened to a dying animal
> It knows not what it is; and gathers me
> Into the artifice of eternity.
> Once out of nature I shall never take
> My bodily form from any natural thing.

Yeats's strange and famous poem "The Second Coming" historicizes this antithesis and envisions the approach of a world spirit signaling a new, post-Christian age.

> Surely some revelation is at hand;
> Surely the Second Coming is at hand.
> The Second Coming! Hardly are those words out
> When a vast image out of *Spiritus Mundi*
> Troubles my sight ...
> ... but now I know
> That twenty centuries of stony sleep
> Were vexed to nightmare by a rocking cradle,
> And what rough beast, its hour come round at last,
> Slouches towards Bethlehem to be born?

How are we to read these difficult images? Is Yeats afraid, or simply struck with wonder? Have the twenty Christian centuries been a nightmare? And how much can we make of the antithesis between "know" and "sleep"? A lot. The rough beast's slumber recalls "Urizen laid in a stony sleep." Yeats, after all, had edited Blake's poems for publication. The turning of the ages was recorded by Yeats, acting as amanuensis to his wife who was in mediumistic trance, and published as *A Vision*. The anti-Christian tone is not unrelated to his involvement in various occult groups while he lived in London and to his membership in The Hermetic Order of the Golden Dawn, which enthusiastically circulated exotic religious writings including gnostic texts.

What Yeats and the Golden Dawn read as "gnostic" were often grecoroman magical texts. He also read gnostic sources in the books published by his long time acquaintance G.R.S. Mead. Mead devoted his life to publishing English translations of the gnostic sources available at the turn of the century. In books like *Fragments of a Faith Forgotten* he promoted an interest in the subject among nonscholarly readers. Mead and Yeats had met as members of the esoteric section of the Theosophical Society, which gathered at the London flat of H.P. Blavatsky in the 1880s.

It was Madame Blavatsky who first claimed the Gnostics as precursors for the occult movement. In her program to divide speculative learning into esoteric and exoteric, truth and religion, the Gnostics were an obvious opposition to what she called "Churchianity." She absorbed the Gnostics, in her universal free-associative style, into a great occult synthesis:

Ialdabaoth, the creator of the material world, was made to inhabit the planet Saturn according to the Ophites. From Ialdabaoth emanate six spirits who respectively dwell with their father in the seven planets.... These seven planets are identical with the Hindu *Sapta-lokas*, the seven places or spheres, or the superior and inferior worlds; for they represent the kabalistic seven spheres. With the Ophites they belong to the lower spheres. The monograms of these Gnostic planets are also Buddhistic, the latter differing, albeit slightly, from those of the usual astrological "houses."

This, from *Isis Unveiled*, is a typical sample of Blavatsky's treatment of the Gnostics. There is an esoteric tradition, Blavatsky felt, within every religion teaching her "secret doctrine." "The Gnosis, or traditional *secret* knowledge, was never without its representatives in any age or country," she writes. The esoteric tradition within Christianity is represented by the Gnostics, but "it is the intense and cruel desire to crush out the last vestige of the old philosophies by perverting their meaning, for fear that their own dogmas should not be rightly fathered on them, which impels the Catholic Church to carry on such a systematic persecution in regard to Gnostics. Alas, alas!"

H.P. Blavatsky and her Theosophical Society wrote the book on secret traditions. Most esoteric movements ever since have found it almost impossible to step outside of her (sometimes unconscious) influence. A few recent groups calling themselves gnostic have appealed to an underground yet pervasive "gnosis" rather than to the ancient historical gnostic sects. This is true of La Asociacion Gnostica which is widespread throughout Latin America, as well as the Los Angeles based Ecclesia Gnostica.

Indeed, in our century there have been several appropriations of gnostic motifs. The psychologist, C.G. Jung, continually refers to the Gnostics in his writings and was often photographed "wearing his gnostic ring." His lifelong interest in the subject was rewarded in 1952 when the Jung Institute in Zurich purchased and presented to him on his birthday a recently discovered gnostic papyrus manuscript. This "Jung Codex" is now our Nag Hammadi Codex I. Jung wrote so much about the Gnostics simply because he liked them. In *Psychological Types* he writes of "the vastly superior [compared to that of the Church] intellectual content of gnosis, which in the light of our present mental development has not lost but has considerably gained in value." He goes on to praise its "Promethean and creative spirit ... we find in Gnosticism what was lacking in the centuries that followed: a belief in the efficacy of individual revelation and individual knowledge. This belief was rooted in the proud feeling of man's affinity with the gods, subject to no human law, and so overmastering that it may even subdue the gods by the sheer power of gnosis."

In 1916, before he wrote his major works, during a period when he believed his house to be filled with parapsychological phenomena, Jung wrote a visionary piece called *The Seven Sermons to the Dead* and ascribed it pseudonymously to Basilides, the second-century Alexandrian Gnostic:

> In the night the dead stood along the wall and cried:
> We would have knowledge of god. Where is god?
> Is god dead?
> God is not dead. Now, as ever, he liveth.
> This is a god whom ye know not, for mankind forgot it.
> We name it by its name ABRAXAS.
> Abraxas standeth above the sun and above the devil.
> It is improbable probability, unreal reality.
> Had the pleroma a being, Abraxas would be its manifestation.
> The dead now raised a great tumult for they were Christians.

But Jung's Basilides preaches on:

> Abraxas begetteth truth and lying, good and evil, light and darkness, in the
>   same word and in the same act.
> Wherefore is Abraxas terrible.
> It is love and love's murder.
> It is the saint and his betrayer.
> It is the brightest light of day and the darkest night of madness.

In the early 1950s Dr. Jung defended himself against an attack by Martin Buber. Under discussion was the entire body of Jung's work, but Buber pointed a particularly snide finger at "his little Abraxas opus." The criticism was that Jung had overstepped the boundaries of psychology into religion, and had located God in the unconsious (rather than in Buber's transcendent "Thou"). This god of the self was, he complained, "the Gnostic god who unites good and evil in himself." Jung took all of this seriously. "Why is so much attention devoted to the question of whether I am a Gnostic?" He apologized for "once having perpetrated a poem, a sin of my [41-year-old] youth ... I am a psychiatrist," he responded, "whose prime concern is to record and interpret his empirical material, to investigate facts and make them more generally comprehensible." Jung's "empirical" defense was later to be complicated by the description in his autobiography of his composition of the *Septem Sermones*. "All my works, all my creative activity, has come from those initial fantasies . . . Everything that I accomplished in later life was already contained in them, although at first only in the form of emotions and images.''

The paradoxical Abraxas of the early poem thus prefigures "the self" which Jung discussed over the next four decades as "a *complexio oppositorum*." Self-knowledge is achieved through the conscious assimilation of the contents of the unconscious, including its dark "shadow" side, towards a goal of "wholeness." Jung, therefore, was deeply interested in the gnostic insistence on evil as an active principle as opposed to the incomplete Christian view of evil as the *privatio boni*, the absence of good. "The Gnostics," he writes with approval, "exhaustively discussed the problem of evil," and he quotes the famous question of Basilides, "Whence comes evil?" Their answer was to oppose "the good, perfect, spiritual God by an imperfect, vain, ignorant and incompetent demiurge." In his book *Aion*, Jung performs a telling psychoanalytic turn on this myth. "The ignorant demiurge who imagined he was the highest divinity illustrates the perplexity of the ego when it can no longer hide from itself the knowledge that it has been dethroned by a supraordinate authority . . . that indescribable whole consisting of the sum of conscious and unconscious processes, the antithesis of the subjective ego-psyche, what I have called the self." Jung pushes this interpretation to claim that "for the Gnostics — and this is their real secret — the psyche existed as a source of knowledge . . . that many of the Gnostics were nothing other than psychologists." C.G. Jung, indeed, saw his own work as "a link in the *Aurea Catena*" (the Golden Chain) from Gnosticism through philosophical alchemy to the modern psychology of the unconscious. The chain had been broken by the Enlightenment with its "devilish developments, anti-christianity and rationalistic hybris." The tradition was then revived "by Freud, who had introduced the classical Gnostic motifs of sexuality and the wicked paternal authority." Freud, however, left out "that other essential aspect of Gnosticism: the primordial image of the spirit as another, higher god who gave mankind the vessel of spiritual transformation, a feminine principle." Jung compensates by reintegrating these motifs and thus creating a version of psychic unity that not only paralleled his reading of Gnosticism, but was inspired by it. Jung's psychology portrays a version of the self that is fragmented, as do many gnostic texts, and like them finds an image of divinity among these fragments. Unlike gnostic texts, however, Jungian psychology does not see salvation as a separation of that divine fragment from the mundane, and its removal to the divine. Rather, Jung takes the entire dualist myth and locates it within the psyche. The result, as his own judgment states, is "that my leanings are therefore towards the very reverse of dualism."

Many of our century's fiction writers have portrayed versions of this psychologized Gnosticism. Herman Hesse's *Demian*, published in 1925, was written right after Hesse had undergone Jungian analysis. The characters and events of the novel constitute an allegory of the Jungian achetypes. The strongest character, Demian, appears to blur all distinctions of age, gender, or ethics. He is "unimaginably different." Demian tells the hero "dismaying" gnostic revisions of scripture to point out that the "people with character tend to receive the short end of the stick in biblical stories." Like a (Jungian) Gnostic also, Demian pushes the hero to transcend his limited view of reality. "Who would be born must first destroy a world," he says, and fly to God, a God whose "name is Abraxas, uniting the godly and devilish elements." That Demian represents an aspect of the hero's own self is clarified as the novel ends by blurring the distinction between the "other" and the "inner." In a mystical, homoerotic vision, the two characters merge into one. Hesse's next novel, *Steppenwolf*, portrays a character dwelling in "this alien world ... the homeless Steppenwolf, the solitary." Steppenwolf, with an allusion to ancient Gnosticism's most stunning image, sees "the whole of human life as a violent and ill-fated abortion of the primal mother, a savage and dismal catastrophe of nature." At conflict with "nature" (Hesse identifies this with "bourgeois convention") is "the spirit ... driven to God." In the course of the novel Steppenwolf is to discover that the conflict is more complicated, that there are not two but a thousand souls clamoring withing him, "a chaos of potentialities and impulses." In answer to his striving, Steppenwolf is given a very psychologizing, very modern message. "You have a longing to forsake this world and to penetrate to a world beyond time. You know, of course, where this other world lies hidden. Only within yourself exists that other reality ..."

These novels of Hermann Hesse are early versions of a genre that has been important throughout this century: stories of conflict between the outer world and the inner reality discovered by journeying through psychological realms. It is not surprising that some of these writings are read as "gnostic." Some, such as Doris Lessing's *Briefing for a Descent into Hell*, are devastating in their criticism of normal life. Rather than promoting any integration towards a total personality, her novel valorizes the hero's dissociated psychic fantasies at the expense of his mental "health." His inner journey takes the hero to mythological lands, to outer space, and back to earth – his "descent into hell" – as a messenger of the gods. The character's struggle to hold on to this reality, against the drugs and shock therapy of his psychiatrists, is described with the classical gnostic metaphors (and with the typically gnostic reversal) of sleeping and waking, forgetting and remembering.

Although they vary in the radicalness of their dualism, all of these psychological writings agree that meaning is not to be discovered in the manifest world. By situating meaning within the human psyche, and implicitly ignoring any transcedent location for meaning, these works are definitely modern. Other types of "immanent" salvation have also been described as "modern Gnosticism." A vast description of modern Gnosticism – including psychology in its scope – was the predominate theme of the political philosopher Eric Voegelin. Beginning in 1952 with *The New Science of Politics* and in many further books such as *Science, Politics and Gnosticism*, Voegelin identifies "the essence of modernity as the growth of gnosticism." He understands Gnosticism to be "the experience of the world as an alien place ... a horror of existence and a desire to escape from it." Rather than the ancient Gnostic achronic salvation from above, however, Voegelin sees modern Gnosticism promising salvation in the future, by means of the historical process. For this radically immanent salvation, without transcendental irruptions, he faults the eighteenth century, and has some harsh words especially for Condorcet and Voltaire. Voegelin proceeds, like some unhinged biblical prophet, to trace and decry the course of modern Gnosticism: Comte, "the first high priest of a new religion, positivism"; Hegelianism (although as early as 1835 Ferdinand Christian Baur had argued for the similarity between German idealism and Gnosticism, calling it "the philosophy of religion, the Godhead's evolving self-knowledge through man"); Marxism, "the self-salvation of man, an intellectual swindle"; Communism, "left-wing gnosticism"; National Socialism, "right-wing gnosticism"; totalitarianism, "the end of the Gnostic search for a civil theology"; progressivism, "scientism and the immanentist pride in the variants of salvation through physics, economics, sociology, biology, and psychology." All, all of this, Eric Voegelin calls Gnosticism. He appeals for "repressing Gnostic corruption and restoring the forces of civilization," and concludes, "fate is in the balance."

Voegelin's writings could be regarded as silly were it not for their strong impact within and beyond his own field of political science. Academicians from various disciplines have gathered at conferences such as "Gnosticism and Modernity," where they discussed such topics as

"The Gnosticism of Lincoln's Political Rhetoric." The literary critic, Cleanth Brooks, having absorbed Voegelin's version of Gnosticism, described Walker Percy's novel *Lancelot* as "modern Gnosticism." The main character of this book, Lancelot Lamar, is confronted by his wife's and daughter's ongoing orgy with a group of sex and drug enthusiasts from Hollywood. In a fury of crazed self-righteousness, Lancelot decides to take matters into his own hands (immanent salvation) and burns down his house with everyone in it. It would appear that Voegelin's influence has removed the distinction between "Gnosticism" and what we call "apocalypticism."

Voegelin portrays Gnosticism as an attempt to solve the ills and evils of this world by the promise of a revolutionary new realm. An ironic complement to this portrait, and a tribute to the complexity and contradictions of the ancient sects, is that the rejection of this world and disentanglement from it is only one gnostic attitude. An ascetic withdrawal is one ethical response to anti-cosmic dualism, and one which characterizes most of the Nag Hammadi texts ("The World Haters," *Time* magazine headlined its report on the present translation project). An opposite stance is to immerse oneself in worldly sins and pleasures, these being, after all, alien and uncorrupting things. This attitude, not found in our texts but attested in ancient descriptions of the gnostic sects, has inspired several recent novels of Lawrence Durrell. His four novels that make up *The Alexandria Quartet* depict a gnostic "cabal" led by a "homosexual goat" named Balthazar. "Indulge but refine" is Balthazar's doctrine, which he claims to be uniquely Alexandrian, "a town of sects and gospels. And for every ascetic she has always thrown up one religious libertine – Carpocrates [the second-century gnostic], Anthony [the Christian monk] – who was prepared to founder in the senses as deeply and truly as any desert father in the mind .... It is the national peculiarity of the Alexandrians to seek a reconciliation (between extreme sensuality and intellectual asceticism). That is why we are hysterics and extremists. That is why we are the incomparable lovers we are." One character, Justine, plays out on this earth the drama of the gnostic Wisdom goddess, "bending over the dirty sink with the foetus in it [like] poor Sophia of Valentinus." Are we, she wonders, "the work of an inferior deity, a Demiurge, who wrongly believed himself to be God? Heavens, how probable it seems." Justine quotes Balthazar, who in turn quotes E.M. Forster. Forster's book *Alexandria: A History and a Guide* was the main source of Durrell's understanding of Gnosticism, with its tragic combination of physical love and theology. Here is Forster's lovely retelling of the creation myth of Valentinus: "He imagines a primal God, the centre of a divine harmony, who sent out manifestations of himself in pairs of male and female. Each pair was inferior to its predecessor, and Sophia the female of the thirtieth pair, least perfect of all. She showed her imperfection not, like Lucifer, by rebelling from God, but by desiring too ardently to be united to him. She fell through love ... and the universe is formed out of her agony and remorse." Durrell went on in later novels like *Monsieur* to describe yet another modern sect of Egyptian Gnostics. In *Monsieur* the amorous interplay of genders and geometries is complex enough to rival any ancient gnostic cosmogony. "I am amazed," wrote Durrell's long time friend, that modern apostle of experience, Henry Miller, "that there has been no revival of this sect." Forster had attempted an answer: "it was pessimistic, imaginative, esoteric — three great obstacles to success."

One interpretation of ancient Gnosticism, combined with an assessment of its modern relevance, has won the favor of many scholarly specialists in gnostic studies. In the 1920s Hans Jonas was a student of both the philosopher Martin Heidegger and the New Testament scholar Rudolf Bultmann. He was thus in a unique position to participate, as a Bultmannian, in this century's investigation of ancient gnostic sources and, as a Heideggerian, in the philosophy of existentialism. Throughout his long career, Jonas has played these two themes against each other. The link between the two is provided by dualism. "Gnosticism," he claims "has been the most radical embodiment of dualism ever to have appeared on the stage of history. It is a split between self and world, men's alienation from nature, the metaphysical devaluation of nature, the cosmic solitude of the spirit and the nihilism of mundane norms." It is "a lasting paradigm of the human condition." Likewise, "the essence of existentialism is a certain dualism, an estrangement between man and the world." Existentialism also contains a "depreciation of the concept of nature." Gnosticism, therefore, has "an analogical modernity." In his book *The Gnostic Religion*, Jonas focuses on one specific image that is used by both the ancients and the moderns to describe "the self-experience of existence," the image of "having been thrown." Here is Heidegger in *Being and Time*: "This characteristic of Dasein's Being ... we call it the 'thrownness' (*Geworfenheit*). This downward plunge into and within the groundlessness of the inauthentic Being, is characterized by temptation, tranquillizing, alienation ...." Jonas compares this to the famous ancient Valentinian formula that freedom is the knowledge of, among other things, "wherein we have been thrown." He made this comparison before the availability of the Nag Hammadi translations, which describe how Yaldabaoth and the archons "threw" mankind into matter and distraction. Jonas expertly draws attention to the dissimilarities as well: "Gnostic man is thrown into an antagonistic, antidivine, and therefore anti-human nature, modern man into an indifferent one." The modern version is more nihilistic, "a dualism without metaphysics." Thrownness is, in both systems, however, "an existential mode of the past," nor is there, he argues, a mode of genuine existence in the future. Genuine existence, freedom, dwells "only in the crisis between past and future, the razor's edge of decision, the existential present of the moment."

Hans Jonas presents a compelling argument, and the similarities between ancient Gnosticism and modern existentialism do seem at least "analogical." We should keep in mind, however, the surprising condemnation of Gnosticism made by Albert Camus. Gnosticism, he claims in *The Rebel*, is conciliatory. It alters the course of metaphysical rebellion by developing the theory of a wicked, inferior god against whom to direct its attack, and exalts a superior god. "The vast number of aeons invented by Valentinus," for instance, "are the equivalent of the intermediary truths to be found in Hellenism. Their aim is to diminish the absurdity of an intimate relationship between suffering humanity and an implacable god."

Existentialist alienation and modern versions of visionary romanticism have combined to give Gnosticism a powerful literary expression. Jack Kerouac and Allen Ginsberg, fellow students at Columbia University in the 1940's, were introduced to Gnosticism by their professor Raymond Weaver. John Tytell, an historian of "the Beat Generation," has shown that an interest in gnostic themes voiced itself in Kerouac's 1959 novel *Doctor Sax*. This mythic reverie of a book ("Memory and dream are intermixed in this mad universe") describes Doctor Sax, "the King of Anti Evil," and his attempts to save the world from "the Great World Snake of evil" with its "moo mouth maw of death." The snake, with its "scaly ululating back," is "an unforgettable flow of evil and wrath and of Satan"; and Doctor Sax, in "his slouched hat" (like Ahab's — Kerouac's professor had been a Melville scholar), searches the world "for herbs that he knew someday he would perfect into an alchemic-almost poison art . . . that would make the Snake drop dead." The novel climaxes in a grand nightmare that seems to draw in every stock character from both sides of the conflict between good and evil. Allen Ginsberg also employs gnostic imagery to voice his hatred of evil in the world. In his nuclear protest poem "Plutonian Ode," written in 1978 after reading Jonas's book on Gnosticism, he confronts our "Radioactive Nemesis ... named for Death's planet." Ginsberg's poem, in the form of an exorcistic chant, evokes the planetary archons of the Gnostics:

> I salute your dreadful presence lasting majestic as the Gods,
> Sabaot, Jehova, Astapheus, Adonaeus, Elohim, Iao, Ialdabaoth, Aeon
> from Aeon born ignorant in an Abyss of Light,
> Sophia's reflections glittering thoughtful galaxies, whirlpools of star-spume
> silver-thin as hairs of Einstein!

   Gnostic motifs have been identified in that most visionary of our modern literary genres, science fiction. Historian William Irwin Thompson sees the gnostic myth in Nicholas Roeg's film *The Man Who Fell to Earth* and in Zena Henderson's novel *Pilgrimage*. Both of these stories are about characters whose sojourn on this planet is a tragic separation from their true home. Painfully alienated, they struggle through memory to regain identification with their higher origins. Superman, too, although he is not homesick, is an alien battling against the forces of evil. Good and evil in "The Myth of Superman," Umberto Eco has written, are "clearly divided into zones of Manichaen incontrovertibility." It is, however, in the science fiction novels of the prolific writer Philip K. Dick that Gnosticism is most consciously employed. In *Valis*, published in 1981, a year before Dick's death, the main character has an encounter with the divine which "fires information into his head by a beam of pink light." The divine is "Mind," but Mind divided against itself, as two contending principles, like the schizophrenic main character of the novel. "From loss and grief the Mind has become deranged," he says. "Therefore we, as parts of the universe, the Brain, are partly deranged." This character, called Horselover Fat, has the following conversation with his therapist:

> "Do you believe man is created in God's image?"
> "Yes," Fat said, "but the creator deity, not the true God."
> "What?"
> Fat said, "That's Yaldabaoth. Sometimes called Samael, the blind god. He's deranged."
> "What the hell are you talking about?"

Fat is talking about *On the Origin of the World* from the first edition of *The Nag Hammadi Library* published in 1977, which Dick quotes elsewhere in the novel. "A lunatic blind creator and his screwed-up world" explained, for Dick, the "irrational, whacked out, psychotic" universe.

In the course of the novel, Fat attempts to recapture, beyond the irrational god (and beyond his own schizophrenia), the true God. This science fiction novel and its sequel, *The Divine Invasion*, tell a cosmic story where mental psychoses play out a drama of madness and intelligence, where fragments of divinity lose and remember themselves in human minds. It might be supposed that the Nag Hammadi texts inspired these novels, but Gnosticism, it seems, is never so simple. "Horselover Fat" is a multilingual pun for the author's own name, and Philip K. Dick claimed that *Valis* was autobiographical, that he, like his character, had an encounter with a beam of divine pink light in 1974. The publication of the Nag Hammadi translations only confirmed his revelation.

A quite self-conscious incorporation of Nag Hammadi texts into a science fiction novel appeared in Harold Bloom's 1979 novel *The Flight to Lucifer: A Gnostic Fantasy*. In it the reincarnated Valentinus and his companions fly to a planet called Lucifer. Quoting our gnostic texts, the heroes wage a violent battle against Saklas, the Demiurge who is worshipped in his "Saklaseum." Bloom, more successful as an interpreter of literature, later confessed that *The Flight to Lucifer* reads as though Walter Pater were writing *Star Wars*. But, then, so does much ancient gnostic writing.

Harold Bloom's strongest appropriation of Gnosticism is in his theoretical books of literary criticism. He describes his "mode of interpreting literary texts as a Valentinian approach," that is, "an antithetical and revisionist way of reading." In a series of books beginning with *The Anxiety of Influence* in 1973 he studies "the anxiety that blocks creativeness" when a writer faces his great precursors. "In Yeats," for instance, the precursor is "the Spectre of Blake." Bloom's argument is that literary influence always proceeds by "a deliberately perverse misreading . . . an act of creative correction, of distortion, of perverse, willful revisionism whose purpose is to clear away the precursor so as to open a space for oneself." A text is therefore "a psychic battlefield" where influence fights to move *backwards*. Bloom's model for this is "Gnosticism, the religion of belatedness." "Valentinus," he argues, "is troping upon and indeed against his precursor authorities, to reverse his relationship to the Bible and to Plato, by joining himself to an asserted earlier truth that they supposedly have distorted." In 1982, in *Agon*, Bloom "misread" his gnostic precursors and claimed them for the latest school of literary criticism: "Gnosticism was the inaugural and most powerful of Deconstructions because it undid all genealogies, scrambled all hierarchies, allegorized every microcosm/macrocosm relation, and rejected

every representation of divinity as non-referential.'' Bloom's willfulness
and enthusiasm bowl the reader over. "Abandon Heidegger for Valentinus,'' he calls out. If his creative misprision is successful, it will be measured by our inability to read these old texts without feeling Harold
Bloom's influence upon them.

By turning reading into an activity upon the text, or rather, by his re-
situating of meaning within the intertextual relationship between texts,
Bloom has shifted the discussion of Gnosticism away from the modern
into the postmodern situation. Ihab Hassan's 1987 book *The Postmodern Turn* draws on Bloom and many other theorists to discuss a
"New Gnosticism" characterized by the dematerialization of existence.
The "New Gnosticism does not revert directly to the ancient cults," yet
it was "prefigured by the ancient Gnostics, authors of a passionate subjectivity." Contempoary philosophy and literary criticsm are on "a
gnostic journey into subjectivity, that leaves texts behind and vanishes
into consciousness." Our own mental constructs, he claims, are our
knowledge. Human beings are becoming "gnostic creatures constituting
themselves, determining their universe by symbols of their own making," and he indicates science fiction and fantasy literature as examples.
As with the ancient Gnostics, the traditional codes no longer determine
our meaning. The traditional canon of texts no longer has authority.
Hassan sees "a vast, revisionary will" at work in our culture, unsettling
and heterogeneous, and he quotes Jean-François Lyotard's now famous
clarion call of postmodernism: "Let us wage a war on totality."

This postmodern appreciation of Gnosticism seems indeed to have an
affinity with ancient sectarianism and revisionary mythologizing. Ihab
Hassan considers "immanence" to be one of the main characteristics of
the "New Gnosticism," a quality of both modern and postmodern
theory. Thus, as Charles Jencks describes postmodern art and architec-
ture, we have personal invented mythology and metaphors with no
shared metaphysical substance. Anatole France (himself a writer who
never made it into modernism) wrote an eloquent version of immanent
gnostic salvation in his 1914 novel *The Revolt of the Angels*:

> The God of old is dispossessed of His terrestrial empire, and every thinking
> being on this globe disdains Him or knows Him not. But what matter that
> men should be no longer submissive to Ialdabaoth if the spirit of Ialdabaoth
> is still in them; if they, like Him, are jealous, violent, quarrelsome, and
> greedy, and the foes of the arts and of beauty? What matter that they have
> rejected the ferocious demiurge? It is in ourselves and in ourselves alone
> that we must attack and destroy Ialdabaoth.

How much do these attempts to see modern, or even postmodern, relevance in Gnosticism help us to understand our ancient texts? or do they misuse the evidence? The evidence, in any case, is conflicting, as James M. Robionson declares in the opening sentences of the introduction to this book. It has also been pointed out that none of the Nag Hammadi texts use "gnostic" as a term of self-designation. Other ancient sources tell us that "gnostic" was used by some sects as a self-designation, but certainly not by all of the various sects that came to be called Gnosticism. We might also notice that the only mention of the famous gnostic heresiarchs in this library (in *The Testimony of Truth*) is as opponents, and "they" are attacked as heretics! With the publication of the Nag Hammadi library the study of ancient Gnosticism has become increasingly problematic, so likewise its relevance. The frequently attempted etymological definition (gnostic comes from the Greek word for know) is frustratingly inadequate. We do better to avoid generalizations and to marvel at the variety of the sources. The variety was brought about more by the mundane issues of time and space, than by theological debates. The first issue was the authority of tradition against revealed interpretations; the other was hierarchical unification against sectarianism. By taking the wrongheaded side of both these issues, the sects and our texts were excluded, and "Gnosticism" became a symbol of heresy. Interpretive appropriations of Gnosticism have all used this element of otherness: the Gnostics as anti-Christians, as visionaries, as esotericists, as symbolists of the psyche, as alienated, and as violent misinterpreters and revisers.

The recent availability of this large number of primary texts has opened up new ways of discussing, new relevances for, the ancient sects we call gnostic. By their skewed readings, by animating the relationship between tradition and imagination, these texts capture our attention. If cultures define themselves not at their calm centers, but at their peripheral conflicts of inclusion and exclusion, then Gnosticism, whatever we mean by it, is more than an antiquarian curiosity. It stands as a continuing testament to difference in the face of our cultural tendencies toward closed homogeneity.